THREE GOLDEN AGES

Also by Alf J. Mapp, Jr.

*The Virginia Experiment: The Old Dominion's Role
in the Making of America*

*Frock Coats and Epaulets: The Men Who Led the
Confederacy*

Just One Man

The Golden Dragon: Alfred the Great and His Times

Thomas Jefferson: A Strange Case of Mistaken Identity

Thomas Jefferson: Passionate Pilgrim

Bed of Honor

In Collaboration

Chesapeake Bay in the American Revolution

Portsmouth: A Pictorial History

Constitutionalism: Founding and Future

Constitutionalism and Human Rights: America, Poland, and France

Great American Presidents, vol. 1

THREE GOLDEN AGES

Discovering the Creative Secrets
of Renaissance Florence,
Elizabethan England,
and America's Founding

ALF J. MAPP, JR.

MADISON BOOKS
Lanham • New York • Oxford

Published by Madison Books
4720 Boston Way
Lanham, Maryland 20706

12 Hid's Copse Road
Cumnor Hill, Oxford OX2 9JJ, England

Distributed by National Book Network

Library of Congress Cataloging-in-Publication Data

Mapp, Alf J. (Alf Johnson), 1925–
    Three golden ages : discovering the creative secrets of
    Renaissance Florence, Elizabethan England, and America's founding /
    Alf J. Mapp, Jr.
        p.   cm.
    Includes bibliographical references and index.
    ISBN 1-56833-113-4 (alk. paper)
    1. United States—Civilization—To 1783.   2. Political science—
United States—History—18th century.   3. Renaissance—Italy—
Florence.   4. Florence (Italy)—History—1421-1737.   5. England—
Civilization—16th century.   6. Great Britain—History—Elizabeth,
1558-1603.   7. Creation (Artistic, literary, etc.)—Social aspects—
Case studies.   8. Social change—Case studies.   I. Title.
E162.M32   1998
909—dc21   98-17124
                                                            CIP

∞ ™ The paper used in this publication meets the minimum
requirements of American National Standard for
Information Sciences—Permanence of Paper for Printed
Library Materials, ANSI Z39.48-1984.
Manufactured in the United States of America.

TO
RAMONA HARTLEY MAPP

CONTENTS

ACKNOWLEDGMENTS

AMONG THE INSTITUTIONS whose helpfulness has made this book possible are the Library of Congress, Washington, D.C., which graciously provided a private study room for part of my research; the Old Dominion University Library; the Library of the Virginia Historical Society; the Virginia State Library; the Norfolk, Virginia Public Library; the Tidewater Community College Library; the Portsmouth, Virginia Public Library; the Earl Gregg Swem Library of the College of William and Mary; the Alderman Library of the University of Virginia; the Library of the University of South Carolina; the Library of the Pentagon; the New York City Public Library; the James Monroe Museum and Library, Fredericksburg, Virginia; the National Gallery of Art, Washington, D.C.; the National Museum of American Art, Washington, D.C.; the New-York Historical Society; the Philadelphia Museum of Art; the Metropolitan Museum of Art, New York City; the Courtald Institute, London, England; the British Public Record Office; the Galleria Degli Uffizi, Florence, Italy; the Frick Museum, New York City; and the Chrysler Museum of Art, Norfolk, Virginia.

Special thanks are due individuals who shared their expertise. Bernard Bailyn, Professor Emeritus of Harvard University, whose writings in American history have earned a Bancroft Award, a National Book Award, and two Pulitzer Prizes, discussed major aspects of this book with me and generously supplied printed source materials. Paul C. Nagel, whose works include three distinguished volumes chronicling the lives of the Adamses, has been helpful in discussing John Adams and John Quincy Adams. Kenneth W. Thompson, Director of the White Burkett Miller Center for Public Affairs at the University of Virginia, author and editor of valuable books on American presidents and on the philosophy of history, has shared insights and supplied encouragement. I have also benefited from discussions with two William and Mary professors, Daniel Preston, editor of the Monroe Papers, and Charles F. Hobson, editor of the John Marshall Papers and one of the best in the whole canon of Marshall biographers. Richard Rorty, Professor of Philosophy at the University of Virginia, and Lewis S. Ford, Professor Emeritus of Philosophy at Old Dominion University, have supplied sources and helpful comments regarding their specialties.

Valuable, too, have been discussions with Jack P. Greene, Andrew Mellon Professor in the Humanities at Johns Hopkins University and formerly Harmsworth Professor of History at Oxford University, who more than anyone else in recent decades has influenced the thinking of professional historians on the regional influences in American history and on relationships among English-speaking peoples in the seventeenth- and eighteenth-century Atlantic world.

Franklin Kelly, Curator of the Department of American and British Paintings, National Gallery of Art, Washington, D.C., was helpful with advice on artistic currents between England and the United States in the great creative period. He suggested about fifty sources and personally furnished some research materials. Lillian B. Miller, Historian of American Culture at the National Portrait Gallery, Smithsonian Institution, and editor of the Peale Family Papers, was generous with time and advice. Her insights as a cultural historian and her expertise in American art were equally useful. I deeply regret that I was unable to tell her fully how valuable her help was before her death in 1997. A. Richard Turner, Goddard Professor of Arts and Humanities, Department of Fine Arts, New York University, and Paul Barolski, Commonwealth Professor of Art History at the University of Virginia, have given valuable advice on Renaissance Florence. John Andrews, editor of two editions of Shakespeare's works and for eleven years editor of the *Shakespeare Quarterly*, has furnished challenging insights on the Elizabethan Age.

Dr. Stephen C. Achuff, David J. Carver Professor of Medicine at Johns Hopkins University and Director of the Division of Clinical Cardiology at Johns Hopkins Hospital, has reviews pages relating to his specialty.

JoAnn Falletta, Music Director of the Virginia Symphony and the Buffalo Symphony and, in the words of the *New York Times*, "one of the foremost conductors of her generation," has supplied information and technical advice on musical problems. Almost all of my advisors have read portions of the manuscript and some have read the entire work.

Jeanne King, a word processor specialist, was responsible not only for the initial typing of a large part of the manuscript and development of the index for this book but also for the unified retyping of the entire manuscript, which had been the work of several typists.

My son, Alf J. Mapp, III, and my wife, Ramona H. Mapp, have rendered skillful service as research assistants. Additionally, Ramona has performed a heroic labor in helping to proof the typescript under terrific pressure.

                                        Alf J. Mapp, Jr.
                                        Willow Oaks
                                        Portsmouth, Virginia

INTRODUCTION

1

THE PERSISTENT QUESTION

WHY WAS THERE such a flowering of talent in one place and one time as in the era of the founders of the United States? Since the appearance of my books *Thomas Jefferson: A Strange Case of Mistaken Identity* and *Thomas Jefferson: Passionate Pilgrim,* this question, with insignificant variations, has been asked me by at least twenty-three interviewers from all parts of the country. Some were from newspapers or magazines, some from radio or television. Some were scholars whose disciplines related to the question; others were simply citizens with an intelligent interest in the American past and its possible implications for our own time.

The frequent expression of such a strong curiosity on this particular point indicates to me that many Americans are asking the question with more than a tinge of nostalgia for an era of greatness that they have known only through history or legend. Some skeptics ask if such an age really existed. They wonder if it now appears golden only because we see it through a sunset mist. But scholars who examine the record are almost unanimously convinced that the Revolutionary and post-Revolutionary generation of Americans was one of giants—humanly flawed people, but giants nevertheless. Their correspondence, and that of their friends and enemies, amply supports that conclusion. And because Washington, Jefferson, Madison, John Adams, and Franklin all wrote their most important letters by hand, and there existed no well-organized public relations industry to transform their images, the evidence is much easier to come by than facts about eminent leaders in our own time.

Another question often asked about the great generation is, Was it unique in its concentration of talent? The answer is no; it was rare but it was not unique. In the history of Western civilization, there were a few with equally impressive records; some would argue, even more remarkable ones. Elizabethan England, Renaissance Florence, Periclean Athens spring to mind. Good cases also could be made for certain eras in non-European cultures, say, for Egypt at favored times in the ninth and eighteenth dynasties, Babylonia under Hammurabi, and China in the time of Confucius. Still, such periods of creative achievement shine like lone stars in the murky night of human history. It is arguable that, in modern history, the generation of America's founders stands with those of Renaissance Florence and Elizabethan England in an exclusive constellation. Interestingly, the three are related in significant ways.

The questions asked me in recent years about America's founders have quickened my interest in a project that I have researched and pondered for nearly two decades—the common characteristics of these three great creative societies and the possible influence of some of these features in their astonishing efflorescence. Without pretending to have all the answers, I do hope that some of these points will prove worthy of consideration practically as well as theoretically. I have researched and written about the founders of the American Republic for thirty-five years. I have also, over a respectable period, researched and written about Elizabethan England. Finally, I have been intensely interested in Renaissance Florence for many years, and have delivered university lectures on its culture, though I have made no original discoveries in the field. Although I claim no personal expertise, I have studied the era systematically in recent years, examining some of its artifacts but relying principally on several hundred generally respected secondary sources, and have conferred with experts in Florentine culture. I perceive in the three great creative societies marked similarities. It is my hope that others may find it worthwhile to expand on some of the things I have found noteworthy, and that experts in the cultures of Egypt, China, and other countries may wish to look for parallels there.

In the pages that follow, I present some common characteristics of modern history's three societies most distinguished by phenomenal creativity, giving primary attention to the one I know best. In the process I focus on the words and actions of representative figures such as Lorenzo the Magnificent, Petrarch, Leonardo da Vinci, Elizabeth I of England, Francis Bacon, Shakespeare, Jefferson, Madison, John Adams, and Franklin. A heterogeneous passenger list for our voyage through time, but all would have found adventure in each other's company—and that fact is one clue to the vitality of the cultures which they personify.

2

THE BOW AND THE LYRE

IN "THE DESTRUCTORS," one of the most profound short stories of the twentieth century, Graham Greene tells of a gang of boys growing up in London after World War II. A single house, a small architectural gem designed by Sir Christopher Wren, stands out amid the surrounding rubble. Its unique perfection, unmarred by the bombings of the Luftwaffe, is an affront to the rebellious spirit of the boys. They determine upon its destruction and accomplish their purpose with relentless efficiency in one day. To their task they bring creative imagination, resourcefulness, organization, discipline, industry, courage, and above all a dedication that spurns material gain and subordinates individual ambition to the objectives of the group. Their triumph is realized when the structure that had survived the war crumbles into a mass of rubble indistinguishable from its surroundings.

Though the story is laced with black humor, only the most insensitive reader could fail to be pained by the reflection that this work of vandalism has commanded the very qualities necessary for constructive accomplishment. The incident assumes the dimensions of universal tragedy when one realizes that the same qualities upon which humanity relies for the preservation and growth of civilization can be employed with equal effectiveness in its destruction. Indeed, a cataclysmic war destroying humankind would command as its tools and weapons the genius, the industry, and the selflessness that are at once the glory and the chief reliance of any advanced society.

A culture that wishes to survive must realize that these cherished qualities are essential, but it must not assume that they guarantee survival. Particularly in our Western cultures, we tend to assume that of themselves they constitute that right which we like to think makes might and therefore will continue to insure our survival despite our forgivably human blundering and its occasionally painful consequences. The virtues exalted by Western civilization are intrinsically no more friendly to survival than fire or atomic energy. They are an arsenal available alike to the forces of life and of death. In considering their influence on the life span of a culture, the accepted virtues are to be viewed less as qualities inherently good in ultimate effect than, by another definition going back to the Old French *vertu*, simply powers. It is true that when a culture has lost its virtues it has lost its powers, but it is also true that virtues are a weap-onry available alike to the forces of construction and destruction. A man may use a gun for survival or for suicide. The life of a culture is dependent not only upon virtues but upon Virtue as defined by Socrates—the informed impulse toward good, the wisdom to see ahead the consequences of our actions.

If such vision was difficult to acquire in ancient Greece, it is even more difficult amid the complexities of modern civilization. On the other hand, if the challenges to our understanding have multiplied with the passage of twenty-four centuries, so have the guideposts. It has often been pointed out that intelli-gence has given the human animal—though condemned to the vulnerability of protracted infancy and even in maturity a feeble swimmer, a nonflier, an unimpressive runner, a frail fighter—the primacy over earth's other creatures. The use of a higher intelligence—a wisdom transcending cleverness—is neces-sary for this dominant creature's survival.

Of course, too glib a trust in human wisdom would be a folly leading to destruction. The ideologue, who thinks he has found the formula to answer the problems of humankind or has compressed the meaning of the universe into a single system, is the enemy of wisdom, for he would exclude the greater portion of the truth.

But there is no harm, and may be some profit, in searching for patterns in human affairs, so long as one realizes that each pattern represents only one aspect of the truth. Sir Winston Churchill, as a young subaltern in India, was lying in a hammock, browsing in a dictionary of quotations, when he was struck with the piercing aptness of one observation, only to come in a moment upon an equally convincing aperçu in support of a diametrically opposite con-clusion. How, he asked, could one possibly separate truth from counterfeit? At that moment, his gaze rested upon the outstretched iridescent purple wings of a butterfly perched upon a shrub. In a second, the insect, by a slight movement, changed to burnished gold. The same surface was visible, but a slight change of the angle of perception had made what was assuredly one color also incontest-ably another. Suddenly he realized that both perceptions were valid. In a flash, he also perceived that truth was multiple and diverse. The truth perceived varied with the angle of perception.[1]

Even one aspect of the truth can be an aid to understanding, so long as we are aware that it is only a single aspect. And if one view is considered in con-junction with even one other, we have gained the depth of binocular vision. Orthoptic exercises with a prism are sometimes used to attain binocular per-spective. The physical process is metaphysically significant. The white light of truth is composed of many colors. Only a fusion of hues seen separately in prismatic refraction produces the "natural" light in which we perceive things in what we regard as their "true" colors.[2]

In this book I wish to explore, in conjunction, two aspects of truth that shed some light on the survival and demise of societies. My subject, therefore, is a life and death matter and consequently one about which I am quite serious. But I am not so fatuous as to propose a formula to insure the survival of any society. It is, however, my hope that some people will find, as I have, intellectual stimulation in considering a few factors that repeatedly have helped to foretell dissolution in nations and other large units of human organization. And I dare to hope that an exploration of some of these influences may be one more aid to decision makers in contemporary societies—a group that in a democracy includes ordinary citizens.

Two factors whose significance I propose to examine in terms of the vitality of a society are the nurturing influence of tradition and the energizing force of exploration. The experience of generations in different parts of the world suggests that the health of a culture is dependent to a significant extent on the proper tension between these factors.

The idea of social or cultural continuity resulting from the interplay of opposites is not new. One thinks immediately of Georg Wilhelm Friedrich Hegel (1770–1831), whose dialectic is familiar in the simplistic form of thesis, antithesis, and synthesis. But Hegel himself traced the origins of his dialectic to the *Parmenides* of Plato five centuries before Christ.

Many thinkers besides Plato and Hegel—among them Vico, Condorcet, Comte, Herbert Spencer, Jung, Spengler, Toynbee, and Alfred North Whitehead—have seen patterns in history and experienced varying degrees of success and frustration in making them visible to their fellow humans. At least one thinker, Gibbon, must have been tremendously frustrated by those who saw everywhere in indelible images the patterns of decay that he had suggested for a much more limited milieu in *The Decline and Fall of the Roman Empire.*

Journalists and politicians continue to read unwarranted patterns into scant evidence in every turn of national fortune or international crisis, but the academic historians of our day are far more likely to avoid recognition of patterns even when they emerge like kaleidoscopic images from chaotic clutter. The twentieth century's increased emphasis on statistics has rescued some branches of scholarship from mere musing but, taken to the extreme, it has resulted in the application of cliometrics to questions too complex and too much compounded of unknowns to admit of easy analysis through compilations of figures. The ethos is lost in the enumeration.

Fortunately, some of the experiences of humankind, communally and individually, are repetitive. Otherwise, regardless of the esthetic and mind-stretching benefits of contemplating the sublime sweep of human experience, the study of history would have no practical value. Equally fortunately, history is not always repetitive; if it were, we could never profit from its lessons.

The concept of the cycle, as dear to the philosopher of history as to the astronomer, the meteorologist, and the business analyst, is essential to any organized search for historical patterns. But the historian's discipline embraces so small a fraction of human experience that he or she cannot know whether a development that appears erratic may be a cyclic repetition of events concealed in primordial mists. The meteorologist, of course, is confronted by the same problem, and to an even greater degree. This year's weather "anomaly" may be, in truth, part of a well-defined cycle not covered by meteorological records that, except for certain spectacular floods, droughts, blizzards, and hurricanes, constitute only a small fragment of history. As a result, long-term meteorologi-

cal forecasts are notoriously unreliable. But short-term forecasts, based on results commonly accompanying certain combinations of factors, are useful in
preparing for disaster or profiting from circumstances favorable to various enterprises. Likewise, the historian, though only speculating on the cyclic characteristics of millennia, may have collected enough observations of human experience to aid in short-term forecasts of some value.

Each of the two factors with which I am primarily concerned in considering societal vitality—tradition and exploration—has been cited separately with
memorable eloquence by a great thinker. Jacob Christoph Burckhardt, the
nineteenth-century Swiss historian, editor, educator, philologist, expert on art
and architecture, and philosopher, was a latter day exemplification of the Renaissance that he made the subject of his most famous work. The Netherlands'
Johan Huizinga and Germany's Friedrich Wilhelm Nietzsche, who perhaps
agreed on little else, agreed on Burckhardt. Huizinga said he was the "wisest
man of the nineteenth century." Nietzsche called him "our greatest sage."
Burckhardt insisted that "man, divorced from tradition, is too weak and too
poor a creature to create greatness out of himself. . . . Without his past man is
a barbarian."[3] Alfred North Whitehead, on the other hand, emphasized experiment as necessary to vitality. Conceding that "the speculative methods of metaphysics are dangerous, easily perverted," he nevertheless concluded, "So is all
Adventure; but Adventure belongs to the essence of civilization."[4]

There is truth in both Burckhardt and Whitehead. Each has cited a force
essential to communal and cultural vitality albeit these two forces are opposed.
We must inevitably conclude that some compromise between them is necessary
to the survival of a culture or a civilization. But the compromise itself is not
the only desideratum. The contest between the forces of tradition and exploration, if sufficiently controlled not to be destructive, is itself a source of vitality.
There is, of course, nothing original in the idea that a contest can be invigorating and sometimes ultimately unifying rather than divisive. Heraclitus, one of
the fathers of metaphysics, observed, "As with the bow and the lyre, so with
the world: it is the tension of opposing forces that makes the structure one."
Goethe, the most universal genius of his time, said in 1832 in his last letter
that "the best genius is that which absorbs" the new "without this in the least
impairing" its inheritance, "but rather enhancing" it.[5]

Apparently, neither Heraclitus nor Goethe cited tradition and experiment
as an especially significant combination of opposing tendencies, but the concept
is inchoate in the idea prevalent in most democratic, and even some oligarchic,
societies that the community is well served when neither the adherents of tradition nor those of change are without opposition. I would say that the principle
is inherent in elemental laws applicable far beyond our planet. In physics, the
opposing forces of attraction and repulsion maintain the universe. Centrifugal
and centripetal are seen in balance. My idea is that, in a society, tradition is the
equivalent of centripetal force, and exploration (or experiment) is the equivalent
of centrifugal.

3

LEGS AND TAILS

ONCE ABRAHAM LINCOLN asked his Cabinet, "If you call a dog's tail a leg, how many legs does a dog have?" When they answered "Five," the president replied, "No, four. Calling a tail a leg doesn't make it one."

I have no notion that, by experiments in nomenclature, I can alter reality. Nor am I ambitious to redefine generally accepted terms. But anyone repeatedly using throughout a book certain variously defined classifications is obligated to explain the sense in which he uses them. The reader has a right to know whether the author is calling a tail a leg.

Two terms that will be employed throughout this work are *culture* and *society*. A *culture* is the way of life of a group of humans. The group may be a primitive tribe, a large nation, or peoples of diverse origins sharing a civilization that spans a continent or rims an ocean. *Civilization* is a subdivision of culture, denoting a way of life distinguished by complex advances in the arts, sciences, and technology, and in which there is sufficient diversification of labor to permit a significant number of people to pursue knowledge as well as (or instead of) game and to cultivate the mind as well as the earth. By *society* I mean a group of human beings sharing a common government, whether it be a township, a nation, or a union of nation-states. Obviously, in a civilization one person is a member simultaneously of several communities, or *societies*, of varying scope. It is also true that among civilized peoples the culture of even a single society may embrace several subcultures determined by ethnic differences and variations in economic and educational level.

References in this book to the tension between tradition and experiment as a source of vitality in both *cultures* and *societies* should not cause the reader to conclude that culture and society are being used alternately and synonymously. The same tension can revitalize both a society and a culture.

One other matter of terminology requires clarification. *Experiment, adventuring*, and *exploration* will be used interchangeably in reference to that spirit which seeks the new, as opposed to *tradition*, which finds sustenance in the familiar.

Vitality itself may seem a nebulous term when applied to a society or a culture. Certainly capacity to survive is a minimal requirement. The ability to grow and develop is a more significant one. *Fruitfulness* is also a measure of vitality. Fruitfulness in a society or a culture is the production of arts, sciences, and ideas that enrich life and that prove—to use a much overworked but irreplaceable word—seminal.

One word of warning is necessary lest anyone be lured by false expectations into reading further. I make no attempt to devise a formula for the proper proportions of tradition and experiment necessary to keep a society or a culture viable. Even if the intensity of collective experience and response were measurable, there would still be too many variables for formulation. I attempt only to record examples of the healthful interplay of the two factors in flourishing cultures and the damaging imbalance of them in waning cultures, hoping that these accounts will suggest considerations pertinent in assessing the vitality of any culture.

Though examples will be cited from many societies, both Eastern and Western, we shall concentrate upon three—Renaissance Italy, Elizabethan England, and the United States in the era of the Founding Fathers. In discussing the development of these three, we shall necessarily refer frequently to a fourth, Athens in its Golden Age. Though we shall discover no magic formula in the School of Athens nor find a talisman in the streets of Florence, London, Williamsburg, or Philadelphia, we shall confer with some of the most brilliant artists and thinkers in four of the most exciting conjunctions of time and place in all of human history. For the writer—and I hope for you, the reader—the experience should be instructive as well as enjoyable.

RENAISSANCE FLORENCE

4

WAKING THE DEAD

W AS THE OLD MAN dangerous or only harmlessly crazy? Like many other fifteenth-century Italian merchants, Ciriaco[1] was an itinerant, ranging far from his native town of Ancona. But his travels were more extensive than those of most of his counterparts. He wandered through Greece and even through Egypt and the Middle East. Was he some sort of spy? Probably not. He seemed to spend most of his time around ancient monuments. He purchased gems and statuettes, and that was understandable. But he was more eager in the collection of old manuscripts and the copying of hundreds of inscriptions from old stones and bronzes. His interest was not likely to be scholarly. He did not have the formal education of a well-trained churchman. He labored in the flawed Latin and Greek that he had taught himself.

Was he seeking esoteric formulas amid the records of magic practiced in forgotten times? Many of his fellow merchants, though they could spare little time for such speculations, were not disposed to dispute the existence of arts of necromancy by which the satanically inclined could control their fellows. More likely, though, Ciriaco was simply insane, foolishly dreaming that he could exercise powers that were God's alone. What better evidence than his own words? When asked why he pursued such unusual interests, he said, "To wake the dead."[2]

Verification of his claim came in the six volumes of copyings and commentary that were deposited in the Sforza Library in Pesaro after his own death. He had indeed been waking the dead, in the sense that he was enabling them to speak again through the writings that he preserved and made available to scholars. But as one of the most active Italians of his time in bringing to light forgotten writings of the ancient Greeks and Romans, he was also helping to wake the living. He was a founder of the Italian Renaissance, one of the liveliest and most fruitful cultures that the world has ever known.

Ciriaco has been overshadowed by later Renaissance figures, including such giants as Botticelli, Raphael, Leonardo da Vinci, Titian, Correggio, Michelangelo, Verrocchio, Giordano Bruno, and Machiavelli. But Ciriaco was sowing some seeds of the Renaissance before these people cultivated it as their garden. And he was so much in the vanguard that his death in 1452 preceded by one year the fall of Constantinople to the Turks, which was once considered the beginning of the Renaissance. More commonly cited now is 1440, the approximate time of the invention of printing. The familiar argument for 1440 could be strengthened a little by citing the fact that it was also the date of the founding of the Platonic Academy in Florence. Of course, ages are not conveniently partitioned in easily recognizable fashion. One might as well attempt to demarcate with straight lines the beginnings and ends of currents of air and water. But there is an appropriateness in Ciriaco's primacy or near primacy. The Renaissance was not simply the creation of professional scholars, artists, patrons, and statesmen. The Renaissance was an ethos to which many elements contributed. The vitality of a society can never be only a prescription promulgated by intellectuals or a priority project of the governing.

Francesco Petrarca (1304–1374), commonly known as Petrarch, is usually hailed as father of the Renaissance. And certainly this poet, scholar, lawyer, ecclesiastic, diplomat, and reviver of classical learning so exemplified the spirit of his age and so energetically gave it impetus that he deserves a special place in any account of the period. A little later, Leonardo Bruni (1370–1444), also called Aretino, gave form and substance to the inspiration of the Renaissance. Through his elegant Latin translations from Demosthenes, Xenophon, and particularly Plato and Aristotle, he made the Greek classics accessible to many of his countrymen. His biographies of Dante and Petrarch helped Florentines to appreciate their own Italian heritage, as did his work as a historian. A true exemplar of Renaissance versatility, he was for seventeen years Chancellor of the Florentine Republic.

But actually the Renaissance had many progenitors—artists, philosophers, business people, politicians, many of them playing more than one of these roles. The age had not only many fathers but also some notable mothers. Witness those who graced the faculty of the very progressive University of Bologna, which in the fourteenth century became the first institution of higher learning to offer classes in anatomy, a fitting symbol of its human-centered curriculum. Novella d'Andrea became one of the leading lights of this great center of learning. And she did not trade on her beauty. Indeed, tradition asserts that it was a handicap. According to an unverified, but persistent, account she had to wear a veil while lecturing so as not to hinder the male students' concentration on her words.

When one talks about periods of unusual cultural fruitfulness, the Italian Renaissance always springs to mind. The suddenness of the burgeoning is sometimes exaggerated because of a mistaken notion that the Middle Ages were barren. But, even allowing for the continuity of medieval influences, it must be admitted that Italy in the Renaissance affords an almost unparalleled example of vigor in almost every field of cultural creativity.

Though Daniel J. Boorstin wittily calls the "Age of the Renaissance" a mid-nineteenth-century invention, he seems to be intentionally hyperbolizing to counter overly enthusiastic interpretations that have made the period the matrix of everything modern.[3] Admittedly, Jules Michelet's *Renaissance* in 1855 and, even more, Burckhardt's *Civilization of the Renaissance in Italy* in 1860, together with other works inspired by these, first made educated westerners conscious of the Renaissance as a defined entity. But the two great nineteenth-century historians found abundant evidence to distinguish the period not only from the Middle Ages but from most other eras. And, within the narrow compass of the Italian city-states, this zenith of creativity was illustrated not only by the domed magnificence of Saint Peter's, the gold, crimson, and cerulean treasures of the Uffizi, the muscular saints and sibyls guarding sarcophagi, and the populous heavens of the Sistine ceiling; the multifold magic of polyphony and the modern musical notations that allowed the eye to speak to the ear; and the poetry whose harmonies rivaled those of music itself. It was marked not only by the beginnings of modern historical scholarship, the revolutionizing of the study of anatomy after twelve centuries of stagnation, and the simultaneously liberating and enthralling advent of what became Newtonian science. Creativity was also signalized by such more mundane changes as the development of cursive writing, the birth of banking and the holding company, and the start of statistical science.

The Renaissance stands apart in other ways. It furnishes one of history's most convincing illustrations of the political institutions of a society reflecting the cultural ethos. For the particular purposes of our investigation, it offers special advantages; there is perhaps no more dramatic revelation of the simultaneous operations of tradition and experiment. In Renaissance Italy are written large the same factors essential to the vitality of any society. If we can discover why the combination of this time and this place presents such a dramatic surge of vitality, we shall have obtained valuable clues that can be applied in the consideration of other societies.

It is fitting that use of *Renaissance* as a proper noun, beginning in continental Europe in the fifteenth century and entering English in the 1840's and in isolated instances in the 1830's, should have given currency to its use in the 1870's and ever since as a common noun. It is not that one period of rebirth should have been memorable enough to separate it from others by capitalization but rather that one period so designated should be so preeminent as an age of renascence as to lead to lowercase applications to other eras sharing some of its characteristics.

Of course, the Renaissance was played out on a larger stage than Italy. All of western Europe was the scene. As Eugene F. Rice, Jr., has cogently observed, "The most remarkable technological innovations of the Renaissance were printing with movable metal type, the use of gunpowder to propel cannonballs and bullets, and important advances in shipbuilding and navigation. In none of these was the contribution of Italy indisputably central."[4] There was a brisk traffic in ideas as well as commerce between northern and southern Europe early in the fourteenth century, and it is impossible to assign sole responsibility for many important creations of the period. Nevertheless, the relative compactness of the Italian theater of developments and the intensive scholarship devoted to them make the Italian Renaissance an almost ideal subject for the study of a burgeoning culture. Besides, it can be argued convincingly that, although northern Europe was then as fruitful technologically as the Mediterranean peninsula, its artistic efflorescence was surpassed by Italy's.

Though the Renaissance reached much of Europe as late as the fifteenth century and continued in England until the middle of the seventeenth century, it began in Italy in the mid-fourteenth century and flourished in the fifteenth and sixteenth, fading rapidly with the dawn of the seventeenth century. Of course, no single factor can account for this extraordinary period of two and a half centuries in Italian history. Scholars have suggested a variety of causes—economic, political, and cultural.

It was once fashionable to ascribe the inception of Italy's Renaissance as much to economic expansion as to any other factor, but this view now seems an overstatement. Eugene Rice has cited this very epoch as an illustration of the fact that "a generalized prosperity is not always" one of "the conditions that nourish periods of cultural brilliance."[5] He and others have pointed out that the bubonic and pneumonic plagues, between 1348 and 1377, "halted more than two centuries of European demographic and economic growth" at the very time that the Renaissance was being born.[6] A sharply diminished population and a decline in markets and production made even the fifteenth century largely a period of economic retreats and rear-guard actions.

So much for the theory that prosperity pushed the Italian states into the Renaissance! But to admit that this was not the case is not to dismiss economic factors. They were quite important and, as is so often true, were inextricably interwoven with the political and cultural.

The old argument frequently ran that, with the formation of well-based governments in the city-states, a period of relative political stability succeeded one of near chaos. This stability, it was said, made possible a flourishing economy that nurtured arts and scholarship. There is a substantial measure of truth in this oversimplified accounting.

Italy was so infested with cruel petty tyrants in the fourteenth century that this period in its history might be called the "Era of the Despicable Despots." Unlike France, Spain, and England, in each of which the feudal system evolved into a centralized monarchy, Italy became a seething mass of independent states—some principalities and some republics—obeying the decrees of the Holy Roman Emperor in spirit only when it suited their own purposes and to the letter only when it might injure their rivals. As Burckhardt said, "The Papacy, with its creatures and allies, was strong enough to hinder national unity in the future, but not strong enough itself to bring about that unity."[7]

Absolute power in civilized societies is a fiction. In any large and complex organization the leader, though perhaps not limited by constitutional provisions, is nevertheless dependent upon the cooperation of some individuals, not all of whom can be coerced through fear. Concessions, even though unstated, must be made by the ruler as well as the subjects. The reign of Louis XIV of France is often cited as a supreme example of absolute monarchy, but an examination of the record reveals that even the Sun King could not always have all that he wanted whenever he wanted it. Nevertheless, when one talks about new approaches to complete autocracy, some of the Italian states of the fourteenth century must be high on the list. And the record does nothing to refute Lord Acton's famous maxim about absolute power tending to corrupt absolutely. The cruelty of the little dictators persisted, in some cases, into the fifteenth century and was whetted by the reverses pushing them to extinction. When the last tyrant of Padua was surrounded by his enemies in 1405, his guards heard him quite literally call upon the Devil as his most likely ally. In 1409 Giovanni Maria, tyrant of Milan and soon to be assassinated, had two hundred of his subjects executed for pleading for peace. He forbade anyone to utter the word; even Catholic priests were required to substitute *tranquillitatem* for *pace* in the regular forms of worship. Such conduct is not especially surprising from a man who kept dogs for sport—not for hunting, but rather for the pleasure of seeing them tear apart the bodies of his enemies.[8] Behavior of rulers in some major states was no less cruel and bizarre. Ferrante of Naples had many of his opponents murdered, some while dining as his guests. But he feared no Banquo's ghost at the dinner table. He had his favorite victims embalmed and kept them, arranged in the clothing they had last worn, as his permanent guests.[9]

Popular revulsion against some of the rulers, together with a struggle for aggrandizement among rival states, resulted in the deaths of some states and annexation of others. New governments emerged from class conflicts of byzantine intricacy. At last there remained only five large and strong political entities: the Papacy, the Kingdom of Naples, the Republic of Venice, the Duchy of Milan, and the Republic of Florence. The old savage tyranny survived in such cities as Rimini, Urbino, Mantua, and Ferrara, independent domains of warlords strong enough to ravage the countryside but too weak to do more than annoy their stronger neighbors.

The pope was honored in his domain as the viceroy of God. But the rulers of the other four great city-states had a more mundane origin. Victors of many years of class strife, they were merchant-princes. The regal accoutrements of successive generations invested them with the aura of aristocracy, but they long remained close to their beginnings in trade. And it was well for their countrymen that they did. Their imaginative concepts of commerce made a far better basis for cultural advancement than an adolescent predilection for unnecessary combat. They were no strangers to the egoism that had sent their predecessors forth to hunt for trophies on the battlefield, but they collected status symbols of another sort, becoming patrons of the arts. They sponsored paintings, sculptures, and works of literature that became their advertisements of achievement in life and their monuments in death. Furthermore, their resourceful response to the problems of dwindling commerce assured the cosmopolitanism of the culture they supported. They encouraged merchant-citizens to seek out new trade routes, to find customers in the whole Mediterranean world, and to bring back to their own people the artifacts of Eastern culture. Ultimately, the exchange of ideas became even more important than the barter of goods.

Though the concept of balance of power among sovereign states may not have found precise expression before the sixteenth century, it was a reality among the Italian city-states early in the Renaissance. The situation was one in

which some artists and scholars suffered professionally and personally for unwise transfers of allegiance from one ruler to another but the bonds of diplomacy were sufficient to make such changes possible for many and advantageous
for some. New learning and new techniques traveled rapidly among the political
communities of the peninsula.

One consequence of contacts with the Arabs in the search for new products and new markets was the rediscovery of Western classics long neglected in
the Christian society of Europe. The church, in many ways the most conspicuous institution of medieval times, had preserved some of the great Greek and
Latin writings, especially those that could be interpreted as prophecies of the
Messiah or otherwise precursors of the New Testament. But Arab scholars had
preserved some that the patient copyists of the monasteries had never seen.
Thus the continued study of classical literature as part of a medieval tradition
was given new impetus by association with the Arabs. As this process involved
viewing a familiar heritage through the eyes of another culture, the effect was
simultaneously to nurture Italian society through a long tradition and to stimulate it with new adventures of esthetics and intellect.

The Italian Renaissance owed its existence to four principal factors: the
rise of city-states ruled by merchant-princes; the necessity and the stimulus for
seeking distant markets, which furnished new ideas as well as new products
(particularly those derived from the Arab countries); the enthusiastic rediscovery of classical writings; and the inclination of the chiefs of state to become
patrons of art and scholarship.

This last factor is important not only because it increased opportunities
for artists and scholars but also because it added secular sponsorship to the
patronage of the church. The church had kept art and learning alive in the
Middle Ages despite the indifference of many and the invasions of barbarian
landsmen and Viking raiders. Though the constructive role of the church in the
preservation and promotion of culture far outweighed any negative aspects, its
censorship was in many instances inhibiting. The secular princes of the Renaissance also insisted that their preferences be honored, but at least they brought
a change of criteria and did not maintain across political borders that uniformity of criteria often so efficiently enforced by the Holy Catholic Church. For
these reasons, the change in sponsorship was liberating.

No one should underestimate the creative strengths of the Middle Ages.
They not only produced important paintings and sculpture but soared to remarkable heights in the illumination of manuscripts and the astonishing glories
of Gothic architecture. But whereas the medieval scholar or illuminator was
almost always a tonsured monk bent over his task in a cell in monastery or
university, his Renaissance counterpart was more likely to be a layman and was
quite as likely to be found in his own study or studio as in any monastic chamber or papal palace. Some were civil servants of highest rank. Their dependence
in so many instances upon the patronage of merchant-princes may have allied
them more often than was desirable with the rich and powerful, but the system
nevertheless fostered a great deal of individuality.

The transition of the Renaissance, however, was not a severance from the

Middle Ages. Typical Renaissance humanists were not in rebellion again religion. They were quite prepared to echo the sentiments of the Hebrew psalmist: "The heavens declare the glory of God; and the firmament sheweth his handywork. Day unto day uttereth speech, and night unto night sheweth knowledge."[10] They wished to read the scroll of the heavens and to study with every device of God-given intellect the greatest work of the Deity—humankind.

5

LORENZO THE MAGNIFICENT

ONFRONTED IN A shadowy alley of his native city, the central
figure of the Florentine Renaissance would have excited the suspicion
of any stranger. Stepping into the brilliant Italian sunshine, he would
have dispelled any lingering doubt that he was a thug. Lorenzo de' Medici's
narrow eyes beneath a frowning brow; his large, twisted, pugilistic nose; the
hard straight line of the uncompromising mouth bracketed by square, muscular
jaws; the belligerently outthrust chin—with these features, he would be perfectly cast as the leader of one of the street groups terrorizing so many Italian
cities of his time.

There can be little doubt that Lorenzo looked like a brawler. The menacing
features of the famous bust by Verrocchio appear also in a bronze medallion
by Bertoldo di Giovanni and are confirmed by a death mask. There is one
smiling portrait, a rondel profile in Nicola Valori's manuscript *The Life of Lorenzo*, which he presented to Pope Leo X. But, while the mouth is relaxed,
nothing modifies the belligerent cast of the rest of the face.[1]

Yet, strangely enough, Lorenzo loved beauty. He was not only a discerning
patron of great painting, sculpture, and literature but one of the better poets of
his day, a writer of sensitivity, sometimes even of delicacy. And in a time and
place of both intrigue and self-glorification, his portraits are sufficient evidence
that he made no effort to censor the artists who transmitted his image to posterity.

While it may be surprising that Lorenzo should look brutal, it is appropriate that he should appear tough. Ruggedness was essential to success in the
politics of a day when removal from office came as often by dagger as by decree. Of course he benefited from being part of a dynasty, but this fact takes
little from his record of personal accomplishment. The man known to his own
generation and to history as Lorenzo the Magnificent was sandwiched in the
order of succession between Piero the Gouty and Piero the Fatuous.

Probably Lorenzo was not seen as ugly by most residents of Florence. A
retinue separated him from them when he walked the streets. More often they
saw him on horseback with his athletic physique dressed in bright silks or shining armor. He probably had the figure and the lithe grace to appear dashing
from a distance when elegantly appareled.

There was glamour enough in his first dramatic public appearance. The occasion was a jousting tournament in February 1469 when Lorenzo was twenty years old. As befitted an event featuring the scion of a fabulously rich family that abhorred waste as much as it practiced generosity, the pageantry was made to serve three purposes. It magnified the future leader in the eyes of his people, celebrated his approaching marriage to Clarice Orsini, and honored his mistress, Lucrezia Donati. Lucrezia was the love of his life. He once wrote that "there was nothing which could be desired in a beautiful and accomplished woman which was not in her most abundantly found." But purely personal attributes, however elevated, were not enough. Her family's status was not truly exalted, though she was descended from Dante's wife, whereas Clarice was of the powerful Orsini clan. The marriage of a Medici had to be dynastically advantageous.

Lorenzo entered the jousting field in a procession including nine trumpeters, eight pages, two armored squires, twelve mounted noblemen, ten mounted cavaliers, sixty-four footmen, and a fife-and-drum corps. There was no danger that he would be overlooked because of the numbers involved. Clad in red-and-white silk and riding a horse caparisoned in velvet of the same colors, he must have seemed like a giant red-and-white centaur. Rubies and diamonds glittered on the gold feather that adorned his black velvet cap but were outshone by the great Medici diamond, mounted on his shield and flashing with every movement. Lest anyone be so obtuse as to miss the significance of his entry upon the public stage, Lorenzo wore over his surcoat a great label suggestive of an allegorical figure in a morality play. The identifying banner was a wide silk one embroidered with roses and studded with pearls spelling out "Le Temps Revient." By "Time Returns," Lorenzo meant to point out more than the cyclic nature of history. Those familiar with the works of Dante and Virgil would have understood the return of a particular time, an ancient golden age.[2]

The quotation was appropriate. It embodied the essence of renaissance, and particularly the Florentine Renaissance, for seldom in history have people anywhere had a greater appetite for both past and future than the people of Florence in Lorenzo's lifetime. And seldom has the tension between tradition and change so strongly stimulated creative energies to fruitful production. Particularly as Lorenzo's personal motto were the words significant, for Charles L. Mee did not exaggerate when he called him "an archetype of 'the Renaissance Man.'"[3]

Was this young Medici's performance in the tournament prophetic of the role he would play in his city-state? The official record would suggest a resounding yes; he fought four challengers and defeated all of them, causing a poet to hail him as the new Achilles. The same healthy realism that made Lorenzo scorn flattering portraits caused him to make due allowance for the weight of his position in the scales of judgment. He wrote, "Although I was not a very vigorous warrior, nor a hard hitter, the first prize was adjudged to me."[4]

Though the tourney was Lorenzo's first spectacular appearance in Florence, he had already rendered notable public service to his city. In the first instance, he was serving his family as well as his community, a particularly happy conjunction for an Italian youth because in Italy, more than almost anywhere else in the civilized world, the family was the most permanent institution of society and the one that commanded the most passionate allegiance. While Piero, the as yet unborn son who would succeed Lorenzo, is perhaps justly remembered as "the Fatuous," the earlier Piero, Lorenzo's father, deserves a better tag than "the Gouty." It is true that his painful affliction—he was sometimes unable to move either hands or feet—curtailed his activity as leader and limited his administration to five years, but he continued his own father Cosimo's patronage of scholarship and art. Except for his physical handicap, he might have attained greatness. That same handicap almost cost him his life when Lorenzo was seventeen years old. It was then that Lucca Pitti, leader of a rival family, failing to unseat Piero by legal means, attempted assassination.[5]

The fact that Piero's illness necessitated his being carried in a litter rather than riding horseback made him particularly vulnerable to attack as he returned to town from his country villa. Apparently, riding well ahead of his father, Lorenzo came upon the would-be assassins, surmised their intentions, and told them Piero would be coming soon. While the boy delayed them in conversation, he sent his father a message to take a different route. Piero and his allies gave the teenaged son full credit for foiling the crime. Piero began assigning him responsibilities of state, dispatching him on a diplomatic tour of other Italian city-states—Pisa, Milan, Venice, Bologna, and Ferrara. Whether he was performing any substantive task or merely spreading a little goodwill and becoming personally acquainted with courts with which he would later deal as the leader of Florence, we do not know. But, upon the youngster's return, Piero sent him on a more consequential mission as a special envoy to the pope to persuade His Holiness to remain aloof from the war threatened by several Italian city-states. Medici strength was great in Florence, and Florence was a great power in Italy, so it was unlikely that the pontiff would risk cooperation with the troublemakers. Nevertheless, an ill-advised word by a clumsy envoy could have complicated relationships. Before Lorenzo returned, Piero said that, without his son, he was "as a man without hands."

Thus, when Piero died in 1469 and Lorenzo succeeded him, the new leader of Florence, though only twenty years old, already had three years of successful experience in statecraft. But that was none too much for dealing with the complex, shifting alliances that kept the Italian peninsula in ferment.

If Lorenzo's own later testimony may be believed, he felt no sense of triumph when the principal men of Florence asked him to assume the post of leadership occupied by his father and grandfather. At this stage of Florentine life, the mantle was by no means automatically his by inheritance. Indeed, though he may not then have known it, it was offered first to a member of the opposition faction. Lorenzo confided to his diary, "Because of my youth, and considering that the burden and danger were great, I consented to it unwillingly; but I did so in order to protect our friends and property; for it fares ill in Florence with anyone who possesses wealth without any control in the government."[6] His statement reminds us again of one of his greatest strengths—

his realism. He did not deceive himself that he had assented in noble sacrifice to some grand abstraction. It was a matter of survival. The Medici had ridden the tiger for two generations. In the interest of self-preservation, they could not dismount.

But Lorenzo cared about Florence, and he cared about civilized values. There was reason to hope that, if he could survive the power struggle, the young man might become a great leader. Part of the reason was that he had been tutored not only in statecraft but also in philosophy and the arts. He was enthusiastic about the revolution in the humanities that was the most exciting development in the Europe of his day. One of his principal teachers was Marsilio Ficino, tiny in body but giant in intellect, a keen student of Greek literature and a philosopher celebrated as the greatest of his day. Plato had never been entirely forgotten, but Ficino is credited with rediscovering him as a thinker of peculiar relevance. Thus Lorenzo's tutor was an architect of the Renaissance. One is reminded of Alexander the Great, a brilliant young man of action studying under Aristotle and acquiring a lifelong veneration for cultural achievement. Of course, Lorenzo never displayed Alexander's military genius. But the balance was not all in the Macedonian king's favor. Lorenzo was an Alexander minus megalomania. One cannot imagine him weeping because he had no more worlds to conquer. His subtle intelligence alerted him to far more complexities in the world of Florence and its neighbors than he could hope to conquer in a lifetime.

A vital part of Lorenzo's education was acquired from other members of his family.[7] Edwin Arlington Robinson expressed the all too prevalent American view of the Medici when he wrote in "Miniver Cheevy":

> Miniver loved the Medici,
>   Albeit he had never seen one;
> He would have sinned incessantly
>   Could he have been one.

Admittedly, there probably were not true saints in the family, even though there were cardinals and two popes, three if one counts a distant relative. But the Medici were on the side of the angels more often than most great families of Renaissance Italy. And some members, at least by comparison with their contemporaries, were model citizens.

Ficino was available as a tutor because Lorenzo's grandfather Cosimo was his discerning patron. A devoted student of Plato's writings, Cosimo had adopted Ficino as a member of his family, providing him with a house of his own and a regular income and commissioning him to translate all of the Greek philosopher's works into Latin. In Cosimo himself, Lorenzo had an example of personal enjoyment, and public patronage, of the arts. The old man was the first great art patron in Florence. He beautified the city with churches and palaces, commissioning the great Brunelleschi, among other architects and artists. He also brought to the handling of the city's finances the same shrewdness that had built his personal fortune into one several times larger than any other in the city. When he died he was affectionately called "the Father of His Country."[8] And, as we have seen, his son Piero, despite his gout, not only continued intelligent patronage of art and learning but also brought knowledge and insight to the conduct of foreign affairs. He made Lorenzo his apprentice and then his invaluable assistant. Lorenzo's mother, Lucrezia, a woman with clean-sculptured features and wise eyes,[9] was devoted to the church, her family, and the arts. She was a competent poet and is credited with influencing her son to become one.

The Medici dated their greatness from Cosimo's father, Giovanni,[10] a businessman and wily politician, who retained the confidence of the common people while building a great fortune, and became the real power in Florence long before assuming the office of gonfalonier of justice, the chief political post. Giovanni left his descendants a banking business that sustained them for generations and a piece of advice that they ignored, none more flagrantly then Lorenzo. The advice was "Be as inconspicuous as possible."[11]

Perhaps the most significant lesson that Lorenzo learned from his family was that the present could learn from the past in order to build for the future. Lorenzo was first a product, and then a molder, of a society that as much as any other in history combined an enthusiasm for tradition with the excitement of fresh discovery. When Lorenzo was an impressionable boy, his father was one of that society's chief exemplars.

In pursuit of his goal of building a Florence as preeminent intellectually and culturally as it was economically and politically, Lorenzo was as flamboyantly conspicuous all his life as he was in the tournament in his seventeenth year. But the performance was a calculated one rather than a spontaneous expression of personality. Those privileged to visit him privately in the palace from which he rode out in such splendor were surprised to see him clad in sober garments in a setting of great simplicity.[12] The public loved a show, and colorful pageantry flourished in Italian sunshine. But beyond all that, it was a means to dramatize the link between old traditions and new adventure. The connection was not always made explicit in words, as in the personal motto on Lorenzo's shield at the tourney, but it was presented repeatedly in symbols readily understood by the populace.[13]

In his second year as leader, Lorenzo stumbled badly in a way that caused many to wonder whether the young man, despite his precocity, was seasoned enough for the job. The Florentine economy depended on wool as much as England's ever did. The thing that placed its woolen textiles ahead of competitors' in world markets was the brilliance of its alum-fixed dyes. Florence and its allies had a European monopoly of alum. When a new alum deposit was discovered in 1471, Florence thought it had no special cause for worry. After all, the mineral was in the area of Volterra, a modest town that was virtually a Florentine fiefdom. Volterra retained a considerable degree of autonomy in strictly local affairs, but both its chief executive and its military commander were appointed by the Florentine government. However, when the town signed a contract to permit mining of alum by a private company from Florence, some of the townspeople rioted. They had visions of the local potential for prosperity being bargained away by the politicians. The town officers wavered, and Florentine authorities intervened for the company. When the rioters did not retreat, Lorenzo, without attempting to negotiate, sent in mercenary soldiers. After a month's siege, the Volterrans surrendered upon the promise that neither the inhabitants nor their property would be harmed. Once within the town, though, the mercenaries broke ranks and became a plundering mob.[14]

The tragedy has continued to darken Lorenzo's name to this date. There are, however, some mitigating circumstances. Several of Florence's tributary provinces were restless and eager to test the mettle of the dominant city's young leader. He could exchange verses with the best of them, but could he trade blows? By a show of force, Lorenzo had ended the threat from Prato, another subject town, shortly before the Volterran revolt. Too optimistically, he hoped for the same result this time. That the Medici chief did not intend to break a promise is evidenced by the fact that the duke of Urbino, who commanded the mercenaries, intervened repeatedly to protect women and children and hanged some offenders under his command. On learning what had happened, Lorenzo rushed to the scene and tried to relieve the suffering of the victims. But little could be done. The futility was underlined later by the discovery that the alum deposits in dispute were practically worthless.

Lorenzo had not acted as a monster, but he had demonstrated fallible judgment. He knew that mercenary armies were notoriously undisciplined and far more given to assaulting unarmed civilians than to attacking their counterparts on the battlefield. In his eagerness to end the revolt before rebels found encouragement in other towns, he shoved this disturbing fact into the back of his mind. Tommaso Soderini, the man chiefly responsible for engineering the smooth succession of Lorenzo to leadership of Florence, had cautioned the young man to avoid such action against the Volterrans. After the fiasco, he said, "To me the place seems rather lost than won; for had it been received on equitable terms, advantage and security would have been the result; but having to retain it by force, it will in critical junctures occasion weakness and anxiety, and in times of peace, injury and expense."[15]

Even when others were most displeased with him, Lorenzo was sustained by the love and labor of his brother Giuliano. Blessed with classically regular features in sharp contrast to Lorenzo's twisted nose and general homeliness, he was considered handsome by many. The brothers' unselfish appreciation of each other was one of their most appealing traits. Of course, the close relationship excited jealously among some who thought they deserved a more favored place in Lorenzo's counsels. Enemies of Lorenzo, aware of his reliance on his brother, believed that both siblings must be eliminated if leadership of Florence was to be wrested from the Medici.

The most powerful enemy of the Medici brothers was Pope Sixtus IV, whose nephews coveted control of Florence. To achieve this end they allied themselves with the Pazzi family, Florentine nobles who resented the prominence of the Medici. Supposedly, the pope gave his blessing (nonprofessionally) to the plot on the condition that no one be killed. Whatever the arrangement, the nephews teamed with the Pazzi to murder Lorenzo and Giuliano. In fact, the Pazzi became so deeply involved that ever since then the conspiracy has borne their name. What the pope's nephews did not know was that, while the Pazzi were delighted to help eliminate the Medici, they were determined that the pope's nephews should not fill the vacuum.

The opportunity for assassination came in April 1478, when the Medici brothers were staying at their hillside villa outside the city. One of the pope's nephews, Rafaello Riario, and his retinue were at the nearby Pazzi villa as the guests of old Jacopo dé Pazzi, head of the family. The Medici brothers unwittingly facilitated the plans for their own assassination when, in a gesture of conciliation, they invited the Pazzi and their guests to a great banquet.

But Giuliano became sick and was absent from the festivities. Killing Lorenzo alone would alert everyone to the plot and still leave his brother unharmed. So the conspirators revised their plans. They told Lorenzo that young Cardinal Rafaello Riario, the pope's grandnephew, was particularly eager to view the fabled art works of the Medici Palace. So Lorenzo invited the prelate and his retinue to return with him to the city, where they would all attend high mass, and afterwards be his midday dinner guests. The scheme was to slay the two Medici brothers when they rose from the meal. But Sunday morning it was discovered that, while Giuliano would make the effort necessary to attend mass, he still felt too sick to be at dinner. It seemed that ill health would yet lengthen Giuliano's life.

The conspirators, however, were determined. Killing the Medici brothers at mass would be particularly difficult, and even to the hardened plotters murder in a sanctuary must have seemed especially revolting. But the religious service seemed to offer the best opportunity. The conspirators had brought along one of the pope's mercenary soldiers to be the chief actor in the homicide. They now instructed him to strike at the instant of elevation of the Host, a convenient signal and one marking the moment when the intended victims would be bent over in worship. The man protested that he could not add "blasphemy" to murder.

Less scrupulous than the hired killer, the pope's nephews and the noble Pazzi proceeded on their own. Two priests in the party accepted the assignment of killing Lorenzo. Cardinal Riario, probably an innocent decoy, walked with him to the cathedral. A little behind came Giuliano with Francesco dé Pazzi, a prancing, primping popinjay whom he probably did not take very seriously. Before they entered the church, Francesco slipped his arm around Giuliano, ostensibly in a gesture of friendship but actually to determine whether Giuliano had taken the precaution of wearing a coat of mail beneath his clothing.[16] He had not.

At the elevation of the Host, the assassins sprang upon their victims. One thug drove his short sword into Giuliano's heart. Francesco dé Pazzi then stabbed him again and again in such a manic frenzy that he accidentally stabbed his own thigh. At the opposite end of the choir the two priests in the plot struck at Lorenzo with their daggers. One gashed his throat, but Lorenzo snatched his ceremonial sword from its scabbard, parried the next thrusts, vaulted over the balustrade of the choir, and took refuge in the sacristy. A pandemonium of shouts and screams echoed through the nave. Someone sucked Lorenzo's wound in case the wounding blade had been poisoned. Except for the possibility of infection, the injury itself was not as bad as it looked. Confused noises reached him and his supporters closeted with him in the sacristy.

Lorenzo sent a boy up the organ loft to report on the scene. The lad told him that Giuliano was lying in a pool of blood. A fierce pounding on the sacristy doors suggested that the enemies were eager to finish their work. But the boy said that the hammering was by massed supporters of the Medici. The would-be killers had escaped. Lorenzo ordered the doors opened immediately. His loyal supporters poured in and carried him safely to the Medici Palace.[17]

Attempting to persuade the people (as he had perhaps already persuaded himself) that the whole murderous plot was an effort to strike down tyranny, old Jacopo de' Pazzi dashed on horseback to a public square, shouting, "Popolo e libertad!" (The people and liberty!). Blocked from entrance to the plaza, he rode to his own house and, finding insufficient protection there, fled to the mountains.

Meanwhile the archbishop, a key figure in the plot, was captured with about thirty of his followers when they invaded the Medici offices to seize the government. The masses, loyal to Lorenzo and his family, roamed the streets to hunt down the Pazzi and their allies. Soon, one by one, the archbishop's attendants were thrown out of the windows of the palace. Finally, the archbishop himself, still clad in his bright vestments, exited an overhead window with a rope around his neck and danced grotesquely in the air as life drained from him. Before long, Francesco, dragged from his bed in the Pazzi mansion, wearing a rope around his neck instead of a brocaded collar, the hair that he had dressed for several hours each day as disheveled as that of any ruffian in the mob, joined the archbishop. Before the largest audience of his life, the prancer pranced his last.

The hill people captured old Jacopo and carried him back to Florence. There he was tortured, probably in an effort to learn details of the plot. The authorities permitted his household servants to take him away for decent burial in his family chapel. But the people's appetite for vengeance had not been glutted. They pulled the body from its grave. Juvenile street gangs became its escort, beating the corpse as they dragged it along. Friends and relatives were startled to hear a knocking on their doors and cries that Jacopo had come to visit them, only to find that the youngsters were slamming the corpse against the panels. Eventually the boys threw the body into the Arno, and crowds gathered on a succession of bridges to see it bob along on its course to the open sea.

But Lorenzo's troubles were not washed away. He had conducted himself admirably both when attacked and later when, despite his fresh wound, he had appeared on a balcony to assure the townspeople that he was alive and un-bowed. The people felt a closer affinity for the Medici than for the Pazzi, partly because the Medici had stressed an affinity with them since the days of old Cosimo. The Medici had not so much flaunted their glory as made it part of a community pageant of shared triumphs. And Lorenzo had called his fellow citizens to a future whose prospect exhilarated, rather than frightened, because it also embraced their past. In fact, Lorenzo was now a hero to Florence. Probably nothing else could have made him so popular overnight as the attempted assassination. But none of these things melted the implacable enemy in the Vatican.

Sixtus IV was frustrated that members of his family had died in an assassination attempt that had failed against its chief target. He was enraged to learn that Lorenzo had consented to the execution of conspirators who had escaped mob vengeance. He was not mollified that Lorenzo had given the pontiff's grandnephew Cardinal Riario the benefit of the doubt and permitted him to return to Rome under escort. The pope first ordered the confiscation of all Medici property in Rome. This was a punishment that the Medici could endure and the citizenry of Florence could shrug off. Next he excommunicated Lorenzo and all Florentine officials. The Florentines did not shrink from them as unregenerate sinners. But eventually Sixtus denied benefit of clergy to all the citizens of Florence. Hell yawned before them—not an abstraction but a sea of flames in which they could be tortured through all eternity.

Lorenzo told his people that, if they wanted him to, he would give himself to the pope as a prisoner in exchange for lifting the papal curse from them. The Florentines refused.

The pope then declared that, if Lorenzo was not surrendered, the Vatican would make war on Florence. The Florentines' civic pride was aroused. The tourneys and pageants of the Medici had fed the citizens' spirit of independence and nurtured an audience response courage. Conscious that they were actors on the stage of history, they defied the pope and prepared to fight.

When war was declared in July 1478, the armies of Sixtus IV and King Ferrante of Naples invaded the Tuscan plains. Florence's allies, Milan and Venice, rallied to her support. Before long most of the small Italian city-states were aligned with one side or the other. The aid of Venice and Milan was more theoretical than real. Venice's war energies were consumed by a struggle with the Turks, and Milan's reigning family were too busy fighting each other to battle anyone else. Florence was defended by an army of mercenaries that, as we have seen, had little stomach for armed combat.[18]

Lorenzo's situation would have been immediately hopeless if the invaders of Tuscany had not been dependent on the same kind of mercenaries. Although Ferrante's army overran a Florentine army camp designed to check their advance and chased Lorenzo's fleeing mercenaries back to the city, they abandoned pursuit to lay siege to a small town along the way. Before the siege was resolved, the traditional fighting season ended and the invaders proposed a truce, which was promptly agreed to by the Florentines. Renaissance Italians were far more aggressive in business, and far bolder in the fine arts, than in war.

Lorenzo the realist had time to ponder his situation. It was perilous for Florence and seemingly ultimately hopeless for him personally. Though the Florentines, even under papal edict, had rallied to him with an ardor almost unprecedented among the Italian states, he knew that the human spirit is much more vulnerable to daily attrition than to sudden threats. And the people were living under the threat of eternal damnation to themselves and the families they loved. Even those who doubted that the pope had limitless influence with the Almighty must have had troubled moments when they were not sure. Their dissatisfaction would grow for other reasons as well. The contending armies had not done a lot of fighting but, in chasing, fleeing, and foraging, they had done a lot of trampling. Crops had been destroyed, food was scarce in the city, and pangs of hunger were more persuasive than twinges of sympathy. On top of these troubles, Lorenzo had had to add to the tax burden to support the war.[19]

Most leaders in Lorenzo's position would have seen no alternative to surrendering to the pope other than the folly of waging war to the death, or to the breaking point of the remarkable loyalty of his followers. But Lorenzo was far more resourceful than most. Seeing clearly that neither he nor his government could survive continuation of the war, he admitted to himself that his personal surrender was the only means to peace but conceived that he need not surrender to the pope. He could place himself in the hands of Sixtus' ally, Ferrante, king of Naples. This might seem an even more fearful expedient than surrender to the pope. This was the same Ferrante known as the cruelest ruler in Italy, the man who kept the fully dressed mummies of his enemies as guests in his home. But Lorenzo had no idea of winding up in the king's mummy collection. The Medici chief had a justified confidence in his own powers of persuasion. He was determined to have a try at convincing Ferrante that his kingdom would be more secure if the balance of power in Italy was not tipped in favor of the pope, as surely it would be if Florence were conquered.

Lorenzo was not on such terms with Ferrante as to make a direct approach to him feasible. But perhaps something could be arranged through Lodovico, newly emerged as the effective head of government for Florence's ally Milan. "The Moor," as he was called because of his dark complexion, was a wily man who, though technically only regent for his nephew, actually was a dictator. He had not been spokesman for Milan at the start of war with Naples, and he had not made himself particularly offensive to Ferrante. First, Lorenzo obtained Lodovico's promise to support his diplomacy if he should surrender to Ferrante. After a while, the Moor reported to Lorenzo that, if he would put himself at Ferrante's mercy, the king would receive him honorably. Unsure how trustworthy that promise was, or whether the king of Naples had any mercy, Lorenzo nevertheless sailed for that kingdom. At least one ambassador from an Italian state had been murdered while visiting at the court to which Lorenzo was headed.

Nothing can take away from the courage of the Medici leader in this bold action. But it must be conceded that he took pains to see that the Florentines would be fully aware of his heroism. On the way to Naples he sent a message back to his own state:

> "It seemed to me that the agitated and disturbed condition of our city demands acts and not words. . . . Seeing that all other endeavors have been fruitless, I have determined to run some peril in my own person rather than expose the city to disaster. Therefore . . . I have decided

to go openly to Naples. Being the one most hated and persecuted by our enemies, I may by placing myself in their hands be the means of restoring peace to our city. . . . Having a greater position and larger stake in our city, not only than I deserve but probably than any citizen in our days, I am more bound than any other man to give up all to my country, even my life. . . . My ardent wish is that either my life or my death . . . should contribute to the good of our city."[20]

If Lorenzo should lose his life on the mission, he would be revered as a martyr, and his parting message would be recited by generations of Florentine schoolboys.

While he may have been covering all foreseeable possibilities with posterity, the Magnificent, as he was increasingly called independently of his name, had no intention of dying at this juncture. And the same words that made a great valedictory for a martyred statesman would also be a highly creditable and useful message for a living politician.

If it seemed impossible that Lorenzo, alone in the court of the enemy that had pushed his regime to the wall, could be in a worse bargaining position, fate soon proved that assumption wrong. In the course of his negotiations, another Florentine town fell to the conquerors.

But Lorenzo began to interest Ferrante. Contemporaries often talked about the Medici leader's rare gifts of persuasion that made people forget the crude face. The surprising thing is that, whereas history records other examples of physically ugly men exuding persuasive charm, in most cases their instrument of success was a musical and appealing voice. Lorenzo's voice was harsh, even gravelly. But his contemporaries recorded that his thoughts were so apt and his words so well chosen that these qualities, together with a personal warmth that seemed genuine, could often transform an enemy into an advocate.

Lorenzo entertained his captors, King Ferrante and his son the duke of Calabria, while he tactfully instructed them in the realities of European politics. His task of convincing them that Naples would not be well served by a conquest of Florence that magnified the pope was made easier by the fact he actually believed what he was saying. Even so, the ruling house of Naples had no idea of granting peace without exacting a price—especially after heavy expenditures for war and when such a settlement would antagonize the pope. Eventually, the prisoner and his captors agreed upon a peace treaty exacting the payment of large sums by Florence and the cession of a little territory more significant symbolically than substantively. Lorenzo was pleased, but after three months the king still had not signed the document. Lorenzo said that he must return to his duties in Florence and told Ferrante good-bye. Ferrante did not force him to remain; such an action would have violated the treaty to which he had agreed and which might yet prove to be in his own interest. But he did send a letter after his erstwhile "guest," asking him to come back. The captor had become the suitor. Lorenzo ignored the message. Ferrante signed.

The Magnificent returned to a great outpouring of enthusiasm in Florence.

He was the savior of their city, the leader who had risked his life for them and won.

This triumph, in February 1480, dimmed a bit when, as months passed, the duke of Calabria failed to evacuate certain Florentine fortresses he had captured that the peace treaty required him to vacate. And the pope, besides being vexed with the king of Naples, was angry with Lorenzo for subverting the papal ally. He was vengeful and he was restive. Acting either separately or in unison, Ferrante and Sixtus IV could consign Lorenzo's diplomatic triumphs to the ash heap. But one day in August the whole situation changed abruptly.

A Turkish fleet appeared off Otranto and landed four thousand soldiers of the emperor Mohammed II. They sacked the city, slew most of the inhabitants, fortified the town as their own base, and sent out cavalry to pillage the countryside.

At news of what had happened, the duke of Calabria withdrew immediately from the Florentine fortresses and moved rapidly to the south. Alarmed at invasion by the dreaded Eastern foe, Sixtus exhorted all Italian cities to forget their rivalries and move in unison against the enemy of their religion and their culture. He offered forgiveness to the Florentines, and they promptly accepted. Lorenzo let the city commissioners represent him at the ceremony in which the triple-crowned pope, august upon his throne, ceremonially welcomed the Florentines back to the fold.

The duke of Calabria recaptured Otranto, and most of the Italian states prepared to settle down to a period of peace. But Sixtus, still determined to acquire a realm for Girolamo Riario, the same nephew who had played a leading role in the attempted assassination of Lorenzo, joined with Venice to attack the city of Ferrara. In a swiftly changing kaleidoscope of loyalties, Lorenzo and Ferrante united to restore peace. Thwarted at Ferrara, Sixtus declared war on his Venetian allies. Lorenzo now assembled representatives of all the contending powers for a conference, which produced a settlement known as the Peace of Bagnolo. When Sixtus learned that all his efforts for the aggrandizement of his nephew and the destruction of Lorenzo had served only to provide his Medici rival the opportunity to become the foremost statesman in Italy, the agony was more than he could bear. The next day he died.

6

SAINTS, SINNERS, AND SEERS

G IVEN LORENZO'S natural gifts, his education, and the foundation laid by three generations of forebears, it is not surprising that he should have become the successful leader of Florence. But that at the age of thirty-five his squint eyes should survey the Italian scene from the highest peak of eminence in the peninsula was far less predictable. As a daring dreamer he himself would always have deemed the achievement possible, but as a realist schooled in history he would have considered it far from a foregone conclusion.

Most impartial observers of earlier generations would have thought it virtually impossible—not primarily because of any lack in the Medici themselves, though they were regarded as upstart products of trade by some of the old nobility, but because Florence seemed to have almost nothing to lift it to preeminence. Indeed, in the middle of the twelfth century, any Florentine rash enough to predict the eventual primacy of his city would have been laughed at for ridiculous chauvinism.

Yet the fantastic dream came true. In *Public Life in Renaissance Florence* (xx), Richard Trexler presents with remarkable concision the case for Florence as a major model of the creative society:

> The language of its great fourteenth-century (Trecento) writers was on its way to becoming the classical literary language of all Italians, the philology of its humanists led the way in the discovery of antiquity, and the canons of representational art established by its fifteenth-century (Quattrocento) artists would last into the twentieth century. Finally, Florence produced the leading political artists of the age, men whose brilliant reflections on the relation between the cultural and the political unity of their city make Florence not only a natural but an exciting choice for this study.

After the start of the Crusades in 1096, communities throughout Italy had felt a quickening of life like a new birth in some cases and a regeneration in others. The crusaders were foiled in their efforts to retake the Holy Land from the Muslims, but they transformed their own countries in the process. They and their followers brought back to their homelands more than income, pilgrims' palms, scallop shells, and tales of valor. They brought also from the East products and processes as exotic as the desert kingdoms themselves. Trade flourished not only between but even during wars. In one community after another in Italy, enterprising people began mining and manufacturing products for which there would be an eager market in the East, products that could be traded for Eastern productions demanded by Europeans. Caravans of Italian merchants followed overland trails, and merchant ships sailed for Byzantium. The great Italian boot, thrust boldly into the heart of the Mediterranean world, placed this part of Europe out front in the ensuing race.

The nobles, whose pursuit of military glory wasted their substance, became heavily indebted to the newly strong merchant class, and the balance of economic and political power in many Italian communities shifted gradually but relentlessly. The Medici had taken advantage of this tide to become the rulers of Florence.

Cultural commerce inevitably followed the barter of goods. The great merchants ventured with their capital, but they also embarked with their followers on a succession of cultural adventures. The cities of Italy grew in population and sophistication, and surged with the energy produced by the challenge of the strange.

It was not remarkable that Florence should share in this general awakening of Italian communities. But there were several important reasons why the city might not be expected to become a leader, much less *the* leader. Generations after the great stimulation of commercial and communal development, Florence not only was insignificant among the cities of Italy but was not even prominent in the province of Tuscany. It was in no degree lifted above such provincial neighbors as Pistoia, Siena, and Arezzo, and was distinctly inferior to Pisa, and even to Lucca and Fiesole.[1] Geography had given some of these cities reasons to dream of greatness. They were Mediterranean ports in times when the inland sea's routes were paths to glory. Florence, on the other hand, was about equidistant from Italy's Mediterranean and Adriatic shores, as far inland as any city beneath the flaring top of the Italian boot could be. Though the city-state that it became embraced within its sphere of influence alum deposits valuable to the wool industry, the town of Florence as originally constituted was woefully lacking in natural resources. Pisa, as a Mediterranean port, easily outdistanced Florence economically and retained its primacy for generations. Lucca, made the provincial capital under Lombard domination, was Pisa's chief Tuscan rival, living partly on ancient prestige and partly on the fine-honed crafts developed in response to the needs of a luxury-loving court.[2]

Its far inland location was not Florence's only geographical disadvantage. Though the lack of a port was the worst handicap an Italian city could suffer, the lack could be compensated in part by an elevated location commanding land routes leading to seaports. Even this compensation was denied Florence. It had grown up in a valley dominated by the heights on which stood the older city of Fiesole. Determined not to grovel in Fiesole's shadow, the Florentines bristled with a hatred toward their neighbor that far exceeded the hostility ordinarily felt by a small community toward a neighboring colossus. But instead of grumbling and enduring the situation, they decided to do something about it. Fiesole had difficulty even imagining its younger neighbor as a rival. But Florence, despite all the obstacles to its development, was determined not only to rival but to surpass the older city.

Florence, while sharing with other Italian communities the excitement of new trading realms, was hard pressed to keep up with other disadvantaged towns and would seem utterly incapable of challenging a well-established and better-placed neighbor. It might, like some other communities, have found the great adventure in the wake of the Crusades stimulating but ultimately debilitating. Such was especially likely to be the fate of a small contender buoyed by no history of past achievements.

But Florence was saved by its belief that it had such a history. There was no historiography in those days. What passed for history was woven from strands of legend at least as much as from threads of fact. The accepted local histories of Florence conceded the priority of settlement to Fiesole but said that the ancient Romans, being a people of superior gifts and strengths, were able to conquer and destroy Fiesole and to leave something better in its place. Those noble Romans of a golden age, so the legend went, had provided a model city in the vicinity, building on the plains beneath Fiesole a duplicate of Rome itself. The new city, Florence, would be the bearer of Rome's proud traditions and would be charged with the responsibility of preserving for future generations in a large part of Italy those customs and excellencies that had made old Rome the greatest city in the world.

Ferdinand Schevill, in his classic history of Florence, says that a belief that the city on the Arno was the heir to the great capital on the Tiber "became the first and outstanding article of the civic faith with which Florence began her existence." Even so learned a Florentine as Dante gave at least emotional allegiance to the legend. Schevill concludes that "the assertion, strengthened by picturesque particulars, of the noble origin of the Florentines and of the vileness of the adder brood of the Fiesolan neighbors is without the least doubt an appreciable moral factor in that amazing energy with which medieval Florence pushed and hacked her way across every obstacle to a lofty, distant goal."[3] So, when Lorenzo stimulated his people by an appeal to adventure while steadying and inspiring them with a sense of the past, he was augmenting a combination of factors that had sustained Florence and propelled it forward for generations.

Of course, any city with access to Roman culture was an heir of Rome in the sense in which it is said that "we are all Greeks." But the very special sense in which the Florentines believed themselves successors to the ancient Romans gave them both a sense of responsibility to live up to a great tradition and the confidence that as a chosen people they had the ability to do so. In the same way, the Founding Fathers of the United States would believe that as the makers of a republic they were the responsible heirs of the ancient Greeks and Romans, that they were divinely chosen to be the custodians of humanity's "best hope." As with the Florentines, this belief energized them and made them bold.

Achieving a viable balance between tradition and experiment was essential to the success of Florence as a fruitful society. And, of course, the combination was peculiarly effective as well as unusually complex, in that many of the new things that appealed to the sense of adventure were elements of rediscovered classical background and therefore representative of tradition. But even this circumstance is not alone enough to account for the rarely paralleled scale of the intellectual and artistic productiveness distinguishing Renaissance Florence.

One of the most important supporting factors was the respect for both learning and creativity that was constantly shown by a succession of top leaders. Cosimo de' Medici, despite his energetic pursuit of business and politics, was not too absorbed in these activities to be the patron of Brunelleschi, Michelozzo, and Fra Angelico and to sponsor the translation into Italian of all the known writings of Plato. Furthermore, he himself became an earnest student of those works. Three chancellors who served Florence in Cosimo's time— Leonardo Bruni, Carlo Marsuppini, and Poggio Bracciolini—were all leading humanists.[4] Most wealthy men in the city patronized art and learning, some from a love of these pursuits and some because wealth devoid of culture did not command a full quota of respect.

Cosimo's son Piero, despite his ill health, was a surprisingly energetic patron of both art and learning. And Lorenzo carried the process a significant step farther, not only continuing the family patronage but himself becoming a creative artist, an able poet and song writer.

No less important than the emphasis Florence's leaders placed on education was the character of the instruction they sponsored. Some teaching was designed to prepare the student for a specific role, as with religious instruction for Christian service and vocational training in painting or sculpture. But the education available to advantaged children of the upper and middle classes, while perhaps including artistic instruction and almost certainly religious teachings, provided also a broad liberal arts background and encouraged philosophical and scientific speculation. While not as insistent on advanced learning for girls as for boys, Renaissance Florence was not as wasteful of female intellect as most communities in history have been. As we have seen, Lorenzo's mother is credited with awakening him to the delights of literature. And some Florentine women of less exalted rank were known for impressive intellectual achievement. Such was the general regard for the humanities and sciences that some exceptional young men apprenticed to learn a single art studied other disciplines on their own until they became polymaths.

One of the chief characteristics of the Renaissance was an emphasis on maximum development of individual potential. Combined with the study of classical models, it led to an impassioned pursuit of excellence. This ambitious striving promoted rivalry, not only with peers of one's own generation but with older associates and even with heroes of the classical past. In a letter to Boccaccio, Petrarch wrote of the desirability of exalted role models, especially when the situation led to competition. "Ahead of you," he said,

> is someone to absorb envy's first blows, to show you the way at the risk of his own reputation, whose steps will teach you what to avoid

and what to follow, someone to rouse you or shake off your numb-
ness, someone for you to try to equal or to wish to surpass, so as not
to see him always ahead of you. These are the spurs of noble spirits
who have often enjoyed amazing success. . . . And surely, if you search
your memory, you will find scarcely a great general, philosopher, or
poet who was not driven by such spurs to achieve that height. . . .
Envy arouses the lover and the scholar. Love without a rival, merit
without a competitor languishes.[5]

One of the most important characteristics of education in Renaissance
Florence was that it encouraged curiosity about everything. A typically wide
range of interest was indicated by one of Petrarch's followers, the great scholar
Giannozzo Manetti, who said there were three books he knew by heart, the
letters of Saint Paul, Saint Augustine's *City of God,* and Aristotle's *Ethics.* Thus
he united Christian and classic pagan teachings in three languages. He cited as
a "marvelous saying" Terence's assertion, "I am a man, and nothing human is
alien to me."[6] But intellectual curiosity went beyond the realm of the human
to that of the inanimate. The culture was much more friendly than most to
learning for learning's sake. Pure research was encouraged. In this respect, the
society stands in sharp contrast to that of Nazi Germany. Nazi insistence that
all extensive research must be for designated practical ends approved by the
state transformed one of the most fruitful scientific cultures on earth into an
arid land where not only was the intellect less well served but even the breadth
of practical invention was sharply narrowed. In the same way, the flowering of
Florentine arts in a society that supported projects as varied as the tastes of
individual or institutional patrons contrasts sharply with the stultification of
literature, music, and the graphic arts in Nazi Germany. As with science, political pressure for uniformity turned a Germany of tremendous achievement, particularly in literature and music, into an unproductive land. Medici Florence,
though a republic, did not enjoy the blessings of a free society. At best it was
an oligarchy and at worst a tyranny. Sad to say, there were even slaves.[7] But
Florence did not enforce uniformity in its intellectual and artistic life. If it had,
there would be nothing about the words *Renaissance Florence* to resonate so
strongly in human consciousness half a millennium later.

Even given the dual forces of tradition and adventure, the strong interest
in learning and creativity, the separation of experiment from the demand for
immediately practical results, and the freedom to pursue varied explorations of
art and science, Florence still could not have achieved its extraordinary place in
history if the Medici had not provided generations of able and dedicated leadership. Cosimo, Piero, and Lorenzo were certainly not immune to the promptings of personal ambition, but their egos had so merged with their patriotism
that they identified with the people they served.

In Lorenzo,[8] greatest of the Medici, this identification was well nigh complete. His people sensed this. After his daring and remarkably successful peace-
making in Naples, they adored him. This did not mean that he could afford to
regard every citizen as a friend. The assassination of his brother and near loss

of his own life in the Pazzi conspiracy had alerted him to a danger that always existed, and the frequent news of political slayings from one Italian town or another constantly reminded him of the threats. Customarily, when he walked the streets that he loved, he had an armed escort of ten men, one preceding him with an unsheathed sword. Some might regard all this as part of the pomp of office. To some degree it was, but it served a far grimmer purpose. There were occasional reminders: when Lorenzo's spies told him that several men were plotting to kill him, he had the offenders hanged. But Lorenzo did not lose perspective. He was extraordinarily popular; even the best-loved Italian leaders were constant targets of would-be assassins.

And if he was not loved beyond the limits of Florence, he did enjoy throughout most of Italy such respect as no other secular leader was accorded. His services as a peacemaker were in demand almost every time the threat of war between states arose anywhere in the peninsula. Under his guidance Florence was not only the leader among Italian cities but also the most prominent politically.

This primacy carried a price. Even Lorenzo's persuasiveness required the support of military and economic pressures that made interstate diplomacy extremely expensive. These charges upon Florentine economy followed a costly war. Furthermore, they came during a recession felt by every economic class in Florence. Those who glibly assume that a society's most creative period inevitably coincides with its highest prosperity err greatly. The Golden Age of Florence, under Lorenzo's leadership, 1469–1492, occurred during a period of economic decline, and sometimes crisis, throughout Italy.

Admittedly, an earlier period of economic growth had helped to make the Golden Age possible. It had made certain cultural amenities attainable long enough for the Florentines to regard them as necessities. And the leaders of Florence were so convinced of the value of education that they were not ready to jettison its instruments at the first sign of a storm. Less precious ballast would have to go. One supreme legacy of the prosperous era was the continuation of commercial, and therefore cultural, intercourse with many other societies. Although commercial activity was reduced, it was still sufficient to insure that Florence would not be an encapsulated world. An equivalent of the second law of thermodynamics operates as surely in human institutions as in the physical universe: a closed system runs down and tends to disintegrate. Witness China in the Ming dynasty and again in the closing decade of the twentieth century. Witness also the fate of the Soviet Union.

Not depending on the fine line between recession and depression to hold back the rising tide of economic woes, Lorenzo adopted drastic measures. The fact that a society could flourish in times of economic decline did not mean that a government could necessarily survive bankruptcy. He boldly dipped into the dowry fund to meet governmental expenses. The action was by no means unprecedented, but on a large scale it was frightening to the Florentines. The dowry fund was a peculiarly Italian institution and reflected the centrality of the family in Italian culture. Fathers paid into the fund when daughters were born and made payments at intervals thereafter. The resulting accumulation plus interest provided a dowry when each daughter was of marriageable age. Few young women would hope for desirable marriages if they did not have adequate dowries. Any threat to the dowry fund was viewed with as much apprehension and anger in Lorenzo's day as would greet tampering with social security in more recent times.

Another bold financial move by Lorenzo was to change the tax structure to favor the great merchants. Land and buildings became the heaviest objects of taxation while the levy on commercial profits was lightened. This change freed money for investment but was unpopular with the mass of citizens. They resented the high interest charged by rich merchants and the means by which those merchants thwarted the higher exactions prescribed for them under a graduated income tax. To Lorenzo's credit it must be said that he did not spare himself; apparently he was taxed up to 66 percent of his income.[9]

Anticipating popular hostility to those financial measures, Lorenzo first strengthened his own authority, making constitutional some powers that he and his father and grandfather had exercised extraconstitutionally, and adding still others. This he accomplished through the recommendations of a special reform committee that he appointed in April 1480 not long after his triumphant return from Naples. Officially in obedience to the group's suggestions, a Council of Seventy was created to be the controlling element in the government. Membership was for life, and the sitting members were empowered to fill vacancies as they occurred. Not surprisingly, the charter members were all, in varying degrees of devotion, Lorenzo's supporters. To make the government less cumbersome, the Council appointed from its own numbers two permanent committees—the Eight, charged with foreign policy and military affairs, and the Twelve, charged with the direction of finance, credit, and trade.

Lorenzo's changes made the government immediately less democratic in practice but probably saved it in the long run from a descent into unrelieved tyranny. At least, that was the fate of other Italian city-states that tried to meet their economic problems without streamlining their governments. Lorenzo succeeded in accomplishing dramatic changes without letting them seem dramatic. Once again, he was expert in conducting Florence along an adventurous course while providing the comfort of the traditional and familiar. Schevill compares the performance of Lorenzo the Magnificent to that of a magician drawing a rabbit from a "magical hat." "This surprise animal," he says, "was a new council, the council of Seventy; intended to supersede all the existing councils without, however, definitely and finally replacing them. In constitutionally conservative Florence nothing old was ever replaced, even though it no longer functioned in any effective sense."[10]

Lorenzo's enemies sometimes accused him of using the powers of government selectively to favor the Medici Bank. Their charges were not documented, but perhaps could not be in an age when conflict of interest was not a well-defined concept. Whatever may have happened when a man might change hats in a twinkling without altering his mind-set, the fact remains that some whose financial interests were tied to the bank believed that he did not serve that institution nearly so well as he did the state. The bank, while still a formidable organization with "business in every country of Europe and the Levant,"[11] was in decline when Lorenzo came to power, and he did not halt its slow descent.

The chief reason for the reduction of Lorenzo's family fortune, however, was his generosity as a patron of learning and the arts. This was not unbridled profligacy in pursuit of a hobby or unthinking surrender to one tempting prospect after another. It was the result of a deliberate policy framed in accordance with his carefully selected proprieties. In the speech young Lorenzo made on becoming head of his family, he acknowledged that large amounts of the family fortune had been spent by his father and grandfather to advance cultural and other projects in the service of the state. And he signaled his own intentions by saying, "Some would perhaps think it would be more desirable to have a part of it in their purse; but I conceive it to have been spent to the great advantage of the public, and am therefore perfectly satisfied."[12]

Lorenzo's first great service to learning and the arts was in providing a peace in which they would flourish. He not only exercised skillful diplomacy to prevent the outbreak of war between Florence and other powers but kept an unremitting watch over even the smallest states in Italy to spot an incipient conflict, internal or otherwise, and intercept the danger. He was conspicuously the chief force in preventing war among the pope, Naples, and Milan, but only long after his death did studies of his correspondence reveal the amazing skill with which he had labored quietly to defuse potential threats from within small states when, to less acute observers, they appeared to be only domestic crises. Even with Lorenzo's best efforts, war was sometimes unavoidable. In 1484 Florence won a small war with Genoa; and in 1487 Lorenzo led a successful expedition against Sarzana. But viewed against a background whether of earlier Renaissance Italian history or of the potential for conflict in the machinations of virtually every government and its opposition in that troubled peninsula, the Medici chief achieved a peace so seldom punctuated by actual warfare as to be almost unbelievable.[13]

Lorenzo used the peace bought by such unrelenting vigilance and strenuous effort to father the learning and arts that have made the name *Florence* ever since a byword for creative culture. His contributions in this regard were made possible by the work of his father, grandfather, and great-grandfather, and by those scholars and artists who had created a climate that fostered his own development and that of many other people sensitive to intellectual and artistic values. The earlier Medici had spent enormous sums to recover manuscripts of forgotten and nearly forgotten Greek and Latin classics. Some had been snatched from oblivion just before the Turkish conquest of eastern Europe following the fall of Constantinople would have made such rescue impossible.

Lorenzo continued the retrieval on an even grander scale. He sent the eminent scholar Giovanni Lascaria to Asia to buy classical manuscripts. Delighted with the results, he dispatched him on a second and even more spectacularly fruitful quest from which the scholar returned with two hundred Greek works, including no less than eighty whose existence had not even been suspected.

The Medici gonfalonier was as active in the dissemination of the works as he was in their acquisition. True to the entrepreneurial traditions of his family, he introduced mass production to scholarship. In a magnified, time-saving version of the old monastic reproduction of manuscripts, he employed what has been called "an army of copyists."[14] And he founded schools and staffed them with scholars to expound the ancient writings. When he was only twenty-three years old, he founded in Pisa in Florence's territory of Tuscany an institution that became one of the world's greatest universities. He did not just wave a wand of office and order the creation. He planned the school himself, hired the faculty, determined the curriculum, and remained a long time in Pisa to direct the institution personally. The surprisingly young Medici's amazingly extensive role in founding a major university is reminiscent of the aged Thomas Jefferson's dominant role in the organization and direction of the University of Virginia. Lacking the American's architectural skills, Lorenzo did not, like Jefferson, design the buildings of his university. But he did have something that Jefferson lacked in his latter years, a large personal fortune, and he poured into the project from his own resources more than twice as much money as was furnished by the state treasury.[15] Lorenzo's wealth, coupled with the intellectual environment of Tuscany, enabled him to attract to the faculty at Pisa some of the most eminent scholars in Europe.

There was danger that, in raising a new university in nearby Pisa, he would precipitate the deterioration of Florence's own Greek Academy. But Lorenzo avoided a harmful rivalry by making Pisa a center for study of the Latin language and those branches of science whose chief texts were written in it, while the school in Florence continued to be the center for study of the Greek language and literature. Indeed, he drew to the Florentine institution a faculty at least as distinguished as that at Pisa and attracted to it as well brilliant students, not only from other parts of Italy but also from France, Spain, Germany, and England. The first English scholars to learn Greek in the fifteenth century studied it in Florence, and one of them, William Grocin, became professor of Greek at Oxford.

The Florentine state was not only a consumer of learning, but also a producer and exporter. Conditions were ideal for a Florence-centered efflorescence of culture. The city-state's consciousness of its past provided inspiration and assurance, while the influx of bright minds from other cultures, as well as the experiences of its own traveling scholars and merchants, brought the challenge of new things. And, as we have seen, study of the great pagan classics, mingled with meditation on the Christian tradition, produced the stimulus of synthesis. The classical heritage was both reassuringly traditional and, in its rediscovery, excitingly new. There was a call to intellectual adventures both on uncharted seas and in waters marked by long-lost treasure maps only recently come to hand. Given these factors and the kind of leadership provided by the Medici, a perceptive observer could have predicted a society of extraordinary cultural vitality.

There was little danger that Lorenzo's support of academic learning would lead that society into the paths of pedantry. He set an impressive example of creativity, not just in statecraft and university administration but as perhaps the best poet in Italy in his time. His was not the heavily rhetorical trumpeting of the statesman turned litterateur. His love songs, though graceful, were conventional, but his lyrics of country life were alive with authentic details of a Tuscan spring, the figure of a circling hawk or of a stolid peasant on the ground. Classical references abound but as part of the life system of one who has digested them and absorbed them into his very marrow. His landscapes are inhabited not by unnaturalized Greek shepherds and coy shepherdesses escaped from classical odes but by robust Italian country folk. And paraphrases of Parnassian eloquence jostle references from the Christian gospels and fragments of folk songs more often heard in a cottage than in a palace.

The most influential thing about Lorenzo's poetry was that it was not written in Latin or any other classical tongue but in the Italian vernacular of his own day. This was a matter of deliberate choice. He had mastered Latin sufficiently to make it his literary language, as had generations of writers in Italy and other parts of Europe. But apparently a love of his native culture and a desire to make his work easily accessible to those of his countrymen who were not scholars caused him to write in the same tongue in which he spoke. His writing was fed by both ancient sources and the life around him and was in a language traditional to his people but excitingly new in literature. It symbolized perfectly the blend of tradition and experiment that vitalized Florentine culture.

Dante, Petrarch, and Boccaccio had all written in Italian but even their illustrious examples had not been sufficient to lift the "vulgar tongue," as it was called, to the status of Latin. The adventurous spirit of the Renaissance had caused some of its poets to write in their native language but the exaltation of newly discovered Latin works inspired efforts to achieve greatness by using the very vocabulary which the ancients had employed. When he was only seventeen years old, Lorenzo had written in a letter that the Tuscan tongue was a perfectly adequate tool for the creation of notable literature and had cited specific examples to prove his point. He argued that it could become an even more effective literary medium if Florentine writers would only labor to make it so. The idea was no mere boyish whim. As a poet of mature talent who also occupied the highest position in Tuscany, he composed all his poems in Tuscan Italian. George Frederick Young goes so far as to say that "it is chiefly due to these efforts of his that the Italian language occupies the position it now does, instead of the lower plane on which it stood in his day."[16]

Some might argue that the literary transition from Latin to the vernacular would have been achieved in Italy eventually, as in other countries, with or without Lorenzo. Perhaps partly because Italian cities prided themselves on being heirs to Rome, they were not in the forefront of the change. Ninth-century England had led all Europe in the development of a literary vernacular, partly through the genius and energy of the learned King Alfred the Great. But Lorenzo certainly accelerated the lagging process in Italy where, besides the fourteenth-century writings of great poets, there were also some thirteenth-century prose writings in Italian. Lorenzo can certainly be credited with one important achievement in this regard: whereas earlier writers choosing Italian instead of Latin had felt constrained to torture the tongue into conformity with

Latin grammar, Lorenzo used the syntax common to cultivated speakers and letter writers in his own day.

Something else was new about Lorenzo's writing. Although he could produce a pastoral in the best Greek or Roman tradition, he often revealed a surprising knowledge of the life of the rural poor. Since ancient times poets had written about peasants, but they were almost invariably comic figures. Lorenzo did not romanticize the peasants; the ones he pictured were more likely to be snoring after a hard day's work and a full meal than cavorting on the green in picturesque dances. But he took them seriously as human beings, empathized with them as they fled rising flood waters or lost their thatched roof to a fire.

A strong factor in the intellectual evolution of Florence under Lorenzo's leadership was that major scholars and writers were not only the principal beneficiaries of his patronage, and guests at court on special occasions as a token of official support of their endeavors; they were his closest friends. Nearest of all were Politian[17] and Pico, count of Mirandola.[18]

Only five years younger then Lorenzo, Politian was nevertheless the Medici chief's protégé. The canon of Florence Cathedral, he was better known outside Tuscany as a leading humanist. Before his eighteenth birthday, Politian produced a celebrated Latin translation of five books of the *Iliad*. At twenty-six he had a continental reputation as a lecturer on the Greek and Roman classics. Nobody did more to advance philosophy to the status of a science. He was a poet in his own right, and some said the best in Italy in his time. Others said he just seemed so because he was "the most perfect ape of antiquity."[19] He was both traditional and experimental.

Pico, also Lorenzo's protégé as well as Ficino's, was fourteen years younger than his Medici patron. In addition to a mind that many considered the most brilliant in Tuscany, he was said to have a noble character, and even the more superficial advantages of a noble bearing and blond good looks. Though not considered as able a poet as Politian, he was regarded as the best all-around man of letters in Italy. He knew twenty-two languages, including such exotics as Arabic and Chaldee. His nobility did not protect him from a tinge of arrogance. When he was twenty-three years old, he posted in Rome a list of nine hundred theses that he was prepared to defend against all comers. The subjects ranged from ethics, theology, and Cabalistic lore to logic, mathematics, and physics.

To two of the scholars among Lorenzo's close friends we are indebted for a particularly intimate knowledge of other chief characters of the age. Vespasiano da Bisticci gave us *Lives of Illustrious Men*. Cristoforo Landino in his *Disputations* allowed us to eavesdrop on some of the scintillating conversations of Lorenzo's coterie.

One should not picture an ideal School of Athens with large-minded men soaring above all pettiness into the intellectual ether. Some were noble spirits but others were beset with jealousy as they vied for Medici favor. Yet, some of the same arguments that struck sparks of indignation also honed their wits.

One of the chief members of the group was Ficino, the great translator of Plato. As Lorenzo's former teacher, he occupied a special place.

Pico, Landino, and Ficino were mainstays of the Platonic Academy. The name Platonic Academy is somewhat misleading. The institution was not a school for formal instruction, nor was it a formal organization, such as Britain's Royal Academy, the French Academy, or the American Academy of Arts and Letters, created to honor individual achievement or set standards in language, science, or the arts.

Its growth had been slow and unplanned. Old Cosimo de' Medici, in 1439 when the General Council of the Church convened in Florence, experienced a conversion—not to Christianity, because he was apparently already a devout Christian, but to Platonism. He was so impressed by the philosopher Gemistos Plethon, who was a participant, and by his enthusiasm for Plato, that he discussed with him the possibility of creating an academy for the study of Plato's philosophy. Though that plan did not materialize, Cosimo remained convinced that a knowledge of the subject would benefit his own and future generations. As we know, when he discovered young Ficino's intense interest, Cosimo financed his education in the Greek language and philosophy and subsidized his translation of Plato's works into Latin.

Before doing all these things for Ficino, Cosimo exacted from him a promise to become an apostle of Platonism. After the old man's death, the work of translating the *Dialogues* continued under his son Piero and grandson Lorenzo until its completion in 1477. Less than a decade and a half later, thanks to the still-new process of mechanically printing books, the translation was disseminated among the intellectually curious of the upper and middle classes throughout Europe.

The Platonic Academy was always an informal gathering, as much social as academic, hardly more structured than the Sons of Ben in Elizabethan England or the Club of Dr. Samuel Johnson in eighteenth-century London. The academy, like each of the two later groups, was held together largely by a single personality—in this case, Ficino. But as Ficino's chief associate in the enterprise was Lorenzo the Magnificent, most powerful statesman in Italy and one of the greatest in all of Europe, the Florentine institution exerted an international influence not approached by any analogous groups. That influence was magnified by the fact that its members were conscious agents of change, none more so than Lorenzo himself.

Though not a professional scholar or an original philosopher, Lorenzo was a scholarly man of philosophical intellect and, as one of the leading poets of his day, he was accepted by the writers as a fellow artist. He was respected as creator as well as patron. With the strength of their versatility and their genius augmented by their leader's power and prestige, the members—through their publications and teachings—exercised an influence that would be felt in every major city in Europe and eventually in every continent.

Central to that influence was the philosophy of which Ficino was the chief expounder. Platonism was its basis. On Plato's birthday the academy held banquets that were feasts of reason as well as of Mediterranean delicacies. At other times there were private readings from the works of the master or public lectures on him or his latter day disciple Plotinus. These larger gatherings were held in a church or civic auditorium, for the Platonic Academy had no building of its own. Prominent visitors from other European cities brought ideas from their intellectual communities and returned to their homes with new ones in exchange.

Ficino dedicated himself to a revival of Platonism and made no pretense to originality. Generations of historians and philosophical scholars accepted his apparent self-estimate, but scholarship of recent decades has revealed that he was far more than a discoverer and transmitter. His was a work of synthesis so far advanced as to be truly original. Like virtually everything else that distinguished the culture of Renaissance Florence, his work was a contrapuntal harmony of tradition and experiment.

Even if Ficino had worked only to revive pure Platonism, that in itself would have been a radical activity. Medieval scholars had so revered Aristotle that they accepted on his authority statements contrary to the evidence of their own senses. Because the ancient Greek, basing his conclusion on dissection of a single abnormal specimen of one species, asserted that the species normally had two hearts, medieval scientists dissecting a succession of the creatures and finding only one heart in each reported that all the specimens were abnormal. To look for guidance to Plato, the teacher against whose precepts the "infallible" Aristotle had rebelled, was still seen by many as wildly adventurous.

But Ficino went even farther. He compounded the element of change by combining classic Platonism with elements of medieval and Byzantine Platonism, and even medieval Scholasticism. He and his associates apparently were not seeking to synthesize Christianity and Platonism, but they were so imbued with Christianity that they were sensitive to all parallels between teachings of their faith and elements of pagan philosophy. Plato's precepts were much more congenial than Aristotle's for the purpose of such a synthesis. Platonic idealism with its doctrine of the ultimate reality as unseen was well attuned to Saint Paul's statement that "faith is the substance of things hoped for, the evidence of things not seen." It was also easy to read Platonism into Paul's statement, "The things which are seen are temporal, but the things which are not seen are eternal." And into his assertion that in temporal vision "we see through a glass, darkly."[20]

Ficino believed that it was his God-given assignment to reveal to his time the tenets of Plato's philosophy so that Christianity could be buttressed among those for whom faith was not enough. Thus the Florentine philosopher was using the new and radical to support ancient traditions of his native culture.

Perhaps the most influential of all the syntheses of Christian doctrine and Platonic precepts effected by Ficino and his followers was that which transformed Platonic love into something apparently never dreamed of by Plato himself. In the new view, as sensual beauty and sensual love were faint impressions of the ideal archetypes imperceptible by the senses, appreciation of physical beauty and of earthly love could be steps through increasingly rarefied stages toward ineffable spiritual beauty and spiritual love. This perception harmonized the very real Renaissance quest for spiritual elevation with the age's delight in amorous poetry and song and in the beauty of the human body as exhibited in painting and sculpture. Certainly this idea would have been at least as foreign to Saint Paul as to Plato. But it made peace between the medieval tradition of loyalty to the church and the exuberant celebration of earthly delights in contemporary art. It also reconciled the search for spiritual wisdom with the pursuit of secular philosophy.

As the printing press made translations of ancient classics available to ordinary citizens, and cathedrals and even humbler churches brought to them the new art in all its seductive charm, the public appetite for cultural riches was excited beyond what previous generations would have believed possible. The growth in both private and public libraries was phenomenal. Hordes of scholars in the employ of merchant princes and institutions descended upon the monasteries with all the avidity of the Viking raiders of earlier centuries. But they received a warm welcome, for they were prepared to pay large sums for manuscripts in which the good brothers had seldom found essential nutriment. Indeed, these paying scholars even rescued from monastery privies Greek and Latin manuscripts otherwise destined for humbler uses than their authors had intended.[21]

The extent to which the influence of these discoveries permeated Florentine society is evidenced not only in the works of scholars and creative writers but also in the diaries, letters, and business and professional papers of other persons. The classical writings were discussed at the dinner table and at parties by women as well as men. Bright schoolboys understood the references by their elders. Attorneys and physicians checked the lessons of their training and experience against the records of their classical predecessors. Sometimes to reinforce their arguments for Christianity, sometimes to refute possible heresies, priests and prelates kept abreast of the new learning.[22]

In this quickening of intellectual and artistic life, the Platonic Academy played a larger role than any university in Europe. Though certainly degree-granting institutions were necessary, one of the strengths of the Academy may have been that it was not one. People spent time in its activities because they were zealous to learn. Excited about the possibilities of individual human development, they strove to be all that they could. Intellectual achievement, as manifested by their words and works, was one of the surest passports to the admiration of their neighbors and one of the most dependable foundations for self respect.

Long before Florence's rise to preeminence, Giotto and Petrarch set the pattern for the energized and energizing Renaissance creator. Though distinguished as an architect and sculptor, Giotto (d. 1337) is remembered today principally as Italy's foremost pre-Renaissance painter. The *pre-* may be a quibble in the same sense that there are no hard-and-fast reasons for persisting in calling William Blake and Robert Burns *pre*-Romantic poets. If it looks like a duck, sounds like a duck, etc.

Some of us would prefer to say that, in his professional career, Giotto bridged the medieval and Renaissance periods. Born near Florence, and probably trained in Cimabue's studio in the city, Giotto on his own studied classical works and labored to revive the old ideals while giving them form in ingeniously innovative ways. He by no means discarded medieval ideas of composition, but in his religious scenes the individual humanity of the figures asserts itself before we become aware of the esthetic pattern. Giorgio Vasari, in 1550, called him the first artist to paint in the "good modern manner," and few art historians since have disputed the claim. For almost half a millennium, Giotto has been honored as "the first of the great Italian masters." He taught Italy a new way to paint, and Italy taught the world. His followers, some of them his pupils, fanned out through the Italian peninsula, making converts everywhere. More than two centuries later, Michelangelo, in spite of his own bold genius, or perhaps because of it, was even more Giotto's disciple than any who had had the benefit of his living tutelage.

In Lorenzo's time Florence still had strong reminders of Giotto's influence. As official architect to the city, he had designed the now world-famous Campanile, which combines the light, soaring quality of medieval Gothic with the order and balance of the classic tradition. When its sounding bells direct the eye upward along its soaring but earth-anchored mass, it is an ideal symbol of the healthy tension between the traditional and the adventurous that was so largely responsible for Florentine glory.

Unlike Giotto, Petrarch was not a son of Florence, but more than anyone else he was the father of the Renaissance in that city and every other in Italy. He is remembered as the first modern lyric poet in any language, but even more as the world's first humanist—one who pursued the study of ancient classical literature, disseminating it for the enlightenment of others, and in the process developing individualistic values and habits of critical thought. Born in Arezzo in 1304, he was the son of a notary who twenty-one months before had been banished from Florence after a quarrel with one of its political leaders. The family became practically itinerant as the father moved from place to place in search of employment that he deemed worthy of his talents. After a general education at Carpentras, at age twelve Petrarch began the study of law at Montpelier. His mother died two or three years later, and the grief-stricken boy told of his love and loss in poems that later became part of the admired Petrarchan canon. It is impossible to know how much their published form owes to subsequent revision, but the teenager was obviously a precocious poet.

Working with legal jargon convinced Petrarch that his future lay with literature instead. He took minor religious orders, a step involving few onerous duties but providing security and the leisure to pursue his writing and studies. He joined the household of Cardinal Colonna in Avignon and had ready access to the intellectual stimulation and worldly glitter of the papal court. Any lingering parochialism was rubbed off in contact with international notables of both ecclesiastical and secular society.

In that place and time, professional service to the church, while forbidding marriage, did not preclude a fully sensual life. Petrarch fathered at least two illegitimate children. But all the idealism in his love for woman was centered from the age of twenty-three on the mysterious Laura whom he saw for the first time on Good Friday of 1327 in the Church of Santa Clara at Avignon.

Whether she was already married we do not know, but for some reason, moral or otherwise, she refused Petrarch's attentions. True to medieval traditions of courtly love, he celebrated his unrequited passion in poetry. Petrarch never did things by halves. In the next twenty-one years he celebrated her laugh, her sighs, her blue eyes, and her golden hair in 207 sonnets as well as in less severely structured verses.

The age was one that loved poetry. Petrarch once exploded that not only lawyers and theologians but even his own valet had resorted to versifying, so that any day even cows might "begin to low in verse." One can easily imagine the excitement caused by Petrarch's love poems, for they were the most beautiful yet composed in Italian, a tongue widely celebrated as the language of lovers. Petrarch was not loathe to learn that his tributes to Laura circulated throughout much of Europe in individual manuscripts. Eventually they were bound into songbooks. On the lips of romantic young swains, the words that could not soften Laura melted the resistance of young women even amid the Alpine snows of Switzerland.

Petrarch was not a conscienceless man. His lifestyle, while not a model of chastity, was more restrained than that of many who carried far heavier ecclesiastical responsibilities. And he was thankful to his God for the gift of life. But his tonsured head was filled much more with the imagery of Virgil, Cicero, and Seneca than with the ruminations of Saint Augustine and other fathers of the church. When he heard or read the name *Rome,* he thought of the *Aeneid* before he remembered the Vatican.

Even his passion for Laura was touched by this still older passion for the classics. Repeatedly he celebrated her as a nymph or dryad. His scholarship and his poetry were both fed by classic springs. He became a diplomat, and his travels gave him opportunities to collect the Latin literature he loved. He personally discovered in Verona a precious lode of Cicero's letters. Although Roman literature led him to its Greek models, these he had to read in translation, for he never mastered the older language. In 1340 he was seen so much as the inheritor of the classical traditions of literature that both Paris and Rome sought to crown him with the laurel wreath of poet laureate. Some unkindly suggested that he had campaigned for both honors, hoping to be granted one, and then found himself with an embarrassment of riches. He, of course, accepted the proffered wreath of Rome.

He was triumphant but not at peace. Kings welcomed him to their courts, but his new-won laurel crown and purple robe made him a conspicuous target for the pointed pens of erstwhile rivals. Several years before, he had fled the dissipation of the court of Avignon for the rustic life of Vaucluse (Closed Valley). There he moved into a cottage, wore peasant clothing, fished and gardened, and lived his version of the simple life, proudly reporting that he managed with only two servants. But he was still restless. Earlier he had climbed Mount Ventoux (6,214 feet) to satisfy an ambition but had not found lasting satisfaction. Now attaining the peak of Parnassus seemed to bring no more contentment.

Longing for the fleshpots of Avignon, he returned to that corrupt city. But another round of dissipation left him with unsated, ill-defined hunger. Much as he prized his classical studies, they were not alone sufficient for his spiritual comfort. He turned back to his Bible, to the writings of the saints of the church and the Scholastic theologians of medieval Europe. He quit his profligate ways and returned to Vaucluse.

He did not, however, abandon his classical pursuits or the writing of beautiful poetry. In letters for publication, he addressed Homer, Cicero, and Livy as though they were his contemporaries. In a sense they were, for he had made himself a product of the environments that produced them. But in his mind they now also lived side by side with the Old Testament prophets and the disciples of Christ. He now saw Plato as an intellectual precursor of Saint Paul, a sophisticated Athenian John the Baptist preparing the way for Jesus. In his own mind, Petrarch reconciled Christianity and classical philosophy sufficiently to find a measure of peace. But in the process there was enough healthy tension to awake his diverse gifts and enable him, as the most influential writer in Europe, to point the way to a society drawing strength from both traditional Christianity in its medieval forms and the excitingly rediscovered classical lore. Perhaps Petrarch had unwittingly foreshadowed this role when, after receiving his laurel wreath in Rome, he placed it on the tomb of Saint Peter.

For the rest of his life, he remained faithful to both Christianity and classical learning and succeeded in reassuring many, though not all, of his contemporaries that there was no conflict between the two. In 1362 his friend Boccaccio wrote him in a state of great perturbation. His regrets about having written the *Decameron* were exacerbated by the deathbed vision of a Carthusian monk who said both Petrarch and Boccaccio would be damned throughout eternity if they did not quit their profane studies. Boccaccio's way of dealing with the problem was interesting. He planned to stop writing, to burn his previous works, *and to give his library to his friend.* Petrarch wrote a lengthy reply appealing to his friend's reason. He concluded:

> What else can I say? I know of many who have attained the highest saintliness without literature; I know of no one excluded from it by literature. . . . [and] while all good men have the same goal, many are the ways to it and great the variety among those headed in the same direction. One man walks more slowly, another faster; one unobtrusively, another more conspicuously; one takes a lower path, another a higher one. All have a blessed journey, but surely the higher, the more conspicuous it is, the more glorious; whence it follows that uncouthness, however devout, is not comparable to literate devotion. Nor can you give me an example of a saint from the unlettered mass whom I cannot match with a greater saint from the other group.[23]

7

GOLD COINS AND
A GOLDEN AGE

AFTER PETRARCH'S DEATH, a century passed before Florence, following his example of amalgamating classical philosophy and Christian tradition, poured into the arts the energy and ingenuity it had hitherto devoted to commerce. Meanwhile the great poet-scholar's influence had quickened artistic impulses in other Italian cities, and elsewhere in Europe, as it would continue to do for generations. The indirect influence is incalculable for, if perhaps no one person deserves the title "Father of the Renaissance" often accorded Petrarch, he was at least the movement's chief catalyst. The lines of direct influence, though, are clearly marked in more than one art, extending to Michelangelo in painting; to Pierre de Ronsard in the revival of the French language in memorable literature; to Friedrich Klopstock and his dramas and epics that changed German literature, as well as to Heinrich Heine, who contributed some of its best-loved lyrics; and to famous English poets as diverse as the organ-toned Milton and the fluting Shelley—not to mention a long line of Italian writers reaching at least to D'Annunzio in the twentieth century.

Of course, Florence had not neglected the arts in the years before Lorenzo. As we have seen, painters, sculptors, poets, and scholars enjoyed the patronage of his father and grandfather and other great merchants. And though Florence had exiled a living Dante for political reasons, it was not disposed to let the world forget that the dead Dante was one of its sons. But, until Lorenzo, no Florentine leader had seen the support of high culture as the principal reason for obtaining wealth rather than as an expensive diversion made possible by its acquisition.

Commercial and political activity had long marched hand in hand in Florence. Probably no community in Europe persisted more steadily in ridding itself of the vestiges of feudalism. A leading historian of the city says that "if Florence may be said to have achieved its independence in the year 1250, it had been steadily moving toward that goal for almost two hundred years before that time."[1] And again: "More clearly than any other Italian commune the Florentine burghers recognized that they were bringing a new social order into the world and that, as a consequence of their revolutionary activity, the emperor, who stood at the head of the traditional feudal system, was their inalterable enemy."[2] Therefore, in the contests between emperor and pope, they consistently sided with the pontiff so as to hasten the process of evolution. They devoted themselves to dangerous games of war, politics, and business, sometimes with zest, but almost always with the hope that, as a result, life would be better for their descendants. The situation recalls John Adams' statement:

> I must study politics and war that my sons may have liberty to study mathematics and philosophy. My sons ought to study mathematics and philosophy, geography, natural history, naval architecture, navigation, commerce, and agriculture, in order to give their children a right to study painting, poetry, music, architecture, statuary, tapestry, and porcelain.[3]

The boldness and ingenuity of the Florentines made their progress to capitalism something more than the toiling evolutionary process that it was in most Italian cities. In Florence, as in other communities, there was the slow transfer of wealth from nobles whose expensive tastes outlived their incomes to enterprising merchants patiently accumulating capital to lend. While the lords kept up the pageantry of power through great tournaments and costly visits with full retinue to the papal and imperial courts, the substance of power passed to the businessmen who quietly lent them money at rising rates of interest. But in Florence, though the opportunities for capitalist growth seemed less than in a score of other cities, progress was suddenly accelerated by a brilliant move.

One by one, Italian cities bent their knee to the emperor and successfully petitioned for the right to coin silver pennies. Eventually, Lucca, Pisa, Sienna, Arezzo, and Volterra each minted its own penny, varying the silver content according to the exigencies of municipal finance. Expert money changers became an unwelcome but necessary third party to innumerable transactions, for specialists were needed to determine the relative values of the fluctuating currencies. Florence had a treaty with Pisa under which it used the sister city's penny in exchange for certain trading privileges. A quarrel between the two led to a brief war in 1222 that ended the reciprocal arrangement. Florence was not content to petition Emperor Frederick II for the privilege of making its own penny. Instead it waited until the years 1234–1237 when the emperor was involved with many problems far from his palace. When he had to rush to Germany to quell a rebellion led by his son, the Florentines seized the opportunity to introduce a coin of their invention. But it was not a penny; it was a solidus, a silver coin equal to twenty pennies.

The Florentines had given solid reality to a monetary unit that until then had existed only as an abstraction. Other cities followed suit, but Florence was first in the field and its leadership was respectfully, if enviously, acknowledged. Furthermore, the quality of the Florentine coin was so scrupulously maintained that it inspired confidence.

Frederick II topped the Florentines by issuing his own gold coin, the first minted in the West since the fall of the Roman Empire. But the imperial mint was closed at his death. Into the breach stepped Florence with its gold florin, equal in value to twenty solidi. Moreover, the city made it an article of faith to maintain the full gold value of the florin through all vicissitudes. The florin became the standard of monetary exchange throughout Europe and even in North Africa.

Ensuing generations of Florentines applied to politics, and eventually to learning and the arts, the same innovative spirit and dedication to quality that enabled their city to forge ahead of numerous well-placed competitors in the race for financial preeminence.

The transition from emphasis on finance to stress on learning and the arts was not abrupt. After all, Florence's great patrons of art were of necessity men of wealth. And some of them pursued scholarship, and even art, in their own right. Several prominent historians were also successful businessmen. Some combined art or science with business to the enrichment of both fields. Paolo del Pozzo Toscanelli (1397–1482) was an astronomer, geographer, and writer, but he was also one of the most prominent Florentine businessmen. He collected the geographical lore of the ancients and amplified it by study of voyages in his own time. He pursued knowledge for its own sake but applied it for practical purposes as well. As early as 1474 he supported with a map his contention that an Atlantic voyage along the latitude of Portugal would be a shorter way to East Asia than the much-vaunted Portuguese route around the Cape of Good Hope. With his knowledge of geography and of celestial navigation, he was able to predict consumer demand and determine the most practical routes so that he built an import-export business linking most parts of the civilized world.[4] He added a giant gnomon to Florence's Cathedral of Santa Maria del Fiore to make astronomical measurements. Thus a church dedicated to one whose birth star had brought astronomers from the East was graced not only by a cross-tipped steeple but also by an instrument of the new humanism that in its way proved again that "the heavens declare the glory of God."

The crowning glory of the cathedral, indeed of Florentine architecture, was the dome designed and constructed by Filippo Brunelleschi (1377–1446). Besides being a great architect, engineer, and mathematician, he was—with another architect, Leon Battista Alberti (1404–1472)—responsible for one of the most revolutionary developments in the history of art. These two developed the concept of geometrical perspective. This made it possible for artists to represent spatial relationships on a flat surface in accordance with an exact geometrical formula. The gain in realism was astonishing. Eventually, proud of this new skill, painters created trompe l'oeil stairs and hallways that seemed to invite intrusion. Heretofore the most sophisticated artists had had no more precise idea of perspective than in a general way to make figures in the background smaller than those in the foreground. Perspective completely dominated painting by professional artists in the Western world until the twentieth century, when some European and American artists became fascinated with what then seemed the novelty of perspectiveless Eastern art. Even so, there have been far more gains for perspective in oriental painting than for Eastern flatness in the works of the West.

Brunelleschi's associate Alberti played the chief part in transmitting a knowledge of Roman architecture to fifteenth-century Europe. He had studied assiduously the drawings and compilations of the ancient Roman architect Vitruvius, and he himself became famous for his own designs in the Roman manner. His role in Italy's transition from the traditional Gothic to a Roman style sufficiently long gone to be, in effect, new was dramatically symbolized in 1450 when he placed over the Gothic structure of the Church of San Francesco Rimini a "Roman skin" of round arches and fluted pillars straight out of Augustan Rome.[5]

In other works Alberti accomplished a blend of the two styles. Originality was prompted in part by the fact that an ancient architecture known chiefly through public buildings dedicated to the uses of Roman religious and civic custom was not immediately translatable into something appropriate to the demands of Christian ritual or domestic comfort. But there was also stimulus in fresh acquaintance with another culture, so that Alberti used considerable ingenuity in creating architectural masterpieces that excited by their novelty yet bore reassuring marks of the familiar. Sometimes, as in the Palazzo Rucellai, which he designed for a great merchant, he leaned more toward the classical style while enlivening it with such devices as Roman orders one above the other as in the Colosseum, a practice then unusual in a private mansion.

At other times, as in the facade of the church Santa Maria Novella, he retained such Gothic features as pointed arches and a rose window while joining the narrow upper story to the broad lower one by the imaginative use of classical scrolls. In several other churches notable in architectural history, he found an animating tension in solving the problem of combining Roman forms with the soaring naves and crouching chapels of his medieval heritage. But, whether he inclined toward the newly rediscovered classical style or to the one more traditional to the culture that produced him, Alberti operated within a narrow zone that included enough of the novel to excite and enough of the familiar to reassure.

For all his brilliant innovations, Alberti was not so original a genius as his colleague Brunelleschi. Young Filippo Brunelleschi received no university education. He was apprenticed to a goldsmith, but this was in a Florentine society that made little distinction between artists and artisans so long as the quality of work was high. And, of course, it was also a society in which there was so much excitement over diverse learning, and so much prestige accorded those who acquired it, that the gifted autodidact had no dearth of inspiration. From goldsmithing, Brunelleschi moved on to sculpture. Fascinated by the relations of volume and space so much a part of this art, he studied not only the esthetic principles involved but also the scientific basis. At the age of twenty-four he competed for the honor of designing bronze doors for the baptistery of San Giovanni and lost to Lorenzo Ghiberti (1378–1455). Within a few years, the victor was recognized as the greatest sculptor in Florence. Nevertheless, the ambitious Brunelleschi scorned to persist in any art where he was only second even in his home town and set out for Rome to study the ruins of antiquity.

The north doors that Ghiberti designed remain today an admired masterpiece, combining the pleasant but perspectiveless flow of medieval design with some attractive classical features. This success earned him a commission to create a set of bronze doors for the east entrance. In the years that passed before the completion of this assignment, Ghiberti, while retaining the graceful line characteristic of the best medieval art, drew on the knowledge of anatomy made available by humanistic scholarship and made use of recent discoveries of perspective to fill his panels with lively crowds. Florence was enraptured, and eventually the world was. These magnificent doors, known as the Gates of Paradise, faced no serious challenge from any other sculptured portals until Auguste Rodin's creation of the Gate of Hell through long labor culminating in 1917, the last year of his life. The French sculptor began with his Italian predecessor's work as a guide and then, influenced by English art of a later date, eliminated the separately formed scenes in favor of an integrated whole. Thus Rodin, like Ghiberti before him, made his work great by combining the strong appeal of tradition with the excitement of innovation.

The painter who made the most dramatic use of Brunelleschi's and Alberti's studies in geometrical perspective was a young Florentine named Tommaso Guidi (1401–1428). Despite the meticulousness of his work, he is remembered today by his nickname, Masaccio, "Sloppy Thomas." Decorating the Brancacci Chapel in the Carmine Church in Florence, he produced some of the world's greatest frescoes and moved that art in one stride from the Gothic of the Middle Ages to the realism of the Renaissance. Many critics have called him "the father of modern art." Among the artists directly and deeply influenced by him are Michelangelo and Raphael. Masaccio's own indebtedness to Brunelleschi is emphasized by his design of the great throne of the Brancacci frescoes in Brunelleschan style. Seldom is the line of descent so clear through a succession of great artists.

When Brunelleschi, defeated in the competition with Ghiberti, left for Rome to study the remains of classical architecture, he was accompanied by another remarkable young man, Donato di Niccolo di Betto Bordi, who called himself simply Donatello (d. 1466). Later Donatello returned to Florence and even served as Ghiberti's assistant in the execution of the doors. But both young men gained in Rome a familiarity with the forms of classical architecture and sculpture that vitalized their work.

Donatello's greatness, and his appeal to his own generation, came from his extraordinary ability to combine traditional forms with bold innovations. The combination expressed not only the universal, but also the particular essence of Renaissance Florence and its humanism. For this reason, Donatello is often called the first modern sculptor. His art was the perfect expression of a human-centered culture. Generations of sculptors before him had consistently produced statues of human beings who were auxiliary to architecture. The male figures leaning or pushing against the walls, or perhaps embedded in them, were as ancillary to the buildings they decorated as the caryatids who supported beams. With his freestanding figures, Donatello proclaimed the individuality, independence, and importance of the individual human being.

This same individuality was expressed in the forcefulness with which he impressed his own personality on the material with which he worked. And the independence was expressed in his professional life as when, believing himself insulted by the patriarch of Venice, he told that exalted politician, "I am a patriarch in my art as you are in yours." The pride of the reply also reflects the honored place of the arts in the sculptor's native Florence.

Though the two friends were both Renaissance pioneers who had profited from the lessons of Rome, in the application of their skills Donatello and Brunelleschi were as different as in personality. A traditional anecdote about the time when they both carved crucifixes is probably factual and certainly representative. Donatello said, "To you it is given to make Christs, to me peasants." While Donatello's men have an earthy or sensuous reality, those of Brunelleschi have an idealized, intellectual quality. It is therefore appropriate that Brunelleschi devoted his best efforts to architecture, which, while one of the arts most influenced by practical considerations, is also one of the most intellectualized.

The most conspicuous example of the intellectual ideal and the practical execution in his art is the great dome of the Cathedral of Santa Maria del Fiore, whose impact on Europe we have already seen. It was a triumph of engineering as well as esthetics. It is not only that Brunelleschi created a dome that presented the essence of the Pantheon in Gothic terms but that, undeterred by pronouncements that he could not erect such a roof without scaffolding, he so combined the medieval technique of outer shell and inner shell with the new science's teachings as to achieve the seemingly impossible. Physically the work was made feasible by a balance of tensions. As such, it was an appropriate symbol of Florentine culture, itself made feasible by a balance of tensions between the traditional and the new. Though not so obviously so, Donatello's sculpture worked because of a similarly healthy tension between the familiar and the Gothic. Most critics are agreed that the tradition-bound sculpture of Florence in the second half of the fourteenth century "was doomed unless it managed to tap a fresh source of inspiration."[6] It did precisely that when Donatello infused his work with invigorating humanism, preserving at the same time enough of the familiar to succeed in stimulating the public without alienating it.

Of all the arts in which Florence excelled in the age of Lorenzo, painting is the one in which its influence has been the greatest. This circumstance is usually attributed to the fact that Florentine painters, while experiencing the stimulus of certain classical principles exhibited in other ancient arts, had access to no Greek, and few Roman, paintings. The art of the brush, particularly in the generations of uncontrolled environment, was a far more vulnerable medium than its sisters. Because of the lack of specific examples from ancient Rome or Athens, painters' allegiance to classical principles could not degenerate into slavish imitation of actual works.

In the absence of such models, Florentine artists turned to the only ones readily available, eleventh- and twelfth-century Byzantine works. The revival of painting in Constantinople in those years had resulted in the production of many icons and altarpieces for Greek Orthodox churches. Some of these were imported into Italy, and some Greek artists, seeing the demand, moved their studios there. Not surprisingly, they soon inspired Florentine imitators. One of these was that same Cimabue to whom Giotto was apprenticed.

As we have seen, Giotto vitalized the beautiful, but stiffly formal, art of the Byzantines. Italian pre-Renaissance and early Renaissance painters applied to the panels and walls on which they worked the same jewel-like colors and rich gilding that characterized the icons and altarpieces from Constantinople. Giotto's paintings bear strong marks of the same influence, but the humanizing techniques by which he transformed patterned friezes into crowds of living individuals, making figures as expressive as faces, were widely and rapidly imitated. A later generation of artists were so much in his debt that they came to be known, a little deprecatingly, as the Giotteschi. Some were to such an extent mere copyists that they threatened the balance of tradition and innovation essential to the continued vitality of their art. A few, however, followed the master's example but also worked in his liberation of spirit, carrying even further the humanization and individualism that Giotto had introduced. Thus they saved Florentine painting from stagnation. Critics have pointed out that the direction in which they moved—in this case toward greater realism—was not in itself significant. The important thing is that they did not stand still.

One of the greatest of the venturing artists was Sandro Botticelli (d. 1510). This Florentine native had been a particular protégé of one of Lorenzo's cousins. Other rich men of Florence vied for the privilege of sponsorship. This competition, if it could have been foreseen, would have been a great comfort to Botticelli's father, who reported on a tax return that his thirteen-year-old son was both backward and sickly. Botticelli was apprenticed to the gifted painter Fra Filippo Lippi (1406–1469), a butcher's orphan raised by Carmelite friars. Lippo, as he was called, showed considerable skill in composition, even in the especially demanding feat of painting on circular panels. The pioneers in perspective had stuck mostly to rectangles. Lippo was in excellent standing with the church until he blotted his copybook by abducting a nun who subsequently bore his child.

Before 1470 Botticelli apparently was affiliated with the workshop of Andrea del Verrocchio (1435–1488), a Florentine painter and sculptor who dared to be innovative in some of the ways opened by bold predecessors. It was in 1470 that Botticelli, then about twenty-five years old, struck out on his own as a painter, capturing the admiration of Florence in general and Lorenzo in particular. His first work to excite great attention was a symbolic figure of Fortitude—appropriately so, not only because he would forge ahead with pioneer boldness but also because symbolic painting would become his particular forte. The symbolism in some of his works is read easily in the context of time and place, but in others it is so subtle as to produce endless disputation among critics.

No great problems are presented by such works as *The Adoration of the Magi*, in which bright-robed members of the Medici family appear as the worshiping kings. The picture presented a traditional event in contemporary guise, but the practice of painting one's patrons into Bible scenes was an old one and may have reflected no more than the painter's desire to flatter those who sponsored his work. A far subtler symbolism began appearing in Botticelli's paintings in the years of his association with Lorenzo and other Neoplatonists. After emulating the styles of various other Florentine painters, Botticelli emerged with a style of his own—one so ethereal and refined and yet so clearly linked to the joys of earth that it seems to embody Ficino's concept of ascending from earthly loves and beauties to the ideals shining in the firmament of ultimate reality. Botticelli's two most famous works are as representative of this spirit as any creation attributed to him. One of these is *Spring*, which some art historians insist is more properly denominated *The Realm of Venus*. The other, one of the most familiar paintings in the world, is *The Birth of Venus*, or *Venus Avienz*, referred to irreverently by some souls still far removed from the Platonic ideal as "Venus on the Half Shell."

Some believe that both paintings were created to commemorate the grand tournament of 1475, in which Giuliano de' Medici made his public debut much as his brother Lorenzo had in the famous one of 1469. Critics have pointed out parallel narrative elements in *Spring* and a vernacular poem by Politian in celebration of that tournament. They have also noted that several years later Politian wrote a poem in Latin in which he assimilated elements from such classical poets as Horace, Lucretius, Ovid, and Columella, and have said that these same inspirations are apparent in Botticelli's picture. Scholars now believe that the painting was executed as a wedding present for one of Lorenzo's young Medici cousins and his bride. The three Graces of classical lore dance in the foreground. In one bit of symbolism presenting no difficulty for the interpreter, Cupid aims an arrow at one of the three. Venus, standing amid orange trees, looks approvingly on her little minion.

Giorgio Vasari, the sixteenth-century painter and architect who became the first modern art historian and critic and to whom we are indebted for so much information on Renaissance artists, appears to have been the first writer to call the painting *La Primavera*.[7] Certainly the springtime setting is evident. Zephyr, herald of the season, blows his breath on Chloris to make the nymph fertile. Mercury, representing among a host of other things May, the month of the Medici marriage, is conspicuous. But, above all, the picture breathes the spirit of spring. It recalls Lorenzo's words that "Paradise, whoever would wish to define it closely, means nothing other than a most pleasant garden, abundant with all pleasing and delightful things, of trees, apples, flowers, vivid running waters, songs of birds and in effect all the amenities dreamed of by the heart of man; and by this one can affirm that Paradise was where there was a beautiful woman. . . ."[8] Lorenzo had dealt with gold all his life, but for him Paradise was far nearer to the traditional bower of Eden than to any vision of streets of gold. Of course, it was also close to the pastoral ideals of classical Latin verse in the days when Rome had become urban enough to see beauty in the bucolic.

Above all there is a springtime lightness in the three Graces that recalls Lorenzo's line in *Corinto*: "I would see your white foot dancing across the

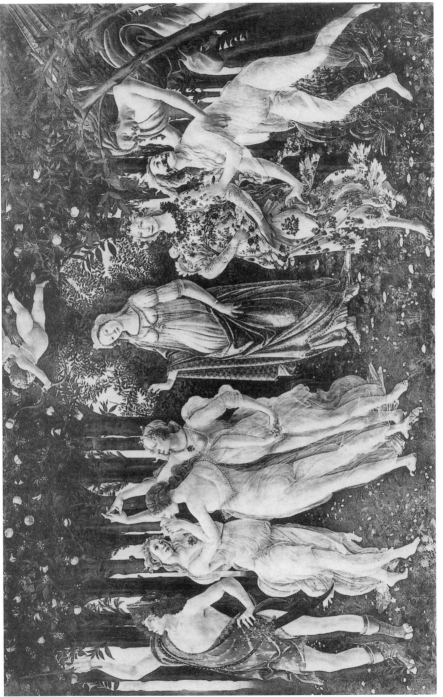

Fig. 1. *La Primavera*, by Sandro Botticelli (1444–1510). Uffizi, Florence, Italy. Alinari/Art Resource, N.Y.

sward, kicking at the wind."[9] Although the classical origins of the figures are evident, they are distinctly Renaissance Florentine creations. Their diaphanous garments reveal sensuously curved but elegantly attenuated figures. In this respect they differ from classical models. They are far less earthbound than the *Venus de Milo*. Though the *Winged Victory of Samothrace* seems capable of soaring into the air, Botticelli's three Graces seem compounded with the air itself. They suggest the Platonic ideals as interpreted by the Heaven-aspiring, earth-loving humanists of Florence.

At the same time, they bear the unmistakable stamp of Botticelli's individual genius. Even some perceptive children who have seen two or more of the artist's paintings from this period can instantly identify his style when encountered elsewhere. His best works are remarkable examples of originality expressed through a harmonious blend of the traditional and the new. And they are even more extraordinary for the degree to which they express both the essence of a community culture and the inimitable essence of an individual creator.

The Birth of Venus excels even *La Primavera* in grace and linear refinement. It is a less cluttered picture. The goddess of love, in the clean nakedness of her beauty, dominates the scene. Though a Roman deity is represented, she is as free of classical restrictions as she is unfettered by clothes. Her gently curving torso and slender limbs are innocent of the requirements of formal anatomy but, in their flowing grace, obedient to the laws of esthetic appeal. The winds, in the guise of two men, blow their breath upon her, stirring her blond tresses as they waft her across the ocean on a scallop shell, one of the most beautiful natural forms. Earth, barefooted but otherwise clad as a dignified Florentine matron, awaits her, holding out a capacious cloak. Is this because pure beauty, as a Platonic ideal, is not in its fullness part of earthly experience? The mundane revelation is necessarily incomplete.

The air has a preternatural clarity, as if it were an ether between earth and Heaven. There is a sense of the space around and behind Venus as with some of the figures in the twentieth-century paintings of Dali and Magritte. A surprising departure from medieval and pre-Renaissance predecessors! Swirling rhythms, subtly implied, push across the canvas until they encounter at the far right boldly vertical trees stalwart as a breakwater. This work is always cited by those art historians who call Botticelli the "inventor" of Renaissance style in the visual arts. Like *La Primavera*, it was a pleasing blend of the traditional and the new, but now the new component was excitingly larger. The result is not only a monument of art history but a living masterpiece of undimmed appeal. Bernard Berenson has praised Botticelli as "a lineal symphonist of a refinement of harmony beyond the achievement of any European artist before or since."[10]

Anyone familiar with *The Birth of Venus* will be surprised, if not shocked, upon seeing for the first time a somewhat later production of the artist, the *Virgin with Christ Child and Six Angels*. It is a circular altar panel whose composition is managed with an adroitness reminiscent of circular paintings by his old master Fra Filippo Lippi. The rhythms, like those of *The Birth of Venus*, are superb. Though eight figures are crowded into one circle, there is nothing

Fig. 2. *The Birth of Venus*, by Sandro Botticelli (1444–1510). Uffizi, Florence, Italy. Foto Marburg/Art Resource, N.Y.

static about the scene. Whereas the *Primavera* and *Venus* were deliberately conceived allegories of neo-Platonism, one apparently based on a poem by Politian and the other on Politian's "La Giostra," the picture of the Virgin obviously derives from the New Testament of the Christian Bible. But the startling thing is that the face of the robed Virgin is that of the naked Venus in the earlier picture. The shape of the head, all the facial features, and the blond tresses are the same. This apparent coincidence may simply arise from the fact that the same model posed as the central figure in both paintings. But Botticelli was an intensely serious and deeply contemplative artist who did few things by accident. He was greatly influenced by the literature and learning of Renaissance humanism and especially by the teachings of his fellow Florentine Ficino. Regardless of how they came to be, the identical faces of the classical love goddess and the Christian Holy Mother are together an appropriate symbol of Ficino's theory, given wide circulation by the Platonic Academy, that even profane love, if refined, may grow toward the love that is divine.

Botticelli's paintings were among the most extraordinary in the history of art partly because of his natural gifts and their development under the tutelage of such masters as Verrochio and Fra Filippo Lippi. But they were also enriched by an intellectual environment that acquainted him with the concept of the Platonic idea and a sophisticated sense of the possible relationship between eros and agape. And the lyrical bent of his painting was enhanced by his knowledge of poetry. He had not been given the formal instruction provided for rich men's sons, but his own questing mind, set loose amid the wonders of Florence, had grown far beyond the narrow bounds of his apprenticeship. His talents and his curiosity had made him a welcome member of the Platonic Academy, learning from some of the foremost scholars in Europe. He was one of those bright youngsters who benefited from the Florentine atmosphere, at its peak in the age of Lorenzo, that encouraged and rewarded intellectual and artistic progress to a degree matched in many societies only by the adulation accorded some athletes and popular entertainers.

It was not always possible for such a gifted young person to acquire a certificate proclaiming that he was educated, but it was quite possible for him to acquire an uncertified education of considerable breadth and depth. The sons and daughters of the poorest citizens had the opportunity to read in public libraries, even amid the personal collections of Lorenzo. And the art galleries of his palace were open much of the time to the general public. Members of the unprivileged classes in Florence had an opportunity to sample intellectual and artistic riches not enjoyed then by the gentry, or even the lesser nobility, in most of the world's cities.

The intellectual and artistic versatility of Botticelli, great as it was, was to be overshadowed by that of another protégé of Lorenzo's—one whose name is often the first to spring to mind at the words *Renaissance man*. Leonardo da Vinci did not seem destined for fame. He was born in 1452 near the Tuscan village of Vinci. His mother's given name was Caterina but her surname is unknown. He was the bastard son of Piero da Vinci, a Florentine attorney, later notary to the Signoria of Florence. The father married in the year of Leonardo's birth, but his bride was not the boy's mother. Piero outlived this wife and married twice more, eventually fathering a number of legitimate children. The first of the legitimate offspring, however, did not arrive until Leonardo was a man. And the father had recognized the illegitimate son from the beginning and had reared him partly at his rural home in Vinci and partly in Florence.

This same Leonardo, at age thirty, left Florence for Milan. Learning that Ludovico Sforza, regent of Milan, sought the services of a military engineer, an architect, a sculptor, and a painter, he applied for all four positions. He explained that he could design bridges; facilitate sieges; make effective and easily transported cannon; build ships that could "resist the attack of the largest guns and powder and fumes"; devise means of arriving at fixed destinations by noiselessly tunneling under an enemy's trenches or even under a river; "make covered chariots, safe and unattackable which, entering among the enemy with their artillery, there is no body of men so great but they would break them"; and "in short, according to the variety of cases, contrive various and endless means of offence and defence."

At this point, one is reminded of the boastful recitative of W. S. Gilbert's "very model of a modern major general." But this was only the beginning. "In time of peace," Leonardo continued, "I believe I can give perfect satisfaction and to the equal of any other in architecture and the composition of buildings public and private; and in guiding water from one place to another."

After listing all these practical accomplishments, he said, "I can carry out sculpture in marble, bronze or clay, and also in painting whatever may be done, and as well as any other, be he whom he may." Knowing that Ludovico wished to erect a noble monument to his father, Leonardo assured him that any work he produced would "be to the immortal glory and eternal honor of the prince your father . . . and of the illustrious house of Sforza." He concluded, "I commend myself with the utmost humility."[11]

Apparently very little humility was possible. Yet Leonardo had not included in his list of accomplishments two that posterity would accord him. He did not say that he was an expert geometrician or that he was one of the world's two greatest anatomists in his century.

All great and versatile intellects are in large part autodidacts. But varied formal instruction, particularly in the early years, is always important. For Leonardo it began at a local school in the Vinci area, where he showed an aptitude for mathematics, drawing, singing, and playing the lute.

Vasari tells us that, when a neighbor asked him to paint a dragon on a shield, the schoolboy carried into his own room a collection of lizards, crickets, grasshoppers, butterflies, serpents, and bats from whose varied forms he composed one "great, ugly creature."

Tradition supported by a fair amount of evidence says that, when Leonardo was about fifteen years old, his father got Verrocchio to take him on as an apprentice. Though there is strong reason to doubt Vasari's story that Verrocchio abandoned painting because of the superiority of his pupil's work, there is ample evidence to support Vasari's assertion that the young man soon surpassed his master. When Leonardo was twenty years old, his father's third wife presented him with his first legitimate child. The young artist moved into Verrocchio's house.

Leonardo's personal notebooks contain many tributes to the human eye. Once he wrote, "Here forms, here colors, here the character of every part of the universe are concentrated to a point; and that point is so marvelous a thing. . . . These [indeed] are miracles. . . . In so small a space it can be reproduced and rearranged in its whole expanse."[12] It seemed that his own eyes were ambitious to accomplish that very feat. He observed everything around him—works of art and works of nature. He would follow an unusual face or figure through the streets until every significant detail of it was imprinted on his mind sufficiently for him to reproduce it in a sketch. As time passed, observation of living bodies was not enough; he dissected cadavers to learn secrets of the human mechanism. He observed the stars and the moving clouds that hid them, studied the flow of water in streams and from pipes, and followed the motions of dogs, cats, and horses. Indeed, he depicted horses with a detailed realism not matched in any earlier works now known. His eye served his science and his art. The two disciplines were not compartmentalized in his mind. His anatomical studies advanced science and improved his painting and sculpture.

Art and science were united in his analyses of geometrical perspective and the whole visual process. Sightings of flora and fauna were important to his scientific cataloging and also enhanced his art. He became a botanist partly in the service of his art but even more in obedience to his intellectual curiosity.

Sometimes Leonardo's ears were united with his eyes in the interest of both art and science. He is the first person known to have perceived that water, light, and sound move in similar waves.[13] He wrote about light spreading outward in concentric circles "just as a stone thrown into water becomes the cause and the center of various circles." Descartes in the seventeenth century saw light as consisting of particles. The lordly Sir Isaac Newton rejected the wave theory outright in favor of what came to be known as the *corpuscular philosophy*. While Robert Hooke and Christian Huygens argued in favor of waves, Sir Isaac brushed aside their suggestions. His was a science of atomism. It appealed to his sense of unity to visualize light as consisting of atoms. Eventually he conceded that streaming corpuscles of light might set the ether into motion, thus creating waves. In the nineteenth century Thomas Young and Augustin Fresnel argued for the wave theory so convincingly that their conception predominated until the twentieth century when, as a result of contributions to a theory of quantum mechanics by Max Planck, Erwin Schrödinger, Wolfgang Pauli, Niels Bohr, and others, the pragmatic decision was reached to regard light in some respects as consisting of particles and in others as consisting of waves.[14]

Successive generations of scientific speculators cannot be said to have settled the question of the nature of light. Science is never definitive. But there is significance in the fact that Leonardo was considering, well ahead of anyone else on record, some of the same factors that have continued to tantalize the world's greatest scientists.

Even in matters more susceptible of definition, however, it was Leonardo's practice to move from one fascinating speculation to another, being caught up in a new enthusiasm before following an earlier one to its logical conclusion. There were exceptions, of course. His dissection of cadavers helped to advance both human and equine anatomy far beyond concepts that had prevailed ever since Galen in the second century A.D. And his researches in perspective expanded the work of Alberti and Brunelleschi beyond pure geometrical principles to matters of color perception at varied distances. But Leonardo's was a restless mind and a restless spirit. Partly it was that "divine discontent" which Plato praised as the parent of both knowledge and invention. But it was also seemingly a matter of temperament.

When Leonardo was twenty-five years old, Lorenzo provided him with a studio in the Medici gardens. The next year, the signoria commissioned him to paint an altarpiece, which after all he did not do, but soon after gave him and Botticelli the assignment of painting full-length portraits of two men hanged for their roles in the Pazzi conspiracy to assassinate Giuliano and Lorenzo. A rough assignment indeed for a man of Botticelli's delicate sensibilities, but it must have afforded Leonardo a welcome opportunity to further his knowledge of anatomy!

When Leonardo was still in his twenties, the monks of San Scopeto commissioned him to paint one of the favorite subjects of Renaissance artists—the Adoration of the Magi. He entered upon the task with tremendous enthusiasm, sketching the contours and appropriate flora of the landscape, the architecture of a nearby building, the forms of horses and a cow, and a rich display of physiognomy and anatomy. The Magi he sketched completely naked, including genitalia, preparatory to robing them for the painting. More than fifty people crowd the final work. But perhaps *final* is the wrong word. Leonardo planned a painting of such scope and variety that he never completed it. Seeing no end in sight, the monks awarded the commission to Filippo Lippi, a man accustomed to meeting his deadlines.

Nevertheless, the incomplete painting by Leonardo is recognized today as one of the world's great masterpieces. He is of the tribe, celebrated by Robert Browning, whose reach exceeds their grasp. This painting is representative of Leonardo's work, its weaknesses and its strengths. It is the sort of creation that William Faulkner had in mind when he praised those "splendid failures" that are greater than most successes because they are grander in concept and more daring in the attempt. In any notable work of art, the concept always exceeds the execution, but this was far more true of Leonardo's creations than of most artists', despite the fact that his mastery of technique has been equaled by few. He tended to conceive things on a grand scale and in almost infinite variety. All respects—esthetic, scientific, and philosophical—were united in his mind, and he tried to give reality to all. The resulting painting, though unfinished, is unforgettable. Its powerful rhythms suggest a unity of all creation—clouds, trees, beasts, humans; and the peace and light surrounding the Madonna and child suggest an all-pervasive spirit, immanent and ineffable. Carpers would say that he had "bitten off more than he could chew." Da Vinci might well retort that his subject was not mere matter for mastication.

It was a year after the excitement and the frustration of work on his *Adoration of the Magi* that he addressed to the regent of Milan his letter of application for the positions of engineer, architect, sculptor, and painter. Soon he left Florence for employment at the Milanese court. The letter doubtless intrigued Ludovico, but the impression that the young man made in person seems to have sealed the deal. Much evidence agrees that Leonardo was tall, graceful, and handsome, with facial features as finely chiseled as those on any of his statues. He was athletic in build and extremely strong, able to bend an iron horseshoe in one hand as easily as an ordinary man might bend one of lead. His speaking voice was extraordinarily musical.

Indeed, music seems to have played a key part in Ludovico's enthusiasm for him. Two tales—each a little different but both centering on music—are told concerning Leonardo's warm reception at the court of Milan. One is that Lorenzo sent Leonardo to the regent to deliver a lute as a diplomatic gift. The implication is that an ability to play the instrument was one of those talents that impressed Ludovico. A second story is that Lorenzo won a musical contest in Milan by singing beautifully while accompanying himself on a marvelous lyre that he himself had made in the shape of a horse's head. Ludovico and his court supposedly were enchanted.

Reports of Leonardo's activities in Milan drifted back to Florence frequently in ensuing years. He planned the architectural transformation of the Cathedrals of Milan and Pavin, and was both architect and interior designer for the Castello. The same hand and brain that planned enduring works of stone also designed in silk and velvet the costumes for pageants and tournaments and flattering gowns for the ruler's wife. But Leonardo always found time to paint and sculpt.

Most notable of his artistic productions was *The Last Supper*. He worked on the painting for three years, sometimes sitting for hours before the wall without wielding a brush. At other times he would dart away from other employment to paint a few rapid strokes, only to walk out immediately afterwards. The Dominican friars whose wall he was painting feared that he would never finish. The prior suspected that Leonardo was lazy and tried by verbal prods to move him faster. Little did the prior realize that some of an artist's most important work is done without a brush or chisel in hand.

Leonardo, who had learned in Florence to appreciate the dignity and importance of a true artist, was thoroughly tired of the prior's interference even before the ecclesiastic prevailed upon Ludovico to speak to the artist about the delays. According to Vasari, Leonardo explained to his employer that, in portraying Christ's Last Supper with his disciples, he faced two great difficulties—finding a face benevolent enough to represent Jesus and another hateful enough to be Judas. But he said that, as he saw more and more of the prior, he began to see the possibility of using that man's face as the model for Judas. Reportedly, Leonardo was permitted to finish the painting in peace.

The tension of the scene and the marked individuality of the faces, which have survived deterioration from the elements, vandalism, and sometimes clumsy efforts at restoration, have helped to make the picture one of the two most famous in the world. The other of this supremely famous pair would also be the work of Leonardo.

Years before Leonardo painted *The Last Supper*, Lorenzo was aware that he had lost to the court of a onetime rival the greatest artist yet produced in Florence. In 1489 Lorenzo was the generous patron of Domenico Ghirlandaio, a native of Florence who, in the true spirit of the Renaissance, painted powerful contemporaries, Roman statesmen, and Christian saints. He was not a genius in creation, but he was a master technician. Lorenzo respected him for what he was but kept hoping for something more. One day he saw in Ghirlandaio's studio the sculptured face of a grinning old faun. It was instinct with life in a way not true of the works around it. Surprised, Lorenzo asked Ghirlandaio whether the faun was his own work.

"Oh, no, Magnificence," the artist replied. "That is the work of one of my apprentices, Michelangelo Buonarrotti. Do you think he has talent?"

"I am sure of it. How old is he?"

"Fourteen."

"Send him to me, then."[15]

Lorenzo presumably praised the boy's skill to his face, but he told him that so ancient a creature as he had portrayed would not have a full set of teeth. The lad immediately knocked out an upper tooth with a single blow.[16] Lorenzo had found another genius, one who might match da Vinci in artistic talent. Perhaps the boy was also potentially a versatile man of parts. If so, he should have every opportunity to prove it. Lorenzo took him into his household and gave him a monthly allowance. Day after day Michelangelo could conveniently study the statuary in the Medici gardens. He could also acquire philosophical depth and learn a host of things by attending discussions in the Platonic Academy.

Only reluctantly did Michelangelo's father consent to these opportunities for his son. The mayor of Caprese, a small town in the Florentine orbit, he was proud of his family. He feared that his son would become a mere stonecutter.

Days in the Medici Palace, filled with the excitement of learning, passed as agreeably as they could for an adolescent of Michelangelo's unquiet temperament. Mealtimes provided a liberal education; he ate regularly with Lorenzo, Politian, Ficino, and Pico della Mirandola. He did carry through life the mark of one altercation in those years. One day, enraged by the youngster's caustic comments, the sculptor Pietro Torrigiano clenched his fist and, in his own words, "gave him such a blow on the nose that [Torrigiono] felt bone and cartilage go down like biscuit beneath [his] knuckles."

Lorenzo, who himself had gone through life with a broken nose, was livid. To escape his wrath, Torrigiano fled to Rome and became a soldier. Making his way to England, he laid aside the sword for the chisel and produced the magnificent tomb of Henry VII in Westminster Abbey. With his broken nose, Michelangelo even looked a little like Lorenzo, not normally to be considered an advantage, but in this case it may have helped to cement the bond between them.

Soon the young artist was imbibing ideas not especially popular with the humanists at Lorenzo's table and in the Platonic Academy. He was enraptured by the sermons of Girolamo Savonarola (1452–1498), a puritanical embodiment of a strong medieval tradition. Savonarola was a black-robed, black-hooded prior whose monumental Roman nose seemed preternaturally fitted for sniffing out sin. His profile was reminiscent of Dante's, but with the sternness of the fourteenth-century poet transformed into ferocity. Dante made the scenes of the Inferno visible to his readers, but Savonarola could make his hearers feel the hot breath of Hell itself. He seemed the embodiment of Death in old woodcuts, a sight inspiring fear in children, awe in the simple, and solemn reflection in the sophisticated.

His appearance invited caricature, but he was a complex person not easily summarized in a tag line. Some of his personal characteristics, as well as those of Florentine society in the Age of Lorenzo, made him extraordinarily persuasive to the young genius Michelangelo and other beneficiaries of humanist culture, not just to the ignorant. Savonarola was the son of a physician and the grandson of the court physician of Ferrara. His parents sent him to the University of Bologna to study medicine. He left after writing back, "To be considered a man [here] you must defile your mouth with the most filthy and brutal and tremendous blasphemies. . . . If you study philosophy and the good arts, you are considered a dreamer; if you live chastely and modestly, a fool; if you are pious, a hypocrite; if you believe in God, an imbecile. . . ."[17]

At home he brooded over sin, writing a poem about vice in Italy, listing popes among the offenders. He fasted so much that he was transformed into the skeletal figure for which he would later be remembered. He pointed the long finger of indictment at one offender after another. When he was twenty-two years old, a denunciative Lenten sermon stirred him to the depths, and he was even more moved by the response of many who threw ball masks, wigs, playing cards, and erotic art onto a great fire in the marketplace.

The next year he stole away from home to enter a Dominican monastery in Bologna, the city where he had been shocked by so much vice in his days as a medical student. In a humble letter, he told his parents where he was and asked their forgiveness for disappointing them. But when they pleaded with him to return, he replied, "Ye blind! Why do you still weep and lament? You hamper me though you should rejoice. . . . What can I say if you grieve yet, save that you are my sworn enemies and foes to Virtue? If so, then I say to you, 'Get ye behind me, all you who work evil!' "[18]

For six years he stayed in the monastery, seeking the humblest tasks, exalted in his humility. Then his superiors decided that he should go forth and preach. In 1481 he was assigned to the Church of San Lorenzo in Florence. Accustomed to the polished eloquence of worldly scholars who believed that nothing human was alien, his congregation was repelled by his narrow and pedantic didacticism. He may not have diminished sin, but he was certainly reducing his audience. So a practical prior removed him from the pulpit and set him to instructing novices.

Savonarola was not one to concentrate on removing the mote from his brother's eye while remaining unaware of the beam in his own. "I am still flesh like you," he wrote to his family, "and the senses are unruly to reason, so that I must struggle cruelly to keep the Demon from leaping upon my back." He pictured himself as the object of a struggle between Satan and the angels. He became convinced that sacred messengers were telling him that he was chosen to be a prophet. His mission was to announce to the world that the Antichrist was now in the ascendant but that, as foretold by the saints of old, the vengeance of God would sweep away the tyrants, adulterers, and atheists. There seemed to be a concentration of all these in Italy.

The prior assigned Savonarola to preach in Lombardy. From the northern hills there came word of this man, calling sinners to repentance and preaching, like John the Baptist, a message of the Christ to come. Thousands flocked to him. Pico appealed to Lorenzo to ask the prior to call Savonarola back to San Marco in Florence. Lorenzo did. Some have suggested that Lorenzo humored his friend in this matter because he remembered Savonarola's sleep-inducing sermons and could not imagine the same dull fellow succeeding in rousing the populace against their leaders. Stirring within the church in Italy was a spirit of rebellion against civil authority. Better to have this voiced with the ponderous awkwardness of the friar he remembered than by some fiery zealot capable of inflaming others.

When Lorenzo attended mass, he was shocked. It was hard to believe that the dynamic prophet with the hypnotic, burning eyes was the preacher of soporific sermons that he remembered from a few years before. Not all was gloom and doom. Savonarola offered the promise of salvation. "Would you see true beauty?" he asked. "Look at the pious man or woman in whom spirit dominates matter; watch him when he prays, when a ray of the divine beauty glows upon him when his prayer is ended; you will see the beauty of God shining in his face, you will behold it as it were the face of an angel."[19]

He contrasted with this true beauty the naked bodies shown in paintings and sculptures populated with pagan gods and goddesses. And he disparaged the lascivious descriptions found in humanist literature as compared with words of biblical truth. These seductive artistic and literary productions, he said, were prized by men who called themselves Christians but in their lives and their preachments had separated themselves from the ways of Jesus. Lorenzo was not comfortable as he listened to such words from a pulpit founded by his grandfather and heavily endowed by himself. His discomfort was increased by the rapt attention of the congregation.

Worse was to come. "Tyrants are incorrigible," said the preacher, "because they love flattery and will not restore illgotten gains. . . . The tyrant is wont to occupy the people with shows and festivals, in order that they may think of their own pastimes and not of his designs, and, growing unused to the conduct of the commonwealth, may leave the reins of government in his hands."

Not only did the congregation as a whole seem spellbound by this eschatological prophet who had targeted Lorenzo almost as surely as if he had called his name or pointed that long index finger. Among those who listened and were moved were two who daily sat at Lorenzo's own dinner table—not only the young genius Michelangelo but also that continental paragon of learning, Pico, who was scarcely less important to the Platonic Academy than Ficino himself.

Pico had been the most adventurously ecumenical of the thinkers close to Lorenzo, even to the extent of having some of his propositions declared heretical by the pope. Perhaps he felt particularly secure because of the early recognition of his genius and because he was a child of wealth, the son of a prince and himself a count. No matter how much he latched onto the new, many people would still see him in the frame of tradition. He eagerly embraced, and linked with Christianity, the Hebrew Cabala and Arabic teachings. He not only reconciled Plato with Christ as many other humanists did but also, to his own satisfaction, reconciled Plato and Aristotle. He then proceeded to reconcile Judaism, Christianity, and Islam. Almost the only popular belief that he had renounced was the so-called science of astrology; this he condemned in a famous essay.

Every year, it seemed, the heritage of medieval Christianity played a smaller part in his thought and teachings. He was maintaining only a tenuous toehold on his native tradition as he stretched and strained to reach out for ideas foreign to his place and time. At first the experience had been invigorating for him and for the Christian society he served. Now many of his compatriots thought he had gone too far too fast, and he was beginning to think so too. He could not compress his expanded intellect into the narrow span of medieval Scholasticism, but when Savonarola preached about simple faith and strict morals—ideals often breached in older times but ideals nonetheless—he touched a responsive chord in Pico.

Ficino, who at first had hailed Platonism as a support for Christianity, now greeted his students as "brothers in Plato" and burned candles before the Greek philosopher's bust. Many lesser humanists not only admired the Greek gods and goddesses in literature, painting, and sculpture but delightedly imitated their notorious morals. They were not unprincipled. They just thought that the esthetic principle was the only one that should govern their conduct.

In the nineteenth century, Matthew Arnold in a different context would label the two forces contending in Renaissance society, giving them "names from the two races of men who have supplied the most signal and splendid manifestations of them . . . Hebraism and Hellenism." He saw Hebraism as emphasizing "duty, self-control, and work"; Hellenism, esthetics and intellectual ideas. Hellenism had an "ardent sense for all the new and changing combinations of [esthetics and ideas] which man's development brings with it, the indomitable impulse to know and adjust them perfectly." Meaning Western civilization when he said "our world," Arnold asserted, "Hebraism and Hellenism—between these two points of influence moves our world. At one time it feels more powerfully the attraction of one of them, at another time of the other; and it ought to be, though it never is, evenly and happily balanced between them."[20]

Some of us would insist that other contests between tradition and experiment also help to determine the fate of various societies, but in the case of Renaissance Florence, Arnold's terminology is particularly apt. The medieval traditions of the city were strongly rooted in the Hebraic tradition of which the old Christianity with its rigorous rules of conduct was a part. The new humanist faith was inspired by Greek esthetics and love of intellectual speculation. Of course, as is usually the case, one cannot insist too strongly on the literal accuracy of the labels. The Hebraic culture that produced the Psalms, the Song of Solomon, the Book of Job, and the Book of Ruth obviously was no stranger to esthetics. Likewise, the Plato who taught that "desire" and "pleasure" should not interfere with justice was not blind to the concept of rigorous morality.

Lorenzo increased his gifts to the monastery, of which Savonarola soon became the prior, but the preacher did not soften his rhetoric. On the contrary, he pointedly said in a sermon afterwards that a faithful watchdog does not stop barking when a bone is thrown his way. When Lorenzo sent five respected citizens to appeal to the preacher to exercise restraint lest public violence erupt, the ecclesiastic instructed them to tell Lorenzo to do penance for his sins. Lorenzo's supporters obtained the cooperation of a Franciscan friar noted for the popular appeal of his sermons, but when he preached at the same hours that Savonarola did, the Dominican drew overflow crowds.

More than any other person, Lorenzo had made Florence great in Italy and in Europe. He had built its cultural legacy with his largesse and his life. He was the peacemaker of the continent. But he was vulnerable to some of Savonarola's accusations. Though his life was less profligate than that of most Italian Renaissance leaders, he had had his share of mistresses throughout his marriage. Though Lorenzo and his Medici predecessors eschewed royal or noble titles, they arranged the marriages of their offspring for dynastic reasons. Love had nothing to do with it. When Lorenzo said that Clarice Orsini had been "given" him as his wife, he spoke quite literally. After an inspection of the prospective bride, the groom's mother had written in the manner of one appraising a broodmare, "The girl is above the middle height, of fair complexion and pleasing manners. . . . she will, I think, be easy to train. . . . I could not see the breasts, as here [in Rome] they are entirely covered, but so far as I could make out they are decently formed."[21] In time Lorenzo became quite fond of Clarice and praised her virtue as wife and mother. But the husband, like many other prosperous Italians of the day, always felt the need of successive liaisons. Savonarola was persuading some of Florence's citizens that such a way of life was neither admirable nor necessary.

Lorenzo was also vulnerable on the count of distracting citizens with celebrations, vain shows, and pageantry while he increasingly circumscribed their liberties. The fact that he governed more fairly than most hereditary rulers of his day, served more sacrificially, and permitted more free expression than was common on the Continent mitigated this circumstance but did not obliterate it.

Lorenzo was tired and ailing, in the grip of that gout which was the curse of his family and which had brought his father to an early grave. He did not have the energy to continue the fight against Savonarola. The succession of his eldest son, Piero, to the leadership of Florence was pretty well assured, but whether Piero would be able to hold it against enemies aroused by the prior of San Marco was another matter. Lorenzo had more hope for a younger son, Giovanni. Despite Lorenzo's early struggle against papal authority, he was ambitious to have a pope in the Medici family.

Giovanni was not especially prepossessing-looking, but Lorenzo himself had not been either. Like the father, the son was highly intelligent. Through diplomacy with Pope Innocent VIII, Lorenzo had contrived to have Giovanni secretly made a cardinal in 1489 at the age of thirteen. Lorenzo correctly conjectured that, with a leg up over potential rivals, such a bright boy would have an excellent chance of gaining the throne of Saint Peter. So Lorenzo, having by his lights done the best that he could for his state and his family, withdrew to the villa at Careggi where his grandfather Cosimo had died. Lorenzo's wife was dead now and he missed her. His best friends were still loyal to him, but he knew that some of them were no longer loyal to the kind of world that he had helped to create. He himself would certainly not outlive that world. Earlier, in this year of 1492, when Giovanni, now sixteen and officially of age, had been revealed to the world as a cardinal, Lorenzo had been too sick to attend the celebration. Only briefly, and then from a litter, did he look upon the great banquet at the Medici Palace before saying good-bye.

He was saying farewell, too, to the banquet of life. In a long conversation with Piero, he cautioned the son to practice certain virtues to which the father had been faithful and others to which he had not. Politian and Pico came to see him. Lorenzo had regrets. "I wish that death had spared me," he said, "until I had completed your libraries."

And now, like every good Catholic, he wished to receive absolution from a priest. He sent for Savonarola. As the gaunt figure in its black habiliments approached, it was as though conquering Death were entering the chamber. According to Pico, Lorenzo refused to meet certain conditions presented by the prior and received no absolution. According to Politian, the dying Medici met every condition proposed by Savonarola and received the absolution he sought. Each "witness" believed what he wanted to. No one would ever know for sure what had happened at this last meeting of the two strong men, but when the black-clad priest strode firmly from the chamber of the dying Medici, a dramatic shift in power in Renaissance Florence was symbolized with all the grim effectiveness of a medieval morality play.

8

BONFIRE OF THE VANITIES

SINGING HYMNS, Florentine men and women late in the final day of Carnival, February 7, 1497, marched through shadowy streets behind four children dressed as angels who carried an image of the baby Jesus. The infant seemed alive; it was the work of the great Donatello. The destination of the procession was the Piazza della Signoria, where a great cone, 240 feet in circumference at the base, towered 60 feet into the sky.[1] It rose in seven stages, the work of carpenters over some days of concentrated activity, and this tiered construction was reminiscent of some medieval conceptions of the Tower of Babel.

Each tier was designed to hold a different category of vanities. Some had been brought by penitent owners. Others had been collected in house-to-house solicitation by children. On the lowest stage were carnival masks and decorations from festive balls. The next tier held books, some by the pagans Aristophanes, Ovid, and Lucian, others by such "renegade" Christians as Boccaccio and Petrarch. There were multiple copies of a risqué and irreverent poem by Pulci in which Lorenzo had delighted. On the level above were diaphanous garments and such instruments of vanity as perfume, false hair, hair curlers, rouge pots, and depilatories. On the next height were lutes, flutes, handballs, and footballs. Then came portraits of courtesans and nude statues and paintings. The next level held wood and wax effigies of Greek and Roman gods, goddesses, and mythological heroes. At the pinnacle was a bearded satyr, the image of sensuousness and unbridled sex. The cone was set afire at four points along the base, and the flames leaped high as though the fires of Hell were reaching toward Heaven. In the red glare, black robed and black cowled like a shadow materialized, stood Savonarola, his face grim, his eyes burning with a fire of their own.

With the celebratory ringing of bells of the Palazzo Vecchio, formerly the site of conferences of humanists from all over Italy, the symbolism was complete. It is easy to see Savonarola as the evil genius of the event, the implacable foe of art and learning and all secular enrichment of life. In fact, some have gone so far as to picture him as the irreconcilable opponent not only of freedom of expression but of all liberty.

This view of the prior is easily supported by selected quotations from his sermons—too easily. In 1990 Marcia B. Hall stimulated what appears to be a long-overdue revision of the Savonarola stereotype. Too many writers have based overconfident evaluations of Savonarola on other people's slender selections from his sermons. Reading them for herself, Professor Hall discovered such humanistic "themes as the dignity of man, the promise of reconciliation and a life freed from the burden of guilt and sin, and the goodness of creation." Certainly at the outset of his preaching upon his return to Florence in 1490, Savonarola was not like Hawthorne's Puritans, who had so concentrated upon the ferreting out of evil that they could not see any good in humanity. Hall finds internal evidence that Savonarola drew directly from the writings of the humanists. "But while he shared the humanist view of human potential," she says, "he confronted his listeners with their constant abuse of that potential."[2]

Savonarola even shared the eagerness of Florentine humanists to adapt the myth of Florence's heroic origins to serve as an inspiration for public service in his own time. He thought the service should be to church as well as state, and of course an earlier generation of humanists believed the same thing.

The Bonfire of the Vanities, as the ritual burning of "vain objects" was called, might lead us to believe that Savonarola was opposed to all scholarship and all art. But such was not the case. He had been at pains to achieve some learning for himself, including some from "pagan" sources. While he abhorred Ovid's poetic advice on the seduction of women, he seems to have been quite comfortable with Plato. After all, Savonarola's preachments were attractive to such a celebrated humanist scholar as Pico. And Savonarola believed that art had a place, even in the church itself. He argued that art should not be pornographic, and especially condemned the hypocrisy of painting a religious picture whose purpose was veiled when its human subject was not—for example, painting in the name of religious instruction an Eve whose erotic charms invited the eye's caress.

As time passed, Savonarola, like most people engaged in a war, became increasingly extreme in his opinions and demands. But even in one sermon when he told the congregants, "You have many books in your houses that you shouldn't have because shameful things are written in them," and asked them to burn their own books of this kind, he admitted that some "pagan" works could "be good and useful in themselves" and said that he did not reject the knowledge they contained. He did protest, he said, the substitution of such writings for Christian Scripture.[3]

No reasonable interpretation can transform Savonarola, even at the outset of his crusade, into a libertarian. He was as much a foe of free expression as most people in the civilized world in his time. But Lorenzo, for all his praiseworthy support of free expression, which was a bold experiment in his day, was no libertarian either. One of the less laudable ways in which he and his Medici predecessors followed the example of ancient Romans was in providing "bread and circuses" to distract a citizenry whose political liberties were being systematically taken from them. Savonarola's accusation about tyrants was on the mark. While Florence buzzed over Lorenzo's latest gift or the next pageant, he had drawn into his own hands all the strings of government. He did not exploit the republic. He loved it as his mother, but in the course of his career his feelings changed from filial to paternal. He believed he knew what was best for its citizens and was determined that they should have it whether they recognized what it was or not. That under his leadership Florence experienced the most remarkable cultural flowering in Europe shows that, whatever other factors were at work, he must in many instances have been right.

But Lorenzo carried his zeal to a great extreme, saying that "without Plato it would be hard to be a good Christian or a good citizen."[4] Some of the scholars at Lorenzo's court were working to create a "Platonic theology."

In the 1970's the great Italian Renaissance scholar Eugenio Garin found in the library of Santa Maria Novella some of Savonarola's manuscripts hitherto believed lost. They revealed him to be a student of Plato and not purely for refutation. The prior complained that "some people want to make all of Plato Christian. Rather, let Plato be Plato and Aristotle Aristotle; do not make them Christians because they are not." Far from shutting his ears to the arguments of Florentine Neoplatonists, Savonarola discussed them with Pico and others at the San Marco library. Reviewing Pietro Crinito's notes on those discussions, Garin says, "Most interesting of all, however, is the effort Savonarola made in Florence to bring himself up to date with fashionable culture."[5]

But disagreement became hostility and, eventually, uncompromising enmity. An understanding of how humanist scholars became warriors in the camp of Savonarola is afforded by the writings of Giovanni Caroli (1429–1503), a Dominican friar who was several times prior of Santa Maria Novella.

Caroli was a dedicated churchman but at the same time drew inspiration in the writing of his biographies from both Plutarch and Virgil. As an eyewitness to the assassination of Giuliano de' Medici and attempted killing of Lorenzo, Caroli was shocked to learn that some clergymen, and indeed the pope himself, had been involved in the conspiracy. Loyal churchman that he was, Caroli put fidelity to the ideals of Christianity above allegiance to the ecclesiastical organization. He therefore saw as fully justified the anticlerical sentiments of the Medici and other leaders in the wake of the violence in the cathedral.

Caroli seems to have been fair minded as well as thoughtful, so that more than common credence may be given his observations. He saw the seeds of destruction in the fullness of the flowering of Florence. He saw corrupt business practices replacing the mercantile methods of earlier days. The problem was magnified by the fact that business, more than ever before, was becoming the religion of Florence. He contrasted the situation with the communal period, in which a sense of community had nourished almost every phase of civic life. Enmity between certain merchant princes had long existed, but now it seemed to be every man for himself.

The ingenuity applied to the arts was impressive, but Caroli thought that increasingly it was exhibited in useless ostentation. Like Savonarola, he deplored the lavish expenditure on costly ornaments and vain shows when many humble citizens were hungry and poorly sheltered. Even developments in church music seemed to him to symbolize contemporary decadence. Towards the end of the fourteenth century, Florence had been the musical center of

Italy.[6] The city's music was further enriched early in the fifteenth century by Franco-Flemish influence. The new vocal polyphony, Caroli thought, was prized more as an exhibition of dexterity than as a heartfelt expression of piety or spiritual love. It even "rendered the liturgical text incomprehensible." Where much was made of religion, he believed, it was more often bigotry than genuine faith.[7]

Most people, it sometimes seems, have a tendency either to romanticize or to denigrate the past. When Caroli turned the clear light of his reason on the past, there was sometimes a golden refraction from mists of nostalgia. But the light of his logic was a penetrating one. He freely admitted the betrayal of some of Florence's noblest traditions, both medieval and Renaissance, by some agents of his beloved church. And, in the historiographical and biographical works for which he is famous[8] he happily combined the forms of classical writing with subjects appropriate to the medieval tradition, producing essays expressive of two traditional sources but experimental in their combination. A compact and striking example of his facility is the dream sequence and dialogue in the *Liber dierum* in which he recasts eschatologically the lines that Virgil puts into Aeneas' mouth upon sighting the walls of Carthage. Caroli's words would be effective even with readers unfamiliar with the Latin classic, but to those with solid humanistic backgrounds, they carried echoes of the past that presented a complex and fascinating polyphony. As Caroli had a classical education and used it to advantage, not only pedantically but creatively, there is great significance in his conclusion that the increasing troubles of Florence at the end of the fifteenth century arose from "its great rejection of the communal past."[9]

Lorenzo's son Piero succeeded to the leadership of the republic upon his father's death. The power was hereditary in all but name. Although Florence was not a kingdom, the Medici family was a dynasty. Piero was twenty-two, by the calendar a year older than Lorenzo on his accession, but in terms of maturity a decade younger. Superficially, the new ruler had one advantage over his father. He had his sire's athletic figure, which in his case was topped with a handsome face instead of the pugilistic countenance of the elder Medici. Piero, too, was fluent, but the flow of his discourse carried less intellectual freight. Also, he did not automatically enjoy the kind of trust that Lorenzo had earned from many of his fellow citizens by a lifetime of service, especially from the time when he had placed himself in the hands of the king of Naples as a hostage for peace. The ailing Lorenzo had been no match for Savonarola, who was formidable both personally and as the powerful symbol of a society desperate to restore the balance between tradition and experiment. It was unlikely that Piero, even given his youthful vigor, could do better.

The young man was shrewd, though. When the new king of Naples attempted to gain a sort of hegemony over him, Piero dealt with the monarch as effectively as Lorenzo had with his predecessor. The wily Alfonso II offered the new Medici chief a title of nobility and an estate to go with it. This would have technically elevated Piero's social status, but the title of course would have been lower than the king's own and would have been derived from him. In appearance Alfonso II would have become Piero's liege lord and could create a public image favorable to the royal interest. The Medici leader replied, "Your Majesty knows that my ancestors have lived as private citizens by their trade and their estates. Nor have I myself any desire for a station above theirs. . . . Forgive me for declining your offer. If you still wish to confer a favor upon me, pray do so in whatever way you think best, through my bank managers."

Piero's answer reveals both the agility that had helped to keep a Medici-led Florence in the forefront of Italian states and the growing greed that increased its vulnerability to Savonarola's moral onslaughts.

Like his younger brother, Cardinal Giovanni de' Medici, Piero had been tutored by some of Italy's foremost scholars and had come to know them, as well as some distinguished artists, as familiar companions of the family. But, whereas Giovanni continued to seek the same sort of company, Piero seemed to have had his fill of them. He preferred acrobatic athletes to men known for their mental gymnastics. People who groomed horses interested him more than those who cultivated their intellects. Quite literally, professional acrobats and grooms claimed a large proportion of his time. One stableman was his most intimate friend and was presumed to be his lover. Only one intellectual, Michelangelo, was a favored friend of Piero. Some have speculated that the young ruler, weary of sycophants, found the artist's frankness bracing.

Piero sought to be a mover and shaker among the states of Italy as his father had been, but without Lorenzo's diligent study and planning. One of his principal objectives was to insure that the new pope, Alexander VI, the former Rodrigo Borgia of Spain, had due respect for Florence and its chief. In the process he embarrassed his brother the cardinal and so far alienated Ludovico Sforza, duke of Milan, as to jeopardize beyond repair the Milanese-Florentine alliance so carefully cultivated by Cosimo and Lorenzo. Ferdinand of Naples demanded that Ludovico abdicate or face the combined armies of his state and Florence. The stability of the Italian peninsula was destroyed. Ludovico appealed to King Charles VIII of France to intervene in the crisis.

Charles had a small claim on the Neapolitan throne, one just large enough to satisfy the demands of voracious ambition. The French monarch not only began planning a campaign to seize Naples but indulged in heady dreams of subjugating all of Italy before retaking Constantinople for the West and eventually planting a standard in Jerusalem. Both Venice and the pope took refuge in neutrality. The king of Naples appealed to Florence for assistance and obtained a commitment, then suddenly died. Besides complicating an already unsettled situation, this event stirred the superstitious, which is to say the majority, by completing fulfillment of Savonarola's prophecy that Lorenzo, Pope Innocent VIII, and King Ferdinand would all die within the space of several years. Supposedly their deaths were Heaven's judgment on tyranny. Piero must have been doubly glad that, recalling Lorenzo's troubles with the prior's eloquent Lenten sermons, he had used his influence with the Vatican to have Savonarola transferred to Bologna for the Lenten season of 1493. Now, with Ferdinand's death in January 1494, many Florentine citizens believed that Savonarola not only had powers of prophecy but also was a sort of "finger man" for God, pointing out deserving targets for Divine wrath. Such leading humanists as Politian and

Pico did not go that far, but they so hungered for the ways of their fathers and so trusted in the prior as a guide that they saluted Charles VIII, a mediocre monarch at most, as a saint sent to rescue Europe from the abyss of sin.

In September, fired with dreams of military glory, Charles personally led his troops across the Alps. He was no Hannibal, but fifteenth century Italy had no Scipio, no Flavius. The French king did not come with trumpeting elephants, but the trumpets of his legionnaires were sufficient to strike terror in the hearts of the peninsula's mercenaries. Renaissance Italy's artists could have given their ancient Roman counterparts a run for their money, but between Renaissance troops and the legions of the Caesars there would have been no contest. The pope quickly forged an alliance with the new king of Naples, Alfonso II, who marched to meet the invader. Alfonso had had more military experience than most of his compeers, but command of mercenaries persistent in avoiding battle and dedicated to diversionary plunder had not prepared him for the disciplined French troops, much less the superbly efficient Swiss infantry attached to them. And while the Italian states had not translated Leonardo da Vinci's designs into actual war machines (indeed, were still firing stones from heavy cannon), the French had highly mobile guns that delivered iron balls on target. Alfonso was quickly routed and returned home to defend his own borders.

Meeting surrender or acquiescence all the way, Charles approached Tuscany. Florence was now the only significant power standing between him and the complete subjugation of Italy. At this moment, two of Piero's Medici cousins, whom he had once had arrested for treason because of a quarrel at a dance, joined the French.

Piero had released them and performed compensatory courtesies once his anger had cooled, but they had not forgiven him. In the end they gave substance to the apparently once empty charge that they were serving Charles. Not only was the Medici family divided in the face of external threat, but other powerful citizens of Florence were moving toward alliance with Charles.

Though Piero lacked the wisdom of his paternal ancestors, he was credited with having their courage. When Charles demanded surrender, he refused and, with a great display of coolness, prepared to fight. Acting on a suggestion from the duke of Milan, the French king evicted the Medici bankers from Lyons. Persuaded that Charles' quarrel was primarily with the Medici family, rather than with the Republic of Florence, many citizens were prepared to accept whatever terms the king offered. Discontent with the Medici because of hostility to the humanist revolution, a feeling exacerbated by Savonarola's preachments, made it easy for many to separate from a family with whom the mass of Florentine citizens had once identified. The living presence of Piero was a reminder that not all of the Medici were godlike creatures.

Soon he shocked even those who, while disliking him, credited him with nerve to match his arrogance. The first French victory in Tuscany sent him running to Sarzanello, where a Florentine force was bravely resisting the invader. There Piero knelt before Charles and begged forgiveness for having resisted him.

Charles let his supplicant know that peace must be costly and humbling.

There must be an immediate loan from the Florentine treasury to finance the siege of Naples and to pay for French administration of Pisa and three other towns until the Neapolitan stronghold was in French hands. This demand was an extreme one put forth for bargaining purposes. Piero surprised the French by accepting at once.

He was so imperceptive that he was caught completely off guard by the steely silence of the Signoria when he returned to Florence and reported the peace terms. In his absence the Council of Seventy had decided to entrust negotiations with King Charles to five ambassadors. One of them was Savonarola.

Piero stormed from the room and returned with armed attendants. The guard at the main door told him that he would be permitted to enter only alone and by a side entrance. He turned on his heel and, with his men, marched back toward the Medici Palace. These events had transpired at the Palazzo Vecchio. The chambers that once had been the scene of humanist dialogues reflected upon all over Europe now echoed to violent threats punctuated occasionally by even more ominous silences.

Back in his palace, Piero discussed with a small group of supporters the advisability of using physical force against the opposition. While they debated, the cathedral bells began tolling. The sonorous waves blended into the roar of a mob. Piero's own secret agents told him that the Signoria had proclaimed him as a rebel and an outlaw. As an outlaw, he was fair game for any angry citizen carrying a club or halberd or even an old sword once drawn in pride in support of his father or grandfather.

Piero's younger brother, the precocious Cardinal Giovanni, now nineteen years old, was waiting quietly within the palace. He had returned to Florence because of dissatisfaction with the pope and concern about developments in the republic. When Giovanni had voted his own convictions in the election of a pope instead of following his older brother's dictates, Piero had humiliated the young man by asking the Florentine ambassador to Rome to prevent him from playing the fool again. But Giovanni did not now gloat over Piero's troubles. Nor did he crouch timorously in the shadows. He armed a group of the household staff and led them into the street shouting, "Palle! Palle!"

This old battle cry of the Medici, referring to the golden balls on the family's coat of arms, had been a summons to victory in the glory days of Lorenzo. Now it provoked shouts of "Popolo e libertad!" (The people and liberty!) from an angry mass vastly outnumbering Giovanni's tiny force.

He led them back into the palace. Piero had already escaped through a rear door and was on the road to Venice. Giovanni shed his raiment for the garb of a simple monk and, with his face partly concealed by the cowl, carried some valuables to Saint Mark's convent. Then, still disguised, he too set out for Venice. No one collected the rewards, offered by the Signoria, of four thousand florins for Piero's head and two thousand for the cardinal's. Some might have argued that Giovanni's head was actually worth a great deal more than his brother's.

If the official rewards eluded the mob, many found compensation. They looted both the palace and the villa at Careggi. So ended more than six decades of Medici rule ostensibly in the service of democracy and genuinely in the service of civilization. The period from the end of 1469 to 1492 has been known since as the "Age of Lorenzo." And the man himself has always been known as "Lorenzo the Magnificent." The title was an honorific bestowed on various citizens of Florence, but with only one has the connection survived; in his case, it has assumed the status of a surname. Under his leadership, for more than two decades, Florence had experienced such a flowering of culture and creativity as to give to the term *Renaissance* a glory that shines as a challenge to successive generations.

On the day the Medici fled Florence, King Charles entered Pisa and told its citizens that they were "free from the Florentine yoke." A Florentine embassy went to the French monarch while he held court there. Chief spokesman for the delegation was Savonarola. Charles was a small man, somewhat deformed, but he sat in all the rich-robed majesty that the most skilled tailors in France could supply. And he glowed in triumph. He had discovered mystical significance in the fact that he bore the same given name as Charlemagne, the greatest ruler on the Continent since ancient times. To all attempts to negotiate an agreement, he replied that when he was inside the "gran villa" he would let the Florentines know what would be.

Savonarola, somber-robed and hooded, moved like a dark cloud between the king in his shining raiment and the transfixed audience. He had prophesied that an invader would come to scourge Italy if its people did not reform, and Charles' arrival was widely interpreted as a fulfillment of that prophecy. The dark eyes burning from within the shadow of the cowl fixed the king in their hypnotic glare. In the voice that had sent chills along the spines of Florentine sinners, the prior warned the sovereign, "You are merely God's instrument for the reformation of his church. If you stray from duty to wreak vengeance on the republic of Florence, the wrath of God will descend upon you."[10] Naked fear wiped the hauteur from the king's face, and he seemed to shrivel within the voluminous habiliments designed to enhance his majesty.

Savonarola turned his back upon the royal conqueror and, unescorted, strode out of the chamber. No one moved to stay him.

A few days later, on November 17, Florence opened its gates to Charles and his army. The heavens were less hospitable. A cold rain drenched the force of sixty thousand, falling impartially on the canopy above the small king dwarfed by a huge white hat; on the knights and marshals by his side; on the richly caparisoned bodyguard of three hundred young men; on the Swiss guards in their rainbow-hued uniforms and their officers in plumed helmets; on the short, wiry Gascon infantry, comprising the bulk of the force; on the cavalry, whose polished armor found no bright rays to reflect and whose sodden banners drooped from their staffs; and on the tall archers from Scotland and other northern countries.[11] The rains beat, too, with the same impartiality on the Florentine citizens who lined the winding streets to shout, half in hope and half in propitiation, "France! France!"

The soldiers were soon quartered about the city in the homes of the people. Charles moved into the Medici Palace. Though gutted by looters, it was still an impressive shell.

The next day he summoned the Signoria to hear formally the abject terms of their surrender. The members told him that they would not accept. The king raged that they would have either his terms or war. The Signoria were fully impressed with the size of the force they had seen the day before. It was the first large, full-time army in modern Europe, and beside it most Italian armies were like local militia. The Florentine leaders knew that Charles meant to call out his soldiers to ravage the city.

But they did not quail when he shouted, "I will sound my trumpets." One of the Signoria, Piero Capponi, shot back, "If you sound your trumpets, we will sound our bells."

Charles knew that the Florentines' bells would be a signal to men throughout the city to attack the soldiers scattered in their midst. Many of his men would be cut down before they had a chance to assemble a sizable unit. Charles laughed, and said that he had only been joking.

Savonarola had taken the measure of the king when he had confronted him before his entry into Florence. It was on the prior's advice that the gates had been opened to Charles' army. The confidence with which Savonarola inspired the Florentines even in their defeat sustained the courage of the Signoria in dealing with the conqueror. When Charles pulled out of Florence on November 27 with many of Lorenzo's beloved miniature bronzes and other Medici curios in his baggage train, he had made significant concessions to the Republic of Florence. There was no undoing of Piero's pledge of an indemnity of 120,000 ducats or of the newly forged alliance between the Florentines and the French. But Pisa, Leghorn, Sarzana, and Pietrassant, though conquered by Charles, would be returned to Florentine jurisdiction. Though he scrupulously refrained from direct exercise of political power, Savonarola was now the real leader of Florence. His prophecy of conquest by France, like his prophecies of the deaths of Lorenzo and other rulers, had been fulfilled. His courage in confronting the French king in his own camp was credited with restraining Charles from general plunder and destruction. Under these circumstances, the king's theft of Medici art could be overlooked.

Charles gathered other trophies on his unresisted progress through Rome, where the pope complied with all his requests, and into Naples, whose king had fled. There on May 12 Charles had himself crowned king, formalizing his long-pursued claims on the Neapolitan throne.

Alfonso II had fled Naples, however, only to make trouble for Charles elsewhere. In Spain he had obtained the assistance of his kinswoman, Queen Isabella, who dispatched an ably led army to help him regain his crown. At the same time, the pope, who had agreed with Charles only to get rid of him, conspired with various Italian princes to strike against the French invader.

An even more insidious enemy was sapping the French army. What remains the most destructive outbreak of syphilis in the history of Europe was bringing crippling pain, delirium, and death. It was rendered even more fearsome by the fact that it had not been known before. Medical historians have debated whether syphilis was carried to the Americas by Columbus' expeditions or brought back by them, or whether the New and Old worlds simply exchanged different kinds of venereal disease. Some have suggested that the *spirocheta pallida* that attacked the French was a recent import; others have speculated that it was a latent strain that flared into one of history's worst epidemics under the particular combination of overcrowding, lack of sanitation, and large scale sexual license accompanying the French occupation. In any event, the concatenation of troubles—political, military, and medical—caused Charles to turn north with his rapidly diminishing force, hoping to reach France before his problems became insurmountable.

Piero de' Medici emerged from the security of his in-laws' home in Rome to join Charles, doubtless hoping that French pikes and swords would restore him to leadership in Florence. The Florentine Signoria, determined to thwart any such attempt, sent Savonarola to remind Charles of his responsibilities as their own sworn ally. In the reprise of his first confrontation with the king, the prior warned him of the consuming wrath of God if he should fail in his duty to Florence. Charles may already have wondered whether the mysterious illness destroying his army was an expression of Divine vengeance. Even apart from this consideration, he was feeling much less like Charlemagne and was eager to quit the scenes of erstwhile triumph. The French troops changed course and bypassed Florence in their northward flight. Piero returned to his in-laws and sought comfort in gambling, gluttony, drunkenness, and prostitutes of both sexes. If Savonarola had cast him in a morality play, he was certainly playing his role to the hilt.

About a hundred miles along the road out of Italy, Charles found escape blocked by the combined armies of the Papal States, Venice, Milan, and Spain. Ferdinand and Isabella were determined to return their kinsman to the throne of Naples. Significant of potential resources was a token force under Maximilian of Hapsburg, son of the Holy Roman Emperor. The imperial father was disturbed by developments south of the Alps. Altogether forty thousand fighting men opposed what had once been the greatest army in Europe, now dwindled through disease and desertion to a mere nine thousand. But the poor coordination of the armies facing Charles permitted him to escape.

Florence was now free to experiment with self-government. Before the end of the year 1495, the Council of Seventy was reduced to a Council of Twenty. In theory there might have been a gain in efficiency that would have provided a better legislative check on any tyrannically inclined executive. In actual practice, the expulsion of the Medici and their supporters left a vacuum in the government.

Mobs were ready to rush into the void. Savonarola dispersed several and prevented others from forming, but he could not be everywhere in an instant, and he was too late to prevent the lynching of the former director of the Office of the National Debt. It is proverbial in a democracy that heads roll in a depression. In a tyranny or a mobocracy, the saying is literally true.

But Savonarola's supporters were strong in the Signoria. There they put through his plan for a Grand Council whose members must be at least thirty years old and must have paid their taxes. The longing for stability anchored in heritage was strong amid the succession of disturbing changes, and it found expression in the requirement that all councillors must be descendants of magistrates. At the same time, the desperate desire for experiment, as well as the apparent belief that short tenure would hobble corruption, limited them to six-month terms. Also elected every six months, from those councillors more than forty years old, would be an eighty-member Senate. The Signoria continued in its old role except that now it had to consult with the Senate at least once a week. Greatly outnumbered by a Senate consisting of about one-third of the qualified voters in the city, the Signoria could be strongly influenced by the legislature whenever they achieved unity as a chamber.

Moved by his passion for reform, Savonarola became the guiding spirit of the Signoria, using his influence in behalf of fairer taxes. Believing in mercy as well as justice, he successfully pressed for amnesty to political offenders. This charity, however, stopped short of the most prominent member of the Medici clan. Savonarola proposed a new court of appeal to hear capital cases, whether the death sentence involved a criminal or a political prisoner. This court should consist of eighty to a hundred members chosen by the Grand Council. Some who had learned politics, though still novices as statesmen, got the prior's proposal amended so that the entire Grand Council, a body about ten times as large as the court Savonarola envisioned, should assume the judicial function. The plot was to make the court so unwieldy and so filled with people lacking special qualifications that its purpose would be defeated and the Grand Council itself would be invalidated. Though Savonarola was shrewd enough to understand what his opponents were doing, he was unable to thwart them.

His practical mind turned to the problem of building up the sagging economy. He fathered legislation to establish a chamber of commerce. Trade associations for various crafts had existed since medieval times, but Savonarola founded an association that cut across occupational lines to promote the general commercial interests of the city. He also dealt with the problem of juvenile street gangs, successfully keeping some of them busy marching and singing in public as a more acceptable expenditure of energy.

The otherwise practical prior was much less realistic in clinging to his notion of Charles and the French as the predestined saviors of Italy. Of course, he had professed to have a revelation that Charles would be both scourge and savior. Most Florentines would concede that the scourge part of the prophecy had been fulfilled. In fact, they thought it was still being fulfilled, as the French king had broken almost every promise that he had made in the treaty with Florence. Florentine suzerainty over other cities had not been restored. The loss of Pisa particularly rankled. Savonarola promised the Signoria that if they would "return to virtue" as evidenced by patiently refraining from action against the French, "I will see to it that your reward shall be Pisa." For a while they complied, but popular resentment rose at the Florentine government's refusal to join the Holy League against France, in which Venice and Milan were playing increasingly significant roles.

This dissatisfaction was exploited by certain lesser Medici who returned to the city under Savonarola's amnesty program. Even an obscure Medici, the prior was learning, could be dangerous. They all seemed to be plotting Piero's return to power. And they found a powerful ally—Pope Alexander himself. His interest in Savonarola was heightened by suggestions from some of his enemies in Florence that the prior might be ambitious to displace the pontiff. Alexander was already aware that Savonarola's criticisms of the Vatican were encouraging dissent among Catholics elsewhere on the Continent and even in England.

On July 21, 1495 Alexander, disturbed by Savonarola's actions and by his influence in keeping Florence out of the Holy League, issued a honeyed invitation for the prior to come to Rome. He said that he was impressed by the reforms wrought by him in Florence and would like to hear directly from him some of his remarkable prophecies. He was also interested in learning how Savonarola knew that his inspiration was Divine.

Savonarola replied that he was ill and asked that the trip might be postponed. The pope appeared to acquiesce but on September 8 ordered the prior to go to Bologna under pain of excommunication. Savonarola, with more firmness than tact, cited eighteen errors in the pope's brief. On October 16 Alexander ordered the prior to stop preaching. The Holy League, he said, insisted upon it.

With the approach of Lent in 1496, ambassadors from Florence requested that the ban be lifted. Though the pope refused formal revocation, he gave them to understand that Savonarola would be permitted to preach a series of Lenten sermons. The prior then delivered his famous sermons on Amos. With unabated zeal and fury, he assailed corruption in the Vatican and further enlivened his discourses with references to what was assumed to be the personal immorality of the pope. Alexander was incensed, but did not pursue the matter further after a college of theologians found the prior blameless. After Lent, Savonarola began a new series of powerful sermons.

Alexander tempted the preacher by offering him a cardinal's hat. Of course, he suggested, it would be inappropriate for a cardinal to be prophesying the doom of the church he helped to govern. Talents such as his could be used more effectively in helping the pope reform ecclesiastical administration. The bearer of Alexander's message was the superior of the Dominican order, the one to which Savonarola belonged. The superior was in the congregation the next time the prior preached. From the pulpit, Savonarola gave an answer as vivid as it was unmistakable: "I seek neither cardinal's hat nor bishop's mitre. I desire only, O Lord, what Thou hast given to Thy saints, martyrdom. Give me a hat, I pray Thee, a red hat, but red with blood."

The contest between the pope, apostolic successor of Saint Peter and commander of the Vatican's legions, military and clerical, throughout Europe, and, on the other side, a Florentine prior armed only with eloquence, burning dedication, and relentless will, would seem on the face of it a ridiculously unequal competition. But Europe looked on in suspense. Savonarola had some material power insofar as he could hold the allegiance of a majority in Florence's faction-torn government. But the republic, as the ally of Charles, who had brought suffering and humiliation to many Italian communities, had waning influence and almost no good will in the peninsula.

The Holy League invited Maximilian I, the Holy Roman Emperor, to Rome to be crowned, just as Charlemagne, the first Holy Roman Emperor, had been. The League and the pope were not so much motivated by a desire to preserve or revive an old tradition as by a wish to bring the imperial ruler to Italy and force Florence to abandon its treacherous ally, Charles, and join forces against him.

If any were so naive as to assume that Maximilian's visit was purely ceremonial, they were soon disillusioned. He besieged Leghorn, over which Florence continued to claim jurisdiction. Venice's excellent navy blockaded the harbor. Death had claimed Piero Capponi, who besides confronting Charles in council with a boldness to match Savonarola's own, had been the republic's leading general. His services were desperately needed now, not only because of the crisis at Leghorn but also because the Florentine army was in retreat from Pisa. When the Florentines looked for a scapegoat, one gaunt figure loomed high on their horizon.

Savonarola responded to the compound emergency by organizing a procession of white-robed penitents to implore Divine intervention. The very idea was ridiculed by some citizens, who argued that, with Florence surrounded and its food supplies almost exhausted, diplomatic overtures to sister cities would be more important than appeals to God. Some even thought that marching in rebellion would be more useful than parading in penitence.

On the day set by the prior, his robed followers wound through the streets, sometimes amid jeers that made a rude counterpoint to their pious chants. Suddenly a horseman arrived from Leghorn with the news that a storm had rendered the Venetian blockade ineffective long enough for ships to arrive in the harbor with provisions for Florence. Later came news that Maximilian had given up his siege and was headed back to Germany. Maybe this strange Savonarola really did have the ear of the Almighty. Anyway, for now, the prospect of a full stomach was more compelling than a call to rebellion.

But the well-fed Alexander, who claimed to be the vicar of God, was moved by no such considerations. With a stroke of the pen, he combined the Dominican convents in Rome with those in Florence and elsewhere in Tuscany and placed them under the supervision of an ecclesiastic in Rome, under the papal eye. The prior thus would be directly subordinate to a hand-picked vicar prepared to send him to an isolated outpost where his sermons might evoke more echoes from the barren hills than they did excited responses from human followers.

Anticipating such treatment, Savonarola formally notified Alexander that he did not intend to move. The pope bided his time, reluctant to give the prior the martyrdom that he sought and hoping that an approaching election would bring to the titular political leadership of Florence someone from an anti-Savonarola faction. Instead Francisco Valori, a loudmouthed supporter of the prior, was chosen. Once in office, however, he probably did the prior more harm than good. He high-handedly banished the Franciscans from the republic because they were rivals of Savonarola's order, the Dominicans. He raised apprehension in some quarters by lowering to twenty-four the minimum age for election to the Grand Council. One of his principal reforms, a graduated income tax, stirred the fervent hatred of business leaders. The prior, though advocating censorship in some matters, was genuinely eager to enlarge the liberties of the citizens. Valori, trading on public hunger for traditional Christianity as symbolized by Savonarola, pushed for autocracy in the name of piety.

The prior was disturbed by increasing evidence that the political chieftain relied ultimately on naked physical force rather than the power of the spirit. He did not like having his fortunes tied to those of such a man. And so it was that Savonarola asserted his own spiritual leadership, quite apart from any political alliances. As we have seen, he called upon the people of Florence to bring to the Piazza della Signoria the material things to which they had given undue homage and to make a huge cone reaching to the sky. We do not know what Savonarola's thoughts were as, black robed and black cowled, he watched through burning eyes the Bonfire of the Vanities. Almost surely he thought back to when, as a twenty-two-year-old, already moved by a Lenten sermon, he had been stirred to the depths by men and women of the congregation who consigned their ball masks, wigs, playing cards, and erotic art to a large fire in the marketplace. Perhaps now, on Shrove Tuesday of 1497, he thought ahead as well as backward. Perhaps he wondered what fires might await him.

9

CYCLE OF FIRE

ONCE AGAIN Savonarola's eyes glittered in the reflection of leaping flames as bells pealed in the Palazzo.[1] Once again shouts went up from an excited multitude. But the events of this Shrove Tuesday, almost exactly one year after the first great Bonfire of the Vanities in 1497, were not a reenactment of that historic occasion. This time, mingled with the roar of celebration, were the insults and threats of enemies and the cries of Savonarola's followers as they fell under the blows of young ruffians.

Much had happened in the year between the two fires.[1] There had been grumbling against Savonarola after what some saw as an orgy of destruction. And Bernardo del Nero, secretly a supporter of Piero de' Medici, had been elected to replace Valori, who as a political chief had rammed through unpopular policies in the prior's name. Doubtless encouraged by these developments, Piero himself had marched to the gates of Florence with thirteen hundred Sienese soldiers. Such was the division of sentiment in the city, however, that Bernardo decided to keep his allegiance secret a while longer. Piero waited outside the locked gates for several hours, hoping for a spontaneous uprising of the citizens at word that their old leader had returned. When nothing of the kind occurred, he turned back and led his troops away.

There was no great movement in behalf of Savonarola either. On the very day that Piero waited outside the gates, there was elected within the city a Signoria even more hostile to the prior than its predecessors. The new chief of state was a leader of the nobles who were his sworn enemies.

Expressing fear that public gatherings would spread the plague, the Signoria banned preaching after May 4. Few doubted that these politicians were less afraid of disease than of Savonarola's eloquence.

The prohibition intensified public interest in the prior's next sermon, as this was supposed to be his last—at least for the foreseeable future. Some young men tried to make the service a failure by bringing rotten meat into the sanctuary beforehand. They also drove nails, point up, into the pulpit ledge. Savonarola, when he warmed to his discourse, was invariably a pulpit pounder. The cruel pranks were discovered in time to wash the foul odor of decay out of the church and to protect the prior's hands.

A much more serious plot had been formed—to infiltrate the congregation and create a riot. In the resulting confusion, armed young men would assassinate the preacher. Savonarola's supporters, however, had gotten wind of this plot also. Armed men of their own number placed themselves strategically amid the worshipers.

The prior was aware of both the assassination and the rescue plans and was prepared to cooperate with his friends. Almost halfway through his sermon, he was interrupted by shouts. He tried to cut through the noise with his strong voice, but the tumult was too much for him. Some of his enemies threw open the doors and ran into the street, counting on being pursued, as indeed they were, by the congregation. This supposedly would give the assassins a free hand. But, instead, a group of the preacher's armed supporters crowded close around the pulpit and then escorted him to the monastery of San Marco.

The prior had been saved. But the more-than-half-superstitious awe with which he had been regarded by many ordinary people was shattered. Many still honored him as a good man, and perhaps an inspired one, but he was vulnerable as other men. Perhaps, then, his prophecies were not infallible.

The city seethed again in August when Bernardo del Nero and four other prominent citizens, one of them a cousin to Piero de' Medici, were convicted of treasonable correspondence with him and were beheaded. Many people blamed Savonarola for not intervening to save them. The government of the republic and Piero's supporters were opposed to each other but could agree on one thing—that Savonarola was a troublesome priest. When he preached a Christmas Day sermon in the cathedral in defiance of a papal ban, attendance was smaller than in the past. When Savonarola's second Bonfire of the Vanities, on Shrove Tuesday in 1498, provoked hurled insults and physical attacks on his followers, not only had his enemies increased in number, but the ranks of his supporters were greatly diminished.

Now was the time for his enemies to unite, some publicly and some secretly. The pope ordered Florence to deliver the prior for trial in Rome. Failure to comply would bring the entire city under an interdict. Savonarola told his congregation that he must submit but, at the same time, urged France, England, Spain, and Hungary to call an ecumenical council to depose the pope.

Once again, fire reappeared as the leitmotif of his life. A Franciscan friar, a member of the order which had once been banned from Florence by a chief of state professing loyalty to Savonarola, now challenged the Dominican prior to prove by ordeal of fire the validity of his doctrines. The Franciscan had said earlier that he challenged any Dominican to submit to the ordeal with him. A Dominican friar loyal to Savonarola insisted that he, not the prior, accept the challenge because Savonarola "has yet to be the protagonist of other, greater affairs." The prior tried in vain to get his loyal follower to ignore the challenge as undignified and without efficacy in determining the truth.

The Signoria made the contest official. The ordeal would determine whether or not Savonarola should be banished from the city. He would be declared the loser not only if the Franciscan were injured and the Dominican remained unscathed but even in the event that both were injured. A platform about seven feet high, ninety feet long, and sixteen feet wide was constructed. A path a little over two feet wide ran the length of the platform. Combustible materials were placed on each side and, at the time of testing, would be lit.

But the Franciscan champion did not appear. He and some of his brethren said they were afraid that the Dominican's clothes had been bewitched to protect him. So Savonarola consented for his man to go into the palace, strip naked, and put on clothes approved by the Franciscans. Then the Franciscans objected that the Dominican's crucifix might be enchanted. Dark was settling on the scene now; and Savonarola, his champion, and the other Dominican friars walked away.

An angry crowd remained in the square arguing over what should be done. Suddenly lightning flashed, thunder rolled, hail fell, and a downpour saturated the fuel for the fires. The crowd dispersed, some in fear that God was expressing disapproval of the proceedings, others in sullen disgust that they had been cheated out of an exciting spectacle.

Among Savonarola's enemies and the hitherto merely disenchanted, hatred of him soared. Even many of his followers turned against him. Some thought he was a coward. Many were angry that he had let them down. He had not exerted himself to create a miracle.

On his walk back to San Marco, Savonarola was protected from vengeful citizens by his guard of pikemen. Even so, he was the target of stones. The next day San Marco was not refuge enough. A mob attacked the building. Its defense was led by Valori, a loudmouth but far more valiant than most of his kind. Realizing that only reinforcements could save the impromptu garrison, he left through a back window and walked toward his home, hoping to escape detection by his enemies. He made it safely into his own street but was then recognized by one of them. He ran fast enough to gain his doorstep but was literally cut to pieces before he could enter the house. His wife, watching in horror from a window above, was felled by an arrow.

That night a mob renewed the attack on San Marco. Once again, fire played a decisive role in Savonarola's life. When the locked gates did not yield to pressure, the attackers set fire to them and gained entrance to the courtyard. The Dominican friars literally fought fire with fire, turning lighted tapers against the invaders. Some dealt punishing blows with heavy crucifixes. As the mob reeled back, friars on the roof poured hot embers on them.

Even as the defenders cheered, a command to surrender came from the Signoria. The armed forces of Florence would not merely remain aloof while San Marco fought off an undisciplined mob. The army would insure that San Marco was conquered. Some monks were for fighting on anyway. Two friars, standing on the high altar, fired harquebuses at all comers, shouting all the while, "Viva Cristo!" The terrible irony of this scene, as well as the futile loss of life, must have been too much for Savonarola. From a side door, he signaled to the fighting friars to follow him. In the library, the prior surrendered. He and two of his supporters were cast into a dungeon.

The next day, and for ten days following, Savonarola was on trial for his life. For most of those days, he was also tortured on the rack. Papal commissioners arrived from Rome in May to hold a new trial. They used fire to torture the desired confession out of him.

On May 22 the death sentence was pronounced, and Savonarola and two followers were led out into the piazza to be hanged. We may be sure that the prior was not blind to the symbolism that suggested the death of Jesus. Suspended from the gallows, the skeletal prior, once his dance of death had ended, seemed more than ever a symbol of Death itself. Men set fire to the faggots piled beneath his lifeless body. As the flames leaped high, he was illuminated as twice before when he had stared at the Bonfire of the Vanities. The assembled crowd watched with a fascination to match their interest in those earlier times.

10

AGE OF GENIUS

ON THE DAY before Savonarola's arrest, King Charles VIII had died. Had he lived, he might have rescued his old ally. The French, under Charles' successor, Louis XII, drove the conniving Duke Ludovico from the government of Milan. Florence was still threatened by three menacing figures in Rome: Pope Alexander VI, his son General Cesare Borgia, and Piero de' Medici. But Alexander died on August 18, 1503, Cesare became ill of a disease to which he later succumbed, and Piero, serving with a French army in desperate flight from the Spanish, drowned in the attempt to escape across a swiftly flowing river. It was as though fate were removing players whose actions had become as tedious as they were predictable, as if it were clearing the stage and tidying up for another act.

It was all part of the same drama, though; and fate, like a skillful dramatist, had placed, in strictly subordinate roles linked to the vanished players, several characters who would be prominent in successive scenes.

Even before Piero de' Medici died by water following the death by fire of his old antagonist Savonarola, another Piero had become the savior of Florence. Piero Soderini was not a flamboyant hero of the sort favored in so much Italian drama. To many, he probably seemed colorless but certainly not inconsequential. He was too strong in his convictions and his integrity to give any suggestion of insipidity. Colorfulness can be the natural expression of a rich imagination, or it can be simply an illusion created by extremism and eccentricity. Soderini lacked the creative individuality to be a colorful personality of the first category and the self-conscious egotism to qualify for the second.

What assets did he have besides conviction and integrity? He had sound business sense and dependable judgment in most practical affairs. He was independent of all the factions that long had torn apart the body politic of Florence. His heritage as the descendant of one of Florence's respected old families provided for him and the citizens a comfortable link with the past. His personal life was said to be blameless and was popularly regarded as harking back to an era of antique virtue. Yet he had declined to join Savonarola's pilgrimage back into the Middle Ages and had opposed attempts to wipe out all the cultural adventuring of humanism. He welcomed the movement away from tyranny to true republican freedom, but at the same time, sought to curb the impatience of those who would discard traditional constitutionalism in the process. In short, he represented the delicate balance of tradition and experiment for which most Florentines yearned after unhappy experience with extremes of each.

As at some other times in the history of Florence, the spirit of the community at this juncture was effectively symbolized by activities at the Palazzo Vecchio. Built about 1300, it had been the seat of government in fact as well as name until increasing domination by one family made the Medici Palace the center of power. Under Savonarola there was a dramatic rise in popular involvement in the government, and the Hall of Five Hundred,[1] then the largest assembly chamber in the area, was added to the Palazzo Vecchio to accommodate the Grand Council. Now, in 1503, the austere atmosphere of the Palazzo Vecchio was being brightened with frescoes. The painter was Leonardo da Vinci, returned to Florence after years in Milan under the patronage of the same Duke Ludovico who, until his ousting, had made so much trouble for Florentine leaders. Leonardo appears to have finished his *Mona Lisa* about this time. Michelangelo soon would join him in painting the frescoes, but first he must finish his statue of David.[2]

The creation of large-scale frescoes for a public building other than a church, in itself, marked a departure from the days of Savonarola's domination. Not that the prior was, as too often has been assumed, insensitive to art. When he sought to explain the power of love, he said, "Love is like a painter, and a good painter if he paints well, greatly delights men with his paintings. In contemplation of the painting men remain suspended and at times appear to be in ecstasy and outside themselves and seem to forget themselves."[3] Savonarola did not believe that the artist's talent should be hidden, but he did believe that, like other human gifts, it should be dedicated to the glory of God. The frescoes in the Palazzo Vecchio were secular art for a secular building. Moreover, they portrayed scenes from Florentine history. As society stabilized after disconcertingly rapid change, it focused contemporary attention on its past.[4]

No less significant than the grand-scale endeavor that commanded the energies of Leonardo and Michelangelo were the individual projects that occupied them before full-time commitment to the public one. Though the *Mona Lisa* may cast a longer-than-justified shadow when seen in the light of Walter Pater's "hard, gem-like flame," it is incontestably one of the world's major works of art. The relaxed air of the sitter and the expressiveness of the hands mark a considerable advance over previous portraiture. These aspects individualized the portrait in an innovative way. In another sense, the painting marked the return to a briefly abandoned tradition. There is no evidence of the painting or sculpting of portraits in Florence between a marble bust dated 1495 and the Leonardo masterpiece, traditionally dated 1503.[5] As Savonarola's battle, first for dominance and later for survival, intensified his ideological extremism, portraits came to be regarded as vanities of the sort destined for bonfires. The *Mona Lisa*, with its emphasis on individual personality, is in the tradition of Renaissance humanism. Michelangelo's *David* is, of course, one of the world's most renowned statues. Its biblical subject would have been acceptable alike to the medieval church and to Savonarola. But its candid celebration of the human body and individual spirit is in the humanist tradition.

Savonarola's influence on Florentine art lingered to various degrees with different artists, always in combination with humanistic influences. The variation was partly generational. The great artist most obviously influenced by the prior was Botticelli, who became one of his disciples. In Botticelli's case, the change was not for the better. Marcia Hall notes, "In these paintings, the urgent, frenetic tone clashes with the message of humanist celebration, joy, and praise of God's creation."[6] For Botticelli, humanism had been liberating, but the prior's influence was constricting. With Leonardo, a contemporary but of a younger generation, the influence was less obvious, but he seems to have found religious subjects a stimulating challenge. For Michelangelo, younger yet, the prior's influence led to liberation and a larger view as the painter found new depths and heights in Christian mysteries. Savonarola may have provided the stimulus, but Michelangelo transmuted it into something grander, subtler, and more appealing.

Hall makes the point that, where Savonarola's direct influence was strongest, the quality of art suffered but that the prior "broke the continuity both of style and of patronage. A successful new style had not been forged, but the old one no longer satisfied. Into this vacuum Leonardo and Michelangelo stepped, introducing the style of the High Renaissance."[7] For these great geniuses, the effect of the new religious content was to free art from simple naturalism. Hall concludes that "certainly the central achievement of the new style was the marriage of the spiritual with plausible reality."[8] Artists did not return to the polished but superficial realism characteristic even of many religious paintings in the last days of Lorenzo and the rule of Piero. At the same time, there was no demand for the simplistic art fostered by Savonarola. When Perugino used that style in 1506 in executing the high altarpiece for Santissima Annunziata, his efforts were ridiculed as backward. Artists and the society they served had achieved a dynamic balance between two interacting forces. Vitality was restored.

It would be a mistake to assume that all that is called "Savonarolan" in art is a result of the prior's direct influence. For few such works is there documentary evidence of a connection. Savonarola was the leader in a Florentine return to many aspects of medieval culture. The movement coalesced around him. Without his remarkable gifts, extraordinary personality, and supreme dedication, the movement undoubtedly would have been more diffuse and hence less effective, but it would have existed nonetheless. It would have taken place in reaction to what many regarded as the excesses of a Florentine humanism moving too far and too fast from a native tradition. Lacking documentary evidence of specific inspiration and dependent on internal evidence from the works of art, we should be chary of saying in most cases that certain features of a specific painting or sculpture are derived from a sermon or writing of the fiery Dominican. But if we use the term *Savonarolan* to refer to a whole movement embodied by the prior, we may sometimes speak with confidence.

Nowhere is the Savonarolan influence in Florentine art subtler or more multiplex than in the creations of Michelangelo. He was too original and too broadly intellectual a genius to be content with simply translating into his chosen medium another's thought. Analysts of Michelangelo's work, from Vasari in the sixteenth century to Erwin Panofsky and Ronald M. Steinberg in the twentieth, have stressed "the creatively synthesizing abilities of his art and intellect." Steinberg sensibly points out that "Michelangelo was as capable himself of abstracting ideas from the early church fathers, associating them with current theological beliefs, and uniting them all with a particular blend of Neoplatonic philosophy as was Savonarola. Both men knew the sources well, and we should not be surprised to find both expounding, on occasion, similar ideas, or using the same kind of imagery to express them."[9]

With true Renaissance versatility, Michelangelo, besides being probably the greatest graphic artist of his generation and certainly one of the very greatest of all time, was also a master of Savonarola's art of verbal communication. He produced a body of poems that has earned him a lasting place in Italian literature. They lack the metrical polish of the many Florentine humanist verses that smoothly exploit the mellifluous qualities of the Italian tongue. But some have a rough-hewn immediacy that has caused subsequent generations to echo the comment of a contemporary that Michelangelo's words were not only symbols but things that could be experienced directly.

Another Florentine for whom literature was a sideline gave promise of achieving lasting fame in that field. One of the most important men in Soderini's government was Niccolò Machiavelli.[10] He was only twenty-nine years old in 1498 when, one month after Savonarola's execution, he was made chief of the Second Chancellery and secretary of the War Committee of Ten. He thus played a role in every phase of domestic policy and some phases of foreign policy as well. His involvement in foreign affairs became far more intimate when he was sent on diplomatic missions to the pope, the king of France, the Holy Roman Emperor, and various less celebrated chiefs of state.

Machiavelli grew so rapidly in sophistication that anyone observing him at this stage of his life might have concluded that his youth had been spent in palaces. Actually, while many of his ancestors over two centuries had enjoyed all the advantages of wealth and had filled some of the principal offices in the republic, young Machiavelli had known of such things only from family tradition and wide reading. His father, though a doctor of laws, was barred from office as an insolvent debtor. His home was distinguished from those of other poor citizens principally by its superior library. Poverty, coming after generations of wealth, must have seemed the more abject by contrast. There was no money to provide Niccolò with an education appropriate to his heritage, and the family was doubtless too proud to accept for him the sponsorship of a Medici or other magnate of Florence. He never studied Greek. His knowledge of the classics came through the Latin that he learned from unfashionable instructors. Altogether, he was his own principal teacher.

Students of his life often have maintained that the autodidact's course, in the words of one of his leading biographers, Marchese Roberto Ridolfi, "saved him from the excesses of humanist erudition." Much of the humanist learning was available to him without the overweening force of intimate association with its more charismatic banner carriers. This was important because Niccolò was a young student in the days when the humanist culture, after stimulating a great fruition of art and scholarship, had gone so far beyond native traditions as to upset the once healthy balance between the familiar and the experimental.

Machiavelli was a brilliant thinker and an earnest scholar. He looked like one whose victories would be on the playing fields of the mind rather than in equestrian tournaments. Of only medium height and thin-bodied, he carried on his scrawny neck a rather large head dominated by a high, broad forehead over which some strands of thinning black hair were combed forward. Once past the bold Roman nose and prominent cheekbones, the lower part of the face was in retreat. A smile as enigmatic as the Mona Lisa's lent, according to some acquaintances, an understated charm; according to others, a look of slyness. The lean features could have been mummified without suffering drastic change.

He was the very embodiment of reflection and speculation. Nothing about him, with the possible exception of his eyes—which, though heavy lidded, were bright—suggested the man of action. But he was that, too. He was very much the activist when he persuaded Soderini, who was desperately seeking some means of ending the draining war with Pisa, to establish a citizens' militia instead of relying on the notoriously inadequate and often treacherous mercenaries. Convincing Soderini was no easy task. The Florentines had become what Napoleon would one day call the English, "a nation of shopkeepers." Except for internecine brawls and occasional riots, they had for two centuries paid other people to do their fighting. When Soderini pushed a conscription act through the Signoria on December 3, 1506, it did not include the urban merchants and their employees. First to be drafted were the peasants, accustomed to physical labor and living in the countryside, the first area to be overrun by an invading army. To Machiavelli went the task of organizing the conscripts.

Now was his great opportunity. In about two years, while continuing to fill his high civil posts and to undertake diplomatic missions, he molded the raw conscripts into an army ten thousand strong. The foreign aid that Pisa had enjoyed as an ally of the pope was being withdrawn; hence, an effective siege force had a chance to succeed. In June 1509, with the surrender of Pisa, Machiavelli was more than vindicated as the planner and the executor. From a friend in Florence came an exuberant report: "Everyone without exception has gone mad with exultation. There are bonfires all through the city, though it is still afternoon. Think what it will be like at night! If I were not afraid of making you too vain, I would say that you have arranged matters so well with your battalions that you alone have restored the fortunes of the Florentine state."

Florence did not long enjoy in peace the fruits of victory. Pope Julius II, a great general, through war and diplomacy had regained for the Vatican the cities of Romagna, lost in some cases by secession but in others to Venetian conquest. Having achieved this objective, he withdrew from the alliance against Venice that he had formed with Milan, Spain, Germany, and France. He then called upon all Italians to evict the French from the Italian peninsula. Florence was still an ally of France.

King Louis XII of France made things more awkward for the Florentine republic by asking its permission to call a council of cardinals to meet in its Tuscan territory. He hoped that such a gathering would find some solution to the crisis short of a war between king and pope. Soderini and his dominant faction, acting over vehement protests from influential citizens, granted the king's request. The council met at Pisa and, far from appeasing Pope Julius, enraged him. The pontiff laid Florence under an interdict. Soderini then asked the king to move the session outside Tuscany. The council reconvened in Milan, but the pope was not mollified. Rome, Venice, and Spain united in a war against France. Louis had the half-hearted support of Florence. Given the military skill of Julius and the strength of the anti-French alliance against Louis, few were surprised when the king's forces were driven back across the Alps.

The day of reckoning for Florence was at hand. Julius sent against the city the troops of his Holy League, principally Spanish soldiers known for efficiency and ruthlessness. Accompanying them was Cardinal Giovanni dé Medici, who had continually risen in eminence and influence since the day when he had been forced to flee his native city. With him were his younger brother and a cousin. The pope's general bore his terms: Florence must dismiss Soderini, pay a heavy indemnity, and allow the Medici to return as private citizens. Surely few were so naive as to believe that the newly enfranchised Medici would be content for long to tend their own gardens when the whole field of public service lay before them.

Soderini refused the terms and sent Machiavelli's militia to oppose the approaching Spanish troops. The two forces met at Prato, about ten miles outside Florence. Machiavelli's men, the celebrated victors over Pisa, were completely outclassed by the Spaniards under Raimondo da Cordona.

General Cordona demanded the surrender of Prato. When the town's Florentine masters refused to submit, he took it by assault the next day. He had only two small cannon, but sent Machiavelli's militia into panic-stricken flight. The Spanish soldiers savagely sacked the city for twenty-one days. Until certain twentieth century horrors, the fate of Prato was sometimes cited as the worst atrocity in modern European history. Some have reported that Cordona made no effort to restrain his soldiers. Others have said that he could not. No building escaped pillaging. The invaders chased men, women, and children through the streets, cutting them down. Some of the women and girls were spared just long enough for a gang rape. Some young women, with the enemy pounding at their doors, dived headlong from balconies to dash their brains out. Mothers drowned their daughters in wells and then jumped in to share their fate. No less than fifty-six hundred townspeople are said to have met violent deaths. The Medici brothers were powerless to halt the carnage throughout the town, but they personally offered shelter to fleeing women and children. According to a contemporary account, "these enormities would have been carried to a still greater excess" if the brothers had not, "at the risk of their lives, opposed themselves to the fury of the conquerors."

Florence was next in the path of the Spaniards. A panicked populace demanded and got Soderini's resignation. He fled. A new government prepared to welcome the Medici and initiated steps to pay the indemnity demanded by the pope, ally itself with Spain, and join the Holy League.

When Cardinal Giovanni de' Medici's younger brother and the late Piero's son entered Florence unostentatiously, there were cheers from bystanders. Two weeks later, Cardinal Giovanni entered in triumph. Never prepossessing in appearance, he had fattened to a degree that made his figure on horseback a sad contrast with the lean majesty of his father. But at age thirty-six he was one of Europe's most respected ecclesiastics and, true to his family tradition, a celebrated patron of art and scholarship. Ironically, he had in his Roman palace the collection of books that Savonarola had safeguarded at Saint Mark's in Florence. The fiery prior had been more often a preserver than a burner of books. Like Lorenzo, Giovanni delighted in music.

The cardinal soon acted in accordance with another family tradition. Without formally occupying any civil office, he assumed the leadership of Florence, abolishing the Grand Council that Savonarola had created. The administration succeeding Soderini's had already nullified the provision that the gonfalier, officially chief of state, should hold his position for life. This did not trouble Giovanni. What did it matter who was gonfalier as long as the cardinal held the power? He shortened the term to two months. To the people of Florence, the Age of Lorenzo seemed to have returned. Violence seemed at an end.

But the peace was so fragile that it was shattered by a fluttering scrap of paper. It fell to the street from the hand of a young scholar. The curious citizen who picked it up saw that it was a list of eighteen names. Something excited his suspicion. This was not hard to do in a time and place rampant with plots and counterplots. The citizen gave the list to the authorities. They ordered that all persons on the list be arrested. These unfortunates were put to the rack to extort confessions. The young scholar and a friend also on the list both broke down and said that they had conspired to assassinate Giovanni's brother and nephew. But they said that the other names on the list were those of people to be approached, people not yet contacted. One of those was Niccolò Machiavelli.

Although the testimony of the two confessed plotters tended to clear the other men listed, the authorities were not satisfied. They ordered that all be tortured. Under the pain of this procedure, most confessed that they had at least heard of an assassination plot. To have knowledge of such a plan and not reveal it was a crime. They were banished. Machiavelli vehemently protested his innocence and did not break under pressure. He and a few others were freed. The two who had confessed to the actual planning were executed.

On the day of their execution, February 22, 1513, Florence received word of another death. Pope Julius II had died. He had lived long enough to drive the French out of Italy with the aid of the Spanish, but not long enough to expel the Spanish. Cardinal Giovanni left at once for Rome. On March 11 he became Pope Leo X. Lorenzo's dream of a Medici pope was fulfilled. In the coronation procession on April 11, Giovanni rode the white Arab charger that

had borne him in battle. The symbolism of the procession and attendant ceremonies reflected the mingling of classical and medieval Christian influences, as
well as Medici patronage of art. Statuary was on display, both cooly classical
ancient Roman figures and contemporary sculptures with distortions expressive of emotion and of Christian theology. In decorations, Apollo, Mercury,
and Athena vied with the apostles.

Once again, the Medici family were operating on an international scale.
Not only was Giovanni on the papal throne as Leo X, but he made cardinals of
his cousin Giulio and his nephew Innocenzo. He also made Giulio archbishop
of Florence, placing him in a prestigious position where he could sustain the
family leadership of the republic. This move was particularly important because
Leo had called his brother Giuliano from Florence to be military leader of the
Holy Catholic Church. The pope's young nephew Lorenzo de' Medici, born
in the year of the great Lorenzo's death and bearing his grandfather's resonant
name, might symbolize a reincarnation of Florentine hopes, but he would need
all the help he could get. In the tradition of other Medici men who had valued
the substance of power more than its appearance, he would be the real chief of
the republic. Machiavelli was desperate to make his peace with the Medici. He
hungered for a return to public office, both as gratification of ambition and
to relieve his poverty. On Giovanni's coronation as Pope Leo X, Machiavelli
composed a "Song of the Blessed Spirits."[11] Neither the pontiff nor his family
were moved. Machiavelli then appealed to a former colleague, now Florentine
ambassador to the Vatican, to intercede for him. But the diplomat was not eager
to help, and this and all other efforts to get into the family's good graces proved
ineffective.

After a while, Machiavelli moved with his wife and children to the family
farm, about ten miles outside Florence. Here he could live more cheaply, and
until such time as he might once again be a part of Florentine public life, he
could escape the frustration of being a bystander.

In a letter to a friend, the same ambassador to the Vatican whose aid he
had sought, he told how he spent his days. Rising with the sun, he would go
into his woods for a few hours to inspect the previous day's work by the wood-
cutters and listen to their problems. Going to a quieter outdoor spot, he would
read the works of two great Florentine poets, Dante and Petrarch, or of one of
their classical predecessors, Tibullus or Ovid. He confessed, "I read their amorous transports, and the history of their loves, recalling my own to my mind,
and time passes pleasantly in these meditations."[12] Though Machiavelli enjoyed
the reputation of a kind father, he, like so many of his contemporaries, had
been a far-from-faithful husband. Now, however, returning home at midday,
he was the perfect paterfamilias as he sat down to a simple dinner with his
family.

If morning and midday of Machiavelli's rural life seemed like a Petrarchan
or Horatian idyll, the afternoon would more appropriately be delineated by the
elder Brueghel. At that time he went to the village inn. "There," he said:

> I generally find the host, a butcher, a miller, and a couple of brick-
> makers. I mix with these boors the whole [remaining] day, playing at

cricca and at *tric trac*, which games give rise to a thousand quarrels and much exchange of bad language; and we generally wrangle over farthings, and our shouting can be heard at San Casciano. Steeped in this degradation, my wits grow moldy, and I vent my rage at the malignity of fate. . . .

Reading this letter is a reminder that Machiavelli had essayed, among other roles, that of dramatist.

While a strong inclination toward the dramatic is apparent in the next part of the letter, one senses also what appears to be sincere revelation. "At nightfall," he says,

I return home and seek my writing room, and, divesting myself on its threshold of my rustic garments, stained with mud and mire, I assume courtly attire, and thus suitably clothed, enter within the ancient courts of ancient men, by whom, being cordially welcomed, I am fed with the food that *alone* is mine, and for which I was born, and am not ashamed to hold discourse with them and inquire the motives of their actions; and these men in their humanity reply to me, and for the space of four hours I feel no weariness, remember no trouble, no longer fear poverty, no longer dread death; my whole being is absorbed in them.

Next he reveals to his friend, who probably did not suspect its significance, the most important activity of his life:

And since Dante says that there could be no science [here the word means scholarship of any kind] without retaining that which is heard, I have recorded that which I have acquired from the conversation of these worthies, and have composed a pamphlet *De principatibus*, in which I plunge as deeply as I can into cogitations upon this subject, discussing the nature of princedom, of how many species it consists, how these are to be acquired, how they are maintained, why they are lost. . . .

This work was the first form of Machiavelli's *Principe* (The Prince), frequently found on lists of the world's one hundred most influential books. In synthesizing classical wisdom with the lessons he had learned from observing leaders of his own time, he was doing in political philosophy what those great Florentine artists Leonardo da Vinci and Michelangelo had done in painting and sculpture, uniting tradition and experiment to produce an original masterpiece.

Of this brilliant reflection on the rise and fall of principalities, Machiavelli wrote, "it should be especially welcome to a new prince, for which reason I dedicate it to his Magnificence Giuliano." The author obviously hoped that his book would speak to generations, but his immediate concern was that it should win for him the good will of the Medici. Again he failed. He hesitated before sending the work to Giuliano, and meantime the intended honoree died. In the hope of gaining some preferment, Machiavelli then rededicated the book to a living duke, Lorenzo of Urbino, who never even acknowledged the tribute.

Various historians and biographers have pointed out that it is well for Machiavelli's fame and influence that he never regained political favor. He went back to his studies and his writing, expanding *The Prince* to the full greatness of his concept. It was not printed until 1532, half a decade after the author's death. If Machiavelli had resumed the kind of public activities that had engaged his time and energy in Soderini's administration, he might possibly have led another army to some now forgotten defeat or victory, but this is unlikely. It is virtually certain that his eloquence would have been exhausted in oral pleas to often blasé princes or would have gathered dust in files of official correspondence.

The cynical tone of Machiavelli's book has given rise to the adjective *Machiavellian*, implying unscrupulous subtlety. The Machiavellian villain in the plays of Shakespeare and other Elizabethan and Jacobean dramatists has caused many people to think of the Florentine political theorist as an Iago. Gloucester in Shakespeare's *Henry VI* refers to "the murtherous Machiavel." The evil Flamineo in John Webster's *The White Devil* takes savage glee in "the rare tricks of a Machivillian (cq)," and Christopher Marlowe's *The Jew of Malta* not only has a Machiavellian villain in the person of Barabas but the prologue supposedly is spoken by Machiavelli himself. English and French willingness to attribute all sorts of vileness to Italians in the seventeenth century caused the Florentine's name to become increasingly synonymous with low trickery. The irony of the situation is that Machiavelli appears to have been regarded as an honest man by most of his respectable associates.

This anomaly springs from his separation of public and private morality. Machiavelli believed that states should not be bound by the laws of ethics binding upon virtuous individuals and that individuals when acting for the state should be free of such restrictions. The concept is that embodied in Sir Henry Wotton's description of an ambassador as "an honest man sent to lie abroad for the Commonwealth." The principle has been denied by many political philosophers and has been vehemently attacked by such practicing statesmen as Thomas Jefferson and Woodrow Wilson. But it has been followed often even by governments that deny it lip service.

Certainly Machiavelli's cynicism is understandable in one who had engaged in the politics of Renaissance Italy when assassination was a favored weapon of statecraft. But one does not have to accept his standards of public morality to testify to the value of his book. It has been a stimulus to the thoughts of brilliant idealists as well as a text of unquestioned acceptance for intellectual pragmatists.

Indeed, some have seen *The Prince* as an idealistic work because, despite the villainous machinations all about him and his own personal reverses in pursuit of a public career, the author continued to cherish the patriotic dream of an Italy united under some leader dedicated to the expulsion of all its foreign enemies. The influence of the book is manifest boldly in Francis Bacon's *Essays* and Sir Walter Ralegh's *Cabinet-Council* and more subtly in the papers and policies of Thomas Cromwell and William Cecil, first Baron Burghley.

Many people may find what appear to be traces of idealism in Machiavelli's writings. He says, "as the observance of divine worship is the cause of greatness in republics, so the neglect of it is the cause of their ruin. Because," he argues, "where the fear of God is wanting, it comes about either that a kingdom is ruined, or that it is kept going by the fear of a prince, which makes up for the lack of religion. And . . . princes are short-lived. . . ."[13] But we cannot assume that these statements are necessarily declarations of personal piety. They are reports on what the author, as a student of history and a holder of public office, has found to work.

"Of all men that are praised," he wrote, "those are praised most who have played the chief part in founding a religion." Next in order were founders of republics or kingdoms, followed by those who by military operations had "added to the extent of their own dominions or to that of their country's." Literary men, he thought, should be added to the list. He concluded emphatically, "On the other hand, those are held to be infamous and detestable who extirpate religion, subvert kingdoms and republics, make war on virtue, on letters, and on any art that brings advantage and honour to the human race, i.e. the profane, the violent, the ignorant, the debauched, the idle, the coward."

Machiavelli did not hold that any formula or code of conduct would insure the success of a state. "Fortune," he insisted, "determines one half of our actions," but far from seeing men as solely pawns of fate, he added, "but . . . she leaves us to control the other half."[14] The person of *virtù*,[15] he was convinced, was more nearly independent of chance than other people.[16] He admonished, "God does not want to have to do the whole thing, for he likes to leave us our free will so we can lay claim to part of the glory by earning it."[17]

He saw force and then guile as essential in the leadership of any society until such time as wholesome customs and habits had gained sufficient ascendancy over the passions of the people. Perhaps the most famous passage in *The Prince* is that in which Machiavelli uses the lion to symbolize force and the fox to represent cunning. The leader of a government, he says, must imitate both, "for the lion does not know how to avoid traps, and the fox is easily overpowered by wolves. So you must be a fox when it comes to suspecting a trap, and a lion when it comes to making the wolves turn tail."[18] This quotation influenced the thought and inspired the title of James MacGregor Burns' famous *Roosevelt: The Lion and the Fox.*

Other political scientists have been impressed by such observations as: "The vast majority of men, so long as their goods and their honor are not taken from them, will live contentedly. . . ."[19] Both scholars and intellectual politicians have found much to mull in the quotation:

a people differs in no wise from a wild animal which, though by nature fierce and accustomed to the woods, has been brought up in captivity and servitude and is then loosed to rove the countryside at will, where, being unaccustomed to seeking its own food and discovering no place in which it can find refuge, it becomes the prey of the first comer who seeks to chain it up again.[20]

There is an echo in the comment attributed to Alexander Hamilton: "Sir, your people is a great beast." Machiavelli's dictum is itself an echo of Plato's reference to the public as a "great strong beast." The Florentine may have been original in picturing the beast not merely as a potential danger but as a creature itself easily victimized.

The Prince is one of the few books of any age deserving the much overworked adjective *seminal*. It is frequently considered the most important work of either scholarly literature or philosophy produced in Europe in a generation. Many see it as marking the advent of objective political science. In the realm of books it is cited, almost as much as the work of Michelangelo or Leonardo da Vinci in art, as an example of the extraordinary cultural vitality of Renaissance Florence. Machiavelli's literary record is even more impressive in light of its versatility. He produced some of the outstanding allegorical verse of his day, his era's most widely quoted treatises on military command and the creation of armies, a highly regarded biography, a history of Florence still valuable to researchers, a distinguished work on linguistics, and *Mandragola*, one of the principal European dramas of the century.

Highly critical of Machiavelli but having much in common with him was Francesco Guicciardini. He, too, was the author of political treatises and histories. In his case also, his commentaries benefited from his own military and political experience. He was more successful than Machiavelli in his efforts to gain Medici patronage. About three years after Cardinal Giovanni de' Medici became Pope Leo X, he appointed Guicciardini governor of Modena, keeping him in one responsible post or another from 1516 to 1534. In *Considerations on the Discourses of Machiavelli*, Guicciardini attacked the author of *The Prince* for giving too much weight to the experience of classical Rome, as opposed to that of contemporary Italy, in attempting to lay the foundations of a science of politics. His own political views, though similar to Machiavelli's, are usually considered more radical.

Guicciardini's greatest accomplishments were as a historian. His *History of Florence* and *History of Italy* are brilliant in both narrative and analysis. Indeed, the second work is a great example of heritage and experiment combining to produce a masterpiece—in this case, one of the principal achievements of European historiography.

Another important writer, an art student of Michelangelo's and a protégé of the Medici, was Giorgio Vasari (1511–1574), whose *Lives of the Most Excellent Italian Architects, Painters, and Sculptors* has been quoted several times in these pages. To this work he brought not only a wide acquaintance among artists and architects of historical importance but also his own considerable skills in painting and architecture, which made him a knowledgeable and sympathetic interpreter. Additionally, his clear style, anecdotal gifts, and warm personality helped to make his book one of the handful of truly great classics in art history.

Art history was being made as well as written. As Pope Leo X, Giovanni de' Medici had the opportunity to be a patron of art on a scale unequaled by any of his ancestors. He was generous in sponsorship of Michelangelo, whose genius as an architect was universally recognized. But his favorite artist was another titan, Raphael (1483–1520). The healthy balance of influence between medieval Christian tradition and experiment inspired by rediscovery of the classics was conspicuously exemplified in this artist's work.

Though a native of Urbino and the son of its foremost painter, Raphael gravitated to Florence, where he lived for three years, becoming internationally famous. He was deeply influenced by Leonardo da Vinci's work, paying in a portrait of Maddalena Doni the tribute of frank imitation of the *Mona Lisa*. Every distinguishing feature of Leonardo's masterpiece appears in that of Raphael—except for the enigmatic smile, and that was not particularly missed. Of course, nobody seems to have concentrated on the Gioconda smile before Walter Pater in the nineteenth century. Soon Raphael met another great Florentine painter, Fra Bartolommeo (1472–1517), and from him learned the magic of rich coloring and softened outlines. During the Florentine years, Raphael was incorporating in his work devices used by both great masters. Those years exuberantly launched him upon a happy eclecticism through which he arrived at a style rich in its borrowings but unquestionably his own.

They also marked the beginning of his career as a beneficiary of the patronage of one member or another of the Medici family, climaxed at last by his support from Leo X. Actually, he had moved to Rome to serve Leo's predecessor, Julius II. The young artist's cousin, the great Bramante, was already in the papal service as an architect and hard at work on Saint Peter's. Michelangelo was making a populous heaven of the ceiling in the Sistine Chapel, and a half dozen other renowned artists and innumerable skilled craftsmen were doing exciting things. Julius commissioned Raphael to adorn some of the walls of his personal apartments and was so pleased with the resulting murals that he called a halt to the work of three other distinguished painters, ordered their creations whitewashed, and asked the young man to cover the surfaces with his own work. To his credit, Raphael persuaded the pope to retain some of the work of his predecessors. Most of the work, however, was done by Raphael, thus gaining not only in excellence but also in unity.

When Julius died with the project still incomplete, the artist wondered if he would be given the opportunity to finish it. But the new pope, Leo X, insisted that the work continue. In concept, the project represented the blend of medieval piety and classicism characteristic of Renaissance Italian civilization at its best. In execution, it became one of the greatest triumphs of that civilization.

Raphael spent four and a half years in covering a semicircular wall with a visual paean to Christianity. The artist was already one of the world's greatest painters of Madonnas, and his ability to blend realism with sublime mysticism was a priceless asset. But never before had he attempted anything on so grand a scale as these monumental figures, not only of the fathers and doctors of the church and the saints but even of the Trinity. Adam, Abraham, David, Peter, Paul, Jerome, Augustine, Ambrose, Thomas Aquinas, Duns Scotus, Dante, and even Savonarola—these and many more, busy at appropriate tasks, composed a symphony of faith extending from ancient Judaism through early Christianity and medieval sainthood into the Renaissance. Raphael's extraordinary gifts as a portraitist enabled him to give a haunting individuality to the separate characters while his aptitude for complex composition enabled him to create of them an unbroken melodic line of interwoven intricacy. An amazing achievement for an artist beginning the task before his twenty-fourth birthday and finishing it in his twenty-eighth year!

Actually, however, great as the scope of the work was, it was only the first phase of a four-phase project. On a wall directly facing the chronicle of faith, Raphael painted *The School of Athens.* It was an institution that had never existed outside the imagination. Nor was it a school in the sense of a group of people representing a dominant concept. In an outdoor urban environment of classical design, about fifty people stroll the streets, stand in clusters, or sit at ease, even sprawling on stone steps, all engaged in conversations or lost in concentration on a problem attacked alone. Of different generations and varying primary interests, they differ with each other on many points.

They are alike in that they are all intellectual representatives of classical Greek thought. Tall, magisterial Plato, lofty browed and white bearded, points upward as if to the realms of ideal thought. He bears such a striking resemblance to Leonardo da Vinci that some believe Raphael, lacking an authentic portrait of the Greek thinker, used as a model his own Italian contemporary.[21] With Plato is his pupil Aristotle, hand extended palm down as if to indicate a more mundane level. Plato's own mentor, stocky, round-headed Socrates, ticks off points on his stubby fingers in dialogue with Alcibiades as faithful straight man. Heraclitus' moving hand tries vainly to make the flow of his writing match the passage of time, fully aware that each discrete moment is irrevocable. Pythagoras, on the other hand, plots the immutable harmonies of the universe, while Ptolemy and Zoroaster each find world enough in a globe. Archimedes transmits to several young students his own enthusiasm for geometric configuration. Diogenes, stretched out nearly naked on steps in the foreground, is perhaps resting after hunting with a lantern for an honest man and is frankly revealing a good deal of anatomical truth. A young boy, the very opposite of Shakespeare's lad who "crept like th' unwilling snail to school," runs up with his books in the kind of eager pantomime beloved in National Education Week posters.

Two smaller walls awaited the artist's brush, each a special challenge because the mural surface was interrupted by a window. One of these walls was devoted to the arts. The scene represented Parnassus, with Apollo seated under the laurel trees and playing a viol. Who can say that viols were not known on Parnassus before mere mortals invented them? A bare-breasted muse is at his side. Homer chants; Sappho plays a cithara. Virgil, Horace, Ovid, and Tibullus are entertaining each other. Mingling happily with them in an environment that knows no generational barriers are Petrarch, Boccaccio, Ariosto, and other Renaissance luminaries. And the same stern-faced Dante that appeared with the philosophers and theologians on the first wall appears again here among artists of song and word. He has impeccable credentials for either group and thus is able to appear in two places at once. Does Dante the artist feel at home with a seminude muse on whom Dante the theologian might cast a disapproving eye?

The window challenge that was overcome compositionally on the third wall was converted into an asset on the fourth. This mural celebrated the rule of law. The window became a divider between civil law and canon law. Such figures as Solomon, the Emperor Justinian, and Pope Gregory IX appeared on this wall or the adjacent ceiling.

The fact that, early in the sixteenth century, Raphael and Michelangelo were simultaneously at work in Rome on their greatest masterpieces is important both symbolically and substantively. Even apart from all the other evidence of artistic and intellectual vitality in Rome at the time, the simultaneous creation there of two of the supreme works of human history would indicate the occurrence of a rare phenomenon. The harmonious mingling of classical and medieval Christian influences with artistic experimentation in each case is completely representative of the vital Florentine Renaissance culture that now was triumphant in Rome. With one of the greatest of the Medici patrons of art and learning on the throne of Saint Peter, and with all roads once again leading to (and from) Rome, the Florentine Renaissance was so truly international as to have outgrown the designation of *Florentine*.

The age produced more supremely great graphic art than it did literature of comparable quality. But the leading producers of scholarly literature (and there were notable ones) tended to be members of the papal court such as Pietro Bembo, a former member of Lorenzo the Magnificent's circle, and Jacopo Sadoleto, a humanist in the Florentine tradition. Rival scholars owing much to direct or indirect Florentine influences held positions at the University of Rome. They found in the healthy tension between heritage and experiment the same vitality that had given birth to the Renaissance.

While Rome coruscated with the brilliance of the culture born in Florence, and Florentine artists created masterpieces there under the patronage of a Florentine pope, the light of Florence itself faded to a dim effulgence. In Florence, patriotic pride had degenerated into insolence, and the excited search for truth had become an effort to reconstruct past glories. In the Age of Lorenzo, Florence had scorned Rome as a city mired in the past. But the life-quickening tides that had once flowed out from the Arno to the shores of the civilized world now, instead, flowed again from old Tiber.

11

WHY THE RENAISSANCE
LEFT HOME

ENAISSANCE FLORENCE is a classic example of the influence on
a society of the shifting balance between heritage and experiment. Of
course only a hopeless ideologue would account for the rise and fall of
vitality solely in terms of a single principle. But a recapitulation of the heritage
and experiment factor at work in fifteenth- and sixteenth-century Florence,
together with consideration of a few of the circumstances tending to modify
that influence, may be worthwhile.

The Italian Renaissance, as I have tried to keep in mind in preceding chapters, embraced far more territory than Florence in its inception and even more
in its fruition. Florence merits special attention because it played a critical role
in that movement.

At the necessary risk of oversimplifying, but without being the least bit
original, I have emphasized that the Italian Renaissance owed its existence to
four principal factors: the rise of city-states ruled by merchant-princes; the need
and the stimulus for seeking different markets, which furnished new ideas as
well as new products (particularly from the Arab countries); the enthusiastic
rediscovery of classical writings; and the inclination of the chiefs of state to
become patrons of art and scholarship. These factors provided the excitement
of discovery of the exotic culture of the Arabs and rediscovery of classical
Western culture. Excitement whetted a sense of adventure, which played against
native tradition and the medieval Christian tradition to provide a tension that
stimulated creativity. The leadership of many of the city-states by merchant-
princes who had the money to vie with each other as patrons of art and scholarship provided the resources to finance creative activity. These patrons had a
different agenda from society's traditional patron, the Roman Catholic Church,
and this in itself was liberating. The combination of all these things, quite pre-
dictably, produced in Italy a period of cultural vitality.

Not so obviously predictable was the fact that it would produce in one of
the least distinguished of Italian cities one of the greatest cultural efflorescences
in history. Florence shared in the general awakening of the peninsula's commu-

nities, but at the start of the Renaissance it was not prominent even in its own province of Tuscany. In a time when the Mediterranean provided paths to prosperity and power, Florence, being equidistant from the Mediterranean and the Adriatic, was highly disadvantaged in comparison with coastal cities. Moreover, the city did not even occupy an elevated position commanding land routes to seaports, but was in a valley dominated by the heights on which the rival city of Fiesole stood. Florence also lacked natural resources. It promised to be one of those communities for which the great adventure in the wake of the Crusades would be temporarily stimulating but ultimately debilitating.

Yet Florence was saved when other cities similarly humble in origin and little blessed by nature found the tidal wave of change too strong to contend with. Florence was rescued and inspired to extraordinary accomplishment by its persistence in regarding itself as the heir to ancient Rome. Virtually all European cities were inheritors of Roman civilization, but Florence regarded itself as peculiarly so. This belief, to quote Ferdinand Schevill again, "became the first and outstanding article of the civic faith with which Florence began her existence."[1] It provided the antithesis to change necessary for a healthy equation of tradition and experiment and, at the same time, provided the basis of a strong patriotism and sense of community—both essential to triumph, or even strong survival, amid a welter of challenging mutations.

The healthy tension between heritage and adventure was central to the vitality and fruitfulness of the Renaissance wherever it transformed society. And, as noted earlier, this effectiveness was increased by a peculiar complexity: the "new" elements of the period were parts of a rediscovered classical background and therefore representative also of tradition. These circumstances have a great deal to do with the transforming power of the Renaissance in Florence as in all other Italian communities in which the phenomenon occurred. But even in combination with the extraordinary patriotism that fueled Florence's aspirations sufficiently to offset severe disadvantages of physical environment, the tradition-experiment equation (while perhaps sufficient to account for her attainment of parity with her sister cities) is insufficient to account for her eventual primacy.

One generally acknowledged factor in Florence's advance was its consistently able leadership from 1421 to 1492. The top post, by whatever name it was known at any point during this entire period, was held by a member of one family, the Medici. Ordinarily this would not be a recipe for effective government or certainly for maximum service to the people. But the period was one in which autocracy prevailed in every community. There was no such thing as being free of tyrants. Despotism was inescapable, and the most fortunate communities were those that had enlightened despots. Giovanni di Bicci de' Medici, first of his family to lead Florence, brought to the task intelligence and a sense of responsibility. The next three generations of his descendants furnished the leadership of Cosimo the Elder, Piero, and Lorenzo the Magnificent, who to these two qualities added intellectual curiosity and an active interest in the arts.

Cosimo, Piero, and Lorenzo all stimulated cultural development by generous and discerning patronage of learning and the arts. All three—but particularly Lorenzo—provided added stimulus to intellectual and artistic progress by personal involvement. Their example made culture both an adventure and a status symbol.

Also highly significant is the fact that while the government of Florence, like all others in Italy, was tyrannical, it did not exploit its citizens to the degree then common even among governments less autocratic in structure. Much emphasis was placed on education for all capable of learning, and the libraries and art collections of the Medici were opened to the public. The emphasis was not just on training citizens for the performance of specific tasks but on opening their minds to culture in the broadest sense. Renaissance theorists celebrated the capabilities of each human being, and Florence's leaders emphasized the ideal of enabling the individual to develop his (and under Lorenzo, her) multifold potential. The dominant philosophy of the Renaissance and the attitude of the Florentine government combined to produce a population including many well-rounded members as well as some of history's greatest polymaths and foremost creative geniuses. The cross-fertilization resulting from individual thought across several disciplines was as important as that resulting from exchange with other cultures. This intellectual versatility was so notable a feature of the period as to give rise to the terms *Renaissance man* and *Renaissance woman*.

Another important attribute of the Medici leaders at their most effective was the skill with which they combined the encouragement of new ideas and practices with reminders of community heritage. This they accomplished by a variety of methods ranging from explicit verbal messages to symbolic pageantry. For a long time, this helped to insure the healthy tension between tradition and adventure and also to build patriotism and confidence in the ability to excel. The Medici chiefs insured their own continuity, in large part, by associating themselves with community traditions cherished by the populace.

A constant revitalizing exchange of ideas and the concomitant growth of Florentine influence were assured by the Tuscan universities and other centers of learning. The republic at its height never closed its mind to new ideas or its gates to the bearers of them. The government did not scrimp on education even in times of economic recession. There was recognition at the top that the economy, as well as the culture, ultimately would profit from an educated citizenry. Indeed, not only was Florentine education at a peak during a recession but so was creativity. Obviously an economy incapable of satisfying basic physical wants would not have left its citizens free to think much about art and higher learning, and certainly patronage of those pursuits would have been impossible without accumulated wealth. But the state of the economy was by no means a barometer of the cultural climate.

Another extraordinary feature of the republic, in view of its being an autocracy, was the freedom of speech and writing permitted in its cultural heyday. Remarkable at any time in the history of autocratic government, this freedom was absolutely astonishing in Renaissance Italy. Striking evidence of its existence is Lorenzo the Magnificent's toleration of the accusations that Savonarola thundered at him from the pulpit of San Marco while the political chief sat in the congregation.

What caused a decline in Florence's cultural vigor? Primarily a serious disturbance of the equation of tradition and experiment. The healthy tension between the attractions of the new humanism and the appeal of medieval Christian tradition was destroyed by the increasing pull of humanism to an extent that separated the political and intellectual leaders not only from the masses but also eventually from the prosperous and educated middle class. Lorenzo and some of his circle laughed over irreverent bons mots that angered many citizens. A Renaissance culture originating in the study of Latin and Greek had moved from the linguistic to the linguinal. Petrarch's laments of a pining heart had been replaced with verses inspired by an aching groin. Some much-applauded art was hostile to spiritual values that once had been combined with secular elements in important artistic creations. Savonarola, who preached a return to medieval spiritual values, not only aroused tremendous enthusiasm among ordinary members of his congregation but won support from some humanists in Lorenzo's own circle, among them the young genius Michelangelo.

With Savonarola's rise to leadership and the expulsion from Florence of Medici leaders more flawed than their predecessors, there was more stable government and a resurgence of creativity. This creativity, as always in Florence, was most manifest in the arts. Here the reinvigoration, resulting from a spiritual infusion upon the revival of some medieval values, was clearly evident.

But some of Savonarola's followers carried reform to extremes beyond anything he had advocated. Finally, the bonfires lit by his eloquence began to consume not only civilization's vanities but also its treasures. This imbalance led to an opposite reaction.

Though the Medici were restored to office in Florence, those in power lacked the discipline and judgment of Cosimo the Elder or Lorenzo the Magnificent. Corruption increased, and people lost faith in their neighbors, their country, and themselves. Weeds of failure were already growing in the fields of triumph when Guicciardini wrote, "[To attempt to rival ancient Rome] with means so inferior as ours is to require of the ass the fleetness of the horse."[2] The ablest of the Medici of the new generation, Giovanni, became Pope Leo X and from Rome fostered an international cultural movement based on a productive balance between allegiance to the traditions of medieval Christianity and involvement with the great intellectual and artistic ventures prompted by the spirit of classical humanism.

While the Renaissance continued to flourish in widening circles, Florence was in decline. There, as we have seen, the quest for glory had become an attempt to repeat the past. The lack of inspired and dedicated leadership hastened the downward trend. So did economic decline. When Florence had had the proper tension between heritage and adventure and had enjoyed able leadership, economic recession had been powerless to curb its cultural vitality. But lacking those two essential elements, the city was devitalized by financial misfortune. The rise of formidable nation-states accelerated the process of decline. Florence had neither the imagination, the initiative, nor the spirit to reach accommodations with them or with her sister cities that would have provided a new lease on life.

In *Renaissance Florence* (pp. 256–257), Gene Brucker succinctly states both the chief reason for the republic's extraordinary creativity and the chief evidence of its decline:

> The achievements of Florentine artists and humanists in the early Quattrocento constitute the most striking evidence for the creative possibilities of this felicitous combination of the old and the new. By the middle decades of the fifteenth century, however, these particular features of the Florentine experience were in eclipse. The most notable characteristic of Florentine (and Italian) history in the later Quattrocento is the spirit of conservatism which pervades every phase of human activity. In politics, in social and economic relations, in religion and culture, institutions have become more rigid, the range of choices and alternatives more limited.

The vitality of Rome at this time, energizing a continent, was a reminder of what could be accomplished by a society, given a healthy balance between tradition and experiment, able leadership, a significant measure of free expression, emphasis on education, and intellectual curiosity that would not accept isolation either geographically or through a too rigidly exclusive, self-imposed specialization. At its best, the Renaissance was now spreading throughout Europe the realization that isolation, either temporal or spatial, is the enemy of both self-fulfillment and realization of community potential. For maximum fruitfulness, there must be an interchange with other times and places. And, while talented people might serve civilized society best by acquiring expertise in one or more specialties, there was growing awareness that mastery of any intellectual specialty is impossible without an informed appreciation of interrelated specialties. Cultural rebirth was exciting, but it was also demanding and not without labor pains.

ELIZABETHAN ENGLAND

12

SAINTS AND
SINNERS—ENGLISH STYLE

FLORENCE'S FRENCH CONQUERORS were impressed with the city. King Charles VIII decided to annex its culture as well as its territory. Not only did he send back to his own realm manuscripts, paintings, tapestries, and thirty-four tons of statuary. He took home an organ builder, goldsmiths, a worker in marquetry, artists in several categories, a landscape gardener, three architects, and (a particularly French touch) a ladies' dressmaker.[1] Evidently the fifteenth century monarch's attitude toward Florence was similar to that a twentieth century United States chief of state, Calvin Coolidge, would have toward Charles' country when he asked, "Can't we get all the art we need from France?"

Apparently Charles had also taken all Florentine knowledge for his province, not by the laborious process of personal conquest but, as became a king, through the armies of scholars and potential scholars at his command. First he looked to the arsenal of learning. The captured manuscripts were a start and he hired Giovanni Lascaris, the Medici librarian, who also would teach classes in Greek. The king's retainers were quick to perceive that the classical studies were "in." Charles had brought along on his Italian campaign his court poet, much as later conquerors would transport favored correspondents to celebrate their victories. Vincent Cronin said that the poet "was ignorant of classical allusions"[2] on entering Italy but before he left the country was hailing his sovereign as a worthy companion of Mars, Caesar, Pompey, and Hector.

In time France developed the spirit, as well as the trappings, of the Renaissance. Guillaume Budé, one of Lascaris' students, eventually succeeded his teacher as royal librarian and also founded the Collège de France, which became a famous center of humanist studies. This activity was under a new king, Francis I, who came to the throne in 1515. An enthusiastic patron of arts and letters, he was a true Renaissance ruler. By this time, Pico and Ficino were studied at the Sorbonne. Soon the French Renaissance had spawned a literary giant of its own, François Rabelais, priest, physician, university lecturer, translator, antiquarian, diplomat, essayist, and novelist. Of course, he earned his greatest fame as the author of *Gargantua and Pantagruel*, in the process adding the words *gargantuan* and *rabelaisan* to the international vocabulary. In the variety of his interests and activities, he exemplified the Renaissance. And though mention of his most famous creation calls to mind astounding physical hunger and thirst, we must not forget that Gargantua also had a vast appetite for less material things; he voiced Renaissance aspirations when he longed to learn every language, read every great book, and acquire all sciences useful to man.

Spain's presence in Italy, where it held Naples as a fief of Aragon, gave access to the Florentine Renaissance. In 1492, the year that Lorenzo the Magnificent died, Columbus planted the Spanish sovereign's standard in the Americas. Spain was simultaneously discovering a New World and rediscovering the Old World of the Greeks and Romans. In the same year, Antonio de Nebrija produced his *Gramatica Castellana*, becoming the first grammarian and the first lexicographer of any Romance language. New World discoveries awakened a sense of intellectual adventure to match the geographical exploration, and this was quickly expressed in Spanish literature.

By 1520 Spain's Renaissance was further stimulated by the writings of Desiderius Erasmus, the prime figure in his country's version of the same movement. He showed the way to the combination of classical rediscovery and Christian tradition that had been so fruitful in Florence at its best.

Centered in the German states was a whole northern Renaissance, rich in both art and practical invention. The star of this movement was Albrecht Dürer, one of the greatest artists in history but also an earnest student of botany and zoology who combined a pious love of Christian tradition with an eager curiosity about the new findings of humanist science. Dürer's rendering of turf composed of many different varieties of grass as seen from ground level is believed to be "the first precise ecological study in botany."[3] He collaborated with a great polymath of the Swiss Renaissance, Konrad Gesner (1516–1565), to produce the then most scientifically accurate picture of a rhinoceros. Gesner, self-educated, produced a Greek-Latin dictionary at the age of twenty. All in all, he wrote some seventy volumes covering many branches of knowledge. His *Biblioteca universatis*, in which he cataloged the works of eighteen hundred authors in Greek, Latin, and Hebrew, made him the father of bibliography. Despite his collaboration with such a scholar, Dürer's position in his native land was not so elevated as it would have been in Florence. The practical-minded Germans, who later would astound the world with their music and other artistic creations of genius, were not yet ready to give full respect to one known primarily as an artist. On a visit to Italy, Dürer wrote, "Here I am a gentleman, at home only a parasite."[4]

When the Renaissance came to England, it produced a more complex and more fruitful culture than it had anywhere on the European continent except in the Italian states themselves. An important factor in the development is that England inherited the Renaissance experience of the whole Continent at the same time that it fell heir to the traditions of classical humanism. The sea and

Channel that served the island nation "in the office of a wall, or as a moat defensive to a house," also slowed the invasion of Continental fashions.

When Florence and her sister states were reveling in the productions of humanism, some Italians spoke scornfully of English backwardness, particularly ridiculing the islanders' failure to produce impressive literature. Some implied that an inborn weakness was responsible. This assumption is ironic in view of the fact that in the seventh century the English monasteries at Wearmouth and Jarrow had been the foremost centers of learning in western Europe. In the eighth century, England's Venerable Bede became, in Wattenbach's words, "the teacher of all the Middle Ages," and Alcuin of York became the chief channel of classical literature to Charlemagne's court and the leading scholar of the Carolingian Renaissance. After the eclipse of English learning early in the ninth century principally as a result of Viking raids, King Alfred himself led a renascence of learning in England, translating Latin classics into English and making a school of his court.[5]

Italian scorn for English literary failings soon seemed even more ironic when the English Renaissance, though falling far short of the Italian in graphic arts, reached literary heights never attained by the Florentine Renaissance. Supercilious boasting is risky. A society proud in the full harvest of its cultural glories may show only intellectual stubble when the seasonal sun moves on to bless a hitherto barren scene.

The connection between the Florentine Renaissance and the English Renaissance was direct. Thomas Linacre, a young Englishman in Florence, had been invited by Lorenzo the Magnificent to study with his own son Piero, under Politian and other prominent scholars. Afterwards Linacre studied at the University of Padua. His Italian experience was so moving that on leaving Italy, in a mood of almost religious veneration, he made an altar of stones at the last Alpine pass. He solemnly dedicated the cairn to his "sancta mater studiorum."

This was no mere youthful whim. Back in England, as the years passed, he continued to reverence that sacred mother. He became a physician, founder and first president of the Royal College of Physicians, and so combined humanist scholarship with his profession that he is often cited as a better example of the Renaissance scholar-physician than any colleague in Italy. He translated some of Galen's famous medical text into a Latin that Erasmus pronounced finer than the original Greek. Pico della Mirandola remained a hero to him. Linacre not only took Pico for a role model but translated a biography of him into English, thus making the Florentine's example and ideas available to other Englishmen.

Renaissance studies became a stronger influence at court when Linacre was appointed tutor to Prince Arthur and, upon Henry VIII's accession, royal physician. England's foremost statesmen and proudest prelates also sought Linacre's medical services, and he advised on many matters other than personal health care.

He influenced education by his benefactions to medical teaching at both Oxford and Cambridge. In the academic world, his scholarly attainments were greatly enhanced by his financial endowments. Not that his scholarly credentials on their own would not stand both the most narrowly pedantic and the most broadly cultural scrutiny. Linacre wrote a Latin grammar and a book on Latin composition. Even more important than any body of intellectual achievement attributed to him was his function as a clearinghouse for ideas among his own countrymen and leading scholarly thinkers on the Continent. He was the close friend of Erasmus, John Colet, William Grocyn, and Sir Thomas More. Many people of his own day almost surely would have thought it extremely unlikely that a few generations later such a man would be almost forgotten by all except specialists in the English Renaissance.

William Grocyn himself provided England another direct link with the Florentine Renaissance. Like Linacre, he had studied Greek under Politian. Whether or not Grocyn was the first Englishman of his day to teach Greek, he was the real establisher of Greek studies at Oxford, bringing the stimulus of classical literature to contemporary concerns. He introduced his students not only to an unfamiliar language but to some of the humanist context. A brilliant student of his, Thomas More, became one of his best friends.

John Colet, after studies at Oxford, had spent three years of study in France and Italy. His Florentine experience had brought him under the influence of the humanism of Ficino and Pico and the spiritual reform of Savonarola. Upon his return to England, he was soon in a position to influence many people. His Oxford lectures on the Pauline Epistles, combining history and theology in exegesis, drew large crowds. Later he was dean of Saint Paul's and founded Saint Paul's School, making the classics an integral part of the curriculum. He personally espoused Neoplatonism of the school of Plotinus, drawing heavily on Ficino and Pico, but attacked ecclesiastical abuses with a zeal reminiscent of Savonarola. Indeed, his fearless denunciations brought him to the edge of punishment for heresy. He worked with Erasmus, Grocyn, Linacre, and Thomas More to promote humanistic values in Europe.

In the communication of Renaissance humanism from Florence to England, Linacre, Grocyn, and Colet all played essential roles as direct bringers of the word. As the chief figure of the northern Renaissance, Erasmus, friend of these English humanists, influenced thinkers throughout western Europe, but his influence became direct in England when William Blount, Lord Mountjoy, who had known him as a tutor in Paris, became his patron. Erasmus' Italian humanism was acquired in Paris. He brought to education a selective advocacy of humanism, writing, "I wished that good letters should find that Christian character which they have lacked in Italy, and which, as you know, ended in glorifying pagan morality." While writing religious works, he translated Pliny and Seneca, and drew on Cicero and Terence. He insisted that, although English was not his native tongue, it was his "natural" one. After leaving England in 1500, he returned repeatedly in the course of travels among Paris, Padua, Venice, Rome, Louvain, and Basel. He stood for a selective and rational use of tradition while making changes necessary for reform. His great masterpiece, *The Praise of Folly*, was written in the home of Sir Thomas More.

Sir Thomas More—the story of the early English Renaissance always comes back to him.[6] Both Colet and Erasmus praised him as the greatest genius in England. Erasmus said that More's household was comparable to Plato's Academy as a center for scholarship and virtue, yet superior to the original because the English residence was also "a school for Christian religion." Such was More's learning and versatility that he would have been a giant even in the Florence of Lorenzo the Magnificent. He stands today as one of the few people in history to be honored in the three capacities of scholar, politician, and saint.

Long before he was so formidable a figure, however, he was a precocious little boy eager for attention. His father, John More, was a prominent lawyer who later was knighted and became an influential judge. Young Thomas was enrolled at Saint Anthony's School and afterwards studied in the household of Thomas Cardinal Morton, where he served as a page. Here he had the opportunity to acquire a good education, and at the same time, attract the favorable attention of nationally important people. When plays were performed at Christmas under the aegis of the cardinal, Thomas "would suddenly sometimes step in among the players and, never studying for the matter, make a part of his own there presently among them." He was so personable that his forwardness, far from irritating his audience, delighted them more than the actions of the regular actors. The cardinal is said to have told his guests, "This child here waiting at the table . . . will prove a marvelous man."[7]

The boy entered Oxford at age fourteen and soon became so fascinated with classical literature that his practical-minded father was alarmed. He withdrew him from the university and sent him at age sixteen to London for legal training. Thomas became committed to the law, but not unwaveringly and certainly not exclusively. At the age of twenty-one, he met Erasmus. Here was a man versed in the classical literature that the young Englishman loved, but completely opposed to the Scholasticism with which some of Thomas' Oxford professors had been imbued. Thomas was hooked on humanism.

At twenty-three, though much involved with legal studies, he still found time to deliver public lectures on Saint Augustine's *City of God.* A monk's cell seemed more attractive than chambers of the law, and he seriously considered the priesthood. Though he continued his secular career, he wore next to his skin a horsehair shirt so abrasive that bloodstains sometimes showed on his top shirt. Increasingly he wrote on religious topics.

But the celibate state seemed to him an unnecessary prerequisite to serving God. He married (twice), fathered children, and entered politics. At twenty-six he was elected to Parliament and so effectively opposed King Henry VII's tax program that the monarch was incensed that "a beardless boy" could be such an impediment. The king insisted on acting as if More were a juvenile, even to the extent of heavily fining, and even briefly imprisoning, the father for the son's offense.

Thomas More became at thirty-one undersheriff of the City of London, actually a judicial office. He became known for learning and discernment, but even more for his refusal of presents from litigants. It was an age when an honest judge was thought of as one who accepted gifts from both sides but decided according to conviction regardless of variations in generosity. He celebrated his thirty-seventh birthday as Speaker of the House of Commons.

Visiting him two years later, Erasmus was enchanted by More in the role of paterfamilias. He seemed the "devoted husband and loving father" beloved of old-time obituary writers. But his dedication as family man was leavened with a good deal of humor. He kept a jester and a monkey in his household although his own proclivity for jokes and pranks would seem to make a hired comedian and a mischievous animal unnecessary. His highly intelligent daughters adored him, probably partly because he took them quite seriously and tried to give them as good an education as would be the lot of a privileged male. Erasmus makes the future Saint Thomas sound like Saint Francis of Assisi when he says that "all the birds in Chelsea come to him to be fed." Erasmus asked, "What did nature ever create milder, sweeter, and happier than the genius of Thomas More?"

More remained in Chelsea, but about six years later moved into one of its great mansions. Here there was ample room for his large family, his many pets, his great library (by the standards of the day), and his private gallery. A pale-skinned, auburn-haired man, quick to smile, a little careless of dress, he strolled the hundred yards of flower-embroidered turf between his house and the river, greeting the members of his menagerie. At such moments, he was the very model of that amiability that Erasmus had praised.

But he was not always that amiable. Henry VII had learned that when the "beardless boy" spoke in Parliament. That king's successor, Henry VIII, had learned it on Evil May Day 1517, when a mob of London apprentices assaulted foreign merchants. More bravely talked the rioters out of further violence and then joined a delegation to implore the king's pardon for the young men. In the same year, he was sent to Calais on a royal mission requiring the same combination of firmness and diplomacy that he had shown in the London crisis, a matter of settling international trade disputes. The king appointed More to his Council. Before the end of the year, he was not just another member of the Council but had specific duties as master of requests.

Henry VIII and More were enthusiastic about each other. The king seemed a reincarnation of Lorenzo the Magnificent, and in More he appeared to have found his Politian and Pico della Mirandola rolled into one, with a more benevolent Machiavelli for good measure. More had written memorial verses on the death of the king's mother and, later, Latin verses on Henry's accession. No mean writer himself, the king was fully capable of appreciating literary artistry. Like Lorenzo, he was both patron and practitioner of the arts. And like his Florentine predecessor, Henry came to power early, in his case at the age of eighteen. He larded his conversation with quotations from the Scriptures and Latin classics. He played a variety of musical instruments and composed two masses as well as simpler songs. He studied the practical sciences of shipbuilding, engineering, fortification, and artillery.

The parallels with Lorenzo were even closer. Henry entered with zest into elaborate pageantry, and so excelled at jousting that the duke of Suffolk was his only serious rival. A superb all-round athlete, he was one of the best archers and wrestlers in England. Like Lorenzo, he had a handsome athletic figure, but unlike Lorenzo he had a handsome face as well.

He also had Lorenzo's ability to captivate people. More said that Henry had "more learning than any English monarch ever possessed before him," evidently forgetting the versatile genius of Alfred the Great. "What may we not expect," he asked, "from a king who has been nourished by philosophy and the nine muses?" Observing the friendship between the monarch and his own friend More, Erasmus wrote, "The King not only admits such men as More to his court, but he invites them—compels them—to observe all that he does, to share his duties and his pleasures. He prefers the companionship of men like More to that of silly youths or girls or the rich."

The king wrote a learned theological essay defending the papacy against Martin Luther and earned from a grateful pope the title "Defender of the Faith," one that has been borne by his successors despite the break with Rome. Since Henry and More both gave allegiance to the church and classical learning, prospects seemed good for achieving in the government and society of England that favorable balance of influence between heritage and experiment that had proved so fruitful in Florence under the rule of Lorenzo.

Under Henry VIII, England was experiencing a surge of nationalism and a stimulus to a national literature drawing on both medieval and humanist sources. This was the same combination that had revivified France half a century before. That movement was still very much alive in the France of Francis I, and the sense of rivalry between the two nations frowning at each other across the Channel, and between the two lusty monarchs, fueled the creative energies of each nation. The first great national classic produced in England as a result of Renaissance learning and Renaissance tensions was Thomas More's *Utopia*. This book was peculiarly pertinent to the problems of the changing society that produced it because its humanist author's subject was his vision of an ideal society.

Utopia, of course, is the Greek word for "nowhere." Using it for a nonexistent country probably appealed to More's sense of humor. It also gave him an escape hatch if his picture of an ideal state angered some of the great powers of England. He could always imply that such a society was an abstraction that could exist nowhere in the real world. Another escape was provided by his adoption of the dialogue form so favored by the ancients. He could record his discourse with an imaginary character, presenting controversial ideas without necessarily revealing his real attitude toward them.

The imaginary character who supplies information about the ideal state is Raphael Hythloday, one of its citizens. More perpetrates the little private joke of having Raphael and himself discover that they have a common acquaintance, the same Cardinal Morton whom the author had once served as a page.

Despite precautions as to the form of his book, the writer nevertheless took serious risks. When More urges Raphael to put his intelligence and learning at the service of the public by becoming counselor to a king, Raphael objects that in "bondage to a king" he could accomplish little. "For, first of all, the most part of all princes have more delight in warlike matters and feats of chivalry (the knowledge whereof I neither have nor desire) than in the good feats of peace; and employ much more study how by right or by wrong to enlarge their dominions than how well and peaceably to rule and govern that they have already."[8]

It was the year after publication of this book that the king appointed its author to his Council. Some have suggested that Henry must not actually have read the book, but this supposition is doubtful in view of his voracious appetite for learning at that time.

The book includes a great deal of social criticism, voiced by Raphael and supposedly based on his observations on a trip to England before the reign of Henry VIII. The reader may decide whether the evils described have persisted into the reign of that monarch. The visitor, as a citizen of Utopia, finds conditions in England distressing. He is appalled by the prevalence of theft, and says that capital punishment for this offense is not only "too extreme and cruel" but utterly ineffective. There is no "punishment so horrible that it can keep them from stealing [who] have no other craft whereby to get their living. . . . Much rather, provision should have been made that there were some means whereby they might get their living, so that no man should be driven to this extreme necessity, first to steal and then to die." The book is surprisingly sophisticated in its attack on the causes of crime.

Raphael denounces one cause of poverty that he considers

> peculiar to you Englishmen alone. . . . Forsooth, your sheep, that were wont to be so meek and tame and so small eaters, now [have] become so great devourers and so wild that they eat up and swallow down the very men themselves. They consume, destroy, and devour whole fields, houses, and cities. For look in what parts of the realm doth grow the finest and therefore dearest wool; there noblemen and gentlemen, yea, and certain abbots (holy men, God wot!), not contenting themselves with the yearly revenues and profits [of] their forefathers and predecessors of their lands, not being content that they live in rest and pleasure, . . . leave no ground for tillage. They enclose all in pastures, they throw down houses; they pluck down towns, and leave nothing standing but only the church to make of it a sheephouse.

Thus More put into Raphael's mouth an indictment of the greed of great landowners who, by enclosing large areas for the profitable raising of sheep to supply the wool trade, deprived their tenants of plots for cultivation, and brought ruin to whole villages. The satire prefigures Jonathan Swift's "A Modest Proposal," published more than two centuries later, in which the ironic Dean pictures absentee landlords as devouring the children of Ireland. Here again, More's book is surprisingly insightful in its attack on the causes of crime.

In Utopia people are cured of the passion for gold. The power of association is used in the process. Those convicted of crimes are required to wear gold necklaces and earrings, and chamber pots are made of the same metal.

Through Raphael, More says:

> The unreasonable covetousness of a few hath turned to the utter undoing of your island. . . . Suffer not these rich men to buy up all, to

engross, and forestall, and with their monopoly to keep the market alone as pleases them. . . . When I consider and weigh in my mind all these commonwealths which now anywhere flourish, I can perceive nothing—so God help me—but a certain conspiring of rich men promoting their own commodities under the name and title of the Commonwealth.

More called for governmental intervention as a protection against monopoly and against conspiracies by employers to keep wages at the lowest possible level. His reasoning was a combination of Christian defense of the poor as found in both the Old and New Testaments and humanist ideas promoting individual potential.

Utopia is pictured as a place where communal ownership has supplanted the concept of private property. This system harks back to some communities of early Christians. In More's supposed conversation with Raphael, he protests that such a system is doomed because, like it or not, the average person is motivated to work only by "the regard of his own gains." Raphael retorts that he has learned differently from living in Utopia. Some Marxists claim More as a cautious exponent of communism. On the other hand, some scholars contend that, as Utopia is Greek for "nowhere" and Raphael Hythloday's surname means "full of poppycock," the author is implying that the communal system, while excellent in theory, would be unworkable. There can be no doubt, however, that whatever More's ideas about solutions may be, he is earnest in his criticism of what he regards as gross inequities in the economic and social systems of his time.

"In their land," More writes of the Utopians,

whoever is found guilty of theft must make restitution to the owner, not (as elsewhere) to the prince; they think the prince has no more right to the stolen goods than the thief. If the stolen property has disappeared, the value of the thief's property is estimated and restitution is made from it. All the rest is handed over to the thief's wife and children, while the thief himself is sentenced to hard labor.

This penance, however, was not served in a chain gang or on a prison-yard rock-pile.

Unless their crimes were compounded with atrocities, thieves are neither imprisoned nor shackled, but go freely and unguarded about their work on public projects. If they shirk and do their jobs slackly, they are not chained, but they are whipped. If they work hard, they are treated without any insults, except that at night after roll call they are locked up in their dormitories. Apart from constant work, they undergo no discomfort in living.

The generally benevolent tone of this passage, despite the provision for whipping, leaves the modern reader unprepared for the revelation that each prisoner has the tip of one ear cut off. Even more shocking is the news that, while friends are allowed to give prisoners food and drink, and clothing so long as it is of the uniform prison color, "to [give] them money is death, both to the giver and to the taker." Prisoners, for the period of their servitude, are known as slaves.[9]

"Premarital intercourse, in either men or women," says More, "if discovered and proved, is severely punished, and the guilty parties are forbidden to marry during their whole lives, unless the prince, by his pardon, alleviates the sentence. In addition, both the father and mother of the household where the offense occurred suffer public disgrace for having been remiss in their duty." The next observation of the narrator seems somewhat at variance with the picture that More's son-in-law William Roper has sketched of him as the happy paterfamilias. More says of the penalty meted out for premarital intercourse, "The reason they punish this offense so severely is that they suppose few people would join in married love—with confinement to a single partner, and all the petty annoyances that married life involves—unless they were strictly restrained from a life of promiscuity."

Not all of courtship in Utopia was so inhibited. "Whether she is a widow or a virgin," says More,

> the bride-to-be is shown naked to the groom by a responsible and respectable matron; and, similarly, some respectable man presents the groom naked to his future bride. We laughed at this custom and called it absurd; but they were just as amazed at the folly of all other nations. When men go to buy a colt, when they are risking only a little money, they are so suspicious that though he is almost bare they won't close the deal until the saddle and blanket have been taken off, lest there be a hidden sore underneath. Yet in the choice of a mate, which may cause either delight or disgust for the rest of their lives, people are completely careless. They leave all the rest of her body covered up with clothes and estimate the attractiveness of a woman from a mere handsbreadth of her person, the face, which is all they can see. And so they marry, running great risk of hating one another for the rest of their lives, if something in either's person should offend the other. Not all people are so wise as to concern themselves solely with character; even the wise appreciate physical beauty, as a supplement to a good disposition.

More does not speculate on the traumatic effect on a lover of rejection following so minute an examination. In real life, he showed in choosing a wife an extreme delicacy that might well have been fraught with serious consequences. He was attracted to the younger of two sisters but proposed to the elder for fear of hurting her feelings if she were passed over.

The Utopians allowed divorce for adultery or for "intolerably difficult behavior." The aggrieved party was permitted to remarry,

> but the guilty party [was] considered disreputable and permanently forbidden to take another mate. They absolutely forbid a husband to

put away his wife against her will because of some bodily misfortune; they think it cruel that a person should be abandoned when most in need of comfort; and they add that old age, since it not only entails disease but is actually a disease itself, needs more than a precarious fidelity.

Many Englishmen were surprised by another revelation about marriage among the Utopians.

It happens occasionally that a married couple cannot get along, and have both found other persons with whom they hope to live more harmoniously. After getting the approval of the senate, they may then separate by mutual consent and contract new marriages. . . . They allow divorce only very reluctantly because they know that husbands and wives will find it hard to settle down together if each has in mind that another new relation is easily available.

Those who see the existence of no-fault divorce in More's *Utopia* as evidence of progressive thought are frequently taken aback to read on the same page, "Husbands chastise their wives and parents their children, unless the offense is so serious that public punishment seems to be in the public interest." Still, we are told, "Women are not debarred from the priesthood." As unsatisfying as it was, the position of women in More's *Utopia* was superior to that of women in England and most parts of the European continent.

Religious toleration, too, exceeded anything known in contemporary Europe. "Though there are various religions in Utopia, . . . all of them, even the most diverse, agree in the main point, which is worship of the divine nature; they are like travelers going to one destination by different roads."

The ruling prince of Utopia is not a hereditary monarch but an elective official, nominated by the people and elected by their representatives. He may legally be removed from office.

The book is full of many other curiosities: provisions for a six-hour workday, uniform building codes, integration of landscape and construction, a municipal water system. Emphasis always is on the welfare of the citizens, not the exaltation or aggrandizement of their government and its leaders. Raphael tells the narrator, "They are absolutely wrong when they say that the people's poverty safeguards public peace—experience shows the contrary. . . . Who is more reckless about creating disorders than the man who knows he has nothing to lose and thinks he may have something to gain?"

The book was a best seller of its day despite the fact that it was written in Latin—or perhaps partly because of it, as Latin was the universal tongue of educated men throughout Europe. More's Latin, like his English, was precise and blessed by the resources of a large vocabulary, which he used for communication rather than ostentation. His anecdotal gifts and use of novelty to gain attention for serious ideas won a large readership.

Moreover, the book's format contributed to its popularity. Not only was dialogue a favored means of exposition in the Renaissance as in the classical period it admired, but the book of travel wonders was the particular delight of armchair adventurers in the great age of exploration accelerated by Columbus' voyage of 1492. The suspension of disbelief was easy for readers of *Utopia*. Its wonders were no stranger than the tales of monsters and weird customs found in books by bona fide navigators and sea captains about lands that could be found between the mermaids and sea dragons on mariners' maps. Some readers said that Utopia was really in America, making a connection between the New World and European imagination that would raise expectations for generations.

So fine a balance does the book strike between the allegiance to heritage and the urge to experimentation that Karl Kautsky, editor of the last volume of Karl Marx's *Capital* has seen it as the forerunner of modern socialism, and R. W. Chambers, a distinguished Anglican medievalist, has perceived it as an adumbration of medieval monastic philosophy. In its time and since, the book has caused people to look back to tradition, if only for the sake of argument, and to explore avidly the possibilities of the untried.

For some of the principal innovators of later generations, such as William Morris in the nineteenth century, *Utopia* has been a major inspiration. It poses questions that can never be answered definitively but that always lead to fresh perspectives, questions that challenge the ideological bias of every age and every country. In its spirit of intellectual inquiry as well as its interweaving of classical and Christian influence, it is representative of humanism at its best.

Utopia is actually composed of two books. The first poses the question of what a well-intentioned and principled person can do to improve the society of which he is a part. What compromises must the hypothetical citizen make with evil in order to survive to combat it? When does compromise become surrender? The second book asks how society can be organized to fulfill the needs of the many, rather than to gratify the lusts of the few. It also asks how much restriction of freedom is necessary to preserve it, recognizing always that, as Plato said, perfect freedom and perfect justice are unattainable on earth. One can easily imagine that the questions posed by these two books would change with changing circumstances, but one cannot imagine a civilized time and place in which they would become irrelevant.

With such a stimulating intellect, fund of humanist scholarship, winning personality, and aptitude for practical affairs, More was well equipped to be the adviser and chief minister of a Renaissance prince in the tradition of Lorenzo the Magnificent. With his classical lore and varied learning, lively participation in the arts, political acumen, and immense popularity with his subjects, Henry VIII seemed even more than at his accession a worthy successor to Lorenzo. With England a larger state than the Florentine republic and a growing power among the nation-states of Europe, there was seemingly the opportunity for More and Henry to work together to build an even more influential society that that of Renaissance Florence.

Erasmus, answering questions about More, wrote a friend that the Englishman was formerly rather disinclined to a Court life and to any intimacy with princes, having always a special hatred of tyranny and a great fancy for equality. . . . He could not even be tempted to Henry the Eighth's Court without great trouble, although nothing could be desired more courteous or less exacting than this Prince. He is naturally fond of liberty and leisure; but as he enjoys a holiday when he has it, so wherever business requires it, no one is more vigilant or more patient.[10]

That Henry enjoyed More's company as well as valuing his counsel was obvious. More's adoring son-in-law William Roper tells us that the king "upon holy days, when he had done his own devotions," used to send for Sir Thomas and "sit and confer with him" in "matters of astronomy, geometry, divinity, and such other faculties, and sometimes of his worldly affairs." And sometimes he kept him up with him at night "to consider with him the diversities, courses, motions and operations of the stars and planets. And because he was of a pleasant disposition it pleased the King and Queen, after the Council had supped, at the time of their [private] supper, for their pleasure, commonly to call for him to be merry with them."

This royal attention was flattering, but when it grew until More "could not once in a month get leave to go home to his wife and children (whose company he most desired) and to be absent from the court two days together but that he should be sent for again," he took pains to repress his animation and deliberately make himself less entertaining. Nevertheless, Sir Thomas continued to grow in the favor of the king although Henry now let him have more time for private life. Even though More's independence was a thorn to Cardinal Wolsey, the king's first minister, it did not affect More's relations with the monarch himself. Sir Thomas grew also in favor with the House of Commons, which made him its Speaker.

Although he did not monopolize More's time as much as formerly, Henry, instead of detaining him at the palace, would sometimes suddenly drop by the house at Chelsea to see him. Once when the king came unannounced and stayed to dinner, he walked with his host in the garden afterward for an hour, his arm around Sir Thomas' neck the whole time. Later Roper, who had witnessed the display of affection, told More that he was indeed fortunate to receive such loving attention from his sovereign. The only other subject he had seen the king be familiar with was Cardinal Wolsey, and that had been only a matter of walking arm in arm.

Roper never forgot his father-in-law's reply. "I thank our Lord, son, I find his Grace my very good lord indeed, and I believe he doth as singularly favor me as any subject within his realm. Howbeit, Son Roper, I may tell thee I have no cause to be proud thereof, for if my head could win him a castle in France it should not fail to go."

As a counselor and diplomat, More had traveled for his king and, on at least one important occasion, with him. In 1520, three years before he became Speaker of the House of Commons, he had been present at the Field of Cloth of Gold for Henry's meeting with Francis I of France. This was probably the most famous meeting of European sovereigns in the sixteenth century and certainly the most bizarrely glamorous. The field was between Guînes and Ardres, near Calais. The castle in each village was almost in ruins, so temporary palaces were erected. Fortunately mild June weather prevailed because beneath the rich tapestries and fine draperies of each was only a flimsy frame.

Nevertheless, the kings tried to impress each other with a luxurious display of fine carpets, exotic wall hangings, and elaborate furniture. Henry was not a whit behind his rival in the game of Renaissance one-upmanship. His palace of cloth covered nearly thirty-six thousand square feet. Its great hall was larger than the one in the palace in London. A number of diverse needs were met. The tent complex included a large chapel with holy water. Outside was a gilt fountain supplying claret and spiced wine. A number of attending nobles bankrupted themselves for finery and display.

The first meeting of the monarchs was held midway between their grand pavilions. Afterwards the two men rotated as hosts. It was recorded as a wonder that the sessions were so congenial although "many persons present could not understand each other." Actually, this communication problem, whatever difficulties it may have caused for the future, may have contributed to the conviviality. On controversial points, people probably tended to hear what they wanted to hear.

Memorable as the meeting has been because of its romantic aura, its achievements were hardly more enduring than the flimsy frames that supported its regal elegance. In about a year, France and the Holy Roman Empire were at war. England entered on the empire's side because of commitments that had been made to the emperor before Henry and Francis had pitched their tents for the carnival of diplomacy near Calais. Appropriately enough, the entertainment then had included jousting and juggling.

Some had thought that England's master juggler was one who wore not the motley of a court performer but a cardinal's hat and robes. Thomas Wolsey was the king's principal minister and, next to Henry himself, the most powerful person in the kingdom. In fact, some people thought that sometimes, when Henry was not paying close attention, Wolsey was the most influential person in England, bar none. This Oxford graduate of modest background had become in quick succession bishop, archbishop of York, cardinal, and papal legate. He had an acquisitive eye on the throne of Saint Peter.

Wolsey's gain in political preferment had matched his ecclesiastical progress. Several years before the meeting on the Field of Cloth of Gold, his skills in organization and negotiation had given Henry military and diplomatic victories over France. Beyond these immediate successes, he had the imagination to conceive of a foreign policy for England that would serve many generations beyond his own. He successfully argued that England should abandon attempts at territorial aggrandizement on the Continent and instead lend her influence to a weaker nation or alliance whenever any power or combination of powers threatened to achieve continental dominance. Henry was pleased at the prospect of keeping England in the forefront of nations without resort to costly wars.

The trouble was not with Wolsey's theory but with his application of it. He had trouble picking losers. In 1525 he caused Henry to side with the Holy Roman Emperor, Charles Hapsburg, in the power struggle with France. It was soon apparent that England, instead of helping a weak empire to achieve military equality with France, had actually augmented a power already stronger than France, enabling Charles to dominate the Continent. Henry was not amused.

The king's displeasure with Wolsey rose when, seeking papal permission to divorce his queen in order to marry Anne Boleyn, Henry asked the cardinal to exercise his diplomatic skills. Wolsey's own ambition to become pope handicapped him as he tried to stay in the good graces of both London and Rome. Impatient with the complications, Henry had Wolsey arrested and forced him to resign most of his political offices. When Anne, who became the king's next wife, fanned his resentment of the prelate's officiousness, Henry had his former first minister arrested for treason. Wolsey died before his trial.

Upon Wolsey's fall, the king named Sir Thomas More to succeed him as chancellor. Now England would have a statesman learned in the law, steeped in the wisdom of humanist scholars and medieval saints, practical in precedent yet dreaming of change. And he would serve as first minister the sovereign who, upon his accession, seemed more likely than any of his contemporaries to fulfill Plato's conception of the philosopher-king.

While More had fulfilled his every promise, Henry had not. His appetite for learning had been outdistanced by his hunger for flesh, both edible and beddable, and his thirst for wisdom had been surpassed by his desire for strong drink and the headiest brew of all, the lust for power. He lost his good looks, becoming heavy jowled and gross in figure, but retained a bluff, hearty manner that charmed the ordinary people, who took it for a kind of camaraderie. Consequently, his tyrannizing was accepted and he built England into a strong nation.

More's service as chancellor was immensely complicated by two major crises, which became entwined. One was occasioned by the strong Protestant reform movement threatening Catholic supremacy, the other by Henry's desire to divorce Catherine of Aragon. The pope's refusal to grant his request caused Henry to divorce her in defiance of the Vatican and to bully Parliament into enacting the Act of Supremacy, establishing the Church of England and declaring the king to be its head. The pope excommunicated Henry, but the king saw that each of his subjects was required to take the Oath of Supremacy, acknowledging him as head of the Anglican Church.

Early in the religious crisis, More retired to private life because he could not in good conscience cooperate with his sovereign's plans. He also refused to take the Oath of Supremacy. Henry imprisoned him in the Tower. When he was tried for treason, Sir Thomas declared, "For this my silence, neither your law, nor any law in the world, is able justly and rightly to punish me."

During his imprisonment, his wife visited him and asked why he who had been always hitherto taken for so wise a man will now so play the fool to lie here in this close, filthy prison, and be content thus to be shut up amongst mice and rats, when you might be abroad at your liberty and with the favor and good will both of the King and his Council, if you would but do as all the bishops and best-learned men of this realm have done. And seeing you have at Chelsea a right fair house, your library, your books, your gallery, your garden, your orchard, and all other necessities so handsome about you, where you might in the company of me, your wife, your children, and household, be merry, I muse what, [in] God's name, you mean here still thus fondly to tarry.

After hearing her arguments quietly and with a cheerful countenance, he said, "I pray thee, good Mistress Alice, tell me one thing."

"What is that?"

"Is not this house as nigh Heaven as my own?"

When More returned to the Tower after further questioning at Westminster, one of his daughters, Mistress Roper, waited about the Tower wharf to obtain his blessing and embrace him one last time. "Without consideration or care for herself," she pressed through the throng and halberd-bearing guards until she could throw her arms about his neck and kiss him. After she had gone a little way from him, she suddenly ran back and hugged and kissed him again. Many in the crowd wept.

The man who informed him on the next day that he would be beheaded that morning wept when he told him. As Sir Thomas mounted the scaffold, his executioner looked disconsolate. More told him, "Pluck up thy spirits, man, and be not afraid to do thine office."

A moment later, one of the wisest heads in Christendom was severed from its body.

Later Charles, the Holy Roman Emperor, told the British ambassador, Sir Thomas Elyot, "If we had been master of such a servant, of whose doings ourself have had these many years so small experience, we would rather have lost the best city of our dominions than have lost such a worthy counselor."

Henry had lost his opportunity to become one of the greatest rulers in history. His subtle mind became the servant of his primitive and often irrational will, devising Byzantine arguments to support the beheading of a long procession of those who stood between him and his desires. More was but the noblest of his famous victims. Two of Henry's wives, Anne Boleyn and Catherine Howard, died by the headsman's ax. So corrupted in the king's service were some of the great nobles that the duke of Norfolk, the premier duke of England, voted for the death of Anne, his own niece. Another victim of beheading at Henry's behest was More's successor as first minister, Thomas Cromwell, who had subdued his conscience to confiscate the monasteries for his royal master but had been inept as his marriage broker. John Fisher, bishop of Rochester, died by the headsman's blow. The head of the Carthusian order in England was one of four monks who met with a more spectacular fate. They were hanged, but while still alive were cut down for disemboweling. Until the process of decay was far advanced, their heads became grim finials adorning the architecture of London Bridge. The cutting edge of justice in Henry's reign was quite literally the well-sharpened blade of an ax.

Yet when Henry VIII died on January 28, 1547, he was sincerely mourned by many for whom he was the fierce focus of a newfound national pride. Englishmen under him had lost a measure of individual freedom but had been repaid in the coin of vicarious vaunting on the stage of Europe. His wars served no worthy goals, and his royal pageantry was as devoid of substance as the glittering maneuvers amid the silken tents of the Field of Cloth of Gold. But during his reign, when several kingdoms of Europe were gaining a heightened sense of national identity, Henry had accelerated the process in England.

The king had thrown away his best chance to build a truly great society when he condemned the neck around which he had earlier thrown his arm in brotherly affection. And he had not gained thereby a single city in France.

There were strong signs of cultural vitality in the kingdom that Henry left. The society had produced Thomas More—and his friends John Colet, Thomas Linacre, and William Grocyn—besides offering a congenial hospitality to Erasmus. Henry's own early scholarship and creative interest in music had reflected growing cultural interests among England's upper and middle classes. So had his patronage of Hans Holbein the Younger, Europe's greatest portrait painter of the time, to whose insightful eye we are indebted for extraordinary likenesses of More, Cranmer, and Henry himself. There was new vigor in English prose, found not only in the writings of More, who met martyrdom in opposing the king, but also in those of Thomas Cranmer, the archbishop of Canterbury who bowed to his sovereign's demands in politics but stubbornly kept the King's English undefiled in penning that great masterpiece the *Book of Common Prayer*.

But in an autocracy, even more than in a freer society, so much depends on the head of government. Would there be a stable regime commanding the allegiance of a freshly patriotic people? And would it be friendly to the arts of civilization?

Henry's successor was his only son, Edward VI, a precocious but sickly nine-year-old. It soon became apparent to those who had not realized it earlier that Henry VIII had exhausted the rich treasury inherited from his father, Henry VII, leaving his own son a bare cupboard. When Edward died less than seven years later, the Howard, Seymour, and Dudley families had fought for control of the kingdom, just as they had jockeyed for a place near the throne in the reign of the child's father. In a twelve-year period beginning before Henry's death and extending beyond Edward's in 1553, each of these families lost two famous heads to the chopping block. At times after Henry's demise, England's independent nationhood was threatened by the combination of a suffering economy, an internal power struggle among great nobles, and an accelerated state-directed drive toward Protestantism that brought change faster than the people could comfortably assimilate it. They felt that a vital part of their heritage was being torn from them at the very time that their lives lacked stability in almost every quarter. For those not prominent enough in Henry's reign to be victims of his wrath, innovation was an adventure. In Edward's tenure, it was a threat.

The boy king was succeeded by his half sister Mary, the devoutly Catholic daughter of Catherine of Aragon. She had been compelled by Henry to deny her faith and consequently carried a heavy burden of guilt. To atone for her lapse, she launched upon a fanatical campaign to force Protestants to convert to Catholicism. In the process she earned the name "Bloody Mary." Her marriage in the first months of her reign to the son of Spain's Charles V, popularly regarded as England's enemy, further frightened and enraged her subjects. Before the end of her rule, she had had to crush rebellion, and had burned three hundred of her subjects at the stake for refusing to abandon their Protestant faith. Her husband, though almost as ardent a Catholic as she, had warned that she was trying to force change too rapidly and too brutally. But she was as driven in her way as her father had been in his. When she died in 1558, bonfires in London burned as brightly as those which had consumed her victims.

The fires had been lit in celebration, but some saw them as the funeral pyres of England herself. Eleven years under the rule of two of Henry's children had brought the country to international humiliation and the verge of civil war. The next heir was Elizabeth, a claimant of questionable legitimacy because of her birth when her father was involved in getting rid of her mother. What hope could England place in this frail Elizabeth?

13

GLORIANA

A SLENDER, GRACEFUL young woman with red-gold hair, Elizabeth marched with firm steps to "the shakiest throne in Europe."[1] Observers noted particularly the brilliance of her eyes, though some disagreed as to their color, and the beauty of her pale, slender hands. Their long-fingered grace signified to some an artistic temperament, but were those hands fit to grasp a scepter and hold it against all comers?

Though the new queen looked delicate and refined, she had not led a sheltered life. On November 28, 1558, when, dressed in purple robes of royalty, she rode through the streets of London, she approached the Tower with emotions different from those of her predecessors. Not only had it been the last residence of her mother, Anne Boleyn, before her beheading. Only four years before her welcome at the age of twenty-five, Elizabeth herself had been imprisoned in the Tower to await death by the ax. She had been falsely charged with complicity in a Protestant plot against her half sister Queen Mary. Most Englishmen believed that another Mary, her cousin Mary Stuart, was the rightful heir to the throne. Only five years before Elizabeth's coronation, Parliament had reaffirmed the illegitimacy of Henry's marriage to Anne Boleyn and therefore the illegitimacy of the child of that union. And did not English law forbid a bastard's succession to the throne? Elizabeth knew that, with a slight twist of fate, many of those lining the streets to cheer her as their sovereign would have assembled to see her head chopped off.

"Bloody" Mary's mercy to her young half sister had saved her life and released her from the Tower, but had not given her freedom. Elizabeth was sent to live under surveillance at Woodstock, where she was when Mary in her last days recognized Elizabeth as her successor.

The young queen's education had not been neglected during her years of sequestration. Far from it. Her chief tutor was Roger Ascham, one of the greatest scholars in the kingdom. He boasted of his pupil, "She talks French and Italian as well as she does English, and has often talked to me readily and well in Latin, moderately in Greek." Many years later a German who had visited at her court reported that she was also fluent in "Spanish, Scotch, and Dutch." Eventually she translated Sallust into English, and produced a notable translation of Boethius, being the first English sovereign to attempt that feat since Alfred the Great. Her Greek improved to the extent that she read Sophocles with pleasure and translated a play by Euripides. As a mature ruler, she read history almost daily and pursued various Italian Renaissance studies to which she had been introduced by language teachers from Italy. She composed both poetry and music and played both the lute and the virginal, though apparently with greater pleasure to herself than to others.

It was good that Roger Ascham had been the strongest influence in her studies in her formative years. Though well versed in the learning of the Italian Renaissance, he was mindful of the harm to its society when the passion for inquiry became an appetite for rapid change at the expense of nourishing traditions. He said of Italy, "Virtue once made that country mistress over all the world. Vice now maketh that country slave to them that before were glad to serve it." According to him, the Italians therefore said that "an Italianate Englishman is the devil incarnate." And he added, "I was once in Italy myself, but I thank God my abode there was but nine days." He insisted that one's Italian learning be placed in proper perspective, complaining of some Englishmen, "They make more account of Tully's *Offices* than St. Paul's epistles; of a tale in Boccaccio than a story of the Bible." He insisted that Englishmen should subordinate Italian Renaissance acquirements to their Christian heritage and the traditions of their own country.

Few of her countrymen found comfort in Elizabeth's book learning or artistic accomplishments when she came to the throne. Word of them was about as reassuring to most Englishmen as reports to passengers of a sinking ship with a mutinous crew that their inexperienced young captain was well versed in Platonism and played a mean hornpipe to boot. Protestants and Catholics lived in suspicion and fear of each other and roamed in armed bands. Many Catholics feared that the young queen would be as zealous in persecuting them as her half sister Mary had been in destroying Protestants. Poverty filled the cities with walking skeletons. The debasement of the national currency was a tragedy to the English and a joke to Europe. The efficiency of the armed forces was as low as their morale. Undermanned forts in disrepair pretended to guard vulnerable coasts. The most comforting thing about the navy was that it did relieve the land by getting rowdy troublemakers out to sea at frequent intervals.

Spain and France threatened to reduce the British to colonial status; French troops were already in Scotland, and Ireland was offering hospitality to Spanish forces. The pope was no refuge of hope. He threatened Elizabeth with excommunication and interdiction. Such threats had inconvenienced her father. But this time the Vatican raised a danger more palpable—invasion by the Catholic kingdoms. Her cousin Mary Stuart, supported by all the Catholic powers of Europe and by most Englishmen's faith in her legitimacy, waited impatiently to displace Elizabeth on the throne.

Fully aware of the dangers that beset her, the young queen met them with courage and outward calm. With great discernment, she chose her councillors and staff. As her chief minister, she selected William Cecil, a lawyer elected to Parliament at the age of twenty-three and a veteran of fifteen years' service to the Crown under Edward VI and Mary Tudor. He had shown considerable flexibility in adjusting to the ideological demands of an era of sudden reversals of political and religious faith, but Elizabeth believed him to be devoted to his native land. In naming him secretary, she told him, "I give you this charge, that you shall be of my Privy Council, and content to take pains for me and my realm. This judgement I have of you, that you will be faithful to the state; and that without respect of my private will, you will give me that counsel which you think best."

Cecil, later Lord Burghley, was a thirty-eight-year-old man of cool sagacity. A member of the advantaged upper middle class, he had mingled with scholars and aristocrats at both Cambridge and Gray's Inn, early had had a nodding acquaintance with the royal court through his father's position as yeoman of the wardrobe to Henry VIII, and before his own royal appointments had, as secretary to Somerset and to Northumberland, learned the ways of England's great noble households. An indefatigable worker, he patiently handled innumerable details without losing sight of the broad vistas of statesmanship. Elizabeth did not always accept his advice, but she learned great respect for the contents of that bearded and balding head.

Soon next in importance to Cecil, but never a serious rival for the queen's regard, was Francis Walsingham. He was at first her ambassador to France, but became even more valuable as the organizer of a secret service that informed her of what her enemies were plotting in Britain and on the Continent.

The queen flirted with handsome young courtiers but was little influenced by them in serious matters. Instead, with the aid of Cecil and other sage advisers, she concentrated on solutions to England's problems. Within the first six months of her reign, she convinced those around her of her earnestness and ability in confronting the major problems of her government, and raised hopes that she could solve them. The great landed magnates and tax-burdened businessmen were impressed that in half a year she had reduced by 60 percent the rate of spending under her predecessor.

Within two years, she had dealt successfully with so many issues that most of her subjects would not have parted with her for any other ruler in the world. Sir Thomas Gresham, who is popularly known for Gresham's Law (which he did not originate) but deserves to be better known for his financial wizardry in other respects, was her expert in international finance. Operating mainly through the great trading centers but also through England's Royal Exchange, which he had founded, he paid off the heavy indebtedness incurred by Mary Tudor. Few would dispute his claim that two years after Elizabeth's accession, her kingdom, so recently the financial laughingstock of Europe, had the best credit record in the Western world.

Though most Englishmen were pleased with their queen, there was still opposition to her and some plotting against her by devout Catholics, especially in the north. Protestants and Catholics were contesting for supremacy. Elizabeth knew that no religious policy she could adopt would truly satisfy both groups. She also knew that either the militant Protestantism of Edward VI or the militant Catholicism of Mary Tudor would infuriate large numbers. The denominational excesses of each of those predecessors had made both groups anxiously watchful of any religious move by the sovereign. Yet, since Henry VIII, the ruler had been officially denominated head of the Church of England and was expected to act in that capacity. The national crisis was exacerbated by the turmoil of Reformation and Counter Reformation then engulfing Europe and sweeping it into a century of religious wars.

Elizabeth faced the fact that she could not please everybody. She did hope to frame religious policies tolerable to most and to maintain them firmly. The most important compromise, she believed, would be a viable balance between the medieval Christian heritage so dear to the Catholics and the new, experimental Christianity appealing to many Protestants and rigorously pressed by the Puritans among them.

She evolved what came to be known as the "Elizabethan Compromise." One of its elements was independence from Rome. This aspect expressed loyalty to her father's policy and undoubtedly was congenial to her own free spirit, but it was at least as much a matter of necessity as of choice. As the Vatican denied her legitimacy, she could not afford to acknowledge its authority in her kingdom. Her first Parliament enacted into law the skeleton of her compromise, and a subsequent one ratified the Thirty-nine Articles, fleshing out the bare bones. Legislation established a Court of High Commission to deal with violations. Such an institution afforded many opportunities for abuse of power, but at first its operations reflected the generally tolerant spirit of the queen herself.

In its independence of the Vatican and in the doctrines (especially the denial of transubstantiation) set forth in the Thirty-nine Articles, the Church of England under Elizabeth was Protestant. But she knew that the mass of people are more loyal to practices than to abstractions, so the rubric of the prayer book remained to some extent familiarly Catholic. The Church of England so constituted was not an acceptable home to unyielding old-guard Catholics or crusading Puritans. But the queen did not demand inward conformity so long as members of the dissatisfied groups refrained from war on their more compromising brethren.

The Church of England did shelter under one roof both High Church adherents, who found comfort in the elaborate ritual of Catholic heritage and the pageantry that conferred significance on the christenings, marriages, and funerals of even the most obscure, and Low Church adherents, who sought to purify worship by elimination of those elements and who regarded vestments as vanities. Congregations of both persuasions comprised the Church of England. The tactful queen knew how to yield a point without surrendering control. In royal documents bearing the sovereign's string of titles like the colorful tail of a high-flying kite, both Henry VIII and Edward VI had included "Supreme Head of the Church." Elizabeth retained the title, but in daily usage substituted "and so forth" for the offending words.

Though Elizabeth maintained an uneasy but fruitful peace between Catholics and Protestants in England, her foreign policy was made both tortuous and torturous by international conflicts between the two groups. She was realistic enough to see that her first task in foreign relations was to end the war with

France into which Mary Tudor's Spanish husband had led her and England. Smarting at the loss of England's last toehold in France, Mary had said that after her death the word *Calais* would be found engraved on her heart. A living Elizabeth deliberately purged it from her own heart and counted it well lost if thereby she could gain a kingdom.

The successes of the Protestant Reformation had prompted the Catholic Counter Reformation, a movement for reform within the mother church led by those who insisted on papal supremacy and certain core doctrines. Italy and Spain, of course, were securely Catholic. The movement kept France (or, at least, most of it) in the papal column, along with the lower Netherlands (later Belgium), Poland, Bohemia, and the states of south-central Germany. Catholic loyalty was both a motive and an excuse for Spanish and French designs on Protestant England. The upper Netherlands (called Holland) was passionately Protestant and, under the leadership of William the Silent, prince of Orange, successfully repelled the efforts of Spain's Philip II to crush it into submission. The long struggle between the Spanish and the Dutch made England's situation more perilous by threatening to explode into a general war from which she could not remain aloof, but at the same time eased direct threats to her by keeping Philip's celebrated infantry occupied on the Continent.

Elizabeth's chief tool of foreign policy was the most celebrated virginity in modern history. Some have pictured her as a model of chastity, while some even in her own day suspected that her reputation owed more to discretion than to abstinence. Ben Jonson had another explanation: "She had a membrane on her which made her incapable of man, though for her delight she tried many . . . there was a French surgeon who took in hand to cut it, yet fear stayed her."[2]

That unyielding integument, real or imaginary, was a barrier to England's enemies. Ambitious monarchs were deterred from attempting to gain by armed conquest a kingdom that might become theirs by marriage. From young womanhood into her late years, Elizabeth kept on tenterhooks a succession of suitors whose passion had more to do with cupidity than with Cupid. In comic opera profusion and variety, she received in the first two years of her reign no less than fifteen matrimonial proposals from eight countries. Her suitors included a prince of Denmark; an Austrian archduke; two brothers of the French royal house, one with a nose of almost Cyrano proportions; a Swedish king of doubtful sanity; and no less engaging a prospective husband than Ivan the Terrible. By keeping alive the hopes and rivalries of various rulers and their heirs, she kept England independent.

This strategy was made more difficult by the reiterated promptings of Parliament, calling upon the queen to marry and produce an heir so that the kingdom would not some day be convulsed by a struggle over succession to the throne. Some thought that Elizabeth was strongly attracted to several of her own countrymen, notable among them Robert Dudley, whom she created earl of Leicester. But all, for one reason or another, were ineligible consorts even if the demands of her foreign policy had not made any marital alliance impossible. Elizabeth herself expressed the situation most pithily when she said that she was "married to England."

Anxiety over the succession was greatly increased by the presence in Scotland of Mary, queen of Scots, once queen consort of France, and rival claimant to the English crown. Her devout Catholicism made her anathema to English Protestants, but a charisma, derived as much from her huge brown eyes and feminine grace as from the aura of royalty, sometimes made normally logical and calculating men venture wild exploits in her behalf. She was most powerful when most helpless.

When Mary was imprisoned in her own realm after a successful Protestant revolt in Scotland, there were daring men to risk their lives in spiriting her across the border to England, where she threw herself upon the mercy of her cousin Elizabeth. The English queen granted protective custody, partly out of benevolence but at least as much because the arrangement simplified the problem of keeping track of a threatening figure. In 1569, only a year later, Mary was the focus and inspiration of two rebellions in England, one led by the Catholic duke of Norfolk to oust Cecil, the other a northern revolt of Catholics determined to reestablish the old faith in their country. The two movements merged, and the revolution climaxed as men wearing the red cross of the Crusades seized Durham Cathedral. The revolt was aborted when Norfolk, sick and apprehensive, left his followers and returned home, and Elizabeth's officers were able to thwart the attempt to free Mary. Until this crisis, Elizabeth, unlike her father and sister, had executed no one for political or religious reasons.

The following year, the pope excommunicated England's queen and branded her a usurper to whom no obedience was owed. With this encouragement, the duke of Norfolk and other Englishmen entered a plot formulated in Italy to overthrow Elizabeth and seat Mary Stuart in her stead. Walsingham's secret police discovered the scheme in time to frustrate it. Norfolk went to the block. Members of Parliament and councillors urged Elizabeth to decree the same fate for Mary, but she refused. Mary, in the Vatican's eyes the rightful heir to England's throne, remained a constant threat to Elizabeth and her government for nineteen years of residence in the realm. Then, alarmed by new plots inspired by Mary's presence if not by her complicity, Elizabeth yielded to the importunities of her advisors and, in a vile humor, signed the death warrant of her troublesome cousin.

The crisis over Mary Stuart further accelerated the deterioration of England's relations with Spain. For a variety of reasons, Spain supplanted France as England's chief enemy. Philip II's efforts to put Mary on Elizabeth's throne were part of his campaign to become Europe's foremost leader in the war on Protestantism. Commercial rivalry intensified the contest between the two nations. Columbus' discoveries in 1492 under the aegis of Ferdinand and Isabella had given the Spanish a head start in the European race for American colonies. Spain had exploited its advantage so energetically that it now controlled most of South America, all of Central America, and a large portion of North America. England, lacking the tremendous wealth of some of the continental powers, watched with envious eyes the great proud-sailed convoys carrying to Spain the largesse of the silver mines of Mexico and Peru.

The Spanish colonies in the New World were for the mother country a source of wealth in other ways as well. She prohibited her colonists from trading with any other nation. Daring English sea dogs were not about to accept the sanctity of the Spanish monopoly, and Elizabeth encouraged them to violate it. The cautious Cecil warned that attempts to breach the monopoly could lead to a war with Spain for which England was not prepared, but Elizabeth chose to play a dangerous game of pretending that she was embarrassed by the froward actions of her mariners. Always she apologized to the Spanish ambassador for their exploits, sometimes lamenting the tribulations of royalty that made a religious hermit's life seem preferable. "This woman," the ambassador reported to his government, "is possessed with a hundred thousand devils; yet she pretends to me that she would like to be a nun, live in a cell, and tell her beads from morning till night." He knew the game as did his king, but Philip II had not yet decided when it was best to go to war.

War with Spain could be disastrous for a small island kingdom. Spain was the strongest nation in Europe. But the danger added spice to the adventure for such mariners as John Hawkins and Francis Drake.

Hawkins, son of a prosperous Plymouth shipping magnate, found serving as captain of one of the company's ships in trading to the Canaries unbearably dull if he must ignore opportunities to make a fortune in trading with the Spanish colonists. He persuaded Queen Elizabeth to lend him a superannuated warship and got many Englishmen to invest in his illegal enterprise. He kept up an ingenious pretense of legality, in which many of the Spanish colonists, hungry for trade outside the Spanish world, happily joined him. Sometimes he would beg permission to enter one of Spain's New World ports because of the supposed exhaustion of his own supplies or the need to repair his vessel. A man who had crossed the ocean for so desperate an enterprise would not balk at crossing the palms of local officials. Sometimes, when they felt that their good names or job security demanded a more obvious excuse for harboring an English ship, Hawkins obliged by firing a few shots into the town. A trading spree followed, to the delight of the colonists, who had "proof" that they had been coerced.

Encouraged by small successes, Hawkins sailed the Spanish Main with a fleet of trading vessels, but had the misfortune to encounter a Spanish fleet of warships while he was in a Mexican port. In the ensuing battle, only two English vessels escaped. Crewmen of the captured ships met a variety of fates, ranging from residence in Mexico with Mexican wives or years of imprisonment to public burning as heretics.

One of the Englishmen who escaped Spanish clutches in the Mexican disaster was Hawkins' cousin Francis Drake. The two ships personally captained by the two relatives were the only ones to evade capture or destruction. Before this experience, Drake had been inspired in his sea career by the prospects of personal gain, the ardent Protestantism instilled by his clergyman father, growing English patriotism, and the excitement of adventure. To these incentives now was added the desire for revenge. While still in his twenties, he became the boldest and most feared scourge of the Spanish Main. Once with two small ships he attacked Nombre de Dios, on the Atlantic coast of the Isthmus of

Panama, looting the town, ambushing a treasure caravan from Peru, and finally abandoning fifteen tons of silver because his vessels were already loaded to capacity.

From a high summit in Panama he had looked westward to the vast stretches of the Pacific and had glimpsed a magnificent opportunity. Spanish colonial ports on the Atlantic were alerted to his raids and those of other English marauders, but those on the Pacific could be caught completely off guard. He outfitted an expedition that sailed from Plymouth in 1577 for this purpose. A secret investor in the enterprise was the queen herself, who warned him not to let Cecil know what they were doing. Elizabeth liked Drake. There are many tributes to his personal magnetism, even from enemies. The queen loved tales of derring-do, especially when told by the blond-bearded adventurer himself. (People persist in picturing Drake as dark of hair and beard, despite contemporary accounts of his blondness; there is a popular belief that all corsairs were dark.) Be that as it may, Drake was no typical corsair. His raiding expedition became a nearly three-year voyage of discovery in which he searched for the western exit of the Northwest Passage and became the first English captain—the first of any nationality since Magellan's expedition—to circumnavigate the globe.

He was equally successful in attaining his more mundane objectives, bringing back in the hold of the *Golden Hind* a rich share of the treasures of Chile and Peru. Elizabeth dined with him aboard his ship and conferred knighthood upon him as he knelt on its deck. With his personal gains he purchased Buckland Abbey, a country estate.

But he did not retire to the life of a country squire. In 1587, when Philip II began massing his warships near Cadiz for an expedition against England, Drake appeared out of nowhere to attack and burn a substantial number of them. Englishmen said that he had singed the king of Spain's beard. The expression was apt. Spain's navy remained formidable, but Drake's impudent strike deprived it of its mystique. It also delayed Spain's attack, giving England precious months in which to prepare.

Important preparations had already been made over a period of ten years. Whereas Drake had become the terror of the Spanish Main after escaping from the Mexican disaster, his companion in arms had sought revenge by another route. Retiring from his career on the sea, Hawkins had become the chief administrator of the Royal Navy. He brought to the task more imagination than any Englishman had since its founder, Alfred the Great. In the style of naval fighting prevalent for generations, in which vessels come alongside each other, firing at close range, with their crews engaging in hand to hand fighting, Spain enjoyed every advantage over her enemies. Spanish wealth made possible the construction of many great floating fortresses with high forecastles and poops that towered above rival ships and rained destruction on their decks from close range. Hawkins found a solution consistent with England's lower budget for construction. He dreamed of revolutionizing naval warfare by building small, swift craft with longer range firepower. The advantage would belong to such vessels. From a distance that made them immune to Spanish shot, they could fire upon Spain's galleons and could then flee the scene before the towering ships could maneuver for pursuit.

Everyone on both sides knew that a great naval battle between England and Spain was in the offing. For more years than most would have believed possible, Elizabeth and Cecil had averted war and had prevented a union of France and Spain. Elizabeth had dallied for five years with the son, twenty-one years her junior, of France's Henri II, preventing him from marrying the Spanish infanta. At last, the young prince had returned from England with no bride and no substantial concessions, bringing only one of the queen's garters. His royal father had expected more. Elizabeth had also distracted Philip II by raising the possibility that she might become his bride, or his son's. The execution of Mary, queen of Scots, however, had put an end to further delays by diplomacy.

In 1588 the time of testing for Hawkins' reconstructed English navy was at hand. So was the testing time for Drake's abilities as a naval commander on the grand scale. And so, too, was the time for England's queen, an adroit diplomat in the days of uneasy peace, to prove herself as a war chief. Though Charles, Lord Howard of Effingham, was lord high admiral of England, he had the good sense to defer to Drake's superior seamanship. Some thought that Elizabeth should similarly defer to some able man. She was now generally popular with her subjects, because they respected her achievements and believed she cared for their welfare, and because she had her father's flair for public relations and had dazzled them with pageantry and public entertainments. But many would have felt more comfortable if a Henry VIII had been their ruler now. He had never risked his life in battle, but on horseback he had been a striking embodiment of masculinity. And masculinity seemed essential in a war leader.

King Philip had assembled a much trumpeted "Invincible Armada" of 130 ships to move against the island kingdom. Aboard were thirty thousand men, twenty-two thousand of them infantry. His plan was to defeat the defending navy and then invade and subdue England. There seemed to be only one glitch as the time of sailing neared, but it was a serious one. The admiral of Philip's great fleet died, and the king replaced him with the rich young duke of Medina Sidonia, who protested quite logically that the commander "ought to understand navigation and sea fighting, and I know nothing of either." He added, "From my small experience of the water, I know that I am always seasick." Philip was not convinced.

Drake was eager for another preemptive strike at Cadiz and other ports where elements of the Armada had gathered, but Elizabeth hesitated too long and the opportunity was lost. In July, Spain's towering sails appeared off England's southwest coast. Aboard was Europe's strongest infantry. Worst of all, the very winds appeared to take sides with the invader, accelerating the approach of the great canvas clouds and at the same time keeping English ships bottled up in Plymouth harbor. With Drake effectively in command, ably assisted by Hawkins, who had forsaken his desk for a quarterdeck, the British towed their small, slim warships into open water. There they harassed the big vessels of the enemy, swiftly dodging retaliation.

The Spanish were disconcerted, partly by the surprising maneuverability of the English craft, but also by the fact that they had not planned to attack England on this day. In obedience to earlier orders, they were on their way to the Netherlands to take on board a viceroy's army that was supposed to participate in the invasion. Accepting the forced change of schedule, Medina Sidonia, the Armada's reluctant commander, headed to Calais, pursued by the English. The Spanish reached the French port, but the English released fire ships among them, spreading panic as well as flames. The Spanish sailed out into the channel, where winds had now risen to gale force.

If those winds had at first seemed to favor the Spaniards, they now proved allies of the English. The Armada avoided being driven ashore on the coast of Flanders, but a wind shift forced them into the North Sea. The English, though now short of ammunition, pursued them. But they became the witnesses, rather than the agents, of the Armada's destruction. The "invincible" force scattered. Wrecks on both the Scottish and Irish coasts marked its erratic flight. Fewer than half of the Spanish ships, and fewer than a third of the men aboard, reached the haven of Spanish ports.

The English lost not a single ship, as compared with Spain's seventy-six; and sixty men, as compared with Spain's seventeen thousand. The elements claimed many victims, it is true, but only after English brilliance in design and tactics had put the Armada to flight. The Spanish had been prepared to defend themselves against any ships trying to grapple with them. But Drake's ships did not play that game. They kept their distance and, with their superior firepower, fired devastating broadsides. When the Spanish returned the fire from their elevated decks, most of the shots passed harmlessly over the low English vessels. One night during the running battle, after Lord Howard had sailed into the center of the Armada, and unscathed, exchanged broadsides with every galleon encountered, the Spanish commander sent the duke of Parma an appeal for help: "The enemy pursue me from morning till night, but they will not grapple. . . . There is no remedy, for they are swift and we are slow."

Parma's ports were so effectively blockaded by the Dutch that the duke and his thirty thousand troops could not come to the rescue of the Armada. But the English did not know this. They massed at Tilbury to await the anticipated invasion attempt. Civilians joined the soldiers. They were armed with any weapon at hand, from muskets and pikes to pitchforks. King Philip had appealed to the country's Catholics to rise against their queen, but his message was drowned in a rising tide of patriotism. Catholics were numerous in the crowd of defenders.

Against the advice of cautious counselors, Elizabeth rode down to the shore to address her embattled subjects. Regal in the saddle, her red hair like an oriflamme of battle, she spoke in clear tones audible to many:

> My loving people, we have been persuaded by some that are careful of our safety, to take heed how we commit ourselves to armed multitudes, for fear of treachery. But I assure you, I do not desire to live to distrust my faithful and loving people. Let tyrants fear. I have al-

ways so behaved myself that, under God, I have placed my chiefest strength and safeguard in the loyal hearts and good will of my subjects.

She concluded,

I know I have the body of a weak and feeble woman, but I have the heart and stomach of a king, and of a king of England too, and think foul scorn that Parma or Spain, or any prince of Europe should dare to invade the borders of my realm. . . . Rather than any dishonor shall grow by me, I myself will take up arms, I myself will be your general, judge, and rewarder of every one of your virtues in the field.

Full-throated cheers acknowledged the queen's sovereignty over her subjects' hearts. The scene at Tilbury might have been the prelude to slaughter. But, of course, the feared invasion did not materialize. Nevertheless, the day's events symbolized a great victory. The queen who thirty years before had succeeded to the throne of a small, strife-torn country on the periphery of world affairs now ruled a united kingdom that had become one of the chief arbiters of Europe.

England and its heroes compelled the admiration even of their enemies. A Spaniard said of Drake, "Were it not that he was a Lutheran, there was not the like man in the world."[3] And Pope Sixtus V, who sent his legion of ecclesiastics with the Armada to aid in deposing Elizabeth, said of England's queen, "If she were not a heretic, she would be worth a whole world."[4]

The Spanish menace did not disappear overnight. England's naval war with Spain continued for sixteen years after the defeat of the Armada. But, as a result of that battle, the balance of power in Europe was changed. For almost a century, beginning in the reign of Ferdinand and Isabella, Spain had been the strongest power in Europe. The great Spanish galleon, with its officers and crew looking down from lofty heights on the vessels of lesser nations, was an appropriate symbol of Spain itself. But Spain had grown complacent. Its government was unwieldy. Its sense of adventure, which had led Spaniards to four continents, was gone. The romance of the conquistadors had yielded to a purely business operation, and Philip II himself was the greatest bookkeeper of all, the chief clerk of royal enterprise. The rich imagination of Spain no longer foraged among the dry facts of the world.

England, on the other hand, was more vital than at any previous time in its history. For many members of the upper and middle classes, life was a personal adventure, the exciting sharing of a national voyage of daring upon uncharted seas, physical and intellectual. Even some of the underprivileged felt stirrings of patriotism never experienced by generations of their ancestors.

The imagination, inventiveness, and daring spirit that, combined with the inspiration of tradition, gave England its naval victories over Spain were evident in almost every phase of the kingdom's life in the Elizabethan Age. English experimentation in design and tactics not only provided triumph over her enemies but revolutionized naval warfare for centuries to come. Grappling and boarding remained the stock tactics of small-time pirates, but cannonading became the practice of navies. The effects of the English naval revolution changed the careers of other nations. The crippling of Spain enabled the Dutch to achieve independence. After Philip had added Portugal to his Spanish dominions, his royal house had monopolized trade and colonization in the Americas. With Spanish withdrawal from one part of the New World after another, vast areas were opened to the competition of England, Holland, and France.

The literature of Elizabethan England pulsed with the excitement of life and soared with aspiration. Christopher Marlowe, in his *Tamburlaine*, wrote lines that could have voiced the sentiments of many a genius of the Florentine Renaissance:

> Nature, that fram'd us of four elements
> Warring within our breasts for regiment,
> Doth teach us all to have aspiring minds:
> Our souls, whose faculties can comprehend
> The wondrous architecture of the world,
> And measure every wandering planet's course,
> Still climbing after knowledge infinite,
> And always moving as the restless spheres,
> Wills us to wear ourselves and never rest,
> Until we reach the ripest fruit of all. . . .

It was appropriate, too, that Marlowe should later choose in *Faustus* a protagonist who longed to encompass all knowledge and all human experience. True to the original legend, the English playwright sent Faustus to his doom as punishment for hubris, but his sympathy for the learned doctor's aspirations is as strong as his horror at his fate.

Shakespeare's Hamlet might seem the antithesis of the Elizabethan hero. On the surface, he is the epitome of ambivalence. In both literary and political parlance, indecisive characters are said to suffer from a "Hamlet complex." Of course, a good case can be made that, under the camouflage of indecision, the Danish prince is one of the most unswervingly purposeful figures in the history of drama. But even if one admits his consistency of purpose, he seems decidedly un-Elizabethan in his lack of appetite for life, balancing life and death by weighing the disadvantages of each. He even says, "And . . . , to me, what is this quintessence of dust? Man delights not me; no, nor woman neither." Yet, in citing the wonders to which he fails to respond, he breaks forth into an exuberant tribute to humankind that is superbly evocative of the Renaissance spirit, whether encountered in the Age of Elizabeth or the Age of Lorenzo: "What a piece of work is man! How noble in reason! How infinite in faculty! In form, in moving, how express and admirable! In action how like an angel! In apprehension how like a god!"[5]

Patriotism and a sense of national duty were also as strong among Elizabeth's subjects as among Lorenzo's people. They find their most famous expression in familiar lines from Shakespeare's *Richard II*:

> This royal throne of kings, this scepter'd isle,
> This earth of majesty, this seat of Mars,
> This other Eden, demi-paradise,
> This fortress built by Nature for herself
> Against infection and the hand of war,
> This happy breed of men, this little world,
> This precious stone set in the silver sea,
> Which serves it in the office of a wall,
> Or as a moat defensive to a house,
> Against the envy of less happier lands,
> This blessed plot, this earth, this realm,
> this England. . . .[6]

It was not martial glory alone that England's sailors brought to the "scepter'd isle." Drake, as we have seen, combined exploration with naval raids in his circumnavigation of the globe. Martin Frobisher, searching for the ever elusive Northwest Passage, discovered the bay that bears his name. Both Drake and Sir John Hawkins made use of stock companies to finance their trading ventures. On New Year's Eve in 1600, Elizabeth inaugurated a new era by chartering the East India Company and awarding it a monopoly of trade in the Eastern Hemisphere between the Straits of Magellan and the Cape of Good Hope. It would exercise both political and military power in each settlement that it planted. Thus was established a new pattern for colonization, one far more democratic—or at least oligarchic—than the royally dictated efforts of Spain and Portugal. Though the system was started in Elizabeth's reign—and continued in that of her successor, James I—to provide the possibility of substantial royal profits at minimal risk, it was actually in imaginative conception a bold endeavor.

No English entrepreneur followed a bolder vision than Sir Walter Ralegh.[7] And no one was more representative of the English Renaissance. Too often he is remembered chiefly as the courtier who spread his cloak over a puddle to keep Queen Elizabeth's feet dry or as the armchair adventurer who sponsored an abortive attempt at colonization in North Carolina. Some English majors recall that he wrote a poem called "The Nymph's Reply to the Shepherd" in rebuttal to seductive verses by Christopher Marlowe. Actually, Ralegh was one of the most versatile people of an extraordinarily versatile age. Of course, he was a courtier, a colonizer, and a poet. But he was not always a stay-at-home adventurer, and his poetry was not merely the self-indulgent hobby of a dilettante. In addition, he was a general, an admiral, an architect, a politician, an amateur musician, a self-instructed chemist, a patron of literature and scholarship, and a historian with an important place in the record of Western historiography.

His life did not begin amid the pomp, pageantry, and political intrigue of courts. He was born on a farm in Devonshire. His father was a squire, his mother the daughter of a knight. His acquaintance with the great world began with his enrollment at Oxford as a teenager in 1568. The next year he left for a rougher school, joining English volunteers led by a cousin of his to fight in France in support of the Huguenots. A few years later, he was a resident of the Temple. He may have sharpened his wits in play with the other law students, and he probably acquired a sophisticated knowledge of London, but he does not appear to have practiced law.

Again he left England in an armed force led by a relative—this time, his half brother Sir Humphrey Gilbert, who was authorized by the queen to take possession of "any remote barbarous and heathen lands not possessed by any Christian prince or people." When Gilbert served his sovereign by attacking the Spanish without her official permission, Ralegh did his part as captain of the *Falcon*, one of Gilbert's ships.

The same recklessness that made him a hero at sea complicated his life ashore. Twice in one year he was arrested for dueling. He then joined his fortunes to those of Robert Dudley, earl of Leicester, whom Elizabeth had once confessed to have loved, but in "nothing unseemly," and whom she had strangely enough offered to Mary, queen of Scots, as a husband. Ralegh was soon a captain of foot in Munster, helping to suppress an Irish rebellion. He suggested assassination as a means of eliminating rebel leaders.

He was sent back to England with dispatches and found himself in a still more dangerous place—the royal court. It was, however, an environment in which he instantly thrived. Whether or not he actually threw down his cloak before his queen, he soon got her attention. His tall figure, bright eyes, handsome beard, and youth were attractive to the aging Elizabeth. In time, he was favored in so many ways by his sovereign that the old nobility often referred to him as "that damned upstart Sir Walter Ralegh."[8]

Donald Davie has said that Ralegh "became the Queen's favorite principally because, in Elizabeth's ceremonious and elaborate and extravagant court, he was the most inventively ceremonious, the most elaborate and extravagant figure of them all." But a much less flamboyant quality played a part as well. With his subtle mind and fluent speech, he was qualified for that amatory fencing with which Elizabeth kept foreign suitors hopeful but at bay and amused herself with her own countrymen. The age was one in which a courtier's jeweled dress-suit literally could cost as much as a small ship, and Ralegh was not one to lag behind in the fashion parade. But the same jeweled shoes reputed to have cost sixty-six hundred gold pieces were filled by feet that had walked a pitching deck and the bloody battlefields of France and Ireland; and the richly plumed hat was rakishly worn on a head that pondered the fate of nations and for answers searched history, ancient, medieval, and modern.

Elizabeth did not appoint Ralegh to her Council, but she did grant him large estates, a profitable patent to grant licenses to tavern keepers, and a license for exporting woolen cloth. She knighted him in 1584 and the following year named him to succeed the earl of Bedford as warden of the nation's tin mines.

He did not regard the appointment as a sinecure but investigated working conditions and improved the lot of the miners.

Ralegh's half brother Sir William Gilbert had a patent to explore and settle sites in North America. It was due to expire in 1584, but Gilbert lacked the funds to exercise his privileges. Ralegh personally advanced the money for Gilbert to lead an expedition to Newfoundland. When Gilbert died in the attempt, the Queen renewed the patent in Ralegh's name.

He turned energetically to exploration and colonization. The promise of proprietary rights to all lands occupied by him or his agents was a major incentive. So was the grand adventure of the enterprise. The only payment required to secure the territory for himself and his heirs would be the regular transfer to the Crown of one-fifth of all precious metals mined.

Captains Philip Amadas and Arthur Barlow, whom Ralegh dispatched to an area of North America far south of Newfoundland, explored the Outer Banks of the future North Carolina and landed on Hatteras Island. The Florentine mariner Giovanni Verrazzano had discovered the same place earlier, but the English captains seem to have been unaware of this fact. In England the name *Virginia* was given to a none too clearly bounded area along the North American Atlantic coast in tribute to Elizabeth's celebrated virginity, which once had been a troubling circumstance of English life but now had come to be regarded by some as a national asset. Amadas and Barlow, however, did not go ashore within the bounds of the later State of Virginia.

Despite explicit warnings in Ralegh's patent against preying on Spanish commerce, his captains took swipes at Spain's ships when they had a chance. There was the assumption that the queen, while maintaining a proper front, would wink at any depredations against Philip's vessels and vassals. Meanwhile Ralegh himself found a new facade of respectability. With anticipatory appropriateness, the old pirate became Member of Parliament for Penzance.

Receiving an enthusiastic report of the Roanoke Island areas from Amadas and Barlow, Ralegh in 1585 dispatched more than a hundred men in seven ships to begin a colony there. Ten months later, starving and surrounded by hostile Indians with whom they had not dealt diplomatically, they seized the opportunity to escape provided by the unexpected arrival of Sir Francis Drake's fleet and returned to England.

Ralegh tried again, sending out a slightly larger company headed by John White as governor. White was a skilled artist whose drawings of life in the New World would include, in the succinct words of Samuel Eliot Morison, "the best portraits of American Indians prior to Catlin, the best flora prior to John Bartram, and the best birds and beasts prior to Audubon."[9] But there was some question as to whether he had enough social prestige to command respect as governor. This was remedied by granting him a coat of arms. Seven other men entrusted with leadership in the colony were also suddenly granted arms, and the garter king of arms designed an appropriate shield for the City of Ralegh, which was to be planted in the wilderness.[10] Sir Walter knew that the stability of a new colony would be sorely strained by the shocks of life in a strange environment; and he was determined to secure for his colonists the traditional landmarks of English society.

Ralegh had instructed White to plant the new colony in the Chesapeake Bay region rather than on problem-beset Roanoke Island. But the master mariner in charge of the ships was intent upon raiding a silver-laden Spanish fleet expected soon in the Azores, and he put the colonists ashore on Roanoke Island and sailed on.

Little had been accomplished toward building the settlement when White was persuaded by other leaders to take advantage of an opportunity to sail back to England to seek supplies and call attention to the colony's needs. White readily persuaded Ralegh to send provisions. Sir Walter was prepared to dispatch one vessel almost at once, to be followed a little later by seven or eight under Grenville. But this was 1588, and the war with Spain soon took priority. Every ship was needed to meet the threat of the Armada. In 1589, despite England's victory, there was fear of another great naval battle with Spain. Though English ships sailed to the West Indies and Brazil, and even to the Far East, in that year no vessels were found to sail to Roanoke.

Finally, in 1590, White was able to return with another captain more interested in raiding Spanish commerce than in carrying relief to his stranded countrymen. After much time spent in chasing and capturing Spaniards, the English vessel came to anchorage off the north end of Roanoke Island on an August night. A forest fire of unknown origin was burning ashore, making a hellish hole in the dark, but revealing nothing. The ship fired its cannon and sounded a trumpet. Those aboard called out in friendly greeting and even sang English songs, apparently as evidence of their nationality. There was no answer.

At daybreak, White, accompanied by other men from the ship, went ashore. There were footprints in the sand, which they assumed to be Indians'. Atop a tree-covered sand dune, the English found carved on the trunk of one in "fair Roman letters" CRO. Coming upon the site of the settlement he had left three years before, White found carved on another tree "in fair capital letters" the word CROATOAN. Grass and weeds grew high against the walls of the houses, and pumpkin vines crawled like invading serpents through doors and windows.

But there were no people. The colonists had been told to carve the name of their destination if forced to abandon the original site, and to carve as well a Maltese cross if they were in distress. White took hope from the fact that there was no cross. As Croatan Island was the home of Manteo, a friendly Indian, there was hope that the colonists were safe. Aside from his concern for the general welfare, White was very personally aware that his daughter Eleanor Dare and granddaughter Virginia Dare, first English child born in America, were part of the vanished community.

The settlers evidently had been gone for some time. Three of the chests left behind by White had been broken into, and the pictures and framed maps that he had intended for the projected executive mansion were "rotten and spoiled with rain." The suit of armor he had intended as a shining symbol of authority when he presided at ceremonies in the City of Ralegh was "almost eaten through with rust."

White was eager to visit Croatoan, but a storm prevented them for an interval. Then the ship's captain insisted on sailing forth in search of Spanish wealth. The searches of other years never revealed the fate of the missing English.

The failure of this second attempt at colonization, though a deep disappointment to Ralegh, was soon superseded by more personal troubles. His ways brought him as many enemies as friends, but he kept the affection of the one who counted most until the day in 1592 when the queen discovered that he had impregnated and secretly married Elizabeth Throgmorton, one of her own ladies-in-waiting. She imprisoned him in the Tower for a short while, then released him but banished him from the court. To the surprise of many, Ralegh proved to be a devoted husband and his wife would later prove her devotion to him in a way that captured the admiration of a nation.

Sir Walter did not spend in an armchair the time between the 1585 expedition to Roanoke Island and his arrest in 1592. By no means was all his adventuring by proxy. In 1588, as vice admiral of Devon, he looked after England's coastal defenses at a vital point, but he also found time for a trip to Ireland. He returned to Ireland the next year as the guest of Edmund Spenser and secured for him a royal pension, in addition to royal aid in publication of the first three books of the *Faerie Queene*. Elizabeth was a sincere lover of literature, but her willingness to help was probably influenced by the fact that the title character (also called "Britomart," "Belphoebe," "Mercilla," and "Gloriana"), though symbolizing glory in the abstract, also signified Elizabeth in particular. The same year, Ralegh sailed for Portugal and participated in an abortive attempt to incite rebellion against Philip II. In 1591 he was preparing for a voyage to the Azores when he was abruptly replaced by Grenville. Rumor had it that Elizabeth feared he might be hurt in a fracas with the Spaniards, or in any event wanted him near her. In 1592 he did sail forth to prey on a Spanish merchant fleet, but the queen called him back to charge him with misconduct regarding Elizabeth Throgmorton.

Ralegh's release was hastened by the eloquent letters he wrote declaring his devastation at finding himself outside the orbit of Queen Elizabeth's favor—not just because she was his queen but because she was Elizabeth. He soon was distributing the treasure that he had taken on his latest raid. But, although he had invested heavily in the expedition, she let him keep only enough to cover his expenses. The rest she claimed for the royal coffers. Partly she may have been expressing her displeasure with the errant courtier, but in financial matters she was much more akin to her paternal grandfather, the acquisitive Henry VII, than to her spendthrift father, Henry VIII.

Though Sir Walter was restored to a large measure of his former favor with the queen, his enemies had tasted blood. And the courtier had no great public popularity to restrain them. He was regarded as arrogant, self-serving, and greedy. An enthusiastic promoter of the tobacco trade, he was frequently seen in a cloud of smoke, but in some people's minds he was associated less with the scent of the burning weed than with the odor of brimstone. He supposedly belonged to a literary group known as the "School of Night" and headed by Thomas Harriot. Once a tutor in Ralegh's household, Harriot had gone on the expedition to Roanoke Island and published a widely circulated *Briefe and True Report of the New Found Land of Virginia.* He had become an internationally prominent astronomer and mathematician. Also included in the group were the brilliant dramatist Christopher Marlowe; the poet, playwright, and translator of Greek classics George Chapman; "the Wizard Earl" Northumberland; and others reputed to be atheists. The charge was almost certainly untrue of Harriot. And it may have been untrue of Ralegh, Marlowe, and others as well, though both were accused of atheism in 1590. All participants were suspected of subversive practices ranging from witchcraft and communion with the dead to speculative discussions.

Probably the group had no formal organization, but to the extent that they met, the last charge was undoubtedly true. The era was as much one of exploration in philosophy and science as in seafaring and the arts. Ralegh was representative of educated Englishmen of his time in combining interest in the past (even the distant classical past) with an exciting sense of history being made in his own time. And, like many of his contemporaries, he was ambitious to be part of history.

With the scholar Lawrence Kemys, reputedly a companion in the School of Night, Ralegh set out in search of El Dorado. To sixteenth-century Europeans the name was not just a symbol for dreamed-of wealth, much less for fulfilled desire, but the designation of an actual city or country loaded with gold. In seeking it, Ralegh was actuated by intellectual curiosity and an adventurous spirit as well as by a hunger for material gain. His studies of Spanish accounts persuaded him that El Dorado was in a part of Guiana now within the borders of Venezuela.

He ascended the Orinoco River for three hundred miles, marveling at the tropical rain forests and savoring the exoticism of its birdcalls. He did not find El Dorado, but he did bring back specimens containing gold. Like other New World explorers before him, he also brought back Indian tales of men who "have their eyes in their shoulders and their mouths in the middle of their breasts."[11] In *The Discovery of Guiana*, which he published the following year, he lamented, "it was not my chance to hear of them till I was come away, and if I had but [heard] spoken one word of it while I was there I might have brought one of them with me to put the matter out of doubt."[12] Ralegh was, however, more cautious than many writers of travelogues. He conceded that, as he had not actually seen the monsters, he could not personally vouch for their existence. Of the riches of Guiana, though, he admitted not a single doubt, arguing that in developing the country, Englishmen could simultaneously enrich themselves and hinder Spain's imperial designs.

He answered the call to direct action against Spain in 1596, commanding a naval squadron and receiving a wound in the capture of Cadiz. This service returned him to the queen's favor. Next he sailed with the earl of Essex on an expedition to the Azores. The two had been friends, but their bond had been frayed by the friction of rivalry for Elizabeth's favor. The earl had moved conspicuously ahead while Sir Walter was under a cloud. Apparently they were at least tenuously reconciled when they set sail, but Ralegh outdistanced Essex and captured Fayal without waiting for him. Sir Walter's victory was dearly bought. Essex exploded in wrath and became an implacable enemy. Sir Walter's quarrel alienated the earl's friends. Ralegh had not lost his habit of alternately charming and alienating people.

Nevertheless, he was appointed governor of the island of Jersey. Shortly after, Essex used his own popularity to form a war party and demand for himself command of the army. Furious when the queen ignored one of his recommendations, he turned his back upon her by way of insult, only to feel her small fists boxing his ears in a surprise attack. "Go to the Devil!" she shouted. Essex grabbed his sword and yelled back, "This is an outrage that I will not put up with. I would not have borne it from your father's hands."

The quarrel passed and she made him lord deputy for Ireland. But being her viceroy did not afford scope for his ambition. After failing in Ireland and angering the queen with his impetuous explanations, he was put in custody at York House until the charges against him could be heard.

When about three hundred of the earl's followers collected in the courtyard, the lord keeper and three other officials demanded an explanation for the illegal assembly. The mob promptly imprisoned them and bore Essex, now more captive than leader, to London for a confrontation with the government. Ralegh helped to rout the rebels. Essex was tried, convicted, and sentenced to die. As captain of the queen's guard, Sir Walter presided at the execution, weeping as the head of his inimical friend rolled. For a year, that head stared from the Tower as a warning to anyone else who might carry in his skull the seeds of revolution.

Ralegh now was again serving in Parliament, making more enemies by his stringent criticisms but, among other things, bravely fighting for religious toleration. Of course, this activity probably gave more ammunition to those who charged him with atheism.

When Queen Elizabeth died in 1603, no powerful person stood between Ralegh and his enemies. Moreover, James I, who succeeded to the throne, was already prejudiced against him. For some, the ascent of this son of Mary, queen of Scots, marks the beginning of the Jacobean Age. But the cultural historians consider James' reign an extension of the Age of Elizabeth. The national vitality that she epitomized and nurtured continued to flourish after her energetic and tempestuous spirit had worn out its shell.

James particularly deplored Sir Walter's eagerness for war with Spain. Besides, the king was repelled by the vainglorious ways of the man and even his personal habits. Ralegh was not only the chief promoter of tobacco in England but also one of its chief users. It was said that one day he was puffing away at his pipe in such a cloud of smoke that one of his servants, thinking he was on fire, threw a bucket of water on him. James was such a fierce enemy of tobacco that eventually he published a pamphlet, the *Counterblaste*, in opposition.

Many Englishmen concluded that James was a fanatic when they read his suspicions that smoking was harmful to the heart and lungs.

In the beginning of the new reign, Ralegh suffered one loss after another. Durham House, from which a bishop had been ousted to provide a mansion for Sir Walter, now was returned to that ecclesiastic. Sir Walter's monopolies were snatched from him, and he was removed from his position as governor of Jersey. Not surprisingly, his long service as captain of the guard was terminated.

Sir Walter was involved with people active in a conspiracy against King James I. For this reason, he was committed to the Tower to await trial. There he tried to stab himself but made only a superficial wound. If he had acted as wholeheartedly and decisively as he did in many situations, he doubtless would have succeeded. He was found guilty, on what many considered insufficient evidence, of participation in a plot to kill King James in intrigue with Spain against his own country. Many people found it hard to believe that this scourge of the Spaniards had suddenly become their ally. Besides, Ralegh's brave and restrained demeanor during the trial gained him some popularity.

Though Sir Walter was sentenced to death, the sentence was not executed; he was permitted to remain in prison year after year. Prince Henry, the king's own son, was reported to have said that he did not understand how his father "could keep so glorious a bird in such a cage."

Though any confinement was particularly vexing to a man of Ralegh's adventurous disposition, his life in the Tower was not as spartan as it might have been, largely because of the prince's quiet intervention. A little house was built for Sir Walter's wife inside the Tower yard, and she eagerly embraced the chance to be with him. Books were provided for his amusement and serious research. He began learning chemistry and even secured chemicals for experiments, which he conducted in a chicken house he converted into a laboratory. It is a wonder that the authorities did not suspect him of a plot to make a bomb. Instead, he produced an elixir whose medicinal merits were never proved but that enjoyed popularity as a stimulant.

He had more time for another kind of production, at which he had long been proficient. He was, in his time, one of the best minor poets in the English language, and some of his best verses are analyzed today in university English classes and enjoyed by the general reader of literary taste.

Disillusionment finds memorable expression in lines from his *The Book of the Ocean to Cynthia*: "Those streams seem standing puddles, which before we saw our beauties in, so were they clear." Whether lured by a legend or informed by reliable report, many Englishmen believed that Ralegh had once seen every puddle as an opportunity if an elegant queen was hesitating before it.

Among his more famous lines, posthumously published but perhaps antedating his imprisonment, and even addressed to Queen Elizabeth, are:

Our passions are most like to floods and streams; The shallow murmur, but the deep are dumb.

The concept may have been old when Quintus Curtius wrote about *altissima quaque* in the first century A.D., but Sir Walter's way of expressing it compares favorably with George Herbert's later reference to "still waters"and even Shakespeare's "Smooth runs the water where the brook is deep."[13]

During his prison years, Ralegh turned also to another genre—historical writing. With true Elizabethan breadth of ambition, he began composing *History of the World*. In the preface he said, "Whosoever, in writing a modern history, shall follow truth too near the heels, it may haply strike out his teeth." Fate had already given him a kick in the teeth, but there was little likelihood that he would suffer another from following truth too nearly into modern times. His book began with the creation of the world and explored the civilizations of Nineveh, Egypt, Judea, Persia, Chaldea, Greece, and Carthage before concluding the hefty first (and only) volume with an account of imperial Rome's conquest of Greece in the second century B.C.

"When a man knows he is to be hanged in a fortnight," Samuel Johnson once said, "it concentrates his mind wonderfully." Though Ralegh, in the twelve years that he worked on his history under sentence of death, roamed in imagination over the delights, delusions, and debris of eight civilizations and more than forty-six centuries, intimations of mortality focused his thoughts as he penned the last paragraphs of his monumental tome. Musing on the cost of "boundless ambition in mortal men," he marveled at human persistence in so destructive a pursuit and attributed it to the fact that "the kings and princes of the world have always laid before them the actions, but not the ends, of those great ones [who] preceded them. They are always transformed with the glory of the one; but they never mind the misery of the other till they find the experience in themselves." He may have been thinking of courtiers as well as kings when he added:

> They neglect the advice of God while they enjoy life or hope it, but they follow the counsel of Death upon his first approach. It is he that puts into men all the wisdom of the world, without speaking a word, which God, with all the words of his law, promises, or threats, doth not infuse. Death, which hateth and destroyeth man, is believed; God, which hath made him and loves him, is always deferred.

Having reviewed, in writing his history, the rise and fall of kingdoms and their leaders, Ralegh quotes Solomon in Ecclesiastes: " 'I have considered all the works that are under the sun; and behold, all is vanity and vexation of spirit.' " Then Sir Walter asks, "But who believes it till Death tells it us?" He cites instances of rulers being moved to rectify injustices only when death confronted them, and concludes, "It is therefore Death alone that can suddenly make man to know himself. He tells the proud and insolent that they are but abjects, and humbles them at the instant, makes them cry, complain, and repent, yea, even to hate their forepast happiness." Ralegh closes with an apostrophe to the great conqueror: "O eloquent, just, and mighty Death. Whom none could advise, thou hast persuaded. . . . Thou hast drawn together all the far-stretched greatness, all the pride, cruelty, and ambition of man, and covered it all over with these two narrow words, 'Hic jacet [Here lies]!' "

These lines might have been Ralegh's valedictory to the world. But they were not. He bribed the duke of Buckingham, the object of the king's amorous ardor, to intercede with James for him. Though he enlisted sentiment in selecting the messenger, Sir Walter appealed to James' self-interest. Still under sentence of death, Ralegh bargained for the chance to return to Guiana and bring back gold. James' coffers were dangerously low. He agreed to let Sir Walter carry out his project and to keep four-fifths of the riches for himself and his partners, provided that one-fifth was reserved for the Crown. There was another proviso: the gold must be taken only from "heathen and savage people." On the insistence of the Spanish ambassador, who protested the arrangement even with this safeguard, James told Ralegh that the death sentence under which he lived would be executed immediately if he should menace the Spanish settlements in Guiana. Ralegh gave written consent to this provision, fully realizing that in so doing he might literally be signing his death warrant.

With his own wealth (now much slenderer than it once had been) augmented greatly by the resources of his friends, he set sail in March 1617 for South America. With him was his son, Wat, who was sometimes irritatingly careless of the personal and family images that Sir Walter burnished so assiduously, but who nevertheless was much loved by his father.

Arrived at the Orinoco, Ralegh found progress up the river barred by a Spanish settlement. Only in the most technical sense could it be said that he kept the pledge exacted from him by King James. He stayed aboard ship while those under his command, including his son, went ashore to find a solution. They attacked the Spanish and burned the settlement. They even killed the governor. The Spaniards fought back with surprising strength, and the Englishmen retreated to their ships.

The leader of the raid was Ralegh's second in command, that same Lawrence Kemys who supposedly had been one of his philosophical companions in the School of Night and who had accompanied him on his 1595 expedition. It was now his distressing duty to tell Ralegh about the raid, its disastrous failure, and the death of Wat Ralegh in the attempt.

Maybe Sir Walter had cherished some unreasonable hope that any Spanish settlement in the way could be circumvented without resort to arms. Or maybe the reality of his son's death and the prospect of his own as a result of what had happened on the Orinoco drove logic from his head. In any event, he harshly reproved his old friend for what had happened. Kemys walked away. He was found later, dead by his own hand.

One by one, ships deserted Ralegh's command, putting the salt winds of an ocean between them and the smell of death. Returned to England and facing execution if he remained, Ralegh attempted to flee to France but was captured at Greenwich and returned to the Tower. The ax that had hung over his head for more than twelve years was about to be lowered.

On the night of October 28, 1618, the eve of his execution, Ralegh, drawing on memory, copied into his Bible a verse that he had composed many years before:

> O cruel Time, which takes in trust
> Our youth, our joys, and all we have,
> And pays us but with age and dust;
> Who in the dark and silent grave
> When we have wandered all our ways,
> Shuts up the story of our days.

Then he added two new lines:

> But from this earth, this grave, this dust
> My God shall raise me up, I trust.[14]

The day of the execution dawned cold and clear, but clouds soon appeared and increased in number as the hour neared. A crowd packed the courtyard to witness Sir Walter's last performance. Across the way and above the heads of the groundlings, ladies and gentlemen of the nobility watched from windows. His tall form clad in black and gray, Ralegh slowly mounted the scaffold and made it his stage. "Honorable lords and friends," he said, "I offer my thanks to Almighty God that he hath vouchsafed me to die in daylight and in the presence of such an honorable assembly and not alone in the darkness."

As he was straining his voice to be heard by them, the lords and ladies forsook their comfortable perches to gather round him on the scaffold itself. As Sir Winston Churchill would observe in another connection, "It doesn't hurt to be polite to a man when you are going to kill him." Ralegh greeted them as if he were welcoming them to his manor house.

He declared his innocence of any treason to king or country and his forgiveness of all men. He explained that he sometimes suffered from a tremor because of illness and hoped that if he should appear to tremble at any stage of the proceedings, no one would attribute that weakness to fear.

At the sheriff's proclamation that all visitors must leave the scaffold, Ralegh excused himself: "I have a long journey to go; therefore I must take my leave." He took the ax from the headsman and felt the edge before returning it. Turning to the master of ceremonies, he said, "Mr. Sheriff, this is sharp medicine. But it is a sound cure for all diseases."

As Ralegh knelt to receive the blow, the perturbed headsman reminded him that it was customary to face east toward the rising sun. "What matter how the head lies," said Sir Walter, "so long as the heart be right?"[15]

The headsman hesitated. Ralegh spoke: "What dost thou fear? Strike, man, strike!"

The ax flashed and the head that had just spoken fell. It was not placed in a sack of the common sort ordinarily used. His loving wife had provided a red leather bag tastefully embossed with his coat of arms.

Ralegh had gone out of public life as he had entered it—in style. Seated on his throne, King James had not half so much style as Ralegh standing on a gallows platform.

But was there substance behind the glittering persona? Though Queen

Elizabeth had kept him near her as a favorite, making him captain of her guard, she never honored his judgment by naming him to her Council. Yet she had named even the impetuous Essex to that august body. Ralegh's New World ventures had ended in failure. To some of his contemporaries his promotion of tobacco culture had seemed a great accomplishment, but other generations have viewed it in a different light. There are other attainments, however. To be a good minor poet is to achieve much more than most writers of verse, but Ralegh did more than this. One of his poems, "The Nymph's Reply to the Shepherd," some four centuries after its composition, is one of the most anthologized works in the English language. Nor are all of Sir Walter's scholarly pursuits matter for jest. True, the most publicized product of his chemical studies was only an elixir that some have called the most popular quack medicine of his day. But his researches in literature, history, and philosophy were more than a dilettante's preparations for midnight sessions of weird hocus-pocus. Some of the best scholars of his day—Harriot and Kemys among them—found intellectual stimulus in his company. And he must be numbered among those who in captivity roamed widely through the realms of imagination and produced a book whose influence extended well beyond his lifetime. For a century after publication in 1614, his *History of the World* was both a standard work of historical scholarship and one of the most frequently cited models of English prose.

Increased information about past societies and improved methods of research eroded its position in historiography. Also its brands of naïveté and prejudice lost currency, yielding to successive brands, and were viewed with the amused contempt that each generation reserves for the philosophical quirks of its predecessors. But as a work of literature it has continued to win the admiration of those alive to the precision, sonority, and supple strength inherent in the English tongue. In the mid-twentieth century, Tucker Brooke, writing in the monumental *Literary History of England* edited by Albert C. Baugh, said that Sir Walter's prose was "of supreme grandeur." He added, "Both in time and in merit Ralegh belongs among the first writers of impassioned English prose."[16] The Devon-born knight who sought a peerage in vain is recognized today as one of the lords of language.

Despite Sir Walter's status in the kingdom of letters, however, his greatest significance today probably derives from his role as a symbol of the Elizabethan ethos. The range of his activities as soldier, sailor, courtier, administrator, explorer, chemist, geographer, poet, prose master, and historian is representative of his era in England. So is the combination of action and contemplation. So, too, the absorption in both ancient lore and contemporary experiment. And, above all, the tremendous appetite for every adventure of life, and the confidence that led him to try not only to colonize a new world but to write the whole history of the old.

14

"ALL KNOWLEDGE FOR MY PROVINCE"

I F RALEGH WAS ambitious in trying to write a complete history of the Old World, his aspiration was dwarfed by that of a contemporary who proclaimed that he took "all knowledge for [his] province." People usually have forgotten that Francis Bacon explained that he harbored no notions of obtaining detailed information on every aspect of intellectual endeavor, but rather determined to acquire the rudiments of every major subject of study in his time. So equipped, he said, he should be able to survey the separate fields and their relationship to each other as if he stood on a high promontory.[1]

Even so, the attempt bordered on hubris, especially when one considers that his project was not the single-minded, lifetime endeavor of a closeted scholar. In true Renaissance fashion, Bacon won fame in law, politics, oratory, literature, history, science, and philosophy.

Born in London in 1561, he had many advantages of heredity and environment. He was the younger son of Sir Nicholas Bacon, lord keeper to Queen Elizabeth and one of her most influential councillors. His mother, Ann, was one of the three celebratedly intellectual daughters of Sir Anthony Cooke. One became the mother of Sir Robert Cecil, Elizabeth's great secretary of state. Another was the mother of Sir Thomas Hoby, Elizabeth's ambassador to France and the renowned translator into English of Castiglione.

When Bacon was just a boy, his precocity drew the attention of the queen, who playfully called him "the young lord keeper." A frail constitution that made him unfit for sports led him into even greater exercise of his intellect. Before he had attained manhood, the extent and variety of his learning were legendary in court circles.

At the age of twelve, he entered Trinity College, Cambridge. At fifteen he was admitted to Gray's Inn for the study of law. He soon left his formal studies, however, to accompany Sir Amias Paulet, named English ambassador to France. Through his uncle, William Cecil, Lord Burghley, the lord treasurer, Bacon applied for royal appointment to some good position in government service. But despite this powerful mediator, the prominence of the young man's father, his own precocity, and the fact that he was personally known to the queen, no job was offered. Upon his father's death, he returned to England, and at the age of twenty-one he became a Gray's Inn barrister. Sir Nicholas had not yet completed purchase of an estate intended for his son, so young Francis found himself heir to a prominent name and little else.

At twenty-three he was elected to Parliament by a Dorset constituency. Undaunted by his previous failure to obtain royal employment, he presumed to compose a "Letter of Advice to Queen Elizabeth." Despite the boldness of its title, the missive was farsighted and reasonable. It called for a larger measure of toleration for those at both ends of the religious spectrum and proposed specific reforms. Some of these were designed to ease the lot of the Puritans. Bacon also addressed the dilemma of Catholics ordered to subscribe to the Oath of Supremacy, acknowledging the sovereign as "the only supreme head" of the church in England. Bacon suggested that there be substituted for this oath so offensive to Catholics one acknowledging the treason of any English subject who refused to bear arms against any foreign enemy, including any pope who might play that role.

Bacon was elected to the next two Parliaments, each time from a different constituency, becoming a useful committeeman in the Commons. But he still did not become a royal appointee. About the time he reached his thirtieth birthday, perhaps trying an indirect approach to royal preferment, he ingratiated himself with the earl of Essex, then Elizabeth's favorite. He became one of the nobleman's confidants and seemed to be in an excellent posture for advancement when he was reelected to Parliament at age thirty-two, from still another constituency. But he spoke against the Crown's request for a triple subsidy to finance the war with Spain, and Elizabeth was still annoyed about that when Essex petitioned her about a year later to appoint his friend to the vacated office of attorney general. Instead, she appointed Sir Edward Coke, who also was heard from later. The next year Essex pressed for Bacon's appointment as solicitor general, and Burghley endorsed the choice, again to no avail.

The queen would sometimes excuse the occasional opposition of young men if they were dashing, as was Essex, and she could reward obedient merit in a homely guise, as with Cecil's hunchbacked son; but there was little hope for preferment at her hands from those who were neither dashing nor pliant. And this was probably how she saw Bacon. Some said that, in that era when women's legs were hidden but men's displayed, she would make an exception for a good pair of legs, but nothing is known for sure about the quality of Bacon's calves. For some reason, however, she did compromise sufficiently to make him a learned counsel to the queen.

Believing that Elizabeth had refused Bacon as a way of insulting himself, Essex made his friend a gift of land as a consolation prize. At first opportunity, he pressed the queen to appoint Bacon master of the rolls. This time she not only refused but showed some irritation. Bacon feared that other actions by Essex would create an irreconcilable breach with Elizabeth. He apparently worried for his friend's sake but was also troubled about his own fate if his noble patron should antagonize the sovereign. He was convinced that Essex was much too reckless in opposing the queen, much too high tempered when she did not follow his advice. He was especially disturbed that Essex was reveling in his role as hero of Cadiz, courting popularity with the soldiers and the people in the manner of one planning rebellion. Not that he believed Essex was hatching such a plot, but the contemplative Bacon feared where the fiery nobleman's impulsiveness might lead. He wrote to Essex, urging him to reconsider his course. He continued to warn him for the next several years, on at least one occasion going so far as to write, "I love some things much better than I love your lordship, as the Queen's service, her quiet and contentment, her honor, her favor, the good of my country and the like."

At this time Bacon was also writing for a much larger audience than the recipients of his private letters. In 1597 he published his *Essays*, besides *Colours of Good and Evil* and *Meditationes sacrae*. Thus he commanded attention by two publications in English and one in Latin. Like most Englishmen of his day, he seems to have used the ancient Roman tongue for the work that he considered most important, but posterity has not agreed with his estimate. Not that the *Meditationes sacrae* is devoid of pithy sayings. One of them, "Nam et ipsa scientia potestas est," became quite familiar when translated into "Knowledge is power." But the *Essays* have made their author one of the most quoted persons in the English language.

Bacon's essays are generally acknowledged to be the first examples of their genre in English. But they are even more innovative than that primacy would imply. Internationally, they mark the debut of a distinct subgenre. Montaigne, credited with originating the form, was said by Hazelton Spencer to have produced a work fitting Samuel Johnson's definition of the essay as "a loose sally of the mind."[2] By the full title of his volume, *The Essays, or Counsels, Civill and Morall*, Bacon announced the seriousness of his purpose and implied that there would be nothing loose about its execution. Bacon himself called the writing a "delivering of knowledge in distinct and disjointed aphorisms." But the sententiousness was deliberate and enhanced the quotability. The omission of interstitial matter made the sentences somewhat artificially discrete, but a complex pattern of symmetries united the whole.

The manner was emblematic of the character of the work, for Bacon combined old ideas and new interpretations with the same measured enthusiasm with which he united classical forms and the eccentricities of an individualistic style. While few would think of Bacon's writing as conversational in tone, Ben Jonson saw it as analogous to his speech, at least on formal occasions. "No man," Jonson wrote, "ever spoke more neatly, more [compressedly], more weightily, or suffered less emptiness, less idleness in what he uttered. No member of his speech but consisted of his own graces. . . . The fear of every man that heard him was lest he should make an end."

Bacon's conciseness conforms to Montaigne's precept that the essay should be more compact than a Platonic dialogue. His product, however, differs radically from the Frenchman's, and from the works of many subsequent English essayists, in that the author's personal whims are withheld from the

reader. Instead, the writer's considered opinions are delivered as solemn assev-
erations dedicated to the serious purpose of preparing an intelligent man for
public service. The compass of the essays is far broader than this concentration
might indicate for, true to Elizabethan concepts, Bacon held that the ideal public servant was one trained in the arts and sciences who complemented book
learning with practical lessons acquired through social intercourse, travel, and
the exercise of responsibility. The volume of essays is not a mere manual. It is
a collection of discourses on subjects as various as gardens, marriage, learning,
and discourse itself.

First he published only ten essays, revealing a ripe wisdom even more surprising in a man of thirty-seven years than the diversity of his knowledge.
Through the years, he added twelve religious meditations in Latin and other
essays in English, until the 1625 edition of *Essays* included fifty-eight separate
compositions.[3] Besides, he had revised and enlarged some of them in ways that
reflected his growing scholarship, practical experience, and literary skill. His
civil and moral counsels owe much to the Old and New Testaments; the history
of Rome, Greece, China, Spain, France, and England; and the writings of Virgil,
Tacitus, Seneca, Cicero, Comineus, Plato, and particularly of Machiavelli. He
deplores what he considers the Italian's low aims but hopes to apply to higher
objects his practical skills in manipulation. Bacon was one of many Elizabethan
writers for whom Machiavelli provided a conduit from the rich traditions of
Renaissance Florence.

Like so many leading thinkers in the Age of Lorenzo and the Age of Elizabeth, indeed like the eponymous rulers of those eras, Bacon stressed the need
for a balance between tradition and experiment. In the essay "Of a King," he
recognized the occasional desirability of changing laws, but said, "A wise king
must do less in altering his laws than he may; for new government is ever dangerous.... [T]hough it be for the better, yet it is not without fearful apprehension." In "Of Innovations" he again favored a balance of tradition and change
but, writing after experience of national leadership, seemed to be more hospitable to experiment: "As the births of living creatures at first are ill-shapen, so
are all innovations, which are the births of time." This is not sufficient reason
to reject them, for "a froward retention of custom is as turbulent a thing as an
innovation; and they that reverence too much old times are but [objects of]
scorn to the new. It were good, therefore, that men in their innovations would
follow the example of time itself, which, indeed, innovateth greatly, but quietly,
and by degrees scarce to be perceived." But he cautioned:

> It is good also not to try experiments in states, except the necessity
> be urgent, or the utility evident; and well to beware that it be the
> reformation that draweth on the change, and not the desire of change
> that pretendeth the reformation; and, lastly, that the novelty, though
> it be not rejected, yet be held for a suspect, and, as the Scripture saith,
> "That we make a stand upon the ancient way, and then look about us,
> and discover what is the straight and right way, and so to walk in it."

While counseling mankind through his formal writings, Bacon was giving particular and pointed advice to his sponsor, Essex. The patron was five years younger than the protégé chronologically and a generation younger in maturity. Bacon used Machiavellian cunning when he proposed to Essex a remedy for "a cold and malignant humor growing upon Her Majesty toward your lordship." He suggested that the earl "never be without some [plans] afoot, which [he] should seem to pursue with earnestness and affection, and then let them fall, upon taking knowledge of Her Majesty's opposition and dislike." Bacon proposed for Essex "the pretense of some journeys, which, at Her Majesty's request, your lordship might relinquish." He also suggested pleasing the queen in "the lightest sort of particulars, which yet are not to be neglected," as in "habits, apparel, wearings, gestures, and the like."

But, of course, the earl did not heed his friend's advice. And when he added rebellion to his offenses and came to trial for treason, Bacon, as queen's counsel, was expected to participate in the prosecution. As we have seen, Bacon had already warned Essex that friendship for him must be subordinate to loyalty to queen and country. Essex's subsequent efforts to abduct the queen and force her to dismiss some of her ministers, he all the while inciting the citizens of London to revolt, were clearly treason. Bacon helped prepare the charges against Essex and, even though he was not commanded to speak at the trial, spoke twice for the prosecution.

Once he said, "I have never yet seen in any case such favor shown to any prisoner; so many digressions, such delivery of evidence by fractions, and so silly a defense of such great and notorious treasons." Bacon may have spoken in anger and disgust with his erstwhile friend for refusing to heed any warnings along the path to treason. Some thought that, viewing the earl's cause as lost, he sided so vigorously with the prosecution in an effort to free himself from the taint of association. Three years later, stung by criticism or nagged by doubt, he published an *Apology* for his part in court proceedings that led to the beheading of his former patron. It was not an appeal for forgiveness but an apologia, an attempt to justify his actions.

Meanwhile, Bacon had courted the wealthy young widow of Sir William Hatton, only to lose out to Sir Edward Coke, whose wife she became. Coke, of course, was the same man to whom he had lost out in his quest for the office of attorney general. There is no way of knowing whether Mrs. Hatton had read Bacon's "Of Marriage and the Single Life," in which he said, "He that hath wife and children hath given hostages to fortune; for they are impediments to great enterprises, either of virtue or mischief. Certainly the best works, and of greatest merit for the public, have proceeded from the unmarried or childless man, which both in affection and means have married and endowed the public."

Even so, Bacon had made in the same essay a less quoted observation: "Certainly wife and children are a kind of discipline of humanity; and single men, though they be many times more charitable, because their means are less exhaust, yet, on the other side, they are more cruel and hard-hearted (good to make severe inquisitors), because their tenderness is not so oft called upon." Bacon submitted to that "discipline of humanity" in 1606, marrying at age forty-five a rich London alderman's fourteen-year-old daughter. No little "hostages to fortune" followed.

By the time of his wedding, Elizabeth was three years dead. Her passing had made many changes in England and particularly in Bacon's life. His development had flourished in the cultural climate of Gloriana's reign, but its rays illumined the England of her successor, and under James I he found the political advancement that had so often eluded him. Bacon was knighted and appointed to the commission for considering union with Scotland. His service in this capacity earned him the office of solicitor general.

A more lasting influence, however, was to proceed from his work in his study than from his activities in the chambers of state. In 1605 he published a volume dedicated to King James, *The Advancement of Learning*. It is one of the ironies of history that the name of King James, certainly no fool but nevertheless a pedant of narrow and crabbed wit, should be associated with two of the most stimulating works in the history of publishing—the most eloquent English version of the Bible and the most influential treatise of scientific philosophy ever produced by an Englishman.

Like the Bible, *The Advancement of Learning* consisted of two books in one cover. In the first, Sir Francis wished to deliver "the dignity of learning . . . from the discredits and disgraces which it hath received." To the charge that intensive secular learning was an affront to God, he answered that no "parcel of the world is denied to man's inquiry and invention." The message of Proverbs 20:27 ("The spirit of man is the candle of the Lord, searching all the inward parts of the belly") he paraphrased as "The spirit of man is the lamp of God, wherewith he searcheth the inwardness of all secrets." Bacon labeled as "ignorance and error" the assumption "that the aspiring to overmuch knowledge was the original temptation and sin whereupon ensued the fall of man." He insisted that it was not "the pure knowledge of nature" as symbolized by Adam's observation and naming of the animals "which gave occasion to the fall." It was instead man's presumption in determining according to his own preferences what was good and what was evil. In the course of his book, Bacon used symbols from the Bible as well as illustrations from the new learning. He brought to his audience a fine balance of enticing discoveries and the reassurance of the familiar.

Sir Francis acknowledged that some "learned men have been heretical whilst they have sought to fly up to the secrets of the Deity by the waxen wings of the senses." Though he also admitted that "a little or superficial knowledge of philosophy may incline the mind of man to atheism," he argued that "a farther proceeding therein doth bring the mind back again to religion." And he warned, "Let no man . . . think or maintain that a man can search too far or be too well studied in the book of God's words or in the book of God's works."

Scholarship had also suffered disrepute, Bacon said, when "men began to hunt more after words than matter." This practice, he said, was the effect of a good thing carried to an extreme. Martin Luther, opposing

> the bishop of Rome and the degenerate traditions of the church, and finding his own solitude being noways aided by the opinions of his

own time, was enforced to awake all antiquity and to call former times to his succor to make a party against the present time. So that the ancient authors, both in divinity and humanity, which had long time slept in libraries, began generally to be read and revolved.

At first this had been a stimulus to creative thinking. But study of the ancient writings necessitated more work—"exquisite travail," Bacon called it—in the languages in which they were composed, "for the better understanding of those authors and the better advantage of pressing and applying their words." This, too, could have been beneficial if it had not degenerated into mere imitation of the elaborate rhetorical devices of the past without cultivation of the spirit of inquiry and invention that had animated the best of the ancients. The pale productions of some who claimed the label humanist had sacrificed vigor to gain only preciosity.

Learning had been further discredited by the excessive contentiousness of those who called themselves scholars, more eager to discover small errors among their colleagues than to discern great truths for themselves.

One of the greatest threats to the advancement of learning, Sir Francis summarized, was

> the extreme affecting of two extremities: the one antiquity, the other novelty. . . . one of them seeketh to devour and suppress the other; while antiquity envieth there should be new additions, and novelty cannot be content to add but it must deface. . . . Antiquity deserveth that reverence, that men should make a stand thereupon and discover what is the best way; but when the discovery is well taken, then to make progression.

Intellectual accomplishment, he believed, was hampered by a common error in education:

> the over-early and peremptory reduction of knowledge into arts and methods. . . . after the distribution of particular arts and sciences, men have abandoned universality, . . . which cannot but cease and stop all progression. For [it is not] possible to discover the more remote and deeper parts of any science if you stand but upon the level of the same science.

Science had a much broader meaning then than now. Any intellectual discipline, even any of the liberal arts, was called a science.

While Bacon deplored the alchemists, who had "made a philosophy out of a few experiments of the furnace," he regretted equally the influence of those prone to "infect their meditations, opinions, and doctrines with some conceits which they have most admired," even if their allegiances were to currently popular myths or biases. An effort to become acquainted with a variety of views on a great many topics would help to counteract this tendency.

Bacon also complained of the lack of originality in studies. He scorned a striving to be original even at the cost of being meretricious. But he thought that too many scholars denied themselves the chance to be original by restricting too much the scope of their endeavors. They became absorbed in minutiae, missing the opportunity for the kind of invention or discovery that comes from broad, as well as deep, observation.

> Whereas the most constant and devote[d] kind of professors of any [study] ought to propound to themselves to make some addition to their science, they convert their labors to aspire to certain second prizes: as to be a profound interpreter or commenter, to be a sharp champion or defender, to be a methodical compounder or abridger; and so the patrimony of knowledge cometh to be sometimes improved, but seldom augmented.

Sir Francis concluded the first book of *The Advancement of Learning* with a warning about "the greatest error of all the rest." This was "the mistaking or misplacing of the last or farthest end of knowledge." Too many people, he said, "sought in knowledge a couch, whereupon to rest a searching and restless spirit," or contrarily a means of obtaining riches or professional advancement. "But this is that which will indeed dignify and exalt knowledge, if contemplation and action may be more neatly and straitly conjoined and united together than they have been; a conjunction like unto that of the two highest planets, Saturn, the planet of rest and contemplation, and Jupiter, the planet of civil society and action." He cautioned, "I do not mean, when I speak of use and action, that end before mentioned of the applying of knowledge to lucre and profession; for I am not ignorant of how much that diverteth and interrupteth the prosecution and advancement of knowledge." He likened the lure of lucre to the "golden ball thrown before Atalanta," who lost her great footrace when she turned aside to pick up the bauble.

In this first book of *The Advancement of Learning*, Sir Francis had discussed the greatest strengths of Elizabethan culture. These were respect and enthusiasm for learning, the acquisition of knowledge from other societies and other times, the encouragement of diverse scholarship and versatility in gifted individuals, faith in personal potential, and the ideal of the man of knowledge and contemplation who is also a man of action. Bacon might well have substituted "person" for "man," because the queen certainly exemplified the combination of intellectual cultivation and public service. Of course, so did Bacon himself. These ideals of Elizabethan England also had been those of Renaissance Florence.

Sir Francis also called attention to major weaknesses of Elizabethan culture. Among these were the tendencies of some scholars to become too absorbed in disputation for its own sake and also to limit themselves to the minutiae of research and speculation. Among some, too, there was a stultifying tendency to let an enthusiasm for past civilizations degenerate into mere imitation. These, too, were major weaknesses of Renaissance Florence.

The second book was one of such scope that few people, even in an age of polymaths, would have had the nerve, much less the competence, to undertake it. It was an attempt to classify all human learning. Central to the effort was the thesis "The parts of human learning have reference to the three parts of man's understanding, which is the seat of learning: history to his memory, poesy to his imagination, and philosophy to his reason." Bacon saw poesy as an attitude of the imagination that could be expressed in prose as well as in verse: "It doth raise and erect the mind by submitting the shows of things to the desires of the mind, whereas reason doth buckle and bow the mind unto the nature of things."

Profiting from his skill in intellectual dissection and in perception of analogies, Sir Francis made generations of scholars his beneficiaries. His classifications were by no means the only possible ones in accord with logic, but they were rigorously logical and so comprehensive as to be useful to researchers in many fields, especially the interdisciplinary studies that he so earnestly advocated. Denis Diderot and his associates in the great French *Encyclopédie* followed Bacon's model of classification, and their work was one of the most seminal of the Enlightenment, influencing not only Europe's greatest scholars in the eighteenth century but also Thomas Jefferson, Benjamin Franklin, and other founders of the United States. Auguste Comte in the nineteenth century drew directly upon Bacon's classification as well as upon the refinements of the Encyclopédists, and many prominent disciples followed his example.

Despite the great compass of Bacon's *Advancement of Learning*, he envisioned it as only the first part of a much vaster enterprise, his *Instauratio magna,* or *Great Instauration.* The word *instauration,* in our time, suggests restoration or renewal rather than creation, a circumstance that may imply something about our time. But in Bacon's day, while having some of those connotations of revival, the word's primary reference was to an act of inauguration or establishment. Sir Francis intended, through the writing of a series of related books, to inaugurate a new way of looking at the universe and to establish a more dependable basis for both science and philosophy than they had ever known.

He produced some related papers in which he announced his intentions in developing various aspects of the *Instauration.* In one of these,[4] adapting two ancient myths for the machinery of exposition, he acknowledged the limits, as well as the potential, of science and discussed the nature of primitive matter and its possible origin. While suggesting new possibilities in research and study, he also acknowledged his indebtedness to two forerunners, one from classical Greece's Golden Age, the other from the glorious ferment of the Italian Renaissance. Democritus he credited with philosophical awareness of the mechanisms of the physical world. To Bernardino Telesio he was grateful for accelerating the transition from accepted authority to empiricism in determining truth. Significantly, in energetically advocating experiment, Sir Francis acknowledged traditions that had led him to this adventurous course.

Though he was proposing a revolutionary procedure in the acquisition, assessment, and organization of knowledge, he knew better than to present his arguments chiefly in his native tongue. The official guardians of academic scholarship still believed that their everyday language was fit only for conveying everyday truths. The great truths should be expressed in Latin, the time-honored language of scholarship.

Of course, Latin was the lingua franca of formally educated people in every European nation and therefore was a suitable medium for addressing an international audience. But Sir Francis was aware that publication in Latin was necessary to obtain a respectful audience from scholars even in his own country. Sir Thomas Littleton's famous *Tenures*, when first published about 1481, initially attracted more attention by the circumstance of its not being in Latin than by the scope of its scholarship. Even so, Sir Thomas had not dared to write in English. It was revolutionary enough that he had expressed his ideas in Law French.[5] In Bacon's time Sir Edward Coke proclaimed the *Tenures* "the most perfect and absolute book that ever was written in any human science."[6] But the work had had to overcome the handicap of presentation in a modern language, albeit an older, highly specialized version of the language.

Bacon, author of the *Essays*, an eloquent and learned guide to managing the practical affairs of life, and an avowed student of Machiavelli, was too shrewd to send forth his revolutionary theories to speak to his compatriots in native accents. Instead, he pushed them into the arena clad in all the habiliments of medieval scholarship and demanding attention in orotund Latin phrases. Meanwhile some of his lesser works presenting some of the same ideas could address in English the understanding of those less proficient in the classic tongue. Bacon knew that, in more ways than one, and for scholars as well as the masses, a revolutionary body of thought should be clothed in reassuringly familiar garb.

Bacon was the first truly influential advocate of the kind of scientific world of education, formal association, and organized research that came to be accepted before the end of the seventeenth century and whose absence became unthinkable for succeeding generations.[7] He urged that students be introduced to laboratory experiment, in which the search for truth becomes a shared enterprise, and that the professor take "his seat, not on a platform or pulpit, but on a level with the rest." His dream of professional organizations for the exchange of scientific ideas, while not realized in his lifetime, was cited as inspiration by the founders of Great Britain's Royal Society. He called for collaborative research, institutionalized and government subsidized. Though the precise system of logical investigation recommended by Bacon was not finally adopted by most scientists, no one in the world did more than he to deliver science from the tyranny of unquestioned Aristotelianism and encourage the testing of every received tenet.

He did not, however, advocate the dumping of Aristotle. He himself was a keen student of the Stagirite and honored him as philosopher, moralist, logician, pioneer biologist, analyst of government, and father of literary criticism—a marvelous example of the versatility that Bacon was always urging. In fact, Sir Francis argued, probably sincerely as well as for purposes of persuasion, that some of his own theories for the reform of science had occurred to

Aristotle even though the Greek had not implemented them.[8] Like most of the great figures contributing to the vigor of Elizabethan culture, Bacon maintained a stimulating balance between tradition and innovation. He argued that Aristotle had earned his reputation by fearless testing of received doctrines, but that modern men were afraid to submit the ancient philosopher's pronouncements to the same testing to which he had subjected the findings of his most distinguished predecessors. Sir Francis warned against "receiving as oracles the thoughts and opinions of one man." Citing the two thousand years that separated Elizabethan Englishmen from the age of Aristotle, he implied that to follow unquestioningly the Greek's mandates would itself be a disregard of heritage, indeed would be "to cast aside not only your own endowments but the gifts of time."

The fine balance Bacon achieved between classical heritage and daring experiment is exemplified by the fact that some scholars still argue as to whether he was indebted more to classical culture or to his own observation and the influence of contemporaries. The argument is fruitless. As has been observed in another context, it is comparable to disputing which is more important to a home run in baseball, the ball or the bat.

Bacon, of course, was not the only man arguing that Aristotle's findings should not be accepted on faith alone. Rodolphus Agricola, Marius Nizolius, Petrus Ramus, and Juan Luis Vives all vehemently urged the same thing. But Bacon was the most eloquent and the best organized of those in the rebel camp, and the only one who offered a science program of truly giant scope to fill the yawning vacuum that would follow an end to Aristotelian dictatorship.

Sir Francis also had a very modern vision of science as a cooperative venture of many people of varying abilities, not just an activity of a few geniuses, and definitely not an arcane pursuit restricted to a small elite. He perceived that its practitioners could learn much from skilled mechanics. And he saw that the wide dissemination of scientific discovery could dramatically increase the rate of further discoveries, not only in a single generation but through successive times as well. In *De sapentia veterum* (On the Wisdom of the Ancients), he cited "the races with burning torches instituted in honour of Prometheus." As Prometheus in bringing fire to earth had brought the inspiration for "arts and sciences," Sir Francis thought that the traditional contests suggested "a very wise admonition . . . that perfection of the sciences is to be looked for not from the swiftness nor ability of any one inquirer, but from a succession." This was important in scientific investigation so "that the victory may no longer depend upon the unsteady and wavering torch of each single man, but competition, emulation, and good fortune be brought to aid. Therefore men should be advised to rouse themselves, and try each his own strength and the chance of his own turn, and not to stake the whole venture upon the spirits and brains of a few persons."[9]

In this instance, too, he was reminded of the need for a balance of caution and celerity to achieve lasting progress. "For the strongest and swiftest runners are perhaps not the best fitted to keep their torch alight since it may be put out by going too fast as well as too slow."

While Bacon was happy to be one of many torchbearers in the race of scientific progress, and urged others to join him, he continued as a loner in the race for political preferment and was eager to be rid of competition. Several years after becoming solicitor general, he was impatient for further promotions and blamed his lack of progress on the jealousy of his cousin Robert Cecil, the very man who had secured a knighthood for him. Now ennobled as the earl of Salisbury and serving as the king's chief minister, Cecil may not have been as fearful of competition as Sir Francis supposed.

In any event, Bacon's hopes for rapid advancement were not realized even when death removed Salisbury from public life. Sir Francis did secure the office of attorney general, but this was not enough to satisfy him. He wanted to exert a strong influence on the king himself. James, however, had new favorites. Sir Francis, although he wrote a series of brilliant state papers full of wise advice, had no part in determining national policy.

Soon he was in conflict again with Sir Edward Coke, who from the King's Bench sought to repel all infringements of the common law, even those originating with the king himself. Despite the somewhat liberal tone of his philosophical treatises, Bacon was a largely consistent defender of royal prerogatives. Many people thought that he had difficulty in bringing to personal situations the objectivity of his experimental science. Some wondered if his ambition blinded him to the merits of the parliamentary side in any disputes between the Commons and his royal patron. He seemed resolved not to repeat with James the course of independent resistance that had earned him the enmity of Elizabeth. In legal disputes between Coke and Bacon, Coke was the framer of the future.

Bacon's loyalty to his sovereign, combined with friendship with royal favorites and undeniably great abilities, paid off. In 1617 he was appointed to his father's old post of lord keeper. Less than a year later he became lord chancellor and, a few months later, Baron Verulam.

As we know, he was energetic in the prosecution of Sir Walter Ralegh. Also, he had been the strategist behind the Privy Council's arraignment of his old rival Coke, partly on charges of disrespect for the king. As a result, Coke was dismissed from the office of chief justice of the King's Bench. Apparently in an effort to gain a powerful ally in a fight for restoration, Coke offered his fourteen-year-old daughter as a wife to Sir John Villiers, brother of the duke of Buckingham. When Lady Coke opposed her husband and hid the terrified child, Bacon helped her. Thus Bacon was hand in glove with the woman he had once courted and lost to the man he now had the pleasure of thwarting. Knowing Sir Francis' success in disciplining all passions except those for knowledge, fame, and wealth, one hesitates to describe her as an old flame, but at least she had once loomed large in his life plans.

Bacon's revenge, however, was short lived. Coke kidnapped his own daughter and compelled her to go through with the marriage. He also staged enough of a comeback to be a member of the Privy Council, the very body that Bacon had abetted in removing him from office, by the time Sir Francis was named lord chancellor.

Bacon really had to watch his step now. His old nemesis was back in power and angrier with him than ever. He could ill afford so powerful an adversary when his support of royal prerogatives had alienated a majority of Commons and his new appointment, highest in the gift of the Crown, placed him in solitary vulnerability on a peak of eminence.

Yet he could look down on his enemies, and he was a nimble-witted fellow well acquainted with the laws of survival in Jacobean politics. The year 1620 saw publication of his *Novum organum*, bringing prophecies of immortality as a scholar and creative thinker. Perhaps he suffered delusions of immortality as a statesman. If so, his confidence probably was strengthened in that title-conscious era when on January 27, 1621 he was created Viscount Saint Albans.

Three days later Parliament met in an angry mood after being out of session for seven years. Bacon urged James to compromise with them on some matters of grievance, but the king knew his divine rights, and he asserted them. Parliament was not yet ready to strike at a reigning monarch, even a Stuart with ingrained notions of sovereignty. But the king's high henchman was a fair target. The Commons moved against the lord chancellor for his complicity in asserting royal prerogatives at their expense, then suddenly dropped this complaint and made a more easily proved charge. Bacon, they said, had accepted bribes.

There was once a citizen of a small community in twentieth century Virginia who admitted he had accepted a two-dollar bribe to vote for a certain candidate in a local election, but boasted that his integrity remained intact because he had voted instead for the man's opponent. The moral vindication claimed by Bacon—learned in the law and with a growing reputation as a philosopher—was no more sophisticated than that of the semiliterate voter. He admitted that he had accepted gifts from parties to chancery suits over which he had presided, but pointed to cases in which he had decided in favor of the less generous litigant. In short, he said that he had accepted gifts, as had long been the custom, but that he had never "had bribe or reward in his eye or thought when he pronounced any sentence or order."

He was found "technically guilty" and removed from office. Afterwards he admitted that he had been wrong in conforming to a custom with such potential for corruption, and made a famous comment: "I was the justest judge that was in England these fifty years. But it was the justest censure in Parliament that was these two hundred years."

In a paraphrase of himself, perhaps a little filiopietistic or at least nostalgic for a youthful ideal from which he had strayed, Sir Francis said he had been "the justest chancellor that hath been in the five changes since Sir Nicholas Bacon's time." Of course, now his political career was over, and he could not even claim, as he might have in Elizabeth's reign, that he was a martyr to principle. It is ironic that the man who sacrificed so much youthful idealism, and so much time and energy from his great intellectual project, to climb the greased pole of politics had repeatedly testified to the primacy of intellectual labors. In 1593 he had written, "The sovereignty of man lieth hid in knowledge wherein many things are reserved which kings with their treasure cannot buy, nor with their forces command."[10] Two years later he wrote that "the monuments of wit survive the monuments of power."[11] In 1605 he wrote in *The Advancement of Learning* and in 1623 repeated in *De augmentis*:

> by learning man ascendeth to the heavens and their motions, where in body he cannot come; . . . the dignity and excellency of knowledge and learning in that whereunto man's nature does most aspire; . . . to this tendeth . . . the strength of all other human desires. We see then how far the monuments of wit and learning are more durable than the monuments of power or of the hands.[12]

Undoubtedly Bacon's fame was greatly enhanced by the political fall that abruptly sent him back full-time to his study. So was Western civilization.

15

THE GRAND DESIGN

"THE CAPTAIN of the Hampshire grenadiers," said Edward Gibbon, "has not been useless to the historian of the Roman Empire." Experiences as a militia captain in his home county had been instructive to the scholar when he delineated the leadership problems of generals and emperors in his great *Decline and Fall*. Although Sir Francis Bacon squandered far too much of his time in the pursuit and administration of offices that could have been filled as well by others, his political experience (much more sophisticated than Gibbon's) undoubtedly enriched his judgment as historian and biographer and added to the practical wisdom of the *Essays*, which he revised over many years. Certainly, however excessive or in some cases ill judged, his political career illustrated one of the great strengths of the Elizabethan Age. In that era, careers of public service attracted many of England's brightest minds.

It was in a spirit of public service, too, as well as in obedience to the promptings of personal ambition, that Bacon at last dedicated himself almost completely to his self-assigned task of classifying human knowledge and pointing the way to its increase. The fact that seven months before his ousting from office he had publicly announced his plan to write the *Great Instauration* testifies to his conviction much more strongly than if the two events had occurred in reverse order. One can only wonder, though, how he expected to complete a project of such scope while occupying the highest appointive post in the land.

Bacon certainly had no lack of confidence. On the title page of his prospectus, he dramatized a purpose that would have been dramatic even in bare statement. Through the Pillars of Hercules (represented by Tuscan columns) and into the foreground, boldly plows a ship with bellying sails. The Strait of Gibraltar had had a special significance for medieval peoples as marking a limit of the known world. Old pictures actually showed the words "Ne plus ultra" (No farther beyond) inscribed on the imaginary pillars, and the warning was implicit even when not spelled out. But Bacon placed beneath and between the columns a contrary sentiment, "Multi pertransibunt & augebitur scientia" (Many will pass through and knowledge will be increased).[1]

The author spoke of himself in the third person: "Francis of Verulam reasoned thus with himself, and judged it to be for the interest of the present and future generations that they should be made acquainted with his thoughts." Complaining that "in what is now done in the matter of science there is only a whirling round about and perpetual agitation ending where it began," he asserts that "there was but one course left, . . . to try the whole thing anew upon a better plan, and to commence a total reconstruction of sciences, arts, and all human knowledge, raised upon the proper foundations."[2]

His sense of responsibility was monumental. Still writing of himself in the third person, he said that,

> because he knew not how long it might be before these things would occur to anyone else . . . , he resolved to publish at once so much as he had been able to complete . . . that in case of his death there might remain some outline and project of that which he had conceived. . . . All other ambition seemed poor in his eyes compared with the work which he had in hand.

Despite his concentration on universal natural laws, he had a true Renaissance faith in the ability of the individual to make a difference. Viscount Saint Alban's faith in this matter was particularly strong when the individual in question was Francis Bacon.

Since this work was an appeal to scholars and other educated persons of intellectual bent, it must be entirely in Latin. Therefore in expanding *The Advancement in Learning*, which classified and defined all studies, and hence was an integral part of the plan, he rewrote it in Latin and published it under the title *De augmentis scientiarum* as the first part of the *Great Instauration*.

The second part, his recently published *Novum organum*, was designed to facilitate a "more perfect use of human reason." It was no accident that the name *Organum* should suggest *Organon*, the title under which Aristotle's treatises on logic were published. Bacon intended to reveal the limitation of the Greek's reasoning methods, so long revered by the academic establishment, and to offer his own improved system.

Third was his natural history,which would summarize what man had learned about the universe from the physical sciences, especially astronomy, biology, and physics.

The *Scalus intellectus*, or *Ladder of the Intellect*, was to be the fourth part. Appropriately named, this portion would present the steps by which problems could be solved and would offer examples of the process.

Prodoni, or *Forerunners*, would be the next part. It would present some philosophical speculations of Bacon's own, arrived at by means other than his new method. These he viewed as forerunners of the comprehensive philosophy that he had dreamed of as the sixth and crowning part of his grand scheme. But he now confessed, "The completion, however, of this last part is . . . both above my strength and beyond my hope." He cherished the consoling idea that others, profiting from his discoveries and ruminations and using his methods, might finish the work that he had boldly advanced.

The method he so strenuously advocated was induction—the process of reasoning from particulars to attain a generalization. The particulars were to be noted by sensory perception, sometimes aided by such empirical processes as measurement. "Man . . . can do and understand so much, and so much only, as he has observed, in fact or in thought, of the course of Nature; beyond this he neither knows anything nor can do anything." This was the opposite of deduction, the method favored by Aristotle, a matter of beginning with a major premise, and then deducing from it subordinate truths. So long as the major premise was true, the subordinate findings would be valid.

Deduction had ruled the world of Western logic for more than twelve centuries. Its reign was about to end, and Bacon was the leader of the revolution. In succeeding decades, this revolution would enlist such giants as Thomas Hobbes, John Locke, John Stuart Mill, and Herbert Spencer. Along the way, David Hume would point out the limitations of induction as well as deduction, but most people would see these doubts as part of his philosophical skepticism, which if taken too seriously could paralyze all human endeavor.

Bacon did not invent induction. Even Aristotle had admitted that it had some uses. Indeed, the very word *induction* was derived from the Latin for what Aristotle called *epagoge*. But Bacon delineated the potential of induction more fully than anyone else ever had and promoted it more vigorously.

In leading a revolution that questioned untested evidence received on authority, Sir Francis was both a shaper and a product of his times. As Anthony Grafton has said, "By the early seventeenth century knowledge had burst the bounds of the library. It now seemed as large and varied as the world itself. It resided in astronomers' reports of telescopic observations, philosophers' reports on their cogitations, mariners' reports of voyages, and physicians' reports of anatomies."[3] Even artisans of experimental inclination contributed irrefutable information contradictory to the writings of Aristotle and other ancient classical scholars.

Even before Bacon's well-organized theorizing lent scholarly respectability to the empirical search for truth, classically trained Europeans were finding their personal experiences in collision with their education. This happened in London, Paris, Lisbon, and Copenhagen, but it was particularly prevalent among those whose adventures carried them to the New World, a hemisphere beyond the ken of the old Greek and Roman philosophers. One of the most dramatic experiences of this kind was reported by José de Acosta, the Spanish missionary who wrote several important books about the Americas. Well versed in the ancient texts, he feared that when he passed the equator he "would not be able to endure the violent heat." On the contrary, he said, "I felt so cold that I was forced to go into the sun to warm myself. What could I do then but laugh at Aristotle's *Meteorology* and his philosophy? For in that place and that season, where everything, by his rules, should have been scorched by the heat, I and my companion were cold."[4]

Throughout western Europe and its New World colonies, men were discovering that Aristotle and other ancient scholars were not infallible. But not all were moved, like Acosta, to laugh at the Greek and Roman pioneers of thought and consign them to the dust heap. As Bacon pointed out, they and their medieval successors had provided all on which his generation had to build. The new learning must connect with something from the past. Indeed, the new learning was a product of the union of tradition and experiment. Innovator though he was, Bacon described himself in *De interpretatione naturae* as "a man that neither affects what is new nor admires what is old."

In the *Novum organum* Bacon warned against certain "idols," or "false notions," that "so beset men's minds that truth can hardly find entrance."[5] He said that they would "in the very instauration of the sciences meet and trouble us, unless men, being forewarned of the danger, fortify themselves as far as may be against their assaults." In some of the most brilliant pages in modern philosophy, he described four principal categories of delusions: Idols of the Tribe, Idols of the Cave, Idols of the Marketplace, and Idols of the Theater.

The Idols of the Tribe

> have their foundation in human nature itself, and in the tribe or race of men. For it is a false assertion that the sense of man is the measure of things. On the contrary, all perceptions, as well of the sense as of the mind, are according to the measure of the individual and not according to the measure of the universe. And the human understanding is like a false mirror, which, receiving rays irregularly, distorts and discolors the nature of things by mingling its own nature with it.

Bacon defined the Idols of the Cave as

> the idols of the individual man. For everyone (besides the errors common to human nature in general) has a cave or den of his own, which refracts and discolors the light of nature; owing either to his own proper and peculiar nature; or to his education and conversation with others; or to the reading of books, and the authority of those whom he esteems and admires; or to the differences of impressions, accordingly as they take place in a mind preoccupied and predisposed or in a mind indifferent and settled.

In support of this argument, which he hoped would change attitudes, he enlisted tradition, citing the observations of the ancient Greek Heraclitus. This was doubly appropriate because Heraclitus had said, "Nothing endures but change," and "All is flux, nothing stays still," summarizing his views in the striking assertion "You cannot step twice into the same river." The river would not be precisely the same as a moment before and, as someone else pointed out, neither would the foot.

The Idols of the Marketplace are those "formed by the intercourse and association of men with each other . . . on account of the commerce and consort of men there. For it is by discourse that men associate; and words are imposed according to the apprehension of the vulgar. And therefore the ill and unfit choice of words wonderfully obstructs the understanding."

Though he blamed vulgar usage for much linguistic confusion, Bacon did not acquit some pedants of major responsibility. Weasel wording of opinions to provide escape from their possible consequences and the use of academic persiflage to protect a scholar from clear commitment on specific points all too often debased language to protect professional reputations. Leaves of the groves of academe were rustled more often by the rolling vibrations of delphic utterances than by fresh breezes of independent thought.

"Words," Bacon insisted, "plainly force and over-rule the understanding, and throw all into confusion and lead men away into numberless empty controversies and idle fancies." Thus, four centuries before G. E. Moore, Bertrand Russell, and Ludwig Wittgenstein discussed the distortions of even meticulously used language, Sir Francis anticipated the central concern of twentieth-century British philosophers.

He characterized as Idols of the Theater those "which have immigrated into men's minds from the various dogmas of philosophies, and also from wrong laws of demonstration." He chose the name "because in [his] judgement all the received systems [were] but so many stage-plays, representing worlds of their own creation after an unreal and scenic fashion." He continued:

Nor is it only of the systems now in vogue, or only of the ancient sects and philosophies, that I speak; for many more plays of the same kind may yet be composed and in like artificial manner set forth; seeing that errors the most widely different have nevertheless causes for the most part alike. Neither again do I mean this only of entire systems, but also of many principles and axioms in science, which by tradition, credulity, and negligence have come to be received.

It seems ironic that Bacon should warn about acceptance of systems of thought while he himself was engaged in setting forth his own system. There was some irony, to be sure, but Sir Francis also was setting forth rigorous methods and standards by which the efficacy of any teachings about the material world, including his own, should be judged. He also advocated, and exemplified in his own life, wide and diverse reading and the study of many systems. "The human understanding," he said, "supposes all other things to be somehow, though it cannot see how, similar to those things by which it is surrounded." Hence the necessity for mentally "going to and fro in remote and heterogeneous instances, by which axioms are tried as in the fire." For such enterprise, however, "the intellect is altogether slow and unfit, unless it be forced thereto by severe laws [of reason] and overruling authority."

Bacon was dedicated to the systematizing of knowledge, but called for a realistic awareness that perfect symmetry could not be achieved. "The human understanding," he wrote, "is of its own nature prone to suppose the existence of more order and regularity in the world than it finds. And though there be many things in nature which are singular and unmatched, yet it devises for them parallels and conjugates and relatives which do not exist. Hence the fiction that all celestial bodies move in perfect circles."

Returning to the Idols of the Cave, he cited those "which have most effect in disturbing the clearness of the understanding." With special emphasis, he wrote, "There are found some minds given to an extreme admiration of antiquity, others to an extreme love and appetite for novelty; but few so duly tempered that they can hold the mean, neither carping at what has been well laid down by the ancients, nor despising what is well introduced by moderns."

These faults he saw as injurious not only to individual understanding but also to the intellectual and practical progress of society. Such predilections, he argued, lead

> to the great injury of the sciences and philosophy, since these affectations of antiquity and novelty are the humors of partisans rather than judgements; and truth is to be sought for not in the felicity of any [one] age, which is an unstable thing, but in the light of nature and experience, which is eternal. These factions, therefore, must be abjured, and care must be taken that the intellect be not harried by them into assent.

He warned against "partiality for particular ages," whether they be our own or some imagined golden age of the past, or even, by implication, a discernible future.

And he admonished his readers not to be led astray through "the predominance [in their considerations] of a favorite subject." His prescription was to acquire an acquaintance with many eras and many disciplines. Do not abandon philosophizing, he urged, but be sure your philosophy is not "based on too narrow a foundation."

Only five years of life remained to Bacon when he was forced out of office in 1621 at the age of sixty, quite an advanced age for men of his generation. The half decade was filled with intellectual activity.

In 1622 he published his *History of Henry VII.* This life of one of England's most influential kings broke little new ground in research but marked a great advance in the art of biography. It changed for succeeding generations the expectations of readers of that genre. Hitherto they had been satisfied with little more than bare chronology decked out with a few encomiums; henceforth, they would look for what Bacon had given them, interpretation of character and the interaction of a personality with the times that gave it birth.

Henry VII was to be part of a vast history of Britain. Sir Francis never found time to write any other part of this projected work; but this volume, besides being important in itself, gives evidence of the great monument of historiography that he was capable of producing. *Monument* doesn't seem quite the right word. The work surely would have proved more energizing than commemorative. When Bacon pressed his feet most strongly on the foundation of the past, it was to thrust himself into the future.

In 1623 appeared his *Historia vitae et mortis* (History of Life and Death) and the Latin translation, with textual additions, of his *Advancement of Learning.* In 1625 Sir Francis published *Apophthegms* and *The Translation of Certain*

Psalms into English Verse. In the twenty-eight years since first publication of his *Essays,* he had kept that book near him, constantly amending the original articles and writing new ones. When he brought forth the final edition in this busy year of 1625, the slim volume of ten essays had grown to fifty-eight.

One of the essays on a topic about which the young Bacon had not written was "Of Atheism." In this valedictory edition, the aging Sir Francis wrote, "I had rather believe all the fables in the legends, and the Talmud, and the [Koran], than that this universal frame is without a mind." As to why the Deity did not respond to challenges to prove his existence, Bacon said, "God never wrought miracle to convince atheism, because his ordinary works convince it."

Though he rejected much of Aristotle and Plato, Sir Francis long had been attracted to theories of the earlier Greek naturalists that the material world consists of an immeasurable number of atoms. Some thought he had flirted with a materialism that did not require God. But in "Of Atheism" he wrote, "Even that school which is most accused of atheism doth most demonstrate religion: that is, the school of Leucippus, and Democritus, and Epicurus, for it is . . . [incredible] . . . that an army of infinite small portions . . . should have produced this order and beauty without a divine marshal."

On a raw March day in 1626, driving through fallen snow, he thought of an experiment in refrigeration to preserve food. He bought a fowl and stuffed it with snow, meanwhile becoming quite chilled. Increasingly ill, he sought help at the home of Lord Arundel, where he was offered the choice of a large and elaborately furnished but cold and drafty chamber or a smaller, simpler but snugger room. He chose the grander surroundings.[6] Before going to sleep he noted that his experiment had "succeeded excellently well." The medical treatment given him did not. Exhausted by fever and congestion, he died on April 9, 1626. It is often said that he died of his own insatiable intellectual curiosity. If so, his illness may have been complicated by his almost equally insatiable appetite for opulence.

The same predilections were responsible for a mixed legacy: for his immediate heirs, heavy debts resulting from a luxurious lifestyle beyond his means; for his fellow countrymen, and eventually for the whole civilized world, the priceless gifts of his fruitful intellect.

One product of his brain saw light only after he himself was entombed. This was *The New Atlantis,* not complete but published in truncated form in 1627. Reminiscent of More's *Utopia* in both purpose and design, it presents many elements of Bacon's political and social philosophy in the form of a fable. The old Atlantis was a legendary Atlantic island, whose earliest known reference in writing was by Plato in his *Timaeus.* Later, in *Critias,* the Greek philosopher pictured the island as the home of an ideal commonwealth. It was appropriate that Bacon, who sought to replace so much of Plato's philosophy, should call his mythical country the *New* Atlantis and place it in the Pacific. Through nomenclature the new location had added significance. The Pacific was by name the peaceful ocean. Bacon's imaginary island was called "Bensalem" (Hebrew for "son of peace"), and it was the home of a peaceful society owing much of its inspiration and useful knowledge to a college "dedicated to the study of the works and creatures of God." Important discoveries and inventions were promoted by government-subsidized foundations and an honorary society of scientists.

In creating a myth, Bacon was turning once again to a field that long had interested him. In *De sapientia veterum* (Wisdom of the Ancients), he had analyzed classical myths and found in them symbolism of a sophistication previously unsuspected. There is still argument over whether Bacon was at least as inventive as he was perceptive in discovering such subtle symbolism. Be that as it may, he set a fashion that has ranged from Freudian and Jungian interpretations of literature and legend to the anthropological analyses of Claude Lévi-Strauss and the skillful popularizations by Joseph Campbell that captured the American public's imagination late in the twentieth century.

Bacon saw a lesson in the story of a voyeuristic Prometheus spying on the secret rites of Bacchus and being condemned as a result to ceaseless and fruitless wandering.[7] He interpreted the tale as a warning to those who sought "by the heights of nature and philosophy" to penetrate the mind of God rather than to study God's works. The devices of science should be devoted to measurement of the substances and forces of the physical world. He admonished, "Men must soberly and modestly distinguish between things divine and human, between the oracles of sense and of faith: unless they mean to have at once a heretical religion and a fabulous society."

Sir Francis detected in the story of Pan a lesson in accord with his own plans for revolutionizing science. Pan's success in finding Ceres when the great gods couldn't was symbolic of the idea that abstract philosophers, dwelling aloft on their lonely pinnacles, were not so adept at acquiring useful knowledge as less pretentious observers of nature. And Bacon used science in interpreting legends. Even the little naked Cupid, armed with a quiver of arrows, became a complex symbol of atomic motion.

Bacon left incomplete not only *The New Atlantis* but also the massive project of *The Great Instauration*. The surprising thing, though, is that, despite his busy public career, he completed so much. Indeed, his public career furnished some grist for his literary mill. His professional knowledge as a lawyer supplied material for his *Maxims of the Law*, republished in 1630 as the first part of Elements of the Common Laws of England, and *The Learned Reading of Sir Francis Bacon upon the Statute of Uses*, published sixteen years after his death. Sir Francis was not as learned in English law as his rival Coke, or so thoroughly versed in the subject as the earlier authority Sir Thomas Littleton or the later Sir William Blackstone. But he was a leading expert on the subject.

Bacon's professional career in the law and as a politician also furnished many psychological insights that enriched the *Essays*, which he revised and edited through many years, frequently after a day of public business. From their brief form in 1597 to the second edition of 1612 on to their final appearance in 1625, they are a fascinating record of the growth of his mind as well as the increasing sophistication of his style. To begin with, the essays were disjointed collections of memorable aphorisms. The author's indebtedness to Machiavelli and others was obvious. In the end the alembic of a brilliant mind enriched by practical experience had transformed his borrowed nuggets into something glowing with the freshness of newly minted gold. In writing the *Essays*, Bacon not only introduced the genre to English literature but produced an enduring literary masterpiece.

As an essayist, he was the forerunner of Blaise Pascal, John Locke, David Hume, George Berkeley, William Hazlitt, Charles Lamb, Thomas Henry Huxley, Loren Eiseley, and Lewis Thomas; he was also the father of a numerous progeny of self-help books ranging from Lord Chesterfield's *Letters to His Son* and Dale Carnegie's *How to Win Friends and Influence People* to the how-to books crowding this week's bestseller list. Of course, Bacon did not invent the genre. The Italian Renaissance humanist Castiglione had produced *The Courtier*, which influenced the conduct of many Elizabethans and the writings of Wyatt, Surrey, Sidney, Spenser, and Shakespeare. But Bacon did give the genre a nobler heritage than it has sometimes manifested.

Bacon's legal scholarship; his interpretation and creation of fables; his production of the first noteworthy English essays; his writing of *Henry VII*, which transformed the art of biography—these things alone would entitle him to a high place on any roster of creative intellects. But all these accomplishments are dwarfed by his contributions to science and philosophy.

Yet superficial consideration might suggest that his influence as both scientist and philosopher was negligible. He was not the father of a complete system of philosophy in the conventional sense, although he philosophized, often in depth, on a wide variety of topics. As a scientist, he is not the author of any law, nor is his name attached to any theory. He never had occasion to leap naked from his bath and run through the streets of his hometown shouting, "Eureka!"

How then can Bacon be ranked among the world's great philosophers and scientists? The most frequent answer is that he is great not for any specific addition to human knowledge but because he devised and disseminated a greatly improved method for the acquisition of knowledge. His leadership in revolutionizing the practice of science has been acknowledged by successive generations. He was hailed as the greatest "wit" in Europe in his time, a time when the term was more synonymous with intellect than with mere cleverness. Later in the seventeenth century John Dryden declared, "The world to Bacon does not only owe its present knowledge, but its future too."[8] Scientists in each generation since have expressed indebtedness to him. They have testified that, even more than the justly exalted Bruno, Galileo, and Copernicus, he was the father of modern science.

Nevertheless, strange to say, no scientist anywhere in the world has used what has come to be known as the Baconian method in making notable discoveries. The precise process of induction he recommended has proved inadequate. He had such faith in it that he believed even mediocre persons using it could produce great results. Ironically, for he was remarkably intuitive, he failed to perceive the importance of intuition in scientific discovery. Without it, the patient accumulation of sensory data would lead nowhere. Only intuition and abstract reasoning could make sense of the bewildering number of discrete facts collected by empirical means in any large-scale research.

There is considerable significance in the paradox that many of the scientists famous for achievements that made no use of the Baconian method have been among the most enthusiastic in his praise. Gottfried Leibniz, the great German philosopher, mathematician, and polymath, acknowledged indebtedness to the "incomparable Verulam," who had led philosophy "to serve mankind on earth."[9] Descartes and Robert Boyle are in the chorus of admirers. Jean Le Rond d'Alembert, Voltaire, and other compilers of a great monument of the Enlightenment, the *Encyclopédie*, saluted Sir Francis as "the greatest, the most universal, and the most eloquent of philosophers." America's most celebrated polymath, Thomas Jefferson, said Bacon was one of the three greatest men in modern history, and he kept his portrait as an inspiration. Darwin saw himself as a legatee of Baconian science.

Why such allegiance from those who did not follow his method? They did not pursue his *exact* method, but they practiced a science that he liberated from medieval Scholasticism and redirected to empiricism. All subscribed to the essential doctrine of his *Novum organum*: "Man, who is the servant and interpreter of nature, can act and understand no farther than he has observed, either in operation or in contemplation, of the method and order of nature." They were the beneficiaries of his warnings to be wary of the idols that distracted or obstructed searchers for truth. It is not surprising that the founders of Britain's Royal Society acknowledged Bacon as their chief inspiration. His view of science as a cooperative venture (despite sometimes bitter competition) has prevailed as the ideal, and his dream of research funded by governments and foundations has been realized.[10]

For a man who early in life took all knowledge for his province, Sir Francis was later reasonably modest in stating his claim to fame. He spoke with satisfaction of the books he had written, saying that they could not be taken from him. He did not claim to be the greatest "wit" (intellect) of his time. He said that he merely "rang the bell that called the wits together." Reverberations of that ringing are heard in our own time. He claimed no particular scientific discovery. He fathered no invention. But, more than anyone else, he did usher in the modern age.

16

THE GREAT MAGICIAN

ALTHOUGH ELIZABETH lent her name to one of the most vigorous and creative eras in the history of any nation and Bacon made that age a vestibule to future centuries, they had a contemporary fellow countryman whose words and thoughts are even better known than theirs throughout the civilized world. Yet strangely enough, though this compatriot produced a body of work astonishing for its variety and transcendent genius, some scholars have persisted in crediting either the Virgin Queen or the philosophizing peer with his entire oeuvre.

These scholars are distinctly in the minority, but even so it is amazing that they should think that either one of the busiest rulers in Christendom or a genius pursuing simultaneously several demanding public and private careers should have found the spare time to produce under a pseudonym the writings of William Shakespeare.[1] Nor are these two luminaries the only ones that some people are eager to credit with writing the plays and sonnets generally attributed to the Stratford writer. In 1920 T. J. Looney put forward the name of Edward De Vere, seventeenth earl of Oxford, and since then the Oxonians (or Looneyites) have been active in behalf of their champion. Some people have even suggested that Christopher Marlowe, who was born in the same year as Shakespeare and became famous earlier than his contemporary, was not killed in a tavern brawl, as was officially reported. Instead, they insist, he was spirited away by friends rescuing him from various entanglements, and from seclusion continued to write, signing his works with Shakespeare's name.

Why are some people so determined to deny Shakespeare the honor of authorship? The reasons are usually cultural naïveté, academic snobbery, or a combination of the two. There is unwillingness to concede that anyone without a university education could have produced works so deep, so noble in diction, so rich in classical allusion as *Hamlet* or *King Lear*, so sophisticatedly polished as *Much Ado about Nothing* or *As You Like It*. And Shakespeare, it must be admitted, had only a grammar school education.

The adherents of rival candidates forget that a genius capable of writing such great plays could not have been kept ignorant once he had learned to read. But even if one counts only formal education, it must be remembered that the graduate of a good grammar school in Elizabethan England had a better grounding in philosophy, and a far better background in classical literature, than the great majority of honor graduates of respected universities today. And the school at Stratford, which Shakespeare almost certainly attended, is believed to have been one of the best in England. It paid its headmaster more than exclusive Eton did, because some educators would accept lower salaries for the privilege of association with future nobles of the realm.

This is no place to rehash the tired arguments put forth in behalf of nominees for "the real Shakespeare." The reader who wishes to pursue these controversies can find abundant literature on the subject.

Of the claims made for Bacon, suffice it to say that they were not advanced until about 170 years after the playwright's death and still seem incredible to most scholars familiar with the works of both men and sensitive to nuances of style. John Dryden said of Shakespeare, "He was the man who of all modern, and perhaps ancient poets, had the largest and most comprehensive soul." Bacon had brilliant insights, but he lacked Shakespeare's astonishing empathy. Furthermore, experts on Elizabethan law say that some legal references in the plays contain small errors readily excusable in a layman but anathema to a lord chancellor. Some have professed to find anagrams for *Bacon* scattered throughout the dramas, but professional cryptologists have pronounced the evidence strained or twisted and have pointed out that the same method can be used to make Shakespeare's pages yield the name *Hemingway*. Undoubtedly Bacon was as incapable of creating a Falstaff or a Beatrice as Shakespeare was of conceiving *The Great Instauration*.

The chief argument advanced for the earl of Oxford's authorship is that he wrote some poems up to the time of Shakespeare's first publication and then ceased. He was not the first or the last young nobleman to write acceptable verses for a decade or so and then abandon the practice, and there is nothing in his known poems to foretell the flowering of genius.

Another earl, William Stanley, sixth earl of Derby, has been suggested as the creator of the Shakespeare oeuvre. He, too, dabbled in verse but produced in his own name nothing nearer to the quality of Shakespeare's lines than many another clever and cultivated man.

I have a special interest in the claim that Queen Elizabeth was the author of the works commonly credited to Shakespeare. In the course of a literary lecture when I was in my early twenties, I dismissed theories of Baconian and Oxfordian authorship, saying, "Next we'll hear that the plays were really written by the queen. It will probably be argued that the queen had written both passable verse and eloquent prose, and that her authorship would explain the playwright's apparent familiarity with courts." That was on a Friday. Sunday's newspapers brought the story of a professor's argument that Her Majesty was indeed the creator of the greatest dramas in the English language. The reasons given were precisely the ones I had assigned to an imaginary scholar. Since then I have learned that creative absurdity cannot exceed the heights, or depths, of earnest speculation.

The claims for Bacon, Oxford, Marlowe, Derby, and Queen Elizabeth all ignore the fact that there is abundant evidence of Shakespeare's being assigned the credit in his lifetime and shortly thereafter by many who knew him well, including those who worked with him in the theater. There is a popular idea that little or nothing is known of Shakespeare's life. The fact is that his life is better known than that of any other Elizabethan dramatist except Ben Jonson.

Shakespeare was born in 1564 in Stratford-upon-Avon, a small country town of which his father became bailiff, roughly the equivalent of a mayor, four years later. The father made his living as a tanner and glover. The mother, Mary Arden, was the daughter of landed gentry, distant relatives of the earl of Warwick and direct descendants of Alfred the Great. Though Ben Jonson once said that Shakespeare had "small Latin and less Greek," Jonson was hypercritical in matters of scholarship and, as we know, the standards were high in good schools. The future dramatist evidently obtained enough classical background for his creative purpose. He also had a keen ear for the speech of his own time, including that of simple workmen and Dogberrys "dressed in a little brief authority" and armed with malapropisms before the term had been invented.

At the age of eighteen, he married twenty-six-year-old Ann Hathaway, only a short while after applying for a marriage bond to wed someone else. A daughter was born less than five months later, followed within two years by twins.

Before long he was on the London stage. Some speculate that he made his acting debut in 1587 in his hometown. In that year the Queen's Men lost a member to death just before the repertory company played in Stratford. The earliest surviving notice of Shakespeare's theatrical career emphasizes his writing more than his acting. In 1592 a rival playwright, probably Robert Greene but possibly Henry Chettle, wrote of "an upstart crow, beautified with our feathers," who "supposes he is as well able to bombast out a blank verse as the best of you" and "is in his own conceit the only Shakescene in a country." The pun on the name *Shakespeare* is obvious. Today Greene is remembered chiefly as the probable author of this attack, and Chettle is recollected largely by the very few who know that the words might be his. In any event, Shakespeare's attacker is known today almost entirely because of his adversarial relationship with England's greatest author.

Shakespeare became a principal member of the Lord Chamberlain's Men, London's leading repertory troupe, which with the accession of James I in 1603 became the King's Men. At the height of his career, Shakespeare drew pay as an actor and profited from his partnership in the company and in ownership of the Globe, London's premier theater. It was there that most of his own plays were produced, and of course he was paid as playwright. He invested much of his earnings in Stratford and its environs, becoming one of the largest property holders in the community. When he had left it for London, the fortunes of the Shakespeare family had been at a notable low. His once moderately prosperous father was believed to have lost most of his savings.

John Shakespeare lost out politically at the same time. Simultaneously there was a rise in the political and financial prosperity of his chief rival in the town government. Many residents of Stratford must have thought the contrast in fortunes was complete when the rival's son went to work in the family business while Mr. Shakespeare's boy Will abandoned his father's trade to pursue a risky career in poetry and an equally uncertain and not quite respectable one in the theater.

William Shakespeare had written several plays, delightful both to the groundlings and to the university wits, before he gained literary respect by publication of the narrative poems *Venus and Adonis* and *The Rape of Lucrece*. The first of these was to run through seven editions in his lifetime, the second through five.

Shakespeare's earliest plays were mostly comedies or histories. The history plays were representative of an extremely popular Elizabethan genre that presented highlights from the reigns of English kings. They were an appropriate expression of the patriotism that was partly the cause and partly the result of venturesome English deeds on land and sea. At first Shakespeare wrote brilliant dramatizations of events recorded in *Holinshed's Chronicles*, also a principal source for many of his rivals. Later he continued to draw from the *Chronicles* but, in addition to narration of the feats of history's greats, he interwove the actions and concerns of far humbler folk, ranging from comic blunderers in *Henry IV* to simple soldiers in *Henry V* pondering their fates on the eve of battle. Shakespeare brought the complexity of real life to his characterizations so that his audiences could simultaneously salute Prince Hal for repudiating the influence of Falstaff, his mentor in dissipation, and feel a pang of sympathy for the rejected old friend.

Through his magnificent history plays, Shakespeare was a conduit for the transmission of nourishing traditions to the English people. These dramas fed pride in "this earth, this realm, this England," and confidence that English soldiers could be depended upon to "show the mettle of [their] pasture"; but they also spoke humbler words about majesty, often effectively (and tactfully) put into the mouth of the sovereign, as in *Henry V*:

> not the balm, the scepter and the ball,
> The sword, the mace, the crown imperial,
> The intertissued robe of gold and pearl,
> The farced title running 'fore the King,
> The throne he sits on, nor the tide of pomp
> That beats upon the high shore of this world,
> No, not all these, thrice-gorgeous ceremony,
> Not all these, laid in bed majestical,
> Can sleep so soundly as the wretched slave,
> Who with a body fill'd and vacant mind
> Gets him to rest, cramm'd with distressful bread.

All comes to a point and poignancy when Henry asks, "Canst thou, when thou command'st the beggar's knee, command the health of it?"[2]

Shakespeare turned for inspiration not only to English history but also to the annals of ancient Greece and Rome. For him, as for many other Englishmen far more at home in their native tongue than any other, Sir Thomas North's vivid translation from Jacques Amyot's French version of Plutarch's *Lives* was the chief window on the world of Pericles, Julius Caesar and Brutus, and Antony and Cleopatra.

Other ancient influences helped to mold Shakespeare's developing art. Seneca's ghosts and magic and bloody action, together with his exalted stoicism contrasted with rhetorical luxuriance, were available to Shakespeare in translation. And the influence of Plautus is almost everywhere in the English playwright's comic scenes. The Roman's Miles Gloriosus breathes again through the bombast of Parolles, Pistol, and one old fellow who exceeds the original in roguish stature as much as in physical girth—Sir John Falstaff.

Shakespeare was the most popular playwright in England when he came to the last decade of his career as a dramatist—popular with the illiterate townsmen in the pit, the solid burghers and their wives, the clever lawyers and university wits, and the sophisticated denizens of the royal court. The popularity was deserved; he had proved himself the most gifted of his country's writers for the stage. Not only would the tragic moments be felt by all elements of his audience, but he had perfected the art of making virtually everyone laugh at the same time. There would be a bit of slapstick or other broad comedy to bring guffaws from the groundlings at the same moment that better educated auditors were chuckling at the subtlety of barbed rejoinders.

Despite these accomplishments, Shakespeare had not yet revealed the true originality of his genius. Of course, he had demonstrated his ability to transform a tired old plot into a compelling narrative, principally through giving the characters a palpable humanity that made the audience care. And in language he never seemed more original than when he was paraphrasing another writer, by a bit of imagery here and there transforming the serviceable prose or competent verse of the original into something sinuous and scintillating. But Shakespeare displayed the full sweep of his creative independence when he overturned received Aristotelian precepts in drama as boldly as Bacon had in science.

The word *received* is important here. Aristotle had not been nearly so rigid in promulgating the unities of action, time, and space as were some self-appointed keepers of the Stagirite flame. Aristotle said in *Poetics* that a play should have organic unity, and observed that the action of most successful tragedies was compressed within a single day. The sixteenth-century Italian critic Ludovico Castelvetro deduced from these observations an "Aristotelian" prescription that the action dramatized should not in real life exceed the time of the on-stage production. A three-hour play should show only events unfolding within three consecutive hours in the world outside the theater. There should be only one setting for all the action. And all events and speech in a tragedy should move toward a tragic end; those in a comedy, to a happy conclusion. Tragedy and comedy could be mixed no more than oil and water, and all playwrights should recognize that fact.

But Shakespeare mixed them to brilliant effect. In *King Lear*, for instance, the Fool's raillery on the heath not only punctuates the long-sustained melancholy before the audience can become inured to its power, but the laughter is all the heartier because of the relief it provides from pent-up emotion. Unity of time is ignored, as in *The Winter's Tale,* when Hermione reappears in the end, supposedly sixteen years after the audience's last glimpse of her. The dramatist is equally free with space. The action in *Antony and Cleopatra* leaps from Alexandria to Rome to Messina, to Rome again and back to Alexandria and, among a mélange of other places, even Syria.

Shakespeare departed from other rules also. In *King Lear* and *Macbeth* he sometimes sacrificed metrical regularity, including the customary five stresses to the line, in favor of the unimpeded flow of emotion-charged language. The results include some of the most memorable passages in both plays, as in Cordelia's words over her sleeping father ("Mine enemy's dog, though he had bit me, should have stood that night against my fire")[3] and Lady Macbeth's invocation ("Come, you spirits that tend on mortal thoughts, unsex me here . . .").[4]

Shakespeare's last great play, *The Tempest,* was produced about 1611. At a later date he either wrote or cowrote *Henry VIII* and apparently collaborated with John Fletcher on *Two Noble Kinsmen* but, although there are noble lines in each of these, particularly the first, *The Tempest* was his last major dramatic effort. In it, as has often been pointed out, the magician Prospero speaks words that might well be the valedictory of his creator:

> Our revels now are ended. These our actors,
> As I foretold you, were all spirits and
> Are melted into air, into thin air:
> And like the baseless fabric of this vision,
> The cloud-capp'd towers, the gorgeous palaces,
> The solemn temples, the great globe itself—
> Yes, all which it inherit—shall dissolve
> And, like this insubstantial pageant faded,
> Leave not a rack behind. We are such stuff
> As dreams are made on, and our little life
> Is rounded with a sleep.

A few lines later, the old magician says, "I'll break my staff, bury it certain fathoms in the earth, and deeper than did ever plummet sound I'll drown my book."

The wizard of language retired to his native Stratford. John Shakespeare's reverses in fortune following his achievements as a business and political leader in the little town had been more than erased by the success of his son. To be an actor in Elizabethan or Jacobean England was to pursue an occupation far less respectable than the elder Shakespeare's trade of glover, but the playwright son was now honored as a man of literature; he had friends among the nobility and was no stranger at court. Like his mother's ancestors, he had acquired property, and he lived in one of Stratford's two largest houses. More important still in that armigerous society, he had a coat of arms in his own surname. It had been granted to John Shakespeare in recognition of offices he had filled, of his family's services to King Henry VII, and of his marriage to one of the genteel Ardens, but it is believed that the son was chiefly instrumental in obtaining it. To William it must have seemed a restitution to the father who had suffered some loss of status, but part of William's satisfaction must have derived from recognition that it was better to be the son of a gentleman than to be the first generation permitted to append that title. Thus, when he returned to a hearth in his native village, the genius who saw all life as an "insubstantial pageant" and envisioned the dissolution of "the great globe itself" drew about him the wrappings of traditional gentility.

He died on April 23, 1616, believed to be the exact anniversary of his birth, thus rounding out his life with a classical unity not always found in his plays. His will provided further inspiration for those who see mystery in everything connected with Shakespeare. Though the quality of the handwriting makes it impossible to speak with assurance, his name appears to be spelled at least two, and possibly three, different ways in that document. My personal theory is that Shakespeare, having spelled his name differently in various transactions over a lifetime, sought to prevent all quibbling over the identity of the maker of his will. Such variations in the spelling of the names of quite literate persons were common in an age that valued phonetic, but not orthographic, consistency.

In any event, the name would be written large for future generations. It is ironic that, before William Shakespeare's birth, a university student named Shakespeare petitioned for a change of patronym on the grounds that a less obscure name would be more appropriate for one of his anticipated status. Long before his death, the playwright's name was one of the best known in England. Though only eighteen or nineteen of his plays were in print at the time of his death, John Heminges and Henry Condell, survivors of his old company, seven years later published thirty-six of them in the *First Folio*. In it Ben Jonson, who had been critical of Shakespeare's "small Latin and less Greek" and of his disregard for the three unities, declared of his old rival, "He was not of an age, but for all time!" Jonson even went so far as to say that his fellow Elizabethan had supplanted such classical giants as Aristophanes, Terence, and Plautus.

Even in the 1660's, when the tension between tradition and experiment that produced the greatest Elizabethan literature had been succeeded by the prosaic and almost unchallenged reign of neoclassical rigidity, many people still loved the plays of Shakespeare. John Dryden, the literary dictator of that age, said in his *Essay of Dramatic Poesy* that Shakespeare, though not always at his best, "is always great when some great subject is presented to him; no man can say he ever had a fit subject for his wit and did not then raise himself as high above the rest of poets quantum lenta solent inter viburna cupressi [as cypresses among lowly shrubs]." Dryden also called him "the Homer, or father, of our dramatic poets."

In the eighteenth century some pedants, caught up in a fashion as restrictive in literature as in landscape gardening, where it imposed geometrical topiary and symmetrical mazes on the free luxuriance of nature, spoke condescendingly of Shakespeare's supposedly primitive art. But the most distinguished

English critics celebrated his virtues. Joseph Addison, most influential of all, asked, "Who would not rather read one of his plays, where there is not a single rule of the stage observed, than any production of a modern critic, where there is not one of them violated?" Playgoers and readers gave an overwhelming answer. They roared their enthusiasm in the theater and gobbled up the sixty editions of Shakespeare's plays published between 1709 and 1799.

Dr. Samuel Johnson, the most celebrated of England's literary dictators, produced his own edition of the master's plays in 1765. Johnson was an ardent classicist, but he was also a man of common sense, and he did not chastise Shakespeare for his departure from ancient models. He said that the Stratford genius,

> above all writers, at least above all modern writers, is the poet of nature, the poet that holds up to his readers a faithful mirror of manners and life. His characters are not modified by the customs of particular places, unpracticed by the rest of the world; by the peculiarities of studies and professions, which can operate but upon small numbers or by the accidents of transient fashions or temporary opinions: they are the genuine progeny of common humanity, such as the world will always supply and observation will always find.

Nineteenth-century Romantics eagerly embraced the "irregularities" and "excesses" in Shakespeare that neoclassicists had been wont to criticize or reluctantly excuse. Samuel Taylor Coleridge, the great English literary critic of his generation, in 1818 said that "the supposed irregularity and extravagances of Shakespeare were the mere dreams of a pedantry that arraigned the eagle because it had not the dimensions of the swan." Forsaking all appearance of impartiality, he added, "The Englishman, who without reverence, can utter the name of William Shakespeare, stands disqualified for the office of critic."

In the same period, Thomas De Quincey insisted that Shakespeare's

> works are not as those of other men, simply and merely great works of art; but are also like the phenomena of nature, like the sun and the sea, the stars and the flowers; like frost and snow, rain and dew, hailstorm and thunder, which are to be studied with entire submission of our own faculties, and in the perfect faith that in them there can be no too much or too little, nothing useless or inert—but that, the farther we press in our discoveries, the more we shall see proofs of design and self-supporting arrangement where the careless eye had seen nothing but accident![5]

With the twentieth century came a tremendous proliferation of Shakespearean scholarship and criticism, with Americans challenging the supremacy of Englishmen and Germans. Shakespeare's plays have been presented on stages around the world, in great metropolises and in jungle clearings. Amid the thousands of productions of certain favorites, some directors have striven for originality by the desperate expedient of costuming the players in every imaginable garb of every known society with the possible exception of Eskimo, the furs being discouragingly hot for the stage of any auditorium comfortably heated for an audience.

Today Shakespeare is honored throughout the English-speaking world as the greatest writer in the language. The critical consensus and popular perception agree. The most commonly reproduced bust of the playwright is instantly recognizable to many people who have never voluntarily read a literary work, and in both advertising and the comic strips is the most widely used symbol of literary excellence.[6]

Many German critics yield him primacy among all the world's authors, ancient, medieval, and modern, and those who do not, usually say that he is second only to their own Goethe. Italians put only Dante and Virgil ahead of him. Many French critics consider him the foremost foreign writer, only a little behind Racine and Corneille in tragedy and Molière in comedy. Though Tolstoy, the man often called the greatest Russian writer, spoke slightingly of Shakespeare, other Russian writers have praised the Englishman as one of a tiny handful of supremely great writers of all time. Greeks have honored him as the foremost dramatist since the time of Aeschylus, Sophocles, Euripides, and Aristophanes. Spain, Portugal, and Latin America have generously accorded him primacy over any dramatist in their own Iberian tradition. Scandinavian playwrights grant him the palm and embrace him as a kindred spirit. Chinese, Japanese, Vietnamese, and Korean intellectuals regard him as the foremost literary figure of the Occident. In most countries where English is not the primary language, Shakespeare is the most admired foreign writer.

Nor is he internationally esteemed for his plays alone. His sonnets are among the world's greatest literary treasures. He did not invent the principal English form of the sonnet, but it bears his name because, more than anyone else, he realized its rich possibilities. Sir Thomas Wyatt apparently is the first English author of a published sonnet. Quite taken with the Italian sonnet, especially as exemplified by Petrarch, he translated some into English and then produced some of his own in his native tongue. Wyatt was then about twenty-four years old and a prominent diplomat. He was precocious: at seventeen he was both a Cambridge master of arts and a husband, and within a year a father besides. Another precocious young Englishman, Henry Howard, earl of Surrey, heir to the duke of Norfolk, was married at fifteen and was as well known for high temper as for high talents. He took the Italian sonnet form and, retaining its fourteen lines, changed the rhyme scheme and transformed the Italian model of octave and sestet into three quatrains and a concluding rhymed couplet. It was this form of the sonnet that came to bear Shakespeare's name.

W. H. Auden said, "Probably, more nonsense has been talked and written, more intellectual and emotional energy expended in vain, on the sonnets of Shakespeare than on any other literary work in the world."[7] People unaware of the extravagant conventions of Elizabethan tributary verse addressed to noble patrons have made unwarranted assumptions about Shakespeare's relationship to the male friend addressed in some of the sonnets. Speculation has been rife about "the dark lady" for whom the poet's passion burns, and A. L. Rowse has made the intriguing suggestion that she was Emilia Bassano Lanier, an Italian musician married to a master of revels at the English court. Even the fractured syntax of the printer's dedication of the 154 sonnets has fostered infinite speculation, much of it more notable for ingenuity than for sober appraisal.[8]

Articles over the past decade in the respected *Shakespeare Quarterly* suggest that, after playing down earlier discussions of Shakespeare's possible homosexuality, many scholars are again professing to find homoerotic elements not only in the first 126 sonnets but also in the plays, citing among other characters the Antonios of *Merchant of Venice* and *Twelfth Night*. This may reflect the growing emphasis among scholars and critics on a search for such elements in all literature. While many respected interpreters of Shakespeare continue to regard as unproved the case for a homosexual bard, the number of those who support such an interpretation is perhaps increasing. At least, that seems to be the current fashion as this book goes to press. Fortunately, an intimate knowledge of Shakespeare's sex life is not essential to an appreciation of his art.

Sir Philip Sidney, with his *Astrophel and Stella*, first made the sonnet truly popular in England. Other sonnet collections—Edmund Spenser's *Amoretti*, Drayton's *Idea*, Daniel's *Delia* among them—gained favor. Subsequently, Milton and Wordsworth produced a few great examples of the genre, and Elizabeth Barrett Browning's *Sonnets from the Portuguese* won great popularity. But to this day Shakespeare towers above all other sonneteers in the English language; some critics would say in any language.

All readers but those hopelessly far gone in bardolatry would admit that not all of Shakespeare's sonnets are great, that indeed some, whether because of hasty writing or inaccurate reproduction, contain awkward and confusing passages. But about a third of the lot are almost indisputably great. No other master or mistress of the form has approached this record.

Shakespeare's elevation among the world's sonnet writers is especially remarkable in view of the fact that the particular model he adopted is the most demanding form of one of literature's most demanding genres. The rigid rhyme scheme and the precisely fourteen lines of any established pattern of the sonnet make it extremely difficult for the writer to avoid artificiality and stilted language. The Shakespearean sonnet's three quatrains and couplet magnify the difficulty. Even in the hands of very skillful poets, the couplet is all too likely to seem a useless appendage grafted onto the body of the poem but receiving no nourishing blood from it. Sometimes this happens even with the man from Stratford. But in his happiest efforts, the concluding couplet is integral to the success of the whole. Sometimes it provides a succinct summary of the preceding verses, at other times a wry comment on them. And sometimes it seems to be addressed to the reader more warmly, or at least more personally, than what has preceded it, as though the author had put aside his manuscript and leaned forward to speak face to face with quiet earnestness.

Well before the end of the twentieth century, Shakespeare had attracted a far larger audience than in any previous era. Of course, the rapidly expanding population of the world and the growth of media have played a primary part, but none of his contemporaries anywhere in the world has experienced a comparable magnification of audience. Every day, whether in an academic setting or a commercial one, Shakespearean dramas are playing in various countries. In his own day, his plays customarily premiered at London's Globe Theater. Today his theater is indeed "the great globe itself."

Would Shakespeare be surprised at the extent of his success? Perhaps not, except for the development of media that he could not have foreseen. In Sonnet 81 he told his love:

> When you entombèd in men's eyes shall lie,
> Your monument shall be my gentle verse,
> Which eyes not yet created shall o'erread,
> And tongues to be your being shall rehearse
> When all the breathers of this world are dead.
> You still shall live—such virtue hath my pen—
> Whose breath most breathes, even in the mouths of men.

The Age of Elizabeth was also the age of Shakespeare. Indeed, as he survived her by thirteen years, it was in part through him that the Elizabethan era was extended into the reign of her successor, making the Jacobean Age part of his temporal empire. In his venturesome exploration of the possibilities of the sonnet, a form still new to his England, Shakespeare was representative of his contemporary culture. In his bold bending of the classical traditions of drama to satisfy the demands of his muse, he was as imaginative as his country's shipbuilders, who devised new and fleeter craft to fight the old galleons, and as Drake, who used the new possibilities with daring flexibility. Yet he was never more Elizabethan than in eschewing change merely for change's sake and instead seeking a happy amalgam of tradition and innovation. Because he was so representative of an age extraordinarily rich in creative energy, he was ironically, as Ben Jonson perceived, truly "not of an age but for all time."[9]

17

BENIGN CONTAGION

I F ELIZABETHAN ENGLAND had produced Shakespeare and Bacon as lone geniuses among a congregation of thinkers and writers of solid but much less impressive gifts, the age would still have stood out for creativity. The simultaneous presence of two such minds in one small country would have been a matter of note. But Shakespeare and Bacon, while too gifted to be typical of their time, or of any other for that matter, were nevertheless representative. They did not work and ponder in splendid isolation above their countrymen. Brilliant minds, in and out of the chosen professions of these two, provided audiences, instructors, and competitors. A benign contagion of creativity was at work in their England.

Even if Shakespeare had never lived, the Elizabethan Age would have to be adjudged one of considerable literary distinction with a rich vein of invention. The contributions of Edmund Spenser, Sir Philip Sidney, Christopher Marlowe, and Ben Jonson would have lent luster to any era in English literature, or any other literature, ancient or modern. Though some of us would pull up short of T. S. Eliot's assertion that George Chapman was "potentially the greatest artist" among Elizabethan playwrights, it must be conceded that a modicum of discipline might have made him one of the greatest writers of all time. As it is, he has memorable lines to his credit and a translation of Homer that excited John Keats' poetic imagination.

Spenser published in 1579 *The Shepheardes Calender*, a collection of twelve eclogues sometimes called the first important work of Elizabethan literature.[1] Very much in the classical tradition, they mark the circuit of the twelve months mostly in dialogues between shepherds. Like their pastoral predecessors in the verses of Theocritus and Virgil, they are an uncommonly eloquent crew. But Spenser makes ancient forms serve contemporary purposes. In two of the eclogues he speaks for himself, once under the assumed name of Colin Clout and another time when he addresses "Elisa," a thinly disguised evocation of Queen Elizabeth. A surprising thing about the *Calender* is its wide range of styles. Sometimes the form is strongly influenced by such continental Renaissance poets as Clément Marot. At least once he writes in Chaucerian vein and declares his intention to abandon linguistic borrowings in favor of fresh draughts of what he was later to call the "well of English undefiled." Tucker Brooke cites the appearance of this book by Spenser as an event comparable to that of Wordsworth and Coleridge's *Lyrical Ballads* in 1798, one of those occasions when, after "the sap seems to have gone out of poetry and the patterns of life have grown too stereotyped, a new writer will sometimes appear like heaven's benediction with the demand for homelier things and a truer poetic language."[2]

In his masterpiece, *The Faerie Queene,* Spenser gives Queen Elizabeth her panegyrical pseudonym "Gloriana." In this long allegorical poem, the character represents both glory and England's ruler. In the course of the work, she appears with many other names, in book 3 as "Britomart," the female knight of chastity, and as "Belphoebe," disciple of Diana, both seemingly appropriate roles for the Virgin Queen.

Gloriana is not the only character who is both an abstraction and the representation of an actual person. Perhaps influenced by association with Sir Walter Ralegh, Spenser tried to celebrate poetically what he believed to be an incipient union of Elizabeth and Robert Dudley, the earl of Leicester. When the earl's independence overstepped the mark and he was condemned as a rebel, Spenser found himself in a difficult position as a result of his meddling. Fortunately for him, the poem was published serially in separate books, so that he had the opportunity to convert his Arthur, recognizable to the cognoscenti as Leicester, into Magnificence, the embodiment of all virtues praised by Aristotle.

The greatness of *The Faerie Queene,* however, does not lie in any of its implied comments on political personalities and events. Spenser was a poet's poet whose chief production, though today usually regarded as caviar for the general, inspired some of the most memorable efforts of more widely favored verse-masters. Some have imitated the nine-line stanza that he invented and that bears his name, notably Burns in "The Cotter's Saturday Night," Byron in *Childe Harold's Pilgrimage*, Keats in "The Eve of St. Agnes," Shelley in *Adonais*, and Tennyson in "The Lotus-Eaters."

Speculation on the origins of this verse pattern is as instructive about Spenser's abilities as is the cataloging of its use by successive versifiers. Some have suggested that it was derived from the ottava rima, which originated in Tuscany in the late thirteenth century and was used skillfully by Boccaccio, Politian, and Ariosto. Others have traced it to the Old French ballade, which owes its existence chiefly to the fourteenth-century poet Guillaume de Machaut. Critics now are disposed to trace the inspiration for Spenser's invention to the greatest English poet of the same century, Geoffrey Chaucer. The point is that assumptions about all of these influences were plausible on the basis of the breadth and depth of Spenser's literary learning.

Spenser's knowledge of other fields was almost as full. *The Faerie Queene* is replete with references to theology, philosophy, and mythology, rich with gleanings from both ancient and medieval times in many nations. Interwoven with his learning from books are the lessons of a busy and varied life. A Cambridge master of arts, he became a courtier, a confidant of great nobles and leading writers, sheriff of County Cork in Ireland by appointment of Her Majesty, and master of Kilcoman Castle, which was burned down by Irish rebels infuriated by his writings against them.

Though the characters in *The Faerie Queene* are allegorical, they also are flesh and blood men and women whose counterparts are known to every reader. Some men armored in three-piece suits go forth daily to slay dragons, it being as routine a business with them as with the Red Cross Knight. Some women still wage quiet wars against Despair, Slander, and Envy. Both sexes dream of bowers of bliss, and resist or succumb to a variety of temptations along the way. Both are compounded in varying proportions of meanness and nobility. In *The Faerie Queene* we see, pursuing their separate and communal tasks, the people of Spenser's time and our own. And few of them are truly ethereal. As Nathaniel Hawthorne said of Anthony Trollope's characters, they are "just as real as if some giant had hewn a great lump out of the earth and put it under a glass case, with all its inhabitants going about their daily business and not suspecting that they were being made a show of."

The reader may be discouraged or even repelled by the archaic style. This is not a problem resulting simply from the passage of time since Spenser wrote. Some of his contemporaries were troubled by it. Ben Jonson said, "Spenser, in affecting the ancients, writ no language. Yet I would have him read for his matter."[3] The poet attempted to reproduce the language of Chaucer, but in the process often produced neologisms with an antique flavor. He argued that this device was necessary to distance from his own time some fantastic occurrences that he described. Those who can overcome initial distaste for this affectation will appreciate not only the author's richness of fancy but also the melody of his verse and the arresting vividness of his sensory impressions.

The most popular of Spenser's works, however, is his *Epithalamion*, a nuptial ode composed as a wedding gift to his bride. It is almost universally acknowledged to be the finest composition of its genre in the English language. Some say it is the finest in any language. The poet took the old Roman form developed by Catullus, used the canzone of Renaissance Italian variations, and so melded those two traditions with the sounds of an English night and the breath of an English morn that there is no jarring note when Phoebus' rising stirs to song an English robin.

Sir Philip Sidney, the friend to whom Spenser dedicated *The Shepherd's Calendar*, was an Elizabethan par excellence.[4] In the union of action and contemplation, of scholarship and creativity, of tradition and experiment, of depth and breadth of culture, as well as in versatility, he embodied the ideals of the society that produced him. It is gratifying that he also lived consistently by the moral code to which many of his contemporaries rededicated themselves in moments of idealism.

Sidney's career was blessed—and threatened—by almost every possible advantage. His father, Sir Henry Sidney, became Queen Elizabeth's Lord deputy in Ireland. His mother was the sister of Robert Dudley, earl of Leicester, for some years the queen's most influential courtier. Young Philip's maternal grandfather was the duke of Northumberland. The young man died before Dudley, but his education was based on the assumption that he would succeed his uncle as earl of Leicester. When Philip was twelve years old he and the old earl accompanied Queen Elizabeth on her progress from Dudley's castle, Kenilworth, to Oxford.

Two years later the boy entered the university there. When he was eighteen, the queen granted him permission to travel on the Continent to improve his skill in languages. A portrait believed to be of him at this age shows a rather handsome but overly serious young man determined to appear mature. His host in Paris was the English ambassador. But the Saint Bartholomew's Day Massacre of Protestants caused the youngster to flee France for Frankfurt. The experience was a traumatic one, and ever afterward he was apprehensive about the designs of France's Catholic royal house.

When he returned to England at the age of twenty-one, he had visited in Heidelberg, Strasbourg, Vienna, Venice, and Prague. Besides becoming fluent in French and Italian, he had also learned a great deal about the intricacies of power politics on the Continent. Everywhere he had gained a reputation for studiousness, courtesy, and consideration for others. But he was also proficient in the martial arts, and he was no pushover. His father's secretary (male, of course) learned this when he received a note from young Sidney saying, "I assure you before God that if I know you so much as read any letter I write to my father, without his commandment, or my consent, I will thrust my dagger into you. And trust to it, for I speak it in earnest."

He was far more diplomatic when, at the age of twenty-three, he was entrusted with an embassy to Vienna. Despite his success, however, the queen did not immediately offer him more permanent government employment. In 1580 he risked the royal wrath to write a famous "Letter to the Queen" protesting Elizabeth's proposed marriage to Francis duc d'Alençon. Vivid memories of the Saint Bartholomew's Day Massacre impelled him to this rash attempt to prevent English union with Catholic France. Indeed, he cherished the dream of his country as an integral part of a European Protestant alliance.

Not surprisingly, his chances for an appointment did not improve. But he was not ostracized from the court. He was knighted in 1583, though for a frivolous reason in which he could not take pride. Prince John Casimir was to be made a knight of the garter but could not come to London for the ceremony. A proxy was necessary. To protect the prince's dignity, it should be someone with a knighthood at least. So Sidney, a very presentable young courtier, was knighted so that he could stand in for the prince.

Sidney was a useful fellow around the court, adding grace and distinction to many of the festivities, occasionally lending an elegant pen to compositions for special entertainments. But meeting Edmund Spenser and the other poets awakened in him a desire to do more serious writing. The lack of public employment gave him the leisure to follow his inclination. Queen Elizabeth's neglect of Sidney was as great a contribution to literature as her patronage of some of his colleagues.

As a writer, Sidney distinguished himself in three categories: sonnets, prose fiction, and literary criticism. That his literary reputation should have advanced rapidly with the impetus of such fine productions does not surprise—until one learns that none was published in his lifetime. Though a bold innovator in literature, Sidney was a conservative adherent of the old social code that frowned upon a gentleman sending forth printed works under his own name. His manuscripts were circulated by hand among his friends, who included some of the foremost writers in the realm. The 108 sonnets of his *Astrophel and Stella* comprise a sonnet sequence surpassed in English only by the works of Shakespeare and Spenser. Sidney produced about forty other sonnets. His work in the genre includes adaptations of French and Latin poetry and virtually every variation known in his time. But they are not merely metrical experiments; they pulse with emotion. *Astrophel and Stella* was inspired by his love for Penelope Devereux, a young woman who married someone else. In one sonnet, he told how, after a beginning of artificial constraint, he caught fire: " 'Fool!' said my muse to me, 'look in thy heart, and write.' " The sincerity of the emotion is in no way compromised by the possible accuracy of Tucker Brooke's observation that "Sidney seems to have looked in his heart only after [Penelope] was promised to another."[5]

Even Sidney's notable prose work *Arcadia* includes much distinguished verse. His *Arcadia* is, of course, not the barren mountainous landscape of the Peloponnesian reality but the idealized pastoral setting of Virgil's *Eclogues*. And the Englishman's prose fiction is punctuated by his own eclogues modeled after the Roman poet's. But he also interpolates poems so diversified as to seem almost a catalog of metrical possibilities. Sidney's work was published, posthumously of course, in two forms, one generally known as *Old Arcadia*, a rather straightforward prose romance, and the other, usually called *New Arcadia*, an incomplete, but greatly enlarged and complicated, reworking of the original. The concept of Paradise in a rural retreat with shepherds and shepherdesses conversing in classically inspired philosophical verse lends itself to precious artificiality. But Sidney's characters are quite corporeal men and women (witness the psychological exposition, as well as the anatomical catalog, of Pamela's charms); and the work has an implicit warning (that could profitably have been heeded by Marie Antoinette and the Petit Trianon crowd) of the dangers that can ensue when royalty plays the rustic shepherd game.

Important as are Sidney's creative writings in both poetry and prose, his most influential work probably was in literary criticism. His *Apology for Poetry*[6] is significant even beyond the fact that it was the chief conduit through which the literary principles of the continental Renaissance reached England. No scholar has successfully refuted Walter Jackson Bate's assertion in 1952 that the book "clearly stands out as the greatest of all Renaissance critical writings."[7] Its brilliant melding of Aristotelian and Platonic tenets with Horatian principles as interpreted and modified by sixteenth century Italians was an act of synthesis amounting almost to original creation. In fact, considering that Sidney deduced literary concepts from Plato's general philosophy as well as drawing them directly from his specific comments on literature, and that he also enriched the whole with gleanings from Christian thought, we may reasonably credit the Englishman with original achievement of a high order.

Sidney said in the *Apology* that poetry then found "a hard welcome in England." He noted that it had not always been so and attributed latter-day indifference to the fact that lately many incompetent versifiers had taken to publishing, "as if all the Muses were got with child, to bring forth bastard poets." The particular impetus for Sidney's book was publication of *The School of Abuse*, an attack on poetry by Stephen Gosson, a Puritan. Sidney's chagrin was multiplied by the frustrating fact that, without seeking permission, Gosson had dedicated the book to him. The Puritan doubtless knew that most people honored Sir Philip as a good man. Gosson may have been one of those who assume that all good men think alike.

The *Apology*, however, is far more than an answer to Gosson. More even than a defense of poetry, it is a powerful argument for imaginative literature of all kinds. It is superior to all other critical writings of the Renaissance—whether Italian, German, French, Spanish, or English—in that it exceeds their generally narrow scope and soars above the level of technical minutiae. Sir Philip argued that those who,

> professing learning, inveigh against poetry . . . go very near to ungratefulness, to seek to deface that which, in the noblest nations and languages that are known, hath been the first light giver to ignorance, and first nurse, whose milk by little and little enabled them to feed afterwards of tougher knowledge. And will they now play . . . the vipers, that with their birth killed their parents?

He showed how, in ancient Greece, poetry not only made the Greeks receptive to other civilizing influences but was actually the tree from which other branches of knowledge grew. In tracing the growth of unwritten literature among Greek, Roman, and other cultures in their primitive beginnings, Sidney was, Bate persuasively argues, "employing an approach that foreshadowed that of modern comparative anthropology."

Sidney left ancient times as he found analogies newer to his own era: "So in the Italian language the first that made it aspire to be a treasure-house of Science were the poets Dante, Boccaccio, and Petrarch. So in our English were Gower and Chaucer."

Sir Philip advanced the point made by some of his predecessors and many of his successors, but never more eloquently than by him, that fiction is not necessarily the opposite of truth. He argued that the best fiction imitates nature. Relieved of the burden of strict adherence to particular facts and a literal rendition of actual incidents, it is free to concentrate on visions of essential truth. He maintained that poetry, or any other form of good fiction, was free to be even "more philosophical" than history. At the same time, because poetry could supply images to vivify the abstractions of philosophy, it could appeal to a wider audience than that discipline. The great value of poetry was its ability to present general truths in an attractive and memorable way. In stating his case,

Sidney went beyond the arguments of Aristotle for imaginative literature as an introduction to ideas, and eagerly embraced Plato's concept of perfect Ideas transcending any individual manifestation.

Horace had said that the maker of literature ideally should both delight and instruct. To this Sir Philip added that without pleasure there could be little learning. He described the ideal poet as one who "cometh unto you with a tale which holdeth children from play, and old men from the chimney corner." The *Apology for Poetry* is too rich and varied an essay to be summarized easily in a few paragraphs as so many other works on the same subject may be. It could have been produced only by one whose knowledge ranged far beyond a narrow specialty. Sidney's informed curiosity in many fields led him to analogies that would have eluded a mind of more restricted experience. His intimate acquaintance with the cultures of ancient Greece and Rome, medieval Europe, Renaissance Italy, and generations of the English background, in conjunction with his involvement with the human relations of practical affairs, suggested questions that did not occur to more conventional critics.

Not the least of his assets as a critic was his ability as a poet. Matthew Arnold's assertion that the creative temperament is not critical, though often quoted, is belied by his own career, though it may be argued that he himself did not become a great critic until he ceased to be an inspired poet. But the literature of the English language supplies still more convincing examples of writers whose creative and critical faculties were mutually helpful—Dryden, Samuel Johnson, Wordsworth, Coleridge, Shelley, Hawthorne, Poe, Henry James, T. S. Eliot, Robert Penn Warren, Rebecca West, John Crowe Ransom, Allen Tate, and Edmund Wilson. Examples spring to mind from other languages as well—Gotthold Lessing, Schiller, Goethe, Rabindranath Tagore, Corneille, though in this last case it must be admitted that the creative faculty was hampered almost as much as helped by the critical.

Sidney apparently completed his *Apology for Poetry* in 1583. He was married in the same year to Frances Walsingham, daughter of the English ambassador with whom he had been staying in Paris at the time of the Saint Bartholomew's Day Massacre. Still fearful of the Catholic alliance, he urged an attack on Spain and sought an active role in the colonial ventures of Sir Walter Ralegh and Martin Frobisher, his devoted friend since grammar school days. He was ready to sail with Sir Francis Drake in 1585 when Elizabeth frustrated that ambition by appointing him governor of Flushing, a Netherlands outpost of British power, which commanded the approach to Antwerp. There he served well, both as an administrator and as advisor to Leicester, commander of English forces in the Netherlands.

In July of 1586 Sir Philip raised English morale by leading a successful raid on Axel. In September, as part of an English detachment to intercept an enemy convoy, he was fatally wounded. His old friend Fulke Greville reported that the dying man "called for drink . . . but as he was putting the bottle to his mouth he saw a poor [wounded] soldier . . . [longingly] casting his eyes up at the bottle." Sidney passed it to him. "Thy necessity," he said, "is greater than mine."

Some historians in recent generations have been inclined to doubt the story, pointing out that Greville was not a witness on the spot. At the time, it was quite generally accepted, often with such exclamations as "How like Sidney!" Elizabeth's court was plunged into mourning, and numerous elegies in Sir Philip's honor were published in England. Special tributes circulated on the continent. The epitaph of his old schoolmate, buried forty-two years later, reads, "Fulke Greville, Servant to Queen Elizabeth, Councillor to King James, and Friend to Sir Philip Sidney." The great regard in which Sidney was held as an intellect and as a human being did much to enhance the prestige of poetry in his generation and the next. Though he was an important poet, a great defender of poetry, and a great patron of poets, his greatest immediate legacy to literature was his life. His personality so impregnated his writings that that life continues today and regularly wins new friends.

A much more inflexible poet-critic, Ben Jonson,was in part the product of the Sidney family's patronage.[8] Jonson was a paradoxical character, as a writer wedded to the classics, tradition, and establishment values, but as a human being so much at war with society as to be jailed several times for violence and once only narrowly to escape execution.

The posthumous child of a clergyman and stepson of a bricklayer, Ben was educated at the prestigious Westminster School under the tutelage of William Camden, a celebrated antiquary and historian so enamored of the classics that he wrote mostly in Latin. Jonson later defined his debt to this teacher as "all that I am in arts, all that I know."

Jonson served in the English army in Flanders, by his own account slaying an enemy champion in single combat. Later he traded the real-life role of an ordinary English soldier for the make-believe one of marshal of Spain, joining a company of strolling players as Hieronimo in Thomas Kyd's *Spanish Tragedy*. In his mid-twenties he worked as both actor and playwright, drawing a prison sentence for "seditious and slanderous" lines. Soon after release from prison, he killed a fellow thespian in a duel but cheated the noose by pleading benefit of clergy. On the face of it, an extraordinary defense in view of his wild, secular career!

Since the twelfth century, English church authorities had claimed with frequent success the right to try and punish in an ecclesiastical court any member of the clergy accused of a capital crime. In the fourteenth century the old provision became a discretionary device by which a royal judge could spare a layman from the full penalty of secular law. This was done by implementation of an old regulation under which one who could read a Latin verse from the Bible was deemed a member of the clergy. Instead of being executed, the accused would be branded on the thumb. This benefit of clergy was extended to women in 1692, and survived in England until 1827. By taking advantage of the provision, Jonson escaped with a mark on his thumb and the confiscation of all his worldly goods. No wonder he always emphasized the importance of studying Latin! Interestingly enough, though he was an actor and playwright at the time of his trial, he was described as "yeoman," and at the time of a later indictment he was still in the eyes of the law a bricklayer and was so described in the official record.

A sophisticated segment of the public, including the clever young lawyers of the Inns of Court, definitely thought of Jonson first and foremost as a playwright. Their fancy was taken by *Every Man in His Humor*, a comedy that debuted with another player-playwright, William Shakespeare, in the cast. Influenced by the vogue of the Italian Renaissance among educated Englishmen, Jonson began with Florence as the setting but later shifted to London. The play, while observing rigid classical concepts of separation between comedy and tragedy, owed much to Italian comedy in plot and manner. It was a satire on superficial attempts to move up in society without the cultivation of inward excellence. Mental fencing between father and son and the stratagems of a servant cleverer than his master, stock elements of classical drama and of Italian Renaissance imitations, were handled with an uncommon skill that lent freshness. As the title indicates, each character embodied a dominant "humor," an exaggerated quirk of character or propensity of personality. One is the boastful coward, another the overly anxious father, and so on. The play was a tremendous success from the first, but Jonson later improved it by introducing the atmosphere of London, a city that he knew well, from the favorite candlelit haunts of the intellectuals to the dark alleys frequented by criminals. The changes brought vitality as well as verisimilitude.

While Jonson satirized with cool rationality the irrational behavior that got his fellow humans into trouble, his own high temper and improvidence continued to make problems for him. Before long, he was again in prison, this time for failure to repay a loan from a fellow actor. Upon payment of the debt plus one pound in damages, he was released. Meanwhile, he was increasing the range of his acquaintance beyond the prison walls in pace with his growing professional reputation. Soon numbered among his friends were titled gentlemen and prestigious scholars. He was energetically turning out plays and masques, some to be performed by children, some soon forgotten.

Again his contentious temperament got him into trouble. He used the stage to satirize fellow playwrights, who retaliated in kind until the conflict escalated into the War of the Theaters. Jonson soon had more than rival playwrights to deal with when he put into the mouths of the performing Children of the Chapel words believed to allude to the relationship of Elizabeth and Essex. The queen let the matter pass, but various persons who believed themselves slandered threatened suit, and Jonson abruptly deserted the muse of comedy to seek safety in tragedy.

Shortly, he determined to abandon the theater altogether in favor of more conventionally literary labor. He left home for several years to be the guest successively of a lord and several other titled gentlemen, apparently forming a close friendship with a lady of the court. Yielding to the commands of the court and the urging of aristocratic friends, he returned to writing plays, confining himself to Roman tragedies conforming to classical models in the antique setting as well as the rules of composition. Notable among his tragedies was *Sejanus*. A self-consciously learned adaptation from the writings of Tacitus, imperial Rome's greatest historian, it nevertheless brought the ancient world to life and attracted a discriminating audience. In the cast was William Shakespeare, preparing to wind up his acting career and devote all his professional labors to writing.

Even now, however, Jonson became the target of fresh attacks from people who, rightly or wrongly, read between the lines of the dialogue critical personal references and slurs on the government. His reputation among his elite friends was not helped by the fact that he had beaten a servant of the earl of Northampton. By now James I, less tolerant than Elizabeth, was England's ruler. Jonson must have known fear when he was called before the Council. Rumor had it that he was accused of treason. Whatever the charge or the resolution, he was soon welcomed to the court—only to be ejected a little later by the lord chamberlain for what was deemed unmannerly conduct!

By the end of 1604, Jonson was not only enjoying royal acceptance after addressing a panegyric to King James and writing a masque performed for him and his queen; he was also so far reconciled to George Chapman and John Marston, his old enemies of the War of the Theaters, that he collaborated with them in writing *Eastward Ho!* a play performed by the Children of the Chapel. But again there was trouble. King James, Scottish born and bred, was displeased by the drama's ridicule of his countrymen. As a result, Jonson and Chapman were soon closer than ever—sharing the shelter of a jail roof. Freed by the intervention of powerful noblemen, Jonson was a guest a little later at a supper given by Robert Catesby for people involved in the Gunpowder Plot. Catesby was the principal instigator of the notorious plan to blow up king, queen, prince, and Parliament in 1605. Though Guy Fawkes, obedient to orders, hid twenty or more barrels of gunpowder in Parliament's cellar, the plot was of course detected, and many times the original volume of explosive powder has been expended in commemorative celebrations on successive recurrences of November 5.

Almost every Catholic was suspect. But despite Jonson's association with the plotters and the fact that he was a Roman Catholic, having converted during one of his prison terms, he got into no trouble over the Gunpowder Plot. Indeed, only two days after the attempt was foiled, he secured a warrant from the Privy Council to meet with a Catholic priest in an effort to secure more information about it and even conferred with the chaplain of the Venetian ambassador. He was soon one of the most respected sources on the scope and organization of the plot. Not only that, he was a great favorite at court, a welcome addition to the company of scholars, and an extremely popular playwright.

In the midst of all this success, he was charged with attempting to convert youths "to the Papish religion." The case was called repeatedly without action, and then there are no further references.

There is no need to continue the record of his mishaps and escapes. The man who shaped his plays to the rigorous demands of reason was temperamentally incapable of leading a well-ordered life. But he went on talking his way into and out of all kinds of trouble. He even talked his way into an extended vacation in France as French tutor to Sir Walter Ralegh's son, although Jonson's knowledge of the language was extremely limited and his pupil was fluent. This proclivity for involvement and escape, however fascinating in itself, is not his claim to fame today.

He is known as the creator of some of the best comedies in English. After decline in popularity in the nineteenth century, his work surged to the forefront again in the twentieth. *Volpone, or the Fox* was a success when first performed in 1606. Today it is a favorite with educated audiences, who have seen it with almost every imaginable variation of costume and setting. Not only the title role, but others as well (Mosca, the fly; Voltore, the vulture; Corvino, the raven) bear labels that make their dominant "humors" obvious. Nevertheless, they come to life with an individuality for which their creator apparently was not striving. Though, as a devotee of pure classicism he scorned originality, he endowed some of these people with characteristics of their London counterparts in trade or society. And he made London itself, more than a setting, at times a dominant character, come to life with an effectiveness that no one would surpass before Charles Dickens. Just as he was temperamentally incapable of subordinating his life to the rules of reason, he was as unable to suppress originality in his work as to hold down with one finger a bobbing cork. This was true even though he deliberately imitated long passages from the classicists and their neoclassical mimics.

Some critics consider *Volpone* the greatest satirical drama in English. Others give the palm to *The Alchemist*, another play by Jonson. *Volpone* is brilliant, but *The Alchemist* is in some ways a more mature work. Its laughter is without bitterness. The three classic unities of time, plot, and place are meticulously observed, but seem more natural than contrived. There is the art that conceals artifice. The drama makes full use of the classical tradition, but presents unmistakably the very London neighborhood of Blackfriars in which Jonson now lived in newfound prosperity. The central event, an epidemic of the plague, was topical, as Jonson wrote in the midst of the great plague of 1610. Each character, in typical Jonsonian fashion, was animated by an obsession—in this case the same for each, the desire for gain without pain, or even effort. While the characters were universal types, the prosperous merchant, the Puritan preacher, and the law clerk were at once recognizably English and distinctly individual. Here was a happy union of cultural heritage and fresh observation of native materials on the contemporary scene.

After *The Alchemist*, Jonson's art did not grow, but his reputation did. *Bartholomew Fair* and *The Staple of News* rival the earlier play in satiric brilliance, but their action lacks its neat inevitability, and they cannot approach its economy of means. Increasingly, his creative energies went into the writing of masques in which the music and costuming together sometimes counted far more than his plotting and words.

Some of his creative energy, too, was consumed in long discourses and fervid arguments at the Mermaid Tavern and other places where the literati gathered. The former bricklayer who never had the advantage of a university education had made the most of his preparatory school tutelage under a distinguished classicist, and now enjoyed the deference of Oxford and Cambridge graduates known for writings in Latin and Greek. At least as intoxicating as the wine was the talk when Jonson, Sir Walter Ralegh, Sir Francis Beaumont, John Fletcher, John Donne, and Shakespeare met around their favorite table. The excitement of those times is captured in one member's verse, "Master Francis Beaumont to Ben Jonson":

> What things have we seen
> Done at the Mermaid! heard words that have been
> So nimble, and so full of subtle flame,
> As if that every one from whence they came
> Had meant to put his whole wit in a jest,
> And had resolved to live a fool the rest
> Of his dull life.

According to Thomas Fuller:

> Many were the wit-combats betwixt [Shakespeare] and Ben Jonson; which two I behold like a Spanish great galleon and an English man-of-war; Master Jonson (like the former) was built far higher in learning; solid, but slow, in his performances. Shakespeare, with the English man-of-war, lesser in bulk, but lighter in sailing, could turn with all tides, tack about, and take advantage of all winds, by the quickness of his wit and invention.[9]

In the eyes of an imaginative Englishman, it was the story of the Spanish Armada and Drake all over again.

Young writers privileged to share table talk with these worthies were grateful for Jonson's interest in them and were proud to call themselves members of the "Tribe of Ben." The great man, somewhat mellowed with age and chastened by the theological studies that he pursued enthusiastically after a conversion during one of his stays in jail, became first avuncular and then paternal. Thomas Randolph, William Cartwright, and Thomas Carew gave him filial respect and affection, and even Beaumont and Fletcher acknowledged his mentorship. His robust personality, as well as his knowledge and skill, augmented his influence.

Jonson is sometimes called a brilliant literary critic, but some of us cannot agree. His most ambitious work in this genre burned while still in manuscript. We know, however, that it was largely derived from Horace. Jonson's published criticism may be found in his prefaces; his *Conversations with* [William] *Drummond*, the Scottish poet; and principally in a collection of notes and essays called *Timber, or Discoveries*, published posthumously. This last work furnishes much ammunition for those who charge the author with a lack of imagination. Some passages parallel ancient and Renaissance sources. Others, as often has been pointed out, are simply translations of passages from Quintilian, Vives, and Lipsius.

But other weaknesses of Jonson's criticism disturb some of us more than this heavy borrowing and imitation. It reveals a literal mindedness surprising in a writer of genius. This trait is especially responsible for a lack of insight in his discussion of Shakespeare. For instance, Jonson ridiculed the reply that Shakespeare has Julius Caesar make to one who says, "Caesar, thou dost me wrong." Jonson says, "He replied, 'Caesar never did wrong, but with just cause,' and such like, which were ridiculous." Jonson attributes this "mistake" to hasty writing.

Fortunately, in his best plays and poems, Jonson is not a slave to literal rationalism, nor does he always follow his own dictum: "Observe how the best writers have imitated, and follow them." He profits from acquaintance with the best who have written before him, but at his own best he adapts rather than imitates, and his London is not merely a pale copy of Rome. Though he somewhat condescendingly says of Shakespeare that "he redeemed his vices with his virtues" and adds, "There was ever more in him to be praised than to be pardoned," he also says, considering Shakespeare's abilities as well as his honesty and "open and free nature," "I loved the man, and do honor his memory (on this side Idolatry) as much as any."

Jonson's masques include many lilting lyrics of great sweetness and freshness that stand in welcome contrast to the unyielding precepts of his formal criticism. When he died in 1637, he left an uncompleted pastoral drama titled *The Sad Shepherd*. In it he casts aside classical restraints as in no previous work, and evidences some of that emotional richness which distinguishes some great Elizabethan works. Perhaps he was on the verge of another period of growth. Jonson the creative artist dwarfs Jonson the critic. However daring in private life, he is not so boldly innovative in writing as the great Shakespeare. But Jonson's best work is a vital blend of received tradition and fresh observation. Perhaps the stultifying pedantry of his criticism is a tribute to the university education he did not have. There is no evidence that the same lack troubled Shakespeare, but the temperaments of the two men were quite different. The former bricklayer was genuinely learned, but he could not wear his learning with the casual grace with which the university wits wore their academic robes.

Jonson was buried in Westminster Abbey. He had written his own epitaph and, true to his classical allegiance, had penned it in Latin: "Orare Ben Jonson" (Pray for Ben Jonson). The stonecutter, thinking the inscription was to be in English, assumed that the first two words had carelessly been run together and "corrected" the spacing. And so today the writer's monument bears the words "O rare Ben Jonson." Many accurately transcribed epitaphs are less truthful.

Of the company that joined Jonson at the Mermaid Tavern, probably none except Shakespeare was more remarkable than John Donne.[10] He is rightly best known to the generally educated public as the author of one of the world's most eloquent and profound observations:

No man is an island, entire of itself; every man is a piece of the continent, a part of the main; if a clod be washed away by the sea, Europe is the less, as well as if a promontory were, as well as if a manor of thy friends or of thine own were; any man's death diminishes me, because I am involved in mankind, and therefore never send to know for whom the bell tolls; it tolls for thee.

At least up to the age of thirty-four, however, Donne was far better known for brilliant and cynical erotic verse than for any serious expressions of faith or spirituality. In the song "Go and Catch a Falling Star," he challenges him who will to search for "a woman true and fair" and let him know when one is found, but concludes,

> Though she were true, when you met her,
> And last, till you write your letter,
> Yet she
> Will be
> False ere I come, to two, or three.

That verse does not illustrate his brilliance, but it does represent the depth of his cynicism. Unless one considers it exceeded by lines in "The Indifferent":

> I can love her, and her, and you, and you;
> I can love any, so she be not true.

Or, from the same poem:

> Will it not serve your turn to do as did your mothers?
> Or have you all old vices spent and now would find out others?

The lines in "To His Mistress Going to Bed" that begin "Off with that girdle" introduce a catalog of erotic attractions and reactions. "The Flea" is in a tradition of venturesome flea poems, a genre to which Europe's poetic lovers turned after exhausting the more modest possibilities of changing places with milady's glove or the harpsichord keys she caressed. Some believe it the cleverest of its kind in any tongue; certainly it is as bawdy as any.

In other poems, however, rather than the mere heat of frottage, there is the purity of a blazing passion that consumes the dross. And occasionally there is an exalted note of a love in which "eyes, lips, and hands" are symbols of a transcending soul love. In "A Valediction: Forbidding Mourning," the poet writes:

> Our two souls, therefore, which are one,
> Though I must go, endure not yet
> A breach, but an expansion,
> Like gold to airy thinness beat.

There was in Donne no abrupt turning from the erotic to the spiritual, and he wrote many poems that combine elements of both. There is "The Good-Morrow," which begins, "I wonder, by my troth, what you and I did, till we loved," and includes the lines:

> For love all love of other sights controls,
> And makes one little room an everywhere.

Donne's pilgrimage of faith was a convoluted one, as sinuous and subtle as the tracings of his mind. When he was only four years old, his father died. The elder Donne, a prosperous merchant, left his family well provided for. The absence of the father increased proportionately the influence of the mother and her family in the child's life. The maternal grandfather and a great-grandfather in the same line had both been writers. Young John's mother's family cherished their kinship with one celebrated for both spirituality and literary brilliance, Sir Thomas More. The growing boy evidently heard much talk about this illustrious relative.

The family was devoutly Catholic. Two of John's uncles were exiled Jesuit priests. One of his brothers was charged with hiding a priest and died a prison martyr to his faith.

Exclusion of Catholics from Oxford and Cambridge would have seemed to bode ill for John's intellectual ambitions, but his precocity was his protection. He entered Oxford quite possibly as a preteen, certainly not past thirteen, an age when his juvenile status precluded his taking the Oath of Supremacy, by which he would have acknowledged the English sovereign as the head of his church. After a liberal arts education, he entered the Inns of Court to prepare for the legal profession, probably learning as much from London nightlife as from his formal studies.

At twenty-four he added another dimension to his experience; he volunteered for Essex's raid on Cadiz. The next year he participated in another of the great adventures open to Englishmen, sailing in Lord Thomas Howard's Island Voyage to the Azores.

Laying aside the sword after that expedition, he took up the pen—as secretary to Sir Thomas Edgerton, a minister to the queen. In this position, he had an opportunity to continue his studies and at the same time was in touch with people who could advance a career in law and government. By this time he appears to have become an Anglican, so religious barriers had been removed.

But then, at the age of thirty, new trouble cost him his job and his freedom. Discovery that he was secretly married to Anne More, Lady Edgerton's niece, enraged his employers. As the young woman was a member of the household, her family felt that Donne had violated a trust. We can be sure also that Sir Thomas was disturbingly aware of Donne's reputation in earlier days as a London rake and the author of erotic verse. The bride's relations had the groom jailed, and tried unsuccessfully to have the marriage annulled.

Donne was soon free but found jobs hard to get. Although the offended uncle, Edgerton, was one of the queen's ministers, Donne had the nerve to seek royal employment. When this effort gained nothing, he applied for secretary-ships in Ireland and the two-year-old Virginia Colony.

But there was help from King James, though not in a direction Donne had anticipated or wished. The young man had been developing a reputation for theological studies, and the king joined church officials in urging him to take holy orders. Donne desperately needed the financial security that an ecclesiastical position could bring, but he demurred, protesting his unworthiness.

Acceding at last, he was ordained a deacon and priest of London's Saint Paul's, an institution with which his name would be indelibly associated. He pursued his duties quite avidly, and his earnest and eloquent sermons became the talk of the capital.

He was faithful as husband and parent as well as priest. He was devoted to Anne and to their house full of children. When she died in 1617 following the birth of their eleventh child, he was devastated. Henceforth the powerful passion that he had felt for her seems to have been transferred to the church that he already loved. Four years later he became dean of the cathedral, and before his death he was slated to become a bishop. But his greatest service to the church was in his sermons, meditations, and spiritual verse. These arresting messages would claim the attention of generations long after most archbishops had been forgotten.

Of course, Donne is remembered still oftener as a maker of great literature. Though most who know his prose know it only from a few striking quotations, his poetry is enjoyed by a great many readers of intellectual bent. He is universally conceded to be the greatest of England's metaphysical poets—a distinguished seventeenth-century group including Abraham Cowley, George Herbert, Richard Crashaw, and Henry Vaughan. He attracts the intelligent general reader as well as the academic explicator writing for professional journals.

It seems strange, therefore, that after exciting great enthusiasm in the seventeenth century, he was neglected in the eighteenth and nineteenth. Indeed, he began to lose his audience even in the latter part of his own century. John Dryden, the literary dictator of that period, said that he himself and his contemporaries, though inferior to Donne and the other metaphysical poets in "wit," excelled them in poetry. And Dr. Samuel Johnson, the literary dictator of eighteenth-century England, complained that the metaphysical poets had not attained the sublime:

> Those writers who lay on the watch for novelty could have little hope of greatness; for great things cannot have escaped former observation. Their attempts were always analytic: they broke every image into fragments; and could no more represent, by their slender conceits and labored particularities, the prospects of nature or the scenes of life, than he who dissects a sun-beam with a prism can exhibit the wide effulgence of a summer noon.

He concluded that Donne and his colleagues had "produced combinations of confused magnificence."

But Johnson conceded: "Yet great labor, directed by great abilities, is never wholly lost: if they frequently threw away their wit upon false conceits, they likewise sometimes struck out unexpected truth: if their conceits were far-fetched, they were often worth the carriage. To write on their plan, it was at least necessary to read and think." And he admitted that Donne was "a man of very extensive and various knowledge."[11]

The comments are probably as generous as could be hoped for from the chief literary critic in England's Neoclassical Age, which discouraged original-ity and pursued symmetry. Any contemporary critic who lacked Dr. Johnson's saving common sense and ultimate sense of fair play would have been much harsher, as indeed virtually all were. But if genius, whether in the arts or the sciences, is in large part a matter of composing arresting metaphors from ob-jects or ideas not ordinarily associated, then Donne is an extraordinary example of the class. And if its proof lies in achieving such effectiveness that the associa-tion will henceforth seem inevitable, Donne belongs in the front ranks.

Other factors contribute to Donne's popularity with intelligent readers. Whether we are addressed by young John the London rake or the reverend dean of Saint Paul's, it seemingly is always with utter candor. There is also his amazing variety, whether the reader seeks sensory delight, an occasional intellectual puzzle, or spiritual admonition. Donne can write with gentle beauty:

> For love all love of other sights controls, and makes one little room
> an everywhere.

Or with horrible specificity describe the convulsive reactions of a head newly severed from the body by the executioner's ax:

> His eyes will twinkle, and his tongue will roll, as though he beckoned,
> and called back his soul.

There is, too, the drama of such opening lines as the lover's plaint at sunrise:

> Busy old fool, unruly sun, why dost thou thus through windows and
> through curtains call on us?

Or a solemn call to attention at the winter solstice: " 'Tis the year's midnight, and it is the day's."

But, above all, there are the magnificent metaphors that prick the mind and stab the heart. Their elements could have been supplied only by a mind that loved both tradition and experiment, that had scavenged the dark places of contemporary London and foraged among the seers of ancient Greece and Rome, the Hebrew prophets, the medieval saints, and the pioneers of the Italian Renaissance. More possibilities of comparison, and hence of creation, are open to the mind challenged to find unity amid temporal, cultural, and geographical variety—a superabundance of dissimilitude. Such was Donne's mind, and it makes him an ideal representative of the Elizabethan Age and its long Jacobean afterglow—and also perhaps of all ages of extraordinary creativity.

Western civilization is indebted to two twentieth century men for rediscovering Donne to an age that was ready for him. In 1921 H. J. C. Grierson, in the introduction to his anthology *Metaphysical Lyrics and Poems of the Seventeenth Century*, pointed out the great merits of the seventeenth century poet, and T. S. Eliot in his review of that volume lent his earnest advocacy and international prestige to the revival.[12]

The Elizabethan Age, especially if we consider its extension into the Jacobean, is filled with a great many other writers who would repay far more attention than they now receive. But so heroic are the proportions of its greatest figures—Spenser, Sidney, Ralegh, Marlowe, Jonson, Shakespeare, Donne—that they overshadow many writers who would be better remembered had they lived in periods of less competition. Yet the fecundity of their era is so proverbial that people seeking to do justice to such a titan as John Milton, who published his greatest work more than six decades after Elizabeth's death—after James' and Charles I's reigns and Cromwell's rule and well into the sovereignty of Charles II—have called him "the last Elizabethan." Though chronologically skewed, the logic is ineluctable.

In some ways, the most representative work of Elizabethan literature was not the creation of Shakespeare, or Jonson, or Donne, or any other individual, however gifted. It was the work of nearly a hundred authors who collectively expressed the genius of an age. It is, more properly, the labor of nearly a hundred authors and one editor of extraordinary industry and competence—Richard Hakluyt.[13] Hakluyt's *Principal Navigations, Traffiques, Voyages, and Discoveries of the English Nation*, commonly known as *Hakluyt's Voyages*, was compiled in three volumes between 1589 and 1600. It consists largely of the personal narratives of those who ventured upon the seas and to strange lands in an age when the appetite for adventure was boundless.

A few of the writers, most notably Sir Walter Ralegh, had well-deserved literary reputations. Some writing in foreign tongues gained literary grace through Hakluyt's translations. Other accounts are by sailors acquainted with few books other than logbooks. But sometimes their labored writing has an immediacy that transcends the medium.

Hakluyt was ideally suited to the task of compilation and editorship. In 1557, when he was about five years old, his father died and he joined the household of a cousin, also named Richard Hakluyt. The elder Richard was a London lawyer whose friends included merchants in overseas trade, geographers, and explorers. The cumulative effect of these influences doubtless would have been a determining influence in young Richard's career anyway, but he dated his dedication from a particular moment. When the boy was curious about a world map in his guardian's Middle Temple chamber, the older man pointed out the kingdoms and territories shown and told him of the "special commodities" of each that supplied the "particular wants" of others. He told him how overseas trade made possible the matching of goods and needs for mutual benefit. Then he led him to his big Bible and called his attention to verses 23–24 of Psalm

107: "They which go down to the sea in ships, and occupy by the great waters, they see the works of the Lord, and his wonders in the deep." "[The] words of the Prophet, together with my cousin's discourse," young Richard later said, ". . . took in me so deep an impression that I . . . resolved, if ever I were preferred to the University . . . I would by God's assistance prosecute that knowledge and kind of literature, the doors whereof were so happily opened before me."[14]

The young man earned a master's degree at Christ Church, Oxford, but a vital part of his education was obtained in conversation with his cousin and his cousin's friends. He was inspired not only to read English accounts of voyages of discovery but also to translate printed works and manuscripts in other languages. His formal training broadened his view and gave him the linguistic tools to convert to his native tongue writings in Greek, Latin, Italian, Spanish, Portuguese, and French.

Though he took holy orders, he chose to serve humanity through education. He returned to Oxford as its first professor of modern geography, and introduced to its students many of the newly corrected maps and globes, hastening their use in the common schools. He continued to learn from manuscripts, but just as assiduously improved his acquaintance with mariners. It was a particularly exciting time for such studies if one was an Englishman. Drake had circumnavigated the globe, and Ralegh, Gilbert, and Frobisher were extending the frontiers of knowledge, and had dreams of extending England's frontiers as well. Soon, in 1607, the first permanent English-speaking settlement in the New World was established in Virginia.

For five years, Hakluyt served with Her Majesty's ambassador to France, where he heard "other nations miraculously extolled for their discoveries and notable enterprises by sea, but the English of all others [condemned] for their sluggish security, and continued neglect of the like attempts." English mariners were already beginning to dare beyond the dreams of their predecessors, but Hakluyt accelerated the process by citing the challenge of other kingdoms' achievements and by trumpeting those of his own countrymen who merited admiration. His publications were both a goad and an inspiration to his own and later generations of English seamen, and to the nation that backed them.

In colonization, he was a maker as well as a recorder of history. It was historically appropriate, and psychologically important, that his great compendium should appear in its first form in 1589, the year after the defeat of the Spanish Armada, when Spanish domination of the seas and of New World colonization was broken and bold-faced English mariners challenged the future with lifted hearts. Hakluyt was an adviser to Sir Walter Ralegh and Sir Humphrey Gilbert in their overseas ventures, and a consultant on colonization to the royal ministers as well as to companies of merchant venturers.

He represented Elizabethan creativity at its happiest, combining prodigious scholarship with imaginative interpretation, the strength of tradition with the freshness of discovery, patient labor with bold endeavor, and patriotic spirit with an insatiable curiosity about all cultures. One of the volumes that he rescued from obscurity was the *Book of Robert Thorne*, published in 1527. Most of that English merchant's writings had been outdated by more than a half century of maritime discovery, but one sentence that Hakluyt republished caught the imagination of Englishmen: "There is no sea innavigable, no land unhabitable."

Hakluyt was an encourager and counselor to those proposing to colonize Virginia. Circumstantial evidence indicates that he took a far larger role even than would be suggested by his energetic work as a publicist for the venture, a principal source on the geography of the New World, and the cataloger of an enticing list of products to be found there. He was, among other things, responsible for bringing together Governor White, the official artist of Ralegh's lost colony, and Theodore de Bry, the Frankfurt engraver. The result was publication of the first reliable pictures of the aboriginal Americans, their habitations, and the flora and fauna of the land. As anyone who has seen White's original sketches knows, de Bry's engravings could not capture their beauty and subtlety, but they did make graphic knowledge of the North American coast accessible to many Europeans. De Bry published Thomas Harriot's report on the land in Latin, English, German, and French, together with White's illustrations. Hakluyt was his collaborator in the English edition and was credited in the French one with being "the cause of the advancement of the present treatise." In the words of George Bruner Parks, "England was discovering a science as well as an art, was preparing itself, by the new interest in geography typified by Harriot's book and White's studies, to take its intellectual as well as its political place among the western nations."[15]

When young Hakluyt seized the opportunity to go to France with England's ambassador, he had been planning instead to embark for America in an expedition headed by Sir Walter Ralegh. Later he was presented with another chance to go to the New World, but was unable either to find a sponsor or to pay his own way. Nevertheless, he was so assiduous and insightful in his study of foreign strands he had never visited that he was called on by royal ministers to corroborate Ralegh's accounts of what he had actually seen and to enlighten the East India Company on what its own agents had observed. Later in life came his opportunity to be an active, on-the-scene participant in one of the greatest and most significant adventures of his time, the planting in Virginia of the first permanent English settlement in America—the transplantation to the New World of the English language, the English Bible, and the English law.

Hakluyt's name is one of seven on a petition leading to the patent of 1606 for settlement in Virginia by the London Company. When preparations were under way for the voyage that carried Christopher Newport, Edward Maria Wingfield, Captain John Smith, and more than a hundred others to the founding of Virginia, a dispensation was granted the Reverend Robert Hunt and the Reverend Richard Hakluyt allowing them "full and free license" to go to Virginia and assume clerical posts without loss of their ecclesiastical positions in England.[16]

The Reverend Mr. Hunt accepted, serving the colonists bravely and generously but, perhaps, unwittingly carrying with him the typhoid bacillus. This infection, together with an inadequate diet, resulting in part from a severe drought, may have been the chief cause of the "plague" that killed so many

Jamestown settlers. But Hakluyt did not go. Why we do not know. He was now fifty-four years old—elderly by the standards of his day. Maybe he did not feel fit for physical adventuring.

Nevertheless, the decade remaining to him was filled with satisfaction and excitement. Two major enterprises for which he had labored—the colonization of Virginia and the development of East Indian trade—were well under way. And messengers from all the great seas weekly brought him tales of adventure to remake the globe.

It was appropriate that Hakluyt should have dedicated *Divers Voyages*, an early and important part of his great work, to his friend Sir Philip Sidney. For the geographer had also created a work of literature, of the imagination as well as of science. Thomas Fuller, in 1662 in his *Worthies of England*, said that "many of such useful tracts of sea adventures, which before were scattered as several ships, Mr. Hakluyt hath embodied into a fleet, divided into three squadrons, so many several volumes. . . ."[17] But there was more to the work than organizing genius. In 1852 James Anthony Froude called *Hakluyt's Voyages* "the Prose Epic of the modern English nation."[18]

18

EXPLORERS ALL

I N 1616, WHEN Richard Hakluyt's death ended his nearly four decades of marking the ocean currents and tracing the courses of navigable rivers, another Londoner began a historic series of lectures on the streams that flowed and the tides that pulsed within every human body. The speaker, William Harvey, being thirty-eight years old, had begun life about the same time that Hakluyt had commenced his researches. Harvey's findings, revealed in his presentations to the Royal College of Physicians and later in a book, were to have as revolutionary an influence in medical science as Hakluyt's had had in geography—and would be far more controversial.[1]

This man who would reverse fourteen centuries of physiology was not a commanding figure as he stood before the College of Physicians. Exceptionally short and round-faced with small eyes, he was not a stereotypical hero. His olive skin was not a help in an age when Englishmen prized blond or ruddy complexions, and when Shakespeare had to explain why he was attracted by a "dark lady." But there was dramatic force in the black brightness of his eyes and in his raven hair, and his animation compelled attention.

He already commanded considerable respect as a physician, and could have moved easily from honor to honor without exciting ire except among a few disappointed rivals. He was physician to Saint Bartholomew's Hospital; to the lord chancellor, Francis Bacon; and to King James I. Harvey's comfortable existence seems to have been threatened only by a nagging curiosity about the functions of the human heart and a great mystery concerning each person's blood supply.

Tremendous patience, as well as great ingenuity, would be required to solve the puzzle. Those who had been Harvey's fellow students might not have been surprised that he would prove ingenious enough to give the first correct answer to an ancient riddle, but probably few would have credited him with sufficient patience. Doubt would have been particularly strong among those who were with him at the University of Padua, where he went after completing six years (beginning at age fifteen) as a medical scholarship student at Cambridge. It was reported of him at the Italian university that he was "too apt to draw out his dagger upon every slight occasion."

But he was respected. His fellow Englishmen chose him as their representative on the institution's multinational council. His teacher, Fabricius ab Aquapendente, made him a member of his household.

Fabricius was one of the world's most celebrated anatomists and professors of medicine. He had studied under Gabriel Fallopius, the great anatomist who had worked with Vesalius and numbered Galileo among his patients. Fallopius had several anatomical discoveries to his credit, especially in sexual categories. Apparently he was the first person to describe the opening of the oviducts, or uterine tubes of the human female, into the abdominal cavity. He named the vagina and placenta and lent his own name to the Fallopian tubes. His discoveries convinced him that Galen, revered since the second century A.D. in Europe and the Arab world as the ultimate anatomist, was nevertheless as fallible as other men. This lesson he impressed on his own student Fabricius, who in turn conveyed it to Harvey.

No other teacher, perhaps, could have prepared the young Englishman so well for his career of discovery. In an age when many mistakes in human anatomy were made or perpetuated because of a scarcity of human cadavers in good condition, Fabricius had built a renowned anatomical theater. It was a theater in two senses of the word—a hall with tiered seats for witnessing demonstrations and listening to lectures, and a center of dramatic activity. Galleries encircling a pit rose six stories, each provided with a balustrade on which students could lean forward and look down to behold a scene in weird chiaroscuro, a pale corpse highlighted amid the gloom by the light of candelabra held aloft by some of their classmates. The lessons learned were memorable. One thing that made an influential impression on Harvey was Fabricius' discovery that small valves in the veins of human limbs regulated the flow of blood to a single direction.

The young Englishman's professional good fortune continued when he returned home. He married the daughter of the late Queen Elizabeth's physician, became a fellow of the Royal College of Physicians, became a lecturer to the college in 1615, and, as we have seen, the following year startled his auditors with an exposition of his revolutionary ideas about the heart and the circulation of blood. He was challenging Galen, still a risky practice, and he was using his old teacher's discovery about the veins of the arms and legs to bolster an audacious theory.

Galen had made an important discovery about the arteries. We are so accustomed to the idea that they carry blood that we are likely to think of it as self-evident. But when the ancient Greek first propounded this theory he was contradicting such established medical authorities as the great Alexandrian physicians Erasistratus and Herophilus. Like Aristotle, they recognized that blood flowed through the veins, but they held that it did not pass through the arteries. These tubes were reserved for the passage of *pneuma*, or "refined air," as Plato had maintained. It was generally assumed that they conveyed the "humors," or spirits, that when cooperating properly kept the body and mind healthy.

Like Aristotle and Hippocrates before him, Galen said that the living and the dead were distinguished from each other by the living's possession of *innate* heat. Heat from the sun or from fire could be transmitted to a dead body, but only with the living was the warmth innate. This heat was centered in the heart. Only the air of the lungs cooled the heart sufficiently to prevent self-destruction by the heat that it produced.

Galen and his successors had referred to the "circulation" of the blood, but they implied only general movement, not a specifically circular motion. Most believed that blood movement was inconsistent in direction. Taking advantage of the transparency of shrimp to examine their bodily processes, and dissecting living oysters, frogs, fish, pigs, and dogs, as well as human cadavers, and comparing his own findings with those recorded by Italian anatomists, Harvey gained unparalleled knowledge of the cardiovascular system. He studied the blood vessels of fetuses, and also compared those of healthy and diseased subjects to determine what purposes were served by the blood vessels.

By Harvey's time, it was generally conceded that the heart was a working, not a passive, organ. But physicians were not agreed upon the heart's intervals of work and rest. Was it working when it expanded or when it contracted? Many thought it was working when it expanded. Wasn't it obvious that it was putting forth effort when it swelled to its maximum size? Harvey established that the heart was a hardworking muscle that worked when it contracted. He posited that this contraction forced blood through the vessels.

He soon was ready with an explanation of the process. As the pulse coincided with the contraction of the heart, it was evident that the ventricles squeezed the blood they contained into the aorta and pulmonary artery. The pulse registered the filling of the arteries.

Galen had noted the septum that divided the heart into separate chambers but believed that it was sufficiently porous to permit the movement of blood from one chamber to the other. Harvey determined that the septum was not porous. Then, in a tremendous advance, he rightly conceived that, as the heart pumped, all the blood in the right ventricle was forced into the lungs and by way of the pulmonary veins to the left ventricle, from which it was then squeezed into the arteries. And from the arteries it was pushed back into the right ventricle. The loop was continuous, and the same fluid filled both the arteries and the veins.

Harvey developed more sophisticated refinements of his theory. But most of his contemporaries were not ready for them. Some were badly shaken by his assertion that the heart and not the liver was the organ that propelled the blood. Aristotle had emphatically said otherwise.

Harvey himself described his findings as "the exact opposite to the commonly accepted views":

The general belief is that the ventricles are being distended and the heart being filled with blood at the time when the apex is striking the chest and one can feel its beat from the outside. The contrary is, however, correct, namely, that the heart empties during its contraction.

Hence the heart movement which is commonly thought to be its dias-
tole [expansion] is in fact its systole [contraction].

After a technical explanation of systole's role in squeezing blood into the arteries and causing them to expand, he gave a beautifully simple illustration: "An
idea of this generalized pulsation of the arteries consequent upon the expulsion
of blood into them from the left ventricle can be given by blowing into a glove,
and producing simultaneous increase in volume of all its fingers." He explained
that "the pulse which we feel in the arteries is nothing but the inthrust of blood
into them from the heart."

In spite of some notable exceptions, such as Immanuel Kant, it seems reasonable to say that a genius for simplification is a generic quality of genius.
Certainly this is true in Harvey's case.

The Englishman credited scientists of other nations and times with some
of the ideas that helped him to his conclusions. He paid tribute especially to
Realdo Colombo, the great sixteenth-century professor of anatomy at Padua,
Pisa, and Rome. One of Vesalius' students, Colombo succeeded him in Padua
and then, to his master's great distress, became one of the chief critics of the
older man's interpretations. Though Colombo did not anticipate the full pattern of circulation that Harvey discovered, he made the important discovery
that blood flowed from the heart through the lungs and returned to the heart.
Also, the Italian determined that arteries dilated when the heart contracted. By
Harvey's own testimony, after many dissections, until he learned these facts
from Colombo's writings, he was "almost tempted" to agree with one of
his predecessors that "the motion of the heart was only to be comprehended
by God."

Aware of Vesalius' finding that the septum between the ventricles was complete and of Colombo's two major discoveries, Harvey combined these facts
with Fabricius' discovery of valves in the veins of the limbs and with his own
observations in vivisection, and envisioned a full circulatory system.

There were intervening steps. Harvey determined the volume of blood
passing from the veins into the arteries. He considered the size of the ventricles
of the heart in light of his conviction that "Nature, who does nothing purposelessly, would not purposelessly have given these vessels such large size." These
considerations convinced him that the common assumption that the body's
blood was the accumulation of juices from food eaten and drinks consumed
was a mistake. "So great a quantity," he said, "cannot be furnished from those
things we eat." He concluded that the blood filling the arteries flowed back
again into the veins. How was this possible? Conceivably, only by means of a
consistent circular movement.

The Dutch naturalist Anton van Leeuwenhoek, born sixteen years after
Harvey enunciated his theory, would observe the capillaries through a microscope of his own invention. But the Englishman had no such instrument. Yet he
confidently posited the existence of "admirable artifices" serving the capillary
function.

Harvey wisely cited scraps from Galen and Aristotle in support of aspects of his theory, even though better evidence was available from other sources—better, that is, from every standpoint except audience psychology. He was scrupulously fair in acknowledging valuable help from the writings of Renaissance Italians. But his principal evidence was derived from his own dissections. He did not disguise this fact, but cleverly summoned tradition in support of bold discovery. "I would say with Fabricius," he asserted, "let all reasoning be silent when experience gainsays its conclusion."

Nevertheless, his teachings in lectures and in his book excited the disbelief and animosity that he had anticipated. Respected physicians and anatomists were slow to join his camp. Not until the nineteenth century did incontrovertible physical evidence exist for all his major conclusions about the circulation of the blood, and only then did some scientists accept them. But before his death at seventy-nine, his theory was accepted by leading anatomists throughout Europe, and he was elected president of the Royal College of Physicians.

In his medical practice, Harvey made practical use of information gained in his study of circulation. Probably the most dramatic instance was when he made a large tumor wither away by tying it off from the arteries that furnished its blood supply.

Although his discovery of the circulatory system was by far Harvey's greatest contribution to knowledge, he also made significant observations in generation and embryology. His ideas were formulated in a broad context relating not only to all aspects of the medical profession but to many other aspects of human culture. He was a favorite intellectual companion of Thomas Hobbes, whom one is tempted to call a giant of the Elizabethan afterglow, except for the realization that there must be a limit to the stretching of chronological boundaries. Harvey was as aware of the currents coursing through the body politic as of those circulating through the individual human body. His awareness of developments in so many fields outside his own particular province, together with his familiarity with the professional literature of preceding centuries, stimulated his analogical creativity. As a result, he produced a seventy-two-page book that changed for the foreseeable future the sciences of anatomy and zoology, and every branch of medical science. The qualities that made him one of the greatest figures in medical history also made him one of the most representative figures of a great era.

Though Francis Bacon and William Harvey towered above all other scientists produced by Elizabethan England, the age gave birth to some who, in periods of only normal creativity, might have been foremost. One of the greatest of these was William Gilbert.[2] Just before his death at fifty-nine in the same year as Queen Elizabeth's, he was generally regarded as the principal scientist in the kingdom. He was her personal physician, but is remembered today for his part in the intellectual ferment of experiment that characterized her reign.

His most important findings are disclosed in his treatise on magnetism, published in 1600. The work includes the record of his experiments with magnets and magnetic bodies. But as with Harvey and other Elizabethans, the breadth of his concerns provided a context suggesting broad, even cosmic, applications. I. Bernard Cohen has called Gilbert's *De magnete* "a work of tremendous importance not merely for the actual scientific discoveries which Gilbert recorded, but also for the progress marked by his clear statement of the scientific method."[3]

Interested, like many before him, in the north-south direction of the magnetic needle and in the mystery of its dipping, he conceived the idea that the entire earth was in effect one great magnet. When the German astronomer Johannes Kepler read Gilbert's theory he thought that this same magnetism could account for the movements of the planets, indeed for all celestial movements. In explaining his view, Kepler concluded that the "celestial machine" was a "clockwork."[4] The term would gain wide usage in the seventeenth and eighteenth centuries. The intellectual line of descent to Newton is clear.

The same Thomas Harriot who was scientific adviser to Ralegh's Roanoke colony and whose "Brief and True Report" of the new land was reprinted in *Hakluyt's Voyages* had several even greater scientific accomplishments. Subsidized by the Earl of Northumberland in those days when some English nobles, like their Italian Renaissance counterparts, were proud to finance the works of scholars, he achieved a lasting international reputation as both a mathematician and astronomer.[5]

Harriot wrote an algebra text that improved notation, using for the first time the signs > (greater than) and < (less than). Even more significantly, in the same work he revealed the relation between coefficients and roots in a way that advanced the theory of equations. His mathematical work had further fruition as a result of its influence on John Wallis, who in the next generation systematized the use of formulas. Harriot's contributions resulted from the action of a venturesome imagination on a store of learning from such earlier and foreign sources as the writings of France's François Vieta, the great correlator of algebra with geometry and trigonometry.

As an astronomer, Harriot studied sunspots and comets. He built a telescope in 1609 at the same time that Galileo was making his more famous one. Apparently at least one, and maybe three, Dutch spectacle makers had a lead of some months on both of them.

Such was the excitement of scientific discovery in the Elizabethan and early Jacobean periods that it attracted colorful adventurers from other fields. Though some of these people were far removed from the dispassionate approach favored by many modern scientists, they nevertheless made significant contributions. John Dee (1527–1608) was a Cambridge graduate who became a foundation fellow of his alma mater, lectured to other scholars in Brussels and Paris, and became warden of Manchester College. Queen Elizabeth depended upon his knowledge of mathematics, navigation, and the physical sciences for hydrographical and geographical reports on newly discovered territories during the great period of maritime expansion. But she also asked him to draw upon his skills as an astrologer to help her choose the day for her coronation. His writings on the particular uses of geometry stimulated a renaissance of mathematics in England. He called for adoption of the Gregorian calendar in his country and made some of the necessary calculations for transition. Yet this man of solid learning and practical accomplishments had enough of an air of mystery and magic to be tried by the Star Chamber for practicing sorcery on Queen Mary. To the judge's credit as well as Dee's, he was acquitted.

The same excitement created by experiments in literature and science attended developments in other fields. Architecture is a prime example. Elizabeth's nobles vied with each other in the building of palaces whose long galleries were of royal proportions. The terms *architect* and *architector* both came into use in 1563. For a while it was difficult to predict which form would prevail, but it was clear that the builder who was also a skilled designer would be recognized as a professional.

Born in Smithfield ten years after this auspicious date was Inigo Jones, a boy who would raise architecture in England to new levels of admiration.[6] Sometime between the ages of seventeen and twenty, he went to Italy at the expense of the earl of Rutland to study printing, and there learned a great deal about both architecture and the theater. In 1605 he was called to the court of James I as a designer of costumes and scenery for masques. Like Leonardo da Vinci and Ben Jonson, here was a genius using his talents to embellish amateur theatricals.

After five years of these transient productions, he had the opportunity to erect walls and create sets that would outlive generations of actors in the most earnest scenes of real life. Early in this period of creating buildings, he studied architecture on a nineteen-month tour of Europe. He was deeply interested in what he saw in Rome, Naples, and Venice, but utterly fascinated with the buildings of a less celebrated city—Vicenza. In this city and its suburbs were the works of one of the most influential architects in world history, Andrea Palladio.

Well versed in Vitruvius' writings and a keen student of the monuments of ancient Roman architecture, Palladio in the sixteenth century gave northern Italy the most exciting new domestic and ecclesiastical architecture in the Mediterranean world. Influenced by the Florentine creations and remodelings of Leone Alberti, he designed facades featuring the interpenetration of different orders and pediments. His work was classical, yet breathed the spirit of the sixteenth century at least as much as that of earlier times.

Jones borrowed from Palladio not only certain architectural devices but also the inspiration to adapt classicism to express the ethos of his own century and his own country. The influence of his pleasing designs was augmented by his prestige as surveyor of the king's works under both James I and Charles I. Partly because the ornate splendor of Italian baroque, which had captured southern Europe, was offensive to English Protestantism, the simpler lines of Jones' buildings were welcomed as an alternative. Architectural historian Norbert Lynton notes, "In England, Palladianism was imposed on a public accustomed to a *mélange* of Tudor and northern Renaissance elements by one man, Inigo Jones."[7] Henry Armand Millon always maintained that Jones had "virtually singlehandedly changed the course of English architecture."

Jones' greatest masterpiece was the Whitehall banqueting house in London. Besides being an esthetic delight, it was the first classical revival public building not only in London but in all of northern Europe. Of course there must have been many considerable talents lost between the cracks of the age's class system, but Inigo Jones, son of an obscure cloth maker, is striking evidence of the opportunities awaiting genius in his time if a deserving youngster caught the attention of one or more of the eager patrons then subsidizing the arts. His success was compounded of native ability, thorough grounding in the traditions of his profession and related fields, and bold venturing to express the culture of his own time and place. Few individual architects in the history of the world have exerted so strong an influence in their nations, or for that matter in half a continent.

English achievements in music more than matched those in architecture. The years from the defeat of the Spanish Armada in 1588 to the end of James I's reign in 1625 are known as the nation's musical, as well as literary, "Golden Age." They produced no composers comparable in stature to such literary titans as Spenser, Shakespeare, or Marlowe, but they did produce William Byrd,[8] often considered England's greatest native composer of all time, and many other creative musicians of lasting international reputations. In fact, the literature and music of the period were intimately connected. Some of Shakespeare's most appealing lyrics derived much of their charm for contemporary audiences from their musical settings. The same was true of songs in the works of other English playwrights.

Just as impressive as the flowering of talent among professional musicians in the Elizabethan Age is the remarkable surge in amateur musicianship. A cataract of sheet music poured from the presses to meet the public demand. Songs introduced in the theater were immediately played on the lutes of young law students and soon on the harpsichords of country houses. In many well-furnished homes, an impressive chest of viols was almost as necessary as ornate chests of linens. The virginal was perhaps the most popular keyboard instrument, and the Virgin Queen was herself one of the realm's most enthusiastic virginalists. Just as nineteenth- and early-twentieth-century America was known for its barbershop quartets, England became a land of barbershop lutists. The ability to play a musical instrument, which in many societies has been a social requirement for young ladies, was then expected of both sexes. A nation of performers comprised an enthusiastic, and in part quite knowledgeable, audience for the suddenly expanding ranks of native composers.

In the early years of Elizabeth's reign, but especially after 1588, Italian madrigals became the favorite musical form. Not surprisingly, composers seeking responsive audiences catered to this taste. At first they turned out quite acceptable examples of the foreign genre largely indistinguishable from the Italian product. But then native genius asserted itself in the production of English madrigals subtly different from their Mediterranean counterparts. One distinguishing feature, their lighter and brighter tone, soon caused them to win greater favor with English audiences than the more somber Italian creations.

One of the most talented of the English madrigalists, and probably as popular as any, was Thomas Morley. The ablest, though far from the most prolific, was John Wilbye. His greatest forte, however, was abstract composition. Morley and Wilbye improved the quality of their works by studying Italian models, but also drew inspiration from the tradition of English part-songs and adapted imported styles to express the ethos of their own society. The boldest innovator among the English madrigalists was the brilliant Thomas Weelkes.

Two other English composers, William Byrd and Orlando Gibbons, composed excellent madrigals but won enduring fame primarily for other kinds of compositions. Byrd had been Morley's teacher and he also became Gibbons'.

Byrd was an exemplar of the versatility in Renaissance Italy and Elizabethan England that produced men adept in both business and the arts. Together with his friend Thomas Tallis, a distinguished musician and composer of an earlier generation, he was granted in 1575 a twenty-year monopoly of English music publishing. This patent included the printing, sale, and importation of music and even the printing of music paper. That he should have been so favored by Protestant royalty may seem remarkable in view of the fact that he was a lifelong Catholic of unquestioned devotion. A broad tolerance was accorded genius. Byrd happily composed both Catholic masses and motets and Protestant hymns. Phenomenally prolific as he was, his church music is even more distinguished for quality than for quantity. Music critics generally agree that in this genre he has had few equals—perhaps none but Rome's Giovanni Palestrina, Munich's Roland de Lassus, and Madrid's Luis de Victoria.

But even this accomplishment is no complete measure of the scope of his achievement. He was a pioneer with the anthem consisting of alternating solo and chorus. His compositions for virginal and organ, at least 150 in all, greatly advanced English keyboard style, and those for viol consort introduced the next dominant genre in English music, the fantasia. Some of his fantasias are deemed comparable to the music of Bach. Thus he was a powerful creative force in secular as well as sacred music. And he wrote for every instrument then in use except the ubiquitous lute. Maybe this medium was too available. For no instrument did he provide more beautiful passages than for the human voice. All in all, few composers have worked so audaciously within a superficially conservative frame.

Byrd's influence in the decades following his death in 1623 was boosted by the activities of his young associate Orlando Gibbons (1583–1625). Though not altogether as great a composer as Byrd, Gibbons carried on the older man's work in fantasia and actually excelled it. This accomplishment has caused him to be called "the last of the Elizabethans." Some might say that John Dowland (d. 1626) was equally deserving of the title. Few works for the viol consort have excelled his *Seven Passionate Pavans*.

Altogether, the Golden Age of English music, both international and indigenous in inspiration, at once traditional and innovative in execution, is one of history's notable expressions of a creative society.

Historic advances were made in another art during the same period—one involving the "genius for compromise" often claimed as a special attribute of the English-speaking peoples. This was the art of law and government. One of the half-dozen most important figures in the entire history of English law was Sir Edward Coke.[9] He was far more than what we have so far seen him to be in these pages, the nemesis of two other heroes of the Elizabethan Age—Ralegh and Bacon.

Stubborn, resourceful, and domineering, he owed his influence as much to larger-than-life personality traits as to his unrivaled knowledge of English law. His rock-solid greatness, looming through all the pettiness that occasionally beclouded his reputation, had its foundation in incorruptibility and an almost religious dedication to the sanctity of the common law.

Admitted to the bar at the age of twenty-six after education at Cambridge and six years at the Inner Temple, he quickly moved forward in his profession, propelled by his own brilliance and pugnacity and assisted by the patronage of Lord Burghley, then Elizabeth's principal minister. Elected to Parliament in 1589, he became solicitor general three years later. The next year, only four years after entering the House of Commons, he became its Speaker. In this office, he adroitly steered the members away from discussion of ecclesiastical matters, a policy perfectly in accord with Her Majesty's wishes.

At this time, as we have seen, his ambitions collided with those of Francis Bacon. Rivalry led to antipathy, exacerbated by temperamental differences between the cautious Bacon and the brusque and impetuous Coke. When both were candidates for attorney general in 1594, Coke defeated his opponent and then thwarted Bacon's efforts to obtain the office of solicitor general as a consolation prize. At least, Coke appeared to be responsible, and Bacon never doubted that he was.

The rivalry became even more personal when Coke, four months after his first wife's death, married Lady Elizabeth Hatton, the very woman that Bacon had been courting. If Bacon alone had believed that Coke had chosen his new mate chiefly to embarrass his political rival, we could attribute this opinion to paranoia. But surprisingly enough, it was the general belief of Englishmen in circles of power that this was the case. As might be expected, the bride was resentful and miserable. Coke's home may have been his castle, but it was no bower of bliss.

He began publishing in 1600 the law reports that would help generations of judges reach objective decisions, and in the same year prosecuted the Earl of Essex with unbecoming zeal. He was equally zealous in prosecuting Ralegh in 1603 and the accused in the Gunpowder Plot two years later.

In 1601 he had received from Queen Elizabeth the favor of a royal visit to his home in Stoke Pogis. A more tangible reward came in 1606 when her successor, James I, made him chief justice of the Court of Common Pleas. Coke had been eager to execute royal commands when they coincided with his own sense of justice, but he soon proved that he was no sycophant. He opposed the king's claim of the right to levy export-and-import taxes and waged a three-year struggle over the royally favored effort to exempt the church from the jurisdiction of common law courts, eventually opposing the move by both archbishop and king to give such jurisdiction to the more easily controlled Court of High Commission. From the bench he ruled against the king's presumed authority to govern by fiat—to make law by proclamation. Such behavior seemed reckless to many. The irascible James cherished theories of the divine right of kings. He was infuriated by Coke's statement, in asserting the supremacy of the common law, that "the King in his own person cannot adjudge any case."

Advised by Bacon, James tempered his wrath and tried to buy Coke's support by appointing him chief justice of the King's Bench, making him a privy councillor, and elevating him to become the first bearer of the title of lord chief justice of England. Well aware of the royal purpose, Coke reluctantly accepted appointment to the King's Bench. But neither this office nor other royally conferred honors blunted his integrity.

His actions were increasingly provocative. Instead of being absorbed into the King's Bench and neutralized by his fellow justices, he was soon dominating its proceedings as effectively as he had those of the Court of Common Pleas. When James, on Bacon's advice, sought to circumvent this domination by consulting separately with each judge, Coke protested the practice. He also maintained vigorously and consistently that the common law was supreme over all individuals and institutions in England except Parliament, which represented the will of the people at any given moment. He challenged head-on Lord Chancellor Ellesmere's attempt to thwart a common law decision. And in the trial of the poisoners of Sir Thomas Overbury, a poet believed to know more court secrets than he could healthily hold, Coke interlarded his comments from the bench with ominous hints of dark doings in high places.

Finally he collided head-on with James. At issue was the king's right to grant commendams (permission to hold more than one benefice at the same time). It had become a favorite way of rewarding faithful courtiers and their families. Yet benefices were often called "livings," and many thought they should be just that, sufficient payment to provide a guaranteed living for one man and his household. James ordered that the court not deal with this matter until he had told them what he wanted done. Instead, Coke and his fellow justices proceeded to act in a case involving this claimed right. Summoned before king and Council, they were instructed to obey without question. Though his fellow justices buckled, Coke answered enigmatically that he "would do what an honest and just judge should do."

After that, as we have seen, Bacon prodded the Privy Council to charge Coke with mishandling a bond, interfering with the Chancery Court, and disregarding the king's instructions regarding commendams. The first charge was a technical matter never proved, and of little consequence if it had been. If the other two were crimes, and they were in the context of Stuart monarchy, Coke was indubitably guilty. He was forbidden to hold circuit courts, and was commanded to correct the "errors" in his *Reports*, the proudest products of his legal scholarship. A few months later, he was dismissed from office.

Coke's next action was both injudicious and unjust. Apparently seeking a powerful ally, he offered his fourteen-year-old daughter in marriage to the duke of Buckingham's brother. We already know about this matter from Bacon's action in abetting the mother in hiding the child. We know that Coke kidnapped her and forced her, despite her lamentations, to marry the man to whom he had promised her. The youth of the bride was not unusual for that day, nor was parental selection of a daughter's husband, but Coke's coercion was cruel by any standards. No matter how often he told himself that he was giving her a great opportunity in spite of herself, rationalization could not erase the wrong.

The surprising thing is that Coke, who though often blunt could be quite appealing when it served his purposes, returned in a few months to both the Privy Council and the powerful Star Chamber. He even entered Parliament, ostensibly as a member of the king's party, but soon demonstrated that the independence of his earlier years was undiminished. He vociferously opposed Prince Charles' contemplated marriage to a Catholic princess from Spain. With zeal and zest, he helped to draw up the charges that ousted his old rival Bacon from office just as he himself had once been removed through Bacon's efforts.

After this petty game of revenge, he concentrated his energies upon one of the noblest works ever undertaken by a member of England's Parliament. He spoke eloquently for parliamentary liberty, and paid for the privilege by serving nine months in prison. But at the end of that time he had to be released. No dishonesty could be proved against him. Sometimes unjust, he was nevertheless always incorruptible. With his matchless knowledge of English legal precedent, the seventy-six-year-old man formulated the bill of liberties that became the Petition of Right. Many people played prominent roles through the generations in transforming the Magna Carta of 1215 from a document certifying the rights and privileges of barons plagued by a tyrannical king into a guarantee of the freedoms of all the English people. But in those centuries of parliamentary history, no individual played a more prominent part than Coke.

As presented to Charles I by the Parliament of 1628, the Petition of Right written by Coke set forth four major principles. No taxes could be levied without the consent of the people's representatives in Parliament assembled. No subject might be imprisoned without being informed of the charge against him. The Crown could not forcibly quarter troops in civilian households. Martial law could not be imposed in time of peace.

The first of these principles would come to be summarized as "no taxation without representation." Though sometimes neglected, it would resurface repeatedly in English history. It would appear in England's oldest American colony in 1652 when popularly chosen representatives[10] of Northampton County, Virginia, asserted the prohibition's applicability to a Commonwealth government under Cromwell as well as to earlier ones under a royal sovereign. Colonel Thomas Johnson gave eloquent expression to this Northampton Protest in a historic oration. More than a century later, as Americans moved toward revolution against the crown, the cry was revived as "No taxation without representation."[11]

The second principle of the Petition of Right was a reiteration of the right of habeas corpus, asserted as early as the fourteenth century and formalized in an act of 1679. It, too, was cherished by England's colonists in North America and became prominent in the rhetoric of the American Revolution. Subsequently it was written into the Constitution of the United States. By extension of the original meaning, habeas corpus is now frequently cited in appealing, to a federal court, a criminal conviction in a state court that the petitioner claims violated his or her constitutional rights.

Few practices not obviously inimical have made civilians feel more threatened than the billeting in their homes of armed and uniformed agents of the government. The quartering of British troops, particularly in Boston households, was one of the most hated practices on the eve of the American Revolution. One item in the catalog of complaints against the king in the Declaration of Independence is the charge of "quartering large bodies of troops among us."

The Petition of Right was a creative production as well as a work of scholarship. Indeed, some portions were more creative than scholarly. The history upon which Coke called in support of the principles enunciated was colored by legend. He interpreted retroactively the intent of the framers of Magna Carta and other milestone documents. As a result, his boldest assertions of individual liberty were not thrust into the world in new-born nakedness but clothed in the majesty of tradition.

Conscious that he had crowned his career with his greatest work, Coke retired from Parliament at the end of the 1628 session, in which the Petition of Right was presented. The old lion lived in peace for six more years. He didn't have to roar anymore. A mere growl was sufficient to discourage interference. But when the lion was dead, officials seized his papers, among them his will, which was never again found.

Whatever his intended disposition of his material possessions, Coke left the world a priceless legacy. Though his greatest gift was the Petition of Right, his *Reports* alone would have been sufficient to guarantee him a high place in the history of jurisprudence. They are more than the name implies; they are commentaries as well as records. In them Coke has drawn deeply on his profound knowledge of the law, but has made medieval jurists support him in ways that would have astonished them. He has made the letter of their law bolster the Elizabethan and Jacobean spirit of innovation. A nineteenth-century successor, Chief Justice William Best, once observed, "I am afraid we should get rid of a great deal of what is considered law in Westminster if what Lord Coke says without authority is not law. He was one of the most eminent lawyers that ever presided as a judge in any court of justice."

Among the most influential of his publications was a volume of *Institutes*, commonly known as *Coke upon Littleton*, published in 1628, the same year that gave birth to the Petition of Right. This, too, was a work addressing the needs of present and future but richly rooted in tradition. The volume consisted of the famous book *Tenures*, the work of the great fifteenth-century jurist Sir Thomas Littleton. Coke was generous in his tribute to this source, calling it "the ornament of the Common Law, and the most perfect and absolute work that ever was written in any human science."[12] Harvard scholar Eugene Wambaugh wrote in 1901, "*Coke upon Littleton*, unrivaled among law books for vast and various learning, has a curious place in the general history of literature, for it presents the most conspicuous example of a masterpiece upon a masterpiece—much as if the plays of Shakespeare were entwined about *The Canterbury Tales*."[13] Littleton's work had had about seventy printings before Coke updated it and enlarged its usefulness. In its new form as *Coke upon Littleton*, it had twenty-six printings by 1903, the four hundredth anniversary of Littleton's original publication.[14] From 1628 until well into the nineteenth century, it was the principal text for law students in both Great Britain and North America. Many, like nineteen-year-old Thomas Jefferson, who rejoiced that he had left "old Coke" behind when he returned home for holidays and called him "an old dull scoundrel," lived to value the work as a reference and from a position of eminence recommend it to others.[15]

Coke was often selfish and egotistical and sometimes a bully, but at least one part of his soul remained inviolate, reverently dedicated to the common law. Few people have left so precious a bequest to succeeding generations.

One of Coke's contemporaries had even more direct influence than he on laws in the New World. Sir Edwin Sandys[16] has been hailed by at least one prominent historian as "the father of colonial self-government"[17] and as the "founder-in-chief of representative government in America."[18] Certainly his position is unique among the builders of America. He was the principal author of the charter under which Virginia originated representative government in the New World, and he was also a sponsor of the settlement at Plymouth. He was a lifelong student of government and a political philosopher of note—one of those splendid Elizabethan-Jacobean characters at home in court, council, and library, adventuring in both ideas and practical affairs.

Sandys was born of the establishment but nurtured in dissent. The conflicts and special insights resulting from these circumstances shaped the exciting life that began with his birth in Worcestershire in December 1561. He was the second son of the bishop of Worcester, and was given his father's first name. The bishop's life had not been an uneventful climb, rung by rung, up the ladder of ecclesiastical preferment. He had once been master of Catharine Hall, Cambridge, but had been removed from office about four years after his appointment. Nevertheless, in the very year of his removal he was named to the much higher office of vice chancellor of Cambridge University. But he risked his life in support of the brilliant but reckless Lady Jane Grey, who reigned as England's queen for nine days in 1553 before being imprisoned and eventually beheaded. The senior Sandys was himself imprisoned, first in the Tower and later in Marshalsea. When released, he wisely fled to the Continent. But he returned to England six years later, was quickly made a bishop, and had held that position for two years when his namesake was born.

When young Edwin was nine years old, his father became bishop of London, and the family moved to the capital, where the boy was enrolled in the celebrated Merchant Taylors' School. The father had already had an impressive scholarly reputation as a translator of the Bishops' Bible, and was capable of providing considerable extracurricular intellectual stimulation for his son. When young Edwin was fifteen, his father became archbishop of York.

Edwin studied at Corpus Christi College, Oxford. Though he never took holy orders, he became acting dean of York. Prospects were good that this scion of England's second highest prelate would become just another privileged beneficiary of the system. His duties in the north were not too strenuous to prevent his obtaining his M.A. from Oxford the following year. At the age of twenty-five he won a seat in Parliament and at the age of twenty-eight obtained a bachelor of civil law degree also from Oxford and entered the Middle Temple to prepare for a career at the bar. After three terms in the House of Commons, he traveled on the Continent for six years. It was pretty late for so extensive a grand tour. Was he becoming a dilettante?

Far from it! In Venice he had met Fra Paolo Sarpi, a friar nine years his senior, a remarkable polymath in the tradition of his country's Renaissance. Theologian, historian, scientist, statesman, Sarpi crowded into his seventy-one years accomplishments ranging from service as procurator general of his order in Rome and counselor of state to the Venetian republic all the way to internationally celebrated experiments in physics and anatomical research. He was credited with discovery of the nature of contractility of the iris. But he was most famous of all for the theological writings that eventually caused him to be excommunicated.

Whether or not Sandys had already conceived the idea of producing a monumental survey of religion in Europe in his time, the meeting with Sarpi at least increased his enthusiasm for the project. Furthermore, the friar's advice was of great help to Sandys in his preparatory studies and in the organization of his material.

Having labored to complete his treatise, "Europe speculum," Sandys decided not to publish it, at least until a time of greater tolerance. If he had been inspired to emulate his Italian friend's industry and scholarship, he was also mindful of the persecution that the friar had brought upon himself.

Several years after returning to England, Sandys resigned his ecclesiastical sinecure and seems to have concentrated on both political philosophy and practical politics. In 1603 he arrived at a critical point in his career. He was member for Stockbridge in the House of Commons, where his ability and industry in committee work had gained wide respect. This was the first English Parliament of James I, and Sandys got off to a good start with the new monarch. He journeyed to Scotland, where James had been ruling as James VI, and accompanied the king to his new capital of London.

James was pudgy, awkward, and physically handicapped in speech by a literally unwieldy tongue, which also caused him to drool. His appearance contrasted with the bold features and neat mustache and beard of Sandys, whose face would have delighted a Rubens or a Van Dyck. But intellectually they had more in common than a casual observer might have supposed. James' mind, like some other narrow instruments, was also a sharp one. His head was full of curious knowledge apart from the rich treasures of scholasticism that it held. The king and Sandys appear to have become good companions by the time they reached London. Proof of royal favor came soon when Sandys was knighted by his sovereign.

In the same month, he received evidence of the respect of his colleagues in the House of Commons. He became chairman of the Commons committee appointed to confer with the Lords with a view to abolishing the court of wards, feudal tenures, and purveyance. This court was a surviving stronghold of the old feudalism. Aside from the obvious opportunities for abuses of power inherent in decisions on wards and feudal tenures, purveyance provided the opportunity for royalty to purchase supplies for its own household at its own valuation. Sir Edwin, eager for abolition, was apparently the sole author of his committee's report. Not surprisingly, hereditary peers were opposed to the proposal and defeated it in the upper house.

Sandys had demonstrated his concern for rights important to his colleagues but had not persisted to the point of angering his king. By adroitness he might have so balanced his relationships with Crown and Commons as to attain one of the most powerful positions in the realm. He accepted chairmanship of a special investigating committee to study business conditions. Even so, it was still possible for this subtle-minded man to compromise in a way that would not cripple his political future. But Sir Edwin emerged as a vigorous advocate of open trade and a stubborn foe of monopolies.

His reputation for dangerous thinking was increased in 1605 when, despite his vigilance, a pirated copy of his book manuscript was published as *A Relation of the State of Religion.* Sandys himself secured an order condemning the book to be burned, but in 1629 it was reprinted at the Hague and eventually circulated in Dutch, French, and Italian.

In 1607 he stirred new controversy by demanding that all prisoners be allowed benefit of counsel. Horror-stricken politicians called his move "an attempt to shake the cornerstone of the law." In the same session, Sir Edwin carried a motion providing for the regular keeping of the journal of the House of Commons—a hitherto unprecedented procedure. It would be harder to retreat from positions officially recorded.

In the next few years, Sandys grew in the esteem of his colleagues in the Commons, but his frequent talk of rights antagonized the king. In 1613, however, Francis Bacon—who knew intellect when he saw it and was also well acquainted with compromise—reported to James that this very bright M.P. had separated himself from the opposition faction and could be quite useful. Evidently to cement Sir Edwin's loyalty, the king granted him a moiety of the manor of Northbourne in Kent.

Returned to Parliament in the same year, Sandys was expected to be a moderating force in the Commons. Great was the astonishment, therefore, when in the first days of the new session he not only attacked pending royally sponsored legislation but also urged that grievances presented to the preceding Parliament be referred to the Committee on Petitions.

His most conspicuous service was as the dominant member of a committee "to consider imposition." He presented the committee's report and in that connection on May 21, 1613 delivered one of the most remarkable speeches in English parliamentary history. The origin of every monarchy, he said, lay in election. The people gave their consent to the king's authority only with the clear understanding that there were "certain reciprocal conditions" which "neither King nor people could violate with impunity." Even those souls so radical or so stolid as not to be shaken by these sentiments were rocked by another assertion, that a monarch who pretended to rule by title other than such a mutual contract might be required to relinquish his throne whenever there was sufficient force to compel his abdication.

The indignation of the Lords may be imagined, but it was nothing compared to the wrath of James. Sandys himself must not have been surprised when, upon the dissolution of Parliament seventeen days later, he was summoned before the royal Council to answer for his statements in the House of Commons. The charges against him were dismissed, but he was not a truly free man. He was ordered not to venture beyond the limits of London without official permission, and to be prepared to give bonds for his appearance whenever demanded. It is a wonder that James let him off this easily. The divine right monarch was so upset by the sentiments voiced by this rebellious House of Commons that he did not convoke another session for more than six years.

In the boldness and sweep of his claims, Sir Edwin was far ahead of his time. He enunciated the social contract theory seventy-six years before publication of John Locke's *Two Treatises of Government*, farther still ahead of the ruminations of Rousseau. Sandys even preceded Hobbes' and, by a dozen years, Grotius' great works on the subject.

Pioneer though he was, Sandys did not pull the doctrine out of thin air. He had combined with his studies of English law wide readings in political philosophy drawn from other countries and other times. Such a theory is implied in some of the writings of Cicero and of medieval Christian philosophers. Contractarian ideas surfaced in French religious wars of the latter half of the sixteenth century and among Dutch rebels against Spanish domination during the same period. It is almost certain that Sandy's survey of the state of religion in Europe played a part, for harried Protestants on the Continent and badgered Catholics in England were appealing to contractarian theories of justice.

These predecessors take nothing away from Sandys. He is to be praised for forging from disparate elements a new instrument for English liberty. Before the end of Sandys' own century, an English Parliament—that of 1689—would charge another King James with "breaking the original contract betwixt King and people."

A more immediate effect of Sandys' "radical" activities was felt in England's colonies, and in the next century it would prove of even greater significance than many major events in the home island. When King James refused to convoke Parliament for more than six years, he deprived Sandys of his principal occupation. This able man then channeled his great energies into the work of colonization.

He had already been active in the field. On March 9, 1607, James had appointed him to the Supreme Council for Virginia, a board seated in England that supervised from afar the operations of colonial government under another council functioning in Virginia. In 1609 Sir Edwin had helped to obtain for the colony a new charter that on its face seemed to tighten royal control but actually provided for less autocratic government. In 1612 he helped to secure another charter that, while continuing the governor and colonial council of Virginia, vested supreme authority for the colony in the London Company. The London Company was a joint-stock company in which Sandys, like others, was a stockholder. Virginia was not adding to England's riches. If Spain or France should seize it, it might not be worth fighting for. On the other hand, it might yet prove profitable. By issuing a charter giving responsibility to a company of private investors, James could wash his hands of the colony at any time. But if it prospered, he could always resume control.

Sandys was active in other colonial ventures. He became a member of the East India Company before August 1614. In 1615 he became a member of the Somers Islands Company. But, increasingly, his interest was concentrated in the London Company, and it was here that he made his greatest contribution to the history of political institutions—one recognized today as of worldwide importance.

The chief officer of the London Company bore the title of treasurer rather than president. From 1612 to 1618 this position was held by Sir Thomas Smith, the choice of the Warwick faction, which favored martial law for the colony and was prepared to stamp out anything smacking too much of democracy. But if Smith had in the earl of Warwick a powerful ally from the nobility, Sandys as leader of the minority had his own noble supporter in Henry Wriothesley, third earl of Southampton. This was the same Southampton famed as patron of dramatic poets, chief among them Shakespeare. He was representative of the Elizabethan Age in the wide range of his interests and in combining artistic and scholarly pursuits with such practical activities as business, politics, and colonization. He shared Sandys' dream of introducing representative government into Virginia.

By the fortunes of internal and external politics, Sandys succeeded Sir Thomas Smith as treasurer, or head, of the London Company and obtained a more liberal charter in 1618. On November 18, 1618 the Supreme Council of the Virginia Company took the momentous step of authorizing a General Assembly, or colonial legislature, for Virginia. The upper house would be the colonial council, chosen by the company in England. But the lower house, to be known as the House of Burgesses, would be elected by the freeholders of Virginia.

On the evening of this decision, a comet appeared in the darkening sky. Superstitious Londoners recalled that, eleven years before, a similar comet had appeared as three small ships had carried colonists to Virginia, which now promised to become, and indeed did become, the first permanent English settlement in America.

However little related to cause and effect, the appearance of celestial portents was appropriate. The formal decision of November 18, 1618 authorized the General Assembly of Virginia which convened July 30, 1619 (O.S.), or August 9, 1619 by the modern calendar. The newly elected burgesses who, incongruously clad in bright silks and velvets, walked down the little dirt streets of Jamestown to take the oath of office in a rustic wooden church, were actors in one of history's great events. They participated in the transfer to the New World of English traditions of representative government. That day, as James Truslow Adams has said, "political self-government was formally inaugurated on the American continent."[19] Today the General Assembly of Virginia is the third oldest representative assembly in the world, yielding precedence only to the parliaments of Great Britain and Iceland.

But this is only part of the story. Virginia's bicameral legislature was built on English traditions but also was responsible for innovations that helped to determine the form and customs of similar bodies in other colonies, and eventually of the Congress of the United States. And Congress has become a model for governing bodies in many other nations. John Fiske did not exaggerate when he called the Virginia assembly of 1619 an ancestor of "the bicameral legislatures of nearly all the world in modern times."[20]

AMERICA

19

"WESTWARD THE COURSE"

A TRAFFIC IN IDEAS linked London's Whitehall with Jamestown's Back Street. And the traffic was not altogether one way. Of course English ships to Virginia were freighted with gifts of inestimable value—not only the traditions of representative government and the common law but also a language and literature rich in ideas. And in England presiding over the flow of ideas to the colony at a most critical period was Sir Edwin Sandys, a man of venturesome intellect and genius for adaptation who was determined to make the colony a laboratory for self-government. But in the little wilderness community on the Chesapeake Bay were innovative thinkers also, at least as endowed with Elizabethan daring as those who guided colonization from London offices and certainly as flexible in practical experiment. In time, Virginians and other American colonists would influence the way some of England's ablest leaders looked at problems of government in the mother country.

Even in the first years of settlement, there were brilliant and cultivated minds within the log stockade of Jamestown. One was George Sandys, a younger brother of Sir Edwin and well remembered today by some literary scholars who cannot identify his sibling who sired self-government in America.[1] George Sandys is still renowned for his translation into English of Ovid's *Metamorphoses* and of book 1 of the *Aeneid*, work which earned him Dryden's praise as "the best versifier of the former age." Dryden had special reason for gratitude. George Sandys was the chief molder of the "closed, antithetically balanced couplet" of which the younger poet made such happy use and which became the favorite instrument of Alexander Pope. Sandys also influenced Milton—in manner and vocabulary and as a source on Mediterranean culture. And just as John Keats learned Homer from reading Chapman's translations, he learned Roman myths from reading Sandys. A significant part of Sandys' translation of Ovid was done at Jamestown. A remarkably adaptable man, Sandys would lay aside his pen to repel an Indian attack and then put aside his musket to return to his literary labors.

He became treasurer of Virginia and a member of its governing Council. He brought considerable sophistication to his service in the colony both as an officeholder and as a reporter to his brother Sir Edwin and other sympathetic leaders in England. Following education at Oxford, he had traveled in Italy, Cypress, Constantinople, Egypt, and Palestine, writing a four-volume *Relation of a Journey* that helped to educate Francis Bacon and many other English leaders in the geography and ethnology of the Mediterranean world.

And George Sandys' practical experience in the New World was a valuable complement to his older brother's philosophical insights. At a surprisingly early stage, some of the Virginia colonists were beginning to think of themselves as a special breed of Englishmen who had much to tell London. In a private letter to two other brothers, Sir Samuel and Sir Myles, George Sandys said that Sir Edwin and his associates were men "of discourse and contemplation and not of reason and judgement."[2]

Another sophisticated resident of Jamestown was the redoubtable Captain John Smith, who was of the Council in Virginia from the beginning and became governor and captain general. He was schooled in warfare and practical diplomacy on three continents. He was the first great cartographer in America and wrote the first American book, *A True Relation*, which disseminated, along with some of his prejudices, more information on the aboriginal inhabitants of North America than most Englishmen got from any other source.

There was John Pory, Speaker in 1619 of the first legislature at Jamestown. He had been a member of Parliament in London and thus had learned firsthand many of the precedents by which America's first representative assembly operated. Among his friends were numerous of England's politicians as well as many of its leading intellectuals and writers, reputedly including Shakespeare. A problem with alcoholism had lowered his prestige somewhat in London, but he was still listened to as a shrewd and knowledgeable observer.

Much of the initiative in England's colonization of Virginia came from some of the settlers themselves. Even so, the major thrust still came from talented and energetic people in the mother country. In no case, however, did the principal push come from King James or his favorite courtiers. And this situation is symptomatic of what happened to England's Elizabethan glory in the reign of King James.

When Queen Elizabeth died in 1603, England had been raised by sound financial management, national confidence, naval prowess, skilled diplomacy, prized traditions, and bold venturing in a score of fields to a position of great respect throughout the Western world. The achievement was a remarkable one for a small island nation lacking the landmass, large population, and abundance of natural resources that were the lot of some other countries.

Elizabethan society was one of the most creative in the history of the world. Its creative energy did not cease with Elizabeth's death in 1603. Shakespeare continued to write, producing at least twelve more plays, including such masterpieces as *Measure for Measure, Othello, King Lear, Macbeth, Antony and Cleopatra*, and *The Tempest*. Francis Bacon published *The Advancement of Learning* and the *Novum organum*. William Harvey presented his findings on the operation of the heart and circulation of the blood and, according to some medical historians, "laid the foundation of modern medicine." Richard Hakluyt continued to add to his *Principal Navigations, Voyages, Traffiques, and*

Discoveries of the English Nation, and his countrymen furnished him ample material by continuing to voyage and discover. Sir Edward Coke molded English law in the reign of James I. Sir Edwin Sandys, reared and educated in the "spacious days" of Elizabeth, brought expansive vision to parliamentary government and colonization amid the narrow concerns of her successor's court.

Provided with efficient government by Henry VII and pointed toward commercial success, unified by Henry VIII and encouraged in scholarship and the arts, preserved by the brilliant diplomacy of Elizabeth, who presided over a Golden Age of culture, England had enough momentum to keep it moving forward even under the timid policies of backward-looking James. Most of the great accomplishments of the Jacobean period derived their impetus from the Elizabethan.

England's experience under Elizabeth paralleled in many ways Florence's under Lorenzo. In each case, the ruler was a brilliant and magnetic person with scholarly and artistic interests and a decided flair for public relations. In each instance, preceding generations of rulers had contributed to commercial development of the state and had been patrons of scholarship and art. Both Lorenzo and Elizabeth were fired with genuine patriotism in addition to desires for personal aggrandizement, and both utilized pageantry not only to glamorize themselves but also to inspire national pride and unity.

Each cherished traditions of the home country, but each also welcomed innovations to meet new challenges. With Elizabeth, this spirit could involve a broad range of projects, from continuing to build a church rooted in Rome but independent of it to fashioning a navy of radically different design to maintain England's traditional maritime strength even in the face of Spanish power.

Elizabeth was not always as decisive as Lorenzo. In the wavering over whether to execute her cousin Mary Stuart, her hesitation was more creditable than single-minded resolution. Her temporizing in some other matters lessened the efficiency of her government, but she was constant in her principal goals—keeping England essentially independent of Spain or any other kingdom, unifying her people, promoting their prosperity, and affording scope and inspiration to their talents. It is remarkable in view of her precarious childhood that Elizabeth could summon at crucial moments the powerful resolution that helped to make her a great ruler.

Not only the careers of the rulers Lorenzo and Elizabeth but also those of their two kingdoms are comparable in many ways. Both Florence and England had seemed poor candidates for international leadership. Their smallness and lack of many obvious natural advantages seemed to doom them to secondary roles at best. Unlike Florence, England had the advantage of ample access to the sea. But, also unlike Florence, England was on the edge of the Continent and, in terms of sixteenth-century communication, far removed from the Mediterranean world, long a center of civilization and commerce.

Both Florence and England were revitalized by a spirit of inquiry that placed their customary ways of life in association, and sometimes stimulating conflict, with a newly exhumed classical culture. At the same time, each state was placed in closer association with differing contemporaneous cultures. The upshot was a reexamination of traditional values in the light of fresh discoveries. Sometimes the people of each state were torn between a native heritage too precious to abandon and new experiences too exciting to forgo. When a viable balance was struck, in individual lives and in the life of the state, there was an impressive release of creative energy.

Creativity in both Renaissance Florence and Elizabethan England was greatly increased, and its productions were made far more significant, by the multiplicity of interests that characterized leaders and thinkers of the day. The very fact that many people were both leaders and thinkers was itself an advantage. Scholarly study and practical pursuits informed each other. And the serious pursuit of literature, art, music, science, politics, and business by gifted individuals provided the cross-pollination of disciplines that often produces fresh analogies and therefore new visions. One who knows only a single art or science is incapable of the bold metaphors that provide sudden vistas of revelation through which understanding leaps ahead. And both Florence and England also had their mercantile metaphrasts who translated the prose of commerce into the poetry of epic accomplishment.

Achievements in virtually every field of human endeavor fed national pride, and that pride itself was a spur to further achievement. Sometimes cynicism and ennui overtake an intellectual class, but in Elizabethan England, as in Lorenzo's Florence, learning was pursued with the sense of adventure that characterized geographical exploration.

Patriotism and a strong sense of community helped England not only to survive, but to triumph over, the challenges of change. Discovery of new lands, new peoples, and new facts about the human body made some old convictions untenable while their successors were still inchoate. Like their rulers, both Florence and England at their height tended toward a healthy tension between heritage and adventure. To England's medieval heritage was added the catalyst of Renaissance culture from the Continent, including especially Florence, and with it of course the reincarnation of the old classical traditions of Greece and Rome.

The able leadership that abetted the success of Elizabethan England was autocratic, as was that of virtually every other state of the time. But, like Florence's in the Age of Lorenzo, it permitted more freedom of expression than was common elsewhere. England utilized the talents of gifted people whether they came from the aristocracy or the rapidly expanding middle class. It was an age when readers were multiplying, as were the number and variety of printed books available to them in their native language. Education became a status symbol.

James' ascension to the throne did not have the immediate and traumatic effect on English culture that it would have had on a less vigorous one. Also, decline was slowed by the fact that many of the great creators bred by Elizabethan society were approaching their zeniths at the time. The imagination of a Shakespeare nurtured ideas and images yet to find expression in some of his chief masterpieces. Bacon's *Advancement of Learning* was not yet ready for the press, and his *Novum organum* was still inchoate in his own skull and not held within the covers of a book. William Harvey had been back in England for only about a year after returning from his studies in Padua and was a dozen years away from delivering his famous lectures on the cardiovascular system. Sir Edwin Sandys, the beneficiary of almost every advantage that Elizabethan England could offer for his intellectual development, began his public career simultaneously with the commencement of James' reign.

Nevertheless, James' succession to the throne set in motion forces that led to a decline from the glories of Elizabeth's reign. The deterioration was obvious first in England's political and military standing in the European community. Elizabeth and her ministers had practiced a brilliant diplomacy involving threats, allurements, and bluff, all backed by a strong navy. James slipped into a timid foreign policy of retreat and appeasement that needlessly sacrificed much of the influence gained under Elizabeth. He even humiliated his people by his humble overtures to a declining Spain. It was as if there had never been a victory over the Spanish Armada. Few Englishmen were as influential at James' court as Count Gondomar, the Spanish ambassador. This arrogant grandee influenced the king's appointments and even played a crucial role in sending the valiant Ralegh to the executioner's block. At times his activities at court threatened the existence of the Virginia colony. His chief appeal to James was made by dangling the possibility that the Spanish infanta might become the bride of the king's son—a possibility extremely distasteful to the mass of Englishmen.

France became the most powerful nation in Europe and the Dutch came to exercise an influence far out of proportion to their numbers while England languished and continually knuckled under to ever diminishing Spain. James even permitted his son Charles, accompanied by the king's favorite, Buckingham, to make a foredoomed pilgrimage to the Spanish court to plead for the infanta's hand.

Spain's respect was to be gained only through strength, and that was being lost yearly through the diminution of England's army and navy. Money was needed to keep up the island's defenses, but such were James' quarrels with Parliament that he seldom convened them to secure the necessary funds.

The king restricted free expression far beyond the limitations of Elizabeth's time. He placed the Church of Scotland under an unwanted episcopacy. At the Hampton Court conference of 1604, he threatened to drive the Puritans from England if they did not conform. Eventually some of the most enterprising ones fled to the Netherlands. James dismissed some of the best minds among England's leaders, including Bacon and Coke, surrounding himself with ineffective sycophants and young men whose physical charms detained his roving eye.

James' beliefs and habits were a far cry from Elizabeth's almost habitual melding of tradition and experiment. Lorenzo's Florence toward the last had been weakened by a too sweeping abandonment of native tradition in favor of the trendiness fostered by some devotees of the humanities, and then in reaction had retreated to a medieval repression that in turn bred rebellion. James weakened his government and English society by his persistent effort to restore medieval belief in the divine right of kings. He discouraged experiment by efforts to revive medieval Scholasticism and to substitute superstitious belief about witchcraft for faith in experiment.

The magnitude of James' offenses against parliamentary government would eventually have the effect of breeding reforms that would limit autocracy in England. Because of his father's legacy, Charles I would pay with his life. James made his son a convert to divine-right doctrine and left him a kingdom torn by dissension and lagging in national pride.

It is ironic that the great King James Version of the Bible should bear the name of this monarch who was usually occupied with narrow enterprises. Aside from its incalculable influence on almost every other aspect of civilization in the English-speaking world, this translation is a compendium of English prose and poetry excelling in volume and eloquence the works of any single writer or coterie. As a ruler of apparently sincere piety, James gladly lent his name to an English version of the Bible owing even more to a succession of sixteenth-century scholars than to the seventeenth-century ones who so ably completed the work.

The other great literary works of James' reign are generally described, quite properly in terms of inspiration, as Elizabethan rather than Jacobean. The seventeenth century would produce other masterpieces, among them John Milton's *Paradise Lost*, published in 1667. But Milton drew inspiration from the English Renaissance and, with justifiable disregard of chronology, has been called by generations of literature professors "the last Elizabethan." As James' reign passed into Charles', there were no monumental works from new writers. A cautious and eventually largely imitative classicism settled upon the land, producing good works still valued. But there were no great adventures in prose or poetry. John Dryden's *All for Love* succeeded Shakespeare's *Antony and Cleopatra*. Thomas Middleton's *Chaste Maid in Cheapside* competed with Ben Jonson's last comedies. Christopher Marlowe's long-hidden *Jew of Malta* was released in 1633 in time to compete with John Ford's new *'Tis a Pity She's a Whore*. In science, John Parkinson's worthy botanical book and William Oughtred's helpful suggestion that X be used as a symbol for multiplication succeeded the sweeping premises of Bacon and Harvey.

England's Golden Age was over. But the seeds of coming greatness lay not too deep for exposure by the excoriating plow of future travail. And some of England's finest seeds had been borne westward to America. Captain John Smith, that redoubtable Elizabethan who led the Virginia Colony, had predicted that the Powhatan River, inappropriately renamed the James, would see the rise of a culture equal to the one that had flourished on the Tiber. To spirited Englishmen disappointed by the course of affairs at home, the Virginia capes seemed like welcoming arms, and the great hook of Cape Cod like a beckoning hand.

"WHERE NONE BEFORE HATH STOOD"

NORTH AMERICA was not nearly as hospitable to Englishmen as some maps and much travel literature in the first decades of the seventeenth century would suggest. Hundreds of immigrants would die in the encompassing arms of the Virginia capes, and Cape Cod would come to seem not so much like a beckoning hand as like a threatening fist.

That Englishmen should have been deceived is not surprising. Michael Drayton, in his famous "Ode to the Virginian Voyage," had hailed Virginia as "earth's only Paradise." Embedded in the soldierly prose of Captain John Smith was his glowing comment on the Chesapeake Bay country: "Heaven and earth never agreed better to frame a place for man's habitation." At least one London drama celebrated a Virginia beach as a literally golden strand. Some plays that satirized the American fever tell us much about popular notions of a felicitous climate and easy wealth in the New World. Even the accounts of voyages edited by the judicious Richard Hakluyt perforce included some narratives too richly colored by mariners' imaginations.[1]

The Jamestown settlers, planting in 1607 the first permanent English settlement in America, found a sense of history not enough to sustain them after a "starving time" in which some had been reduced to eating their own horses. One provident colonist was convicted of "salting away" the body of his dead wife to insure his own survival. In 1610 the settlers voted to abandon the colony, but the timely arrival of a new governor with three supply ships reversed the decision. In 1622 a concerted Indian attack killed 347 men, women, and children in Virginia. Except for the warning that an Indian youth gave an English friend after half a night of wrestling with conflicting loyalties, the capital itself probably would have been destroyed.[2] But by that time Virginia had had representative government for three years and had discovered within itself a surprising resilience.

In 1620, thirteen years after the founding of Jamestown and one year after the establishment of representative government in Virginia, Puritans who had fled persecution in England and then sojourned in the Netherlands arrived in

Massachusetts and started that colony. Intending to settle in Virginia north of Jamestown, they were blown off their course and landed on Cape Cod.[3] Nearby, on the site of an abandoned Indian village, they founded Plymouth. A decade later, a larger colony of Puritans settled at the present site of Salem. Eventually, the two settlements merged in the Colony of Massachusetts.

The Massachusetts settlers profited from the experiences of the Virginia colonists, and benefited from the unity born of consciousness of being a persecuted minority. But, like so many victims throughout history, they themselves became oppressors, nailing Quakers' ears to boards and exiling as heretics such notable religious leaders as Roger Williams and Anne Hutchinson. They, too, had their starving time, when there were scarcely enough survivors sufficiently strong to bury the dead.

Much nonsense has been written about the early settlers of both Virginia and Massachusetts.

Captain John Smith was a brave and resourceful man to whom the Virginia Colony in large part owed its life. But as the writer of the first history of the colony, he glorified himself by picturing most of his associates as scheming, lazy, inept, or a combination of all three. Consequently, the early Virginians except for Smith often were seen as a sorry lot. This view prevailed until a reassessment based on other accounts revealed that Smith, though probably the most valuable colonist, did not have a monopoly on either ability or goodwill. Nineteenth century romancers rewrote history to picture the first Virginians as younger sons of lords, almost to a man, wading ashore waving pedigrees of prodigious length as their title deeds to leadership. Twentieth century reaction to this caricature has produced portraits of the Jamestown settlers as illiterate wastrels and refugees from Newgate prison.

Filiopietistic New Englanders pictured the settlers of Plymouth and Massachusetts Bay as colonies of saints enduring the hardships of a wilderness to be nearer to God and to save the souls of the aborigines. This picture was later modified to present those early Americans as imperfect, but quite superior, human beings. In the twentieth century, some historians who should have known better described the Massachusetts colonists as a sturdy, intelligent, and virtuous middle class in contrast to a Virginia population consisting of a few foppish aristocrats and an indolent mass of the deprived and depraved.

Actually the settlers of Virginia and Massachusetts were not markedly dissimilar. There was one major difference in the passengers brought to Virginia in 1607 aboard the *Susan Constant*, *Godspeed*, and *Discovery* and those who came in 1620 on the *Mayflower*. There were no women among the first people at Jamestown, the theory being that men should take the first steps toward subduing the wilderness before women were exposed to its dangers. On the other hand, women were among the English who settled Plymouth. But this difference soon disappeared. As English women filtered into the Virginia Colony, they quickly proved as durable as the men. By 1620, the year that English people settled in Massachusetts, the number of women at Jamestown had increased dramatically as a result of special efforts by the London Company to encourage their emigration.

Between 1607 and the "Great Muster," or first complete census of the Virginia Colony, in 1624, there came to Jamestown a fairly representative sample of England's population. There were laborers and artisans of various sorts, but with a larger proportion of the privileged element than would be typical of an English community. The disproportion was most evident with the first voyagers. Of the slightly more than one hundred pioneers on the three small ships, forty-eight were listed as gentlemen. Though socially and educationally privileged, they were not effete. A goodly number had been soldiers in the Low Countries. Though the proportion of the advantaged decreased after the first voyage, they continued to be more numerous than one might have expected.

Among the Virginia settlers before 1624 were a number of sophisticated people, some educated at Oxford, Cambridge, and the Inns of Court, who knew the great world and were known by it.[4] Besides such leaders as John Pory, George Sandys, and the self-made sophisticate Captain John Smith, there was Sir George Yeardley, who presided over the first representative legislature in America about six months after becoming governor. Lady Yeardley was of the distinguished Flowerdew family. Also there was the colony's secretary, William Strachey, author of an account of the wreck of the Virginia-bound *Sea Venture* in a Bermuda hurricane, a vivid piece of writing that apparently influenced Shakespeare's *Tempest*. One early governor, Sir Francis Wyatt, scion of one of England's great families, was accompanied by his brother the Reverend Haute Wyatt, who remained to rear a family of his own.

Persons of sophisticated background other than appointees to high office also came. Among them was Charles Harmar, nephew to one John Harmar and brother to another, both distinguished professors of Greek at Oxford University. Edmund Scarburgh, a Cambridge alumnus, and his son of the same name moved to Virginia. Staying behind in England was another son, who as Sir Charles Scarburgh, royal physician, proved a helpful intermediary at court for his colonial relations. Sarah Offley, wife of Adam Thorowgood, one of Virginia's richest residents, was the granddaughter and great-granddaughter of lord mayors of London. Captain Henry Woodhouse was the grandson of Sir Nicholas Bacon, lord keeper of the seal and father to Sir Francis Bacon. The four sons of Sir Thomas West, second Baron De La Warr, all came to Virginia. Their mother was first cousin to Queen Elizabeth.

In the 1630's came more Englishmen of distinguished backgrounds, notable among them Colonel Nathaniel Littleton, brother to Sir Edward Littleton, Baron Littleton of Mounslow, England's chief justice of Common Pleas. The colonel was the son of Chief Justice Sir Edward Littleton and the grandson of Chief Justice Sir Edward Walter, and a direct descendant of Justice Sir Thomas Littleton, author of *Tenures*. More than fifty of his ancestors have separate biographical sketches in a current edition of the *Encyclopaedia Britannica*. He was descended in multiple lines from William the Conqueror, King Alfred the Great, and the emperor Charlemagne. Many other representatives of England's ruling classes came to Virginia, so many that Governor Sir William Berkeley said in his *Discourse and View of Virginia*, "Men of as good families as any subjects in England have resided there, as the Percies, the Berkeleys, the Wests, the Gages, the Throgmortons, Wyatts, Digges, Moldsworths, Morrisons, Kemps, and hundred others, which I forebear to name, lest I should misherald them in the catalogue."[5]

Though almost all of Plymouth's *Mayflower* settlers were plain folk and illiterate, some people of education and sophistication emigrated to Massachusetts in subsequent years, especially, after 1630, to Massachusetts Bay.[6] Herbert Pelham, the first treasurer of Harvard University, was a grandson of the first Lord Delaware and a descendant of English royalty. Grace Chetwode was the daughter of Sir Richard Chetwode and a descendant of the Plantagenets. Major Richard Saltonstall was a descendant of the great Percy and Neville families. Edward Carleton was descended from English kings. Margaret Tyndal, wife of Massachusetts Bay governor John Winthrop, was the daughter of Sir John Tyndal and a descendant of some of England's greatest nobles. Governor Thomas Dudley, whose family remained in Massachusetts after his service was over, was almost certainly a descendant of English royalty and Charlemagne.[7]

So in Virginia from the first, and in Massachusetts somewhat later, there were aristocrats and members of England's burgeoning upper middle class. They were distinctly in the minority, but they were numerous enough to provide a considerable leavening. They had seen something of the world, some in military service on the Continent, some in the political and social conclaves of London. A fair number of these privileged ones had studied the classics at solid preparatory schools or even at Oxford and Cambridge. Some had matched wits with other bright young law students at the Inns of Court. These were people who read books and sometimes wrote them. Their journals reveal that they saw American colonization in the context of discoveries elsewhere in the world and in the light of history.

The fact that most of these people became colonial leaders on one level or another magnified their influence beyond their numbers. Conscious of their heritage, they drew nurture and inspiration from it. But also they were committed to change; otherwise they would not have taken the long and perilous voyage to a strange land.

The backbone and sinews of colonization in both Virginia and Massachusetts were English yeomen—men and women. Many of them could not read and write, but more could than historians once believed. It used to be assumed that any person signing his will with an X was illiterate. Since then it has been noted that some of these same people had earlier signed their names to other documents; many of the wills were deathbed papers. Twentieth century scholarship has also revealed that some English colonists who could not write were able to read print. Illiterate or not, the English masses had come a long way since the days when, as Thomas Hobbes said in *Leviathan*, the "life of man" was "solitary, poor, nasty, brutish, and short." Even the most disadvantaged who came to early Virginia or Massachusetts were animated by dreams and aspirations. They were eager for change, but did not wish to overthrow the social or economic system prevailing in England. They merely wanted to improve their position in it.

The dichotomy of motivations commonly assigned to the Virginians and the Massachusetts colonists is simplistic. Because the Puritan element was much larger in the northern colony than in the southern, many people have concluded that most of the Massachusetts immigrants were motivated solely by religious considerations. The desire to live freely in accordance with their own religious views but in an English environment was the chief motivation of the *Mayflower* people and of some later arrivals. But a desire for economic opportunity was present also and was dominant among some. And the Virginia colonists were not motivated solely by personal ambition and dreams of riches and empire. An idealistic patriotism and loving concern for their posterity mingled with more narrowly selfish aims. Individual writings and the records of the London Company reveal that some had a serious interest in Christianizing the Indians; it apparently was the chief motivation of at least two prominent leaders among the early Jamestown settlers.[8] Besides there were some Puritans in Virginia, some of them officeholders, including at least one governor.[9] Indeed, at times Puritans seem to have constituted a sizable minority on Virginia's Eastern Shore, and at Bennett's Creek on the western shore there was a Puritan community.

Admittedly, the approach to religion varied somewhat in the two colonies even among the dedicated. There was condemnation of maypoles among some of the Massachusetts leaders, but that very condemnation is proof that maypoles were raised among them. Sea captains returning to Massachusetts communities after voyages to Virginia sometimes complained that the sensuous temptation of musical instruments had been insinuated into Sunday worship in the southern commonwealth and that Christmas there was profaned by the singing of carols.

But life among the Puritans was not always so drab as subsequent generations have supposed. Illustrators and other artists, reflecting the popular conception and also reinforcing it, have depicted the Puritan's existence in shades of gray—gray woods, gray ocean, gray costumes, an almost universal gray relieved only occasionally by a touch of snow, whitecaps on angry waves, or a stiff white collar above a dark cloak. But portraits from the period show Puritans adorned in bright colors, and there are records of clothing made from red cloth. Even among the *Mayflower* passengers there were some people of education, such as Governor William Bradford, an autodidact who knew more literature and languages than many university graduates. And, of course, the language of the Mayflower Compact is ample evidence of the literacy of some others. Among later immigrants was a fair sprinkling of the liberally educated who appreciated beauty as well as austerity.

Though the better educated in both Virginia and Massachusetts exercised an influence far out of proportion to their numbers, leaders began to emerge from the yeomanry of both. Some of the illiterate labored to provide educations as well as estates for their children. A man who made his mark literally in lieu of a true signature sometimes lived to see his son make his mark figuratively in the life of the colony.

Still, though John Smith had dreamed of development in Virginia to rival ancient Rome, and John Winthrop of a Massachusetts government with God at its head, most Europeans, as the seventeenth century neared its end, found little reason to anticipate great leadership from America. Certainly there was little reason to suspect that it would be in the vanguard of individual freedom. Virginia struggled with a series of tyrannical governors, one of whom, Sir William Berkeley, originally one of the most promising, thanked God that there were neither printing presses nor free schools within his bailiwick. Even the Massachusetts Bay Colony, once more advanced in freedom than Plymouth, was a theocracy. And one of its ablest governors, John Winthrop, had set the tone for generations by his declaration that democracy was "the meanest and worst of all forms of government."[10]

Nevertheless, as the seventeenth century yielded to the eighteenth, there were signs in Virginia and Massachusetts, and in other colonies stretching along the Atlantic seaboard, that the Englishmen who now increasingly called themselves Americans had a fighting chance for greatness.

21

WHERE THEY WERE IN 1760

THE PROMISE OF AMERICA as a great creative force in the world was no more evident to most eighteenth century Britons than to their counterparts of the preceding century. Of course, there had been believers from the first in Virginia and Massachusetts, men and women whose faith helped them to survive, some whose belief in America's future was intensified by the necessity for passionate denial that their sacrifices had been in vain. But confidence in America's destiny was uncommon among those who came to the New World as observers and then returned to their native island.

There were some exceptions. Richard Rich sailed to Virginia with Captain Christopher Newport in 1609 and upon returning to England published the next year his *Newes from Virginia*, containing the lines:

> God will not let us fall . . .
> For . . . our work is good,
> We hope to plant a nation,
> Where none before hath stood.

And when the eighteenth century had run half its course, the great Anglo-Irish philosopher George Berkeley wrote in his book *On the Prospect of Planting Arts and Learning in America*, "Westward the course of empire takes its way; . . . Time's noblest offspring is the last."

Some exceptionally keen British observers failed to anticipate any remarkable creative efflorescence in North America even on the eve of what would be known as the era of the Founding Fathers. Among the oblivious ones, despite his strategic location as a professor at the College of William and Mary in Williamsburg, Virginia, was William Small.[1] He lived in the capital of England's most populous North American colony, where he was a frequent guest of the royal governor and a prominent member of the intellectual community. William and Mary was second only to Harvard in age among American colleges and had chosen to assume the role of a university, inaugurating courses in science and secular philosophy at a time when the older school had chosen to forgo university status rather than risk leading astray the potential ministers among its students. Moreover, Williamsburg was on a main route connecting Boston, New York, Philadelphia, and Annapolis in the north with Charleston and Savannah to the south. Its taverns and drawing rooms were full of the talk of lawyers and businessmen fresh from other places where American public opinion was being molded.

Small's lack of awareness was not due to a deficiency of curiosity. In profile he was an ideal symbol of inquisitiveness. His long, pointed, boldly outthrust nose was emphasized by a receding brow and chin, as though the eagerly probing proboscis were outrunning the rest of the face. There were those who believed that the prominent nose was thrust into too many places where it had no business. The college administration thought it was much too often poked into its operations, and a largely clerical faculty thought it too frequently probed those processes of nature that should be beyond the profane inquiry of man. Of course, Small's skepticism and investigative zeal made him a favorite with his students. When, standing all alone, he opposed the faculty decision that any professor might punish any refractory student by any means the teacher deemed appropriate, he became a hero.

Small's investigative activities were not confined to the contemporary and the mundane. A product of the Scottish enlightenment, he was a mathematician and physical scientist whose learning led him into philosophical disquisitions.

Partly because of differences with the college administration, Small took two extended leaves of absence in England before finally resigning when his candidacy for president of the school was rejected. But, above all these considerations, he was glad to quit a little colonial outpost of British culture for the intellectual riches of England itself, out of which he firmly believed would issue the thoughts and theories determining the course of events in much of the world.

Ironically, among Small's students at that time was a young man destined to become a world leader of opinion, who would be cited by scholars of later generations as one of the two best exemplars of the Enlightenment—Thomas Jefferson.[2] And these same scholars would cite as the other member of this remarkable pair another American, a retired Pennsylvania printer, now deputy postmaster for the colonies, who had not enjoyed the advantage of a college education. His name, of course, was Benjamin Franklin. When the seventeen-year-old Virginian entered college, the fifty-four-year-old Pennsylvanian was absent from his Philadelphia office. The Pennsylvania legislature had sent him to London to plead with the home government to enforce taxes on proprietary estates. Franklin was a persuasive man. For years he had been persuading his fellow citizens to work for innovations he favored. In the year of Jefferson's birth, the Junto Society, which Franklin had founded more than a decade earlier, had become the American Philosophical Society. Besides these accomplishments, Franklin was a good representative to send abroad because his reputation had already preceded him. He had invented an improved stove that bore his name. And his experiments in electricity were much discussed in Europe, especially the one in which he had flown a kite in an electrical storm.

George Washington in 1760 was a member of the House of Burgesses,

which met in Williamsburg in the capitol, at the other end of Duke of Gloucester Street from the college. Except for these legislative sessions, he lived the life
of a prosperous farmer on his Mount Vernon estate. Only the year before, he
had married a rich widow, Martha Custis. At the time of Braddock's defeat and
fatal wounding at Monongahela in 1755, the twenty-three-year-old Virginian
had attracted international attention by intervening to save the army of British
regulars and colonials from rout. He enhanced his reputation as a fighting colonel in the French and Indian War until 1758. When, as a newly elected burgess,
he was confronted with the unforeseen necessity of replying to a House resolution supporting him as a brave defender of British America, his celebrated courage deserted him. The tall young colonel's face flushed, and he stammered until
Speaker John Robinson interrupted. "Sit down, Mr. Washington," he said,
"your modesty is equal to your valor, and that surpasses the power of any
language that I possess."[3]

Twenty-five-year-old John Adams was plump but not jolly. He was trying
to make a name for himself as a Massachusetts lawyer, but he sometimes worried that he should have chosen another career. Sometimes he thought he
should have been a minister. He had considered becoming a doctor but was
afraid that he would vomit amid the grosser scenes of medical practice. Meanwhile he studied many subjects, including history, classical and English literature, physics, and philosophy. He had resolved, "I will rouse up my mind and
fix my attention. I will stand collected within myself and think upon what I
read and what I see. I will strive with all my soul to be something more than
persons who have had less advantages than myself."[4] He was courting the
sprightly and saucy Abigail Smith. When a raging storm prevented their getting
together as planned, he wrote her that nature's wrath might be a blessing "to
you, or me, or both, for keeping me at *my Distance*. . . . Itches, Aches, Agues,
and Repentance might be the Consequences of a Contact in present Circumstances."[5]

Law was also the profession of John Dickinson, like Washington twenty-
eight years old when Jefferson entered college. Three years into practice after
studying law in London, Dickinson entered upon his public career at this time
in Pennsylvania. That state and Delaware would be home bases in a political
life of national significance. His serially published *Letters from a Pennsylvania
Farmer* was still some seven years in the offing. For a while he would be, even
more than Jefferson, the penman of the Revolution.

David Rittenhouse, born in the same vintage year as Washington and Dickinson, was a watchmaker and mechanic in Pennsylvania. His political career
had not even begun, and in 1760 the public did not yet know him as a student
of that vast clockwork—the universe.

James Madison, future "Father of the Constitution," was a nine-year-old
boy in Orange County, Virginia. When he was ready for college, his parents
would seek Jefferson's advice.

John Marshall, whose judicial decisions would in effect rewrite much of
the Constitution, was a five-year-old boy. One of Jefferson's numerous Virginia cousins, he would be a rival and opponent in crucial times.

Five-year-old Alexander Hamilton was living in the West Indies with his unmarried parents. His grandfather was a Scottish laird, and the disparity between the boy's distinguished paternal ancestry and his own dubious status embittered him from early years onward. "My blood," he would say, "is as good as that of those who plume themselves upon their ancestry." His great precocity would occasion wonder long before he was old enough to enter King's College in New York, later Columbia University. Washington would come to regard him as a surrogate son, Jefferson would see him as a bitter rival, and John Adams would privately refer to him, with technical accuracy but malicious connotation, as a "bastard."

George Mason was a thirty-five-year-old Virginia planter, a neighbor of George Washington. When he was ten years old he had suffered the death of his father, but since then he had seemed to lead a sheltered life. Instead of attending school, he had a private tutor. He read law with a relative, attorney John Mercer, but did not practice. The paperwork had little attraction, and he detested speaking in public. In fact, he almost fainted whenever he attempted it.

Nevertheless, impelled by a sense of responsibility, Mason made himself one of the most useful men in the county, serving as vestryman, a position that then involved civic duties, and as one of the local justices. His quietly effective work as one of the founders of the town of Alexandria increased his fellow citizens' regard.

Loving the peace and security of his farms and his house, not one of the largest but one of the most beautiful in the colony, he also delighted in his fine library, where he educated himself in history and philosophy and the constitutional law of many nations over many centuries. His son said that Mason sometimes became so absorbed in his studies that he "absented as it were from his family sometimes for weeks together."[6] Nevertheless, as a widower who had suffered greatly from the loss of his mate, he especially cherished the affection of his motherless daughters. For all these reasons, he was reluctant to leave home and at first resisted the idea that he become a candidate for election to the House of Burgesses. But a year before our meeting him in 1760, he had yielded to the demands of his neighbors.

Mason would be a member of the lower house of Virginia's legislature for the next twenty-eight years. It was his highest public office—with the magnificent exception of his service as a delegate to the Convention of 1787 that produced the Constitution of the United States. There, though he nearly fainted every time, he was one of the five most frequent speakers and, in some long periods, rose to speak more often than anyone else except James Madison.

Fellow delegates were impressed with his wisdom and vast knowledge, and he became one of the principal molders of the Constitution of the United States. Earlier, in the crisis of 1776, he had drafted the Virginia Constitution and, even more important, the Virginia Bill of Rights, which became a model in thought and language for the United States Bill of Rights and similar documents throughout the world.

Appropriately the medallioned profile of this lawyer who never practiced the legal profession appears in the capitol of the United States with those of Hammurabi, Lycurgus, Justinian, and other great lawgivers over a period of nearly four thousand years. But if Professor William Small met George Mason in 1760—and he well may have during the session of Burgesses in the little town of Williamsburg—he could be forgiven for not recognizing the shy planter as potentially a historical figure of international stature.

Though Small had come from Scotland, he had had no opportunity whatever to know one of his fellow countrymen, also a product of the Scottish Enlightenment, who would be one of the giants among the founders of the American Republic. In 1760 James Wilson was only eighteen years old, and he would not arrive in America until 1765, just in time for all the Stamp Act excitement. A teacher of Greek and rhetoric in Philadelphia, he soon began studying law under John Dickinson and eventually became the leading lawyer in Pennsylvania. At the age of twenty-six, Wilson wrote his magisterial *Considerations on the Nature and Extent of the Legislative Authority of the British Parliament*, which was published in 1774 on the eve of revolution. The work envisioned a British Commonwealth of Nations such as would come into existence in the twentieth century. As one of the leaders of the Constitutional Convention of 1787, and as a member of the first Supreme Court of the United States, he brought a broad and deep knowledge of philosophy and law to the problem of providing strong government simultaneously at both the local and national levels.

One future Founding Father was Small's fellow teacher and frequent dinner companion, but the Scotsman probably did not envision him in that historic role. Already a Virginia burgess in 1760, George Wythe taught an impressive array of subjects. At William and Mary he would become America's first law professor attached to any college. He would be a signer of the Declaration of Independence written by his prize pupil, and would be a strong member of the Constitutional Convention in 1787. One of his greatest services was in reforming and revitalizing legal education more than anyone had in centuries, through inauguration of the moot court system of having students act in realistic dramatizations of court cases. Perhaps his strongest influence of all was exerted as the teacher of a galaxy of future leaders, including John Marshall (although for only a few months), Henry Clay, and especially Thomas Jefferson.

Both Small and Wythe appreciated the brilliance of young Jefferson. They obviously preferred his company to that of many of their older colleagues. The youngster often was with them as a fellow guest when they dined at the Governor's Palace. Governor Francis Fauquier was not only a polished man of the world but also sufficiently scholarly to be a fellow of the Royal Society. Apparently young Tom Jefferson first appeared at the Palace as a violinist, one of the student musicians invited to provide entertainment for the governor and his guests. Tom was a proficient amateur musician, but the quality of his talk eclipsed that of his playing, so that he soon was invited principally for his conversational powers.

Young Jefferson's appreciation of Small and Wythe was perhaps even greater than their admiration of him. In later years he wrote, "It was my great good fortune, and what probably fixed the destinies of my life, that Dr. William Small of Scotland was then professor of mathematics, a man profound in most of the useful branches of science, with a happy and enlarged and liberal mind.[7]

Jefferson was attributing to his old teacher even greater learning than many modern readers might assume. In Jefferson's day, "science" could be any field of scholarship. To ascribe to anyone profundity "in most of the useful branches of science" was to make an astounding assertion.

Jefferson continued:

> He, most happily for me, became soon attached to me and made me his daily companion when not engaged in the school, and from his conversation I got my first views of the expansion of science and of the system of things in which we are placed. Fortunately, the philosophical chair became vacant soon after my arrival at college and he was appointed to fill it *per interim,* and he was the first who ever gave in that college regular lectures in ethics, rhetoric, and belles lettres.[8]

Wythe had a large head with bulging forehead, appropriate symbolism for the man whose cranium was chock full of facts about law, history, literature, and philosophy. Equally appropriate was his benevolent expression. For many years he would be to Jefferson an inspiration and revered avuncular presence.

A third person, very different from the two professors, contributed heavily to Jefferson's education before the young man completed his studies in Williamsburg. The year was 1765, and the town, like Philadelphia, to which James Wilson came at the same time, was electric with arguments over the Stamp Act. Only strong self discipline enabled the twenty-two-year-old Jefferson to concentrate on his lessons while crowds gathered and excitement mounted a mile away at the other end of Duke of Gloucester Street. There, in the capitol of Virginia, the House of Burgesses was in session to consider "steps necessary to be taken in consequence" of the act of Parliament requiring the purchase of special stamps for legal documents, insurance policies, ship's papers, licenses, and a great many other things, ranging from playing cards and almanacs to newspapers, pamphlets, and broadsides. This was the first direct tax ever levied on the American colonies. Many people feared it would not be the last.

Word had spread that Patrick Henry, a new young legislator who claimed the allegiance of many of Virginia's western settlers, was going to speak. His activities as a lawyer had already gained him notoriety as a foe of privilege. Jefferson's older Randolph cousins, venerated pillars of the establishment, had pronounced Henry a dangerous radical. Jefferson greatly admired his cousins, but at this stage of his life few things could have so excited his curiosity about the newcomer as their vehement disapproval.

Too late to find a place in the crowded chamber, Jefferson stood just outside the open door. When the tall, dark-haired burgess stood to claim the floor, his plain, dark clothes contrasted conspicuously with the bright colors worn by his colleagues. He had the starkness of an Old Testament prophet. His voice was deep, melodious, and commanding as he asserted that, under two royal charters granted by King James I, the Virginia colonists were entitled to all the rights of Englishmen "as if they had been abiding and born within the Realm of England." The right to self-government, he insisted, had "never been forfeited or in any other way given up." He concluded by introducing a resolution that "the General Assembly of the Colony have the only and exclusive right and power to lay taxes and impositions upon the inhabitants of this colony and that every attempt to vest such power in any person or persons whatsoever, other than the General Assembly aforesaid, has a manifest tendency to destroy British as well as American freedom."

When Henry sat down, veteran legislators vied for the chance to reply. In the voting that ensued, his first four resolutions passed, the fourth by a margin of only two or three votes. The fifth—proclaiming the Virginia General Assembly's exclusive right to tax the colony's inhabitants—needed all the oratorical help that its author could give it.

As Henry rose this time, his face was flushed and his voice throbbed with controlled excitement. Self-taxation, he said, was essential to freedom. As his extraordinary voice rose to a roar, then sank to a whisper, it was almost like a multitude of voices rushing down the winds of time. He made his fellow legislators see themselves as actors in a universal drama. Charging that the Stamp Act was an act of tyranny, Henry, his voice vibrant with emotion, declared, "Caesar had his Brutus, Charles the First his Cromwell, and George the Third . . ."

"Treason!" shouted the Speaker.

"And George the Third," concluded Henry, "may he never have either."[9] Almost certainly, no one will ever know whether Henry had originally intended to end his sentence in that way. In any event, he had adroitly freed himself from charges of treason without leaving a scintilla of doubt about his implied threat. Henry's motion carried by a single vote.

Jefferson was startled when his normally placid cousin Peyton Randolph, rushing past him in exit, exclaimed, "By God, I would have given five hundred guineas for a single [additional] vote."

Governor Fauquier wrote authorities in London that the "young, hot, and giddy" had prevailed. Jefferson later wrote of Henry at this moment, "He seemed to me to speak as Homer wrote."

There was a new breed of leader in the colonies in the second half of the eighteenth century, and Jefferson had seen in action one of the most impressive specimens. He had heard what was then almost surely the most eloquent voice in American politics, certainly the most eloquent voice of the frontier. Not that Henry was an untutored, self-made son of the wilderness. International interest in his career coincided with a quickening interest in the natural man, and Lord Byron saluted him as a "forest-born Demosthenes," but he had had important elements of a classical education. His principal teacher was his father, Justice John Henry of the Hanover County Court, an alumnus of Scottish universities and probably the best-educated person among the parents of all who would come to be known as Founding Fathers. Patrick Henry's mother, Sarah Winston Henry, was praised by Colonel William Byrd II, a Royal Society member sometimes called the premier gentleman of America, as the most fascinating female conversationalist in Virginia. Actually, Henry's connections gave him entrée to Tidewater planter society, and his home county was not nearly so far west as Jefferson's Albemarle. By no stretch of the imagination could Hanover's hills be described as mountains. But Henry voiced the aspirations of the small farmers, the hill country men, and the western settlers. He articulated the concerns of the frontier.

Also, in others of the thirteen English colonies south of Canada on the Atlantic littoral, there were those who derived their ideas of freedom from English traditions and classical learning and those who found them in the rough and ready egalitarianism of pioneer life. In the clash of these forces, there was the likelihood of much waste of human potential. In the union of them, there was the possibility of realization on an impressive scale.

22

"BEFORE WE WERE THE LAND'S"

HOW DID THE HUTS of Jamestown and Plymouth nurture the civilization of Williamsburg and Boston? How was it that by 1775 the erstwhile frontiers of European culture had become its bastions? The European population of the thirteen colonies totaled about two and a half million, fully a third as many as Great Britain could claim. Nor were they all from the British Isles, though its emigrants predominated. The Dutch had founded Albany and New Amsterdam. Though both settlements had surrendered to England, the Dutch remained an important element there and along the Hudson River, where great estates were occupied by still powerful patroons. The Swedes had occupied the shores of Delaware and New Jersey. The German nations had not established settlements, but German Protestants had founded Lancaster, York, and Bethlehem in the English Quaker colony of Pennsylvania.

The thirteen colonies—New Hampshire, Massachusetts, Rhode Island, Connecticut, New York, New Jersey, Pennsylvania, Delaware, Maryland, Virginia, North Carolina, South Carolina, and Georgia—stretched along the Atlantic littoral. No towns exceeded Williamsburg and Boston in influence, but others rivaled them in various ways. New York City (the former New Amsterdam), Charleston, and Savannah were flourishing ports, each with its own distinctive brand of English culture, and Philadelphia, with a population of forty thousand, was the second largest city in the British Empire, eclipsed only by London.[1]

These port cities, as well as Baltimore and Norfolk, prospered in a trade consisting largely in the export of American raw materials and the import of European finished products. Far more impressive than the growth of these centers of trade was the changed character of the commerce of ideas between America and Europe. Increasingly, Americans were importing the raw materials of European thought about a free society and sending them back in altered form. America had become a creative partner in intellectual exchange with the Old World.

The physical rusticity of early settlements in Virginia and Massachusetts can be misleading when one marvels at their nurturing of the vital culture of the early American Republic. Cabins in both colonies housed minds not cabined and confined. Some of the pioneers of the American wilderness were acquainted, through reading or personal association, with pioneers of thought in the Old World. There were times in the history of seventeenth century Virginia when one might have assembled a small chapter of Oxford alumni. And one might have organized in the Massachusetts Bay Colony a rival chapter for Cambridge. Besides, there were some Cantabrigians in Virginia and some Oxonians in Massachusetts, and in both places alumni of preparatory schools providing a solid background in the classics. The educated were by no means so numerous as to be typical of society, but they certainly weren't that plentiful in Europe either. And we have seen, as in the case of George Sandys, there were even among the early colonists a few examples of internationally significant scholarship. Two seventeenth-century colonists, John Winthrop, Jr., of Connecticut and Colonel William Byrd II of Virginia, received the high tribute of election as fellows of the Royal Society of London.

Of course, creative minds could grow in cabins. From the seventeenth century until well into the nineteenth, American life would be enriched by those who spent their formative years in cabins, their horizons enlarged by their natural surroundings and a few great books—the prospect of a distant mountain enhanced by stories of Moses and Parnassus, the waves of ocean or bay mingling with the cadences of Homer or the King James Bible.

But changes in architecture would signal the increasing sophistication of colonial societies. Jamestown began with wattle and daub houses inside a palisade. They were dwellings of a sort quite common in medieval England, and still not unusual in rural sections of the old country. But in Virginia they were quickly joined, and soon succeeded, by more complex structures. These, too, however, were of medieval design. People often incorrectly assume that most domestic architecture of a historical period reflects the designs of the most famous architects of the era. Actually, most people tend to build houses not radically different in style from those they knew when growing up. Few seventeenth-century Englishmen in the home country or in the colonies built dwellings in the style of Inigo Jones or other great Elizabethan and Jacobean architects, just as few twentieth-century Americans have chosen houses in the style of Frank Lloyd Wright.

Many of the houses in early Virginia were in the Tudor style, which had developed in the reign of Henry VIII.[2] Some were half-timber, with a portion of the wooden skeleton showing through the plaster, in a style much favored for Christmas card scenes since the nineteenth century. Some had one or more broad-based pyramid chimneys with crowstep shoulders. Diamond-paned casement windows were popular with those who could afford them. Some houses were of frame construction, often with a single room and a loft above. The original structure might be added to as the family grew.

Some houses were brick. A bricklayer found employment at Jamestown in 1607, the year of first settlement. Three years later, there were houses with brick ground-floors and timbered second stories. Glazing varied the pattern of some brick walls. In 1611 Jamestown, tiny settlement in a wilderness, had streets of row houses, all contiguous, most about twenty by forty feet in inside measurements—exactly the specifications in medieval building codes for English cities! Such was the strength of tradition.

But some other settlers mixed a little experimentation with traditional forms. They learned from the Indians that bark shingles could provide cooler roofing than wooden ones or thatching. They learned, too, from the aborigines that straw mats with bright designs could lighten dark interiors. Indian building skills commanded respect. The treasure house of Powhatan occupied 3,000 square feet as compared with 2,413 for the Governor's House at Greenspring, the largest English mansion in Virginia in the seventeenth century.

On the Eastern Shore of Virginia, the peninsula separated from the rest of the colony by Chesapeake Bay, settlers developed their own style of domestic architecture—an elongated structure consisting of big house, little house, colonnade, and kitchen. Many such dwellings were one room deep. Front and back windows would be placed in line with each other so that, in that land swept by the winds of both bay and ocean, and where no place was more than five miles from tidal water, full advantage could be taken of summer's cooling breezes. In 1724 Hugh Jones, a professor of mathematics at the College of William and Mary (founded 1693), wrote of its principal edifice, "The building is beautiful and commodious, being first modeled by Sir Christopher Wren, adapted to the nature of the country by the gentlemen there. . . ."[3] So much for the sacrosanct authority of the surveyor of the king's works, who was also England's greatest architect! By the end of the seventeenth century, a great many public buildings in Virginia were being "adapted to the nature of the country by the gentlemen there." So were the institutions that the buildings housed.

The story was much the same in Massachusetts. The first housing was crude indeed, but the structures that evolved from it are enough to disprove the canard that Puritans cared nothing about esthetics. The best of the cottages were for a while in the style of old England, medieval and Tudor. Houses with an overhanging second story, a type sometimes found in Virginia, proved especially popular in New England.

The Dutch, who acquired Manhattan in 1624 and established New Amsterdam, brought with them the town architecture of their homeland. They built in brick or stone, or sometimes a combination of wood with one of these more durable materials. Curvilinear gables with round cusps appeared on their brick houses. A few appeared in Virginia, too, apparently not as a result of the Dutch colony's influence but as a direct copying of some English houses that followed Holland's architectural lead.

Houses in Maryland and the Carolinas were much like Virginia's adaptations of English models. Pennsylvania, founded late, in 1680, tended to begin with English designs more recent than the medieval, and sometimes selected very sophisticated models. After the turn of the century, German settlers in the southwestern part of the colony introduced the gambrel-roofed style that came to be known as Pennsylvania Dutch.

The Swedish colony, founded on the Delaware in 1638, though shortlived, brought to America a domestic architecture that proved so popular that many came to regard it erroneously as the most distinctive American contribution to house building. This was the log cabin constructed of round logs notched at the corners for a tighter fit. As the frontier marched westward, the log cabin moved with it. This Swedish contribution was proudly cherished as an indigenous American creation. In the American Republic, "log cabin candidates" for the House, the Senate, and the presidency multiplied rapidly, and one overzealous politician was accused of claiming that he had been born in a log cabin that he had built with his own hands. In the twentieth century, western films would make the log cabin even more of a cultural icon. As the United States became increasingly urban, many Americans, nostalgic for what they assumed to be a simpler era, built log houses as vacation homes and even as year-round dwellings. A few were constructed in the traditional way, but more were prefabricated structures with machine-turned, symmetrical logs, as alike as cigarettes, constituting an extremely uniform effort toward individuality.

By paths as varied as their dwellings, colonial Americans moved toward the creation of an independent nation. For a long time, they did not realize that it was what they were doing. Nor was it even a distant, dreamed of goal. As Robert Frost wrote:

> The land was ours before we were the land's.
> She was our land more than a hundred years
> Before we were her people. She was ours
> In Massachusetts, in Virginia,
> But we were England's, still colonials. . . .[4]

By the time, however, that these colonists found themselves on the threshold of independence, they had created a distinctive subculture of the European world, one infused with tremendous vitality. Within their homes and taverns, their stores and schoolrooms, their county courts and statehouses, they had thought and spoken for generations in the largely unconscious process of building philosophies that would energize the new nation at the moment of its birth.

23

THE VIRGINIA PATH

IN POLITICAL MATTERS as well as in physical pioneering, the seventeenth century Virginia settlers were finding paths through a seemingly trackless wilderness. From their old homes they brought familiar tools, some that proved helpful, some that became too burdensome to keep, and others that were useless until refashioned for the new environment.

Two of the tools brought by the Jamestown settlers were put to use immediately after their first landing. This was at Cape Henry, at the mouth of Chesapeake Bay, where they went ashore before moving up the James River to the place where they would build their palisaded village. Though by their own account they were "ravished" by the sight of "tall, goodly trees" after more than four months at sea, and they had to take time to plant a stout wooden cross amid the sand dunes, there was another duty to which they were urged on by both royal command and their own curiosity even before they could enjoy the luxury of exploration. King James I had entrusted to the adventurers a small sealed box that was not to be opened until they had set foot upon the soil of Virginia.[1]

It was known in a general way that the box contained instructions for the new government. There was therefore an air of tense expectation on that day in May 1607 (late April by the Old Style calendar) when the seal was broken, a document was withdrawn, and someone began reading from it. The colonists were to be governed by a Council of seven and their president. No particular surprises in that. But there was reason for surprise that no president had been named. And especially surprising, disconcerting to some, was the fact that Captain John Smith was one of the councillors.

This stocky, lush-bearded twenty-eight-year-old had come to the New World in chains. He had sailed as a free man, but officers of the expedition said that they had made him a prisoner to keep infuriated fellow passengers from throwing him overboard. Not that Smith had done anything criminal but, as tempers had flared among the crew and more than one hundred passengers crowded aboard three tiny ships, he had been ready with advice at every juncture, and he could illustrate the wisdom of his counsel by citing his own heroic experiences on land and sea in Europe and Asia. His fellow travelers could not claim that his advice had gotten them into trouble; they regularly ignored it. The irritating thing, apparently, was that Smith was so often proved right.

First things first. Captain Christopher Newport had commanded them at sea. Now that they were on land, they did not have a government to deal with the problem of Smith or anything else until they had a president. As this officer had not been chosen for them, they must choose him for themselves. And so, making use of one of the tools they had brought with them from England, they held an election. Captain Edward Maria Wingfield was chosen, but more important than the selection was the process itself.

Then the colonists could deal with the problem of Smith. They were not eager to welcome this offensive fellow to the Council, but the king might not take kindly to the rejection—and, worse still, the arrest—of one of his appointees. This was the time for another tool brought from home. In the first recorded jury trial on American soil, Captain Smith was found innocent, and all impediments to his holding office were removed. In this instance, the decision may have been even more important than the process. Various persons, in England and Virginia, contributed to the survival of Jamestown, but no one saved the settlement more often than the boastful, but brave and resourceful, captain.

Sixteen nineteen frequently is called the "red-letter year" in Virginia history.[2] The reasons are threefold. It was then that women first arrived in the colony in large numbers. The fact that any man marrying one of the "young maids" had to reimburse the London Company 120 pounds for her transportation has given rise to the erroneous story that the planters bought their spouses. Actually, the young women were carefully screened for character and general fitness by the company and were free to decline all proposals of marriage if none suited them. Most seem to have been of solid yeoman stock, but some were orphans of gentle birth. The worth of some is hinted at by the later tribute to one: "She placed her little foot upon the soil of Virginia and the wilderness became a home."

It was also in 1619 that blacks first came to Virginia. It is often said that they were slaves, but available evidence seems to indicate otherwise. The term *slave* was then sometimes used interchangeably with *indentured servant.* The name was applied to anyone—black or white—who agreed to serve another, or the colony itself, for a stated period in exchange for transportation to Virginia and a gift of tools of a trade, or some other significant desideratum, on completion of indenture. Unfortunately, black slavery did evolve from indenture and was legally recognized in Virginia in the 1630's. It had already been accorded such recognition in Connecticut. The first legally recognized slaveholder in Virginia was Anthony Johnson, himself a black.

The third great event of 1619 in Virginia was the convening in Jamestown of the first representative assembly in the New World, an occasion that we have already reviewed from the perspective of Sir Edwin Sandys and others in Elizabethan England. This great precedent, especially significant because it provided an example for each of England's other colonies in North America, embraced a host of smaller ones. The legislature that met in the little wooden church at Jamestown was, like England's, bicameral, even though at first the two houses sat together. As the Council, or nonelective body, was the upper chamber and had existed since 1607, it corresponded to England's House of Lords, which antedated the Commons and was appointive and hereditary. On the first day, Virginia's legislature, acting as the judge of its own members' qualifications, refused to seat the burgesses from Martin Brandon because they were from the bailiwick of one who exercised many of the privileges of a feudal baron.

The legislators were quick to exercise the power of taxation, establishing the first poll tax levied by an American government. But they went beyond this action, asserting the exclusive right to levy general taxes. In doing so, they foreshadowed the doctrine of implied powers, which would play a major role in United States constitutional history. The Virginia legislators argued that, although authority to levy general taxes had not been expressly granted them, they had been given "power to make and ordain whatsoever laws and orders should by them be thought good and profitable for our subsistence."

Other precedents also were more the product of exigency than of deliberation. The colony survived the challenge of masterful campaigns, one led by Powhatan and one by Opecancanough, both brilliant Indian chiefs, in 1619 and 1622. But in 1624 a crisis erupted within when James I, charging the Virginia Company with mismanagement, revoked its charter. Fortunately, Virginians were already so wedded to representative government that they would not let it die, and at least two royal governors, Sir George Yeardley and Sir Francis Wyatt, connived with them in its preservation. The governors went so far as to convoke legislative sessions without the king's assent. The crisis quickly deepened, however, in 1629 when John Harvey became governor.[3] During his six-year tenure, Harvey committed a series of "executive offenses" ranging from striking a councillor in the teeth to permitting a man with a commission from the king to seize another man's skilled servant for his own labor force, and finally to detaining a petition to the sovereign from the people's representatives.

Oppressed by a tyrannical governor and deprived of royal remedy, the Council arrested him and compelled him to listen to a recital of grievances. Their spokesman then said, "Sir, the peoples' fury is up against you and to appease it is beyond our power, unless you please to go [to] England, there to answer their complaint." Harvey refused and attempted to reassert his authority. Failing, he agreed to sail for England on the first ship available. The Council named an interim successor to serve "till the King's pleasure [was] known." The Council then obtained confirmation of its actions from the House of Burgesses.

Although this solution was in response to immediate need and not the result of long planning, it proved an effective one. Harvey filed charges against the Virginia "conspirators," but their representatives won the sympathy of officials in England. The colonists' accomplishment was a remarkable one. Without the shedding of blood, they had achieved a complete overturn of executive authority. Moreover, while taking action unprecedented in an English colony, they had shown scrupulous regard for traditional English legal principles. And

the Council's appeal to the Burgesses for confirmation, though intended primarily to enlarge their own base of support in an emergency, advanced the
dimensions of representative government in Virginia.

This almost spontaneous reaction to crisis was every bit as significant as if
it had been the result of long calculation. New spontaneity had been made
possible by a subtle change in political attitudes and philosophy in the less than
three decades of English settlement in Virginia. One does not have to accept all
the premises of Arnold J. Toynbee's *Study of History* to agree with his assertion
that institutions transported across an ocean undergo a "sea change." One aspect of the change was visible in 1624 when local government in the colony, in
obedience to conditions imposed by the dispersion of population under the
plantation system, began to assume forms quite different from the English
models of municipal government advocated by royal authority. Another clue
to the changing climate of opinion in Virginia appeared in the same year when
the colony's legislature, instead of enacting verbatim the provisions for the established church which prevailed in the mother country, provided for "uniformity in our church *as near as may be* to the canons in England" (italics mine).

When the king revoked the Virginia Company's charter, Virginians, seeking a substitute for diocesan authority, turned to their own civil government—
legislative as well as executive—and authorized still greater institutional departures from the English model. The dramatic ousting of Governor Harvey in
1635 was the culmination of a series of changes marking a significant shift to
admit a larger proportion of innovation in the equation of tradition and experiment.

But sometimes the legislature itself had to be held in check, or prompted
to reform, in defense of the rights of transplanted Englishmen. In 1652, after
parliamentary commissioners from England informed residents of Virginia's
Northampton County that they would be required to pay a poll tax, Colonel
Thomas Johnson, a prominent planter, urged resistance in a fiery oration. Representatives of the people drew up the Northampton Protest, declaring the "law
which requireth and enjoineth taxations from us to be arbitrary and illegal,
forasmuch as we had neither summons for election of Burgesses nor voice in
their Assembly." Nobody has successfully refuted Ralph T. Whitelaw's claim
in 1950 that the "Northampton Protest against taxation without representation
. . . is noteworthy as being the first expression in the English colonies of one of
the principles ultimately involved in the American Revolution."[4] Though the
General Assembly delayed action on the protest until 1653, and then fined
Colonel Johnson and others for their part in it, representation was granted to
Northampton County in that same year and Johnson was elected a Burgess.
Thus the resistance to tyranny that Virginians had begun under royalty was
continued under Cromwell's parliamentary regime.

During the eight years of parliamentary rule beginning in 1652, the Burgesses almost constantly gained in influence. Though the governors in this period were in some cases actually Puritan, and in all instances nominally so, they
governed in a spirit of compromise foreign to their Massachusetts counterparts.
Virginia had demonstrated such loyalty to the fallen House of Stuart as eventu-

ally would earn it the designation "the Old Dominion," and Cavaliers fleeing Cromwell's England were sure of a warm welcome in the colony. While religious freedom was not expressly guaranteed, as in Roger Williams' Rhode Island, the Calverts' Maryland, or William Penn's Pennsylvania—all founded by oppressed minorities—the atmosphere was generally tolerant as compared with that of most of the other colonies. Few talents were lost to the community because of religious persecution.

When royal government was restored in 1660, Virginians eagerly greeted the return as governor of Sir William Berkeley, who had served as governor immediately before the triumph of the parliamentary regime and had continued to live among them after stepping down. Berkeley had been as popular as any chief executive in the colony's history. The genial temperament manifested in his first tenure had not prepared them for his harshness now. Berkeley was an intelligent and sophisticated aristocrat, the author of a drama that had played successfully to London audiences. But he had always been an ardent royalist, and the execution of his king had been a traumatic experience. He now saw every opponent of royal measures as a potential regicide. When he, a representative of the king, was faced with opposition, he believed that the entire fabric of society was threatened.[5]

Virginians were not awed by even so impressive a royal governor as Sir William. The memory of the ousting of Harvey was still strong. And the General Assembly was so strong after eight years of Puritan governors' dependence on it, that it offered the office to Berkeley when the outcome of the power struggle between Cavaliers and Roundheads in England was still uncertain. It justified its action by asserting that "by reason of the late frequent distractions" there was "in England no resident absolute and generally confessed power." The offer of the governorship to Sir William was contingent upon his pledging allegiance to whatever power established itself as the home government.

After Sir William's appointment was confirmed by Charles II under the restored monarchy, the governor made himself increasingly independent of the General Assembly. He did not neglect any sign of respect for the Burgesses, but he used his influence to secure the election of members favorable to his views. The councillors were likely to share most of his philosophy anyway, but he carefully cultivated their friendship as well as that of the lower house. Many measures were first decided upon at social gatherings at Greenspring, the governor's estate, rather than in open debate. Meanwhile, the yeoman farmers felt increasingly far removed from the decision making that circumscribed their lives. The gap between the prosperous and the poor steadily widened, and those whose fathers had dreamed of advancement for themselves or their children despaired now of progress for any of their foreseeable progeny.

A series of natural disasters hit agriculture hard, all but wrecked the economy, and brought disproportionate suffering to the small farmers. As they labored in their meager fields, they were not inspired with loyalty when the governor, having pocketed his annual bonus from the General Assembly, rode past in his great coach from Jamestown to his mansion with its great hall, numerous servants and slaves, seventy horses, and fifteen hundred fruit trees.

Adding to the economic squeeze on Virginia was the strengthening of the hated Navigation Acts instituted by Cromwell's regime. No American, Asiatic, or African goods could legally enter England except aboard English ships of which the owner, the master, and three-fourths of the crew were English. Worse still, all commodities produced for export by England's American colonies could be shipped only to England or its dominions. The Americans not only were denied the opportunity of seeking the most profitable markets for their products but also were required to pay higher freight rates than were offered by the Dutch, England's great competitors in transatlantic trade. These provisions were a severe irritation to Virginia, and to England's other American colonies: Massachusetts (including the province of New Hampshire and the district of Maine), Connecticut, Rhode Island, Maryland, Carolina, the West Indies, and Pennsylvania (including the Swede-settled province of Delaware). The Dutch colony of New Amsterdam had been added to England's roster by conquest and renamed New York. An increase in taxes to support war with Holland exacerbated dissatisfaction in all these colonies.

In 1673 Governor Berkeley wrote that many Virginia farmers were so desperate that he feared they would be lured by the Dutch to "revolt to them in hopes of bettering their condition by sharing the plunder of the country with them." The next year he reported that he had "appeased" two mutinies "raised by some secret villains who whispered among the people that there was nothing intended [by a new levy] but the enriching of some few people." In 1675 a concatenation of omens heightened the desperation of the superstitious—a large element in any seventeenth century society. They saw a comet "streaming like a horsetail westwards." Afterwards there settled upon them with the heaviness of fate a flight of pigeons so numerous that the limbs of large trees broke under their weight; the same phenomenon had occurred before the "massacre of 1644." A third event of 1675 heightened anxiety. Biblical accounts of plagues of locusts sprang to mind when clouds of insects rose out of the ground and devoured the leaves of the trees.

When parties of Susquehannocks and Doegs moved southward into Virginia and fighting broke out between the Indians and the English, many colonists thought that the prophecy of the omens was about to be fulfilled. A blunder on the part of some of the settlers who mistook friendly tribesmen for enemies escalated the warfare. Virginians petitioned their government to authorize a large-scale counterattack before invading numbers increased. One of a group of petitioners from Charles City County identified himself to Governor Berkeley as "one of your honor's subjects."

"Fools and loggerheads!" Berkeley exploded. "You are the King's subjects and so am I. . . . Pox take you." After that, he denied the right of petition when defense was concerned.

An Indian attack near the falls of the James devastated plantations in the area, alarmed all of Virginia, and raised the determination of many settlers to organize for their own defense. Among those raided by the Indians was Nathaniel Bacon, who suffered not only heavy property loss but also the loss of his overseer, who was as well a valued friend. Bacon repeatedly applied to the governor for a commission to lead troops against the Indians but was denied every time. When the enemy were reported to be concentrated at a point fifty or sixty miles above the falls of the James, men of Henrico and Charles City counties assembled in determination to become an army. When word spread that Bacon was willing to lead them and he appeared in their midst, he became their commander by acclamation.

The new leader undoubtedly had more prestige than any other that they could have gotten to oppose the policies of the governor. Twenty-nine years old, he had been in Virginia only two years but already had been a member of the Council half that time. His advancement was helped by his fluent speech, his extraordinary charisma, and his impressive connections. He was cousin to Berkeley's wife, to a veteran eponymous member of the Council, and to the late Sir Francis Bacon. Though highly intelligent, young Bacon did not share the scholarly predilections of his celebrated relative. He was a master of arts from Cambridge, but reportedly had rollicked his way through the university. He had taken the continental tour customary for young Englishmen of his class and had studied law at Gray's Inn. His marriage to a Suffolk knight's daughter against her father's will had caused her to be disinherited, and a financial scheme of his own had gone sour. So, like many of his countrymen, he emigrated to Virginia for a fresh start. But, unlike most of them, with the help of a generous father, he purchased two plantations on arrival.

Nathaniel Bacon, when he accepted command of his makeshift army, appears to have been motivated chiefly by anger at the destruction of one of his plantations and the killing of his friend. An impatient man by nature, he was frustrated by the governor's caution. There is no indication that he intended to lead a political reform movement to deal with legal and economic inequities afflicting the ordinary people. But his newfound followers had learned to regard the governor's rejection of their appeals for protection as part of a long pattern of disregard of their needs. They were determined to demand correction of the whole package of abuses. Bacon listened and became their spokesman.

Historical estimates of Governor Berkeley vary widely to this day.[6] Some agree with the contention of Bacon's followers that Sir William was profiting from the fur trade and was reluctant to sever business relations with his Indian allies. Others think that he was sensibly trying to prevent a long period of costly warfare when there was still a chance to settle a conflict born of rash actions on both sides. Regardless of his intentions, he had long ago let communication atrophy between him and the people. For his part, he was disposed to see as treason any opposition to the policies of His Majesty's viceroy.

Bacon tricked several tribes of Indians into fighting each other, and in two days of brutal battle won a major victory in which he destroyed a great division of the Susquehannocks, while wiping out many Occaneechees, killing their chief, and laying waste their trading post. Whether or not with his approval, some of Bacon's men slaughtered hostages.

Hoping to avert the battle just concluded, the governor had proclaimed amnesty for the rebel and his followers if they would lay down arms immediately and "return to their duty and allegiance." Berkeley personally led three hundred mounted volunteers to intercept Bacon before the battle, but was too late. Sir William now suspended Bacon from the Council and "all other offices civil and military." But he let the proclamation of amnesty stand for all but two particularly active followers of the rebel if they would abandon their leader. Bacon himself was no longer promised amnesty. Rumor had it that Sir William intended to hang him.

Long-festering discontent erupted into mutiny in almost every part of the colony. Personal confrontations between Berkeley and Bacon were everything that one could have expected from two high-tempered opponents, one a septuagenarian governor who had triumphed as a London playwright, the other a charismatic young leader who had just discovered his talent for public performance. In one meeting, Sir William, throwing up his arms and rolling his eyes heavenward, exclaimed, "Now I behold the greatest rebel that ever was in Virginia." Bacon's reply was so effusive that the governor declared, "If there be joy in the presence of the angels over one sinner that repenteth, there is joy now, for we have a penitent sinner come before us." The tableau ended with Sir William rising from his chair as the rebel dropped to one knee before him.

A subsequent confrontation saw Bacon and his army on the statehouse green, with the governor rushing out to the young officer. Berkeley, tearing open his coat to expose his white-shirted chest, roared, "Here, shoot me 'fore God, fair mark!" Drawing his sword, he demanded, "Let us settle this difference singly between ourselves."

Bacon replied in a chivalrous speech appropriate to a drawing-room scene, but all the while his followers kept their guns trained on the windows of the state house, where the Burgesses hastily enacted legislation to meet rebel demands.

The laws so obediently passed were far more democratic than anything previously adopted in America, or for that matter anything enacted even decades after the Revolution. They repealed the law of 1670 that had restricted the vote to men owning real estate, and granted suffrage to all freemen. They repealed another law that had exempted councillors from certain taxes. The office of justice of the peace had often been passed on from father to son; the new legislation provided that the popularly elected representatives from each county sit with the justices when those officials assessed taxable property. Councillors, however, would specifically be prohibited from sitting with the justices. And other officers would be more frequently accountable to the voters than before. The term of the sheriff, a powerful county official, would be limited to one year. In those days of the established church in Virginia, vestries had civil as well as ecclesiastical responsibilities. They had been self-perpetuating, but under one of the new laws they would be chosen triennially by the voters of each parish. Other legislation prohibited anyone from holding more than one of the following offices at a time: sheriff, clerk of the court, surveyor, and escheator.

The struggle resumed, with Berkeley briefly regaining control of Jamestown only to lose it again to the rebels. Unable to hold the capital, Bacon burned it. He died of a fever before he could see action again. Berkeley's return to power occasioned so many executions that he was summoned to the court of Charles II to defend his own conduct. England had had enough of bloodletting in its civil war. Charles said, "That old fool has hanged more men in that naked country than I did for the murder of my father." Berkeley died before he could have an audience with his sovereign.

The revolutionary legislation enacted at gunpoint in Virginia was repealed. But it was not forgotten. Marylanders, like Virginians, had suffered under England's Navigation Acts. Inspired by Bacon's example, residents of that colony's Calvert County took up arms and proclaimed "the liberties of the freeman of Maryland." The rebellion was put down, but was the first of a series of insurrections that, merging with a strong spirit of militant Protestantism, helped end the Calvert Proprietary and accustomed Marylanders to the idea of fighting for liberty in defiance of royal authority. The example of Bacon's Rebellion also led to insurrection in Carolina's Albemarle County.

In 1676, exactly a century before the American Declaration of Independence, Virginia rebels went to war against an imperial government whose Navigation Acts seemed to exploit the colonies and whose royal authority was too distant for understanding, too intrusive for toleration. Yeomen learned that in such a struggle they could find leaders in the ranks of the privileged. When Virginians and other colonists went to war for independence in 1776, Bacon's Rebellion was cited as a precedent. It came to be called "the false dawn of American independence." Zodiacally, the false dawn is the glow that appears over the horizon but vanishes before the coming of the true dawn. It does not cause the dawn, but it is caused by some of the same factors and is its herald.

But the greatest long-time influence of the rebellion was not through the lawyerly compilation of records of like occurrences to justify contemplated actions but in the power of myth to infuse with fire the dreams of people in a crisis of freedom. Plato believed myth so important to the proper functioning of his ideal Republic that he advocated the deliberate creation of a suitable mythology. No true historian can justify conscious mythologizing for the supposed good of society, but the spontaneous accretion of myth over generations can sometimes help to inspire a society and focus its aspirations. In such cases, the myth is not an artificial tool manufactured to facilitate societal transitions advocated by "those who know best." It is instead a symbolic expression of a people's longing for fulfillment.

It is their larger-than-life self-portrait. And if the ideals be noble, when the early reality is shed like an outgrown mask, as with Beerbohm's Lord George Hell or the protagonist of Hawthorne's "Great Stone Face," the new reality bears a striking resemblance to the old dream. One thinks of the Renaissance fulfillment of Florence's myth of itself as principal heir to the heritage of ancient Rome. Bacon had not been dead long when ballads and odes and legends began to glorify him and his followers. Dreams of greater liberty and opportunity had brought many immigrants to the new world. However much some Americans might try to deny freedom to their fellows, a native mythology was emerging in which those who struck for freedom strode as giants across the landscape of the land of the second chance. A self-fulfilling legend is an inchoate truth.

24

ROYAL ROAD TO LEARNING

SOMETIMES GIANTS walked only in the landscape of the imagination, and the steps toward freedom were small and hesitant. But with a place in the sun at the right hour, even an ordinary figure can cast a giant shadow. The decades immediately succeeding Bacon's Rebellion brought to Virginia no comparable high drama; but in a multitude of ways scarcely discernible, from year to year, the colonists were building a society that was more than a pale copy of England. Massachusetts, New York, Pennsylvania, South Carolina, and other colonies were experiencing similar incremental change. Along the Atlantic littoral from Maine to Charleston, Americans were inching forward toward independence of mind long before a formal declaration of separation.

Between 1677 and 1689, England certainly did not send giants to govern Virginia. But the failings of the royally appointed administrators led to important successes for representative government. Some eras with more honors have much shorter records of achievement. Charles II in 1677 appointed Thomas, Lord Culpeper, a royal favorite, to succeed Sir William Berkeley as governor. Culpeper was so reluctant to exchange the delights of the court for the rigors of a burned-out capital that he did not arrive until nearly three years later. Meanwhile the colony was led by two interim executives, both of whom lacked the prestige of full appointment and the second of whom became senile. Under these circumstances, the legislators were emboldened to defy executive authority.[1] After the Lords of Trade and Plantations, the London-based overseers of colonial government, described a message from Virginia legislators as "seditious, even tending to rebellion," the king ordered Culpeper to Virginia to deal personally with the crisis. Arriving in July 1680, the governor conferred with the Council as to how best to administer punishment. Undoubtedly, he was staggered when these royal appointees rigorously defended the lower house and unanimously recommended that he not comply with the king's order. The Council was composed of Virginia's elite—politically, financially, and socially the king's most prestigious subjects in the colony. What could the governor do in the face of such united opposition?

He explained his problem to London. The Privy Council advised His Majesty that the spirit of resistance was strong among all classes in Virginia. The implication was that there might be in the offing a rebellion that would make Nathaniel Bacon's foray look like a minor civil disturbance. The king rescinded his order to the governor but, in an attempt at retroactive face-saving, commanded that all references to the affair be "razed out of the books of Virginia." He could not, however, erase it from the minds of Virginians.

Growing among all classes of free Virginians was the idea that citizens had certain rights that nobody, not even the sovereign, could set aside. Resistance to any denial of these rights was itself a right. This idea was not far removed from the concept of "unalienable rights" that a Virginian, voicing the consensus of colleagues from New England to Georgia, would write into the Declaration of Independence nearly a century later.

The next crisis came when royal threats forced through the House of Burgesses an act imposing a duty on each hogshead of tobacco exported from Virginia. The sticking point for the legislators was the provision that the revenue obtained would not be administered by them, but would go directly into the royal treasury. Hard times ensued when a glut of tobacco lowered prices for this chief money crop. When the acting governor convinced the legislators to appropriate money for a standing army to remain in Virginia but forbade consideration of the tobacco depression or any other business, infuriated farmers destroyed the tobacco in their own fields and then banded together to slash the plants of neighbors not willing to go along. There were suspicions that some of the great planter class had given not only sympathy but leadership.

Ordered back to Virginia to deal with the problem, Culpeper antagonized many people in carrying out royal instructions to punish offenders. Later the colonists were able to get him removed on the basis of frequent absences and almost habitual inactivity.

His replacement was another peer, a much more forceful one, Francis Howard, Lord Effingham. In the small pond of the Virginia colony, Culpeper had been like Aesop's King Log. Frustrated by his inertia and frequent absences, the Virginians longed for a more active chief. But like the denizens of the fabled pool, they were given an activist in spades and almost came to regard his predecessor's reign with wistful nostalgia. The activities of this reactionary petty tyrant did far more to school Virginians in the philosophy and subtle stratagems of resistance to autocracy than could have been accomplished by the guidance of the most enlightened royal appointee.

In the August heat of the contentious year 1686, the governor, in obedience to the king's personal order, dissolved the General Assembly. Because the Burgesses retained the power of taxation, Effingham could not do without them indefinitely, but he said, "The public debts being paid, . . . I shall not for the future have so frequent Assemblies."

The Burgesses, convened again in 1688, promptly charged the governor with seizing legislative prerogatives in imposing fees by fiat. Most hated was what now appears to have been a forerunner of the Stamp Act that later roused Americans to revolution. It was "a fee of 200 pounds of tobacco for the seal affixed to patents and other public instruments." The Burgesses were also disturbed by Effingham's action in restoring by proclamation a certain law that had been repealed many years before. They feared that a governor, particularly this one, might "by proclamation revive all the laws that for their inconveniencies to the country have been repealed through forty years since."

The legislators directly petitioned the king, Charles II's successor, James II. The king received the petition, but was busy with an emergency of his own. William of Orange, ruler of Holland, grandson of Charles I and son-in-law of James II himself, was preparing to invade England. The crisis was precipitated by the birth of James' first male heir, a product of his marriage to an Italian Catholic. Associating Catholicism with the long-standing threat of Spain, prominent Whigs and Tories in England united in welcoming William, leader of Europe's Protestant coalition.

Some Virginians were quick to react to news of division in England. Effingham reported to London that "Unruly and disorderly spirits, laying hold of the motion of affairs, and that under the pretext of religion, . . . betook themselves to arm." It was all disturbingly reminiscent of Bacon's Rebellion. Veterans of that war were still active in the colony, and probably were among the dissidents. Saber rattling gave way to noisy celebration when word arrived in March of 1689 that William and Mary had been proclaimed king and queen.

Known as the "Glorious Revolution," the bloodless transition in England is commemorated as a historic constitutional change—the shift of the governmental center of gravity from the throne to Parliament. The influence of this event was stronger than that of any precedents set during Cromwell's rule under the Commonwealth. This was true, first of all, because it combined parliamentary leadership and monarchy, an institution that most Englishmen were not ready to abandon. At least as important was the fact that the new rulers owed their titles to a Parliament that had changed the order of succession to clear the way for them. Supremely important was the fact that, before being crowned, they had subscribed to the Declaration of Rights. In this document, they acknowledged the illegality of any royal attempt, without the consent of Parliament, to make or suspend laws, levy taxes, or maintain a standing army.

For recognition of these principles, Virginians had been battling—sometimes in the field and more often in the legislative chamber—for almost half a century. It had begun with the colony's own small, but highly significant, "bloodless revolution" when Governor Sir John Harvey, who had misunderstood the temper of the new land, was expelled by its citizens acting through responsible representatives and officers of government.

By a happy synchronism, a culmination of events in Virginia's struggle for legislative government had occurred at the very time that parliamentary government under the Crown achieved a dramatic advance in the mother country. The newly crowned William acted on the petition presented to his predecessor by the Burgesses' representative. He ordered the Lords of Trade and Plantations to investigate the Virginians' complaints and see that justice was done. After consideration of the charges and of Effingham's personally delivered defense, the Committee recommended that the governor's tax for affixing the seal to patents be discontinued. They also recommended abandonment or compromise of other controversial practices by the governor. A few months later, the Committee heard further reports from the Burgesses of misgovernment and oppression by Effingham. Not completely abandoning one of their own, the Lords involved in the weighing of evidence decided that Effingham should retain the title of governor and presumably a large portion of the emoluments of the office. But he was ordered to stay away from the colony, and the actual powers of his position were assigned to a resident lieutenant governor.

By now, in kingdom and colony, "bloodless revolution" was not an event but a continuing process. Representative government in America, and specifically in Virginia, had been born in the brain of an idealistic and scholarly Englishman, Sir Edwin Sandys, working in the bright afterglow of Elizabethan glory. It had been implemented by men in America for whom it was more a matter of acceptable solutions than of ideological crusading. It had been helped along by friendly, fair-minded governors such as Sir George Yeardley and Sir Francis Wyatt, but also unwittingly by such autocratic successors as Sir John Harvey and Lords Culpeper and Effingham.

Though the Virginians' concept of individual freedom, remotely originating in Greece and Rome, was imported from England, the colonists' pursuit of that ideal would not keep them in close filial association with the mother country. The lines of legislative evolution in kingdom and colony, like other parallel lines, would not merge.

As early as the ousting of Harvey in 1635, the necessity of struggling in Virginia for rights taken for granted in England gave the colonists the feeling that the king, the peers, and sometimes the Commons conspired to deny them the "rights of Englishmen." The colonists perforce had come to think of themselves as having interests apart from those of the mother country. This feeling grew in Berkeley's second administration into a strong conviction on the part of many men that they were justified in opposing royal power by force of arms in defense of these colonial interests. Even some gentlemen who chose not to enlist under Bacon's banner excused or sympathized with those who did. Governor Culpeper's lethargic autocracy, combined with his frequent absences, allowed Virginians to get into the habit of resisting royal directives with impunity. Having had a "log" for a ruler, moreover one that was always floating away in times of crisis, the colonists were ill prepared to endure quietly the aggressive autocracy of an Effingham. As they found themselves constantly in contest with His Majesty's representative, the consciousness of interests separate from those of England intensified.

A more subtle change had also come about since Bacon's Rebellion. Many great planters of the colony had come to regard the rights for which the yeomanry contended as identical in most cases with Virginia's interests. The drive for greater colonial independence no longer divided, but rather united, all classes in Virginia. The movement drew its impetus from the yeomanry, but increasingly attracted leadership from the aristocracy.

25

"ARISTOCRACY WITH THE DOORS OPEN"

GREATLY SIGNIFICANT in the story of America, and ultimately in world history, is the fact that the growth of political autonomy in Virginia was accompanied by marked cultural progress. As a result, the achievement of American independence, in which Virginians played a prominent role, would be virtually simultaneous with a cultural efflorescence endowing some of these same leaders with the intellectual tools and the eloquence to speak memorably to an international audience.

The man sent to Virginia in 1690 to perform the duties of governor while Effingham remained in England and held the title was Lieutenant Governor Francis Nicholson. He was high tempered and tactless, but he was a highly energetic administrator with enthusiasm for education and civic projects. He was also farsighted. He initiated some important endeavors, and energized others that he found languishing.

Early efforts to found a college in Virginia had been thwarted by the Indian wars of 1622. The project was resuscitated in the 1660's but perished amid the troubles of Berkeley's administration. Nevertheless, some had cherished the dream through the years, and in 1690, the year of Nicholson's arrival, some of the great planters joined with him and the Reverend James Blair to secure funds and obtain a royal charter. It is a wonder that two such headstrong people as Nicholson and Blair worked well in tandem, even for a while. Blair had come to Virginia as a missionary in 1685 and four years later had become the commissary, or official representative, of the bishop of London, whose diocese included Virginia. Each thirty-five years old in the year of their collaboration, each energetic, determined, and supremely confident of his own rightness, they were united in their determination to found a college in the colony.

While these two men became the principal movers in the founding of the college, much credit should be given to a cultural milieu that had been building in Virginia. John Jennings points out, "English university graduates among the planters and within the professional classes increased, strengthening public sentiment in favor of the establishment of schools and colleges."[1]

A Scot with a master of arts degree from Edinburgh as well as being the trusted subordinate of a bishop who had been a leading candidate for arch-bishop of Canterbury, Blair had helpful connections in Great Britain. He trav-eled to London to enlist aid from many people. In direct appeals to the king and queen, he won their enthusiastic support as well as the issuance of a charter for a college named in their honor. The College of William and Mary was chartered in 1693, and the cornerstone of its famous Wren building was laid in 1695.

Blair became its first president under conditions that might well be the envy of most college heads today. He was the General Assembly's choice, and the charter specified that he should be president "during his natural life." Moreover, he was elected rector, or chairman, of the college's governing board. William and Mary was an institution of both church and state, the training of ministers being one of its functions, so an appeal from the board could be addressed either to the governor and Council or to the highest ecclesiastical officer in the colony. The king intervened to make Blair a member of the Coun-cil; the president was allied by friendship, and eventually by marriage, to some of the other members. If recourse was made to the ranking ecclesiastic in Vir-ginia, that was Blair himself. So if anyone wished to appeal from the lifetime president to the board, Blair would preside over the matter. If it should be appealed from the board to either church or state, he would have an influential voice at that stage.

When the cornerstone of William and Mary was laid in 1695, Nicholson was no longer Virginia's chief executive, having been replaced by Sir Edmund Andros, who had been governor of both Massachusetts and New York. Andros resented Blair's influence with the General Assembly, particularly in securing funds for the college. The commissary's energetic leadership coincided with a period of increasing enthusiasm for education on the part of Virginia's leaders.

Blair also was resourceful in obtaining money from other, sometimes less conventional, sources. As J. E. Morpurgo said, he drew on both "piety and piracy."[2] Blair persuaded trustees of the estate of Robert Boyle, famous scien-tist and cofounder of the Royal Society, that a gift to the nascent college would fulfill the great man's bequest "for the advancement of the Christian religion." Blair also cooperated with his own lawyer to obtain freedom for four captured pirates in exchange for their donating to the school a portion of their booty.

When Blair could not convert Andros to support of the college, he deter-mined to get rid of him. The minister became one of the most effective king-makers and king-breakers in Virginia history. In fact, when one considers that in this period all the governors were royal appointees, Blair's record of influ-ence in this regard is without parallel in the Old Dominion and perhaps in all of British America. Andros was the recalcitrant governor on whom Blair cut his teeth, but he was only the first of a succession of chief executives appointed or removed through the commissary's influence during the fifty years that he served as president of William and Mary. Blair made full use of a network of associates extending throughout the settled part of the colony and reaching across the Atlantic to the palaces of the bishop of London, the archbishop of Canterbury, and Their Royal Majesties.

Blair used his influence not only to secure Andros' recall in 1698 but also to have his old coworker Francis Nicholson appointed as successor. Nicholson returned to Virginia to find the statehouse at Jamestown in ashes. It had burned shortly before Andros' departure. What many men would have viewed as an extraordinary misfortune, particularly given the timing, Nicholson seized as an opportunity. Though Jamestown was built on lower ground than was desirable for a capital, this disadvantage had been offset in the early days of settlement by its access to the spacious waters of the James River, nearly five miles wide a little downriver from the site. The first settlers were thankful that their town was not deeper in the wilderness. Although the waterways still were the main thoroughfares in a day of good boats and bad roads, the lines of settlement no longer clung to the coastal rim but, concentrated largely along the rivers, reached inland eighty to one hundred miles. Besides, Jamestown had never completely recovered from its destruction in Bacon's Rebellion. Fate had provided an opportunity to build a proper capital on a suitable site.

Nicholson had such a location in mind. Middle Plantation, the site of the young College of William and Mary, was on relatively high ground about seven miles inland from Jamestown. It was not on the water but was only a short distance from landings on both the James and York Rivers. Nicholson proposed that the new capital be named Williamsburg.

The building of the town was exciting and significant for reasons beyond the immediate cause for interest in Virginia. The project introduced the concept of municipal planning to America. In many ways it would be superior to the haphazardly developed towns of England. The 1699 Act of Assembly condemned buildings occupying the three-hundred-acre site. Duke of Gloucester Street, the broad main thoroughfare, would stretch a straight mile between the college and the projected capitol. In a bold step reminiscent of the municipal building codes in Renaissance Florence, specific standards were imposed for any structures, business or residential, to be erected on this street. Within the provisions there was room for ample expression of individual tastes. Nicholson encouraged the construction of substantial public buildings, even to the extent of making contributions from his personal fortune.[3]

He was equally generous in support of primary education. He called for public schools in various communities, offering to pay part of the salaries of clergymen willing to double as schoolmasters.

Nicholson was just as vigorous, and just as much personally involved, in protecting the colonists from organized crime. He himself led successful assaults on gangs of pirates infesting the Chesapeake Bay and some of Virginia's creeks and rivers.

This man of action had a gentler side, as shown by his concern for the welfare of slaves. He not only encouraged their Christianization but also their education in reading, writing, and other basic skills. One could not have expected him in that era to advocate emancipation.

Though a man of many virtues, Nicholson also had a grievous fault. His

temper flared whenever he was opposed. The councillors, proud men accustomed to deference, bridled at what they considered his insults. Nicholson's
temper became his undoing in the spring of 1700 when the forty-five-year-old
governor conceived a grand passion for a prominent planter's teenaged daughter. The young lady was already betrothed to a man quite acceptable to her
parents and presumably to her. The governor swore that, if she married her
intended, he would cut the throats of the groom, the justice who issued the
license, and the clergyman who performed the ceremony. Recovering himself,
he wrote the bride that he hoped God would make her "one of the happiest
and fortunatest women in all respects." But the harm to his reputation was now
irreparable. It was easy for Blair, who had had disagreements with him, to get
rid of him now.

Thus Nicholson's folly, abetted by the intrigue of his enemies, brought to
an end one of the most useful gubernatorial careers in the British colonies.
But the College of William and Mary remained, ironically enough, as a joint
monument to him and Blair. And the city of Williamsburg is itself a memorial
to Nicholson's vision, initiative, resolve, and capacity for innovation within a
framework of tradition. The support that Virginians gave to his and Blair's
favorite projects was a tribute to the abilities of these remarkable leaders. Even
more important, it testified to the creative society that Virginia was becoming
as it entered the eighteenth century.

For a decade or two, Williamsburg was a battlefield for the struggle between rusticity and elegance, but elegance was winning. With the handsome
Georgian buildings of the college and the capitol, Duke of Gloucester Street
was anchored in elegance at either end. An H-shaped structure with large,
round towers and a graceful, flag-topped cupola emblazoned with the royal
arms, the capitol is still considered one of the most attractive public buildings
ever erected in America.

When Alexander Spotswood became governor in 1710, he continued the
building program launched under Nicholson.[4] He submitted his own design
for a new, graceful Bruton Parish Church on Duke of Gloucester Street and
offered to pay personally for twenty-two feet of brick wall. He also designed
the colony's architecturally distinctive armory and powder magazine. The
building of an official residence for the governor, inaugurated under Nicholson,
was completed by Spotswood, who added handsome walls and gates, outbuild-
ings, and terraced gardens. The name "Governor's Palace" was not at first official nomenclature, but was bestowed by groaning taxpayers. Nevertheless, the
building was so handsome—its design has been attributed to both Inigo Jones
and Sir Christopher Wren—that it became a matter of Virginia pride.

Great planters and their wives who were entertained at the executive mansion emulated some of its interior and exterior features in their own homes.
Architectural historian Thomas Tileston Waterman says, "The Governor's Palace initiated the great period of Virginia building which produced a larger number of fine Georgian mansions than any of the other English colonies."[5] He also
says that "it initiated a period of mansion building unequalled in the history of
England's colonies."[6] Some Virginians may have obtained home plans from

English architects or copied plans directly from English architectural books, but most builders of elaborate dwellings appear to have altered book plans to suit their own requirements or to have relied on native builder-architects who followed the same procedure. Thus creativity within traditional forms was introduced.

Spotswood worked to strengthen the economy that supported the colony's growing elegance. With tobacco as chief pillar of that economy and even the principal means of exchange, he saw the need for enforcement of strict standards for the product. But he also saw the need for the diversification of production and the promotion of industry. He took the lead, mining iron and operating a foundry.

His humane spirit worked hand in glove with his promotion of prosperity. As in all the other American colonies, there were many people who thought that war to the death was the only solution to the problem of frontier relations between the English and the Indians. Spotswood thought that integration of the native and colonial economies could bring peace and a better life to both groups. To this end he founded the Virginia Indian Company to regulate and stabilize the fur trade. He also encouraged cultural integration by offering remittance of the annual tribute from defeated tribes as an inducement to send their youths to the school in Williamsburg. He founded a school farther west for the Indians there, and paid the expenses himself.

With imagination and flair, Spotswood promoted the settlement of Virginia's western lands. John Lederer, a German immigrant, had explored the Blue Ridge Mountains of Virginia as early as 1670, and a few other adventurous souls had followed. But reports of their findings had invited skepticism, and the area remained a terra incognita. Spotswood organized and personally led an expedition across the mountains. It included veteran rangers and Indian guides, a few great planters, and eager young men on horseback from some of the colony's most prominent families. They all drank toasts on the crest of the Blue Ridge and then went on beyond the routes taken by Lederer. They returned with tales of great herds of stilt-legged elk and shaggy-coated buffalo. They told of a land exciting in its beauty and majestic in its expanse, and most of all a habitable land of great opportunities for the hardy and the persistent.

One early result of all the adventuring was the creation of a new county as a buffer against France's expanding North American empire and its Indian allies. In the spirit of the jolly expedition that had included young cavaliers with classical educations, the new county was named for their leader by making a Latin pun. It became "Spotsylvania," or "Spot's wood."

There was enough glamour mixed with the practicality of the transmontane trip to stir popular imagination. Spotswood acted to insure against its fading. The governor gave each of the mounted volunteers who had accompanied him a tiny golden horseshoe studded with diamonds, and dubbed each of them a "Knight of the Golden Horseshoe." Here, too, humor was mixed with sentiment. The emblem was a memento of the delay early in the expedition when riders who had ventured into rocky terrain with shoeless horses accustomed to sandy soil had to stop for shoeing. The little souvenirs were cherished by their owners and passed down to generations of their descendants.

Spotswood and leaders of the General Assembly were worried over the growth of slavery in Virginia. With the governor's support, the legislators in the session of 1710–1711 tried by heavy taxation to curb the importation of blacks. But the attempt was vetoed by the trade-conscious Crown.

Spotswood was actually aware that the British colonies in North America were interdependent in matters of economy and defense. On northern trips to negotiate with the Indians, he conferred with other colonial leaders on common problems. His influence was also felt to the south. He intervened to restore order when rival candidates for governor of North Carolina resorted to the sword. And he sent troops and arms to South Carolina when it was hard beset in a war with the Yamasees.

Sufficiently able and magnetic to become perhaps the greatest of Virginia's colonial governors and to exert beneficent influence beyond the borders of the colony, he was not strong enough to remain in office in 1722 when Commissary Blair disputed with him on a question of civil versus ecclesiastical authority.

Though ousted from the governorship, Spotswood remained in Virginia, enjoying the respect and affection of most of its citizens. Later he was appointed postmaster general for England's American colonies and, probably to nobody's surprise, soon established efficient postal routes between Williamsburg and New England.

Although his twelve years as governor were ended, the Spotswood legacy lived on in Virginia. It not only survived but grew because, besides being the originator of many beneficial things, Spotswood was the author of policies expressive of the ethos and aspirations of the society he served. He became a permanent resident of Virginia, for it was already his spiritual home. Numerous philosophical ties bound him to the governing class to which some Virginians belonged and many more aspired.

Spotswood had not at first expected to feel so much at home among the Virginians. Early in his administration, he complained that the councillors "looked upon all persons not born in the country as foreigners."[7] The Burgesses stubbornly insisted on the validity of precedents established within their own borders, whether or not such precedents existed in Great Britain. One might have expected the royally appointed councillors to be more appreciative of royal custom than the popularly elected members of the lower house. Spotswood therefore was particularly surprised that the councillors departed from their oaths of office and ignored the king's wishes "when these interfere[d] with the ease of the people or the liberties which, by a long custom, without any lawful foundation, they [had] been used to." They would accept "no jurisdiction, civil or ecclesiastical, but what [was] established by laws of their own making."

After twelve years as governor, Spotswood, while loyal to the Crown, knew what it was to feel himself a Virginian and not just a Briton who happened to live on the outer reaches of the empire. The prevailing attitude favored independent experiment among a people still loyal to important elements of English culture and tradition. Like the college and some of the public buildings planned in England for Virginia, some of the political, ecclesiastical, and social institutions derived from England were "adapted to the nature of the country by the gentlemen there." There were incentives to creativity in the art of government.

What Ralph Waldo Emerson said of Victorian England was true of eighteenth-century Virginia: it was "an aristocracy with the doors open." Of course, they were not open to everyone. The portals were not only closed but barred to blacks. Escape from servitude was quite possible, and the number of free blacks was slowly growing. Opportunity for paid employment on the side enabled some slaves to purchase their own freedom as well as that of spouses and other family members. As we have seen, the first legally recognized slaveholder in Virginia was a mid-seventeenth-century black planter on the Eastern Shore. Afterwards, many other Virginia blacks would win their freedom, and some would fulfill long-cherished ambitions of becoming slaveholders themselves. This practice would continue until 1865. But no degree of prosperity could gain them admission to the aristocracy.

Whites, whatever their gifts, ordinarily could not make the transition from yeoman to aristocrat in a single generation, as some had in the early days of settlement. But an energetic yeoman might become a planter of the middle sort. And the acquisition of substantial acreage, a contracting of the proper marital alliance, valuable service to the community, and good manners might lift a planter of the middle sort into the aristocracy. A woman, unless her manners were execrable, almost always assumed the social status of a husband whose station before marriage had been above hers. People who had risen to the upper class in a single generation might occupy a tenuous position in the eyes of some resentful gossips, but their children would have the proper bloodlines on one side and one generation of personal accomplishment on the other, plus respectable estates. Another generation of personal accomplishment combined with prestigious marriages would make their children's positions unassailable.

There were enough familial links among the classes that even some of the councillors were not completely removed from the colony's humbler folk. There was a sense of common cause when councillors, Burgesses, and ordinary petitioners joined to fight for their rights.

Even descendants of those who had entered the colony as white indentured servants did not constitute a breed apart, as is sometimes supposed. Indentured people were employed in a wide variety of jobs, ranging from menial house-and-field tasks to plantation administration and the teaching of Latin.

Their backgrounds were also various. Adam Thorogood, an indentured servant in Virginia in 1624, was "Captain Adam Thorogood, Gentleman" in 1626, and a county justice in 1628.[8] In 1635 he received a grant of 5,350 acres for transporting 120 people into the colony at his own expense. This former indentured servant had been no stranger to polite society. He was the son of a vicar and nephew of a knight. His own son became a county justice, sheriff, and burgess, and married the daughter of Governor Sir George Yeardley. Nicholas

Granger was one of seventy-five young boys found "running wild in the streets" of London, "sleeping under stalls" and begging, who were shipped to Virginia in indentured service. He became a respected plantation owner, and his son married the widow of a man of prominent family. His descendants included professional men of national and international reputation.[9] It must be admitted, however, that the lives of most of the other "*Duty* boys," as they came to be called from the name of the ship that brought them, remained obscure.

Some Virginia immigrants were indentured to uncles or older brothers. A grant of fifty acres awaited the sponsor, and the "servant" would be apprenticed to his own relative to learn farming, house construction, shipbuilding, or some other trade. Members of the same family living under the same roof, proprietor and indentured servant were not considered members of different social classes. But even when there was no kinship to soften the relationship, the indentured one was not necessarily degraded. At least once in the seventeenth century, a Virginian protested to county officers that he had been denied the designation "gentleman" on official rolls while his indentured servant was accorded the honorific. He was told that his servant was a gentleman, but he himself was not.

At one time in the seventeenth century, about twenty members of the General Assembly had once been indentured. Indenture was more often an opportunity than an oppression. It was a way for people to emigrate to Virginia who could not otherwise afford the journey. At the end of a period of indenture, they received property or the tools of a trade. As the eighteenth century waxed, the indentured proportion of Virginia's population decreased. Also, the opportunity to enter the colony poor and become rich declined correspondingly. But economic differences were not insuperable barriers to political cooperation. Partly responsible were the mingling and mixing of earlier generations, coupled with the memory of times when great planters on the Council and their more modestly propertied counterparts among the Burgesses had stood shoulder to shoulder for colonial rights.

Nevertheless, the great planters early into the eighteenth century had a lifestyle that distinguished them from their neighbors, and exercised an influence economically, politically, socially, and culturally that dwarfed that of fellow citizens. By midcentury their preeminence in Virginia was comparable to that of the nobility in England. Their status was recognized in what became the popular, but strictly unofficial, designation of "river baron." The James, York, Rappahannock, and Potomac Rivers that penetrated deep into the mainland, and the creeks and inlets of the Eastern Shore, were the principal avenues of travel and commerce. The homes of the great planters dotted the banks of these streams, and to their wharves came not only boats engaged in Chesapeake trade but also ships from New England, London, Liverpool, and sometimes Amsterdam and Lisbon. When Durand de Dauphiné, the Huguenot exile, approached one of the large plantations, so great was the aggregation of big house, dependencies, barns, workshops, and tenant houses that he mistook it for "a rather large village."

The same traveler wrote, "The gentlemen called cavaliers are greatly esteemed and respected, and are very courteous and honorable. They hold most of the offices in the country, consisting of twelve seats in . . . [the Council], six collectors [of Customs], the rank of colonel in each county, and captains of each company." As for legislative duties and judicial service, he said, "They sit in judgment with girded sword."[10] The cavalier image was especially vivid in the case of such river barons as Councillor Ralph Wormeley of Rosegill, who surveyed his plantation from a saddle of crimson velvet.

But, though some of the great planters dressed with elegance and panache and many delighted in sports, they were not merely leather-lunged, jolly fox hunters. In this "land of gauntlet and glove," many held learned volumes as easily and familiarly as they did the reins of spirited horses. Wormeley, an Oxford alumnus, had in his library such classics of political philosophy as Cicero's *Prince*, Sir Walter Ralegh's *Maxims of Government*, Henri duc de Rohan's *Treatise on the Interest of the Princes and States of Christendome*, John Locke's *Two Treatises of Government*, and Francis Bacon's *Elements of the Common Laws of England*. Besides, there were volumes of history, biography, and science, and more than thirty dictionaries, grammars, and other works concerning the English, French, Spanish, Greek, and Latin languages. And among the poets represented by separate volumes were John Donne, George Herbert, Edmund Waller, Virgil, Ovid, Horace, and Terence.

Wormeley was far from unique among the river barons in his appetite for literature and scholarship. A fellow councillor, Colonel William Byrd II, had studied law at London's Middle Temple. While in England for his education, he had so impressed some of its most distinguished scholars that he had been inducted into the Royal Society at the age of twenty-two. His personal library probably was one of the two largest in the American colonies, and his scientific observations on Virginia's flora and fauna were attentively read in Europe. In dealing with lighter subjects, he was one of the most graceful prose writers in North America in his time. Before coming down to breakfast each day, he customarily read a selection from Hebrew, Greek, or Latin unless he was feeling lazy, in which case he read in a modern language.

Robert Carter of Corotoman, called "King Carter" because of his extensive property and regal ways, was the richest man in Virginia. His estates comprised a duchy of three hundred thousand acres, and he had power to match, becoming Speaker of the House of Burgesses, then councillor, and serving as rector of the College of William and Mary and acting governor of Virginia. His library, in English, Latin, and French, was strong in law, theology, and philosophy, and included the same classical poets favored by Wormeley. Carter notified the English schools attended by his sons of errors that he had discovered in the Latin texts they used.

Councillor Richard Lee, patriarch of a Northern Neck family rivaling the Carters, had a library in English, French, Latin, Greek, and Hebrew, including the works of some of the world's greatest thinkers. Not only were such ancient classics as Aristotle, Xenophon, Plutarch, Epictetus, Livy, Suetonius, and

Homer represented, but so were such later writers as Erasmus, Thomas à Kempis, Descartes, Montaigne, and Francis Bacon.

Of course, the presence of certain books in a private library does not guarantee that they are read. Some archeologists of the future might conclude that most twentieth-century Americans were avid readers of the Bible and Shakespeare. And, of course, these works have been better read than most books. But many Bibles gather dust between annual spring-cleanings, and the pages of some of the most ornate editions of Shakespeare remain unclipped. The true test of familiarity is in range and frequency of quotation. And this test the river barons passed with flying colors, whether we examine their public papers, their private correspondence, or their personal journals.

Many river barons were aware of Plato's ideal of the philosopher-king. And many were the sort to identify with it. All of them wielded magisterial power, and the most prominent of them searched history, philosophy, theology, and classical and Renaissance literature for guidance. Some were lawyers as well as planters. Some, in accordance with time-honored English custom, were judges without having been lawyers. But law books tended to be fairly numerous in their libraries, and virtually all were acutely aware of the power of precedent.

Nevertheless, the broad reading of some led them to be innovative within the framework of tradition. Colonel William Byrd's studies in religion, history, and science led him to disapprove of the institution of slavery and to believe that its existence boded ill for the colony. His studies and observations also led him to suspect that the abilities of some blacks were much greater than most white Virginians and Londoners assumed. His readings about self-government in earlier societies whetted his skill and zeal as an advocate of American liberties. As official liaison between the colony and London, he became so persistent a pusher of colonial rights that the royal government abolished the office. Richard Lee summoned the rich resources of varied learning to support the dictates of his independent conscience, which once led him to refuse to recognize the sovereignty of King William and Queen Mary. In the eighteenth century, Virginia's most influential rebels were members of its elite.

The councillors were not isolated from the Burgesses and the county commissioners. Most councillors were county commissioners before attaining their more exalted offices, and some continued in their county offices even after appointment to the Council. Many served as burgesses before their final elevation, and afterwards many had sons or brothers serving in the lower house.

But there can be no doubt that the councillors were the most powerful leaders of an oligarchy. Theirs was largely a self-perpetuating body because royal governors and the government they served came to recognize that things went more smoothly in Virginia when appointments to the upper chamber were made with due deference to those already seated. Spotswood, stronger and more independent than most governors, explained in 1713 that he preferred the appointment of certain men to fill three Council vacancies because all the other qualified men were "related to one particular family, to which the greatest part of the present Council [were] already near allied."

Privileged Virginians carried in their heads their own *Almanac de Gotha.* They emulated Elizabethan ideals of noblesse oblige. Books ranging from Castiglione to English manuals for the nobility were found in their libraries. The evidence is fairly clear that they imitated an ideal of the nobility rather than the actuality. As a result, in culture and in responsibility, they generally excelled English nobles of the period. The responsibility was demonstrated repeatedly in their acceptance of the idea that, to justify their prerogatives, they had to render genuine service.

It is difficult to generalize about people as fiercely individualistic as Virginia's great planters. But we can say that they were compounded in varying degrees of certain traits whose desirability, or lack of it, was largely a matter of proportion. One of their most obvious characteristics was pride, individual and family, that when properly restrained helped to keep them honest and dignified in business and government. Carried to excess, the same trait became arrogance. They were acquisitive. Within limits, their acquisitiveness enabled them to accumulate the means for graceful lives of culture. Out of control, it could lead to rampant greed. "King" Carter saw the weakness in himself as well as in some of his friends. He wrote to one of them:

> I wish both you and I were more mortified to . . . [the world] than we are. The thoughts of having a little more white and yellow earth than our neighbors would not puff us up with so much vanity and insolence, nor make us so uneasy when we meet with plain dealing. . . . We are but stewards of God's building: the more he lends us, the larger accounts he expects from us, and happy they that make a right use of their Master's talents.

Carter was no more moved than the "rich young ruler" of biblical fame to surrender all his wealth. But such reflections did cause him to build handsome Christ Church in Lancaster County, to labor hard for the College of William and Mary, and to provide funds for the education of those less fortunate.

The leaders of Virginia were hardworking. We should not be misled by the legend of indolent planters sipping mint juleps on broad verandahs while a squadron of house servants, in number almost rivaling the field hands, scurried about in obedience to their master's sybaritic desires. There were undoubtedly some indolent planters, but they were neither successful farmers and businessmen nor political leaders. The owner of a large plantation governed a small community, among whose members were distributed not only agricultural jobs but many trades, such as carpentry, blacksmithing, mill operation, shoemaking, and textile weaving. Usually he had at least a sloop, but sometimes he had one or more oceangoing ships engaged in coastal or transatlantic trade.

A society in which each large plantation was a separate community placed a high priority on versatility. This factor was strengthened by the fact that a great planter characteristically functioned at various times as farmer, businessman, judge, militia officer (sometimes also naval officer), architect and builder, and legislator. He was expected to know at least one language besides his native

English, to be acquainted with classical literature, and the history of the ancient Greeks and Romans, medieval and modern Europe, Britain, and North America.

Pride in their personal success in Virginia, coupled with the realization that, despite their attainments, most Londoners regarded the planters as provincials, fostered a Virginia-centered patriotism. Leading Virginians, when they referred to "my country," were likely to mean the colony rather than their ancestral home. The supercilious attitude of some in the home government bred resentment and defiance that blossomed into patriotism for the planters' native soil. Pride in English traditions, strengthened by proud lines of descent (in some cases authentic and in others imagined), warred with Virginians' impatience with English failure to understand their needs or respect their knowledge of their own environment. This situation produced in Virginia a ruling class torn between a love of tradition and a demand for innovation.

Such a tension between heritage and experiment, if kept within a favorable balance, could be vitalizing and creatively productive—provided the society did not remain too insular. In the second half of the eighteenth century, forces were at work that would end insularity—that would make Virginia an actor, not merely a property, on the world stage.

In the 1740's England was at war with Spain. In 1742 a Spanish fleet of thirty-six ships attacked Georgia, but was driven off by Scots under the command of General James Oglethorpe. Colonies to the north feared similar attacks. Norfolk, Virginia, on the great natural harbor of Hampton Roads, would be a tempting prize. Its citizens carried guns to church as their pioneer ancestors had in time of war with the Indians, and the Anglican rector preached with a pistol on the pulpit. In 1744 when the war between England and Spain was caught up in the vortex of the War of Austrian Succession, England found herself perforce at war with France. A New England expedition seized the French Canadian fortress of Louisbourg, but it was returned to France in 1748 when the Treaty of Aachen officially ended the war.

Actually, however, what succeeded was not peace but an armed truce between England and France. Nowhere was undercover continuation of the conflict more evident than in North America, and in few places was anxiety about it so great as in Virginia. The Ohio Territory was Virginia's by royal charter from London. But Paris also claimed it as part of the French Empire. The diplomats negotiating the settlement at Aachen had not agreed upon a boundary separating the rival claimants.

The situation heated up in 1749 when the French governor of Canada sent the chevalier Céloron de Bienville to reinforce his country's claims to the disputed territory. He proceeded from Lake Erie to Lake Chautauqua, down the Allegheny River and the Ohio, and up the Miami before returning to his point of departure. Visiting many Indian tribes, he told them that the English intended to steal the land of the aborigines as well as Ohio, which he said belonged to his own nation. In the name of the French king, he would warn the English to retire. In the course of his journey, Céloron ordered various British traders to cease "trespassing."

When Robert Dinwiddie arrived in Virginia in November 1751 to assume his duties as royal governor, he was determined to do something about the French threat. Nearly sixty years old, quite elderly by eighteenth-century standards, the heavy-jowled, double-chinned executive with the big nose and prominent paunch was one of the most energetic leaders the colony had ever had. In twenty years of dynamic political administration, including a term as surveyor general of customs for the Southern District of America, his life of action was marked by a paper trail comprising a correspondence among the most voluminous on the continent.

Dinwiddie's undoubted patriotism in opposing French designs on the Ohio Territory was augmented by his concern as an investor in the Ohio Company, which sought to develop the area. He dispatched three diplomats to Pennsylvania to secure ratification of the eight-year-old Indian treaty of Lancaster, including confirmation of the English right to build two trading posts on the Ohio River and erect settlements south of that stream. He instructed his representatives to cultivate amicable relations with the Six Nations.

The governor hoped that the French in the Ohio valley were for the most part only traders, but he feared that they were backed by a "great army of French among the lakes." With the advice of the Council, he divided Virginia into four military districts, each commanded by an adjutant. In the southern district, which included all of Virginia south of the James River and east of the frontier, this post was filled by young George Washington. That he should receive such a command and the automatic rank of major before his twenty-first birthday was a tribute to his ability to impress Dinwiddie. The fact that he was the half brother of the late Lawrence Washington, adjutant for all of Virginia, and the grandson of Colonel John Washington, a famous Indian fighter, subtracts little from the dimensions of his personal achievement. It is even more remarkable in light of the fact that, although he was an outstanding frontier surveyor who had added two thousand acres to his ancestral estate, he had no military experience beyond local militia drills.

When Washington learned that fifteen hundred French troops had been landed on the southern shore of Lake Erie and had built forts and roads there, he was pleased to hear that Dinwiddie intended to warn the French commander to leave English territory. The young Virginian volunteered to deliver the message. The governor accepted the offer, and instructed him to determine the strength and position of French garrisons. The major was to demand a reply from the Frenchman. He was to wait not more than a week for the answer and to request a French escort back to the English settlements. Meanwhile, King George had granted Dinwiddie authority to build forts to prevent French seizure of the Ohio country. Moreover, the governor was empowered to seek the cooperation of other colonies in opposing the French menace. Dinwiddie dispatched letters under the king's seal to his fellow governors in English America and called the General Assembly of Virginia into special session.

Washington returned to Dinwiddie with a reply from the French commander evasive in every way except for its assertion of French rights to the Ohio country and determination to make a prisoner of every English trader on its waters. The Frenchman also paid tribute to Washington's "quality and great merit."

The governor asked the major to prepare a written report for delivery to the Council the next day. Thanks to his careful keeping of a daily journal, the young officer was able to present a detailed, unusually informative, seven-thousand-word document.

Dinwiddie's energy and efficiency, united to Washington's high competence and valor, produced effective resistance to French encroachment in the west. Though Governor Sharpe of Maryland was made acting commander-in-chief of the military forces being assembled in England's American colonies, Dinwiddie held the even more important job of civilian coordinator of intercolonial cooperation. South Carolina and the Jerseys were tardy in furnishing supplies. Even more disappointing was the failure of Pennsylvania, a rich colony as much imperiled as any. Its legislature announced that it would remain aloof because no French forts had been built within its boundaries. Many persons in other colonies called the struggle "Virginia's war." They were not eager to compete with the Old Dominion's primacy in this effort.

It was at the Battle of Monongahela, at the site of the present city of Pittsburgh in Pennsylvania, that a large force of English and colonials under British Major General Edward Braddock was defeated by the French. The chief reason for the near debacle was the general's insistence on using formal European tactics in a frontier situation. Washington, now a colonel, had tried respectfully to warn him of the need for innovation to meet the demands of the terrain and of Indian involvement, but Braddock persisted in the old ways and lost not only the battle but also his life. When Washington, more than any other officer, kept the retreat from becoming a rout, his name became famous throughout the colonies and in England. His actions strengthened the growing belief among many Americans that, in their own territory, they, not the leaders of the mother country, knew what was best. It was appropriate that this should be Washington's role at a climactic moment because it was he who had fired the first shot in what was coming to be called the French and Indian War.

He was made commander in chief of all Virginia military forces. But, by this time, the war was clearly a problem far beyond Virginia's borders. Not only had Braddock been defeated in Pennsylvania, but in the same year Governor Shirley of Massachusetts had failed in an attempt to take Fort Niagara from the French, and William Johnson in an effort to seize Crown Point on Lake Champlain. Johnson did win a small battle with the French on Lake George, and was knighted for it, but it was England's only victory in North America that year. From the site of Braddock's defeat, Dumas, the architect of that French triumph, exulted, "I have succeeded in ruining the three adjacent provinces, Pennsylvania, Maryland, and Virginia, driving off the inhabitants and totally destroying a tract of country thirty miles wide."

The war was no longer confined to North America. Ironically, all the action of 1755 had occurred while England and France were officially at peace. Far-flung as the North American struggle was, it soon was subsumed by what we now know as the Seven Years' War. Austria came to the support of France, while Frederick the Great of Prussia came to England's aid. By 1761 France, Austria, Russia, Sweden, Spain, and most of the German states were at war with England, Prussia, and Portugal. One of the most decisive events of the contest was the coming to power in England of William Pitt. He perceived that the struggle was a world war and conceived its strategy on a global scale. With Prussia fighting under Frederick in Europe and the British navy keeping French ships in port, he concentrated England's armies in America, making it the principal theater of the war. The excellent generalship of Geoffrey Amherst, whom he made commander in chief in North America, and the brilliant victory of another of his appointees, Brigadier James Wolfe, over Louis Joseph Montcalm at Quebec, together with the triumph of a provincial force under Massachusetts' Colonel Dudley Bradstreet, proved the wisdom of his decision.

Victories of Great Britain and her allies in Europe and India completed a roster of triumphs so great that in the *annus mirabilis* of 1759, as Horace Walpole reported, the bells of London were worn with the pealing of victories. With the fall of Montreal the next year, the French knew they had lost. Less perceptive in this instance, Spain entered the war against England in 1762 and lost both Havana and Manila. Before the Treaty of Paris brought a formal end to the war in 1763, England had captured or destroyed nine-tenths of all warships flying the flag of France.

Voltaire wrote, "Such was the complication of political interests that a cannon shot fired in America could give the signal that set Europe in a blaze." From the perspective of more than a century later, William Makepeace Thackeray observed:

> It was strange that in a savage forest of Pennsylvania a young Virginia officer should fire a shot and waken up a war which was to last for sixty years, which was to cover his own country and pass into Europe, to cost France her American colonies, to sever ours from us and create the Western Republic; to rage over the Old World when extinguished in the New, and of all the myriads engaged in the vast contest, to leave the prize of the greatest fame with him who struck the first blow.[11]

With the Treaty of Paris in 1763, British imperialism was fully launched upon its course on the oceans of the world and in three continents. But at the same time, events signaled that America could be an initiator as well as a follower. Virginia's Governor Dinwiddie had won the Crown's support for extensive operations to combat French expansion in North America. He had also initiated and coordinated communication among the colonies in preparation for large-scale conflict. A young Virginia officer, George Washington, and the Virginia militia prevented England's first major campaign in the war from becoming an unmitigated disaster. Later, with North America as the principal theater of conflict, Virginia and New England together bore the brunt of the colonial struggle, helping to change the course of a war that England had been losing. Pride in American achievements and capabilities soared.

At the very time that imperial potential set English imaginations afire, the

Americans kindled to a new sense of independence and of the possibilities of united effort. John Richard Green, in his monumental *Short History of the English People*, maintained that in the French and Indian War "began the history of the United States." As England prepared to write a great deal of history in English for generations to come, her American colonies awakened to a new sense of their own potential. Out of such disparate dreams, conflict was inevitable. Would London achieve the balance of heritage and innovation that could hold together an empire including North America? Or would the viable proportions be achieved by statesmen compromising for survival in some future capital on the Atlantic littoral that fringed that continent's vast frontier?

26

PURITAN COMMONWEALTH

JOHN WINTHROP was disappointed and sorely troubled.[1] The habitual gravity of his long, dark-bearded face accurately portrayed his mood. In 1630, in his forty-third year, the country squire of Groton in Suffolk had left England with nearly a thousand emigrants bound for Massachusetts. He had not embarked lightly upon this adventure. As the master of a manor purchased by his grandfather with profits from the clothing industry, he had a substantial, but dwindling stake in English society. Before sailing, he weighed carefully the likely effect on his fortunes of leaving or remaining.

As an intelligent gentleman farmer with a good education, occupying a minor public office, he might in another time have looked forward to increase in income and higher levels of public service. But three of his sons had come of age and claimed their patrimony, thus drawing away half of his estate. Though his means were cut in half, his expenses, because of the sad state of the economy, remained the same. "With what comfort can I live," he asked, "with seven or eight servants in that place and condition . . . ?" The prospect of diminished comforts for his wife and children was, he wrote her, "one great motive" to impel him to emigrate.[2]

He was also concerned that his Puritan loyalties would inhibit a career of public service in England. With an apparent mixture of idealism and ambition, he had dreamed of such a career.

When Winthrop finally made up his mind to embark for New England, he seemingly was convinced that God had guided him. He wrote to his wife, "I am verily persuaded, God will bring some heavy affliction upon this land, and that speedily." England, he believed, had provoked the Lord "more than all the nations round about us: therefore he is turning the cup towards us also, and because we are the last, our portion must be to drink the very dregs which remain."[3]

Even before leaving England, his choice had gained him a higher office. And that was important to him. As justice of the peace for the manor at the age of eighteen, ruling on disputes between humbler neighbors, he had acquired a taste for authority. Like his father, he had practiced law in London, and that experience and his nearly two years at Cambridge fully qualified him for his

attorneyship at the Court of Wards and Liveries, but this he had lost because
of his known Puritanism.

His new, higher office had come to him through a brief series of improbable circumstances. The Massachusetts Bay Company, like the Virginia Company and other mercantile organizations interested in New World settlement, was a joint-stock corporation centered in England. It was managed by directors known as "assistants" and by a governor, both of whom were elected by the freemen, or stockholders. The governor was not a political official but the chief executive officer of a business corporation with headquarters in London. Some leaders of the company conceived the bold idea of transferring the charter and government of the organization from old England to New. Their dream was to make the charter an instrument for the creation of a Puritan commonwealth in America. Such a metamorphosis was possible because of a surprising omission from that document: there was no proviso for a meeting place for the conduct of company business. Samuel Eliot Morison, as distinguished as any historian who ever wrote on the subject, concluded that the lack might be attributable either to accident or to someone's "greasing the palm of some government clerk."[4]

In any event, leaders of the corporation agreed to transform the London-based business into a New World commonwealth, but discovered that their governor was not prepared to emigrate to America, nor was any assistant willing to become governor. Those willing to emigrate and live under the charter said that they would accept only John Winthrop as their governor. They would not follow anyone else to New England. So Winthrop became governor. Why he was chosen, beyond the important facts that he was intelligent and had a reputation for integrity, no one knows today. He was not even a member of the Massachusetts Bay Company.

Within nine months, sixteen vessels were assembled to transport about a thousand Puritans (some seven hundred in the first contingent) under the transformed charter. In physical size this expedition of 1630 dwarfed that of the Jamestown settlers of 1607, with little more than a hundred colonists aboard three ships and that of the Plymouth settlers of 1620, aboard the single ship *Mayflower*. When the Massachusetts Bay Puritans embarked at Southampton, the farewell sermon was preached by the Reverend John Cotton on the text of 2 Samuel 7:10: "Moreover I will appoint a place for my people Israel, and will plant them, that they may dwell in a place of their own, and move no more; neither shall the children of wickedness afflict them any more, as beforetime."

Coupled with the preacher's emphasis on the great new beginning, and the implication that he addressed a chosen people, was an admonition to remember the mother country and all that was good in their national heritage: "Forget not the womb that bore you and the breasts that gave you suck. Even ducklings hatched under a hen, though they take the water, yet will still have recourse to the wing that hatched them. How much more should chickens of the same feather and yolk?"[5]

Out upon the ocean, Winthrop himself preached to his fellow voyagers. "The end," he said, is to improve our lives to do more service to the Lord . . . that ourselves and posterity may be the better preserved from the common corruptions of this evil world. . . . We have taken out a Commission; the Lord hath given us leave to draw our own Articles. . . . If the Lord shall please to hear us, and bring us in peace to the place we desire, then hath he ratified this Covenant and sealed our Commissions, [and] will expect a strict performance of the Articles contained in it.

He added, "We shall find that the God of Israel is among us, when ten of us shall be able to resist a thousand of our enemies; when he shall make us a praise and glory that man shall say of succeeding plantations, 'The Lord make it like that of NEW ENGLAND.' For we must consider that we shall be as a city upon a hill. The eyes of all people are upon us. . . ."[6]

The same note was to be sounded again and again in the declarations and documents of Massachusetts history. There was the praiseworthy thirst for righteousness and the inspiring faith in their own high calling as a chosen people. A society based on these beliefs could be expected to evidence high dedication, courage, and willingness to work. It would combine the sustenance of tradition with the healthy exercise of experiment. It would know the energizing fervor of patriotism. There was also the danger that zeal occasionally would lead to a holier-than-thou attitude and that sense of responsibility as a chosen people could degenerate into a tendency to prescribe *the* way for all peoples. There was, too, the chance that so strong an alliance between church and state could lead to identity of political and ecclesiastical administration. One thing, however, was beyond dispute. A great transforming force was being planted on the North American continent.

Winthrop was a stern taskmaster—for others, but most of all for himself. But he had a tender side as well, not revealed in any of his recorded sermons or public utterances, but in private correspondence. Representative is the letter that he wrote his "faithful and dear wife" from aboard the *Arbella*, then riding at the Cowes, which would take him and his two sons to America. She remained behind to take care of unfinished business and would join him later in their new home. He told her that their boys were "well and cheerful."

They lie both with me, and sleep as soundly in a rug (for we use no sheets here) as ever they did at Groton, and so I do myself (I praise God). . . . And now, my sweet soul, I must once again take my last farewell of thee in Old England. It goeth very near to my heart to leave thee; but I know to whom I have committed thee, even to Him who loves thee much better than any husband can. . . . Oh, how it refresheth my heart to think that I shall yet again see thy sweet face in the land of the living—that lovely countenance that I have so much delighted in, and beheld with so great content!

In subsequent lines, he reminded her of an agreement that was a strange blend of romanticism and disciplined precision. "I hope," he wrote, "the course we have agreed upon will be some ease to us both. Mondays and Fridays at five of the clock at night, we shall meet in spirit till we meet in person." It seems strange that even the relief of spiritual intercourse, obviously a matter of great importance to him, should be restricted to two days a week. One also wonders whether, in specifying the exact hour of 5:00 in the evening, he was mindful of the time zones that lay between him and his love.

He concluded his letter with an eloquent outburst of emotion:

> Yet, if all these hopes should fail, blessed be our God, that we are assured we shall meet one day, if not as husband and wife, yet in a better condition; let that stay and comfort thy heart. Neither can the sea drown thy husband, nor enemies destroy, nor any adversity deprive thee of thy husband or children. Therefore I will only take thee now and my sweet children in mine arms, and kiss and embrace you all, and so leave you with God. Farewell, farewell. . . . Thine whereso-ever, John Winthrop.

On June 8, 1630, those aboard the *Arbella* entered the Gulf of Maine under bright blue skies. Offshore breezes brought them "a sweet air . . . like the smell of a garden."[7] On June 14, they entered Salem harbor. John Endecott, who had served as governor of the small settlement of Salem for about twenty-one months, came aboard to welcome the newcomers and learned that his office was now obsolete, superseded by Winthrop's gubernatorial leadership of the whole newly created Massachusetts Bay Commonwealth.

Winthrop thought settlement should be concentrated at Newtowne, site of the present Cambridge. Compactness would facilitate communication and permit protection by a single fort. But the diverse preferences of his flock proved too strong for his channeling. They spread out along the coast north of Plymouth. In the next six months or so were founded the towns of Medford, Watertown, Roxbury, Dorchester, Lynn, and Boston.

The halcyon weather that had marked the colonists' arrival yielded to a winter reminiscent of the "starving time" at Jamestown twenty-three years before. As in that hard year in Virginia, the people subsisted largely on a steady diet of shellfish. In Massachusetts this native fare was augmented largely by salt junk and hardtack left over from the provisions of their voyage. As many as 180 indentured servants had to be forced to forage for themselves. Their masters could not feed them. Like their Virginia counterparts, the Massachusetts colonists in great numbers succumbed to scurvy and a mysterious fever. They were saved, first of all, by the eleventh-hour arrival of a ship that Winthrop had sent back to England for supplies. Then a shipment of grain from Virginia and another from Ireland provided not only immediate relief but also the seeds for a harvest of their own. Nevertheless, discouraged by what they had suffered, many settlers returned to England in provisioning ships. A few hundred new colonists came in 1631 and 1632.

But in 1633 came the Great Emigration, spurred by William Laud's appointment as archbishop of Canterbury. He had long called for the imposition of more restraints on the Puritans. He used his new powers to force High Church rituals on every English parish, to suppress Puritan tracts, and to gag Puritan speakers. Convinced that they were now persecuted as ancient Israel had been, Puritans fled old England for New. Sometimes as many as a dozen ships bearing the incoming faithful rode at anchor in Boston harbor.

In 1635 several English lords of Puritan persuasion proposed to emigrate to the Massachusetts Bay Colony if its leaders would assure them that the commonwealth would be "reformed" to consist of two classes, gentlemen and freeholders, the first group forming a hereditary house of lords, and the second electing from its own number a house of commons. The leaders of Massachusetts Bay replied that they would be glad to elect to office anyone from a "noble or generous family with a spirit and gifts fit for government," but totally rejected the idea of hereditary office. No matter how able emigrating peers might be, "if God should not delight to furnish some of their posterity with gifts fit for magistracy," it would be unwise "if we should call them forth, when God hath not, to public authority."[8]

A shrewd reply indeed! And an impressive rejection of the hereditary principle that was a time-honored feature of English society. But hardly the occasion for three lusty cheers for democracy. The Massachusetts Bay Colony had its own rules for excluding from power, or even from participation, all but a favored elect.

Such restriction necessitated much boldness and some ingenuity to circumvent a charter that was truly democratic. It provided for annual election of a governor, deputy governor, and eighteen assistants by the General Court, which should consist of all freemen or stockholders of the corporation. The same body should exercise supreme legislative power. It had abrogated unto itself supreme judicial power as well, and had gotten by with it because its first judicial action was to order the deportation of Thomas Morton. The mass of Puritans apparently felt more threatened by Morton's activities than by the tyranny of their fellows. He sold firearms and liquor to the Indians, admittedly a dangerous practice. Moreover, he and his friends had erected at his home, Merry Mount, future site of Quincy, an eighty-foot maypole, "drinking and dancing about it many days together, inviting the Indian women for their consorts, dancing and frisking together like so many . . . furies," and indulging in "the beastly practices of the mad Bacchanalians."[9] Hopes for true self-government in Massachusetts Bay resided in the fact that the General Court, exercising supreme legislative and judicial power, must include all freemen. The reality, however, was that no freeman who was not an assistant had been included among the first colonists.

Soon, though, other freemen arrived from England, and still others entered Massachusetts Bay from other New England settlements. At the meeting of the General Court in October 1630, 108 such freemen demanded voting privileges.

Winthrop supported their enfranchisement at the next meeting of the General Court, in May, and 116 were duly admitted. The concession quieted the current complainants, but was more than offset by the General Court's declaration that no other man could become a freeman, and therefore a voter, unless he was a member of one of the local Puritan churches. Church membership was not available to anyone merely for the asking. An applicant had to convince the communicants that he was in truth one of God's "visible saints." From the Puritans' viewpoint, the choice was really God's, not theirs. God's election would prevail. The Massachusetts Bay Colony was a Bible commonwealth. Who would question God's ability to judge the qualifications of his own "saints" and thus of the citizens of His ideal commonwealth?

James Truslow Adams estimated that at the time of the October meeting, when the compromise was made, all political rights in a community of about two thousand persons were limited to "a tiny self-perpetuating oligarchical group of not more than a dozen citizens. Ninety-nine and one half percent of the population was thus unenfranchised and unrepresented, and even denied the right of appeal to the higher authorities in England."[10]

Though Winthrop supported the enfranchisement of more than a hundred of those previously barred from voting, he did not view with equanimity even this modest increase in electors. He saw it as a step toward democracy. There "was no such government in Israel," he pointed out. "Democracy," he said, was "amongst most civil nations, accounted the meanest and worst of all forms of government."[11] His views were shared by John Cotton, the former vicar of Saint Botolph's, who had preached the farewell sermon to Winthrop's colonists as they left England, and then had joined them in Massachusetts upon the ascension of Laud as archbishop. There Cotton's learning and eloquence had made him at once a leader. "Democracy," he said, "I do not conceive that ever God did ordain as a fit government either for church or commonwealth. If the people be governors, who shall be governed?"[12]

So strong and determined were the freemen that in 1632 they compelled the assistants to allow them full participation in election of the governor and deputy governor. Some assistants cherished the hope that the results would be the same despite the enlarged electorate; John Cotton preached an election sermon arguing that those elected to office should always be reinstated unless there were just complaints against them. Despite this argument, the independent-minded freemen ousted Winthrop, electing Thomas Dudley in his place. Winthrop had prepared to celebrate his anticipated reelection with a banquet at his house. He graciously went ahead with his plans, having the new governor and assistants as honored guests.

This generous spirit was one of the reasons that Winthrop was so often returned to office. For the twenty years between his first election as governor and his death in 1649, he held that position half the time, and for the other ten years he was deputy governor.[13]

The shift from Winthrop to Dudley opened no ideological chasm. Winthrop later described Dudley as "a very wise and just man, and one that would not be trodden under foot by any man."

Before relinquishing his office, Winthrop dealt with a problem that changed the composition of the legislature over which his successor would preside. Residents of Watertown protested against paying a tax levied by the assistants alone rather than by vote of the freemen or their direct representatives.

They declared that it was "not safe to pay" taxes so exacted, for there was danger "of bringing themselves and posterity into bondage."[14]

Summoned before Winthrop and admonished by him, the protesters were thrown a sop. The governor and assistants offered Watertown, and every other town in Massachusetts Bay, the opportunity to appoint members of an advisory committee on taxation. Suspecting that the freemen had been guaranteed rights and privileges not revealed by the colonial leaders, those of Watertown appointed deputies to this committee and requested that their deputies be permitted to examine the charter.

Much mystery attached to that document. On state occasions it was carried in procession in a great, closed, leather-covered box. Apparently it was intended to evoke a solemnity reminiscent of the carrying of ancient Israel's Ark of the Covenant. The desired effect was not always achieved. Mischievous Thomas Morton of Merry Mount said that the mass of colonists thought it was a musical instrument case. Mindful of Puritan warnings against the seductive influence of well-tuned strings, he suggested that they thought it contained a favorite fiddle preserved from the days of the governor's youth.

Examination of the charter produced ample justification of the freemen's demands. The General Court was confirmed in the right of electing the governor and deputy governor. Four General Courts would meet each year and could be dissolved only by majority vote. "In the Court of elections every freeman was to give his own voice."[15] Held in the spring, the Court of elections, besides engaging in the usual legislative work, would choose the governor, deputy governor, and assistants. In 1637, a new statute, while confirming the privilege of any freeman to appear personally in Boston to vote, provided that those who wished to avoid the journey could fill out ballots in the form of proxies to be cast by their towns' deputies. Some freemen cast paper ballots and some signified their choices by dropping different kinds of beans into the box.

In 1642 a lost sow ultimately left the leaders of Massachusetts Bay as confused as she herself was. The case of *Sherman v. Keane* is one of the most important ones in New England history. A poor widow sued in a lower court for recovery of her lost sow, which was held by a prosperous shopkeeper. She lost before the local magistrates and appealed to the General Court. The assistants in that body voted to sustain the lower court's decision. But a majority of deputies voted to reverse it. Winthrop said that the defendant "was of ill report in the country for a hard dealer." This fact may have influenced the deputies, whose interests were more closely allied to the mass of people's, and who may have sympathized with the needy woman. An ambiguous clause in the charter was unclear as to whether the assistants had the authority to veto a judgment of the General Court if the majority of the court reflected only the opinion of the freemen and deputies.

The assistants claimed the power, arguing that they were magistrates while the other members of the General Court were not. Governor Winthrop argued that the language of the charter conferred a "negative voice" upon these magistrates. "If the negative voice were taken away," he said,

our government would be a Democracy, whereas now it is mixed. . . .
Now if we should change from a mixed Aristocracy to a mere Democracy, 1st, we should have no warrant in scripture for it: there was no
such government in Israel. 2nd, we should voluntarily abase ourselves
and deprive ourselves of that dignity which the providence of God
hath put upon us, which is a manifest breach of the fifth commandment.[16]

After a two-year struggle, Winthrop and the assistants won. Their victory
was signalized by an act of the General Court of 1644, which provided that the
assistants and deputies sit in separate chambers and that the concurrence of
both houses be necessary for enactment of any measure. Concurrence would
also be necessary "in matters of judicature."[17] As virtually all judicial functions
of the General Court involved the hearing of appeals from decisions of the
assistants, the new arrangement enabled them to veto all appeals from their own
judgments.

Later, though, the hearing of appeals by the General Court under these
rules proved so futile and farcical that the demand for reform could not be
denied. In 1649, therefore, the judicial provisions of 1644 were repealed. In
"matters of judicature," the two houses—Assistants and Deputies—would sit
together and decisions would be made by a majority of the combined membership.

The assistants had already had to retreat from another attempt to perpetuate and increase their authority. In 1636, some leaders had persuaded the General Court to establish a "council for life, for that it was showed from the word
of God that the principal magistrates ought to be for life." Three perennial
holders of high office—Winthrop, Dudley, and John Endecott—were elected
to the council. But only three years later, rebellious rumblings among the freemen were so strong that the whole idea was abandoned. Nevertheless, the practical effect remained much the same. We have already seen that Winthrop was
governor for half of the twenty years he served the Massachusetts Bay Company and deputy governor in the other half. Dudley's record was almost as
consistent. When he was not governor, he was always deputy governor or at
least an assistant. Endecott became governor in 1649 and was governor for all
but one of the next fifteen years. In the lists of assistants for the first two decades of Massachusetts Bay, the names Bradstreet, Nowell, Humphrey, Pyn-
chon, and John Winthrop, Jr., the governor's son, constantly recur.

As their letters, journals, and even public utterances make perfectly clear,
the leaders of Massachusetts Bay continued to think of themselves as the chosen
elite of God's chosen people. They conceived that it was not only their right
but their obligation to remain tightly in control of a Bible commonwealth committed to them by the will of God. On the few occasions when any of them
thought about separation of church and state, it was with abhorrence of something unnatural and essentially wicked. They therefore resorted to numerous
devices to retain domination of the colony despite any compromises that might
be forced upon them by the increasingly restive freemen.

One such device was to leave vacant at all times some of the eighteen positions for assistants provided in the charter. While a full complement of assistants might seem to be an aid in resisting demands by the more numerous deputies and far more numerous freemen, the few leaders constituting the nucleus of power did not see it that way. They saw any increase in the number of assistants as a dilution of the purity of a tiny group that, however much they might indulge in petty squabbles among themselves, usually united against any opposition from outside. In 1647 they even secured enactment of a law limiting to seven the number of candidates for assistant that the freemen might vote for.

The influence of the assistants was greatly magnified by the fact that, besides sitting as members of the General Court when it functioned as the highest appellate court in the colony, assistants sat as magistrates in each of the subordinate courts. The function of the assistants as judges of the county courts assumed greater importance still from 1641 to 1664, when the General Court assigned those local tribunals the duty of deciding which colonists should be admitted to the status of freemen. They not only controlled the admission of people to the electoral process but also dominated the appointive system. They directly appointed many petty officials and exercised a veto on the election of militia officers. They were empowered to levy certain rates and taxes independently of the General Court.

In performing their many functions, the assistants worked hand in glove with the clergy. The life of the colony was dominated by two institutions, church and state, which were really one body in two guises. The lay leaders of the congregations were also the holders of civil office. The clergy could help the political chieftains by disseminating information and opinions deemed important by the little band of leaders, and by giving expert advice on theological aspects of governance. At the same time, this working relationship increased the clergy's influence. The clergy and the assistants enjoyed a symbiotic relationship that augmented the power of the tiny elite-within-an-elite whose authority within the colony was sometimes little short of absolute.

As the Massachusetts colonists had been bred in English traditions of freedom, it is not surprising that many of them, especially those brought to America more by desire for personal advancement than by religious zeal, were determined to curb the power of the assistants. Nor is it astonishing that, reared on traditions of Runnymede, they thought of a legal document as the proper curb. Winthrop and the other leaders conceded "that some men should be appointed to frame a body or grounds of laws in resemblance to a Magna Carta, which, being allowed by some of the ministers and the General Court, should be received for fundamental laws." The committee of four that was appointed included Winthrop and Dudley. Later the Reverend Mr. Cotton and three other clerics were added.

The assignment of the enlarged committee was "to make a draft of laws agreeable to the word of God, which may be the Fundamentals of this Commonwealth, and to present the same to the next General Court. . . ."[18] But the code, drawn up by Mr. Cotton and presented at the next session, was not accepted. For three more successive years, the General Court appointed committees to draft a suitable body of laws and each time failed to adopt the document submitted. Two excuses were given. One was that a new legal corpus should be developed through experience as was the English common law, not suddenly created by a legislative body. The other was "that it would professedly transgress the limits of our charter, which provide we shall make no laws repugnant to the law of England."[19]

The charter itself was the subject of contention. In 1631 the Reverend Roger Williams had come to New England and, three years later, after service in the Plymouth church, had become pastor of the Salem church. A protégé of Sir Edward Coke, the great English jurist and legal scholar, he had graduated from Cambridge and had become an Anglican priest. His association with Puritans, among them Oliver Cromwell, led to his emigration to Massachusetts Bay, where he soon became a controversial figure because of his insistence that the magistrates, as agents of civil government, had no right to enforce the religious code of the Ten Commandments. He also argued that the Massachusetts charter was invalid, among other reasons because it violated the land rights of the Indians. He excited further resentment by urging the Salem congregation to separate from the other churches of Massachusetts.

The General Court in 1635 refused to seat the delegates from Salem until they repudiated Roger Williams. The next day the General Court banished the preacher from the colony, but said that he could remain over the winter. Williams had fewer fears of the frozen landscape than of the adamant assistants and fled, spending the winter with friendly Indians. In the spring of 1636, he purchased from them land on the western bank of the Sekonk River. There he founded the town of Providence, dedicating it as a shelter for "persons distressed for conscience." Many came and he welcomed them all, even the Quakers, though he disagreed particularly strongly with the tenets of their sect. From the settlement grew the colony of Rhode Island.

Banishment of Roger Williams did not end attempts to have the charter revoked. Thomas Morton of Merry Mount, following his own deportation, joined with Sir Ferdinando Gorges, a prominent patentee and founder of Maine, New England, to obtain revocation. The Lords of Trade and Plantations, a committee of the Privy Council in London, ordered recall of the charter on the grounds of the deception practiced in omitting designation of a meeting place for the corporation, thus making it possible to transform it into a government and transfer it to America. The King's Bench ordered cancellation, and dispatched Gorges with a writ demanding surrender of the document. In addition, King Charles I granted Gorges, together with Captain John Mason, a commission to govern New England. The ship in which Gorges was to sail to America cracked up at its launching, delaying his departure. When Governor Winthrop learned of the order to surrender the charter, he mounted ordnance to oppose any forces from England, alerted the militia, and had a beacon set on what is now Boston's Beacon Hill to signal the colonists to repel invasion. At this time the occurrence of a national revolt in Scotland forced the king to deal with a much closer and more ominous rebellion, so that what might have been punished as treason in Massachusetts Bay was ignored.

Winthrop and the assistants, however, could not prevent the invasion of ideas. Any newly arrived immigrant might carry the infection. The case of Anne Hutchinson was often cited as an example. A housewife, daughter of a Lincolnshire clergyman, she came to Boston in 1634, when she was in her early or middle thirties. Something about her excited suspicion from the first. Initially she was denied church membership.

Soon, however, she gained the friendship and high respect of the women. Her generous and efficient services as a nurse won a following. Frustrating for a woman of her intelligence and leadership abilities were the Thursday meetings at which church members discussed the previous Sunday's sermon. Women might attend, but were warned to remain silent. Determined to do something about this situation, she found scriptural justification in Titus 2: 3–5, which enjoined Christian women to teach younger women the ways of righteousness. She started holding meetings for the women on the same days that the men met. Even some of the ministers and magistrates started attending. Whatever their original motivation—curiosity, hostility, the collection of evidence—some eventually shared her views.

In England she had been one of John Cotton's parishioners. Now she told the audience at one of her Thursday meetings that, whereas Mr. Cotton and her brother-in-law John Wheelwright preached a "covenant of grace," all the other ministers in Massachusetts Bay preached a "covenant of works."

Winthrop said "no man could tell (except some few, who knew the bottom of the matter) where any difference was." But of at least one thing, Winthrop was sure. He did not seek enlightenment from a female. This fact he made generally clear in his dealings with Anne Hutchinson and specifically clear in what he wrote in his journal a little later about another woman:

> Mr. Hopkins, the Governor of Hartford upon Connecticut, came to Boston, and brought his wife with him (a godly young woman, and of special parts), who was fallen into a sad infirmity, the loss of her understanding and reason, which had been growing upon her divers years, by occasion of her giving herself wholly to reading and writing, and had written many books. Her husband, being very loving and tender of her, was loath to grieve her; but he saw his error, when it was too late. For if she had attended her household affairs, and such things as belong to women, and not gone out of her way and calling to meddle in such things as are proper for men, whose minds are stronger, etc., she had kept her wits, and might have improved them usefully and honorably in the place God had set her.[20]

Mrs. Hutchinson, according to Winthrop, was "of a haughty and fierce carriage, of a nimble wit and active spirit, and a very voluble tongue." Obviously, he had not fallen under her spell.

But Winthrop was not governor when Anne Hutchinson's influence reached its height. In 1636 he was deputy governor. The governor was a twenty-three-year-old wonder boy, Henry Vane, who had been elected almost as soon as he arrived in the colony. A long-faced, beak-nosed, tight-lipped portrait of him at a somewhat later date shows little of the charm with which he has been credited. The fact that his father, Sir Henry Vane, was privy councillor to Charles I and a newly appointed commissioner for the colonies may have increased the son's appeal.

Young Governor Vane became a convert to Mrs. Hutchinson's teachings. This conquest encouraged others to join her study group. The theological matter that Winthrop considered so abstruse soon became a matter of general argument. "It began to be as common here," he said, "to distinguish between men, by being under a covenant of grace or a covenant of works, as in other countries between Protestants and Papists."[21] The more sophisticated characterized Mrs. Hutchinson as an Antinomian, one who believed that faith, even unaccompanied by works, was sufficient for salvation. This was the grace of God, the unmerited love and favor extended to human beings as the gift of a generous Creator.

The Antinomian concept was a threat to the theocracy that ruled Massachusetts Bay. It presumed that a believing individual might learn the truths of God through direct revelation independent of interpretation by the clergy or of the civil rulings of those that they advised. Fear and anger seized the colony's leaders at the words of such Hutchinson proselytes as the man who told Captain Edward Johnson:

> Come along with me. I'll bring you to a woman that preaches better gospel than any of your blackcoats that have been at the ninny-versity, a woman of another kind of spirit, who hath had many revelations of things to come, and for my part, I had rather hear such a one that speaks from the mere motion of the spirit, without any study at all, than any of your learned scholars, although they may be fuller of scripture.[22]

In the ensuing division, the magistrates and most of the ministers argued that Mrs. Hutchinson should be silenced. A notable exception among the clergy was John Cotton, who had attended some of her parlor meetings and was regarded by some as one of her followers. The Boston congregants also supported her almost unanimously. When the clergy called a meeting to discuss the best way of disposing of Mrs. Hutchinson, Governor Vane angrily spoke up in her defense. Not many months before, Vane had joined with Hugh Peter, a contentious immigrant who had once been pastor of a church in Rotterdam, to convince Winthrop and others that they needed to be stricter and more rigorous in enforcing all religious requirements. That his erstwhile ally should now be under the spell of so bold and dangerous a woman was more than Peter could bear. He rebuked Vane for presuming to speak from the base of so short a life and such limited experience. The governor replied, "The light of the Gospel brings a sword."[23]

The Puritan establishment struck first at Anne Hutchinson's brother-in-law, the Reverend John Wheelwright. He had preached about bringing a sword rather than peace, probably taking as his text Matthew 10:34: "Think not that I am come to send peace on earth: I came not to send peace, but a sword. For I am come to set a man at variance against his father, and the daughter against her mother, and the daughter-in-law against her mother-in-law. And a man's foes shall be they of his own household." This talk of allegiances transcending earthly loyalties was upsetting to the magistrates. The biblical text may have been disturbingly close to Vane's statement, in the context of the debate over Mrs. Hutchinson, that "the light of the Gospel brings a sword." The magistrates convicted Wheelwright of sedition.

Bostonians protested the effort to muzzle the preacher and suggested that today's troublemaker may be tomorrow's saint. They said, "Paul was counted a pestilent fellow, as a mover of sedition, and a ringleader of a sect."

Balloting was hot on election day, May 1637, between the Blue Coats, as the supporters of Governor Vane were called, and the White Coats, who wanted to unseat him and elect Winthrop. In many ways, the fight was more over Mrs. Hutchinson than over either of the two candidates.

Realizing that support for her was concentrated in Boston, the magistrates moved the central polling place from that town, its customary location, to Cambridge. In a closely contested election, a change of site could determine the winner. Winthrop won, but a bitter Boston denied him the usual armed escort when he proceeded to the capitol to assume office. Instead, he was attended by two of his servants bearing borrowed halberds.

The vanquished Vane returned to England. Like his father, he would be knighted, and would know many triumphs and defeats. He would become leader of England's House of Commons and would be chiefly instrumental in abolition of the Protectorate before being imprisoned, exiled, and eventually executed. John Milton would salute him in verse for brave services to liberty. But in 1637 he was a bright young man worsted in combat with his elders and deeply sunk in disillusionment.

Just a few days after his victory, Winthrop's government moved against other enemies seen as impeding the progress of their God-ordained commonwealth. They, together with Plymouth and Connecticut, declared war on the Pequot Indians and slew great numbers of young and old of both sexes. Reverend Thomas Shepard, a Cambridge master of arts, and a stout pillar of the Winthrop faction, described the victory as a "divine slaughter." The Puritan fathers added a neat profit to the fruits of triumph by selling the remaining Pequots into slavery.[24]

The magistrates—even Winthrop, who often was described as the "gentlest" of them—had learned to look upon all who opposed their designs, or even criticized their handiwork, as enemies of God. In his journal, Winthrop told of a ship, some of whose passengers spoke disdainfully of New England as they approached old England. Immediately, strong winds tossed them about like a cockle shell, and they begged the Lord's pardon for speaking ill of Massachusetts. Aboard was George Phillips, a minister who had refrained from criticism of New England. His prayers therefore were acceptable to the Almighty, and saved the ship. But those who had said bad things about the region and its governments were not spared. "The Lord followed them on shore," Winthrop says. Some were renounced by friends. One lost a child to the plague. The complaints of John Humfry, one of the founders of New England, the husband of an earl's daughter, and a sometime magistrate, must have been particularly offensive, perhaps because he had been able to survey from a high position the society that he lambasted. One of the Humfry daughters, Winthrop reports, became insane, and two others, both children, were "often abused by divers lewd persons."[25]

In full confidence that they were the viceroys of God, the Puritan hierarchy of Massachusetts Bay proceeded to deal with the threat to their dominance posed by Mrs. Hutchinson. A synod of the New England churches convened in Cambridge. Presiding was the same Thomas Shepard who had praised the killing of Pequot men and women as a "divine slaughter." The session condemned "erroneous opinions," citing no fewer than eighty, together with "unwholesome expressions." At this point, some of the Bostonians walked out.

With those remaining, the leaders attempted to find some sort of unity. The sentence on Wheelwright had not yet been executed, and by compromise he might yet have avoided punishment. But he would not yield. Cotton, who so far had fared better at the hands of the hierarchy, found compromise possible.

Wheelwright was banished, as were two General Court members who had supported him. The synod adopted resolutions condemning rebellious meetings of churchwomen. Mrs. Hutchinson would ignore this condemnation at her peril.

Her defiance brought her to trial before the General Court with Governor Winthrop presiding. She acquitted herself well in the first part of the trial, and Cotton was a strong witness for the defense. Then she told the court of the revelations she had received from the Lord. The magistrates admitted the possibility of individual communication with God, but held that no revelations of doctrine had been transmitted since the last chapter of the Apocalypse. Her claims, therefore, were blasphemous. Specifically, she was charged with violating the fifth commandment, "Honor thy father and thy mother." She had dishonored the "fathers of the Commonwealth." Because of "the troublesomeness of her spirit" and "the danger of her course among us," she was banished from the colony.

Thomas Shepard, who had declared Anne Hutchinson's protestations of innocence unsatisfactory, and had reminded her judges that "any heretic may bring a sly interpretation upon any of these errors," seemed to rank her conviction with the subduing of the Indians as equal blessings to the commonwealth. "The churches here are in peace," he gloated, "the Commonwealth in peace, the ministry in most sweet peace, the Magistrates (I should have named first) in peace; all our families in peace. We can sleep in the woods in peace, without fear of the Indians; our fear is fallen upon them."[26]

Not all of New England, however, was frozen in peace. The General Court could banish Mrs. Hutchinson from Massachusetts Bay, but not from its neighbors. Thrust out of the commonwealth, she went to Rhode Island, where Roger Williams and his followers had founded a far more tolerant colony, one whose leaders were willing to explore new ideas, or at least to be exposed to them. With her went some of her followers, some of whom had been fined, some disfranchised. There also were those who had not personally felt the hand of oppression, but had seen more than enough of its effects. She did not tarry at Providence, the settlement founded by Williams, but started one of her own at what became Portsmouth.

Four years later, upon the death of her husband, described as "a peaceable man," she moved to Long Island. There she and her entire household, sixteen persons, were killed by Indians. Learning of her fate, Governor Winthrop called it a providential act of God.

Banished from Massachusetts Bay, John Wheelwright founded the town of Exeter in the future New Hampshire. There he continued to preach. In 1639 he and his followers signed an Exeter Compact inspired by the Mayflower Compact. In 1643, after Portsmouth, Dover, and Hampton all had acknowledged the sovereignty of Massachusetts Bay, Exeter followed suit. Wheelwright moved to Maine. Declaring that he repented preaching doctrines condemned by the Massachusetts General Court, he applied for and received remission of his sentence of banishment. Later, without moving from Maine, he found himself living in Massachusetts again. Threatened with annexation by the bay colony, the government of Maine appealed to the English Parliament in December 1651. Nevertheless in May 1652 the Massachusetts General Court declared that Maine was part of their colony. Historians and constitutional lawyers alike have echoed Herbert L. Osgood's statement in his monumental *American Colonies in the Seventeenth Century* that the claim was "more clearly an usurpation than was any later act of the crown which affected New England."[27] Nevertheless, Massachusetts proceeded to force settlement after settlement into unconditional surrender until it had annexed the more than forty thousand square miles of the Province of Maine.

The success of the General Court in establishing domination both inside and outside their government's legitimate borders encouraged the magistrates to intensify their tyranny. Not only was there the occasional excommunication and banishment of a church member, but there was also the daily persecution of the large proportion of the population—probably about four-fifths—who were not of the elect permitted to be members of the Puritan churches.[28] Upon this group particularly fell the law providing that anyone who should "spend his time idly or unprofitably" would be subject to such punishment "as the court shall think meet to inflict."[29] With no specific definition of the crime and no exact prescription for the penalty, enormous discretion was left to the magistrates. Massachusetts had indeed a government of men and not of laws.

Massachusetts Bay was acquiring an unenviable reputation in England, even among Puritans. The Reverend John White, who had had so much to do with the launching of the colony, urged Governor Winthrop to "have an eye to one thing, that you fall not into that evil abroad, which you labored to avoid at home, to bind all men to the same tenets and practice."[30] And Winthrop's brother Stephen, on a trip back to London, wrote the governor, "Here is great complaint against us for our severity against Anabaptists. It doth discourage any people from coming to us for fear they should be banished if they dissent from us in opinion."[31] Another Winthrop connection, Sir George Downing, reported growing resentment in England against Massachusetts because of the "law of banishing for conscience which makes us stink everywhere."[32]

Perhaps word of the revulsion of Puritans in the home country strengthened the resolve of their long-suffering brethren in Massachusetts. Local demands for a curb on the judiciary became more vociferous. Still Winthrop resisted. But perhaps the extremity of his response provoked bolder action than some of the colonists would otherwise have taken. In rejecting a request for specific penalties for specific offenses, he said that, as "judges are Gods upon earth," their power should not be more limited than that of God himself.[33]

When refusals and even procrastination seemed likely to provoke rebellion, Winthrop and the magistrates considered a code of laws prepared by John Cotton. This minister had retreated so far from his brief excursion into liberal theology in the company of Anne Hutchinson that he was now a leading pillar of clerical despotism. He prepared a code known as "Moses his Judicials" because it was based largely on Mosaic law.

Cotton's code eventually was rejected by the magistrates in favor of the Body of Liberties, adopted in December 1641. This was the work of Nathaniel Ward, who, in Samuel Eliot Morison's apt words, flashed "across [Massachusetts'] early history like a cock pheasant in the gray November woods."[34] Yet, at least superficially, Ward would seem to have been a Puritan among Puritans, born and bred. A Puritan minister himself, he was the son of a Puritan minister, the brother of two Puritan clergymen, and the father of another. The father's Latin epitaph at Bury Saint Edmunds, in England, was translated:

> Grant some of knowledge greater store,
> More learned some in teaching;
> Yet few in life were holy more,
> None thundered more in preaching![35]

If the elder Ward wrote his own epitaph, as some people have, it bespeaks a sense of humor more than it does a spirit of Christian humility. In any event, Nathaniel Ward, who emigrated to Massachusetts Bay in 1634 at about the age of fifty-five, was a man of both humor and piety. Samuel Eliot Morison, one of the most learned and indefatigable diggers into Puritan history, cited him as the "one wit" he had "managed to excavate" from "the generation of Puritan founders."[36]

The famous minister Increase Mather testified to hearing "a hundred witty speeches" by him.[37] A few years after writing the code, Ward, under the pseudonym Theodore de la Guard, published a humorous book called *The Simple Cobler of Aggawam.*

Much of this book, though, has a serious purpose—the dissemination of his intense prejudices. He called fashion-conscious women "ape-headed pullets."[38] He confessed (or perhaps boasted) his desire to "talk as loud as [he] could" against religious toleration. "Poly-piety," he said, "is the greatest impiety in the world." He feared that a "universal toleration of all hellish errors" would make "Christ's Academy the Devil's University." Noting that some persons had said "that men ought to have liberty of their conscience, and that it is persecution to debar them of it," he said, "it is an astonishment to think that the brains of men should be parboiled in such impious ignorance."[39]

This last comment seems ironic in that Ward himself had left his English pastorate and begun life in the New World at what was then an advanced age, all because he had been denied freedom of conscience. Originally an Anglican minister, Ward, because he could not conscientiously "subscribe to the articles established by the canon of the church," had been deprived of his living and excommunicated by Archbishop Laud. Apparently, to Ward's mind, the difference was that whereas he knew the preferences of God, the archbishop did not.

From such a man as Ward one would not expect a gentle and flexible code of law that allowed for diversity. Yet the code that he produced was considered much more liberal than that proposed by Cotton.

The magistrates of Massachusetts Bay would have denied at any time that they perpetuated a government of men rather than of laws. They would have said that, as men in God's service, they simply enforced God's laws. But many observers from both inside and outside the colony had no assurance that the magistrates were especially privy to the will of God. They believed that Massachusetts Bay was governed by fallible men who, in the absence of provisions for specific punishments for specific crimes, glibly, though probably sincerely, filled the vacuum with their own prejudices and predilections.

Ward's proposed code addressed this problem. He accepted the proposition that all just laws were derived from God and specifically referred to Christianity as a major source. But his specific citations were more often from the English common law than from the Bible.

The code was not designed merely for the exigencies of a decade or even a generation. It cited the "liberties, immunities, and privileges . . . due to every man" as always the source of the "tranquility and stability of churches and commonwealths" and "the denial of them" as "the disturbance, if not the ruin, of both." In a rhetoric worthy of some of the great public documents of the later American Revolution, Ward declared, "We hold it therefore our duty and safety whilst we are about the further establishing of this government to collect and express all such freedoms as for present we foresee may concern us, and our posterity after us, and to ratify them with our solemn consent." The "rights, liberties, and privileges" listed were to be "impartially and inviolably enjoyed and observed throughout our jurisdiction forever."

The catalog of protections was extensive: "No man's life shall be taken away; no man's honor or good name shall be stained; no man's person shall be arrested, restrained, banished, dismembered, nor any way punished; no man shall be deprived of his wife or children; no man's goods or estate shall be taken away from him, nor anyway endamaged under color of law or countenance of authority, unless it be by virtue or equity of some express law of the country warranting the same, established by a general court and sufficiently published. . . ."[40] Perhaps as a necessary concession to diehards, the sweeping nature of the assertion was slightly compromised by eighteen additional words: "or in case of the defect of a law in any particular case, by the word of God."

The list of capital offenses in Ward's Body of Liberties was the same as in Cotton's code. Both codes were easier on robbers, burglars, and larcenists than the laws of England. But death was prescribed for certain offenses—adultery, "unnatural vice," and blasphemy—that were not capital offenses in the mother country. Cruel and barbarous punishments were forbidden but, as in most constitutions today, cruelty and barbarity were not defined. Torture was permissible to obtain from a convict the names of accessories to a capital crime.

There is a surprisingly humane provision: "No man shall exercise any tyranny or cruelty towards any brute creatures which are usually kept for man's use."[41] In the act of removing the yoke of tyranny from the shoulders of men, Ward and his allies were mindful of creatures lower in the chain of being.

Foreigners were guaranteed equal protection of the laws with citizens. Basically, this was an enlightened provision, although no alien could be comforted by the promise of protection equal to that afforded resident Quakers, or even resident Puritans who believed they had received individual revelations from God.

Despite all the talk and writing about the prescription of specific punishments for specific crimes, such specificity applied only to capital offenses. Judicial discretion in sentencing for lesser crimes has been lamented as backward or hailed as progressive in different periods of various western cultures.

More clearly a reform measure was assertion of the right of freemen to elect any of their number as magistrates, and to refuse to reelect them without needing to cite any misfeasance or malfeasance on the part of the officeholder.

Church councils and synods were forbidden to interfere with congregational government. Regarded then in Massachusetts as a protection for religious freedom, this provision would be regarded in some other societies as a restriction on it.

Several specific provisions of the Body of Liberties marked an advance over guarantees of freedom in England. One of these was a prohibition against the granting of monopolies. Another was Article 80: "Every married woman shall be free from bodily correction or stripes by her husband, unless it be in his own defense upon her assault."[42] At that time in England, the law permitted a husband to chastise his spouse with a "reasonable instrument." Such an instrument had been defined from the bench as "a stick no bigger than my thumb." Though perhaps not written into law, as has often been asserted, this interpretation seems to have prevailed in most of English America as the colonies moved into statehood. It is ironic that a reform in this particular area should have been sponsored by Nathaniel Ward, a known misogynist who in nonjudicial moments accused many women of having "squirrels' brains."

A curious provision in the eyes of most Western societies was one prohibiting anyone from accepting pay for defending another in court. This prohibition practically eliminated the profession of law. Apparently, Ward and others thought that law was too important a matter to be left to lawyers.

Progress in the law frequently has come through people little, if any, freer of prejudice than the common run of humankind. But they have had either a reverence for the principle of law, lifting them at times above their own prejudices, or sufficient common sense to realize that even their own freedom to indulge prejudice was imperiled if there was no extension of legal safeguards. Some reformers have been moved by both considerations. It is ironic, but not anomalous, that the chief agent for legal reform in Massachusetts Bay was Nathaniel Ward, who seldom bothered to conceal his contempt for both women and the Irish and his utter abhorrence of religious toleration.

Ward later returned to England, where he enjoyed greater freedom than in Massachusetts Bay. As James Truslow Adams pointed out in *The Founding of New England*, the Puritan fathers of the bay colony

> having changed their place from members of an opposition to members of a government, their new responsibilities would tend to foster even more strongly [a] fear of innovation. . . . [O]f the tiny group who now claimed absolute sway over two thousand subjects, rapidly increasing to sixteen thousand, none had held any position of administrative importance in the old country. Some of them had, indeed, occupied offices, but they were rather of a nature to encourage . . . intolerance of contradiction, and tendency to arbitrary action upon a small stage.[43]

One does not have to imagine every petty official as a Dogberry or Verges (some of those in Massachusetts had decent educations), but even in the case of some of the cleverer ones, their experience as a "people of the book" within their sectarian fold may have tended, as Samuel Johnson said of the study of the law, to "sharpen their minds by narrowing them." It is not strange that, lacking a cross-fertilization of ideas, Massachusetts Bay had no flowering of creativity. Nathaniel Ward was a courageous man of more than ordinary intelligence, but only the barrenness of the landscape made him seem a towering oak. There is praiseworthy eloquence in some passages of the Body of Liberties, among much that is trivial or merely eccentric, but his one book offers little variety, and its vaunted humor is distinguished more by its anomalous status in Massachusetts Bay than by any subtlety. Any vividness of style that it attains is largely the product of vigorous cantankerousness and lively prejudice.

As history shows, however, creativity in New England was not a lost cause. Connecticut and Rhode Island, and sometimes the Plymouth Colony, nurtured ideas. Some of these were force-fed to the magistrates of Massachusetts Bay by residents excluded from the inner circle and hence more likely to believe that the status quo was not ideal.

In England, as an opposition in the minority, these migrating Puritans had not only kept themselves mentally in fighting trim, but, like Toynbee's outnumbered predators among the North Sea herring, had kept the majority flexible and vigorous as well.[44] Now, transferred to Massachusetts Bay and heavily seated on their patch of earth, they were as adamant as a New England boulder and almost as incapable of evolution except in geological time. The Body of Liberties, therefore, effected no sudden revolution.

In fact, in 1644, three years after adoption of the code, residents of Massachusetts Bay vainly begged the General Court to allow those who were not members of Puritan congregations to participate in the government. The injustice was compounded by the fact that the church leaders, who were also political leaders, denied membership to many who wished to join. In 1646, a formal petition for the civil rights of thousands of disfranchised residents was presented by seven citizens. They pointed out that, although large numbers of citizens were denied the right to vote, they were required to pay taxes and serve in the military.

The identities of several of the petitioners were significant. One, Dr. Robert Child, a recent arrival, was a graduate of the University of Padua. He came with fresh views of the outside world and after exposure to the intellectual currents of Europe. Another petitioner, Samuel Maverick, was an "old planter," a settler in the territory of Massachusetts Bay even before the arrival of such founding fathers as Winthrop and Endecott. Because of that priority, he had a legally guaranteed status as a freeman, and hence a participant in the government. Maverick had exactly the same names—first and last—as the nineteenth century Texas rancher whose surname has become a byword for independence. The eponymous seventeenth-century settler was equally independent. Though he was a freeman, the only one not a Puritan church member, and was secure in his rights, he intervened to secure the same opportunities for the less privileged. He harked back to an earlier tradition of English rights in English America.

Another petitioner was David Yale, a stepson of Theophilus Eaton, co-founder of New Haven, a settlement of Massachusetts Bay people who successfully resisted all attempts to keep them within the older colony. New Haven had become the richest colony per capita in New England. Its houses, the handsomest in the region, symbolized the prosperity of their owners. When the original planters of New Haven voted to restrict participation in government as severely as in Massachusetts Bay, Eaton's was the lone voice of protest. Eaton was not Yale's only link with independent minds. His brother-in-law was Edward Hopkins, governor of Connecticut, a colony governed according to the Fundamental Orders, a quasi-democratic document framed largely by the Reverend Thomas Hooker, who had led his congregation out of the tyranny of Massachusetts Bay. Yale also maintained connections with the great world in England. He was attorney in New England for the earl of Warwick.

The Massachusetts Bay Colony was insulated from its neighbors and from Great Britain. Its vital signs appeared only when that insulation was penetrated. Connecticut, New Haven, and Rhode Island had been established without authorization from England. In fact, the fundamental laws of Connecticut and New Haven contained no reference to any earthly power outside their borders. Because of the crisis of civil war in England, Governor Winthrop of Massachusetts Bay had gotten by with his refusal to return his colony's charter. It was even easier during the same period for the neighboring colonies, which had never been chartered, to conduct their affairs without regard to decisions in London. Thus all of these four New England colonies were becoming freer in the sense of growing independence from the mother country. In Massachusetts Bay, however, there was no corresponding growth in individual freedom.

Massachusetts residents who found the lack of personal freedom unbearable tended to move to other colonies rather than struggle for reform where they were. Sometimes, as in the cases of Roger Williams and Thomas Hooker, they became influential leaders, even founders of new communities whose relative freedom made Massachusetts Bay residents envious and restive. Those who resisted from within, like Child, Maverick, and Yale, tended to derive ideas and inspiration from the bay colony's more freedom-minded neighbors.

The demands of the Massachusetts Bay petitioners were not extravagant. They requested admission to the Puritan churches for "members of the Church of England not scandalous in their lives and conversations." But they also wished to end the requirement that a citizen be a member of a Puritan church in order to vote. They asked that "civil liberty and freedom be forthwith granted to all truly English, equal[ly] to the rest of their countrymen, as in all plantations is accustomed to be done, and as all freeborn enjoy in our native country."

In replying to the petition, Winthrop and Dudley dodged the quite valid contention that the Massachusetts Bay colonists did not enjoy the liberties and degree of religious toleration that would have been theirs if they had remained at home in England. The irony of the situation was particularly bitter in that, besides seeking economic opportunities, many of the settlers had dared the perils of the Atlantic Ocean and the North American wilderness in the hope of finding a level of freedom and toleration not yet available in Great Britain.

Governor Winthrop, nevertheless, considered the appeal intolerable. The General Court agreed, fining all of them and imprisoning two. Child and some of his fellow petitioners, believing that their best recourse was a resort to English law as interpreted by courts in England, prepared to sail to Great Britain. Just before departure, they were arrested on orders of some of the magistrates. Agents of Massachusetts Bay searched their baggage and their homes. The magistrates ordered them imprisoned. The judges had taken no chances about securing a majority for the verdict. Some of the magistrates who had not concurred in the original fining of the petitioners were not even apprised that their colleagues were meeting again. Another of the petitioners, John Dand, was imprisoned when it was discovered that he had advocated appointment of a royal governor. Two petitioners, Thomas Fowle and William Vassall, succeeded in getting to England but found the realm too busy with internal strife to consider the problems of Massachusetts Bay.

Winthrop and his colleagues indulged in no easy optimism that their troubles with rebels were over. Edward Winslow, who had served as agent for both Massachusetts Bay and Plymouth, wrote him not to assume that "all of the troubles of New England" were confined to the governor's bailiwick. Citizens of Plymouth had petitioned their General Court "to allow and maintain full and free tolerance of religion to all men that would preserve the civil peace and submit unto government." They had met with a friendly reception from many of the General Court. "You would have [marveled]," said Edward Winslow, "to have seen how sweet this carrion relished to the palate of most of the deputies!"[45] But this potential support did the petitioners no good. Plymouth's governor refused to allow the General Court to vote on the proposition. Thus the Pilgrims of Plymouth were denied not only the rights that they had enjoyed in their native England but also those that had been available to them even as aliens during their twelve-year residence in Holland.

In spurning the petition of Child and others that they be accorded the rights of Englishmen, the General Court had declared, "Our allegiance binds us not to the laws of England any longer than while we live in England." Departures from the English common law were evident in an amplified code adopted in 1648. Rhode Island, which the year before had adopted a code firmly based on the laws of Great Britain, seemed a lonely holdout as other northern colonies were increasingly influenced by Massachusetts statutes. In 1652 the Massachusetts General Court established its own mint and began producing its own currency, the pine-tree shilling. It also declared Massachusetts an independent commonwealth. This gauntlet of defiance was hurled not at the foot of the throne but against the door of the Puritan Parliament that had assumed authority in form as well as substance after securing the execution of King Charles I.

Most of the leaders of Massachusetts were not evil men. Winthrop, the most influential and sometimes called the "noblest of them all," was conscientious and, within the limits of his imagination, caring. Roger Williams, in a testimony to Winthrop's character that is inadvertently at least as great a tribute to his own, said that the friendship between the two men survived their differences and even Williams' banishment. But the Massachusetts magistrates always knew what was best for their people, and for the people of other colonies as well. And, as Judge Learned Hand observed, "The spirit of liberty is the spirit which is not too sure that it is right."[46]

The influence of Massachusetts on her neighbors was increased by association in the New England Confederation, which had been formed in 1643 to combat threats from the Indians and the Dutch. Organized at a convention in Boston and known formally as the United Colonies of New England, the confederation was composed of Massachusetts, Plymouth, Connecticut, and New Haven. They mutually guaranteed each other's territorial integrity. A Commission consisting of two members from each colony was to coordinate all military activities of the confederate colonies. The consent of at least six of the eight commissioners was necessary for the waging of war, defensive as well as offensive. The costs of war were apportioned among the colonies according to the number of male inhabitants of fighting age in each. If agreement could not be reached among six commissioners on any major matter, the disputed question would revert to the general courts. Rhode Island was not taken into the United Colonies. Its people were too independent to be dominated by Massachusetts. Maine was not invited to join either. To have done so would have been to recognize her as a sovereign community, and such recognition would have been an impediment to Massachusetts schemes. Ten years after formation of the confederacy, Massachusetts, with no legal justification, annexed Maine.

Interstate disputes, the extradition of fugitive servants and criminals, and relations with the Indians were all placed within the Commission's jurisdiction. But Commission convocations became committee meetings, rather than executive, legislative, or judicial sessions. Regular annual sessions ceased in 1664. The coming of King Philip's War in 1675 temporarily provided a renewed incentive for united activity, but the United Colonies of New England disbanded in 1684. Before the organization ended, it had taught the participants something about intercolonial cooperation. But having abandoned it, they were not disposed to try it again until confronted by a perceived external threat of impressive magnitude.

Meanwhile, the leaders of Massachusetts Bay were always discovering internal threats. In 1656 two Quakers, Mary Fisher and Ann Austin, arrived in Boston. Scenting danger, the Bostonians examined them as to their beliefs in a session presided over by Deputy Governor Bellingham. The revelations proving unsatisfactory, another kind of examination was prescribed. The women were stripped and searched. They were imprisoned for a time and then shipped out of New England.

Far from remonstrating with the Boston officials for their handling of the situation, the General Court of Massachusetts Bay formally approved. Alerted by the crisis, they adopted a statute providing a fine for any ship-master convicted of transporting Quakers to the colony, and prescribing imprisonment and whipping for any Quakers who gained entrance. Any Massachusetts Bay citizen who defended Quaker views would be fined and banished.

The authorities proved three years later that these enactments were not mere bluster. They hanged a woman and two men for worshiping as Quakers, and later executed another man for the same offense.

Edward Burroughs, an English Quaker, informed Charles II of the persecution and warned that the bloodletting in Massachusetts, "if it were not stopped, would overrun all." The king wrote a letter ordering an end to all persecution of Quakers and, obviously with conscious irony, had the missive delivered to Governor John Endecott by one of their number who had been banished from New England.[47]

Quaker views were not popular in Rhode Island either. But the leaders of that colony had been both more humane and more sophisticated than their Massachusetts counterparts. As early as 1657, they had informed the bay colony's General Court that they made no effort to punish the Friends for their beliefs, holding that "they are like to gain more adherents by the conceit of their patient sufferings, than by consent to their pernicious sayings."[48]

Beginning in 1636, there was a development that could have led to greater tolerance and ideological diversity. The General Court of Massachusetts appropriated the sum of four hundred pounds "towards a school or college." Competition for the site was vigorous among various towns. Newtown won because it was considered remarkably free of the Antinomian heresy for which Anne Hutchinson had been expelled. Probably because of hopes that the new institution would become a New World version of their English alma mater, some of the magistrates got the winning community's name changed to Cambridge. The college opened in a clapboard building in the summer of 1638. John Harvard, a teaching elder of the church, died and left the school his library and half the value of his modest estate. In 1639, the grateful General Court named the new institution Harvard College.[49]

Though the founding of a college might seem to offer an antidote to the narrow conformity of Massachusetts society under Puritan rule, many years would pass before Harvard's influence would have that effect. Governor Winthrop, Deputy Governor Dudley, Thomas Shepard, and other leaders of the repressive government were dominant members of the Harvard Board of Overseers. The chief purpose of the new school was to create future ministers of the Gospel in the image of those then wearing the seal of approval in the bay colony. It was to be one more instrument to perpetuate the governing philosophy then in control under the alliance of Puritan lay leaders and clergy. As Jack P. Greene points out in his brilliant revisionist *Pursuits of Happiness*, the leading citizens of Massachusetts and most of their followers had not come to America to replicate the England that they knew or even to anticipate the England of the future. Instead, they were determined "to move in precisely the opposite direction of the world they had abandoned in old England."[50] Harvard College would for a long time be one more instrument of a reactionary purpose.

It was the first college in English America and, with the exception of William and Mary in Virginia, would be the only one established in the seventeenth century. But, while a little formal learning can promote conformity, it also can whet the appetite for independent study. And the acquisition of knowledge freely sought to satisfy individual curiosity can frustrate ultimately the most earnest propaganda efforts of totalitarian regimes, whether pursued cynically, as in some times and places, or with the passionate sincerity of the Massachusetts Puritans. Harvard eventually would provide an example of this truth.

27

THE CLOUD-VEILED SUN

THE MASSACHUSETTS PURITAN oligarchy did almost everything in its power to prevent Harvard from becoming a true liberal arts university encouraging independent thought. The chief purpose of the college was twofold: to train ministers for Puritan congregations and teachers for schools inculcating Puritan principles in the young. The dominant coterie in Massachusetts believed in education, but were convinced that its greatest value lay in enabling people to study the Christian Gospels and the interpretations of them prepared by right-thinking Puritan ministers. They rejected the belief of some of their English brethren that young Puritans might acquire even from Anglican instructors the tools that they might use in promulgating a purer faith. The colonial Puritans identified with the biblical Israelites, a chosen people battling constantly not only against avowed enemies but also those in the guise of helpers. William Hubbard, one of the most prominent Massachusetts ministers, spoke for the colony's rulers when he said, "It is not meet that the Israelites should always go down to the Philistines to sharpen their weapons, which they are to use in fighting against the enemies of God's Church, or for whetting their tools they must use in tilling God's field."[1]

There was nothing unique in the seventeenth century about the Massachusetts leaders' belief that education should serve religion. In other American colonies the Anglicans, Lutherans, Presbyterians, Baptists, and Dutch Reformed adherents pressed their particular articles of faith upon students submitted to their guidance at the primary, secondary, or collegiate level. But in no other colony was every part of the educational process so dominated by a single sect; moreover, by a sect whose leaders also exercised the chief political authority. If Harvard could inculcate the "proper" beliefs in the future ministers and political chieftains of Massachusetts, and in the schoolmasters who would prepare the young for admission to the college, the system of control would seem to be foolproof.

But, though some of Harvard's founders could recite numerous dates and events from antiquity onward, accompanying them with precise citations, they had not read one of the important lessons of history. They had not learned that young and eager minds frequently apply intellectual tools to experiments for which they were not designed.

Also, they did not allow for the varying influences of individual personalities in teaching and administration. Their rigid system for certifying faculty could not guarantee that one of "correct" views would have the character and personality to become an effective role model, nor could it predict the continued orthodoxy of a teacher whose charisma might make him a Pied Piper introducing wild notes from outside the walls.

The first head of Harvard was certainly not what the godly examiners had bargained for. Nathaniel Eaton flogged his charges with a cruelty notorious even by the standards of seventeenth-century pedagogy. He fed them spoiled beef and moldy bread. Nor were the students his only victims. With a cudgel, he delivered two hundred blows to his assistant while the man was held helpless by two servants. When the governing board dismissed Eaton, he absconded with college funds.[2]

His successor, Henry Dunster, provided a refreshing change. He not only improved student morale but secured able teachers, copied some courses from the curricula of English universities, and extended to four years the time for earning a bachelor's degree. Religious preparation still had primacy, and the study of the *Abridgement of Christian Divinity* was required. But religiously oriented instruction included the reading of the Old Testament in Hebrew and of the New in Greek. A student proficient in translating the Greek Gospels might be attracted to reading pagan philosophy in the same tongue. Astronomy was also added to the curriculum. The heavens that declared the glory of God were sure to make some stargazers impatient with the confining dome of Puritanism that shut them from Heaven.

Unfortunately, education at Harvard and at preparatory schools in Massachusetts did not remain stimulating for long. Soon it was in such a torpid state that it satisfied neither the entrenched leaders who had counted on its help in maintaining the status quo nor those rebels who had looked to it hopefully as an agent of change. The low state of education in the commonwealth was about the only thing on which the two groups could agree. The Reverend Samuel Torrey, an enthusiast for witch trials and very much a pillar of the old order, lamented in 1674, "If we do consider how much both civil and religious education is neglected, and if we look upon the sad face of the rising generation and see how much of ignorance . . . doth already appear in the countenance of it, . . . our hearts may well tremble to think what will become of the worship and ordinances of God in the next age."[3]

In the same year that Torrey issued his warning, the synod reported that schools "and other public concerns" were "in a languishing state."[4] In the two preceding years, the Reverend Thomas Shepard, Jr., son of one of the chief denouncers of Anne Hutchinson, had declared that there was "a great decay in inferior schools," and the Reverend Urian Oakes, an establishment figure preaching the Election Sermon, warned that "the nurseries of piety and learning and liberal education" were "languishing" and might "die away."[5]

The primary and secondary schools were indeed dying away for want of proper teachers. Harvard was the chief provider of instructors, and from 1661 to 1670 there were on average seven graduates a year.[6] Subsequent classes were not quite so small, but many graduates preferred to begin work as church-appointed ministers or to enter the family business without spending any time as teachers. Harvard clearly was not supplying enough teachers to keep the schools open.

Of course, while public schools, in the American sense of tax-supported institutions open to the public, were an accepted part of life in Massachusetts, they were still an anomaly in most of the other colonies. But whereas a few youngsters in some of them, especially Virginia, were sent to England for preparatory schooling and university training, Massachusetts did not have the benefit of such a leavening. Contamination from the old homeland was feared. The mother's milk in England might carry infection to the babes of Massachusetts. Even newcomers trained in the English universities were suspect because of that fact. Conditions varied from area to area in the North American colonies, but *some* of Virginia's "old field schools," and comparable institutions in other colonies, furnished more intellectual stimulation than most of the free schools of Massachusetts.

The colony's repressive society all but smothered the lamp of learning. And at Harvard the flickering flame was tended by a succession of inept keepers. The head must be a minister, and few clergymen of prestige or unusual ability were eager to endure the penury of the post and the dictation of scornful overseers when they might instead become the powerful ministers of large congregations. But, as Thomas Jefferson Wertenbaker has pointed out, this circumstance

> proved a blessing in disguise, for it weakened the grip of the conservative group of clergymen who wished to make the college a mere feeder for the Churches and a bulwark of the old order rather than a liberal arts college. Had Harvard, in the years from 1660 to 1724, been presided over by a series of such commanding clergymen as Increase Mather and Cotton Mather, and had these men given to it all their time and energy, it would not so soon have become a center of liberal thought.[7]

Increase Mather did serve as president, consenting to occupy the position temporarily following the death of one occupant and the refusal of the proffered post by a succession of ministers.[8] But he agreed only to give the college whatever time he could spare after completion of his daily duties as pastor of a Boston church.

Mather's keen mind and forceful character were beyond question. The holder of a master's degree from Dublin's Trinity College, he was well grounded in the classics and published more than a hundred books. But his intellect, character, and phenomenal energy were dedicated to perpetuation of a Puritan culture already antiquated when he began his career. Most of his writings espoused the narrowest of Puritan theologies. He founded a scientific society in Boston, but within it experimental thought was severely circumscribed by the tenets of the Massachusetts churches.

Mather in 1683 opposed the royal order to return the old Massachusetts charter, not because he loved republican government but because he was determined to preserve the Puritan despotism. In 1688 he went to London to represent some of the colony's congregations in their plea for retention of the old charter. Two years later, he was made an official agent of the colony in England. He argued, as he did about so many things he opposed, that to relinquish the document would be a sin. Still, he was not able to block return of the charter, but did secure a compromise that restricted freedom under the new one.

Meanwhile, Increase Mather had been first a part-time president of Harvard and then an absentee one. In the circumstances, direction of the college was left to two faculty members, John Leverett and William Brattle. Both worked to broaden the curriculum and to introduce ideas afloat in the great world but usually doomed to shipwreck on Massachusetts' rockbound coast.

At length, the General Court, displeased with Mather's representation in England and with the scant time that he spared for Harvard on his return, adopted a resolution requiring the president to live in Cambridge. Mather then demanded of the governor, "Should I leave off preaching to 1500 souls, for I suppose that so many use[d] ordinarily to attend in our congregation, only to expound to 40 or 50 children, few of them capable of edification by such exercises?"[9]

Nevertheless, when the General Court insisted that he must move to Cambridge or resign from Harvard, he moved. But late in 1700, on the threshold of a new century for which he was ill prepared, he returned to Boston. Cambridge, he said, was not good for his health. Maybe the General Court should name a new president. Instead of begging him to remain on his own terms, the General Court resolved, "For as much as the constitution requires that the president reside at Cambridge, in case of Mr. Mather's refusal, absence, sickness, or death," his duties should be assumed by a vice president.

After three more unhappy months in Cambridge, Mather informed the governor that he would no longer live there and that the General Court therefore should name a successor. He admonished, however, that "it would be fatal to the interest of religion if a person disaffected to the order of the Gospel, [as] professed and practiced in these churches," should be appointed.

When without hesitation the General Court accepted his resignation and named an interim successor, Mather was shocked. His resentment was exacerbated by the fact that the interim appointee was permitted to spend five days a week in Boston. Increase Mather's son Cotton, himself an unrelenting minister in the old Puritan tradition, blamed Councillor Samuel Sewall for the authorities' action. That man, he said, had treated the elder Mather "worse than a neger."[10] Sewall tried to placate the Mathers by sending the father a haunch of venison and asking the son to consider whether his attack was consistent with the younger man's own book *The Law of Kindness for the Tongue*. An unrepentant Cotton "charged the Council with lying, hypocrisy, [and] tricks."

A review of the controversy would be no more edifying now than the actual arguments were then. Suffice it to say that, in the midst of contention, the interim head of Harvard resigned because of ill health. The Mathers and their adherents were now confident that either father or son—they being the two foremost scholars of the Massachusetts Puritan old guard—would be named president. Instead, the post was offered to John Leverett, who was known to have truck with ideas from the outside world and who was not even a minister. The defeat of the Mathers was further dramatized by the fact that in 1700 they and their allies, viewing Leverett as a subversive, had ousted him from the college.

That the Mathers deemed Leverett subversive by no means implies that he was a libertine or even a liberal by the standards of most societies. Increase and Cotton had been partly responsible for enactment of a law to punish "provokers of the high displeasure of the almighty God." They had no doubts about what violations of the Sabbath provoked Divine wrath. All persons of both sexes above fourteen years of age who were guilty of "uncivilly walking in the streets and fields" on Sunday, or "travelling from town to town" or "going on shipboard," were to be admonished or fined.[11] If unable to pay, they were to be whipped by the constable. Bowling and shuffleboard at places of public entertainment were forbidden every day of the week.[12]

There probably was truth in the claim that Leverett made the Massachusetts brand of Puritanism seem less attractive to many students. At least one of them in later years said that Leverett and Brattle had "made more proselytes to the Church of England than any [other] two men ever did that lived in America."[13] While inviting critical thinking about church policies as about all other aspects of life, they emphasized "righteousness, faith, and charity."

Leverett was the son of an attorney of ill repute and the grandson of another John Leverett, who had been an officer in England's parliamentary army before becoming major general of Massachusetts forces and then governor of the colony. The first John had been very much a giant of the old guard and had been one of the commissioners sent to Maine in 1652 to tell its people that they were being annexed by Massachusetts.

When the younger John Leverett was ousted from Harvard in 1700, he had studied law and was serving his first term in the General Court as representative from Cambridge. He had scheduled pupil recitations for five o'clock on winter mornings so that he could be in his seat when the General Court convened in Boston. He immediately had become an attorney. And in the very year of his ousting, he had become Speaker of the House. Here was strong evidence of restlessness among the legislators. Six years later he was elected to the Provincial Council from Eastern Maine, where he owned property in the area formally annexed through his grandfather's activities as a commissioner.

In Leverett, Harvard had as president not only a scholar and politician but also a businessman and diplomat—all skills useful to a university head in any era. He organized the Lincolnshire Company for settling and developing the large property in Maine that he had inherited. Governor Joseph Dudley sent him on diplomatic missions to the Iroquois and to the governor of New York. Dudley also dispatched him to lift the morale of participants in the Port Royal expedition.

Impressed by Leverett's services, Governor Dudley reciprocated by revalidating the Harvard Charter of 1650 and using it to eliminate the president's opponents from the board of overseers. The president used his authority to make only a few changes in the curriculum, but they were significant ones. French was offered as an elective. Courses in theology included contemporary Anglican teachings. Extracurricular activities were introduced. A club was formed, and students started a publication of their own. Cotton Mather, who persisted in calling Leverett the "pretended president," reported in horror that the students were reading "plays, novels, empty and vicious pieces of poetry, and even Ovid's Epistles, which have a vile tendency to corrupt good manners."

The student body increased so greatly that a new building had to be added. And graduates left to become influential teachers, preachers, and elected officials in Massachusetts and elsewhere in New England. Many of them combined a solid grounding in the classics and other traditional learning with a healthy curiosity about intellectual trends in their own time. And when their open-mindedness brought them into dangerous conflicts in the communities they served, the increasingly prestigious Harvard president was a faithful ally. Leverett's reputation extended beyond North America. In 1713 he was elected a fellow of Britain's Royal Society.

In that same year occurred an incident that placed him at odds with the governor with whom he had worked so successfully. When the position of college treasurer became vacant, Dudley's son applied, but the College Corporation turned him down. About the same time, the eccentric but influential Judge Samuel Sewall, who had begun waging war against the growing custom of wearing wigs, attacked Leverett for supposed neglect of religion at Harvard. The Mathers increased the volume of their criticism. Cotton Mather launched an investigation of Harvard in 1723. Leverett was hard put to prevent the College Corporation from being packed with foes. The new governor, Colonel Shute, gave his strong support. This advantage, together with Leverett's political acumen and the well-earned loyalty of former students, enabled him to win his victory before his abrupt death on May 3, 1724. Thanks to that victory, he was succeeded as president by Benjamin Wadsworth, who continued the policy of stimulating intellectual curiosity and defending a modicum of academic freedom.

Such stout pillars of reactionary and isolationist Puritanism as John Winthrop and Samuel Seawall loom large in most accounts of colonial Massachusetts, and even culturally oriented histories of the colony seem to be dominated by the likes of Cotton and Increase Mather. Whatever these people's limitations, they all had qualities that demand respect. But in terms of creative influence in building in Massachusetts a viable culture that would enrich the new American nation, Leverett was a greater giant than any of them. There is no reason to believe that Samuel Eliot Morison exaggerated when he said, "It is largely owing to Brattle as tutor and to Leverett both as tutor and President that Harvard was saved from becoming a sectarian institution, at a time when the tendency of most pious New Englanders was to tighten up and insist on hundred-per-cent Puritanism in the face of infiltrating ideas that heralded the Century of Enlightenment."[14]

As scholar, attorney, politician, diplomat, and educator, John Leverett typified the versatility characteristic of so many of society's energizers. He was also representative as one who drew nurture from tradition and excitement from discovery. He was a major force in transforming a moribund culture into a vital one.

The results are important not only to regional history but also to the history of the United States and of a world molded in part by American influence. It was important to the future of America that, before the end of the first quarter of the eighteenth century, New England should move culturally and socially nearer to England's other colonies. In his brilliantly conceived and executed *Pursuits of Happiness: The Social Development of Early Modern British Colonies and the Formation of American Culture* (1988), Jack P. Greene successfully challenges "those who have assumed that the history of [colonial British American social] development can be told within a framework derived from the New England experience." He holds that "New England's influence in shaping American culture during the colonial era has been exaggerated." Within the framework of colonial British America, he has "emphasized the atypicality of the experience of orthodox puritan New England and the normative character of that of the Chesapeake. . . ."[15]

The same historian supports with many contemporary citations his contention that "In the century after 1660, the societies of the orthodox puritan colonies seemed to many of their leading figures to be coming apart. . . ." Virginia and its neighbor Maryland, on the other hand, "were moving in precisely the opposite direction, becoming more settled, cohesive, and coherent."[16] He also points out that the New England colonies in the late seventeenth and early eighteenth centuries were becoming more "contentious" and beset by self-doubt at the very time that Virginians were "becoming less contentious and growing in healthy self-confidence."[17]

As we have seen already, once past the division of Bacon's Rebellion, Virginia entered upon an era of public spiritedness and cultural aspiration symbolized by the founding of the College of William and Mary and by the planned city of Williamsburg and its elegant new structures. Meanwhile, Massachusetts seemed in disarray. It had to deal with its own problem of division, deeper than Virginia's in Bacon's Rebellion, before it could move forward as a creative society. That was the division in every town and village, and in the councils of the capital, between those confined within the old Puritan hegemony and those prepared to pursue an idea whenever and wherever its gleam punctuated the dark frontier. Church leadership, often inseparable from political and cultural leadership, was passed from generation to generation in a laying on of hands. But enlightened Puritanism, sometimes a revitalizing force in England, had become a cramped creature in its Massachusetts cell. The hand that was laid on New England was a dead one, twitching occasionally, but with rigor mortis rather than life.

Ironically, Harvard, designed as a stronghold for the old Puritanism, became an outpost of change. Through it were disseminated some of the intellectual products of the seventeenth century as well as "subversive" creations of other ages. Controversial ideas quite understandably bred controversy, expressed in litigation as well as in public debate. The bitter argument over ideas that Massachusetts people called "Rhode Islandism" became characteristic of Massachusetts itself.[18] Puritanism's old guard fought hard for self-preservation and also in many cases from a sincere conviction that in fighting ideas they were combating Satan.

The populations of Massachusetts and Virginia were similar in composition, chiefly English. The Massachusetts settlers, however, had been in rebellion against the supposedly wicked ways of England, whereas the Virginians had been trying to build in America a greater England with more opportunity for all people of enterprise.

The major demographic difference in the two colonies was in the greater proportion of black slaves in Virginia. Indian slavery had come to Massachusetts under Governor Winthrop. Black slavery followed quickly and expanded, though not so rapidly as in Rhode Island, which, like New York and New Jersey, for most of the decade from 1700 to 1710 had a higher proportion of slaves than the Chesapeake colonies of Maryland and Virginia had had between 1660 and 1680.[19]

Though the manufacture of flour and iron had become important in Virginia, manufacturing was not nearly so important as in Massachusetts. Nevertheless, per capita wealth in the southern colony was substantially greater than in the northern one. The extremes of wealth and poverty, however, were generally greater among the free citizens of Massachusetts than among their Virginia counterparts.

Religious and political tolerance in most of Virginia in the late seventeenth and early eighteenth centuries was not as prevalent as in some times and places, but set a high standard for the contemporary Western world. By contrast, on this score Massachusetts had a lot of catching up to do if an environment favorable to creativity was to be attained. The denial of freedom of expression directly inhibited both philosophical and artistic creativity. Indirectly, they were also hindered by the lack of stimulating variety that is another cost of enforced conformity. But Massachusetts was narrowing the gap that separated her from her more advanced neighbors. Far more than any other agency, Harvard was sending forth the builders.

Their growing strength was demonstrated by the ferocity with which the threatened Puritan oligarchy struck at them and at rationalism itself. In 1681 some New England clergymen assembled for the specific purpose of combating rational views by calling attention to "strange apparitions, or whatever else shall happen that is prodigious, witchcrafts, diabolical possessions, remarkable judgements upon noted sinners, eminent deliverances and answers of prayer."[20] The most influential of the clerical group was Increase Mather, whose detailed accounts of witchcraft in his *Essay for the Recording of Illustrious Providences* spread fear in almost every element of society. The zeal and influence of Cotton Mather soon equaled his father's. Children, notoriously susceptible to the power of suggestion, accused one adult after another of taking them on wild midnight rides and torturing them by supernatural means. Cotton Mather had his own explanation of why so many instances of witchcraft appeared in New England. He wrote in *The Wonders of the Invisible World*, "The New Englanders are a people of God settled in those which were once the devil's territories."[21]

The hysteria climaxed in 1693. Salem was the foremost center of witch trials, and Samuel Sewall was one of the most prominent judges. When the hysteria had subsided, Sewall repented his part in it, "asking pardon of men and especially desiring prayers that God . . . would pardon that sin."[22]

Before it had run its course, the witchcraft mania had so dominated Massachusetts courts of law that scores of men and women were charged on "spectral evidence" and nineteen were executed. Hanging was the favorite method of killing these unfortunates, but at least one woman was pressed to death.

The fight against witchcraft hysteria gained its most powerful ally when some youngsters testified to the spectral activities of Lady Phips, wife of Governor William Phips. He forbade the judges to commit "any more . . . accused without unavoidable necessity, and those that have been committed I would shelter from . . . the least suspicion of any wrong to be done unto the innocent."

But the old-line Puritan clergy did not give up immediately. When the governor was away on a trip, a plan was devised to conquer a coven of witches with a convention of clerics. The General Court considered a proposal that the ministers be summoned to advise the lay leaders of government on the "right way as to witchcraft." The proposition was defeated by a four-vote margin. In 1693, with the governor still absent, Deputy Governor William Stoughton convened the General Court to deal with more charges of witchcraft. Fifty-two persons were indicted, but true bills were found against fewer than half. Only three were convicted. Frustrated at the escape of so many, Stoughton ordered the "speedy execution" of these three, together with five people convicted by the preceding General Court. Eight gaping graves awaited them, but were filled again when a messenger from Governor Phips arrived with reprieves before the hangman had done his work.

Deputy Governor Stoughton was presiding over the Court when word arrived that the prisoners had been spared. Rising in his wrath, he said that the clergy had missed the opportunity to rid itself of witches and that those responsible had advanced the designs of Satan. "The Lord have mercy on the country." And he strode out.

In his absence, the General Court acquitted others accused of practicing witchcraft. But in the spring Stoughton returned to the bench and tried to bully a jury into indicting a young woman for practicing the black arts. When they refused to comply, Stoughton sent them back to reconsider. When they returned, they again refused to indict. Public opinion sustained them. Soon all Massachusetts prisoners awaiting trial for witchcraft were released.

This only sent the Mathers into a frenzy of activity to recoup lost ground. Accompanied by thirty to forty people, they entered the home of Margaret Rule, a seventeen-year-old girl who claimed to have been assaulted by supernatural beings "in a manner too hellish to be sufficiently described." Cotton Mather sat on the bed where she lay, and he and his father questioned her.

Leading questions elicited answers that rekindled the fading hysteria as the crowd spread out from the house like sparks in a breeze. But even this circulation was not enough for Increase Mather, who prepared an account of the interrogation titled "Another Brand Pluct Out of the Burning." Governor Phips had prohibited publication of anything about witchcraft, but Mather circulated his manuscript by hand. The old Puritan oligarchy, which had fastened its censorship on Massachusetts, was still influential, but times had changed indeed when its most powerful members had to resort to an underground, when the high priest himself had to establish his own samizdat.

At least one of the witnesses to the bedside interrogation of Margaret Rule was no help to the Mathers in spreading fear of witchcraft. Robert Calef, a Boston merchant, had entered the house with the rest of the crowd specifically to check on the methods of the Mathers. He circulated his own account, emphasizing the role of leading questions and domineering techniques.

Cotton Mather denounced Calef as "one of the worst of liars," preached against him, and told him that he would have him arrested for slander. The merchant invited discussion with Mather over what Calef regarded as the harm done by the minister in reviving the witchcraft controversy "after the sorest affliction and greatest blemish to religion that ever befell this country . . . , [particularly] after his Excellency had put a stop to executions, and men began to hope there would never be a return of the like." But Mather had him arrested. Nevertheless, when Calef appeared in court, no one, not even Mather, appeared against him.

Calef, however, had not finished with Mather. Not that he sought to convict him, but to convince him. He fired off a succession of letters designed to show him the error of his ways. Now Mather was on the defensive, sending Calef affidavits from those who supposedly had witnessed levitation and other happenings in connection with Margaret Rule that could be explained only as the work of evil spirits. Neither man convinced the other.

In official circles, most people had wearied of the contest. Court actions had ceased. In 1694, however, many of the Massachusetts clergy joined in a last stand against rationalism. They set out to catalog, among other supernatural manifestations, "apparitions, possessions, enchantments." Though some Harvard men rode to the rescue, the institution's influence was not always undividedly cast against superstition. A circular requesting information on these weird phenomena bore the imprimatur of the Fellows of Harvard. And for generations, even as the sun of the Enlightenment rose over Europe and cast its beams upon America, a fear of witchcraft lingered in some dark places in Massachusetts.

But the important fact is that there were bearers of light in Massachusetts, and they determinedly searched out the shadowy corners. These were not always the professional scholars or those professionally charged with responsibility for social uplift. Indeed, some prominent members of these categories, such as the Mathers, served, always unwittingly, often conscientiously, the forces of darkness. Some of the most effective leaders of intelligent reform were essentially men of practical affairs, businessmen who shared John Leverett's vision of versatile learning combined with purposeful activity as one way to a fuller life.

Though some of these people were branded atheists by the clergy, they seem in most cases to have been as deeply religious as the ministers, though less doctrinaire, much less sure that they had specific and unchallengeable answers to which the mass of men were not privy. Robert Calef was one of this breed. The Boston cloth merchant's intellect ranged far beyond the bolts of material dispensed in his store. He wrote a book revealing the fallacies in preachments about witchcraft, and the lack of objectivity in Massachusetts clerical investigations. He gave it a title sure to attract attention: *More Wonders of the Invisible World*. When no printer in Boston would risk publishing the book, he secured a London publisher. Increase Mather had a copy burned in the Harvard Yard, but this dramatic signal of disapproval probably increased circulation.

An even more remarkable example of the influence of merchant-scholars was William Brattle's brother Thomas. Before entering upon his business career, Thomas Brattle graduated from Harvard and traveled abroad extensively. Afterwards he prospered, and was generous with both time and money in the pursuit of truth. He was the principal founder of Boston's Brattle Street Church, whose minister and congregation often opposed the designs of the Puritan old guard. For twenty years he was treasurer of Harvard. He became a mathematician and a distinguished astronomer.

Ultimately, he had a greater influence on the intellectual life of New England than both Mathers combined. Cotton Mather praised Sir Isaac Newton as "the perpetual dictator of the learned world,"[23] but it was Thomas Brattle whose observations of Newton's comet, based on fixed stars, enabled the celebrated genius to test Kepler's laws. Newton used some of Brattle's findings in the *Principia*.[24] Brattle's observations of two solar eclipses and a lunar eclipse were published in the Royal Society's *Philosophical Transactions*. For thirty-three years before his death in 1713, the scientific world of two continents gave respectful attention to his astronomical and mathematical data. Upon his death, the Royal Society requested for its archives not only his observations in these fields but in music as well.

Brattle's career is reminiscent of those businessmen of Renaissance Florence who ventured as boldly in intellectual realms as in commerce. Massachusetts society early in the eighteenth century could boast other men of practical affairs who, though not quite so conspicuously, knew and helped to preserve the best of classical and medieval traditions while latching onto exciting ideas brought from foreign shores by the winds and currents of change. In them, as much as in any of the citizens of Massachusetts, lay the colony's opportunity to be part of the great creative epoch toward which some areas of America already were moving.

SCIENCE ENSLAVED

S AMUEL ELIOT MORISON indignantly repudiated Charles Francis Adams' characterization of the century of New England history from 1640 to 1740 as a "glacial period." Morison positively bristled at the same writer's assertion that, after the expulsion of Anne Hutchinson and the death of John Cotton, "a theological glacier . . . slowly settled down upon Massachusetts" with the result that for a century and a half, except for Cotton Mather's writings, "absolutely nothing" worthy to be designated literature was composed in the colony.[1] Morison contended that, after Charles Francis Adams used the term "glacial period," "Brooks Adams, James Truslow Adams, and a host of others used it as a cover to their ignorance of, or lack of interest in, what went on in the New England mind for a century or more." Like the Adamses, Morison was a historian of impeccable Massachusetts genealogy. He observed that "it is curious how the recession of this 'glacier' always seems to coincide with the rise of the Adams family."[2]

Perhaps the truth lies somewhere between the two contentions. For a century following 1640, New England creativity does seem largely to have been smothered by a great "theological glacier." Beginning early in the eighteenth century with John Leverett's enlightened administration of Harvard and the intellectual courage of a few ministers and businessmen, there were occasional thawings. After decades of the frozen theocracy's expansions and contractions, it became apparent that overall the glacier actually was receding, but until about 1740 the movement was indeed glacial.

It would be a mistake to assume that Harvard gave Massachusetts a bracing shot of democracy. Although students at first were ranked according to academic performance, this practice was superseded about 1720—just when the college was winning the battle against the Puritan oligarchy—by one based on the students' parentage. The sons of royal governors and councillors were placed first. The next honored group also owed its position to heredity; it consisted of the sons of college graduates.[3] The practice in Harvard was no more democratic than in Elizabethan England or even Renaissance Florence. It did not create in advance a healthy ambiance for the ideas of the founders of the American Republic expressed in the Declaration of Independence and the Constitution of the United States. But Harvard did transmit to certain favored persons the Western intellectual heritage, while also making available to them some of the currency of ideas from other contemporary societies. The opportunities were not presented on the scale that transformed Renaissance Florence or Elizabethan England, but they were sufficient to advance a hitherto tentative and sporadic process of transformation. Harvard's graduates augmented in intellectual preparation, as well as in numbers, the small group of New Englanders prepared to engage in dialogue with some society other than their own. Out of this healthy interest in ideas came a culture sufficiently creative to contribute importantly to the vital society that dominated America in the Republic's early years.

Some ideas current at Harvard were circulated by means of a press established in Cambridge, Massachusetts, in 1638. The Reverend Jose Glover, a militant Puritan ousted from an Anglican pulpit in England, had sailed for the colony with the intention of becoming a printer of religious materials. Beset by difficulties in getting their works printed in their own country, English Puritans had resorted to having them printed in the Netherlands. The bay colony's Bible commonwealth seemed a likely location for such an enterprise.

Glover died on the voyage, but his wife, who had accompanied him, set up the press in Cambridge. She married Henry Dunster, president of Harvard. On her death, the press became his property. Eventually, it was installed in a lean-to attached to the president's official residence, which was built in 1645. Thus began the connection between Harvard and publishing.[4]

Productions of the press in the first decade of its operation were not substantial either quantitatively or qualitatively. From it came haltingly only twenty-three imprints. Most were almanacs, commencement broadsides, and other ephemera, but there was a famous work, the *Bay Psalm Book*, which gained great popularity in New England and even in some Puritan circles in the mother country. It was the work of tin-eared translators who converted the majestic poetry of the Old Testament to a sound no more mellifluous than the creaking of a gallows sign in a nor'easter.

Of course, the Harvard press much later would publish many scholarly works respected throughout the world, but in its infancy it was not the chosen vehicle for those launching works of any learned or literary pretensions. Not only did such theologians as Richard Mather, John Cotton, and Thomas Hooker tend to favor English publishers, but so did those rare authors of belle lettres such as Anne Bradstreet.[5] Eighteen years old in 1630 when she sailed for Massachusetts with her husband and her parents, except for her strong spirit she was ill prepared for life on the frontier. Reared in the comfort of the earl of Lincoln's estate, where her father, Thomas Dudley, was steward, she was physically delicate and suffered a recurrent illness that her physicians never fully understood. Though reared in strict Puritanism, she, like another Anne, Anne Hutchinson, was a woman of independent mind.

Unlike Mrs. Hutchinson, she did not publicly challenge the views of the Massachusetts theocracy. It would have been extremely awkward if she had, because her father succeeded John Winthrop as governor. As it was, an initially secret vice of hers eventually caused some prominent Puritans to look askance at her. She performed the traditional duties of a housewife, including the rearing of eight children. But all the while, it turned out, she had been writing poetry. The fact that she was the governor's daughter made the offense all the more conspicuous. She herself described in verse the disapproval she engendered:

> I am obnoxious to each carping tongue
> Who says my hand a needle better fits.

At least one Puritan preacher, however, approved her writing. The Reverend John Woodridge, her brother-in-law, carried copies of her poems with him on a trip to England. There, unbeknown to her, he secured publication of them in 1650. The book was titled *The Tenth Muse Lately Sprung Up in America, or Several Poems, Compiled with Great Variety of Wit and Learning, Full of Delight . . . by a Gentlewoman in Those Parts.*

The surprise was not an altogether happy one for the author. In the verses were awkward places made more so by misprints. Mistress Bradstreet referred to her book variously as an "ill-formed offspring" and "my rambling brat in print." But the chief weakness of the poems was something that many of her contemporaries saw as a virtue. Many lines were reminiscent of English translations of the works of Guillaume du Bartas. Others echoed Francis Quarles, George Herbert, and other honored versifiers. No plagiarism was involved, but her poems were imitative.

She continued to write poetry, however. In 1678, six years after her death, the new poems were published in a second edition of her work. Many of these poems were in a fresh voice, mingling common idioms with biblical diction, reflecting the wild American landscape at least as frequently as English meadows and lawns, drawing its imagery more often from simple household tasks than from the habits of court or cloister.

In subject and viewpoint even more than in tropes and metrics, Mistress Bradstreet's later poems reveal her independence of Massachusetts theocracy. Occasionally she questions Puritan tenets. Sometimes she questions the relevance of any religious faith, but in these instances reflection always leads back to trust in God, usually more from reading Nature's book than from perusing the essays of bay colony divines. And a full-bodied tribute to her marriage partner, Simon Bradstreet, appears in the poem headed "A Letter to Her Husband Absent upon Public Employment." It begins:

> My head, my heart, mine eyes, my life, nay, more
> My joy, my magazine of earthly store,
> If two be one, as surely thou and I,
> How stayest thou there, whilst I at Ipswich lie?

It concludes:

> Flesh of thy flesh, bone of thy bone,
> I here, thou there, yet both but one.

Another secret poet among the Massachusetts Puritans kept all but one of his verses hidden during his entire life. He even forbade his heirs to publish them. The manuscripts were discovered about two centuries after the author's death, and publication followed in 1937 and 1939. They would have created great excitement if they had been released in the poet's lifetime, for he was Edward Taylor, strict Puritan pastor of a frontier church about a hundred miles inland from Boston.[6] He was a Harvard graduate who seemed to have imbibed during his student days no questioning spirit or tolerance of variant ideologies. Apparently no departure from the narrow path of orthodox Massachusetts Puritanism was observed by the little community that he served for fifty-eight years as both physician and preacher.

Far stranger than the fact of such a man writing poetry is the kind of poetry that he wrote. As one might expect, much of his verse declares a strong Christian faith. There is even one poem titled "The Joy of Church Fellowship Rightly Attended." But there are others reminiscent of the Song of Solomon, though carrying the imagery a step further. The church, the Bride of Christ, is pictured as having "trussed up" breasts

> like stately milk pails ever full and [that] flow/with spiritual milk to make her babes to grow.

He even pleads:

> put these nipples then my mouth into/and suckle me therewith I humbly pray.

Many verses are erotic and some boldly scatological. His poem "Huswifery," on the other hand, is free of such references, but uses a simple spinning wheel as a complex and extended metaphor for the relationship between God and the worshiping author. At his best in this vein, he suggests, without imitating, some of the metaphysical poems of George Herbert and even John Donne. He does not equal them, but certainly his verses are as good as any that we know were produced in colonial North America. In his preface to *God's Determination*, he anticipated by some six decades the powerful style of William Blake's "The Tyger," writing:

> Infinity, when all things it beheld
> In nothing, and of nothing all did build,
> Upon what base was fixed the lathe, wherein
> He turned this globe, and riggaled it so trim?
> Who blew the bellows of his furnace vast?
> Or held the mold wherein the world was cast? . . .
> Who spread its canopy? Or curtains spun?
> Who in this bowling alley bowled the sun?

Publication of Taylor's poetry in his own lifetime would have produced for him a personal crisis, but it might have encouraged other writers of originality.

Much more acceptable to the Puritan oligarchy were the writings of another Harvard graduate who also served as both minister and physician. Michael Wigglesworth was thirty years old in 1661 when he published his most famous poem, "The Day of Doom." In 224 stanzas it depicted God's mercy on Judgment Day, but detailed more memorably the punishments awaiting blasphemers, hypocrites, apostates, heathens, and unbaptized infants. Though Edward Taylor's own poetry was very different from this, he joined the many extravagant admirers of Wigglesworth's masterpiece, rejoicing that Mrs. Taylor quoted it so often. "The Doomsday Verses," he said, "much perfumed her breath."

A rival best-seller was written by a woman who had passed through a living hell and cataloged her observations with a thoroughness and particularity rivaling Mr. Wigglesworth's.[7] Mary Rowlandson was the wife of a minister in the frontier village of Lancaster, Massachusetts, and the mother of four children. On the morning of February 10, 1675, she and her family found themselves under attack by Indians: "Some in our house were fighting for their lives, others wallowing in their blood, the house on fire over our heads, and the bloody heathen ready to knock us on the head if we stirred out."[8]

Both she and her six-year-old daughter were wounded and captured. On the third day of their journey in captivity, Mary Rowlandson's little girl died in her lap. The mother recorded, "I cannot but take notice how at another time I could not bear to be in the room where any dead person was, but now the case is changed; I must and could lie down by my dead babe, side by side all the night after."[9]

In stark language with occasional biblical echoes, she narrates the events of nearly three months of captivity until her freedom was purchased through a public subscription conducted by Boston women. The story was an exciting one and the conclusion pious enough to satisfy Puritan didacticism. "The portion of some," she said,

> is to have their afflictions by drops, now one drop and then another; but the dregs of the cup, the wine of astonishment, like a sweeping rain that leaveth no food, did the Lord prepare to be my portion. Affliction I wanted, and affliction I had, full measure (I thought), pressed down, and running over; yet I see when God calls a person to anything, and through never so many difficulties, yet He is fully able to carry them through and make them see and say they have been gainers thereby.[10]

Motivated by a strong desire to communicate her experiences to those who might profit from them, and apparently innocent of literary vanity, Mary Rowlandson nevertheless founded a genre. Hers was the most immediately popular, and the most enduring, of the many tales, both fiction and nonfiction, that became one of the staples of American literature. The locales moved westward with the march of settlement, but the stories themselves moved eastward as well, enthralling the Old World with New World adventures.

It is noteworthy that the most creative literature in seventeenth-century Massachusetts was not produced by pillars of its Puritan establishment. Neither Thomas Shepard, Michael Wigglesworth, nor any of the three Mathers— Richard, Increase, and Cotton—published anything that speaks to successive generations through its creative power.

Instead, the books of creative vitality were the work of marginal, though privileged, members of Puritan society. Anne Bradstreet, though the well-edu-cated daughter of a Massachusetts governor and wife of a prominent citizen, was nevertheless a marginal member of that society by virtue of her sex. She was fortunate in having a loving husband who respected her writings and a brother-in-law who was their enthusiastic promoter. But, as we have seen, she herself wrote that, because she was a housewife, her writing made her "obnox-ious to each carping tongue." And her own verses reveal occasional doubts about Puritan orthodoxy. Edward Taylor, as pastor of a Puritan congregation, might seem part of the establishment in the Puritan theocracy, but his church was on the frontier, far removed from the power centers of Massachusetts. And as a not so smoothly assimilated product of his environment, he withheld his verses from publication. How he must have been torn between the promptings of his own independent spirit and his allegiance to the tradition within which he worked, forbidding his descendants to publish his writings, yet not able to summon the resolve to destroy them himself! As for Mary Rowlandson, her position, living as she did on the frontier, was geographically marginal. And having been, however unwillingly, part of a society branded savage, she was marginal in other ways that being a heroine did not erase.

There is nothing in Puritanism per se that militates against literary and intellectual creativity. Indeed, a vigorous Puritanism forced to contend and sometimes compromise with a differently oriented society can be a stimulus to imaginative achievement. Witness the examples of Andrew Marvell and, most especially, John Milton. But the Puritanism of the bay colony was much more moralistic than anything England itself knew in the same century.

The existence of independent creative minds in Massachusetts even under the stultifying conditions of its society suggested, though, that there might yet be found within its borders enough rebels to build a great tradition. The popu-lation included a number of highly intelligent people. And even the oppressive oligarchy strongly encouraged classical learning. Their efforts to transmit the classics, shorn of a humanistic outlook, were doomed to frustration. Their task was as impossible as that of some totalitarian states who sought in the twentieth century to acquaint their citizens with the technology and science of freer peo-ples without exposing them to the concomitant awakening of intellectual curi-osity.

With the Restoration of the Stuart monarchy and the beginning of the reign of Charles II in 1660, there was no longer a Puritan commonwealth in England to welcome sermon manuscripts from the Puritan Commonwealth in Massachusetts. Bay colony divines who earlier had bypassed their own little Cambridge press now quite readily entrusted to it their election-day sermons, farewell exhortations to churches they had served, and funeral elegies on departed officials.

But the press could boast of truly notable productions as well. Foremost were the volumes of the Indian Library, the inspiration and largely the work of John Eliot. Dedicated to fulfillment of the biblical admonition to carry the message of Christ to all peoples, he studied the language of the colony's Algonquin Indians, preached to them in familiar accents, and trained some among them as teachers and evangelists. He founded an elementary school for each Christian village of Indians that he organized. Though the pupils studied the English language, Eliot also saw that they were instructed in their own, and he created texts in the native tongue. He climaxed these efforts by translating the Bible into Algonquin. The New Testament was published by the Cambridge press, by then located in the Indian school at Harvard, in 1661. The Old Testament followed in 1663.

An additional printer, Marmaduke Johnson, was imported from England to apply his expertise to the monumental task. The schedule of the project was threatened when Johnson, who had left his spouse behind in England, paid court to a local maiden and was haled before the judiciary by her irate father. The judges fined the offender and ordered him to return to England after production was complete. But they were saved from moral compromise when they learned that Johnson's wife had rendered him technically innocent by running away with another man. A Puritan pillar reported that Johnson "hath been very much reformed."

Production of a twelve-hundred-page translation of the Bible into a language in which it had never appeared before was a signal accomplishment. Though financed by an English Puritan missionary society, the project had the approval of the Massachusetts oligarchy and was executed in the colony. Although it was designed to mold rather than interact with another culture, a certain amount of interaction was inevitable. The new Bible was the product of new learning applied to ancient heritage. It was both a sign of vitality within the colonial Puritan culture and the promise of a stimulating association.

Some of the attention attracted by the press's success was unwelcome to its operators. In 1662 the General Court prohibited printing outside Cambridge and established a licensing board consisting of the president of Harvard and the ministers of Cambridge, Charlestown, and Watertown. Even this safeguard eventually proved insufficient in the eyes of the General Court, who in 1669 countermanded the licensing board's approval of a book and halted work on it although it was already in press.

The book was a great classic of piety, *De imitatione Christi*, generally attributed to Thomas à Kempis. It had been translated into English as early as the fifteenth century, but the Massachusetts press was preparing a new translation. Thomas à Kempis had been an Augustinian monk, and therein lay the rub. The General Court, "being informed that there is now in the press, reprinting, a book . . . written by Thomas a Kempis, a Popish minister, wherein is [sic] contained some things that are less safe to be infused among the people of this place," called for "the more full revisal thereof, and that in the meantime there be no further progress in that work."

The licensers were unwilling to supervise a revision, so Massachusetts missed the opportunity to produce a proof of lively scholarship and make accessible to its people a religious classic outside the narrow canon of bay colony Puritanism. Nevertheless, the fact that an effort had been made was significant.

Unfortunately, this event signaled the beginning of a more systematic censorship than Massachusetts had known before. The tide of censorship would ebb and flow through generations, but the colony, and later the state, would be cited time and time again for rigorous suppression of printed matter. Boston eventually would have a Watch and Ward Society famous for its aggressive protection of public morals, and in the twentieth century "banned in Boston" became a distinction eagerly sought by publishers in quest of best-seller status in the rest of the United States.

Boston nevertheless became a publishing center. Printing in the city was licensed in 1675. There appeared the first American edition of John Bunyan's *Pilgrim's Progress*, an admissible book even by the most stringent Puritan standards. There, too, was published Mary Rowlandson's *Narrative*.

Boston competition proved too much for the little press in Cambridge, and it closed down. The Harvard press of later years was a revival, not a continuation.[11] But from the colony's original Cambridge press descend, through various mutations, some of the leading publishers of the Northeast.

The government of the Dominion of New England, founded in 1686 when Sir Edmund Andros became governor simultaneously of all New England colonies except Connecticut and Rhode Island, was not friendly to free expression. Neither, of course, was the Puritan oligarchy, but the governor's views of what was fit to print did not coincide with theirs. Puritan writers were inhibited by what he as a royal official deemed appropriate. Even the usually prolific Cotton Mather was hindered. Benjamin Harris, a publisher of the *New England Primer*, launched a newspaper, but its first issue was its last. The Council joined Andros in strangling it at birth. Whether an attempt to publish a newspaper would have met a similar fate in each of England's other American colonies is beyond conjecture. But at least none had a newspaper at the time.

The ending of the Dominion of New England in a few years permitted official Puritan savants to run unvexed to excess. The champion producer of literary progeny was Cotton Mather. In the last year of the seventeenth century, he published seventeen books, bringing his lifetime total to 450.[12] Samuel Eliot Morison has calculated that about 30 percent of all books printed in Boston and Cambridge during the century's last decade had been penned by the Mather family.[13]

As John Greenleaf Whittier later wrote, Cotton Mather's most famous writings consisted of "all strange and marvelous things, heaped up huge and undigested."[14] Increase and Cotton Mather deserve credit for an interest in science, one that they were able to share with only two or three Massachusetts people except for their own relatives. But Increase wasted much of his ingenuity in an attempt to prove that the time of a comet's appearance was completely unpredictable. And Cotton used much of his cleverness to teach his readers how to detect witches in their midst. Cotton Mather was an especially voracious reader, but read mainly to confirm his prejudices. For the most part, the Mathers' books were quite brief, but even so they represented a considerable expenditure of mental effort and physical energy. If such resources were ever freed from a narrow servitude to Puritan prejudice, there might indeed be a flowering of New England.

The intellectual community of Massachusetts received two important additions in 1686 when Charles Morton and Samuel Lee arrived from England. They were prominent dissenting ministers frustrated by the established church who hoped to find a more congenial society in New England. Both had been students at Wadham College, Oxford, when Christopher Wren, Robert Boyle, and Robert Hooke formed there the organization that became the Royal Society. It was then the best place in England to obtain an education in science, and they took advantage of the opportunity.

After serving as a rector and being ejected for nonconformity, Morton became master of the Dissenters' school at Stoke Newington, one of the most prestigious of such institutions in England. Among former pupils who later lauded him as a teacher were Samuel Wesley and Daniel Defoe. Morton emigrated to Massachusetts in the hope that he could teach there with greater freedom and in the belief that he would become president of Harvard. But dissension among the college's governors denied him the presidency. And, after he was prosecuted for preaching a "seditious sermon" in Charlestown, Massachusetts, the college's leaders, although he was acquitted, were unwilling to let him teach. Nevertheless, he was made vice president of Harvard in 1697. He returned to the classroom, carrying with him manuscript copies of *Natural Philosophy*,[15] his own compendium of scientific articles extracted principally from the *Philosophical Transactions* of the Royal Society. He seems to have made no additions of his own to the selections, and sometimes has been accused of not fully understanding the implications of some of the materials he included, but nevertheless he provided for Harvard a science textbook greatly superior to anything it had used before. Yale adopted the same text. Unfortunately, Morton's record of service to science is marred by his endorsement of Salem's witchcraft trials.

Morton apparently also was a pioneer in another way. He seems to have been the first minister in Massachusetts to perform a marriage ceremony. That privilege, heretofore, had been "reserved to the civil authorities." It is ironic indeed that, in a society in which the clergy played so large a role in most civil matters, they were prevented from performing what was normally regarded in other places as an ecclesiastical function.

Samuel Lee had been a fellow of All Souls and dean of Wadham College, besides serving as minister to several London congregations. Lee preached in Massachusetts, but probably exerted his widest influence as the author of such pamphlets as *Joy of Faith* and *Day of Judgement*. It has been pointed out that the titles would attract a Puritan audience whose thirst for theology seemed unquenchable, but that the brew so labeled was compounded of the scientific as well as the sacred. The labeling was not false, however. Lee constantly cited the scientific wonders of creation as evidence of the greatness of the Creator.

Lee's attitude was at least as ancient as that of the Hebrew psalmist who sang, "The heavens declare the glory of God."[16] Though most Puritans who accepted Lee's exposition of this idea drew their inspiration from the Bible, the concept voiced by him was also an echo of the Italian Renaissance.

Paul Dudley, a Harvard student when Morton introduced his science text-book and when Lee was writing of science as a sacred book of revelations, became enthusiastic about the new studies. In 1721 his researches would win him election to England's Royal Society. But he was definitely an exception among the students of his day, not only in proficiency but also in zeal. He himself lamented that, "as to more experiments, our people don't much care for making them."

Nevertheless, seven residents of Massachusetts were elected fellows of the Royal Society before the American Revolution. The nearest competitor in this category among the American colonies was Virginia, three of whose citizens achieved this distinction in the same period.

Except for theology, science was about the only field that the bright young minds of Massachusetts were encouraged to enter. In that closed society, there was no room for political speculation except as an adjunct to theology. And even then, builders of the City on a Hill had best be careful not to embellish too much the plans that the Puritan fathers believed they had received directly from God. But these same tribal elders had claimed science as boldly as they had initially claimed the wild coast of Massachusetts. In fact, they had enslaved science and made it the servant of their theological purposes. Thus science in colonial Massachusetts was protected and even nurtured, but was denied independent growth. The bay colony's arbiters in scientific matters were the same divines who so effectively transformed their pulpits into political rostrums.

A perfect example of this fact was Cotton Mather. He was elected to the Royal Society. Though astronomy, among seventeenth century churchmen in much of the world, was the most controversial of all sciences, challenging the flattering and comforting concept of an earth-centered universe, Mather not only gave the study his blessing but personally pursued it avidly. He also was excited by the possibilities of the microscope and eagerly read medical books from England. He embraced the germ theory when it was still widely disputed, and advocated inoculation for smallpox when it was still opposed by many physicians. Yet he insisted that in the final analysis the findings of science must conform to the framework of his particular theology. And, of course, he summoned science to the business of detecting witches. To science he gave the care lavished on a particularly valuable slave that could be depended upon to do his bidding.

Probably the leading scientist in New England in the seventeenth century was John Winthrop, Jr. He was the son of the famous Massachusetts governor and served as an assistant during about eight years of his father's administration. When he arrived in New England, he was an alumnus of the Bury Saint Edmunds Grammar School, Trinity College in Dublin, and London's Inner

Temple. He was also a veteran of the duke of Buckingham's expedition to relieve the beleaguered Protestants of New Rochelle. He founded the town that is now Ipswich, Massachusetts. Then he moved to Connecticut and served as its governor for one year. After returning to England for about two years, he came back to Massachusetts and founded ironworks at both Lynn and Braintree. He moved back to Connecticut, obtained from London the charter joining the New Haven colony to Connecticut, and through annual reelection was Connecticut's governor for the last nineteen years of his life.

These accomplishments testify to his success as entrepreneur and politician. But his significance was greater than these facts alone would suggest. He was in the Renaissance and Elizabethan mold of the man of affairs who is also a cherisher of traditional wisdom and an eager advocate of the new learning.

When he first appeared in the New World at the age of twenty-five, he brought with him a large library for the times, one particularly rich in scientific interest. Because of the system of classification used at the time, it is difficult to say exactly how many of his books would today be classified as scientific. For example, fifty-two volumes were classified as pertaining to chemistry, twelve to astronomy, astrology, and the occult. One cannot even be certain about the scientific relevance of all of the thirty-three volumes listed under medicine. One can accept with more confidence the scientific listing of twenty-seven books assigned to mathematics and physics.

Winthrop's library was not just a stimulus to abstract speculation. He was a practitioner in most of the fields covered. As a physician who personally compounded many prescriptions for his patients, he studied with a practiced eye, and an eye to practice, the tomes on chemistry as well as those on medicine. As an active amateur astronomer, who incidentally gave a telescope to Harvard, he had practical use not only for the volumes on astronomy but also for those on mathematics and physics. Books on metallurgy would probably have been useful to him in his prospecting and assaying in connection with his ironworks. His interest in astronomy led logically to a study of optics.

The most intense of his many intellectual interests, however, was in a field whose value was disputed by some serious scientists. The close alliance, indeed ancestral connection, between chemistry and alchemy caused some to think of the younger study as tainted. At the same time, their attitude was resented by others who proudly called themselves scientists as they searched for the philosopher's stone that would turn base metals into gold.

In the general freedom of his scientific speculations, John Winthrop, Jr., departed from the norm for Massachusetts intellectuals. But, then, he had become one of the Connecticut men. And, like Rhode Islanders, they always were different.

In Connecticut, Winthrop found at least two friends to share his scientific interests. Jonathan Brewster, son of the prominent Elder Brewster of the Pilgrims, operated a trading post on the present site of Norwich. But when he was not at the counter weighing pelts or handing out provisions, he was likely to be measuring and mixing chemical ingredients in his laboratory. And though the Reverend Gershom Bulkeley concocted sermons in the study of his Connecticut parsonage, he labored over other concoctions among the beakers and mortars of the laboratory. With these two men, Winthrop shared his books and his thoughts.

Born in Connecticut in 1703, twenty-seven years after the death of John Winthrop, Jr., was one whose intellect profited greatly from the scientific interest that the governor had fostered. Jonathan Edwards is important both as an example of cultural transition in New England heralding an age of more vigorous creativity and as a pre-Revolutionary American whose influence extended far beyond the borders of his native region. The pivotal nature of his role is illustrated by the fact that he has been saluted as "the first modern American" and "a prophet of modernity." He also has been called "a great anachronism" and "America's last medieval man."[17] As this circumstance would suggest, Edwards' creative energy owed much to the tension produced by contending forces—the nurturing influence of tradition and the call to adventure of new ideas. We have observed the productive influence of such contention, in proper balance, in Renaissance Florence and Elizabethan England, both in those societies as a whole and in the lives of their most creative members.

It was appropriate that such an innovator as Edwards should be born in Connecticut, which enjoyed more freedom than Massachusetts from the palsied hand of conformity. But it was also appropriate that Massachusetts, which had so long dominated New England, should become his home during his time of greatest influence.

Jonathan was the fifth child and only son of Timothy and Esther Edwards. The father was a Harvard graduate and ordained minister of inherited wealth. The mother was a daughter of the Reverend Solomon Stoddard, who "dominated the Connecticut Valley and contested the ecclesiastical leadership of New England with Increase and Cotton Mather."[18] Jonathan's grandmother was the elder Governor Winthrop's niece. The boy's paternal ancestry was equally colorful, but in a disturbing way. His grandmother Edwards was believed to be mentally sick. This diagnosis could have resulted from her husband's invoking a council of ministers to endorse his petition of divorce when she gave birth to another man's child. She was not the only member of her family to have a bad day in court. Her brother was hanged for murdering another sister with an ax. Still another sister killed her own child.

With so gloomy a family heritage, and growing up in a Puritan society sulfurous with breathings of Hell and damnation, Jonathan Edwards not surprisingly was often steeped in melancholy reflection. Encouraged by intellectual parents, he was precocious in both his studies and his musings.

His precocity, however, was not quite so startling as has been assumed by some biographers. They have made much of the fact that he entered Yale before his thirteenth birthday. This fact is less impressive when viewed in the context of his times. Thirteen was then the customary age for matriculation at the Connecticut college. Jonathan entered in September and became thirteen on October 5. Thus he was only a few days short of the standard age.

Some biographers also have cited as an example of juvenile genius an essay on "flying spiders" that he was believed to have written at age eleven or twelve.

They have praised the acute powers of scientific observation displayed. The subsequent revelation that Edwards probably was in his twenties at the time he wrote the paper transforms the supposed work of genius into one of solid competence with some distinguishing qualities of style.[19] Edwards was, however, a highly intelligent child who developed into a more conspicuously brilliant adult. Nevertheless, the efforts to picture the young boy as another William Godwin or John Stuart Mill are unjustified.

Though Edwards was not a child prodigy, in the course of his adult career he evidenced rare intellectual gifts. Even before the end of his college days, he had embraced the two great principles of his philosophy. The rest of his life was spent in reconciling them. One principle was that of the Newtonian universe, a mechanistic affair governed by unalterable natural laws. The second was a kind of Berkeley idealism that held that all things perceived had no independent existence but depended upon a perceiver.

Some of Edwards' admirers have maintained that he conceived the essence of Berkeley's philosophy before reading about it. This is quite possible, but somewhat unlikely in view of the intense contemporary interest in the bishop's views and the availability of comments on them.

In any event, Edwards, as the years passed, showed considerable ingenuity in the reconciliation of what some considered quite disparate ideas. He accepted a deterministic view of the universe but, in common with the Deists much criticized by his fellow Puritans, saw God as the great Determiner. And though he accepted the idea that perceived things, whether objects or ideas, existed only in perception, he thought that this existence was ultimately in the mind of God.

Actually, Edwards' scientific investigations and philosophical speculations were all in bondage to his theology. And his theology was that of the Massachusetts theocracy. Beginning with the premises of Massachusetts Puritan teachings, he sought their confirmation in scientific observation of the natural world and in the pages of philosophy. He relentlessly ignored any evidence that did not support his preconceptions, and he resolutely turned his face from any avenue that might tempt him from the narrow, well-worn circle of his thoughts. Astronomy interested him because it seemed to bolster the ideas of an orderly, God-directed universe. Observations of flora and fauna were pursued insofar as they confirmed his concept of a benevolent Creator. He could safely peruse the pages of Nicolas Malebranche and George Berkeley, secure in the knowledge that their "theocentric metaphysics" would filter out any questions seriously challenging his own beliefs. Unlike the Hebrew psalmist or the Renaissance thinkers who discovered in a burst of euphoria that "The Heavens declare the glory of God," Edwards began with an inherited claim to a share of God's glory and searched for validation through the phenomena of the universe like an attorney ferreting through a mound of documents in pursuit of a title deed.

Even when Edwards was twenty years old and strongly attracted to teenaged Sarah Pierrepont, whom he later married, his approach seemed more theological than romantic. It might have inspired apprehension in a young lady less dedicated to the Puritan ethic. "They say," Edwards wrote with coy indirection,

> there is a young lady in [New Haven] who is beloved of that Great
> Being who made and rules the world, and that there are certain sea-
> sons in which this Great Being, in some way or other invisible, comes
> to her and fills her mind with exceeding sweet delight, and that she
> hardly cares for anything, except to meditate on Him—that she ex-
> pects after a while to be received up where He is, to be raised up out
> of the world and caught up into heaven; being assured that he loves
> her too well to let her remain at a distance from him always.

Edwards was fortunate to secure a helpmeet of such pious predilections.
When he was seven or eight years old, he had responded to the religious excitement of his village church by going into the woods as John the Baptist had gone
into the wilderness, and there praying to God. He and some of his schoolmates
even built "a booth in a swamp, in a very retired spot, for a place of prayer."[20]
"My affections," Edwards later recalled,

> seemed to be lively and easily moved, and I seemed to be in my ele-
> ment when engaged in religious duties. . . . But in process of time,
> my convictions and affections wore off; and I entirely lost all those
> affections and delights and left off secret prayer, at least as to any
> constant performance of it; and returned like a dog to his vomit, and
> went on in the ways of sin.

But often an uneasiness seized him, as he recalled, "especially towards the
latter part of my time at college, when it pleased God to seize me with the
pleurisy, in which he brought me nigh to the grave, and shook me over the pit
of hell." Not long after recovery, he reverted to his old ways.

> But God would not suffer me to go on with any quietness; I had great
> and violent inward struggles, till, after many conflicts with wicked
> inclinations, repeated resolutions, and bonds that I laid myself under
> by a kind of vows to God, I was brought wholly to break off all
> former wicked ways, and all ways of known outward sin; and to apply
> myself to seek salvation, and practice many religious duties; but with-
> out that kind of affection and delight which I had formerly experi-
> enced.

Nevertheless, "I made salvation the main business of my life." But he
sought it in "such a miserable manner" that afterwards he was "ready to doubt
whether such miserable seeking ever succeeded."

The impediment to acceptance was a cardinal belief of the Puritan oligarchy in which he was raised. "From my childhood up," he said, "my mind had
been full of objections against the doctrine of God's sovereignty, in choosing

whom he would to eternal life, and rejecting whom he pleased, leaving them eternally to perish, and be everlastingly tormented in hell. It used to appear like a horrible doctrine to me."

But later, through some process that he never fully understood, Edwards became "convinced, and fully satisfied, as to this sovereignty of God, and his justice in thus eternally disposing of men, according to his sovereign pleasure." In fact, he would become so satisfied with this doctrine that he would write, "The misery of the damned in Hell is one of those great things that the saints in their blessed and joyful state in Heaven shall behold and take great notice of through eternity."[21]

At first, Edwards' audience was limited. After two years of theological study in New Haven following graduation from Yale, he became minister to a Presbyterian congregation in New York City. Eight months later, despairing of supporting an anticipated family on his slender pay, he resigned his post. In 1724 he returned to Yale as a tutor, but suffered a long illness in the following year and resigned in 1726 to become associate pastor of the Northampton, Massachusetts, church ministered to by his grandfather Solomon Stoddard.

There was little reason to assume that Edwards would become a famous preacher. He seemed to be a very bright young man plagued by health problems, both physical and emotional, and at age twenty-three was quite fortunate to be rescued from poverty by the intervention of a respected grandparent.

Not that Edwards was lazy. Far from it. He rose at four o'clock every morning, and daily devoted thirteen hours to study. He meditated during long woodland walks, sometimes deriving ideas from his observations of nature, sometimes from reflections on his reading. Lest he forget any of the thoughts crowding fast upon him, he wrote each on a slip of paper and pinned it to his coat. This frail, willowy young man must often have returned to town looking like a "sparsely feathered chicken."[22]

His life was governed by seventy "resolutions" that he had compiled as a teenager. Swearing to such resolutions was not unusual in Edwards' time. His contemporary Benjamin Franklin did the same thing, though Franklin's resolves were not that numerous. Each boy, the young Puritan and the young Deist, used this method in a determination to achieve perfection. With all the agitation over problems in colonial society, there was an underlying confidence that perfection was an attainable ideal. Both Edwards and Franklin pledged to conquer self-indulgence, but there was one marked difference in their recipes for improvement. Unlike Franklin, Edwards believed that humility was essential. He also admitted that he lacked it. But he seemed to have no notion of how to acquire it. His whole way of going about it revealed the extent of his problem. He resolved to become the most humble person in his community.

Yet, while Edwards often seemed unable to achieve humility in relation to his fellow humans, he did prostrate himself before his God. From childhood onward, there was a powerful esthetic impulse in Edwards that sometimes troubled his Puritan sense of propriety. Like many others of his faith, he believed that beauty was an appropriate part of life, but he feared that sensual attunement to beauty could lead to grossness. He solved this problem to his own satisfaction. He early came to think of holiness as a divine beauty, and hence the supreme experience esthetically as well as religiously. Seeing God in every natural wonder kept him mindful of the supreme beauty and majesty of the Creator. Edwards was seized by a desire "to lie low before God as in the dust; that I might be nothing, and that God might be all."

He began to view God's disposal of souls to Heaven or Hell as the supreme example of His elevation above all creation and therefore the most beautiful and thrilling expression of the Divine will. Edwards' wife had frequent religious experiences whose intensity matched his own.

The grandfather that Edwards assisted in the ministry of the Northampton church apparently was deeply religious also, but in a more relaxed way. Indeed, his relaxation of rules for certain observances was evidence of a recent tendency in several of the congregations of Massachusetts, one vehemently condemned by some of the old-guard Puritans. Originally, church membership in the Old Bay Colony was supposed to be limited to "visible saints"—those who professed to have experienced salvation by grace, and were fortunate enough to be chosen by those already sure of their own sainthood. The Synod of 1662 had acknowledged a "covenant membership" for those who professed an intellectual conviction of the rightness of Christianity and a willingness to assume the duties implied. Grandfather Stoddard had dramatically lowered additional barriers. He admitted to the sacrament of the Lord's Supper all in his parish who wished to participate. He did not view the ritual as a privilege denied to any but the elect, but rather as a means of outreach to the unsaved.

In Edwards' eyes, such a policy was dangerously near to Anglican practice. It opened the door to the Arminian theology embraced by many Anglicans, the belief that salvation was dependent on individual conduct as well as God's grace. The threat was intensified by the recent defection to the Anglicans of three officers of Yale College, among them the rector himself. As Arminianism attracted one prominent New Englander after another, Edwards feared that he saw its symptoms among his own relatives. Particularly disturbing was the attitude of his cousins the Reverend Solomon Williams and Solomon's brother Israel. Their influence could be very harmful, he thought. Solomon had the influence of any preacher plus powerful connections. Israel had so much wealth and political power that he was called "Lord of the Valley." Their quarrel with Edwards intensified in 1729 when the young man succeeded his grandfather as pastor of the Northampton church.

The major point of contention was Edwards' belief in the worshiping individual's access to the "immediate power and operation of the spirit of God." Solomon and Israel Williams, and many other conservative Massachusetts Puritans, believed that the way to religious truth was solely through theology. Though they may not consciously have acted from such motivation, many of the clergymen had a vested interest in the purely theological approach to salvation. Indeed, it was for some a cumulative inheritance from generations of clerical forebears, and for all a bequest from professional antecedents.

In arguing for direct revelation of God's truths through emotional experiencing of the Holy Presence, Edwards was taking a position similar to that which had gotten Anne Hutchinson into trouble with the Puritan old guard. One major difference was that Edwards, though he insisted on the validity of such direct communication with God independent of theological studies, was formidably equipped to split theological hairs with any clergyman in New England. Of course, the most important difference between Edwards and Anne Hutchinson was that he was a man and thus, whatever his threat to the religious status quo, no danger to the established concepts of male and female roles in society. Edwards therefore was not expelled from the colony. But he was ousted from his pastorate.

This dismissal, however, did not come until twenty years later when he had repeatedly preached his views in defiance of powerful people in his congregation and, by the extraordinary effect of his sermons on the emotions of his hearers, had raised alarms among many clergymen and lay leaders throughout New England.

Not all the church people of Massachusetts were content with an approach to their Maker through a theology interpreted by their leaders. Some were excited by the revival movement that, beginning in 1734 and stimulated by the American tour of the magnetic British preacher George Whitefield, had swept through the colonies. Aflame with religious fervor, they were impatient with those who wished to smother their radiance in the wrappings of cold reason.

The revival gave Edwards the opportunity to appeal to his congregation to throw themselves upon the mercy of God and receive His saving grace. Edwards lacked the orotund voice and commanding physique of some preachers. By all accounts, he was slender and appeared frail. If we may trust a portrait of him, probably painted about 1740 and variously attributed to John Smibert and Joseph Badger, he had a long face with a long nose, an angular jaw, and a straight, thin mouth—a physiognomy unremarkable except for refinement and severity. But the piercing eyes were fierce as an eagle's. And he had two things more important for his purpose than any physical attribute—supreme moral earnestness and a rare gift of compelling imagery. There were countless unsaved to whom God offered His gift of grace. Edwards could make them feel the horrors of the Hell that yawned beneath them.

In his famous sermon "Sinners in the Hands of an Angry God," he said, "Whatever some have imagined and pretended about promises made to natural men's earnest seeking and knocking, it is plain and manifest that whatever pains a natural man takes in religion, whatever prayers he makes, till he believes in Christ, God is under no manner of obligation to keep him a moment from eternal destruction."

"So that," he continued,

> thus it is that natural men are held in the hand of God, over the pit of Hell; they have deserved the fiery pit, and are already sentenced to it; and God is dreadfully provoked. His anger is as great towards them as to those that are actually suffering the executions of the fierceness of his wrath in Hell, and they have done nothing in the least to appease or abate that anger. Neither is God in the least bound by any promise

to hold them up one moment. The devil is waiting for them, Hell is gaping for them, the flames gather and flash about them, and would fain lay hold on them and swallow them up; the fire pent up in their own hearts is struggling to break out. . . . In short, they have no refuge, nothing to take hold of; all that preserves them every moment is the mere arbitrary will, and uncovenanted, unobliged forbearance of an incensed God.

By now sobs would come from many parts of the sanctuary. And then the preacher would stop talking in the third person about "natural men" and, fixing his auditors with a piercing stare, would address them directly:

Your wickedness makes you as it were heavy as lead, and to tend downwards with great weight and pressure towards Hell; and if God should let you go, you would immediately sink and swiftly descend and plunge into the bottomless gulf, and your healthy constitution, and your own care and prudence, and best contrivance, and all your righteousness; would have no more influence to uphold you and keep you out of Hell than a spider's web would have to stop a fallen rock.

Now repressed sobs yielded to loud weeping. Minutes later, the preacher warned, "The bow of God's wrath is bent, and the arrow made ready on the string, and justice bends the arrow at your heart, and strains the bow, and it is nothing but the mere pleasure of God, and that of an angry God, without any promise or obligation at all, that keeps the arrow one moment from being made drunk with your blood."

Undeterred by screams from some of the congregation, the preacher pressed on.

The God that holds you over the pit of Hell, much as one holds a spider or some loathsome insect over the fire, abhors you and is dreadfully provoked. His wrath toward you burns like fire; He looks upon you as worthy of nothing else but to be cast into the fire; He is of purer eyes than to bear to have you in His sight; you are ten thousand times more abominable in His eyes than the most hateful venomous serpent is in ours.

Sometimes the preacher would have to pause because his own voice was drowned by the wails of his hapless hearers. Soon he would say:

You have reason to wonder that you are not already in Hell. It is doubtless the case of some whom you have seen and known, that never deserved Hell more than you, and that heretofore appeared as likely to have been now alive as you. Their case is past all hope; they are crying in extreme misery and perfect despair; but here you are in the land of the living and in the house of God, and have an opportunity to obtain salvation. What would not those poor damned hopeless souls give for one day's opportunity such as you now enjoy? . . . Therefore, let everyone that is out of Christ, now awake and fly from the wrath to come. The wrath of Almighty God is now undoubtedly hanging over a great part of this congregation. Let everyone fly out of Sodom. Haste and escape for your lives, look not behind you, escape to the mountain, lest you be consumed.

Edwards emphatically was not a "God is love" preacher. Not only did he not see the love of God for His people as a thing to be expected; he did not believe it was in the nature of natural man to love God. Love for God was an attribute only of the reborn, Christ-mediated man or woman. Edwards tried to convince the unsaved that their souls were in danger because they were guilty of hating God. He would say:

You object, against your having a mortal hatred against God, that you never felt any desire to kill him. But one reason has been that it has always been conceived so impossible by you, and you have been so sensible how much desires would be in vain that it has kept down such a desire. But if the life of God were within your reach, and you knew it, it would not be safe one hour. . . . When you come to be a firebrand of Hell . . . you will appear as you are, a viper indeed. . . . Then will you as a serpent spit poison at God and vent your rage and malice in fearful blasphemies.

After convincing many of his hearers that God loathed them and was eager to torture them through all eternity, Edwards frequently was able to convince them that they hated God. Then he could play upon their guilt feelings to bring them to submission.

It was by a masterly use of psychology that Edwards brought so many of his fellow colonists to the state of acceptance. His skilled use of sensory effects and of suspense also was an impressive literary achievement. It is not surprising that he was in wide demand wherever Massachusetts adherents of the Great Awakening sought an inspiring revival leader.

Nevertheless, he could not hold the allegiance of a majority of his own congregation. Men whose formal education matched his own argued that enthusiasm alone did not provide a proper foundation for lasting faith. The building blocks of reason, they argued, were essential. But Edwards could not be deterred from what he believed to be his God-given mission. Complaints from leaders in his congregation and in the community caused him to redouble his efforts. He believed that the Great Awakening might be "the dawning, or at least a prelude" to the millennium with its fulfillment of the divine promise to the world. He thought that the millennium probably would come first to America, perhaps first of all to Massachusetts. How could he slacken his efforts now?

At the height of the revival of 1735, when Edwards was inspiring weeping and even screaming confessions of faith, his own uncle, Joseph Hawley, publicly opposed his methods. When Hawley asked his nephew's forgiveness, Edwards replied that "the town and church" lay "under great guilt in the sight of God," and warned, "Abuse of God's messengers has commonly been the last sin of an offending, backsliding people." He said that Hawley would be made aware of "God's frowns."

On the first Sunday in June of 1735, Hawley committed suicide by slashing his throat. In a letter about what he called this "thing of a very awful nature," Edwards explained that his uncle

> had been for a considerable time greatly concerned about the condition of his soul; till, by the ordering of a sovereign providence he was suffered to fall into deep melancholy, a distemper that the family are very prone to; he was much overpowered by it; the devil took the advantage and drove him into despairing thoughts. He was kept very much awake anights, so that he had but very little sleep for two months, till he seemed not to have his faculties in his own power. He was in a great measure past a capacity of receiving advice, or being reasoned with. . . . Satan seems to be in a great rage at this extraordinary breaking forth of the work of God. I hope it is because he knows that he had but a short time. . . . We have appointed a day of fasting in the town this week, by reason of this and other appearances of Satan's rage amongst us poor souls. I yesterday saw a woman [from Connecticut] who says there is a considerable revival of religion there.

New England church members had become sharply divided over revivalism, some exulting that it had waked a sleeping denomination, others lamenting that it had produced an unhealthy enthusiasm that left apathy in its wake. Growing opposition throughout the region to what some regarded as hysteria bolstered those within Edwards' congregation to oppose him more emphatically on matters of doctrine as well as methods of conversion. He gave a personal grievance to many of his parishioners when he announced from the pulpit that he had been told of the circulation of unfit books among the young, appointed an investigating committee, and read aloud the names of those whose testimony would be sought. The list included both witnesses and accused without making any effort to separate the sheep from the goats. Named were representatives of most prominent families in his church. The investigation ended abruptly.

Edwards' ministry ground slowly to its conclusion. Denied the right to present his views in a special series of sermons, he offered them in writing. He wrested from church leaders the opportunity to have his case judged by a council consisting of delegates from ten churches. By a one-vote majority, the ad hoc council declared that Edwards' pastorate should be terminated at once if his congregation so desired. Of the 230 voting members (women were not permitted to vote), 200 balloted to dismiss the pastor. Preaching his farewell sermon July 1, 1750, Edwards said that Jesus Christ, "before the whole universe," would endorse his position in the Northampton controversy. He warned, "The devil will undoubtedly seek to make his advantage" of the dismissal.

Thus ended Edwards' connection with the church he had served twenty-three years. He wrote a friend, "I am now thrown upon the wide ocean of the world, and know not what will become of me, and my numerous and chargeable family." He was then almost forty-seven years old, a far more advanced age for his day than for ours.

The minister to whom he addressed his letter about not knowing what would become of him offered to help Edwards to obtain a pulpit in Scotland. Some of Edwards' writings had attracted an admiring audience there, but he hesitated to venture upon a career so far from home. Meanwhile, as his old congregation searched for a new pastor, it occasionally called upon him to fill in. He did, willingly, until after several months the protests of diehard opponents ended this supply work. In August 1751 he answered a call to the missionary outpost at Stockbridge, Massachusetts. Here he would minister to a congregation of Indians and a few pioneers. The environment was a strange one for the frail scholar who used vivid imagery to frighten his audience, but daily lived amid the abstractions of complex philosophy.

The small church support available for the outpost was augmented by mission funds from the Massachusetts Assembly and the London Society for the Propagation of the Gospel in New England, as well as from prosperous individuals in London. There was a grant from the king himself for the education of Indian boys. Even so, until his Northampton home could be sold, Edwards had insufficient funds to support his family. His wife and children painted fans and produced fancy needlework for sale in Boston.

Before long, Edwards was expanding the mission to include a school for girls and introducing superior organization for the whole enterprise. He got the Assembly to appoint three trustees to administer the funds. But this seemingly wise move had unfortunate consequences. Ephraim Williams, a member of the same clan of Edwards' relatives that had been in bitter conflict with him in Northampton, was an influential merchant in the Stockbridge area. He was as eager to curb the preacher's influence as other Williamses had been. Two members of the family secured appointments to the Boston Commission for the London Society for the Propagation of the Gospel in New England. They engineered appointment of another relative as director of the girls' school. One of the three trustees appointed through Edwards' efforts married one of the hostile Williamses, and appeared in Stockbridge to assume overall direction of the mission.

When Edwards reported a conflict of interest because of the mingling of Williams mercantile interests with Williams administrative activities, his enraged relatives tried to have him ousted. They even determined to buy out the lands of those who supported him. But the preacher moved quickly and boldly, lining up the colonists, the Indians, a majority of the Commission, and the Assembly. He won his battle.

For the rest of his career, most of his battles were waged in print. He continued to fight Arminianism, but he also wrote other philosophical works read in Great Britain as well as in America.

Some of his philosophical essays contrasted strangely with the harsh tone of such sermons as "Sinners in the Hands of an Angry God." As to why the universe and all its creatures, including human beings, had been created, Edwards posited that

> the diffusive disposition that excited God to give creatures existence, was rather a communicative disposition in general, or a disposition in the fullness of divinity to flow out and diffuse itself. Thus the disposition there is in the root and stock of a tree to diffuse and send forth its sap and life, is doubtless the reason of the communication of its sap and life to its buds, leaves, and fruits, after these exist. . . . Therefore . . . we may suppose that a disposition in God, as an original property of His nature, to an emanation of His own infinite fullness was what excited Him to create the world. . . .[23]

Thus Edwards saw God as the supreme artist and viewed creation as an esthetic process. His own esthetic excitement in the presence of beauty was evident in many lines.

He earned the respect of philosophers as well as theologians by publication of a book with the formidable title *A Careful and Strict Enquiry into the Modern Prevailing Notions of that Freedom of Will Which Is Supposed to Be Essential to Moral Agency, Virtue and Vice, Reward and Punishment, Praise and Blame.* The work owed much to John Locke's influence, and some readers might see sophistry in Edwards' argument that, while the mind can freely choose, the "origination" of such choice is predetermined. Nevertheless, Edwards argued his case with considerable intellectual subtlety. It was this work, perhaps more than any other, that caused Francis A. Christie in the twentieth century to hail him as "the first great philosophic intelligence in American history."[24]

Some of Edwards' sermons and essays dealt warmly with the theme of Christian love. And there were those who saw its workings in the preacher himself. Travelers who spent the night in his home praised his thoughtfulness. Many from Massachusetts were impressed by his kindness in riding out on the road some distance with departing guests. The custom was followed in some other colonies but apparently was not a habit in theirs.

Special academic recognition came to Edwards in 1757, at the age of fifty-four, when he was asked to accept the presidency of the College of New Jersey, later Princeton, an office made vacant by the death of his son-in-law the Reverend Aaron Burr. At first Edwards declined, citing the low ebb of his energy and his reluctance to lose time from his writing. The urging of his fellow ministers, however, caused him to accept. He assumed his duties in January 1758, teaching one course as well as heading the administration and preaching regularly.

The career of this man who clung so tenaciously to many elements of the old theology was ended by his adherence to a controversial practice of the new science. He chose to be inoculated against smallpox, and as a result died of infection.

Edwards had not lived long enough to leave his impress on Princeton University. The prominent president of another college, Ezra Stiles of Yale, predicted that Edwards' essays and sermons would be forgotten. Stiles, who was right about many things, was mistaken in this. Some of the preacher's philosophical essays are still the subjects of masters' theses and doctoral dissertations, and the sermon "Sinners in the Hands of an Angry God" still appears in anthologies for college use.

But the Enlightenment, which came to dominate philosophy and academic studies in the eighteenth and early nineteenth centuries, was not sympathetic to his pronouncements, and the relativism of the twentieth century was even less so. Most scholars who write about Edwards do so in tones of regret for what might have been. The prevalent view is that he wasted much ingenuity and assiduity on things whose time was past. It is not that things spiritual have faded from concern, as was once predicted by some materialists, but that the narrow theology of Edwards and some of his followers finds today virtually no adherents among major thinkers, whether clerical or secular.

The claims that Edwards was a prodigy in science melt under the light of examination. It is not just that his essay on spiders turns out to be a work of early manhood rather than childhood. His interest in science was commendable. Especially praiseworthy was his insistence that friends of religion should not fight the revelations of science. But his initial curiosity about natural phenomena eventually was channeled into a narrow search for secular support of religious concepts. He sometimes is hailed as a pioneer American botanist, but his activities in this field fade into insignificance beside the internationally recognized accomplishments of Virginia's John Clayton, Pennsylvania's John Bartram, New York's Cadwallader Colden, and South Carolina's Alexander Garden. Indeed, Edwards' achievements in botany or any other natural science would have attracted little notice if he had lived in either the middle colonies or the South. In these disciplines, New England lagged far behind the other two sections. His activities in natural science were less notable than those of his fellow Massachusetts clergyman Cotton Mather.

Edwards' intelligent interest in science, however, was important. More conspicuously than anyone else in Massachusetts in his day, he sought to unite the faith of his fathers and the new science. He also tried to join the rigorous demands of intellectual Puritanism to the emotional fervor of the Great Awakening, which, brought from England by George Whitefield, excited worshipers in every colony from New England to Georgia. The degree to which he combined within himself the opposing claims of the traditional and the challenging, the indigenous and the imported, makes him the most appropriate symbol of New England as it entered the second half of the eighteenth century.

Alfred Owen Aldridge has said that the great mystery about Edwards is not how a man of his intellect and studious habits failed to become a more complete philosopher, but rather "how a philosopher of any eminence at all could have sprung from the provincial intellectual milieu of New England in the first decade of the eighteenth century." He provocatively points out, "Benjamin Franklin, only three years Edwards' junior, whose life presents intriguing parallels and contrasts, rose from essentially the same environment but escaped at an early age to a more cosmopolitan atmosphere."[25]

Once when Edwards was young he moved to New York, but he did not stay long. When he became president of Princeton at age fifty-four, middle-aged by the standards of our time but elderly by those of his generation, was he too old for further growth? History presents examples of people who continued to grow at more advanced ages. Edwards, who in his youth had formed thirty-four resolutions for self-improvement and later increased their number to seventy, made one more in the last year of his life—to keep abreast of contemporary findings in science. Perhaps the great tragedy is not so much that Edwards did not live to leave his impress on Princeton as that he did not survive long enough to be influenced by the New Jersey environment.[26]

The middle and southern colonies were both much more open to free discussion than New England, especially Massachusetts. Later, as quarrels threatened the union of Great Britain and her North American colonies, it was quite conceivable that Massachusetts might be the leader in pressing the dispute to the point of separation. From the seventeenth century on, the Old Bay Colony had asserted its independence whenever colonial dissatisfaction and English vulnerabilty or preoccupation with other concerns presented a suitable opportunity. But the intellectual foundations of a new American government, if one were found, seemed likely to be more the work of Virginians, South Carolinians, and citizens of New Jersey, Delaware, and Pennsylvania, than of New Englanders. People of the middle and southern colonies had been honing their wits on the great questions of the day while the Massachusetts men all too often had been sharpening their barbs for internecine warfare in theology.

The great city of Philadelphia, so dominant in the affairs of Pennsylvania, was itself dominated by mercantile interests that counseled reconciliation in all contests between the colonies and the mother country. Pennsylvania, therefore, might be more reluctant than most of her sisters to sever the bonds with Britain. But there were thinkers in Pennsylvania who participated actively in the debates that engaged the Atlantic world. Pennsylvania's spokesmen would probably urge compromise after other colonies had given up. But if they once accepted the idea of American independence, they might well be prominent among the framers of any new government.

On the basis of the tensions between heritage and innovation in the separate colonies, and of their troubled relationships with the parent nation, one might then have predicted that Massachusetts would be first in pushing the conflict between England and America, but that Virginia would not be far behind. One might also have forecast that Virginians, New Yorkers, Jerseymen, and South Carolinians would be prominent in the intellectual leadership of the new nation being formed. And it might have been foreseen that Pennsylvania, however reluctant to rebel, if it took the final step, would also play a prominent role in the creation of an American philosophy of government. Massachusetts, however, would not at first contribute so richly to what one of her distinguished sons, John Adams, would call the "war for men's minds." Still, with its long tradition of bookish leaders also skilled in the practical affairs of life, Massachusetts might experience an intellectual awakening that would furnish some of the most important leaders in the founding of the Republic.

Of course, a wise observer, in the second half of the eighteenth century, would never have assumed that independence would come in this way, or even that it would come at all. Actual events seldom fit so neatly the patterns of our theories. But the law of averages allows for an occasional textbook case or laboratory demonstration in the flow of real events.

THE PHILADELPHIA WIZARD

W HEN JONATHAN EDWARDS lay dying in Princeton, he questioned why God had led him to accept a college presidency in New Jersey if he would not let him live to serve. Then he peacefully submitted to the Divine will. At this time another former resident of Massachusetts was in London celebrating a milestone in his own career. Benjamin Franklin early had accepted the Deism that Edwards had fought against most of his life, and Franklin had dedicatedly pursued the science that always had intrigued Edwards.[1] Franklin's efforts had been spectacularly successful. In 1758, at the age of fifty-two, three years younger than the dying preacher, Franklin had the honor of seeing his book *Experiments and Observations on Electricity* published in German. First printed in English, it also had appeared in French. He was famous in Europe, perhaps even more than in America.

Franklin had come to London the year before to represent the Pennsylvania legislature in its attempts to tax lands of the Penn family, designated as proprietors under the colonial charter. Such taxation would be possible if the Penns consented. If they did not, it would be necessary to obtain from the British government a change in the charter. Either way, superb diplomacy would be required, and Pennsylvania could claim no more effective practitioner.

The tax money was needed for defense of the colony. Some of Franklin's earlier actions had gotten him intimately involved in the problem before he became an emissary to London. In 1755 when British General Edward Braddock led his army against the French at Fort Duquesne in Pennsylvania territory claimed by the British Crown, authorities asked the farmers to furnish horses and wagons to supply the troops. In his effort to overcome their reluctance, Franklin not only assured them that they would be recompensed for any losses but promised that, if the government should fail to do right by them, he would reimburse them personally. When Braddock's expedition ended in defeat that would have become a rout except for the clear-headed bravery of the young provincial Colonel George Washington, some of the Pennsylvania farmers lost both horses and wagons. When two months passed without official restitution, Franklin faced an unanticipated debt of twenty thousand pounds, a huge sum at that time.

Fortunately for Franklin, the government paid its debts. But two months of anxiety had cured him of recklessness in assuming financial responsibility.

He already had an impressive record of responsible citizenship. One high point had come the year before, when he was a member of the Albany Congress, composed of delegates from New England, New York, Pennsylvania, and Maryland. The meeting had been called to consider the British government's advice to make a treaty with the Iroquois as a preliminary to fighting the French in North America. Three years before, Franklin had composed a plan of union for the colonies. He now seized the opportunity to present it to the Congress. Franklin's plan, with a few amendments, was adopted.

Before the conference convened, he had geographically presented his most urgent message through a cartoon that he published in the *National Gazette.* The earliest known American cartoon, the now famous picture showed a snake in separate pieces designated as New England, New York, New Jersey, Pennsylvania, Maryland, and Virginia. The caption was "Join or Die."

Franklin came to Albany with a more detailed exposition of his views, a manuscript titled "Short Hints towards a Scheme for Uniting the Northern Colonies." Represented at the conference were New York, Massachusetts, New Hampshire, Connecticut, Rhode Island, Pennsylvania, and Maryland and the Six Nations of the Indians. The commissioners from the several colonies resolved that colonial union in some form was needed and appointed a committee to study the matter and make recommendations. Franklin's influence as a member was evidenced not only by the contents of its first report but also by its nomenclature.[2] Its proposals were offered as "short hints."

Discussion of these suggestions led to adoption of a Plan of Union, a lightly amended version of the proposals offered by Franklin. It called for a union of all British colonies on the Atlantic coast of North America except Nova Scotia and Georgia. Heading it would be a president general who, like the various royal governors, would be a Crown appointee paid from the royal treasury. The legislature of each colony would elect delegates to a grand council to legislate for the colonies on those matters assigned to its jurisdiction. The hand of the canny author of *Poor Richard's Almanac* is evident in the provision that the number of delegates from each colony, varying from two to seven, be determined not by population but by the size of each colony's payments to the general treasury. Both the president general, and ultimately the Crown, would have veto power over legislation. The union would have jurisdiction over Indian affairs, but it was concluded that this responsibility would necessitate regulation of real estate purchases in territories "not now within the bounds of particular colonies."

Approved July 10, 1754 by the Albany conferees, the plan ultimately was rejected by the assemblies of individual colonies. It was also rejected by the Board of Trade on behalf of the Crown. Admitting, however, that some change was needed, the board proposed appointment of one commander in chief for the armies of all the colonies and one commissary of Indian affairs. Franklin once said of his plan that "Its fate was singular; the assemblies did not adopt it, as they thought there was too much *prerogative* in it, and in England it was judged to have too much of the *democratic.*"³

Franklin's participation in the Albany Congress came six years after he had retired from private business to devote more time to scientific pursuits. His prominence in the deliberations was an indication of the extent to which public business had filled up the time gained. The man who had drawn the world's attention to his experiments with electricity, helping to add *positive* and *negative, plus* and *minus,* to the vocabulary of the subject, and proving the suspected identity of lightning and electricity by his famous experiment with kite and key in a thunderstorm, was now involved with the muttering thunder of approaching conflict on both sides of the Atlantic.

His involvement seemed almost total in 1757 when the Pennsylvania assembly sent him to London to plead its case against the proprietors. These absentee landlords, heirs of William Penn holding title deeds granted to their ancestor, appointed the colony's governors. Even more offensive than this exercise of power was a related one, their refusal to allow the governor to endorse into law any appropriations for defense unless their own huge baronies were exempted from taxation.

Even Franklin's famous powers of patient persuasion were at first unequal to his assigned task. But by 1760 he had successfully asserted the right of the Pennsylvania Assembly to tax the proprietors' estates. Only unsurveyed "waste lands" were still exempt. Franklin remained in London partly because the precarious character of his hard-won victory demanded continued vigilance. Equally influential, however, in his decision to stay until 1762 was his delight in the society of one of the world's intellectual capitals. In acquiring friends among Britain's leading thinkers, he was both winning allies for colonial causes and finding stimulus and instruction for his own intellect.

Among his principal newfound friends was Joseph Priestley, the nonconformist clergyman and chemist who shared Franklin's interest in electricity and would soon be recognized for important discoveries in the field. The term "Priestley rings" would memorialize his observations of the effect of electrical discharges on metallic surfaces. These activities excited Franklin, who had set up in his own London quarters an apparatus for electrical experiments. Priestley's historic discovery of oxygen would make his own name a household word.

Franklin found another influential friend in John Fothergill, a physician who was England's foremost authority on diphtheria but who was even better known throughout Europe for his richly varied botanical garden. A keen observer of his country's politics and a sharer of Franklin's hopes for reconciliation between Britain and the colonies, he could give the American good advice.

Another English friend was William Strahan, copublisher of Dr. Samuel Johnson's *Dictionary,* and eventually publisher to Hume, Adam Smith, Gibbon, William Robertson, and Blackstone. With this autodidact book-lover, who had been a printer before he was a publisher, Franklin had much in common.

A true polymath among Franklin's English friends was Peter Collinson. His position as a fellow of the Society of Antiquarians testified to his accomplishments as a preserver of the national heritage, just as his membership in the Royal Society paid tribute to his fresh discoveries about plants and insects. His signature on articles in learned journals carried as much weight as it did on contracts in the North American trade, where he was a great merchant.

Franklin shared friends with Lord Kames, the great Scottish jurist and philosopher, and with Dr. Samuel Johnson, and corresponded with both, but seems never to have met either face to face. One longs in vain for a confrontation between the pontifical Grand Cham of Literature and the artfully self-effacing American diplomat, with the faithful Boswell recording the encounter.

Before attaining adulthood, Franklin had calculated that through wide reading and diligent study he could obtain a better education than many young men received at Harvard. Before he left the colonies for London, he had received the imprimatur of Harvard and two other American colleges—Yale and William and Mary, all three had conferred upon him the degree of master of arts. Immediately before his departure, he was elected a member of the Royal Society. In Britain, he was awarded an LL.D. by Saint Andrews and a D.C.L. by Oxford.

While abroad, he had evidenced his learning not only by his detailed and cogent answers to governing bodies and his reports on electricity but also by republication of an earlier essay titled "Observations on the Increase of Mankind: The Peopling of Countries." On the basis of this article, originally written in 1751 and published in 1755, Carl Becker and others have credited him with anticipating some aspects of the Malthusian theory of population nearly a half century before Thomas R. Malthus' publication of the first edition of his *Essay on the Principle of Population as it Affects the Future Improvement of Society.*

So enchanted was Franklin with the "sensible, virtuous, and elegant minds" of Great Britain that when he returned to Pennsylvania in 1762 he was consoled by the hope of returning "in two years at farthest." He wanted to become a permanent resident if he could "persuade the good woman to cross the seas." The "good woman" was Deborah Read, his common-law wife. She was the daughter of his first landlady in Philadelphia. Marriage in a formal ceremony was impossible because she was the legal mate of a deserting husband. She not only could not comprehend the intellectual matters to which Franklin was devoted but was too illiterate for conduct of many of the ordinary affairs of everyday life. Nevertheless, she was a loving spouse, proud to bear two of his children but not too proud to give maternal affection to at least one of his children borne by other women. Poor Richard was a model of domestic sobriety, but Franklin was his literary creator, not his alter ego.

"Debby" remained in Philadelphia when Pennsylvania's legislature sent her husband to London again in 1764, this time to petition the Crown to assume government of the colony as a royal province. There could be a larger degree of self-government under a king with responsibility for a whole empire than under colonial proprietors with monarchical yearnings.

Franklin's mission was swamped by the storm over the Stamp Act. In an interview with George Grenville, chancellor of the exchequer, the Pennsylvanian warned of dangers inherent in Parliament's unprecedented levying of a direct tax on Americans. Without boldly attacking the proposed measure as unconstitutional, he suggested that the London legislature stick with the "usual constitutional method" of raising revenues in the colonies.

Franklin soon concluded that resistance was useless. He wrote his friends in America, "We might as well have hindered the sun's setting. . . . But since 'tis down . . . let us make as good a night of it as we can. We can still light candles." Franklin did not perceive that the spark of controversy had already lit the fires of revolution. Indeed, when Grenville asked him and other colonial agents to nominate Americans suitable for employment as stamp distributors, Franklin put forward the name of a personal friend in Philadelphia.[4] And when protests arose, Franklin advised that friend to perform his official duties "with coolness and steadiness." Far from balking at compliance with the new regulation, Franklin shipped stamped newspapers to be sold by his business partner.

His fellow citizens in Philadelphia felt betrayed. They long had saluted his public spirit, manifested in the creation of agencies ranging from a fire department to a public library, and had elected him to their colonial legislature even when he was in England. The ocean between him and his countrymen created a gulf of misunderstanding. Some accused him of having facilitated passage of the act in order to gain financial advantage. Hostility was so high that friends feared for the safety of Franklin's Philadelphia home and his family.

Only a dramatic event could restore his popularity. At the first opportunity, he engineered one. As a newspaper editor, Franklin had sometimes published pseudonymously letters of his own composition. Some that praised his editorials he wrote with great care for their effectiveness. Other letters attacked his own editorials, and these missives he filled with ignorant diatribe. This double role in public controversies was only the prologue to a far more demanding enterprise.[5] Now he would write dialogue for a drama in which he would be a principal player. And the Atlantic world would be his amphitheater.

In February 1766, probably with his own connivance, Franklin was summoned before the House of Commons, then sitting as a committee of the whole to consider a proposal to repeal the Stamp Act. In an examination lasting ten days, he replied to 176 questions.

Proud Americans gloried in their countryman's ability to answer all inquiries clearly, concisely, and informatively. Many Englishmen also were struck with admiration at his performance. The *Gentleman's Magazine* commented, "The questions . . . are answered with such deep and familiar knowledge of the subject, such precision and perspicuity, such temper and yet such spirit, as do the greatest honor to Dr. Franklin, and justify the general opinion of his character and abilities." Edmund Burke said that the American was like a schoolmaster interrogated by schoolboys. When the Stamp Act was repealed two weeks after the conclusion of Franklin's testimony, many Americans were disposed to see a simple case of cause and effect.

The Pennsylvanian's performance was impressive even if one saw it, as some did, as a "brilliantly stage-managed affair."[6] Some of his best answers were given to questions asked by friends, and perhaps supplied by the answerer. But he had also anticipated questions to be asked by enemies, and he answered them promptly, supplying statistics and other exact data from a capacious memory.

After this success, Franklin was prepared to return to Philadelphia and savor his restored popularity. But the Pennsylvania assembly renewed his commission as agent and insisted that he remain. His responsibilities increased. In the next four years, first Georgia, then New Jersey, and finally Massachusetts commissioned him as their agent. He was no longer merely a spokesman for Pennsylvania; he was the representative of New England and the mid-Atlantic colonies. Increasingly, Englishmen thought that he spoke for America.

By now his dealings were as often with skeptical or hostile English politicians as with admiring scholars. His disenchantment was obvious in 1768 when he wrote of the English public, "Some punishment seems preparing for a people who are ungratefully abusing the best constitution and the best King . . . any nation was ever blessed with, intent on nothing but luxury, licentiousness, power, places, pensions, and plunder." He had lost patience with the people, but he had not lost his faith in monarchy.

Just as Franklin had complained after the Albany Congress of 1754 that his Plan of Union had been too "democratic" for the proprietors but not democratic enough for the colonial assemblies, so now he complained in 1768 that in England he was considered "too much of an American, and in America . . . too much of an Englishman."

With his predilection for pragmatic compromise, Franklin worked hopefully for reconciliation between England and her colonies until Parliament passed the "coercive acts" of 1774. Already, in fact as early as 1770, he had deplored the expression "supreme authority of Parliament." He argued that Americans should base their claims of autonomy on the theory that the union of England and her North American colonies corresponded to that of England and Scotland before the 1707 Act of Union. Their union had consisted solely in their allegiance to the same sovereign.

As early as January 1774, Franklin had strong personal reasons to be discouraged about the possibilities of reconciliation. His own efforts to achieve that goal included an attempt to show that misleading information from royal representatives in America had a great deal to do with London's oppressive colonial policies. As London agent for the Massachusetts House of Representatives, Franklin sent to Thomas Cushing, Speaker of that body, six letters that Thomas Hutchinson, the colony's chief justice, had sent to an English cabinet minister.

Though Franklin admonished Cushing that the letters should not be published, or even copied, but simply shown to some persons, Samuel Adams in June 1773 read them aloud to the Massachusetts House and later had them published. When the House petitioned the king to oust Hutchinson from office, a scandal broke. It resulted in a duel in December between two prominent Englishmen. To exonerate one of the duelers, Franklin on Christmas Day said that he himself was solely responsible for procuring the letters and sending them back to Massachusetts.

In January a committee of the Privy Council conducted hearings on the

Massachusetts House's petition to remove Hutchinson. During the hearing, news of the Boston Tea Party arrived, and inflamed the English inquisitors. Franklin disapproved of the destruction of private property in the now celebrated episode, but was looked upon as one of the incendiary Americans. The British solicitor general branded him a "thief." As the case of the purloined letters assumed tremendous proportions, Franklin was dismissed from his office as deputy postmaster for America. The solicitor general, entranced by his own wit as a punster, predicted that Franklin would "henceforth esteem it a libel to be called a man of letters."

But the American was sustained by the faith and loyalty of English friends. William Pitt led the Whigs in efforts toward conciliation, and Franklin helped him. But in March 1775, perceiving that war was imminent, the Pennsylvanian sailed for home. Ironically, three days later, his friend Edmund Burke delivered one of the world's most eloquent orations, his speech on conciliation with America—all in vain except for its inspiration to future generations.

On May 5 Franklin returned to the familiar brick buildings and narrow residential streets of Philadelphia. Then, also, this man, who thirteen years before had pondered the advantages of permanent residence in England, entered upon a new role as a leader of the American Revolution. The very day after his return, he was elected a delegate to the Second Continental Congress. Though he joined reluctant rebels in a petition to the king offering "one opportunity more of recovering the friendship of the colonies," he said of Britain, "I think she has not sense enough to embrace [it], and so I conclude she has lost them forever."

He returned to new phases of familiar tasks, devising a new Plan of Union for the colonies and organizing an intercolonial postal system, becoming the first postmaster general. Long an advocate of correspondence among the colonies and with English sympathizers, he accepted appointment to a committee to correspond "with friends in Great Britain, Ireland, and other parts of the world."

Appointed to the committee to prepare a Declaration of Independence, he made minute suggestions, which Thomas Jefferson, as principal author, gratefully accepted. When other delegates demanded major deletions and alterations, Franklin sympathized with the suffering writer and said that he had long ago made up his own mind never to prepare another paper for submission to a public body. He told the younger man an anecdote about a hatter who had altered his elegant signboard so many times in response to individual criticisms that eventually it bore only his own name and a picture of a hat.

Seventy years old, Franklin was an avuncular presence in the Congress and well on the way toward becoming one for the newborn nation. Though he was not a Quaker, he was the foremost citizen of the Quaker city and, with his portly figure, simple and sober garb, and benign countenance framed by shoulder-length hair, he seemed the very model of Quakerly virtue. And was he not, as Poor Richard, a preceptor almost as concerned as a parent but happily more tolerant? Of course, there were some in the Congress who knew his reputation abroad. After all, he had been convivial with some of Europe's less inhibited noblemen, and was reported to have been several times a guest in England's Hellfire Club, where some of the ladies wore exquisite masks and nothing else. To young colleagues in the Congress, he was a worldly uncle who had been a traveling salesman for American ideas, one who could wink knowingly at some of the peccadilloes of his nephews and nieces, but who could be depended upon in a crisis to put the family's interest above his own.

The popular image of Benjamin Franklin was as much his own creation as his bifocals, the lightning rod, the stove that bore his name, or the Franklin glass harmonica, for which both Mozart and Beethoven composed. His image-building began for commercial advantage before he entered politics. By his own admission, as a young printer he trundled supplies of paper through the streets in a wheelbarrow instead of having them delivered, hoping thereby to impress people with his industriousness.

Back of the image was much solid substance. Franklin used to say that he became an inventor because he was a lazy man always looking for an easier way. But, though he had no love for unnecessary physical exertion except in the sport of swimming, his energetic mind seemed to be at work every waking hour. Not only was he busy as an inventor and an improver of other people's inventions; he was also an enthusiastic student of electricity, hydrodynamics, hydrostatics, chemistry, geology, physiology, and psychology.

Meanwhile, he was presented an opportunity to polish his skills in diplomacy. Hoping for substantial support from France in the struggle with Britain, the Congress named a committee of three to negotiate a treaty in Paris. Franklin was the most famous of the triumvirate—and the oldest. "I am but a fag end," he said in accepting, "and you may have me for what you please." That "fag end" soon became one of the brightest threads in the fabric of French society. The capital was still strongly influenced by Rousseau's theories of the natural man's superiority. Wearing his fur cap just often enough to attract maximum attention, Franklin seemed a true son of the American wilderness. Yet he could discuss authoritatively the latest findings in a variety of sciences. Besides, like a wizard, he had "snatched the lightning from the sky." So far as Paris was concerned, Franklin was a made-to-order Enlightenment hero.

About two years later, when John Adams arrived in France to replace one of Franklin's fellow commissioners, he found the Pennsylvanian's face staring at him from shopwindows, adorning living-room walls as a domestic icon, gleaming from proudly worn medallions, adorning a snuffbox drawn from a satin-clad dandy's pocket, and winking from the bracelet on the slender wrist of a gesticulating coquette. The Bostonian said:

> His reputation was more universal than that of Leibnitz or Newton, Frederick or Voltaire, and his character more beloved and esteemed than any or all of them. . . . His name was familiar to government and people . . . to such a degree that there was scarcely a peasant or a citizen, a *valet de chambre*, coachman or footman, a lady's chambermaid or a scullion in a kitchen who was not familiar with it, and who

did not consider him as a friend to human kind. When they spoke of him, they seemed to think he was to restore the Golden Age.[7]

Adams was given to aggressive hyperbole, particularly in discussing colleagues he believed to be overrated. But when Jefferson joined Franklin and Adams in France in 1785, he was every bit as sweeping in testimony to the Pennsylvanian's reputation. He found "more respect and veneration attached to the character of Dr. Franklin in France than to that of any other person, foreign or native."[8]

Franklin's popularity among the French was of great practical value to his country. It made it much easier for the government in Paris to sign on February 6, 1778 not only a treaty of commerce with Britain's rebellious colonies but also a treaty of "defensive alliance . . . to maintain effectively the . . . independence absolute and unlimited of the United States."

Franklin's own effectiveness as diplomat and keen analyst of European events more than compensated for the disadvantage of his nepotism. But the abilities of an ordinary public servant would not have. He appointed as secretary for his diplomatic mission William Temple Franklin, the illegitimate son of the old man's own illegitimate son, New Jersey's ardently monarchist royal governor William Franklin. Temple proved inefficient in almost every duty and made a hodgepodge of the accounts. Franklin also appointed his nephew Jonathan Williams to the sensitive post of United States naval agent at Nantes, where he was an utter failure.

Franklin was adroit in obtaining loans from the French government and, as Carl Becker has said, persuading Foreign Minister Vergennes "to overlook irregular methods and to honor debts for which the French government was in no way obligated." To lessen British power was France's chief motivation, but Franklin's personal friendship with influential men—and women—greatly augmented his influence. Even his scholarship and scientific experiments helped. He was a guest of learned societies and was elected to the British Royal Academy of Medicine. The Enlightenment was in vogue, and even hardened politicians gave more attention to a man with impressive intellectual credentials.

After the Congress of the United States sent John Jay as a representative to Spain and John Adams to Holland, Franklin served as a coordinator for American diplomats in Europe, meeting bills of exchange drawn on him by them, by American ship captains using European ports, and by the Congress itself. His diplomatic colleagues frequently carped about the way he carried out his duties, and plotted to have him recalled. Franklin anticipated them by resigning on the grounds that overwork was menacing his health. When Congress implored him to remain at his post, he consented. He said, "I call this continuance an honor . . . greater than my first appointment, when I consider that all the interest of my enemies, united with my own request, were not sufficient to prevent it."

In 1781, four months before Cornwallis' surrender at Yorktown, Franklin was named with Adams and Jay to negotiate a peace with Great Britain. The British were not receptive to his suggestion that they give Canada to the United

States. But when negotiations were stymied by Jay's insistence on a technicality and Adams' demand that American fishermen be permitted to dry fish on British coasts, Franklin saved the day. Drawing a paper from his pocket and saying that "the first principle of the treaty was equality and reciprocity," he demanded compensation for goods carried off from Boston, Philadelphia, and the Carolinas, as well as for "the burning of towns." The British then acknowledged the claim that Adams had advanced in behalf of fellow New Englanders in the fishing trade.

At first, Franklin resisted Adams' and Jay's determination to negotiate with Britain without keeping Vergennes informed as promised. But eventually he acquiesced. Afterwards, Franklin had the task of appeasing the Frenchman, who was either genuinely incensed or a master of histrionic wrath. Franklin's apology was so successful that in the process he obtained from the Frenchman's government a loan to the United States of six million livres.

Having completed his official duties in Europe, Franklin sailed from France in July 1783. Characteristically, he employed himself on the voyage in maritime observations and the writing of a treatise "The Causes and Cure of Smoky Chimneys." Back in Philadelphia, he became president of the Executive Council of Pennsylvania. He left the minutiae of administration to others, but was the guiding spirit of the state government. His reputation as a wise man, one attuned to the laws of the universe but mindful of homely matters, was strong throughout Western civilization in 1787 when he became a member of the Constitutional Convention that drew to his hometown the delegates from every American state.

30

"THE GREAT LITTLE MADISON"

BENJAMIN FRANKLIN brought to the Constitutional Convention of 1787 a carefully devised agenda, the product of more than a half century of experience in government and in the contemplation of its intricacies. It called for a single legislative chamber and an executive board rather than one chief executive. Franklin insisted that all executives of the national government be unpaid.

No one in America could rival the Pennsylvanian's combination of theoretical and practical knowledge of the ways of men and governments. Who could block the adoption of his agenda?

Probably no one in the convention could have prophesied who would provide the most formidable opposition. It was not George Washington, a celebrated lieutenant colonel at age twenty-two, a Virginia legislator at twenty-seven, the commander of the armies of the United States in the Revolution, and at fifty-five the statuesque figure now hailed as the "Cincinnatus of America." Nor was it Robert Morris, whose combination of acumen and forcefulness had made him the "financial dictator" of Continental government. It was not even such a formidable debater as Gouverneur Morris, James Wilson, Roger Sherman, or that master politician Elbridge Gerry.

The chief impediment in Franklin's path was a frail-looking man only a little more than five feet tall and weighing only about a hundred pounds. He looked far younger than his thirty-six years; in a miniature portrait painted four years earlier by Charles Willson Peale, he appeared no more mature than many teenagers.[1] He had no oratorical tricks to compensate for his unimpressive appearance. When he rose to speak in his uncommanding voice, he held his hat before him with both hands and read quite obviously from notes concealed in the crown.

But those notes were based on wide and deep learning assembled by a master of logic. Holding the note-laden hat as if it were a wheel, he steered through the Convention's debates like a master pilot sensitive to the winds and currents of opinion and never swamped in the wake of the mighty dreadnoughts on every side. He was, as Dolley Payne Todd, his future wife, would say, "the great little Madison."[2]

James Madison was a stranger to the fiercely competitive worlds of business and journalism in which Franklin had thrived.[3] And he had not had the tempering experience of representing a third-rate power in the capital of one of the world's greatest empires. Altogether, he seemed an unequal match for the older man, either as respectful opponent or as compromising ally.

Madison had had political experience before his election as a delegate to the Continental Congress, but most of his elections appear to have been dignified contests with gentlemanly opponents. His defeat for reelection to the Virginia assembly has been attributed to a failure to solicit votes personally and to provide the customary entertainment for the voters.

But he was wise in the theory of government and knowledgeable about its practice in different societies throughout history. He was, like Jefferson and Franklin, a polymath. Like these leaders at the time of the founding of the United States, and like so many leaders of Renaissance Florence and Elizabethan England, he was a master of several intellectual disciplines and a student of even more.

Though he had the educational experience of growing up in a cultured household, his formal schooling began late—at age twelve. But soon, under the tutelage of Donald Robertson, a Scottish schoolmaster in Virginia's King and Queen County, he was reading Greek and Latin classics and studying Spanish and French. He later told of his embarrassment at discovering when speaking with Frenchmen that his pronunciation of their language was far from adequate. He would say jocularly that, from the burred speech of his Scottish teacher, he had learned "Scotch French."

After further study under the Reverend Thomas Martin, an Episcopal minister in his home county of Orange, Madison entered the College of New Jersey (now Princeton University) at the age of nineteen, not young for matriculation but still only seven years after the beginning of his formal education.

The college, under President John Witherspoon, provided one of America's most intellectually stimulating environments. An earnest student of history and government, Madison distinguished himself not only in the classroom but also in extracurricular leadership. He was a founder of the Whig Society, a debating club whose name indicated the political bent of its members. The student body was anti-Tory and had made the sins of British imperialism almost an additional course. Some student gatherings seemed to be symposia of resistance bordering on rebellion.

Madison graduated in 1771, but remained one more year to study both ethics and the Hebrew language under President Witherspoon himself. Whether or not he seriously considered entering the ministry, as some have supposed, his interest in theology was no passing fancy. Back home in Virginia, he entered upon a self-directed course of reading in the subject.

Before he had begun his collegiate education, his parents had consulted with a planter and former lawyer in a neighboring county who had a wide reputation for learning. At that time, neither the young student nor the planter eight years his senior suspected that each eventually would become the other's best friend and remain so until death claimed the elder. When Madison entered upon his self-directed studies, first in theology and then in government and political philosophy, he increasingly consulted his friend. He was flattered when the friend, in turn, began consulting him. He had reason to be, for the friend was Thomas Jefferson.

More and more, Madison seemed to pursue his studies with no long-term objective. He stayed at home, spending part of the time, as he said, in teaching his brothers and sisters "some of the first rudiments of literature." Curiosity alone, unaccompanied by zest, impelled him to study. A dark cloud of melancholy settled upon him, and he became convinced that his life would be short and plagued with illness. He thought it was useless to launch upon any important enterprise.

At last indignation burst through his melancholy. He was impelled to action by what he considered the tyranny of Great Britain and the bigotry of Virginia's Anglican legislators who did nothing to discourage religious intolerance. His own Presbyterianism made him critical of Anglican assumptions of superiority, and his sympathies extended beyond his own denomination to Baptists, Methodists, and Lutherans. There was no official persecution in Virginia comparable to that in such states as Massachusetts, but members of churches other than the established one were denied certain privileges while being forced to support the religious establishment with their tax payments. And while some Anglican legislators expressed contempt for ruffians who threw hornets' nests and snakes into Baptist gatherings, few showed any zeal to provide legal protection. Madison had seen more religious tolerance in Pennsylvania than in Virginia, and he burned to improve the situation in his own colony.

The recluse became an activist. He attacked religious intolerance as "diabolical" and "hell-conceived." He also resumed criticism of British policies, a practice in which he had joined enthusiastically at Princeton. He was elected to his county's committee of safety, a body with counterparts throughout Virginia, which organized local resistance to British measures regarded as oppressive.

In 1776 he was sent as a delegate to the Virginia Convention, the body that proposed a declaration of independence to be framed by the thirteen colonies acting in unison. There he was a member of the committee for a constitution and declaration of rights. George Mason, another intellectual planter who disliked speaking in public assemblies, was the prime mover in both projects. Indeed, he is justly regarded as the author of the Virginia Declaration of Rights, one of the world's most eloquent statements about human freedom. It was not the last time Madison and Mason would work as partners. America and the whole cause of human rights would profit from their association.

Even more important than Madison's committee work was his boldly offering from the floor a resolution declaring the free exercise of religion to be a right, not merely a privilege. His resolution was amended by other delegates. If it had been adopted in its original form, it would have deprived the Anglican denomination in Virginia of its status as an established church.

Madison was a member of the first legislature elected under the new state constitution. As an institution antedating the transition from colony to state, the Virginia assembly, in its 157th year, was the second oldest legislative body in the English-speaking world. As a member, Madison was working with some of the ablest political figures in North America.

It was upon completion of his first term that Madison was defeated for reelection because he balked at some of the campaign customs of his day. But he had won the respect of his fellow legislators, as was shown in 1778 when they elected him to the Governor's Council, and two years later when they chose him as a delegate to the Continental Congress.

In its sessions, he had the opportunity to measure himself and his colleagues in Virginia assemblies against a national assemblage of representative citizens. Though strongly impressed with the abilities of delegates from the other states, he did not find wanting either himself or his earlier associates. Speaking in public was still an ordeal for him. He knew that, as in so many Virginia meetings, he lacked the more obvious oratorical talents of some of his colleagues. But he had no reason to believe that he could not think as well as any of them in matters of public policy, and none among them had given more time to studying the long-range purpose and effects of government.

Madison's aversion to public speaking, which did not prevent him from speaking out when important issues were at stake, was one aspect of a basic shyness. Until set afire by what he saw as the arrogance of British colonial policy and by his hatred for religious intolerance, he had become almost a recluse after completing his studies at Princeton. His shyness was increased in 1783 when Kitty Floyd, daughter of a congressional colleague from New York, broke her engagement to marry Madison. The wound was deep. Any reference to the romance always upset him, and he tried to erase any record of it. In the same year as the breakup, Madison completed his congressional term and retired from Congress.

Some intimate friends cherished his witty table talk, which, when ladies were not present, included risqué humor. But most people who saw him socially thought of him as a quiet little man withdrawn from conversation beyond the minimum required for politeness. Silently, he would observe the scene through large, solemn eyes.

Madison's congressional service, though brief, was by no means negligible. His journal testifies to his own diligence and has provided historians with one of their most valuable resources for reconstructing debates. Recognizing the need for a stronger federation, he repeatedly called for duties on imports as a means of raising national revenue. His foresight was also evidenced in the arguments for free navigation of the Mississippi by the United States that he included in the official instructions he composed for John Jay, then American minister to Spain. And shyness did not keep him from speaking out with Hamilton against the action of the United States commissioners in violating a pledge and instructions to keep the French allies informed of peace negotiations with the British.

The balance of his judgment was impressive. At the same time that he vigorously asserted Virginia's claims to western territory, a sore point with many of the smaller states, he also played a major role in the compromise of 1783 in which the Old Dominion, in a superb example of enlightened self-interest, ceded the Northwest to the general government.

Another stand that he took has invited considerable dispute about its wisdom, but leaves no doubt about the extent of his influence. When his colleagues seemed locked in endless argument over a proposal to substitute population for land values as a basis for determining individual states' financial contributions, Madison provided an acceptable solution. Some of the states that had few slaves insisted that bond servants not be counted in working out a population formula, while states with many slaves maintained with equal vehemence that they were part of the population and should be counted as such. Madison's proposal that five slaves be counted as the equal of three free persons won general acceptance. Later, the framers of the Constitution adopted the same three-fifths formula for determining representation in the lower house of Congress. Succeeding generations have criticized the formula as unrealistic and insensitive, but many northerners and southerners in Madison's generation believed that without such a compromise there would have been no American Republic.

Even if Madison's engagement to Kitty Floyd had not come to a humiliating and traumatic end, there were many things in 1783 to make continuation in Congress an unalluring prospect. While he was considering the basis for determining the contributions of individual states to the general government, his own state often failed to pay his salary. Virginia's performance was not uniquely deplorable. Many of Madison's colleagues were sustained, as he himself was, by the generosity of Haym Salomon, a patriotic Jew who loaned money to the delegates without charging interest. Such an arrangement would have rendered both him and them suspect in a later age, but it enabled talented men who were not rich to continue in the service of their country.

Even this solution could not buy material comfort. Madison wound up his term not in Philadelphia but in Princeton, sharing with a fellow delegate "a room not 10 feet square without a single accommodation for writing." The words are Madison's own and are eloquently suggestive of his priorities. Congress had not fled Philadelphia to escape the British. General Cornwallis had surrendered to Washington at Yorktown in October 1781. Though the British had the strength to resume the war with other forces if they believed it practicable, and Washington warned that they might, the invaders were no longer pressing the Americans. Peace negotiators had been meeting in Paris in a state of uncertainty. But the real menace that drove the Congress from Philadelphia was the threat of a mutinous army sure that it had won a war and eager to return home. The situation highlighted some of the young nation's chief problems as 1783 drew to a close.

Family problems conspired with public frustrations to make a return home seem appropriate. Madison's father was markedly in physical decline. The son, in the formal way in which he referred to personal matters, described himself as moved by "the solicitude of a tender and infirm parent."

Back in Orange County, he began the study of law, apparently impelled as much by idealistic as by practical considerations. He said that he wanted to "depend as little as possible on the labor of slaves."

Law was not his only study. He followed his friend Jefferson in the paths of the sciences, devoting time especially to natural history and chemistry. In Paris as United States minister, Jefferson found rare books and recent publications to feed the younger man's intellectual hunger. Madison also obtained through Jefferson books in a category in which he was proving at least as profound a scholar as the sage of Monticello. He sought "whatever may throw light on the general constitution and droit public of the several confederacies which have existed." Like many other thoughtful Americans, he had concluded that his country could not survive without a stronger central government. The building of one would probably be the most important task of their generation, and he meant to have a part in that labor.

In the interim, he served nearer home as a member of the Virginia House of Delegates, the lower house of the state legislature. Even as exhibited on this narrower stage, there was nothing parochial about his interests. During the three years of his service, he was one of the most influential of a group of able and energetic legislators pushing for development of the commonwealth's natural resources and expansion of its commerce, at the same time preserving its credit amid naive efforts, typical of the times, to solve financial woes by almost unlimited printing of paper currency.

With his quietly persistent arguments, he thwarted the oratorical efforts of Patrick Henry to fasten an established church onto the newly reformed body politic. Henry shrewdly attempted to guarantee sufficient votes by suggesting that a general assessment be levied not only for support of the Episcopal clergy but also of the Methodist, Presbyterian, and Baptist. Jefferson earlier had written Madison that their best hope was "devoutly to pray for [Henry's] death."[4] But this time Virginia Baptists were the great orator's nemesis. They said that if, as they had maintained, it was wrong for the Episcopalians to be an established church, it was equally wrong for Baptists. With the cooperation of the Baptists and some other dissenters, Madison not only defeated Henry's plan but also officially disestablished the Anglican Church, a consummation for which Jefferson had worked and of which he had dreamed for years.

Like Jefferson, Madison foresaw the significance of the West in the nation's future. He proposed measures to improve transportation and communication between Tidewater and Piedmont Virginia and the mountains and valleys to the west. He called for admission of Virginia's Kentucky district as a separate state. As when he had prepared, for the Continental Congress, arguments that John Jay could use in insisting on the United States' right to free navigation of the Mississippi, he again defended that claim, calling it a "natural right."

He pursued another of Jefferson's dreams—the establishment of a system of public schools. But most of his fellow legislators found this idea, like his proposal that Americans pay their pre-Revolutionary debts to British merchants, too idealistic for serious consideration.

One of the most influential things that Madison did as a Virginia legislator had a significant effect on the development of the American Republic. He was convinced that America, even after winning political independence, would remain an economic colony unless the central government was empowered to pursue commercial policies for all of the member states. Without such an arrangement, there could be no realistic hope for commercial concessions from foreign powers. Accordingly, Madison called upon the legislature to grant to Congress the power to regulate commerce. The "commerce clause" would become an important part of the new Constitution. Not only would the call for it provide the impetus for a strong federal government and transform American trade, but it would be interpreted by the courts in successive generations to make federal power more nearly all-pervasive than most of the founders had envisioned.

Beginning with a call to give Congress the power to tax imports, Madison was defeated in that effort, but then broadened his campaign to embrace a demand for general congressional power to regulate commerce. Defeated in this effort also, he then succeeded in getting Virginia to invite her sister states to an interstate commercial convention in Annapolis in September 1786.[5]

Ironically, though the meeting was conveniently held in her own capital, Maryland did not send delegates. Neither did Connecticut, South Carolina, or Georgia. And the delegates from four other states—New Hampshire, Massachusetts, Rhode Island, and North Carolina—arrived too late to take part. Thus the meeting consisted of representatives from only five states: New York, New Jersey, Pennsylvania, Delaware, and Virginia.

Despite the discouragingly small attendance, Madison and Alexander Hamilton both urged the scheduling of another meeting with even more extensive objectives. Those present adopted a document drafted by Hamilton that called for a convention in Philadelphia on the second Monday in May 1787 to discuss all things necessary "to render the constitution of the Federal Government adequate to the exigencies of the Union."

Many people found little reason to celebrate a tentative proposal from five of the thirteen states, particularly when all had had an opportunity to participate. But Madison, who once had been mired in melancholy, now saw things differently. When the General Assembly of Virginia voted unanimously to accept the invitation, he wrote General Washington that at last there was "some ground for leaning to the side of Hope."

Madison returned to Congress in February 1787, serving until the opening of the Constitutional Convention in May. By his own later testimony, his otherwise reluctant return to Congress was induced by his desire "to bring about, if possible, the canceling of Mr. Jay's project for shutting the Mississippi." Jay had agreed with Spanish officials that the United States should forgo for twenty-five years its right to navigate the Mississippi. In exchange for this tremendous sacrifice of national interest, Spain would make commercial concessions sought by seven northern states. Madison introduced resolutions to substitute Jefferson for Jay in the negotiations and to curb the influence of the northern bloc. Neither resolution passed, but in the debates a crack appeared in northern unanimity, and the proposal to sacrifice American rights to the Mississippi for a quarter of a century landed in history's dustbin.

Another happening had a much greater effect on the proceedings scheduled for Philadelphia in May. Impoverished farmers in Massachusetts blamed their troubles on the state government. Explosive town meetings were followed by an insurrection led by Daniel Shays, a former captain in America's Revolutionary forces. When insurrection was crushed in the eastern part of the state, it erupted in the western. As late as February 1787, the men of Shays' Rebellion almost succeeded in seizing the arsenal in Springfield. As a result, political leaders in many states were far more willing than heretofore to consider measures for strengthening the central government.

Not that there was unanimity on how to deal with the threat of anarchy! Some politicians believed that it would not be possible, now that the War of Independence was over, to unite under one government three communities as disparate as the North with its fisheries and commerce, the middle states with their modest farms and shops, and the South with its plantation society. And some officers who had attained high rank in the Revolution and now were active in the Society of the Cincinnati were quite ready to run roughshod over states' rights in the interest of law and order. No less a Revolutionary hero than General Henry Knox warned, "The state systems are the accursed things which will prevent our being a nation. . . . [T]he vile state governments are sources of pollution which will contaminate the American name for ages—machines that must produce ill, but cannot produce good. Smite them, in the name of God and the People."[6]

James Madison was the first delegate to arrive in Philadelphia for the Constitutional Convention of 1787.[7] He was even ahead of the delegates from Pennsylvania. Indeed, he was in the city eleven days before the conferees were gaveled to order. The extra time was not wasted. By May 14 all the delegates from Virginia and Pennsylvania were on hand, and they were the only ones who were. Combined, the two delegations included the two most distinguished members of the Convention—George Washington of Virginia and Benjamin Franklin of Pennsylvania. Madison was well acquainted with Washington. Franklin, now eighty-one years old, he was meeting for the first time, though the Virginian had been one of the strongest defenders of the Pennsylvanian when some other members of the Continental Congress had tried to oust him from his post in Paris.[8] If Madison could enlist leading Pennsylvanians in the federal cause to which his fellow Virginians were committed to one degree or another, the gain could be crucial.

Among the Virginians were such notables as George Wythe and George Mason, both famous for erudition, and Governor Edmund Randolph, a master of polished persuasion. Three famous Virginians—Patrick Henry, General Thomas Nelson, and Richard Henry Lee—were conspicuously absent. They had been clear about their lack of enthusiasm for a new constitution. Another Virginian, who had authored America's most famous political document so far, was also absent, but not from lack of interest. Thomas Jefferson wanted to be at the Convention in Philadelphia, but he was held fast in Paris by his duties as minister to France. Nevertheless, he was in Philadelphia in more than spirit. He was there as an influence. He was the favorite confidant of Madison, who seemed certain to play a prominent role in the proceedings. Jefferson had recommended and supplied much of the younger man's reading over a period of years. In a lively correspondence, the two had discussed the problems of national union. A little before the historic meeting, Madison had asked Jefferson to send him the names of some good books to read in preparation. Jefferson had replied with a list of more than two hundred.[9]

THE OTHER JAMES

O N THE EVE of the Constitutional Convention of 1787, many people might have predicted that a Virginian and a Pennsylvanian would exert the greatest influence on the proceedings. And they would have been correct. But if asked to name the particular individuals, they would have erred. George Washington and Benjamin Franklin, as the most respected delegates, would have been the popular choices. It must be granted that they performed essential functions, for no one else could have presided with Washington's authority, and no one else could have matched Franklin's healing diplomacy. But the Constitution-maker who did most to shape the new government was a Virginian of far smaller reputation than the venerated Washington—James Madison. And the next most influential shaper of the Constitution was not the famous Dr. Franklin, but a Pennsylvanian of much smaller public stature—James Wilson.[1]

Of the two Jameses foremost in the proceedings, Madison today is justly celebrated as Father of the Constitution. But Wilson is a shadowy figure whose name brings scarcely a glint of recognition even from many generally well-informed Americans. An examination of his career provides convincing evidence of his importance and at the same time suggests reasons why he has been denied posterity's accolades.

Physically, Wilson was more imposing than Madison—a distinction that he shared with virtually every other delegate. On some people, he made a strong, favorable first impression. One of these was John Adams. The New Englander met Wilson at the Second Continental Congress in 1775. Though Adams at that time praised Franklin as "a great and good man . . . composed and grave," he nevertheless doubted that the elder statesman was the younger Pennsylvanian's equal "in fortitude, rectitude, and abilities."[2]

Wilson's eyes were those of a man given to speculation, either philosophical or commercial. The lift of his right eyebrow added a quizzical touch. When he looked over his spectacles, his gaze became professorial. His chin, his mouth, his nose, and his jaws were firmly molded. The face was strong in outline but unweathered, almost lineless.[3] Those who trusted physiognomy as a delineator of character might have had their faith confirmed by a knowledge of his career.

As for philosophical speculation, Wilson had been schooled in one of the world's great nurseries of metaphysical debate. Born in Scotland in the vicinity of Saint Andrew's University, he had matriculated there at the age of fifteen, going next to the University of Glasgow, and finally to Edinburgh, then the most prestigious university in the English-speaking world. He appears not to have obtained a degree there, not from any deficiency of scholarship but perhaps because he was more interested in obtaining an education than in collecting certificates.

His professorial gaze was appropriate to one who, arriving in Philadelphia at the age of twenty-three, soon joined the College of Philadelphia faculty as a teacher of Greek, Latin, and rhetoric. Now seeing the value of a diploma, he applied to his employers for an honorary master of arts degree and obtained it about three months into his teaching career.

Philadelphia, like other American cities, was torn by the Stamp Act controversy when Wilson arrived in 1765. It was, as he quickly perceived, a great time for lawyers. Wilson entered upon the study of law in the office of John Dickinson, who was not only one of Pennsylvania's leading attorneys, trained in London's Middle Temple, but also a Pennsylvania representative at the Stamp Act Congress and author of the declaration of rights and grievances that it adopted. During the approximately two years that Wilson studied with him, Dickinson became famous throughout the American colonies for his *Letters from a Farmer in Pennsylvania*. These missives, first published in newspapers, helped to crystallize colonial resistance to Britain's Townshend Acts.

While reading law, Wilson was writing a series of essays in the manner of Joseph Addison for the *Pennsylvania Chronicle*. Dr. Samuel Johnson said, "Whoever wishes to attain an English style, familiar but not coarse, and elegant but not ostentatious, must give his days and nights to the volumes of Addison." On both sides of the Atlantic, many young men of literary predilection improved their styles by perusing *The Spectator*. Two of those who benefited most lived in Pennsylvania—Benjamin Franklin and James Wilson.

In 1768 Wilson opened a law office in Reading and soon had a good practice among the German farmers. Larger opportunities in Carlisle, coupled with difficulties in his romantic relationship with a Miss Rachel Bird, caused him to move to that Scotch-Irish settlement. Within a few years, he was an attorney in nearly half the cases in the county court and had clients in seven other counties as well. Like many another Pennsylvanian on the way up, he signaled his ascent by buying a home, livestock, and a slave. And he completed the role of solid burgher by acquiring a wife, his sweetheart of former times, Rachel Bird.

Despite his demanding profession, he lectured on English literature for six years at the College of Philadelphia, exploring some of the most eloquent expressions of philosophy in his native tongue. But not all of his speculations were philosophical, not even his most zealous ones. As his law practice expanded into wider areas of Pennsylvania and even into New Jersey and New York, he poured his earnings into speculative land purchases and, caught up in the fever for big profits, borrowed heavily against future earnings.

In spite of his daring conduct of his personal finances, he rapidly acquired a reputation for wisdom in the public business.

In 1774 his reputation soared. Being named to head the Cumberland County Committee of Correspondence, which maintained communication with other communities concerned about the erosion of American liberties, was followed by election as a delegate to the first provincial conference of Pennsylvania and then to the First Continental Congress. This swift succession of events provided the impetus for him to revise a manuscript he had begun six years earlier and have it published in time to circulate among his colleagues in the Congress.

His treatise was called *Considerations on the Nature and Extent of the Legislative Authority of the British Parliament*. Behind this low-key, academic-style title lay an explosive proposal. Wilson argued that "all the different members of the British Empire are distinct states, independent of each other, but connected together under the same sovereign." He anticipated the concept of dominion status that reached full fruition in the British Commonwealth of Nations. Two other Americans, Thomas Jefferson and John Adams, inspired (like Wilson) by personal observation of provincial assemblies and study of Greek, Roman, and Enlightenment philosophers, published about the same time essays advocating dominion status.

Wilson was not only in a small vanguard. He was one of its most radical members. At the Pennsylvania provincial conference of January 1775, he argued as an extreme Whig that the Parliament in London had no authority over the American colonies. He insisted upon the corollary that an act of Parliament could be unconstitutional. He was one of the makers of the American doctrine of judicial review, which went back at least as far as 1652–1653, when Virginia's Colonel Thomas Johnson and his Eastern Shore of Virginia associates declared in the Northampton Protest that taxation without representation was illegal.[4] It had gained further force on November 23, 1765, when the twelve judges of Frederick County, Maryland, repudiated the Stamp Act, and in February 1766 when the justices of both Northampton and Accomack counties in the Old Dominion declared the Stamp Act illegal and therefore void.[5] When the Constitution of the United States proposed in 1787 was submitted to the states for ratification, many members of ratifying conventions anticipated judicial review. The practice was firmly established by the action of the Supreme Court under John Marshall in *Marbury v. Madison* in 1803.

Wilson was ready in 1775 for practical application of the theories he had so boldly expressed in his pamphlet the year before. At the provincial conference, he introduced a resolution declaring the Boston Port Act unconstitutional. Most of his colleagues were not ready to support such drastic action. But his pamphlet gained a wide audience, not only in America but in Britain as well.

As the conflict between England and her colonies grew more heated, Wilson was elected colonel of a Cumberland County battalion. But three days later his services were preempted for a job more in line with his training and proven skills. He was elected to the Second Continental Congress. His duties included meeting with western Indians in a fruitless attempt to cultivate friendly relations.

Allies, or even dependable neutral neighbors, were vital to colonists increasingly aspiring toward independent nationhood. In 1776 Wilson sought "to lead the public mind into the idea of Independence." To this end, he addressed an appeal to his fellow Americans in all the thirteen colonies. But he did not publish it. Sentiment for independence grew so rapidly that Wilson, so recently in the forefront, found himself in the rearguard. Indeed, on June 8 he joined with his old mentor in the law, John Dickinson, and others to obtain a three weeks' delay in action on the proposal. This conservative action was prompted not so much by any change of sentiment on Wilson's part as by his awareness that many of his constituents were not yet ready for a break with Britain.

Nevertheless, many Americans, especially in Pennsylvania, assumed that Wilson was backing away from the independence toward which he so recently had urged them. He was the target of so much vilification that twenty-two of his congressional colleagues came to his rescue, issuing a sympathetic exegesis of his position.

On July 2 Wilson voted with the majority for independence, but he was in a minority in the Pennsylvania delegation. Only two of the colony's seven delegates stood with him at this crucial moment. Some of his constituents had reviled him when he appeared to be wavering in his support of independence. Probably an equal number were now angry with him for rallying to the cause.

Dickinson was among the Pennsylvania delegates who declined to sign the Declaration. As revolutionary sentiment grew, many Americans scorned him for not taking a step at which they themselves had hesitated.

Wilson was a powerful figure in the Congress of the new nation. He was one of the most active members of the Board of War besides being chairman of the standing committee on appeals. Frustrated by the weakness of the new confederation, he called upon the states to yield revenue and taxing powers to the Congress. He also urged the states to relinquish to the national government their claims on the undeveloped western lands. He advocated proportional representation in Congress based on the free population. In the Congress itself, he called for votes by individuals rather than state units.

At the same time that he served as a leader of the Congress, Wilson waged a bitter fight against Pennsylvania's new constitution. Political power in Pennsylvania was divided between conservatives allied with the great landed interests and a radical party fueled by the aspirations and frustrations of frontiersmen and immigrants. The radicals removed Wilson from Congress in February 1777 but saw him returned in eighteen days when a successor could not be found. He continued to blast the new constitution as "the most detestable that ever was formed."

Once again, in September 1777, the radicals removed him from Congress. Feeling against him ran so high that he fled to Annapolis. Early in his career, he had fought against the forces of tradition that he believed held Pennsylvanians in thrall to an empire. Now he found his strongest enemies among those who called for wholesale destruction of traditional institutions. In his own life, he moved toward a new balance of heritage and experiment. Before the end of 1778, he made his home in Philadelphia and became a leader of the Republican Society, actually a political party opposed to the excesses of the radicals.

Alarmed by what he had seen of radicalism under the Pennsylvania faction led by George Bryan and still embarrassed by the earlier necessity for fleeing to Annapolis, he converted to conservatism with a speed that made some people suspect his motives. Philadelphia corporations replaced egalitarian frontiersmen as his clients. He would have starved if he had depended upon finding pioneer farmers in the metropolis. But, of course, the concerns and views of his clients influenced his own attitude. His social contacts were increasingly with the landed aristocracy and captains of commerce. He became still more closely allied with the status quo when he left the Presbyterian Church to become an Episcopalian.

Some former supporters could not understand when the erstwhile crusader for independence served as legal counsel for Loyalists associated with exploitative schemes. In 1779, influenced by high prices during a food shortage, popular discontent exploded into violence. Circulation of a handbill urging the militia to "drive off from the city all disaffected persons and those who supported them" incited armed men to seize some citizens especially conspicuous for profiteering and Loyalist sentiments. When they started after "those who supported them," Wilson, as one "who had always pled for such," was high on the list.

When his appeal for governmental protection brought no immediate response, he transformed his mansion into a fortress garrisoned by fellow speculators. He barricaded the doors through which elite guests had entered on happier days. Attacking militiamen arrived ahead of any protective force. Shots were exchanged and there were several casualties before cavalry arrived under the personal command of Joseph Reed, president of the Supreme Executive Council of Pennsylvania. The attackers withdrew.

At this time, the success of the American Revolution was in doubt. Both militiamen and Continental soldiers in many areas were reduced to a prisoner's diet of bread and water. The uniforms once so proudly worn were oftentimes barely distinguishable from the rags of long suffering beggars. Indeed, many soldiers had not had money in their hands nearly so recently as street-corner mendicants. Some had not been paid for months. In the camps, mutinous murmurings were more common than patriotic songs.

Hard-pressed to preserve the discipline of his troops when in their misery they learned of the huge profits made by speculators, Washington exploded, "I would to God that one of the most atrocious [speculators] of each state was hung in gibbets upon a gallows five times as high as the one prepared for Haman. No punishment in my opinion is too great for the man who can build his greatness upon his country's ruin."

Among many Americans, especially in Pennsylvania, Wilson's role as a patriot was overshadowed by his activities as a speculator. Doubtless, few would have wagered that, if the United States succeeded in establishing its independence, he would be among its leaders.

When some of his countrymen were fleeing to escape the British, Wilson went into hiding to evade the justice demanded by his fellow citizens. He returned a few days later to post a bond of ten thousand pounds. Later the legislature solved pressing problems for him, his allies, and his attackers by enacting an act of oblivion for those on both sides of what some called the "Battle of Fort Wilson." The violent acts of both provocateurs and attackers were officially forgotten.

Wilson's political rehabilitation proceeded faster than that of his old mentor John Dickinson. After all, Wilson had signed the Declaration of Independence and Dickinson had not. And Wilson had worked hard to carry out difficult assignments in the Second Continental Congress. When patriotic conservatives regained power in Pennsylvania in 1782, they wanted the advantage of his intelligence and industry. He was reelected to Congress.

Still, none of his contemporaries regarded him as a starry-eyed idealist. When he urged the founding of states in the western lands, a proposal consistent with his early advocacy of relinquishment of those lands by claimant states, he was accused of being concerned chiefly with advantages to large land companies. When he advocated a general revenue plan as a means of strengthening the Confederation, his colleagues followed him, but many suspected that his zeal was fired by a desire to have interest paid on the loans of the Bank of North America.

Business had become so important a part of Wilson's life that it was crowding out law except for a few particularly lucrative parts of his practice. He did find time to serve from 1779 to 1783 as France's advocate general in America in maritime and commercial matters and to be the great financier Robert Morris' counsel in establishment of the Bank of Pennsylvania.

While business interests caused Wilson to withdraw from the general practice of law, they did help to educate him in some of the legal problems of government in relation to commerce. And, even in pursuing the most pragmatic approaches to these problems, he was still a political philosopher. One product of his concentration on business problems in a broad context was the publication in 1785 of his *Considerations on the Power to Incorporate the Bank of North America*. It was in large part a sophisticated study of sovereignty, a question with which makers of a national constitution would have to deal.

Wilson had not forsaken politics, but he still had not made up his mind to be a statesman. In the three years since the official ending of the Revolution by the Treaty of Paris, he had shown a willingness to advance good government when it was consistent with self-interest, but there was little evidence of dedication to the commonweal. He had been impressive in defending Pennsylvania's claims against those of Connecticut before congressional commissioners; but even his friend Joseph Reed, who had led the cavalry to his rescue in the "Battle of Fort Wilson," tempered his praise with realism. Reed said that Wilson had "taken much pains, having the success of Pennsylvania much at heart, both on public and private account." Reed knew that his friend had poured a lot of cash into the acquisition of Connecticut land.

At the same time that Wilson was speculating in Connecticut lands, he was active westward in several land companies, serving as president of the Illinois and Wabash Company. With a partner, he purchased a manufacturing conglomerate including a rolling-and-slitting mill, gristmill, sour mill, and furnace. Within two years, he tried to borrow from Dutch businessmen a large sum for expansion of those facilities. Shortly afterwards, he offered the Dutch his services in a two-million-florin land speculation, promising to make his profession subservient to business interests. Apparently he already had. One of those reading law under his tutelage said that "as an instructor he was almost useless."

That Wilson had the intellectual capacity and the unflagging industry to achieve greatness no one could deny. But he had shown little disposition for the compromise that many deemed essential to ultimate success in democratic assemblies. And of the delegates elected to the Constitutional Convention of 1787, few brought so much baggage of complicated business interests and byzantine involvement in speculation.

32

HEROIC HYPOCHONDRIAC

THE SQUIRE OF Gunston Hall was wrestling with his conscience. Usually his conscience eventually won—with the help of exhorting neighbors. The bouts were fought whenever George Mason was urged to accept public office that would take him far from his five-thousand-acre plantation in Fairfax County, Virginia.[1]

Not that he was lazy, though his corpulent figure suggested a sedentary life. More appropriate symbols were the large, dark, bright inquisitive eyes, alertly aware of details but seeming to look beyond the surface.

Certainly his career belied any suggestion of lethargy. He personally managed his extensive farmlands without the aid of the chief overseer customarily employed by extensively propertied gentlemen. Beginning at the age of twenty-nine, he had served for twenty-five years as a trustee of the nearby town of Alexandria. He was still, and had been for some years, one of the gentleman justices of the Fairfax County Court—an important job but one that did not require his comprehensive knowledge of the law. From the age of twenty-three, he had been an Episcopal vestryman of his parish in an age when vestries administered relief to the poor and were charged with some governmental responsibilities. He had performed many services for his community, including the interesting but onerous task of supervising the building of Pohick Church.

He was an active, hardworking planter and public-spirited citizen. He had the initiative and the spare energy to become a member of the Ohio Company and to serve as its treasurer. He was interested in the land speculation that was the company's chief business, but he never succumbed to speculative fever as James Wilson had. Perhaps the most important result of Mason's participation in this business came when London regranted the Ohio Company's land to the Grand Company of Pennsylvania. Defending Virginia's claims to the Northwest Territory, he produced his first state paper on a constitutional theme.

Although Mason was a model of active citizenship in Fairfax County, he was notoriously reluctant to accept responsibilities that would keep him from home more than a day. His perpetually delicate health, manifested in a complex variety of symptoms, could account for some of his hesitation. Then, after the death of his wife in 1773, concern for his nine motherless children played a large part. Two years later, he cited "the duty I owe to a poor little helpless family of orphans to whom I must now act the part of Father and Mother both."

But, even in 1759 when his wife was living, considerable community pressure was required to get Mason to stand for election to the House of Burgesses. Sorely disappointed with the assembly's proceedings, he did not stand for a second term. But, without often leaving his home county, he did exert an increasingly strong influence on public events throughout Virginia and beyond. In 1765, at the prompting of his neighbors George Washington and George William Fairfax, he devised a legal means of circumventing some of the payments exacted by the Stamp Act. The following year, he wrote resolutions to form a nonimportation association as a protest against duties imposed under Britain's Townshend Acts. Introduced in the House of Burgesses by Washington when it reconvened on its own after dissolution by the royal governor, they were submitted to the Continental Congress, where they formed the basis for united action. Thus, the Virginia Association, Mason's brainchild, was the prototype of the Continental Association, which was the most important instrument of resistance forged by the First Continental Congress. In 1774, when Parliament passed the Boston Port Act to punish Massachusetts for the Boston Tea Party and other offensive acts, Mason wrote the Fairfax Resolves in protest against what he regarded as an unconstitutional exercise of power. These resolutions were adopted by the Fairfax County Court, the Virginia Convention, and the Continental Congress in Philadelphia.

Of course, in 1775, at the age of fifty, Mason lost another bout with his conscience and his neighbors, and was persuaded to serve in the Virginia Convention. Moreover, he was the second highest in the balloting when the convention elected an eleven-member Committee of Safety to govern the colony as an executive committee until a new constitution could be devised following the flight of the royal governor, Lord Dunmore. The only man to top Mason in the vote was Edmund Pendleton, whose acute intellect, prodigious diligence, and great powers of persuasion made him an excellent choice for chairman. Another distinguished member was Richard Bland, erudite in both history and law. Two others, Carter Braxton and Thomas Ludwell Lee, were future signers of the Declaration of Independence. Another, John Page, was a future governor.

One of Virginia's most respected citizens, George Washington, was unavailable for civilian office. He was in Massachusetts trying to weld a disciplined Continental Army out of disparate elements whose principal common characteristic was individualism.

In a letter in the autumn of the year, Mason gave Washington his estimate of the convention's proceedings. Some observers at the time, and many historians since, have praised the perspicacity of the men who began the task of transforming a colony into a commonwealth. But Mason saw things differently. "I never was in so disagreeable a situation," he wrote,

and almost despaired of a cause which I saw so ill-conducted. . . . Mere vexation and disgust threw me into such an ill state of health, that before the Convention rose, I was sometimes near fainting in the House. . . . However, after some weeks the babblers were pretty well silenced, a few weighty members began to take the lead, several wholesome regulations were made.

Mason had to feel better about the work of the 1776 convention, if only because he himself took the lead in so much of it. The Virginians voted unanimously to declare their colony an independent state, and to instruct their delegates in the Continental Congress

to propose to that respectable body to declare the United Colonies free and independent States, absolved from all allegiance to, or dependence upon, the Crown or Parliament of Great Britain; and that they give the assent of this colony . . . to whatever measures may be thought proper and necessary by the Congress for forming foreign alliances and a confederation.

This was a bold step, one which no other former colony dared to take. The North Carolina convention had instructed its delegates to the Continental Congress to support a resolution for independence if one should be offered in Philadelphia, but did not empower them to initiate one.

The Virginia resolutions for independence provided also "that a committee be appointed to prepare a Declaration of Rights, and such a plan of government as will be most likely to maintain peace and order in this colony, and secure substantial and equal liberty to the people." Mason was appointed to this committee, and through his erudition, eloquence, and firm convictions soon became more influential than its chairman or any other member. Two important documents were produced as a result of this assignment—the Virginia Declaration of Rights and the Constitution of Virginia. Mason wrote the first and was the principal author of the second.

He presented his draft of a Declaration of Rights just ten days after being appointed to the committee. But he had dedicated the greater part of a lifetime to its preparation. His studies in Greek, Roman, and British history; his concentration on the laws of England and Virginia; his absorption of the philosophies of Montesquieu, Francis Hutcheson, and John Locke—these things, together with his thoughtful participation in government at various levels over several decades, had prepared him to produce one of the great state papers of world history. His eloquence contributed as much as his erudition to making it memorable.

An eminent twentieth-century legal scholar, Dean Roscoe Pound of the Harvard Law School, said:

The Virginia Bill of Rights of 1776 is the first and, indeed, is the model of a long line of politico-legal documents that have become the staple of American constitutional law. . . . Moreover, in actual application in the courts, the Bills of Rights, both in the Federal and in the State constitutions, are the most frequently invoked and constantly applied provisions of those instruments. Nor has the Virginia Bill of Rights been conspicuous only as a model. With all allowance for the historical documents that went before it, it must be pronounced a great creative achievement.[2]

Historian George Bancroft aptly summarized the uniqueness of Mason's contribution:

> Other colonies had framed bills of rights in reference to their relations with Britain; Virginia moved from charters and customs to primal principles, from the altercation about facts to the contemplation of immutable truth. She summoned the eternal laws of man's being to protest against all tyranny. The English petition of rights in 1688 was historic and retrospective; the Virginia declaration came out of the heart of nature, and announced governing principles for all peoples in all time. It was the voice of reason going forth to speak a new political world into being.[3]

The voice was a clear and mellifluous one. It declared "all men are by nature equally free and independent, and have certain inherent rights." It said that "all [political] power is vested in, and consequently derived from, the people," and that "government is, or ought to be, instituted for the common benefit, protection, and security of the people." Among the rights of humankind set forth was "the enjoyment of life and liberty, with the means of acquiring and possessing property, and pursuing and obtaining happiness and safety."

Besides voicing noble principles, the Virginia Declaration of Rights spelled out provisions necessary for their implementation. It emphasized such safeguards of freedom as an independent judiciary, free and regular elections, trial by jury, and a free press. It rejected general warrants, excessive bail, cruel and unusual punishments, hereditary office, and taxation without representation.

Mason was consciously writing for other countries and generations as well as his own. His colleagues shared his awareness. Edmund Randolph, a fellow delegate from Virginia, said later that the responsible committee had undertaken the task so that "a perpetual standard should be erected, around which the people might rally, and . . . be forever admonished to be watchful, firm, and virtuous" in "all the revolutions of time, human opinion, and government."[4]

Some of the phrases echo in the Declaration of Independence, the Constitution of the United States, Lincoln's "Gettysburg Address," Franklin D. Roosevelt's "Four Freedoms," and the Atlantic Charter subscribed to by President Roosevelt and Prime Minister Churchill. Some of Mason's phrases were themselves echoes of statements on liberty drawn from many societies whose creativity had enriched Western civilization. His own extraordinary creativity was revealed in the bold adventuring he brought to a reconsideration of the heritage that nourished him intellectually and spiritually. For this corpulent, soft-voiced man, so reluctant to leave home, so afflicted with a multitude of illnesses physical and perhaps even hypochondriacal, was in truth a bold sailor on uncharted oceans when the great tide shifted and the warring winds rose to a howling gale.

After this stormy voyage, Mason went into port again, pleading the needs of his family, augmenting with personal counsel to various leaders the brave words that he had launched on the seas of seventy-six. But in 1780 he married again and, after an interval, increased his involvement in public affairs. In March 1785 he and Madison were influential members of the Virginia delegation that met with Maryland commissioners at Alexandria to discuss navigation problems concerning the Potomac River and Chesapeake Bay and then adjourned to Mount Vernon for further discussions with George Washington as their host. The conferees went so far as to draft an agreement recommending to their legislators uniform commercial regulations and imposts, annual conferences on common commercial problems, and even a uniform currency. Of course, none of this activity necessitated Mason's leaving Fairfax County.

But the Mount Vernon Conference was a catalyst that so accelerated the movement toward interstate unity that Mason was subjected to unaccustomed pressures. Maryland and Virginia agreed to invite Pennsylvania and Delaware, who also had a strong interest in the Chesapeake Bay, to a future conference. At Madison's instigation, Virginia's legislature invited all the states to send delegates to a commercial conference at Annapolis in 1786. Mason, who was again a burgess, was named to the Virginia delegation. He agonized and in the end did not go.

Inadequate attendance at the Annapolis Convention caused the participants to curtail their discussions. But in a statement drafted by Alexander Hamilton, those present asked the states to send delegates to a convention at Philadelphia in 1787. They said that this meeting should be to "discuss all things necessary to render the constitution of the Federal Government adequate to the exigencies of the Union." In a more restrained mood, the Continental Congress found "expedient" a convention "for the sole and express purpose of revising the Articles of Confederation and reporting to Congress and the several legislatures such alterations and revisions."

Many men, inside the Congress as well as out, perceived that the loose government by committee under the Articles of Confederation was inadequate for peacetime crises, which did not evoke the patriotic responses of wartime.

Virginians wished to send to the 1787 Convention their own great constitutionalist. But the man who had balked at going to Annapolis dreaded even more a journey to more distant Philadelphia for a more attenuated session. So he sat amid the comforts of family in the elegant interior of Gunston Hall and wrestled with his conscience. He admitted to himself and a few friends his fears that, without stricter regulation of commerce, the states were headed for economic destruction. The new nation could not remain free either in a state of economic chaos or of economic dependency.

Though he had a strong sentimental allegiance to states' rights, Mason was convinced that a strong central government was essential to survival.

His head was crammed with ideas of what should be done. He had no right to stay away from Philadelphia. He would attend and make his ideas known. He greatly admired oratory and forceful speech. Captured by Patrick Henry's conversational gifts as well as oratorical flair, he thought him perhaps "the first man on the continent." How persuasive such talents could be! But Mason knew that his own great skill with a pen was not matched by vocal eloquence. Nevertheless, he did have knowledge, and it must be imparted. He still felt faint whenever he rose to address an assembly. But however light-headed he might feel and however much his feet might pain him, he would rise as many times as necessary to place his views before the Constitutional Convention in the great northern metropolis. He would enter the field as an already wounded soldier, but he would be a fighting one.

33

THE SUN ON THE PRESIDENT'S CHAIR

THOMAS JEFFERSON and James Madison were two best friends who seldom disagreed vehemently about anything. But they differed sharply over a vital matter in 1787. So great was their difference of opinion that Madison, although he had sought Jefferson's advice before the meeting in Philadelphia and continued to seek it throughout the Convention, must have been thankful that his friend's duties in Paris frustrated his desire to be part of the conclave.

Madison was one of those who persuaded the conference that their deliberations should be behind closed doors with nothing divulged to outsiders except by general consent. This policy, he argued, would remove an impediment to free discussion and would "save both the convention and the community from a thousand erroneous and perhaps mischievous reports." Jefferson's estimate of the decision was vociferous. Irving Brant summarized it in one word: "abominable."[1] Madison was not convinced. Long afterward he told historian Jared Sparks, a future president of Harvard, that if the debates had been made public, the delegates would have failed to produce a constitution.

Another circumstance not generally considered favorable to the efficient performance of deliberative bodies contributed to the ultimate effectiveness of the Philadelphia conclave. Though they were scheduled to convene on May 14, the only delegates present on that day were from Virginia and Pennsylvania. Only after eleven days had the delegations of five other states joined them to form the prescribed quorum. As we know, Madison, the best prepared of all the participants, had arrived eleven days ahead of time. He had had time to plant some ideas among the Pennsylvanians, and then among other delegates as they arrived. He had had the opportunity to answer individually in friendly conversation some of their objections or troubled questions. His influence was magnified by the specificity and certainty with which he urged his ideas upon those whose theories were still amorphous.

Of course, there was general agreement that the Articles of Confederation, under which the thirteen states had maintained a central government since

March 1, 1781, were inadequate. The delegates' presence in Philadelphia was testimony to that fact. New Hampshire and Rhode Island, the only states that preferred to continue under the unreformed Articles, had signaled their attitude by failing to name delegates even by the May 14 deadline for convening. New Hampshire relented in time to send delegates straggling in on July 23, but Rhode Island remained "adamant for drift."[2]

The official designation of the government, "The United States in Congress Assembled," pointed to a central weakness. In place of a true executive, the Confederation had a legislature functioning as a huge supervisory committee. This Congress was unicameral, which of course facilitated executive decisions more than if agreement between two houses had been required for action. But many legislative purposes would have been served better by a bicameral Congress, one chamber for stability and another for change.

Apart from these considerations, the Congress often was paralyzed by the requirement of nine affirmative state votes for many actions and seven for the rest. For all practical purposes, the absence or abstention of four, or in some cases six, states could veto a measure favored by a majority of the states. Each state delegation's vote was cast as a unit. As each delegation was appointed by the legislature of its state, and each delegate could be recalled by the body that appointed him, the federal government was an ungainly puppet whose tangled strings were pulled by the legislatures of thirteen states.

As a delegate from Virginia, the most populous of the thirteen, Madison was acutely aware of another flaw in representation. Balloting by units gave equal representation to each state. Tiny Delaware's vote equaled that of the Old Dominion, sixteen times larger.

The great curse of the Confederation was its impotence. It had no power to tax people or corporations directly. It had to requisition the states for funds for operation, and frequently they did not comply. It had no power to regulate commerce; this lack not only complicated relations between the states but also made it difficult to obtain commercial treaties with foreign nations. Though each state had its own system of courts, the Confederation itself had no judiciary except in the maritime sphere. There was nothing wrong with the provision that all powers were retained by the states unless expressly delegated to the Confederation, except for the fact that there was no procedure for enforcing the expressly delegated powers. Why, one might well ask, had the states tolerated for six years a system so inefficient? Any amendment required unanimous consent.

In any event, Madison was convinced that the time for amendment was past. A loose organization of states, however inefficient, might in a war for independence command sufficient loyalty to get by. It could not long survive amid the rivalries and discords of peace. Madison believed that the Convention must create a constitution providing for a strong central government and submit the document to the states for ratification.

The titular head of the Virginia delegation was Governor Edmund Randolph. The governor believed that the Confederation could be transformed sufficiently by amendment of the Articles. This view gave Madison serious concern not only because Randolph's influence was needed in the Convention in support of a new government but also because it would be important in the subsequent struggle for ratification in Virginia. Madison despaired of taking Virginia farther along the road to federalism than Randolph was willing to go.

Randolph could be a most engaging advocate.[3] Darkly handsome, his aquiline profile was a reminder of the strain from Powhatan and Pocahontas that mingled in him with the bloodlines of English kings. Now thirty-six years old, he had an easy assurance, the result both of his personal accomplishments from an early age and his membership in one of Virginia's most powerful clans. In 1776, at the age of twenty-five, he had helped to found the new Commonwealth of Virginia and had become its attorney general, occupying the same office that his grandfather, uncle, and father had held under the colonial regime. His father, a Loyalist to the core, had returned to England when revolution was imminent. Edmund's Uncle Peyton became the first president of the Continental Congress, and Edmund himself became an aide-de-camp to Washington, a leader of the Virginia Convention of 1776, and a member of the Continental Congress.

A graduate of the College of William and Mary, well versed in the classics and widely read, he wrote and spoke in a style at once graceful and lively. His intellectual attainments helped his political advancement in a society, both in Virginia and in the broader context of American leadership, that highly valued such accomplishments.

Madison was determined to change Randolph's mind, to convince him that the Articles of Confederation, even if much amended, would still be a thing of patches and tatters. He wanted to convert the governor to the extent that he would become an earnest advocate of a strong central government, bringing to the cause both the weight of his office as chief executive of the most populous American state and his own personal persuasiveness as a polished speaker and attractive personality.

After the Convention had adjourned, Randolph said that conversation with the most knowledgeable delegates had convinced him "that the Confederation was destitute of every energy which a Constitution of the United States ought to possess." Chief among those conferees was Madison. Another was Washington, Randolph's former chief, who had learned the Confederation's weaknesses the hard way when he commanded its armies. Others were colleagues whose aid Madison had enlisted, or whose convictions he had boosted.

Randolph presented what was known from the first as the Virginia Plan. He enumerated the weaknesses of the Confederation and suggested that, if the next step was not toward centralization, it would be toward anarchy. He did not blame the framers of the Articles for the paper money crisis, the failed treaties, and the revolt in Massachusetts. He conceded that, given "the jealousy of the states with regard to their sovereignty" at the time of the Confederation's inception, "perhaps nothing better could be obtained."

The actual plan that he presented in the form of fifteen resolutions was largely Madison's work. Madison is not known ever to have admitted authorship, but the parallelism, and sometimes the identity, of constituent statements with his own notes reveals his hand. One rather vague statement designed to advocate a central government without calling it one is the only serious departure from Madison's words and thoughts.

The fifteen resolutions of the Virginia Plan, as was soon noted, could be organized into four groups. The first three dealt respectively with legislative, executive, and judicial powers; the fourth, with interrelationship of the three.

The Virginia Plan proposed a bicameral national legislature in the tradition of England, a system familiar to Virginia since the inauguration in 1619 on its soil of the first legislative assembly in the New World. Other colonies had followed the same pattern. Under the Virginia Plan, representation in each chamber would be proportional to state population. The lower house would be elected directly by the people. Individual state legislatures would nominate candidates from whom the national lower house would elect members of the national upper chamber.

The executive for the national government would be chosen by the national legislature.

A national judicial system would be topped by a supreme court.

The proposed governmental organization was one of checks and balances, made more complicated by a fourth provision. A council of revision would have the power to veto acts of the national legislature. This council would consist of the executive and several members of the judiciary.

Following Randolph's presentation, young Charles Pinckney of South Carolina rose to present an imitative, but less well organized, plan. Madison's discussions of the ideas that he expressed in the Virginia Plan had been so full, and had included so many of his colleagues, that many of his thoughts and phrases found their way into other people's arguments. He was much more concerned with circulation than with attribution.

Both the Virginia Plan and Pinckney's proposals were referred to the Committee of the Whole, but no action was taken on the South Carolina presentation. The Virginia Plan, on the other hand, was discussed seriatim on May 30. Upon consideration of the first clause, the one saying that "the Articles of Confederation ought to be so corrected and enlarged as to accomplish the objects proposed by their institution," portly, peg-legged Gouverneur Morris of Pennsylvania rose to protest that it would not suffice. This was the vague statement substituted for Madison's original first clause in order to placate Randolph. The temporizing governor had been willing to propose a strong central government only if he could introduce the plan as an alteration of the Articles.

Morris was an outspoken man whose stately style was enlivened with barbed witticisms. Despite his acerbic comments, he had a powerful personal charm that melted hostility. Underneath the hard crust was a humanitarian. Earlier, as a resident of New York and member of its constitutional convention, he had fought hard to abolish slavery but had been defeated by prosperous New Yorkers unwilling to part with the institution. He did secure a provision for religious toleration. Morris distrusted democracy but ardently supported American independence and believed that a strong central government was essential to preservation of the nation. He was right when he insisted that the first clause of the Virginia Plan was an inappropriate introduction to any plan for a strong central government.

Randolph conceded the point immediately and substituted a resolution "that a *national* government ought to be established, consisting of a *supreme* legislative, executive, and judiciary." Almost surely these were the words originally proposed by Madison.

Randolph had rightly surmised that such bold words would alarm many delegates. Some questioned whether the Convention was empowered to go beyond amendment and actually abolish the Articles. Others asked whether proponents of the Virginia Plan contemplated abolition of the states themselves. Randolph replied that such was not their intention; the states would continue to exist but would have to yield when in conflict with a national government exercising powers specifically granted to it.

Morris insisted that the Articles of Confederation, "a mere compact resting on the good faith of the parties," was insufficient to carry out the functions for which a federal government had been created. The creation of a truly supreme national government, he said, was legally permissible because it provided the only means of fulfilling the responsibilities assigned to the existing government. Failure to act in this regard would be to invite anarchy, and anarchy inevitably prepared the way for a tyrant. "We had better take a supreme government now," he said, "than a despot twenty years hence—for come he must."

Morris would speak many times throughout the Convention, always riveting attention by his quick intelligence, reservoir of knowledge, verbal skills, and commanding presence. Sometimes his stands would hinder the purposes of Madison and his allies. At other times, as now, they would bolster the Virginian's efforts.

Eight state delegations were present to vote on the resolution for a supreme national government, with each delegation voting as a unit on a motion to delete the words "national" and "supreme" and officially found the new government on "the design of the states in forming the convention." The vote was four to four. If need be, Madison was prepared to argue that, even with the weakened introduction, a strong government could still be created. But certainly the tone set by such deletions would not be favorable to the development of a supreme government.

The tie was broken by one whom hardly anyone would have expected to do such a thing. Robert Yates of New York was part of the majority within his delegation that caused that state to be aligned with those who favored the eviscerating deletions. At first, Yates had been rather contemptuous of Madison and had had trouble getting his name straight. Then, as he noted the Virginian's persuasive powers in conversation and even on the convention floor, he began to fear his influence. Yates decided to vote for rejection of the deletions, in hope that the stronger form of the resolution would prove unpalatable to some who now favored significant strengthening of the central government.

But Yates' scheme backfired. The division within the New York delegation was sufficient to permit adoption of the strong resolution. Yates fired increasingly futile salvos as the Convention progressed until finally, long before adjournment, he picked up his grapeshot and left.

Presided over by George Washington, the most respected American of his generation, and including such learned luminaries as Madison, George Mason, Alexander Hamilton, Gouverneur Morris, James Wilson, and Benjamin Franklin, the Convention was one of history's select gatherings. Franklin, as he said, had lived all his life in capitals—Boston, Philadelphia, London, and Paris. He had met with sharp intellects and powerful personages on two continents. But he pronounced the group now convened in Philadelphia "the most august and respectable assembly" he "ever was in."

The perspective of time tends to ratify his estimate. But very little time was required to prove incorrect his supposition that the conferees would proceed easily in great unanimity. Madison's industry and ingenuity had created an impression of unity that exceeded the reality.

There were small-state delegates to whom the distant despot envisioned by Morris in the absence of a strong central government was not nearly as imminent and palpable a threat as the domination of the large states if such a supreme authority were created. They were alarmed by the Virginia Plan's provision for proportional representation in both houses of Congress according to the free population. An alternative Virginia proposal to apportion representation according to the volume of taxes paid to the national government brought no comfort. Either method would mean domination by the large states.

On June 15, William Paterson, New Jersey's forty-two-year-old attorney general, offered a plan on behalf of the small states. The New Jersey Plan was born chiefly out of small-state frustration with the Virginia proposal for representation according to population, but it included other provisions designed to close the power gap. While it would in effect continue the old Confederation, it would strengthen it by giving it the authority to tax and to regulate foreign and interstate commerce. United States treaties and acts of Congress would prevail over state statutes. Like the Virginia Plan, the New Jersey one would empower the national legislature to elect the executive, but the executive would specifically be plural and would not exercise any portion of veto power. The plan offered by Paterson, like that presented by Randolph, included a Supreme Court. The most controversial of the New Jersey resolutions called for a one-house national legislature with equal representation for each state regardless of population.

For three days, the Convention debated whether to strengthen the Articles of Confederation by revision or to form a new government. In the end, they voted seven states to three to attempt construction of a truly national government along the general lines of the Virginia Plan. The victory was an important one for Madison and his allies, but virtually all delegates realized that compromise between the two plans would be necessary to win strong support from the Convention. Even though the government outlined by the Convention would be consistent with the major purposes of the resolutions prepared by Madison and presented by Randolph, there would have to be important concessions to the small states.

Like Madison, Paterson was unimpressive in physical appearance. He was short and sharp-nosed in a way that, to unfriendly observers, suggested a genteel rodent. Beyond the borders of his own state, his reputation was small, but it gained quickly from his able performance at the Convention. Next year he would be elected a United States senator. Later he would serve as governor, and eventually he would be named by George Washington to the United States Supreme Court. A city in New Jersey would perpetuate his honored name.

Luther Martin, the "Maryland Bulldog," made a snarling, snapping attack on the Virginia Plan. A tough, unrelenting attorney, for three days he treated the Convention to a pyrotechnic show of exploding temper. Little versed in the Enlightenment philosophy familiar to many fellow delegates and sometimes lapsing from their standards of grammar, he was nevertheless a shrewd master of rough-and-tumble combat. He insisted that state equality was "essential to the federal idea" and that the preservation of the states was the national government's only excuse for being.

Madison replied with cool logic that the small states need not fear consistent domination by a bloc of large states; the diverse and sometimes conflicting economic interests of the giants would prevent them from becoming a monolithic power.

Many delegates were far more heated in debate than Madison. Disturbed by the threat of growing acrimony, Franklin proposed that each session be opened by a prayer by a clergyman. Thirty-two-year-old Alexander Hamilton, impatient and more than a little arrogant, sarcastically told the elder statesman that the Convention was under no "necessity of calling in foreign aid."

Whatever his internal stress, Franklin remained outwardly calm. He saw his dream of a unicameral legislature go glimmering and soon perceived that he had hoped vainly for a national government whose officers served without pay, but he supported Madison's efforts to convince the Convention that a central government's chief strength would lie in reliance on the people. With his long-practiced diplomacy, he averted or ameliorated any conflicts.

Hamilton demanded a supreme government of such sweeping powers that he may have made Madison's recommendations seem far less drastic than they otherwise would have. For his part, Madison made his views more acceptable when he became as concerned about democracy as about stability and efficient operation. Some other delegates changed even more rapidly. New York's Rufus King, an eloquent master of parliamentary tactics, was converted from advocacy of a weak federalism to active support of a strong central government.

Even though the Convention voted on June 19 to accept the goal of a central government as set forth in the Virginia Plan, the effort still could have foundered on the question of equal versus proportional representation. Several people deserve major credit for preventing this disaster. James Wilson was Madison's strongest ally. Both were scholars of the law and of history who could interpret the heritage of various lands and eras in terms of personal political experience. Both were completely committed to the necessity for a strong central government even if it meant acceptance of unpalatable details. Both were aware of the vulnerability, as well as the strengths, of democracy and recognized the need for built-in safeguards against the tyranny of the majority.

By no means were all the great talents on the side that ultimately triumphed. Hamilton's private writings reveal that he not only wanted a much stronger central government than most delegates would accept but that there also was a monarchist cast to his concept of the executive. In contrast, Randolph and Mason shared the distrust of executive power that haunted many Americans as a result of their experience under royal governors. Two South Carolina cousins, General Charles Cotesworth Pinckney and the much younger Charles Pinckney, were not monarchists, but their concept of a national legislature squinted toward England's House of Lords, preferably in the days before an assertive Commons. They were products of the strong aristocratic tradition of South Carolina, where apparently there was not as much communication between great planters and small as in Virginia. The general, though, did advocate the abolition of religious tests for public office, a policy that his state would not accept for many decades. Young Charles was celebrated for varied learning. He so valued his reputation for precocity that he pretended to be younger than his thirty years. He also prepared a journal of proceedings at the Convention that for a long time caused many persons, including some historians, to assume that he had determined the course of events in Philadelphia.

Though Gouverneur Morris was more autocratic than democratic, his cynical wit penetrated many weaknesses in the arguments of those who favored democracy and caused them to act from a more solid philosophical foundation.

As one who had gone within a single session from weak federalism to strong centralism, Rufus King had a unique ability to persuade wavering delegates at some junctures. His learning and eloquence amplified this ability. He was one of the briefest speakers, and one of the most effective. With one pointed observation, he could puncture the argument that another delegate had spent an hour inflating.

Paterson was nominally the leader of the small-state bloc. The resolutions he had presented on behalf of the small states were usually known as the New Jersey Plan, but some called it the Paterson Plan. Concentrating almost exclusively on the issue of legislative representation, he preserved a force that a less sagacious leader would have dissipated in pursuit of multiple objectives.

But the master strategist of the small states was not Paterson, nor was he even a New Jerseyman. He was a dark-suited, solemn-faced, lantern-jawed Connecticut man who seemed prepared to conduct the obsequies if the Virginia Plan was buried. Roger Sherman, mayor of New Haven, was then sixty-six, an advanced age for his generation. Despite the time that he gave to a local office, his reputation was national. In 1776 he had served on the committee to frame the Declaration of Independence and had signed the document. He had been a member of the committee that drafted the Articles of Confederation. He enjoyed seniority in the Continental Congress. Educated briefly in a small country school, he had learned the cobbler's trade from his father and then improved his lot by becoming a surveyor and, after a spell of reading law, an attorney.

The paucity of his formal education had not kept him from becoming treasurer of Yale. He brought to leadership of the small states great shrewdness, infinite patience, and a thoroughly realistic sense of what could and could not be accomplished.

Sherman on June 11 advocated what came to be known as the Connecticut Compromise, a proposal that representation in the lower chamber be based on population, while in the upper each state would have one vote. A grand committee appointed July 2, and including members from all the states, rejected the plan, but Sherman did not give up. Three days later, the committee reversed its stand. The proposal accepted by the committee had been amended in several significant ways. The lower house would consist of one representative for each forty thousand inhabitants, with five slaves counted as three people. All states would be equally represented in the upper house, but each would not necessarily be restricted to a single vote. Each state could have two voting senators. The fact that a large part of the slave population would not be counted was somewhat reassuring to small-state delegates who dreaded the prospect of an increasing slave population in the lower South. Some large-state delegates were correspondingly reassured when Franklin moved that all money bills should originate in the lower chamber, with the upper empowered to accept or reject them but without alteration.

Madison assailed this last provision, arguing that it was not a significant concession to the large states but could produce stultifying conflicts between the two houses. He hinted that the large states might form their own union, realizing that economic pressures and other forces eventually would compel the small states to join.

Gouverneur Morris, impatient with temporizing, deplored a policy of weakening the federal government through concessions to small states. "This country must be united," he said. "If persuasion does not unite it, the sword will . . . and the gallows and halter will finish the work of the sword. . . . State attachments and state importance have been the bane of this country. We cannot annihilate; but we may perhaps take out the teeth of the serpents."

In July, Washington wrote to Hamilton, who had absented himself for a while from the Convention, "In a word, I *almost* despair of seeing a favorable issue to the proceedings of the convention, and do therefore repent having had any agency in the business. The men who oppose a strong and energetic government are, in my opinion, narrow-minded politicians, or are under the influence of local views."

Just when the Convention seemed almost hopeless even to its stouthearted chairman, forces quietly at work turned the tide. Common sense dictated the necessity of a solution, and far-ranging intellects devised the means. On July 12 the Convention accepted the committee's proposal for representation in the lower house. Four days later, it accepted the proposal for equal representation of all states in the upper house. Now that the large states were confident of power in one chamber and the small states of strength in another, events moved rapidly. The Convention drafted twenty-three "fundamental resolutions" embodying what it believed should be included in the projected constitution.

There was one threatening moment when someone moved to appoint a committee to draft a constitution and General Pinckney warned that he would vote "Nay" unless there was assurance that the new government would not emancipate slaves and would not tax exports. Probably as a sop to the general and fellow South Carolinians, John Rutledge, a former governor of South Carolina, was appointed to a committee to draft the constitution and was elected its chairman. He was an able man and had the reputation of an honorable one, but his agenda was feudal. Not only was he an ardent defender of slavery, but he had urged that legislative representation be according to recognized social classes and that high property qualifications be set for officeholders.

Serving on Rutledge's committee were Randolph, Nathaniel Gorham of Massachusetts, Oliver Ellsworth of Connecticut, and James Wilson, the most influential of all. Wilson's knowledge and abilities were so great, and his views and Madison's had come so close together, that his membership on the committee was a greater guarantee of preservation of the spirit of the Virginia Plan than the presence of Randolph, who had introduced it.

The committee drafted a constitution and submitted it to the Convention on August 6. Debate continued until September 10. In August the Convention decided on two-year terms for members of the House of Representatives, as the lower chamber was called, and six-year terms for senators. In the same month, they voted to empower Congress to regulate foreign and interstate commerce. They also prohibited bills of attainder. Attainder was a practice by which a government not only could deprive a convicted criminal of his property but, claiming that his blood was attainted, could also deprive his descendants of their legacies. Often in English history, bills of attainder had been used against those convicted of political offenses. A bill of attainder was a legislative act for attainting a person without judicial trial. On the same day that the Convention prohibited bills of attainder, it also prohibited ex post facto laws.

In September the Convention settled upon a term of four years for the president of the United States. Other proposals had included a seven-year term and even (this was favored by Hamilton) presidency for life.

The Convention appointed a Committee on Style and Arrangement to prepare a final draft of the Constitution. Dr. William Johnson of Connecticut, not one of the great leaders of the Convention but a delegate whose verbal precision had been praised, was chairman. The other members—Madison, Hamilton, King, and Gouverneur Morris—were both leaders and word masters.

Madison, so often plagued by frail health, had been ill since the beginning of the last week in August and had little time and energy for this final committee work, but he managed to drag himself to every regular session of the Convention. Anyway he already had done more than anyone else to shape the new Constitution. On September 10, Morris was asked to draft the document. Though he was unenthusiastic about some of the provisions agreed upon, he believed passionately in the general spirit of the Constitution. Working with great ability and surprising speed, he completed his task within two days. Madison, justly called the Father of the Constitution, wrote forty-three years later,

"The finish given to the style and arrangement of the Constitution fairly belongs to the pen of Mr. Morris. . . . A better choice could not have been made."

Morris' spirit typified that of most of the delegates. Even when frustrated in some of their wishes for the new government, they continued to work on the structure. In the course of the long labors and constant arguments from May 25 to September 17, 1787, only thirteen members had abandoned the Convention. Hamilton had left in disgust but had returned for the last arguments and to help polish the document. Though dissatisfied with many aspects of the new Constitution, he was prepared to work hard for ratification in the hope that it would hold the states together until succeeded by a government more to his liking.

Elbridge Gerry of Massachusetts refused to sign the Constitution, but his reluctance had been consistent from the first. More disturbing was the unwillingness of Mason and Randolph. Mason was one of America's great geniuses and one of its most profound scholars of constitutional law. Psychologically a blow to the cause of ratification was the refusal by Randolph, the man who had introduced the Virginia Plan, which was the principal basis for the Constitution. And if any of the states did not ratify the Constitution, the accomplishments of the Convention would be wasted.

But now friends of the proposed government had far more reason for celebration than for apprehension. When the rambling document of twenty-three articles sent from the floor to the Committee on Style and Arrangement returned to the Convention, it had been transformed by Morris into a coherent masterpiece of only seven articles. Most delegates were eager to conclude the business.

Even so, they made a last effort toward complete unanimity of those still attending. Madison lent his powerful endorsement to Mason's demand that the Constitution contain a warning against standing armies. Trying to gain Randolph's signature, the Convention amended the provision for one representative in the lower house for every forty thousand persons to one for every thirty thousand. Washington, who as chairman had refrained from making any speeches in the Convention, intervened to speak in support of the motion. Still both Mason and Randolph said that regretfully they could not go along.

The Convention was not so considerate about appeasing Mason and Randolph's call for a bill of rights and Charles Pinckney and Gerry's demand for a guarantee of freedom of the press. Pinckney and Gerry's request was largely ignored. Mason and Randolph's proposal for a bill of rights was put to a vote and turned down by every state. Probably most delegates were unaware that the issue was vital to Mason. Madison said later that, except for the fatigue and impatience of the concluding hours, the Convention probably would have been more attentive to satisfying Mason. With grave anxiety, Madison recorded Mason's declaration that "he would sooner chop off his right hand than put it to the Constitution as it now stands." If the author of Virginia's great Bill of Rights had called earlier for a national equivalent, the proposal might have had smooth sailing.

With Mason and Randolph unable to accept the new Constitution, Madison worried about the chances of ratification in his own State of Virginia. The fact that Virginia's two most powerful orators, Patrick Henry and Richard Henry Lee, had even refused to participate in the Convention increased his anxiety.

But doubts retreated momentarily when George Washington signed the new Constitution and more than half a hundred delegates filed past to add their signatures.

On the last page of the notes that he so faithfully kept of the Convention proceedings, Madison preserved for posterity a historic moment in the life of the Constitution:

> Whilst the last members were signing it, Dr. Franklin looking toward the President's chair, at the back of which a rising sun happened to be painted, observed to a few members near him that painters had found it difficult to distinguish in their art a rising from a setting sun. I have, said he, often and often in the course of the session, and the vicissitudes of my hopes and fears as to its issue, looked at that behind the President without being able to tell whether it was rising or setting; but now at length I have the happiness to know that it is a rising and not a setting sun.

34

"THE MOST REMARKABLE WORK"

WHEN THE CONSTITUTION of the United States was a century old, William Ewart Gladstone, the great British student of political philosophy and master of practical politics, wrote: "I have always regarded that Constitution as the most remarkable work known to me in modern times to have been produced by the human intellect, at a single stroke . . . in its application to political affairs."[1]

The accomplishments of the Convention of 1787 make that year not only a pivotal one in the story of America but also one of the high points in human history. It is one of the world's best examples of fruitful compromise. It is cited also as one of the most impressive examples of the collective application of creative energy.

Yet even this creativity was exceeded by that shown in subsequent months as Americans argued over ratification and proposed ingenious solutions. It was in some ways equaled by the Northwest Ordinance, which the government of the Articles of Confederation brought forth in the last days like a dying apple tree producing its richest harvest. And, of course, the leaders of the 1787 Convention and their associates, and a younger generation shifting their weight in the wings while their elders still occupied center stage, all would prove their resourcefulness in an outpouring of energy for nearly four decades. Their bold and imaginative actions in the halls of Congress, the office of the president, and the chambers of justice would command the attention of three continents in their own time. Eventually, these actions would be argued about, and often imitated, in every part of the civilized world.

The Northwest Ordinance was by far the most important achievement of government under the Articles of Confederation. The ordinance was adopted by the Congress on July 13, 1787, at the very time that the Constitutional Convention was debating the form of a government to replace the one under which the congressmen served. In fact, passage came only three days before agreement on the Connecticut Compromise opened the way for adoption of a modified Virginia Plan that became the basis for the new government.

Timing was not the only ironic aspect of the Northwest Ordinance. Even more unusual is the fact that its chief creator was not serving in either the Congress of the Confederation or the Constitutional Convention. He was across the Atlantic in France.

This man was Thomas Jefferson. He had exerted some influence on the Convention through his longtime exchange of ideas with Madison, the Father of the Constitution, as well as through the reading he had suggested to his friend and his continuing correspondence on specific issues. There is more concrete evidence of his contributions to the Northwest Ordinance.

The ordinance provided for government of the territory northwest of the Ohio River, east of the Mississippi, and south and west of the Great Lakes. From it later would be carved the states of Ohio, Indiana, Illinois, Michigan, and Wisconsin, and part of Minnesota. Portions of land comprising the Northwest Territory were claimed by Virginia, Massachusetts, New York, and Connecticut. Between the years of 1780 and 1786, these states relinquished their claims to allay the fears of small states, anxieties that were an impediment to true union. Governance of the territory then became the responsibility of the Confederation.

The basis of the Northwest Ordinance, also called the Ordinance of 1787, was Jefferson's Ordinance of 1784. It was a most enlightened document, embodying a concept that he had enunciated even before the Declaration of Independence—that the states should not subject the western lands to the same colonial status that they themselves had fought to escape. In his plan, new states organized in the Northwest Territory would be equal partners of those on the Atlantic seaboard. The United States would voluntarily renounce imperialism in its continental expansion. There were provisions for evolution to statehood through a prescribed series of orderly steps with self-government at every stage.

Jefferson's draft was enlightened in an equally important way; it provided that after 1800 slavery should not exist in the new states. Unfortunately, this provision was defeated by a single vote.

Surprising was the defeat of another provision, one that would have prohibited hereditary titles in the new states. Despite all the talk of democracy, some ambitious Americans evidently were not yet ready to cancel the possibility of the trappings of hereditary privilege.

Altogether, Jefferson's experience as the author of the Ordinance of 1784 was a frustrating one. Though finally adopted by the Confederation Congress, it was mangled by amendments and was never implemented.

But in 1787 it was resurrected in nearly its original form and, with largely harmless modifications, became the foundation of the historic Northwest Ordinance. The Congress did not eagerly seize the opportunity. With Jefferson's Ordinance of 1784 never having gone into effect and a 1785 ordinance having only vaguely provided for division and sale of lands in the Northwest Territory, the Ohio Company's application to buy a large amount of land in the area forced the Congress to provide a more specific plan. To their credit, they returned to the vision that had inspired Jefferson.

Under the Northwest Ordinance, the territory would be governed at first by a governor, a secretary, and those judges appointed by the Congress. When there were five thousand free adult males within its boundaries, an elected bicameral legislature would be established, and the territory would be permitted to have a nonvoting representative in the United States Congress.

Three to five states could be carved from the territory. When the free population of any part of the territory reached sixty thousand or more, they could apply for admission as a state. The new states would be "on an equal footing with the original states in all respects whatsoever." The Northwest Ordinance provided that, even before the creation of states, no one born in the territory should be placed in involuntary servitude except as a punishment for crime. Religious freedom and right of trial by jury were guaranteed. So was public financial support for education.

It is good that in most cases Jefferson's choices for names of the new states were not followed. Though his suggestions for Illinoia and Michigania proved serviceable with slight modifications, such tongue twisters as Assenisipia and Polypotamia were rejected. His choices, though, are symbolic of the sources of thought that led him to produce so creative a plan. Strange hybrids of native American and classical origin, they reflected his adaptation of ancient traditions to the challenges of a new environment.

A striking accomplishment, the ordinance was made possible not only by Jefferson's creativity but also by the society that had fostered it, and by the imagination and idealism of many members of even so moribund an institution as the Confederation Congress. Of course, this creativity and idealism did not flourish in a bell-jar environment protecting them from the selfish and sordid. The push for passage of some sort of territorial ordinance came from eager speculators among stockholders of the Ohio Company, and from their chief lobbyist, Manasseh Cutler, one of the company's leaders, who also obtained approval of a huge land sale to his Cutler-Sargeant-Putnam syndicate. He and his associates gained six million acres by agreeing to resell a third of the land to a member of the Treasury Board and his associates, and by pledging support to the president of Congress in his effort to be first territorial governor.

Cutler certainly was representative of the versatility that helped to make his time a creative one in the United States. Besides being a lobbyist, a land speculator, a politician, and a Congregational clergyman, he was at various times a teacher, a lawyer, a physician, and a scholar whose investigations in astronomy, botany, and meteorology won him membership in several learned societies. Some of the Congress compromised with his materialism; many were inspired by his gleams of idealism. It is good that creativity sometimes is a sufficiently vigorous plant to transmute and transcend the dirt of its environment instead of being smothered by it.

Both idealism and practical politics were necessary to secure ratification of the Constitution produced by the delegates who labored in Philadelphia from mid-May to mid-September of 1787. Madison, of course, said that, except for the opportunity to debate in secret, enabling men to compromise without losing face before their constituents, the delegates would have been unable to produce the plan of government. But the secrecy of the Convention had raised fear on which opponents of ratification capitalized. Ironically, journalists and letter writers sometimes took refuge behind pseudonyms while playing on public fears of what had transpired in hidden deliberations.

On September 20, three days after formal adjournment of the Convention, the Congress of the Confederation received the Constitution designed to make it obsolete. Demands that the Congress "censure the Convention for exceeding its authority" were overridden, and that body voted to send a copy of the Constitution to each state legislature. Each state's assembly was expected to submit the document to a specially called ratifying convention within its borders. Advocates defended what we now see as one of the great documents of history—great in creative boldness and in continuing influence. But creative boldness itself created problems for those working for ratification; it imposed upon them the task of advocating the untried.

If the task was demanding, the abilities involved were transcendent. The Constitution, which Gladstone later called the greatest political achievement "in modern times to have been produced by the human intellect at a single stroke," was partly a product of the times but equally the result of a remarkable concentration of talents. Many political theories advanced by outstanding thinkers were circulating freely in Western civilization, but extraordinary ingenuity was necessary for their integration and implementation.

Citing particularly the studies of historian Robert B. Morris, Silvano Arieti reminds his readers that "many historians agree that if a small group of people consisting of Benjamin Franklin, George Washington, John Adams, Thomas Jefferson, John Jay, Alexander Hamilton and James Madison had not lived and emerged at the same time, the American Revolution and the writing of the American constitution could not have taken place." Arieti, who has drawn on a rich background of Continental European culture in producing the twentieth century's most provocative work on creativity, adds a few other names, including James Wilson, and says, "it is difficult to think of comparable leadership in any other country." Arieti discusses impressive examples of aggregations of talent in France and Italy, but cites the founders of the United States as his principal example from modern history of the "interaction of significant persons" in "socio-politico-historical creativity."[2]

Such a gathering was possible only in a society that exalted excellence and public service and shared Bacon's belief that "knowledge is power." It was also made possible by a society that valued intellectual and practical versatility, as well as classical learning and contemporary experimentation, so that capacious minds were afforded ample opportunities for comparative observations across disciplinary lines. Furthermore, while they brought to their association the stimulus of cultural variety ranging from the urban metropolis of Philadelphia to the towns of New England and the plantations of the South, and descended variously from French, Dutch, Swedish, and German as well as British stock, they shared a common culture molded in England and modified by American experience.

One of the most exciting aspects of the conflict over ratification was that it pitted against the brilliant advocates a roster of opponents rivaling them in stature. The opposition could boast a George Mason, a Patrick Henry, and a Richard Henry Lee. The great questions of constitutional government would be debated by worthy antagonists on both sides. There would be some uninspired carping, fear mongering, and demagoguery, but the debate would be dominated by highly intelligent and informed people who disdained to talk down to the public. Makers of local opinion in even the smallest village listened attentively to disquisitions that would engage only an elite in our time. As late as the Lincoln-Douglas debates in the next century, ordinary audiences would continue to be fascinated by intelligent arguments concerning the body politic.

Some giants of the opposition expressed their views in publications still studied by political scientists. Notable were several Virginians.

Richard Henry Lee, a former president of the Continental Congress, published his pamphlet *Observations Leading to a Fair Examination*, a work more inspired in the writing than in the titling. A scion of the Virginia family that John Adams said had produced more men of worth than any other clan he knew, Lee had been educated at schools in the colony and in England. The most important part of his learning in preparation for public life had been acquired through intensive reading that tapped the principal sources of Western culture. Such was his polished oratory that he was called the "Cicero of Virginia," even by those who, entranced by Patrick Henry's more perfervid orations, called the "liberty or death" man "the Demosthenes of America." Though he kept a black handkerchief wrapped around a hand maimed in a hunting accident and suffered various illnesses, including a form of epilepsy, Lee gave the impression of strength and vigor. In the Congress, he had introduced the motion for independence and had signed the Declaration. He led the forces for passage of the Northwest Ordinance, delighting particularly in the prohibitions against slavery north of the Ohio River. He had spoken forcefully against slavery as early as 1759.

George Mason published his *Objections to the Proposed Federal Constitution*. Both he and Lee joined with Henry to fight against the Constitution in the Virginia ratifying convention.

Skilled penmen produced pamphlets in support of ratification. One of these was John Dickinson, who published *Letters of Fabius*. As Dickinson had opposed separation from Great Britain and refused to sign the Declaration of Independence, his advocacy now of a strong, independent national government carried special weight. Besides membership in the Continental Congress, he had been in immediate succession president of the State of Delaware and president of the Pennsylvania Executive Council. He was cofounder of Dickinson College.

Two Connecticut natives bearing the same patronym but apparently unrelated were prominent in the war of words. Noah Webster, the celebrated lexicographer and textbook author, penned *An Examination into the Leading Principles of the Federal Constitution*. Pelatiah Webster, Congregational minister, industrialist, Philadelphia merchant, and political economist, wrote a proratification pamphlet titled *The Weakness of Brutus Exposed*. In 1783 he had envisioned a strong national government in a work called *A Dissertation on the*

Political Union and Constitution of the Thirteen United States of North America.

Most important of all the works produced on both sides of the controversy, however, was *The Federalist*. As Ben Jonson said of Shakespeare, it "was not of an age but for all time." It has appeared on many lists of the most influential books in the English language and on some lists of the most influential in any tongue.

We are so accustomed to the sight of *The Federalist* as a substantial volume on a shelf of classics that most people think of it as a leisurely literary production, intended from the first for immortality between hard covers. In reality, its origins are quite different. Seventy-seven of the eighty-five essays published in two volumes as *The Federalist* (March-May 1788) were written at white-hot speed for publication in New York newspapers between October 27, 1787 and April 2, 1788. The immediate purpose was to influence public opinion to press for ratification while the New York state convention was in session. The secondary purpose was to influence other ratifying conventions through republication in the newspapers of other states.

Posterity was the third audience under consideration. But personal fame was not the spur. Madison, Hamilton, and John Jay were the three writers of the essays, but each signed his work "Publius." The Latin nomenclature assumed by the *Federalist* authors, as well as by their opponents and many of their allies, was a reflection of the classical culture in which America's intellectual leaders were steeped. As writers and as statesmen, they saw themselves as counterparts of leaders of the ancient Roman republic.[3]

At the time of first publication, most Americans did not know who was writing the essays signed "Publius," and many probably assumed that there was a single author. Even after it was known that each essay was written by Madison, Hamilton, or Jay, the public could not match each work with its author. In fact, eventually Hamilton himself was uncertain of attribution in the case of some essays. The question was not settled until 1944. Hamilton wrote fifty-one essays, Madison twenty-nine, and Jay five.[4]

Like Hamilton, a New Yorker and King's College (Columbia University) graduate, Jay had served the Confederation both as a president of the Continental Congress and as a diplomat in Europe. He had earned respect for his legal learning but had alienated many Americans, especially in the South, when he recommended giving up free navigation of the Mississippi for twenty-five years to placate Spain. Once a slave owner and purchaser, he had later become first president of the New York Society for Promoting the Manumission of Slaves. He was scheduled to write many more than five of the essays, but ill health intervened.

Alexander Hamilton wrote the introductory essay of *The Federalist*. Published in the New York *Independent Journal* on October 27, 1787, it announced the intention to discuss the usefulness of the Union, the inadequacy of the existing Confederation, and the need for vigorous government to meet challenges to national survival. A little strange after Hamilton's expression of near-monarchial sentiments in the Constitutional Convention, and fully royalist ones in private correspondence, was his promise to reveal the Constitution's conformity to republican principles and show how it would bolster republican government and liberty as well as property rights.

Jay wrote the next four articles, drawing on his experience as foreign secretary of the Congress and as a diplomat in Europe to stress the need of a strong Union to deal with foreign threats and with problems of sectional conflict that otherwise might divide the states and make them easy prey for European imperialism.

In the next four essays, Hamilton used his financial expertise to discuss the worsening threat of commercial rivalries among the states. These and conflicting territorial ambitions could foster armed strife between individual states and perhaps even a division of the Confederation into warring confederacies. A strong national government under the proposed Constitution would be the best protection against such a disaster.

Hamilton, in number 9, produced one of the most quoted of his contributions:

> it is impossible to read the history of the petty Republics of Greece and Italy, without feeling sensations of horror and disgust at the distractions with which they were continually agitated, and at the rapid succession of revolutions, by which they were kept in a state of perpetual vibration, between the extremes of tyranny and anarchy. . . . If momentary rage of glory break forth from the gloom, while they dazzle us with a transient and fleeting brilliancy, they at the same time admonish us to lament that the vice of government should pervert the direction and tarnish the luster of those bright talents and exalted endowments for which the favored soils that produced them have been so justly celebrated.

He continued:

> From the disorders that disfigure the annals of those republics, the advocates of despotism have drawn arguments, not only against the forms of republican government, but against the very principles of civil liberty. They have decried all free government, as inconsistent with the order of society, and have indulged themselves in malicious exultation over its friends and partisans. Happily for mankind, stupendous fabrics reared on the basis of liberty, which have flourished for ages, have in a few glorious instances refuted their gloomy sophisms. And, I trust, America will be the broad and solid foundation of other edifices not less magnificent, which will be equally permanent monuments of their errors.

Hamilton readily admitted that the records of some republics of the ancient world would be sufficient to discourage later advocates of republican government if political science had not subsequently devised certain protections that would be effective within such a framework.

> The regular distribution of power into distant departments—the introduction of legislative balances and checks—the institution of courts composed of judges holding their offices during good behavior—the representation of the people in the legislature by deputies of their own election—these are either wholly new discoveries or have made their principal progress towards perfection in modern times. They are means, and powerful means, by which the excellencies of republican government may be retained and its imperfections lessened or avoided.

At the time that Hamilton wrote, opponents of the new Constitution had, as he said, "with great assiduity cited and circulated the observations of Montesquieu on the necessity of a contracted territory for a republican government." In New York and her sister states were lawyers, physicians, merchants, farmers, and skilled craftsmen who venerated the French philosopher and quoted his writings at either firsthand or second.

In the face of reiterations that Montesquieu had insisted that republican governments were effective only on a small scale, Hamilton boldly asserted that one of the best safeguards of liberty within a republican system was "the enlargement of the orbit within which such systems are to revolve." Hamilton argued that the largest of the existing American states already, as separate entities, exceeded the dimensions recommended by Montesquieu as suitable for a republican community. The New Yorker says:

> Neither Virginia, Massachusetts, Pennsylvania, New York, North Carolina, nor Georgia can by any means be compared with the models from which he reasoned and to which the terms of his description apply. If we therefore take his ideas on this point as the criterion of truth, we shall be driven to the alternative either of taking refuge at once in the arms of monarchy, or of splitting ourselves into an infinity of little jealous, clashing, tumultuous commonwealths, the wretched nurseries of increasing discord and the miserable objects of universal pity or contempt.

A better student of Montesquieu's works than most of the ratification opponents quoting him, Hamilton informed them that the Frenchman "explicitly treats of a CONFEDERATE REPUBLIC as the expedient for extending the sphere of popular government and reconciling the advantages of monarchy with those of republicanism." Hamilton quoted Montesquieu's definition of a "confederate republic": "a kind of assemblage of societies that constitute a new one, capable of increasing by means of new associations till they arrive to such a degree of power as to be able to provide for the security of the united body."[5]

The Frenchman argued, "The form of this society prevents all manner of inconveniences." He urged:

> If a single member should attempt to usurp the supreme authority, he could not be supposed to have an equal authority and credit in all the confederate states. Were he to have too great influence over one, this would alarm the rest. Were he to subdue a part, that which would still remain free might oppose him with forces independent of those he had usurped, and overpower him before he could be settled in his usurpation.

Likewise, he contended, "Should a popular insurrection happen in one of the confederate states, the others are able to quell it. Should abuses creep into one part, they are reformed by those that remain sound."

In maintaining that a huge territory could be governed without threat to republican principles as long as the government was a federation, Hamilton was echoing the assurances of James Madison in Convention debates and repudiating his own insistence in Philadelphia that a continent could be ruled only by a concentration of national power barely short of monarchy.

Hamilton sought to reassure those who blanched at the words "subordination to the general authority of the Union":

> So long as the separate organization of the [member state] be not abolished, so long as it exists by a constitutional necessity for local purposes, though it should be in perfect subordination to the general authority of the union, it would still be, in fact and in theory, an association of states, or a confederacy. The proposed Constitution, so far from an abolition of the state governments, makes them constituent parts of the national sovereignty by allowing them a direct representation in the Senate, and leaves in their possession certain exclusive and very important portions of sovereign power.

He quoted Montesquieu on this point too: "The confederacy may be dissolved, and the confederates [states] preserve their sovereignty."

In other words, the states had the right to secede from the Union, but so long as they remained in it, they must accept subordination to the national government. In 1803–1804 some influential politicians in Hamilton's home state of New York would seek to join with others in New Jersey and the five New England states to secede from the Union and, under the leadership of Massachusetts senator Timothy Pickering, to found a Northern Confederacy. They feared that, when new states were created from the Louisiana Territory, the balance of power in Congress would shift from the North to the South and West. Hamilton was influential in defeating the proposal. In 1860–1861 some southern states, fearing northern domination of Congress, would secede and form the Confederate States of America.

Hamilton cited ancient Lycia in Asia Minor as a nearly perfect federation.

Such was the intellectual context of the debate over federalism in the United States, and such the attitude of many in the audience, that this analogy was the clincher in his final paragraph.

As the contest between Federalists and Anti-Federalists warmed in New York, it also grew heated in Virginia. With Governor Randolph, Patrick Henry, George Mason, and Richard Henry Lee all opposing ratification, Madison's friends begged him to return to Virginia and assume leadership of the ratification forces in the Convention. He hesitated, but then yielded to the suggestion of Hamilton and Jay that he join them in writing the series of articles signed "Publius" for publication in New York newspapers. He concluded that he could best serve the cause of ratification by participating in a series designed to influence the outcome in New York, but which also would be reprinted in Virginia and other states and play a part in decision making there.

Madison's first essay, number 10 in the series by Publius, followed Hamilton's famous number 9 and exceeded it in reputation. Indeed, it has become the most famous essay in *The Federalist*. The essay is a perfect example of the "sweet reasonableness" with which Madison addressed most topics, including some that were potentially quite incendiary.

"Among the numerous advantages promised by a well-constructed Union," he says at the outset,

> none deserves to be more accurately developed than its tendency to break and control the violence of faction. The friend of popular governments never finds himself so much alarmed for their character and fate as when he contemplates their propensity to this dangerous vice. He will not fail, therefore, to set a due value on any plan which, without violating the principles to which he is attached, provides a proper cure for it.

Madison admits that "the instability, injustice and confusion introduced into the public councils have in truth been the mortal diseases under which popular governments have everywhere perished." He notes that "they continue to be the favorite and fruitful topics from which the adversaries to liberty derive their most specious declamations." He readily concedes that American governments, those of the states as well as that of the United States, "are too unstable; that the public good is disregarded in the conflicts of rival parties; and that measures are too often decided, not according to the rules of justice, and the rights of the minor party, but by the superior force of an interested and overbearing majority."

Madison defines a faction as "a number of citizens, whether amounting to a majority or minority of the whole, who are united and actuated by some common impulse of passion, or of interest, adverse to the rights of other citizens, as to the permanent and aggregate interests of the community."

He recognizes "two methods of curing the mischief of faction: the one by removing its causes; the other by controlling its effects." He likewise acknowledges "two methods of removing the causes of faction: the one by destroying the liberty which is essential to its existence; the other by giving to every citizen the same opinions; the same passions, and the same interests." The first remedy, he said, was

> worse than the disease. Liberty is to faction what air is to fire, an aliment without which it instantly expires. But it could not be a less folly to abolish liberty, which is essential to political life, because it nourishes faction, than it would be to wish the annihilation of air, which is essential to animal life, because it imparts to fire its destructive agency.

The second recourse, attaining uniformity of opinions, passions, and interests, he brands "impracticable." Of course, many of his own generation, or preceding ones, who made no claim to philosophy would have said the same thing. But Madison analyzes the reasons in a provocative way.

> As long as the reason of man continues fallible, and he is at liberty to exercise it, different opinions will be formed. As long as the connection subsists between his reason and his self-love, his opinions and his passions will have a reciprocal influence on each other. . . . The diversity in the faculties of man from which the rights of property originate is not less an inseparable obstacle to a uniformity of interests. The protection of these faculties is the first object of government. From the protection of different and unequal faculties of acquiring property, the possession of different degrees and kinds of property immediately results; and from the influence of these on the sentiments and views of the respective proprietors, ensues a division of the society into different interests and parties.

Madison makes a sharp point and drives it home. He says that "the most common and durable source of factions has been the various and unequal distribution of property. Those who hold, and those who are without property, have ever formed distinct interests in society. Those who are creditors, and those who are debtors, fall under a like discrimination." His development of this theme has caused some to see him as a forerunner of Karl Marx, as an earlier author of the communist philosopher's doctrine of economic determinism.

Irving Brant has wisely pointed out that Madison and Marx were alike only in recognizing the socially motivating force of economics. Whereas Marx "produced the dictatorship of the proletariat" in the hope of ending economic injustice, "Madison thought too much of liberty to sacrifice it to any economic goal. . . . He would fight the harder for democratic self-government the more it was assailed . . . while Marx treated it as a destructible pawn in a campaign to destroy private property."[6]

Madison was fully aware of the variety and complexity of economic influences:

A landed interest, a manufacturing interest, a mercantile interest, with many lesser interests, grow up of necessity in civilized nations, and divide them into different classes actuated by different sentiments and views. The regulation of these various and interfering interests forms the principal task of modern legislation and involves the spirit of party and faction in the necessary and ordinary operations of government.

Admitting the existence of these separate interests, Madison acknowledges the danger posed in the legislative process.

No man is allowed to be a judge in his own case, because his interest would certainly bias his own judgment, and, not improbably, corrupt his integrity. With equal, nay with greater reason, a body of men are unfit to be both judges and parties at the same time; yet, what are many of the most important acts of legislation but so many judicial determinations, not indeed concerning the rights of single persons, but concerning the rights of large bodies of citizens, and what are the different classes of legislators but advocates and parties to the causes which they determine?

He argues that in a sizable republic, representative government can deal with the problem of factionalism far better than a pure democracy. The system of pure democracy, wherein citizens determine all matters by direct vote, he saw as inefficient beyond the level of the small community. First, representatives are virtually sure to be above the dead level of the general population in education and ability. Second, the competing local factors involved in decision making over an extensive geographic territory increase the likelihood that some factional interests will counterbalance others.

No cockeyed optimist, however, Madison foresaw that unfavorable economic factors would intensify to create serious problems for the whole world. He predicted the growth of poverty on a global scale as a result of an increase of population exceeding increase of the means of production. He was writing eleven years before publication of Malthus' famous *Essay on the Principle of Population*. The heir of a sizeable estate, Madison rose above personal interest to assert that, although the right of the prosperous to defend their property should be recognized, it was not as fundamental as the right of the poor to vote. The franchise should not be limited to protect economic privilege.

The Virginian anticipated a variety of factional troubles that almost certainly would afflict the Republic, but believed that they would be ameliorated by the geographical scale of the Union served by such a government.

The influence of factious leaders may kindle a flame within their particular States, but will be unable to spread a general conflagration through the other States: a religious sect may degenerate into a political faction in a part of the Confederacy; but the variety of sects dispersed over the entire face of it, must secure the national Councils against any danger from that source: a rage for paper money, for an abolition of debts, for an equal division of property, or of any other improper or wicked project, will be less apt to pervade the whole body of the Union, than a particular member of it; in the same proportion as such a malady is more likely to taint a particular county or district, than an entire State.

He concludes, "in the extent and proper structure of the Union, therefore, we behold a republican remedy for the disease most incident to republican government." He has reinforced by repetition and specific examples one of Hamilton's principal arguments in essay 10, and at the same time has enriched it with specific predictions that over the course of American history have evidenced his remarkable prescience.

Relying on his previous research plus a few notes from Hamilton, Madison discussed the character and fate of confederations from ancient to modern times, leaving readers free to draw parallels from contemporary experience and thus convince themselves of the need for the strong Republic envisioned by the Constitutional Convention. Hamilton concentrated on weaknesses of the Confederation.

By December 12, 1787, the twenty-two *Federalist* essays so far published had been reprinted in nine newspapers in New York, Massachusetts, Rhode Island, Pennsylvania, and Virginia.[7] Fortunately, all the contributors had quick and orderly minds. Madison said that the essays "were written, most of them, in great haste, and without any special allotment of the different parts of the subject to the several writers. . . . It frequently happened that while the printer was putting into type the parts of a number, the following parts were under the pen, and to be finished in time for the press."

Between December 5 and 18, conventions in three states ratified the proposed Constitution. In only one of these, Pennsylvania, where the vote was two to one, could *The Federalist* be considered a factor. *The Federalist* had not even been published in Delaware and New Jersey, both of which ratified unanimously. Rhode Island was doubtful, Massachusetts scarcely less so. In Virginia, whose sons had taken the lead in producing the Constitution, ratification seemed more imperiled than anywhere else. And, without Virginia, the vital middle link in the chain of states, there could be no effective Union.

Both Hamilton and Madison drew energy from urgency. In most of seventeen successive articles, the New Yorker concentrated on taxation and military matters, in both of which he was knowledgeable. Meanwhile, Madison concentrated on proving that the Constitution, described by some as an instrument of tyranny, was actually true to all essential principles of republicanism. This he did in twenty-two essays published consecutively between January 15 and February 22, 1788.

These writings by Madison, together with his number 10, constitute one of the most important commentaries on government in the history of the world. Number 44 includes the most influential statement of the doctrine of implied powers: "No axiom is more clearly established in law, or in reason, than that wherever the end is required the means are authorized; wherever a general power to do a thing is given, every particular power necessary for doing it is included." Two aspects of Madison's authorship of this sentence are ironic. First, the doctrine of implied powers is associated much less often with him than with his writing colleague Hamilton. Second, Madison would regret writing this succinct and forceful statement when he grew more fearful of centralized government. This regret would be especially acute in 1819 when Chief Justice John Marshall paraphrased his fellow Virginian's sentence in writing the famous decision in *McCulloch v. Maryland* that opened the way to increased expansion of federal power.

Anticipating the verdict of posterity, Jefferson, at the very time of publication, pronounced *The Federalist* "the best commentary on the principles of government which ever was written." How could such a masterpiece of intellectual learning, assimilated experience, and brilliant ingenuity be produced in rapid-fire installments whose timings were dictated by political exigency and journalistic deadlines? Part of the answer lies in the genius of Hamilton and Madison. But another part, an essential one, lies in the society's emphasis on an intellectual curiosity going far beyond any immediate interest or pragmatic purpose. The writers spent their earlier lives in preparation for the great task.

Certainly, learning was conspicuous in the careers of such beneficiaries of advanced formal education as Madison, a graduate of Princeton, and Hamilton and Jay, both alumni of King's College (Columbia). It was evident in John Dickinson, who had studied in London as well as Philadelphia; John Adams and John Dawson, both Harvard trained; Edmund Randolph and John Page, William and Mary graduates; Oxford graduate Charles Cotesworth Pinckney; Princeton alumnus Benjamin Rush; Yale man Noah Webster; and a host of other debaters on both sides of ratification, men whose proclivity for assuming classical pen names bespoke an attachment to classical learning.

It was reflected even in the intellectual discipline of such noncollegiate types as Patrick Henry, who was tutored by a father trained in the Scottish universities, and George Mason, who was initiated into formal learning by private tutors but who found his Pierian spring in his guardian's large and select private library.

An admiration for intellectual achievement so permeated American society in the time of the founders of the Republic that it inspired printer Benjamin Franklin to become a world-renowned polymath. And even Roger Sherman, the Connecticut shoemaker and self-trained lawyer who became a state supreme court justice and engineer of the Connecticut Compromise—this patriot, who eschewed a classical pen name in favor of the designation "A Countryman"—wrote knowledgeably about Magna Carta and evidenced so much learning in other ways that Yale presented him an honorary degree.

The founders of the United States, it must be admitted, were sometimes vain about their learning. But they never succumbed to the vanity of feigning ignorance and wearing it as a badge of honor.

35

A GENIUS FOR GOVERNMENT

AS HE ADDRESSED the delegates to Virginia's ratification convention in Richmond in June 1788, holding his hat before him like a ship's wheel as he steered through treacherous currents, Madison must have felt that he was back in Philadelphia in the previous summer. Once again, he was looked to as captain of the forces favoring a strong Constitution. Once again, he was dependent upon profound knowledge and an aptitude for quiet persuasion as he faced opponents far more skilled in the pyrotechnics of debate.

Spectators as well as delegates packed the New Academy on Shockoe Hill. The setting was an appropriate one. Founded under the leadership of the Chevalier Alexander Maria Quesnay de Beaurepaire, a veteran of Revolutionary service in Virginia and grandson of Quesnay, the famous philosopher and economist, the institution was modeled after the French Academy and dedicated to the arts and sciences. It was intended to be both national and international, with branches in Baltimore, Philadelphia, and New York and affiliations with the royal societies of London, Paris, and Brussels. Conceived by Virginia's lieutenant governor John Page, one of Jefferson's closest friends, it was to have 25 resident scholars and artists and 175 nonresident associates from North America and Europe. Its own printing press would disseminate the learned productions of those people.[1]

The French Revolution would put an end to this project so dependent on support from Paris. But the ratification convention in the New Academy was a glittering assembly including some of America's most brilliant and cultivated minds, exactly the sort of people from whom associates in such a project would be drawn. Though all participants were from a single state, the assemblage was one of the most distinguished in American history.

Individual faces and distinctive voices must have heightened Madison's sense of déjà vu. There was the swarthy distinction of Governor Randolph's aquiline profile and the polish of his modulated speech. Full-faced George Mason was familiarly passionate and acidulous. Great-headed, bulging-browed George Wythe brought to the proceedings in Richmond his accustomed demeanor, that of an alert and courteous schoolmaster. And there was John Blair, with Washington and Madison one of those Virginians who had signed the Constitution in Philadelphia.

But there were others at the Virginia convention who had not been at the Philadelphia meeting, statesmen whose stature was such that their absence from the national conclave had been the subject of much speculation. Chief among these was Patrick Henry, "the American Demosthenes," generally recognized as the greatest orator on the continent.

There were others whose names are still remembered by historians and, in some cases, by an informed public—Benjamin Harrison, George Nicholas, John Tyler, Sr., Theodore Bland, James Innes, and Henry "Lighthorse Harry" Lee—each of sufficient ability to have been among either the foremost leaders or the ostracized in an era of less distinction. And there were young men of some accomplishment and even greater promise, such as James Monroe and John Marshall.

Washington and others let Madison know that he was the chief reliance of those hoping for ratification by the Virginia convention. In the brief interval between his return to Virginia and his participation in the debates in Richmond, Madison walked or rode horseback daily to regain strength that he had lost through illness from overexertion in Philadelphia. He also spent time in a subtle effort to convert Randolph to ratification. The governor had refused to sign the Constitution before leaving Philadelphia. But Madison took hope from the fact that Randolph had introduced the Virginia Plan at the Constitutional Convention, using his prestige, forensic gifts, and personal charm to secure support for the principal basis of the document adopted.

On the eve of the Richmond conclave, Madison wrote Jefferson, "The Governor is so temperate in his opposition and goes so far with the friends of the Constitution that he cannot properly be classed with its enemies." In conversations with Randolph, Madison stressed points on which the two agreed and, rather than directly rebutting the governor's objections to ratification, led him to "discover" answers to the problems raised. Madison also honed a negative weapon. He knew that in his heart Randolph did not trust Patrick Henry, Virginia's most powerful opponent of ratification. Without being so vehement a critic as to lose his own credibility, Madison seized every opportunity to exploit that distrust.

Randolph was far more capable of seeing both sides of a question, to the point of presenting a meticulous exposition of the strengths and weaknesses of each, than of making up his mind between alternatives. When, early in the proceedings in Richmond, he rose to speak, each faction expected him to espouse its cause. Some delegates, not solidly committed to either camp, thought that he might join the ranks of those who did not absolutely oppose ratification but insisted that it should come only after certain amendments to the Constitution had been approved. Madison knew that the governor had been leaning this way, and he consistently worked to counteract the influences that impelled Randolph to such a view. Madison believed that trying to get separate states to agree on amendments and perhaps to participate in another Constitutional Convention before ratification would be to kill all hope for the proposed new government without the ignominy of actually wielding a murder weapon.

As Randolph, on gaining the floor, launched into a defense of his failure to sign the Constitution, Henry's antiratifiers brightened. When Randolph explained that he still wanted amendments to the document that had been signed in Philadelphia, the foes of ratification were mightily encouraged.

Then the governor said that, although he still wanted amendments, he believed that they should follow rather than precede ratification. In the rest of his remarks, he followed the views expressed by Madison in conversation and in *The Federalist*. The enemies of the Constitution were greatly disappointed, but not dismayed. After all, they had Henry on their side—an orator so persuasive that he sometimes gained his way in the legislature without either making a speech or politicking, but simply by threatening to speak if anyone should propose anything contrary to his preferences.

The next day Henry, ordinarily almost as conspicuous for brevity as for eloquence, cast aside all time restraints and, through an entire day's session, delivered what was probably the longest speech of his career.[2] This sustained cannonade was not directed against separate parts of the Constitution, but targeted the first three words of the preamble:

> I would make this inquiry of those characters who composed a part of the late Federal Convention. . . . I have the highest veneration for those gentlemen; but sir, give me leave to demand what right they had to say, *We, the people*? My political curiosity, exclusive of my anxious solicitude for the public welfare, leads me to ask who authorized them to speak the language of "We, the People" instead of "We, the States"? *States are the characteristics and soul of a confederation.* If the state be not the agent of this compact, it must be one great consolidated government of the people of all the states.

Henry anticipated that the friends of ratification would invoke the revered name of Washington, who had not only signed the proposed Constitution but presided over the Convention that devised it. Speaking still of the Virginia delegates, who had played such prominent roles in Philadelphia, he said:

> I would demand the cause of their conduct. Even from that illustrious man who saved us by his valor, I would have a reason for his conduct. That liberty which he has given us by his valor tells me to ask this reason; but there are other gentlemen here who can give us this information. The people gave them no power to use their name. That they exceeded their power is perfectly clear. . . . I wish to hear the real, actual existing danger which should lead us to take those steps so dangerous in my conception. Disorders have arisen in other parts of America, but here, sir, no danger, no insurrection or tumult has happened; everything has been calm and tranquil.

The last observation was no exaggeration. Though rebellion had erupted in some other states, notably in Massachusetts where it was a formidable threat to the government, Virginia had been free of such disturbances. In effect, Henry was asking his fellow Virginians why they should sacrifice a large measure of their freedom to create a government capable of quelling revolt elsewhere. "The Federal Convention," Henry said, "ought to have amended the old system. For this purpose they were solely delegated; the object of their mission extended to no other consideration."

By a strict interpretation, he was entirely correct. But the influence of his speech was not derived solely—or even principally—from this fact. His magnificent voice was itself, independent of particular words, a force to soothe or thrill. But his power of mesmerism was compounded of a hundred subtle arts. Madison, many years later, said that "when he had made a most conclusive argument in favor of the Constitution, Henry would rise to reply to him, and by some significant action, such as a pause, a shake of the head, or a striking gesture, before he uttered a word, would undo all that Madison had been trying to do for an hour before."[3]

With no weapons but the prosaic ones of knowledge and cool logic, Madison had to reply to this giant sorcerer. Historian Hugh Blair Grigsby, who by his own testimony had "often heard of Mr. Madison's mode of speaking from members of the Assembly of 1799," said that "the Father of the Constitution" had the physical qualities of an orator in a less degree than any of his great contemporaries. His low stature made it difficult for him to be seen from all parts of the house; his voice was rarely loud enough to be heard throughout the hall; and this want of size and weakness of voice were the more apparent from the contrast with the appearance of Henry. . . ." Madison's style, as in the Constitutional Convention in Philadelphia, seemed eccentric. When speaking, he would always hold his hat, seemingly a strange proceeding until one learned that he kept his notes in it, hoping to maintain the illusion of "expressing some thought that had casually occurred to him. . . . The warmest excitement of debate was visible in him only by a more or less rapid and forward see-saw motion of his body."[4]

Madison presented the same carefully thought-out arguments that he had used in *The Federalist*. He also got Hamilton to send him many extra copies of the published essays. Many of the delegates, including some of the hostile as well as the undecided, listened to Madison's arguments by day and studied his and Hamilton's written arguments by night.

As the debates continued day after day, Mason, whose greatest strength lay in philosophical perspective and intellectual argument, joined Henry in emotional scare tactics. Under such conditions, one might well expect that the state convention would cease to be a deliberative body, that the debate over the particular applications of universal principles would degenerate into a brouhaha.

Through all the welter of angry disagreement, however, Madison maintained his calm demeanor and gave courteous consideration to every opposing argument. A large number of delegates, probably the great majority, became even more earnest students of the issues than they had been at the outset.

Eventually, Henry, who had given Americans the slogan "Give me liberty or give me death" in their War of Independence, and Mason, who had given to

Virginia and ultimately the world a historic Bill of Rights, concentrated on the need for amendments to protect civil liberties. Madison argued that ratification might become fatally complicated if it had to wait upon amendments, but pledged that, if Virginia and her sister states ratified the Constitution, he would work hard to obtain the addition of amendments constituting a bill of rights.

As the convention in Virginia moved toward final votes, leaders of both the Federalist and Anti-Federalist factions believed that victory would be theirs. Both agreed that the vote would be close. Neither side felt completely sure of the outcome.

Ratification had gotten off to a roaring start in little Delaware, whose ratification convention on December 7, 1787 approved the Constitution by unanimous vote. In Pennsylvania, despite Franklin's influence and the fact that Philadelphia had been host to the Constitutional Convention, the Federalists were hard put to overcome the delaying tactics of their opponents, but on December 12 won a two-to-one victory. In New Jersey, reflecting the general satisfaction with the compromise obtained by William Paterson to protect small states from domination by large, the convention on December 18, after only one week of deliberation, voted unanimously for the new instrument of government. In 1788, on the second day of the new year, Georgia ratified unanimously. A week later, Connecticut approved with a lopsided vote of 128 to 40.

Suddenly, though, the tide seemed to be turning. Informal polling and prognosticating at the Massachusetts convention indicated that Anti-Federalists outnumbered Federalists 192 to 144. Moreover, the Constitution's foes in that state were led by Sam Adams, a formidable agitator who had played as large a role in whipping up popular frenzy leading to the Boston Massacre as his cousin John had in quelling it, and had been the chief instigator of the Boston Tea Party. With him, conciliation was not a habit. But Federalists proposed that amendments be offered with ratification, and Sam Adams acquiesced. The letter of the agreement was kept. Nine amendments were submitted along with the instrument of ratification. But ratification, by a vote of 187 to 168, was made unconditional.

The ratification effort in Rhode Island proved a fiasco. Ultimate failure had been foreshadowed when it, alone among the thirteen states, had declined to send delegates to the Philadelphia Convention. Nevertheless, when the Constitution was submitted, urban leaders in Rhode Island strove valiantly to pressure the legislature into calling a state convention. Instead, the assembly called for a popular referendum on March 24. Indignant, the Federalists refused to vote. The only surprise was that on the appointed day even as many as 1 in every 102 participants voted for ratification.

With nine ratifications required to form the new government, and only six obtained so far, no loss was trivial. But the smallness of Rhode Island and its nonstrategic location (it would not make a break in the coastal chain of ratifiers) made its loss more bearable than most.

Maryland's ratification on April 28 by almost six to one was heartening to the Federalists, but soon there was disturbing news from South Carolina. On May 12 the resolution for a state convention squeaked through the legislature by a single vote. But surprisingly, only eleven days later, the newly named delegates voted 149 to 73 for ratification.

The hope of Federalists everywhere was that New Hampshire would provide the crucial ninth endorsement. But there the issue was heavily in doubt. On June 18, the New Hampshire convention reconvened after adjourning in February following a week's work that had brought no consensus. Only three days after being gaveled to order, the resumed convention voted 57 to 47 for ratification.

The official requirements for founding a new government had been met. But Virginia, New York, and North Carolina had not yet acted. North Carolina was a valuable addition in itself, but even more important was the fact that without it South Carolina and Georgia would be separated from the contiguous union of coastal states. Nevertheless, if Virginia and New York joined the Union, North Carolina might soon be drawn in.

The great worry was about Virginia and New York. Without these powerful states, the new Union was doomed. Even the loss of Virginia alone might make success impossible. Its position linking (or separating) the northern and southern states, its comparatively large population, and its influential role in American affairs could make a failure to ratify fatal to the Federalist hopes for a strong Union.

Despite the doubts about Virginia's course, Alexander Hamilton had faith in Madison's predictions of victory. Certainly the chances for triumph in the Old Dominion appeared stronger than in Hamilton's own state of New York, where Governor George Clinton, a consistent foe of federalism in the Philadelphia Convention of 1787, led Anti-Federalist forces constituting a clear majority. Hamilton used extended discussion and various other parliamentary tactics to delay action in the hope that New Hampshire, and especially Virginia, would ratify in time to sway his own state toward the same course.

With Hamilton, discussion was not merely a delaying tactic. Like Madison in the Virginia convention, he used arguments from *The Federalist* to convince the wavering.

For Madison, the struggle was a wearing one. He had never recovered fully from his exertions in Philadelphia. His swaying as he talked might now be due as much to weakness as to elocutionary habit. Henry, by contrast, was at the top of his form. When he talked about the manacles being forged for free men by advocates of the Constitution, some delegates involuntarily stared at their own wrists, as if to reassure themselves that they were not yet enslaved. An astute observer, Spencer Roane, even after he was freed from the immediate spell of Henry's orations, said that there were parts of them that would almost have put Demosthenes and Cicero to shame. Yet, when Virginia's vote came on June 25, it was 89 for ratification to 79 opposed. Proposals for a bill of rights and twenty other amendments were attached to the resolution of ratification, but they were by no means prerequisite to endorsement.

Hamilton made the most of the psychological effect on the New York convention. On July 25 he and his followers beat back a proposal for conditional ratification. The next day, ratification with no strings attached passed the convention 30 to 27.

The Congress had formally recognized the adoption of the new Constitution when its president, Cyrus Griffin of Virginia, had announced on July 2 that the necessary nine ratifications had been obtained. On September 13 the Congress made arrangements for the first presidential and congressional elections in the new Republic. North Carolina and Rhode Island seemed certain to be drawn into its gravitational field. The fact that five ratifying states had called for a bill of rights and that Madison and other Federalist leaders had pledged to work for one made this reform virtually certain.

Great credit is due Madison and Hamilton for their brilliance and persistence in persuading conventions in their respective states to ratify the Constitution despite initial opposition by majorities. Particularly extraordinary was Madison's achievement, because he opposed in George Mason one of the world's great constitutional lawyers and, in Patrick Henry, one of its most charismatic orators.

John Marshall, a young delegate to the Virginia convention who argued ably for ratification, often indicated, after he had for decades listened to leading orators, that Henry was the most exciting he had ever heard. But on at least one occasion, while recognizing the captivating magic of Henry's performances, he said, "Eloquence has been defined to be the art of persuasion. If it includes persuasion by convincing, Mr. Madison was the most eloquent men I ever heard."[5]

The achievements of Madison and Hamilton in securing ratification by their state conventions are almost as much a credit to their fellow delegates as to themselves. Only intellectually sophisticated audiences would have chosen logic over the exhortations of passion and fear. Only people versed in political tradition and, at the same time, acquainted with current theories and experiments in governance could have comprehended the distinctions on which hinged crucial parts of the debate. Of course, the majority of citizens were not knowledgeable in these complex matters, but their leaders were to a surprising extent—not only those whose influence was statewide or national but the locally prominent figures.

Nor was this sophistication, though conspicuous in Virginia and New York, to be found only there. In varying degrees, it existed in most of the states. Leaders were representatives of a creative society that did not scorn the currency of finance but honored also the currency of intellectual communication and the coinage of concepts.

Madison and Hamilton had persuaded not only those whom they had addressed in person but also the multitude that they had reached directly or indirectly through *The Federalist*. Many who never attended a ratifying convention read the essays of Publius and communicated their reactions to those who did. They helped to create a society that held in tenuous, but fruitful, balance devotion to civilized traditions and eager response to the lure of discovery and experiment. It was a society that encouraged genius, and Americans of the time had discovered a genius for government that found many exemplars.

36

WAS WASHINGTON IGNORANT?

T HE FIRST PRESIDENT of the United States, George Washington, was an "ignorant" man. At least according to his vice president, John Adams.

Yet Adams had been tremendously impressed with Washington when both were delegates to the First Continental Congress in 1774. What he knew of the Virginia colonel's bravery and unflappable leadership in the French and Indian War was reinforced by conduct in Philadelphia that revealed him as a "solid, firm judicious man." In fact, it was Adams who nominated Washington to be commander in chief of the Continental Army.

One thing about Washington puzzled the New Englander for a long time. Someone had mistakenly told Adams that Washington had "made the most eloquent speech at the Virginia Convention that ever was made."[1] The Massachusetts man kept waiting for an example of such eloquence. He could have waited a lifetime without gratification. Washington spoke seldom in public, always briefly and to the point, and was always glad to regain his seat.

How did one in whom Adams had reposed so much confidence become in his eyes an ignorant man? Abigail Adams, after reading her husband's praise of the Virginian, had had the opportunity to meet the general when he assumed his command in Boston. "I was struck with General Washington," she wrote her spouse. "You had prepared me to entertain a favorable opinion of him, but I thought the one half was not told me. Dignity with ease, and complacency, the gentleman and soldier look agreeably blended in him. Modesty marks every line and feature of his face. . . ."[2] The Adamses were a devoted couple, but John frequently felt inadequately appreciated by the world at large and often was irritated when Abigail lavishly praised some other man. The situation vis-à-vis Washington worsened when it became obvious that the little Adamses thought the tall soldier in blue and buff uniform with gold epaulets was more heroic than their rotund little father in his dark suits.

Adams' feelings about Washington were ambivalent. He admired his character, but when even Adams' own Massachusetts seemed to idolize the man to an absurd degree, the Sage of Braintree comforted himself with the reflection that the Virginian was greatly his inferior in learning.

How ignorant was Washington? All persons living in a complex civilization are ignorant in terms of the ratio of individual knowledge to the sum of knowledge available to the society. Adams was specifically critical of the president's lack of a classical education. Certainly the general lacked the classical scholarship of John Adams, who could match Jefferson chapter and verse in citations from the Romans. But Washington's personal letters, as well as official comments, abound in classical references, many of them "cliches" but, significantly, the common references of the formally educated.[3]

Details of young George's formal education are unavailable, and speculation has been wild. Douglas Southall Freeman made the most sensible suggestion, pointing out that the boy's father had provided English educations for his two older sons and doubtless would have provided the best early schooling available for his promising youngest son.[4] It is a known fact that George's mother was unwilling to have him leave home, and that this feeling intensified when at the age of eleven he lost his father. There was a presumably good grammar school conducted by an Anglican minister a mere ferry-ride away in Fredericksburg.

We know that Washington was taught geometry and some elements of astronomy. Apparently he enjoyed mathematics and may have pursued the study beyond formal instruction. Somewhere he learned trigonometry. He probably received some of the most important parts of his education from association with his older half brother Lawrence, whose English education and bright mind had prepared him for a precocious role in Virginia public life.

Other important elements came from frequent association with in-laws. Lawrence had married a daughter of William Fairfax, cousin to Thomas, sixth baron Fairfax, and the American agent for his lordship's estates, which included five million acres in Virginia. Washington spent much time at Belvoir, a Fairfax home in his neighborhood. His sister-in-law was a cultured product of England's great world.

Lord Fairfax himself left England and moved to the area. Though an Oxford graduate and former contributor to *The Spectator*, his lordship was a less than sparkling conversationalist, but another member of the family, George William Fairfax, only six years George's senior, imparted through conversation some of the education he had acquired in England. George William's wife, the vivacious Sally, won a special place in the young Virginian's heart and contributed to his sophistication.

But he was by no means dependent solely on English immigrants for his cultural development. The early deaths of his father and Lawrence deprived him of some valuable influences. But his mother's family, the Balls, were leading residents of the Northern Neck, the peninsula between the Rappahannock and Potomac Rivers that was his birthplace and boyhood home. Episcopal Bishop William Meade recorded that, because of the distinction and culture of its sons, the Northern Neck was called "the Athens of Virginia."

Probably Lord Fairfax's greatest contribution to the broadening of Washington's horizons came when he hired the sixteen-year-old boy to help survey some of his wilderness property. The youngster's diary records many learning experiences ranging from discoveries of the majesty of untamed nature to, in his own words, trying to sleep in a frontier hostelry under "one threadbare blanket with double its load of vermin." To spare the feelings of his host, George waited until the man had departed, and then slept on the floor.

One year later, at age seventeen, he was licensed as a surveyor by the College of William and Mary.[5] This was his most intimate association with an institution of higher learning until at age fifty-six he became chancellor of the same university.[6] George quickly put his license to use, becoming official surveyor of Culpeper County while still seventeen.

Washington's practical education included, besides his profession as a surveyor, the management of the superb Mount Vernon estate to which he fell heir at age twenty upon the death of Lawrence and Lawrence's daughter; the military and diplomatic commission in French-occupied territory beginning when he was twenty-one; the saving of Braddock's army at twenty-three; command of all Virginia troops at twenty-six; and service in the House of Burgesses, as a county justice of the peace, and in the Continental Congress. All of these experiences helped to prepare him for such national roles as commander in chief of the Continental Army, president of the Constitutional Convention, and president of the United States.

But Washington's education beyond grammar school was not entirely a matter of practical experience. He was an autodidact in the best traditions of the Italian Renaissance, Elizabethan England, and the colonial America of his youth and young manhood. In a lifetime of study, he accumulated a vast amount of detailed information on many subjects. When Patrick Henry after the Continental Congress of 1774 was asked who had been the greatest member, he replied, "If you speak of solid information and sound judgement, Colonel Washington is unquestionably the greatest man on that floor."

Like Jefferson and many another giant public figure in the Virginia of his day, Washington proudly listed his occupation as farmer. It was not just an attempt to identify closely with a predominantly agricultural constituency. Jefferson and Washington literally depended on the soil for their livelihood, but they also looked to it for the nurture of their spirits. Long before the Enlightenment yielded to Romanticism, they, like some of their European contemporaries, had a great faith in people who lived close to the earth. Like other heroic ages, the Early National Period was a mythopoeic one. Washington's contemporaries—mindful of the Roman patriot who had left the plow and taken up the sword to lead his people in battle, but had returned to his farm after rescuing the republic—delighted in calling him "Cincinnatus." He was fully aware of the significance.

One of the most important aspects of Washington's career as a farmer, however, is the fact that he became one of the most efficient farmers in America. Entering upon the ownership and management of a substantial agricultural estate at the tender age of twenty, he became, despite many distractions of public service both civil and military, not only a highly successful farmer on a truly large scale but an influential model of sound agricultural practice and an enricher of the science of agronomy. He studied botany and introduced fruits and vegetables foreign to his native soil. He kept abreast of experiments on farms in other parts of America and in Europe and duplicated them under varying conditions, contributing his own reports to the international literature of scientific agriculture. He was so much in the vanguard that he even attempted to set up controlled experiments. It is appropriate that Antoine Houdon included a plowshare with his great statue of Washington.[7] Not only was it a symbol of his career as a farmer; like Jefferson, he was the inventor of an improved plowshare. Washington added a device that automatically dropped seeds into the furrows.

Washington was also largely self-taught in military science. He independently studied manuals on the subject, and as a young provincial officer in the French and Indian War learned all that he could of European professionalism from British general Braddock and his staff. But he also perceived many things that his often arrogant preceptors did not. He saw ways of blending their Old World traditions of discipline with some of the lessons that he had learned on the frontier. He was not too proud to learn from the Indians some valuable lessons of warfare in a wilderness.

While the British officers were wedded to parade-ground tactics used on the open fields of the long-cultivated European continent, Washington futilely but determinedly urged that they take advantage of the natural cover available alike to themselves and their enemies. Braddock's defeat, which would have become a rout if Washington had not intervened when the general was fatally wounded, vindicated the young American's arguments.

As commanding general in the Revolution, Washington evidenced the courage and resolution expected of him but also demonstrated a creativity whose existence had been largely unsuspected. He added the sophistication of European methods to "the type of hit-and-run raid he had often seen the Indians achieve during his previous war."[8] He gained surprise by clever stratagems. When short of artillery, he even employed such imaginative devices as placing logs at ill-armed points in imitation of cannons so that the enemy would avoid them and attack the strongest American positions. He made some mistakes, as virtually all generals have, but it was said that he never made the same mistake twice. At Yorktown, aided by a French fleet under Admiral the Comte de Grasse and a large measure of luck in the weather and in timing, he used masterly strategy to bottle up Lord Cornwallis' army and win the crucial battle of the Revolution.

As a member of the House of Burgesses, Washington became a self-taught student of the law as well as a lawmaker. He did not become a true legal scholar, such as those other two Georges, Mason and Wythe, but he prepared himself for the legislative role by giving diligent attention to the statutes of Virginia and the traditions of the English common law. In preparation for the Constitutional Convention of 1787, and as its presiding officer, he was an attentive listener and reader of the statements prepared by delegates of broad and deep learning in legal history.

Political history—especially that of England and its American colonies— also claimed his attention. His writings show a familiarity with leading characters and episodes. In applying what he had learned to the events of his own time, he was able to integrate politics and economics.

Though as president he sometimes relied on ghostwriters, notably Madison and Hamilton, to provide graceful expression of his own thoughts, he was the master of a remarkably lucid writing style. Many of his sentences were too long and complex for popular taste in his own time and even more so in recent generations. But it is impressive that one with so little formal schooling was able to create sentence after sentence of great length and complexity but nevertheless free of structural flaws. His syntax reflected the organization of his well-ordered mind. Many of his reports also reveal keen observation, retentive memory, and effective use of significant detail.

Many persons impressed by evidence of Washington's pragmatic intelligence would probably picture him as blind and deaf to esthetics, more appreciative of a straight corn row than of the cyma curve of painter or sculptor, more delighted with the blast of a hunting horn than with any orchestral sound of brass or woodwind. He certainly took pleasure in neat fields and foxhunting, but he was enthusiastic about painting, sculpture, and music. Twenty-one paintings and engravings hung in his banquet hall alone. In defiance of prevailing fashion that prized portraiture but scorned landscapes, he was a committed purchaser of skillful renditions of natural scenes, occasionally commissioning works to his taste. Independent of the artistic fashions of his time, he insisted on indigenous forms rather than neoclassical embellishments in American landscapes. James Thomas Flexner, an art historian as well as a Washington biographer, says, "Washington anticipated by several generations the mid-nineteenth-century conceptions of the Hudson River School."[9]

He enjoyed classical concerts and maintained at Mount Vernon a music room whose furnishings at one time or another included a spinet, pianoforte, harpsichord, violin, and German flute. Though he once modestly protested to Francis Hopkinson that he could "neither sing one of the songs nor raise a single note on any instrument," there are reports of his practicing on the flute. Certainly his references to concerts indicate that he was not just keeping up with the Joneses, Lees, and Carters in a musically conscious Virginia society, but was truly charmed by classical harmonies.

The great house at Mount Vernon was itself symbolic of another interest, one that united esthetics and practicality. Washington's boyhood home was the nucleus of his mansion. He rented it from his half brother's widow before it became his own property. It was a neat but modest home, much like many others in Virginia. A story-and-a-half structure, it presented between two end-chimneys a face of typical fenestration—a front door flanked by pairs of windows, with three dormer windows. In 1759, anticipating his marriage to the wealthy widow Martha Custis, he raised the roof and inserted a second story. In the 1770's and after the Revolution, he widened this house to one hundred feet, surmounted it with an attractive cupola and added a classical pediment on the back and a full-length portico on the river side.

Transforming a conventional house by successive stages into a mansion distinctive when created but widely copied since was far more difficult than abandoning the old structure and building a completely new one. Some writers have wondered why Washington assumed the hard task of integrating the earlier structure into his new plans. Since the old house had been his boyhood home and then the home of his beloved brother Lawrence, sentiment would seem to account for his choice.

Washington not only played an important role in the planning of the final mansion but also carefully superintended many aspects of the execution. One visitor noted that he even personally did part of the measuring, not entrusting this task entirely to the builders. One notable feature of the finished structure was the shaping and rustication of the exterior boards to counterfeit stonework. The effect was heightened by the application of sand to freshly painted wood. Rustication was used in other buildings in Great Britain and America, but the radical extent of its use at Mount Vernon has been called unprecedented. Architectural historian Thomas Tileston Waterman also says, "Precedent for the portico, which is unique of its period, is unknown."[10] Researchers recording the Mount Vernon restoration have said, "The most striking architectural feature of the mansion is the high-columned piazza, extending the full length of the house, a splendid adaptation of a design to setting and climate. It seems to have been a complete innovation and would, in itself, entitle George Washington to distinction among architects."[11]

In Washington's time, the contractor who built an imposing home was also frequently the architect. It was once thought extremely unlikely that Washington was the sole architect for the final version of Mount Vernon. But construction records and his correspondence on the subject suggest that he played the dominant role in design. After a study of all the evidence now available, James Thomas Flexner concludes, "he was his own architect."[12] Sometimes when public duties kept Washington from home, others supervised construction for him. But when he was on the scene, he even made minute observations of his carpenters' methods of cutting boards, noting wasted motions that could be eliminated. Flexner observes that this was "a work-time study more suited to the twentieth century."[13] In building a house, as in building a government, Washington favored a happy blend of tradition and experiment, and insisted on efficiency.

He also embellished the setting of Mount Vernon with elegant landscaping. The long portico looked out on the Potomac River, and he wisely left the sweep of lawn on that side unadorned except for a few trees. But elsewhere he put to use ideas that he got from illustrative plates in his books on the great gardens of England and continental Europe. With an unerring eye, he imported plants whose colors and shapes would complement those of native shrubs. He even planned ornamental paths and hedges for his vegetable gardens.

Flexner stresses that the esthetic sense that "found its great expression in the design of Mount Vernon" and its gardens was a passionate concern that also "could manifest itself in the spacing on a page of a letter or of a survey."[14]

This interest extended to literature. Washington's personal library included quality fiction. He was familiar with great poetry. Fired by adolescent love, he produced some verse acrostics hammered out with the rhythmic regularity of an anvil chorus. By his early twenties, he appears to have abandoned the creation of poetry. Surviving verses reveal some familiarity with classical history but do not suggest that his devotion to military and political careers impoverished the realm of literature. He appears never to have lost his appreciation of poetry. He once arranged for a reading to his staff by Phillis Wheatley.

When located near a theater, as in Williamsburg, Philadelphia, or New York, Washington was a frequent patron. His enthusiasm ranged from classical drama to puppet shows.

How ignorant, then, was George Washington? Certainly he lacked the extensive classical background of his fellow founder John Adams, who called him "ignorant." And he could not match the broad scholarship of Jefferson, Madison, Mason, or Franklin. But his interests ranged from agronomy, landscaping, architecture, military science, and government to economics, music, poetry, and drama. In the first five of these fields, he was a creative performer. Jefferson, analyzing Washington for posterity, said, "His mind was great and powerful, without being of the very first order." Then he revealed his own standard for mentality of "the very first order": "his penetration [was] strong, though not so acute as that of a Newton, Bacon or Locke."[15]

Washington brought to his role as first chief magistrate of the Republic under the new Constitution the inquiring intellect, diverse interests, and creative approach that Lorenzo brought to the leadership of the Florentine republic and Queen Elizabeth to her reign over England. If Washington were president today, most members of the media who favored his politics would hail him as a prodigious intellect.

Unlike some of his successors in office, and many leaders in other lands, he was not afraid to recruit dazzling intellects as his chief lieutenants. He filled the two principal cabinet[16] posts by appointing Jefferson as secretary of state and Hamilton as secretary of the treasury. Both had been deemed precocious from their adolescence. As a college boy at William and Mary, Jefferson had been a favorite intellectual companion of the learned Professors George Wythe and William Small and the delight of distinguished guests in the Governor's Palace. As a youngster in the British West Indies, Hamilton won acclaim as the author of much-admired newspaper articles. As mature men, both brought to Washington's cabinet brilliant creativity stimulated by a richly varied intellectual diet.

Jefferson was not just one of the greatest American secretaries of state (some would say the greatest); he was also one of the greatest foreign secretaries of modern world history. The author of policies inspired by tradition but inventively pursued, he became a role model for diplomats in his own and other countries. He and Washington, who shared his love of both stability and experiment, were severely tested by the war between England and France. Highhanded actions by both contenders repeatedly threatened to shatter the American policy of neutrality. This is not the place to survey in detail the means by which Jefferson, aided by Washington's perception, understanding, and flexibility in the service of inflexible resolve, thwarted every attempt to draw the United States into armed combat.

Particularly brilliant was Jefferson's handling of the international crisis when French ambassador Edmond Genet dedicated his energy and resourcefulness to the accomplishment of American involvement. John Quincy Adams, son of John Adams and (before becoming president) one of Jefferson's ablest successors as secretary of state, said that in the Genet crisis the Virginian had "triumphantly sustained and vindicated the administration of Washington without forfeiting the friendly professions of France. . . . Mr. Jefferson's papers on that controversy present the most perfect model of diplomatic discussion and exposition of modern times." George Canning, one of Britain's most brilliant foreign secretaries, paid an extraordinary tribute in 1823. At that time, taking his country out of the Holy Alliance in order to steer an exacting course between contending powers, he told the House of Commons, "If I wished for a guide in a system of neutrality, I should take that laid down by America in the days of the Presidency of Washington and the Secretaryship of Jefferson in 1793."[17] The creative foreign policy pursued by America's federal government in its thirtieth year became the model for the venerable parent government in Great Britain as it dealt with a major crisis under the leadership of one of its greatest statesmen.[18]

To understand the significance of the measures initiated by Hamilton as secretary of the treasury, it is necessary to consider his philosophy of representative government. He succinctly stated its central tenets during a debate on June 18, 1787 in the Constitutional Convention. "All communities," he said,

> divide themselves into the few and the many. The first are the rich and wellborn, the other the mass of the people. . . . The people are turbulent and changing; they seldom judge or determine right. Give therefore to the first class a distinct, permanent share in the government. They will check the unsteadiness of the second, and as they cannot receive any advantage by a change, they therefore will ever maintain good government.

Superficially, Hamilton's statement is not far removed from John Jay's assertion that the country should be run by the people who owned it. Viewed in any light, Hamilton's declaration that the people as a whole "seldom judge or determine right" and that leadership should go to "the rich and wellborn" has been unacceptable to most Americans in subsequent generations and indeed frequently was so in his own. Hamilton's combination of distinguished ancestry and illegitimate personal origin made him preternaturally sensitive to the virtue of aristocracy. His marriage into New York's great Schuyler family increased the orientation, while the Schuyler wealth and his own success as a banker encouraged him to regard riches as not just a personal blessing but also a criterion of fitness.

That Hamilton should have held such elitist views is in no way remarkable. A minority in every state had similar ideas. Hamilton stood apart from most of the other great founders of his generation in the accuracy of his vision of America's future. He voiced more forcefully than any of his colleagues and

competitors the idea that the United States was destined to be an urban-domi-
nated nation dependent for prosperity on manufacturing and international
trade and requiring the support of a complex financial structure.

Jefferson also envisioned the growth of large cities, but regarded it as a
possibility rather than a necessity, and in any event saw such a development as
one to be dreaded. His vision also was accurate when he predicted that the
growth of great cities would mean an increase in disease, crime, and a poverty
more brutalizing than that of the countryside. In many ways, Jefferson had a
broader vision than Hamilton, one more empathetic with almost every element
of the population. And great as Hamilton's intellect was, Jefferson's was even
more far-ranging. But Hamilton was supremely realistic in his perception that
America could not live out an agrarian idyll in sequestration from the rest of the
world. He was aware that, if the United States did not compete in international
commerce, it would lose its independence.

To prepare America for the role that he envisioned, Hamilton advanced
measures calculated to strengthen the federal government, and to develop a
strong, truly national financial structure. One of the most controversial of these
was his proposal for dealing with the debt that was the federal government's
unwelcome legacy from the Confederation. His recommendation to fund the
foreign debt at par, permitting creditors to exchange, at face value, depreciated
securities for newly issued interest-bearing bonds, drew no significant opposition. But his proposal to handle the domestic debt in the same way was an
entirely different matter. It consisted in part of the Confederation's arrears of
interest and unliquidated claims and in part of the debts piled up by the states
during the Revolution. Debtors and farmers were incensed at a move that necessitated sale of their securities at a huge loss.

Whereas this proposal divided the nation into opposing economic and occupational groups, the plan for the federal government to assume the state debts
separated the country geographically. The New England states had the heaviest
record of unpaid debts and therefore rejoiced in the opportunity to unload
them on the central government. The southern states had gone a long way
toward paying their debts and were furious at a proposal that would now tax
their people to pay the debts of those who, it appeared to them, had been less
provident.

Virginia, which had paid nearly all of its Revolutionary debt, led the opposition. Its James Madison led a chiefly southern coalition, which defeated the
proposal in the House of Representatives by a margin of two votes.

In the long run, Hamilton's program tended to advance his two principal
objectives: establishing public credit on so firm a foundation as to inspire confidence in the new federal government among its own citizens and in the community of nations; and bolstering and stabilizing that government by strengthening the bonds of common interest among the business and commercial
groups that Hamilton believed to be the hope of the Republic.

Despite the House's initial rejection of assumption, Hamilton eventually
won on the issue—but at a price. He delivered enough northern votes in Congress to locate the permanent national capital on the Potomac River instead of

in Philadelphia, in exchange for Madison's pledge of enough southern votes to permit passage of the narrowly defeated provision for assumption. Each side gave up something it wanted for something that mattered to it even more. The brilliant theorists of *The Federalist* were also masters of practical politics.

Not all southerners accepted the compromise. Patrick Henry produced a list of resolutions charging that assumption of state debts by the federal government established a moneyed interest and guaranteed its perpetuity, and was subversive of the very republican and federal interests it purported to support. Henry and other Virginia signers of these resolutions protested that they found "no clause in the Constitution authorizing Congress to assume the debts of states."

Undeterred by these and other strict constructionists, Hamilton, as secretary of the treasury, submitted to Congress another proposal designed to strengthen the federal government. It called for a national bank to be known as the Bank of the United States.

When Washington requested written opinions from members of his cabinet, Jefferson wrote that the national bank measure was unconstitutional. He based his opinion on the Tenth Amendment to the Constitution, still ten months from final adoption but nevertheless a foregone conclusion. It provided: "The powers not delegated to the United States by the Constitution, nor prohibited by it to the states, are reserved to the states respectively, or to the people." Hamilton argued that provisions for a national bank were constitutional because Congress was empowered to collect taxes and regulate trade, and creation of such an institution would facilitate the execution of both responsibilities. He then made one of the most famous and influential statements ever attributed to him: "If the *end* be clearly comprehended within any of the specified powers, and if the measure have an obvious relation to that *end*, and is not forbidden by any particular provision of the Constitution, it may safely be deemed to come within the compass of the national authority."

This doctrine of implied powers was not original with Hamilton, but he invoked it so often and so forcefully that it became more closely identified with him than anyone else. As early as August 1787, Jefferson, who for all his zeal was more a pragmatic idealist than a hidebound ideologue, had departed from his usual strict constructionism. When some insisted that Congress lacked the power to enforce levies on the states, he had argued that no express grant of authority was necessary. "When two parties make a compact," he said, "there results to each a power of compelling the other to execute it." The great philosophical difference between Jefferson and Hamilton was that, whereas the secretary of state accepted the necessity in the national interest of rare departures from strict construction, the treasury secretary advanced the doctrine of implied powers in a deliberate effort to strengthen the central government.

In the instance of the proposal for a national bank, Washington—ordinarily a decisive man—had difficulty choosing between the opposing views so ably presented by Hamilton and Jefferson. But finally, theorizing that in such cases more weight should be given the opinion of the cabinet member whose department was most intimately involved, he sided with Hamilton.

Repeated differences of opinion between the secretaries of state and treasury led to heated rivalry between the two. The competition between them was exacerbated by their striving for Washington's approval. Hamilton's principal biographers believe that he saw Washington as a father image. This need for the president's approval may have been all the stronger because of Hamilton's self-consciousness about his illegitimacy. Though Jefferson was only eleven years younger than Washington, his attitude toward the older man also seems to have been tinged with filial sentiment. As a hero who combined wilderness surveying with a public career, Peter Jefferson, who died when Thomas was fourteen years old, may have seemed to the son very much like the Father of His Country.

The secretaries of state and treasury, however, were separated by philosophical differences that ran deeper than matters of taste and temperament. While Jefferson believed with almost religious fervor that America's strength must lie in farmers who owned their own land, Hamilton believed that it should be based on a diversified economy dominated by manufacturing, commercial, and financial interests. While Jefferson advocated a broad diffusion of wealth and strongly sympathized with debtors, Hamilton urged governmental encouragement of business even if it led to greatly increased wealth for the most enterprising, and his sympathies were with the creditors. Though the Virginian believed that all functions that could be performed efficiently by local or state governments should be left to them, the New Yorker tried to strengthen the central government at every opportunity and to enhance the power of the chief executive within it. Jefferson maintained that the people, acting through representatives, were the best arbiters of their own interests, but Hamilton insisted that they seldom judged rightly and, as we have seen, said that important matters should be decided by an elite.

Arguments between Hamilton and Jefferson, and between their followers in Congress and in the press, helped to educate the public regarding their widely divergent philosophies. As in the debates over the Constitution, the voters were exposed to a mass of information ranging from the structures of the classical Greek and Roman republics and their Italian Renaissance successors to the sweep of English parliamentary history and the analysis of contemporary problems.

Not that argument was always conducted on a high level. Hamilton hid behind a pseudonym in writing published attacks on Jefferson. And Jefferson, in reply to Washington's efforts to make peace between the two cabinet officers, described his rival as "a man whose history, from the moment at which history can stoop to notice him, is a tissue of machinations against the liberty of the country which has not only received [him] and given him bread, but heaped its honors on his head."[19]

Yet, when Jefferson was hard pressed in a down-to-the-wire contest for the presidency in 1801, Hamilton wrote to leader after leader of his own party saying that the Virginian was preferable to Burr. And Professor George Tucker of the University of Virginia said that when he and others expressed surprise at seeing a bust of Hamilton at Monticello facing one of the owner, their aging host remarked that he and Hamilton would be " 'opposed in death as in life,' in a tone and manner that showed that no vestige of ill feeling was left on his mind." The professor added that the former president was not "slow to acknowledge the virtues and talents of Alexander Hamilton."

The rivalry between Jefferson and Hamilton, and the crystallization of support around each, hastened the development of a phenomenon which the usually realistic Washington hoped that the United States would be spared—the growth of political parties. But, even though the contest for national leadership inevitably descended to personalities and prejudices, and the unwarranted maligning of the public motives and personal morals of even the most upright founders, it also frequently rose above that level. Many American voters were prepared to read and listen to lengthy discussions of the issues. And the leaders of both the Federalist and Democratic-Republican parties were men whose mental activity ranged far beyond practical politics and provided a broadening and allusion-rich context for their debates. When Jefferson and Madison traveled through New York State in 1791, conferring with the other potential leaders of their party, they combined the politicking with "botanizing."

Philip Freneau, editor of Philadelphia's *National Gazette*, the most influential Anti-Federalist newspaper, was not only a brilliant polemicist but also America's leading poet. In such poems as "To a Wild Honeysuckle" and "The Indian Burying Ground," which still delight discriminating readers, the insights inspired by native flora and fauna and the wisdom of the aborigines are combined with traditional European elements to create a truly American poetic literature. In the *Farmer's Weekly Museum*, a prestigious New Hampshire journal, columnist Royall Tyler, celebrated author of the play *The Contrast* and later chief justice of Vermont, mixed political satire with literary comment. In its advice to aspiring politicians, the *Maryland Gazette* summarized journalistic expectations of American leadership: "Keep always before your eyes the steps by which a Jefferson and Madison have gradually ascended to their present preeminence of fame. Like them you must devote your whole leisure to the most useful reading. Like them you must dive into the depths of philosophy and government. . . ."

Naively, the paper added to the list of qualifications "keeping and holding fast, as to the rock of your political salvation, their unshaken integrity and scorn of party." Jefferson and Madison held fast to their integrity but, about two months after publication of the Maryland editor's advice, they were conferring with New York political leaders on moves that led to formation of the Democratic-Republican Party.

The movement of political events had swept Madison from Washington's side with a rapidity that few would have envisioned at the start of the first presidential administration. The first president, though the master of a clear and logical style, relied on ghostwriters for his principal formal addresses. Madison was the author of his first inaugural message. As a member of the joint Senate-House inaugural committee, he also wrote the House's official reply to the president. Then, at Washington's request, Madison wrote the president's formal reply to the House. Washington turned to Madison again in 1792 for help in preparing his "Farewell Address," when he hoped to retire from office after one term. On the insistence of the public, he returned for four more years. The growth of political parties and the changed relationship with Madison are symbolized by the fact that, when Washington wished to update his "Farewell Address" for use in 1798, he turned not to Madison but to Hamilton.

Jefferson's resignation as secretary of state, effective December 31, 1793, because of Washington's increasing reliance on Hamilton's advice, even in foreign affairs, underlined the political divisions that had beset the once united band of patriots. Gone were the days when Washington presided over a Constitutional Convention framing a new federal government, with Madison taking the lead in determining its character while seeking Jefferson's advice in correspondence, and Madison and Hamilton later joining talents to fight for ratification. The Virginian and the New Yorker had together produced that great masterpiece of political wisdom, *The Federalist*, and Washington and Jefferson had both applauded. Now politics had made "Federalist" a label cherished by Washington and Hamilton but rejected by Jefferson and Madison.

But monolithic governments do not foster freedom. They certainly do not promote creativity. It was not only inevitable that the nation would divide into political parties; it was also desirable. And it was fortunate in those formative years that the leaders of both parties were brilliant, educated men who, however great their ambitions, however passionate their partisanship, were still capable of subordinating personal desires to the national interest. A government was blessed when it could claim a Washington as its president, a Jefferson as its secretary of state, a Hamilton as its secretary of the treasury, and a Madison as a leader of the House.

The president himself is rightly regarded as the least intellectual of these four, but in diversity of interests, earnest studiousness, and creativity he was the superior of most chiefs of state in most eras in most countries. His greatest strength, as the public has rightly assumed, was in his character. But ancillary to it were various abilities of a high order.

As first president of the United States, Washington—scarcely less than the framers of the Constitution—made the presidency what it became. His every public action produced a precedent.

This fact was illustrated by the evolution of the president's cabinet. The Constitution made no provision for such an institution. Washington began his first administration with the aid of heads of three executive departments—Foreign Affairs (renamed "State"), War, and Treasury—established between July 27 and September 2, 1789. Congress created the office of postmaster general on September 26, and in May 1795 created a department for that officer. The Federal Judiciary Act, besides providing for the organization of the federal court system, also established the office of attorney general. Washington quite naturally consulted with the five department heads on matters of their particular purviews. He sometimes sought the opinion of each on the same question, as in October 1789 when he weighed the pros and cons of a presidential tour of the United States. But he conferred with them individually.

In November and December of that year, he varied his policy, meeting three times with department heads as a group to discuss the connected issues of foreign policy and military preparation. The next year he held several more such meetings. At the end of his eight-year presidential tenure, Washington had established a precedent of cabinet meetings that has been followed by all of his successors.

Washington had done much to determine the character of the American presidency before he was elected to the office. The Articles of Confederation had provided for legislative government, and the various state constitutions had accorded few powers to their own chief executives. Experience of executive tyranny before the Revolution had caused a recoil. Except for the presence of Washington at the Constitutional Convention of 1787, always prominently in view as the presiding officer, the government agreed upon might well have begun life crippled by a fettered executive. But there was a general understanding among the delegates that Washington was virtually certain to be the first president and that he could have the job as long as he wanted it. And there was firm faith in his ability as well as character. He had been tested in the snows and fires of Revolution. There was confidence that he would be strong without being tyrannical. The framers of the Constitution provided for a president whose renewable tenure of four years, barring impeachment, was independent of both the legislature and the judiciary. In foreign affairs, and in quick response to a military emergency, his powers were almost limitless. The office of the presidency was molded to the Constitution-makers' image of Washington.

In turn, Americans saw Washington as the embodiment of what they liked to believe were their own virtues—intelligence, courage, versatility, patriotism, and the proper balance of daring born of a sense of adventure and prudence bred by respect for tradition.

THE PHILOSOPHER-KING AND THE NEW REPUBLIC

AMERICAN POLITICAL CREATIVITY in the years immediately following Washington's retirement from the presidency in 1796 was not to be found in the administration of his successor, John Adams. Nor was it evident in the legislation of the Federalist-dominated Congress. It was manifested instead in the ingenuity of the Democratic-Republican opponents of the Federalist chief executive and his party's majorities in House and Senate.

The threat of war with France in Adams' administration tended to separate him from some of the leaders of his own Federalist Party, notably a prowar faction led by Alexander Hamilton. The president's diplomatic efforts forestalled a declaration of war and bought an uneasy peace following two years of undeclared naval war between the two countries.

A more lasting effect of Franco-American conflict was the hostility to France, and to foreigners in general, that influenced the Federalist-led Congress to pass harsh legislation applicable to immigrants. Between June 18 and July 6, 1798, the Senate and House passed three acts designed to curb the activities of resident aliens. The Naturalization Act increased the residence requirement from five years to fourteen. The Alien Act authorized the president to expel from the United States any alien that he even suspected of activities or inclinations broadly and amorphously delineated as "secret." The Alien Enemies Act empowered the president to imprison or expel any alien in time of declared war.

Some congressmen voting for these measures were motivated by genuine fear for their country's sake. But some Federalists appear simply to have seized the opportunity presented by the apparent imminence of declared war; they counted on Francophobia to countenance the arrest or banishment of immigrant journalists numbered among the principal Democratic-Republican publicists.

Having placed stiff control on aliens, the Congress on July 14 enacted legislation that threatened the liberties of American citizens. The Sedition Act of that date provided for the imprisonment of citizens joining with aliens to oppose execution of a federal law, obstructing a federal officer's performance of his duties, or aiding "any insurrection, riot, unlawful assembly, or combination." More disturbing were provisions for the fining and imprisonment of anyone convicted of publishing or printing "false, scandalous, and malicious" criticisms of the federal government, the president, or either house of Congress. This act was scheduled to expire in March 1801 and would not be subject to renewal. But the Democratic-Republicans (or simply "Republicans," as they increasingly were called) were well aware that nearly three years of such draconian measures could negate First Amendment guarantees of free speech and a free press.

To John Adams' credit, he never used any of the powers granted him under the Alien Acts. But, at various levels of government, the Sedition Act was used to punish legitimate opposition to the Federalist Party. Federalists prosecuted twenty-five persons for "false, scandalous, and malicious writings" and succeeded in convicting ten, all by an interesting coincidence, Republican editors or printers.

Alarmed for their party but even more for their country, the two leading Republicans, Jefferson and Madison, struck back. With individual liberty at stake, they moved to interpose between the central government and the individual citizen the only power available to them—that of the states.

In so doing, Madison, as the Father of the Constitution and therefore of the federal government of the United States, invited the charge of inconsistency. In reality, however, he had been quite consistent. He had worked for a federal system as a much stronger protector of the American experiment in individual freedom than the manifestly inadequate Articles of Confederation. He subsequently had worked to secure a Bill of Rights as a bulwark against the potential tyranny of the central government, not only in order to obtain votes for ratification of the Constitution but also because he was sincerely devoted to individual liberty. It was that devotion that now led him to counter a threat from the government he had helped to build.

Madison had foreseen the problem and the means of its coming. On May 13, 1798, he had written to Jefferson, "Perhaps it is a universal truth that the loss of liberty [at] home is to be charged to provisions against danger real or pretended from abroad."[1] Jefferson was the chief initiator of the measures taken to combat the Alien and Sedition Acts. He was the anonymous author of the Kentucky Resolutions, adopted by the Kentucky legislature, which asserted that the Constitution was a compact among the states delegating special powers to be exercised by the federal government. Under the terms of the Constitution, the federal government was to be supreme over the states in foreign policy but not in domestic. If the federal government assumed domestic authority not granted to it in the Constitution, such assumption would be unconstitutional and therefore void.

Madison was the author of the Virginia Resolutions, adopted by the Virginia legislature. They were a milder but more precise expression of the theory set forth by Jefferson in the Kentucky Resolutions. Jefferson had to remain anonymous because he was vice president of the United States; many doubtless would have deemed it inappropriate for the holder of that office to write resolutions protesting the activities of the government of which he was officially a part. The Kentucky and Virginia Resolutions became important documents in American history, the most quoted expressions of the strict constructionist, or states' rights, theory of government. Followed by learned and complex exegeses, they were cited on pivotal issues by governors and state and national legislators into the middle of the twentieth century.

Creativity, in March 1801, moved from opposition to incumbency. Jefferson was inaugurated as the third president of the United States. His walk from the boardinghouse to the capital for the ceremony, in striking contrast to the formality of Washington's and Adams' regal rides by coach to their oath takings, signaled a changed mood in the presidency. At the start of the new government, elaborate ceremony deeply rooted in tradition gave a needed sense of continuity. But with the federal government having become oppressive in Adams' administration, more from congressional zeal than from his initiative, the informal note was important in establishing a nonthreatening presence. And, in its own way, it suggested stability. Boisterous trumpets were not needed to clear the path for the chief magistrate of a well-established republic.

Determined in opposition, Jefferson was conciliatory in victory. In his inaugural address, he said, "We have called by different names brethren of the same principle. We are all republicans; we are all federalists." Those who heard the new president speak these words thought he sounded like a peacemaker. Many who read his statement seized upon the significance of his leaving "republicans" and "federalists" uncapitalized, generic terms rather than partisan labels.

There was a difference of spirit in other ways equally significant. Seventeen days after his inauguration, Jefferson wrote to an old friend, Joseph Priestley, one of the celebrated alien intellectuals whose settlement in America had alarmed some Federalists. Dissenting clergyman, teacher of the classics, a scientist admitted to the Royal Society as an expert on electricity and now even more famous as the discoverer of oxygen, he was a Renaissance man whose high hopes for the new nation had been dimmed but not extinguished during the Adams years. In this first year of the nineteenth century, and first month of his presidency, Jefferson exuberantly wrote Priestley, "We can no longer say there is nothing new under the sun. For this whole chapter in the history of man is new. The great extent of our republic is new."[2]

As a conservative who had become a rebel through conviction prodded by circumstance, Washington exemplified the tension between tradition and experiment that helped to make the period of the founders of the United States such a creative one. As a product initially of a conservative family tradition and subsequently of the adventurous Enlightenment, Jefferson embodied the same productive tension. Though he quarreled with successive English governments, he cherished his British heritage and took inspiration from Francis Bacon, John Locke, and Sir Isaac Newton, whom he considered the three greatest figures in modern history. And he delved into Anglo-Saxon history in seeking guidance for the development of democratic institutions. He instituted a course of Anglo-Saxon language and literature at the University of Virginia, and composed an innovative text in the subject, thus combining in one project his reliance on tradition and his delight in experiment.

Though Jefferson was an enthusiastic disciple of the Enlightenment, much of his light came from the lamps of Greece and Rome. When he wanted Virginia legislators to approve his design for a capitol, he stressed his plan's indebtedness to a classical model rather than its significant variations. He knew that people are much more willing to accept the new and strange when familiar aspects are emphasized. He used the same technique in presenting political ideas, citing both Athenian and Anglo-Saxon experience in arguing for an enlarged electorate, and drawing upon his capacious memory to present at least a partial precedent for each legal reform. But this approach was not solely artifice; it was also the one most congenial to his own spirit with its dual allegiances. More than anyone else, he was responsible for the classical revival in American architecture. When Pierre L'Enfant was proposing boldly original designs for the new federal city of Washington, Jefferson wrote to President Washington, "Whenever it is proposed to prepare for the Capitol, I should prefer the adoption of some one of the models of antiquity, which have had the approbation of thousands of years. . . ."

In nation building as well as in architecture, Jefferson was skilled in adapting traditional structures to contemporary and future needs. His patriotism, his experience in statecraft, his wide knowledge of both traditional Western culture and the new science, his stimulating friendships with some of the most brilliant thinkers in both America and Europe, the sweep of his vision, and his eloquence in communicating it, all combined to make him one of America's greatest presidents. This is no place for even a condensed history of his two terms, 1801–1809, but rather for a consideration of the most creative aspects of his tenure.[3]

No one should underestimate Jefferson's role in restoring America's threatened freedoms, or in managing the government's economy with uncommon wisdom and restraint—something he never achieved in his personal affairs. Both of these accomplishments helped to clear the way for bold initiatives. And Jefferson, like Washington, but unlike some of their successors in later generations, did not fear to bring truly brilliant intellects into his Cabinet. Of course, he served a society whose leaders prized intellectual excellence. Jefferson's secretary of state was his old friend Madison, possessor of one of the world's most incisive political minds, whether *political* be defined narrowly as pertaining to "the science of the possible" or philosophically in reference to the human role as "a political animal." For his secretary of the treasury, Jefferson chose Albert Gallatin, a brilliant student of economics and a Republican leader of proven effectiveness in the House of Representatives. Nevertheless, it took courage to name him to the second highest post in the cabinet, and Jefferson waited until Congress had recessed, because an interim appointment did not immediately require senatorial assent. The major obstacles to approval were Gallatin's Swiss nativity (he was a scion of Switzerland's ancient nobility), heavy French accent, and darkly Mediterranean features—all repugnant to the many Francophobes among Federalist senators.

The most imaginative of Jefferson's presidential accomplishments involved the American West. This is ironic in view of the fact that he never traveled more than fifty miles west of his Virginia birthplace. Together with reluctance to be long away from Monticello, tendency to motion sickness made Jefferson refuse diplomatic missions abroad until convinced that duty demanded his presence in Europe. The same feeling would have made traveling over rugged western terrain a torture.[4] But imagination and study carried him where he could not go physically. Born on the frontier, though exposed to the elite society of Tidewater, he gloried in the tales of wilderness adventure told by his father, Peter Jefferson, a surveyor and in his time one of North America's two most famous cartographers. Indian chiefs who came to dinner at his parents' table further whetted his interest in the West.

As Jefferson matured, his theories of the frontier's stimulus to democracy and his hopes that new states carved from western lands could begin life free from the curse of slavery united to reinforce his earlier romantic interest in the region. His concern with geopolitics antedated by more than a century the label's entrance into the English language, and he warned that acquisition of the vast Louisiana Territory was essential if the United States was to be more than a second-rate power. He was one of the first to foresee that Spain would cede that territory to France, enabling Paris to deny the young Republic free access to the Mississippi. Possession of the territory by the United States would guarantee American navigation of the Father of Waters and provide "more cultivable land" than was available to any other "civilized nation." Ultimately, acquisition was made possible by Napoleon's needs and frustrations, but it was Jefferson's actions with the cooperation of James Monroe, on the scene in Paris, that made it a reality.

Jefferson, as an advocate of strict construction, might have been stymied by the lack of a constitutional provision for purchase and assimilation of foreign territory. But he had earlier conceded that a true emergency might at times justify the assumption that the Constitution's provision for such an essential as defense implied the granting of powers necessary to performance of that duty. The need for speed led Jefferson to reach agreement with Napoleon on the Louisiana Territory before explicit authorization, but he said that he must submit his actions to the Congress for confirmation or rejection. Thus Jefferson risked his own political career, but did not place the Constitution in jeopardy.

Without the shedding of blood, by the stroke of a pen he doubled the size of the United States. An opportunity greater than the one he had sought suddenly presented itself when Napoleon offered more than was asked. Jefferson's superb knowledge of international relations and long study of available information on the western lands enabled him to grasp the scope of the opportunity and to match it with the range of his own daring and flexibility.

Even before conclusion of the Louisiana Purchase Treaty with France, Jefferson had submitted a secret message to Congress requesting a twenty-five-hundred-dollar appropriation for an expedition to ascend the Missouri River to its source and proceed from there to the Pacific. Officially, the expedition would be "for the purpose of extending the external commerce of the United States." The statement was true as far as it went. The fur trade, important to the American economy, moved from the Missouri country to the Pacific over Canadian routes frozen in the winter and even at best involving many portages. Discovery of a southern route across territory soon to be acquired by the United States would facilitate transport and would stimulate commerce not only on the Mississippi and the Ohio but also on such eastern rivers as the Susquehanna, the Potomac, and the James. Jefferson was eager for the United States to attract the profitable Canadian fur trade away from England. He also wanted to promote development of the Louisiana Territory as an integral part of the United States.

But he had a third motive as well, one even more expressive of his Enlightenment interests and creativity. He hungered to add to the sum of human knowledge. Jefferson picked Meriwether Lewis as leader of the expedition and, on Lewis' insistence, accepted as a coleader William Clark, younger brother of the great Revolutionary general George Rogers Clark. Lewis was twenty-nine years old, Clark thirty-three. Both were Virginians.

Lewis was a native of Jefferson's own Albemarle County and from a family well known to him. A captain of the First Infantry, U.S.A., he had been on detached duty since Jefferson's first inauguration, officially serving as the president's secretary. Actually, instead of working in that capacity, he had lived in the Executive Mansion, studying under Jefferson's supervision to prepare for his role as explorer.

Really his preparation had begun years before he knew he would have the assignment. His military training was valuable, as were his wilderness experience and boating skills. Since Jefferson wanted a detailed report on flora and fauna, it was important that Lewis had studied botany and zoology in Philadelphia, then the American center of scientific investigation. His study of celestial navigation in the same city obviously would be helpful in exploration. Besides, he had studied commercial and diplomatic factors pertinent to North America's development. As if his qualifications were not already almost too good to be true, he topped them off with a passionate devotion to abstract reasoning and philosophical contemplation that enabled him to provide for Jefferson the same combination of factual and speculative knowledge that he himself had sought in his European travels. In his own way, Lewis was as much a product of the creative society of the time, with its emphasis on versatility, as was the president himself.

Clark's expertise as engineer and geographer, together with his extraordinary skill in trading and negotiating with the Indians, superbly complemented Lewis' more formally intellectual qualifications. The two leaders rendezvoused in Saint Louis in December 1803, preparing to spend the rest of the winter planning and training for the expedition.

With them when they moved westward on May 14, 1804 were nine young Kentuckians; fourteen volunteers from the United States Army; two French watermen; an interpreter and hunter; his Indian wife, Sacajawea; and Clark's black servant, York. Sacajawea's role as a guide has been exaggerated, but there has been insufficient recognition of her importance as a diplomatic intercessor with the Shoshone, an advisor on tribal protocol, and an inspiration to the men as she cheerfully bore the hardships of exploration. The giant stature of the dependable York was matched by his courage. Lewis and Clark, like leaders of the Virginia settlers of 1607 and their Massachusetts counterparts of 1620, were aware that their small band was making history. Both Lewis and the president who sent him had the intellectual perspective to view that fact in the light of many disciplines and against the backdrop of twenty-three centuries of civilization.

On November 15, 1806, Lewis sent back to Jefferson the restrained report "In obedience to your orders we have penetrated the Continent of North America to the Pacific Ocean." But thrilled with the sight of the great western sea, he exulted in his journal, "O Joy!"

Lewis arrived in Washington on December 28 with an extended report of a mission accomplished and with a richly varied sampling of flora and fauna to delight the president, one of the world's great collectors of natural curiosities. Lewis could count his two years of special training and twenty-eight months of toil and danger well worth the cost. He and his companions had discovered that the mountain country was filled with beaver and otter, and that Americans using the Columbia River could transport pelts for the China trade much faster than the British moving through Montreal. They had looked upon buffalo grazing on seemingly endless prairies that could someday sustain herds of cattle and sheep. It was clear that the explorers' findings would eventually stimulate settlement and commerce in the vast Louisiana Territory.

The expedition was an odyssey of the mind as well as an adventure of body and spirit. Moving with respect and sometimes reverence across a majestic continent, dealing in enlightened and humane fashion with its aboriginal inhabitants, the explorers brought back enough information and enough specimens for analysis to stimulate the thoughts of great scientists and other intellectuals for generations. Benjamin Franklin, David Rittenhouse, and other Americans had proved to the Old World that the young Republic had sons capable of adding significantly to the world's scientific knowledge, just as the creativity of such political philosophers as Madison, Hamilton, and Jefferson had drawn the admiration or the ire of European thinkers. But here was an organized venture of government into the realms of the intellect as well as the hidden places of physical geography. The Old World had mounted no expedition exceeding it in intellectual significance—not even the justly celebrated journeys of Captain James Cook and Alexander von Humboldt. The Lewis and Clark expedition, uniting traditional European scholarship with frontier skills regarded as peculiarly American, had realized the dream of Thomas Jefferson, the world statesman of the day who most nearly epitomized Plato's ideal of the philosopher-king.

38

HOMEGROWN SOLOMON

"WHO MOST INFLUENCED the style of your judicial opinions?" The question was addressed to Chief Justice John Marshall, the most celebrated jurist in American history, the man whose opinions were so influential that he was said to have "rewritten the Constitution."[1] Whom would he name? Littleton? Coke? Blackstone?

"Alexander Pope," was the startling reply. Marshall had not named a jurist, but a poet. Of course, Pope was a very special poet, England's most eminent in the eighteenth century. The future jurist could have chosen less appropriate models. Pope's *Essay on Man* was destined to be a favorite with scientists and philosophers, including Immanuel Kant. There are times when a judge needs to remember that man is

> Placed on this isthmus of a middle-state, a being darkly wise and rudely great. . . . Created half to rise, and half to fall; Great lord of all things, yet a prey to all; Sole judge of truth, in endless error hurl'd; The glory, jest, and riddle of the world!

Sir Winston Churchill, who had wide experience of the wisdom and folly, cowardice and courage, of humankind, quoted those lines with guttural relish.

Many judges, too, could profit from imitating Pope's pithiness. The most significant aspect, however, of Marshall's citing the poet as his chief model for judicial expression is the insight it affords into the mind of a great practical founder of the Republic. The age was one in which those who governed and judged might find inspiration and wisdom in creative literature at least as readily as in code books. Successive generations of legal experts have praised Marshall's opinions for "lucidity" and "vigor." Some have argued that their persuasiveness sometimes owed more to literary artistry and psychological insight than to detailed legal analysis.

Marshall's formal training in the law was brief. In 1779, at the age of twenty-four, concluding his service as an officer in the American Revolution, he entered the College of William and Mary. There he attended the law lectures of George Wythe and the natural philosophy lectures of the college's president, James Madison, cousin of the statesman.

Wythe's were the only law lectures then available in America, he being the first professor of the subject in a United States institution of higher learning. Before his pioneering, would-be students of the subject had gone to England or had read law under the guidance of a licensed attorney until they were prepared to pass a bar examination.

No one could have done a better job than Wythe in training young men for legal and political careers within the broad context of a lively culture. This revered teacher of Marshall, Jefferson, President John Tyler, and Henry Clay was, of course, famous for legal erudition and for the mock courts and legislative assemblies with which he supplemented his lectures in law and government. But his range of interests and of active instruction went far beyond these two disciplines. His legal researches carried him into Roman and Saxon law, and he studied other aspects of those two civilizations. His own initiation into Latin and Greek was under the tutelage of his mother, Margaret Walker Wythe, a strong-minded woman who had once appeared before the House of Burgesses to protest that her husband interfered with her right to worship as she pleased. Wythe later studied the ancient classics on his own and became a teacher of literature, including "approved English poets." He also taught mathematics. And he applied his theoretical knowledge in a flourishing career as an attorney and judge of Virginia's High Court of Chancery, and in political pursuits that made him a leader in the House of Burgesses and the Continental Congress.

Dr. Madison, Marshall's other teacher at William and Mary, was a former law student of Wythe's and was as much a polymath as his mentor. Natural philosophy, the subject in which Marshall heard him lecture, was the academic label for the physical sciences, which embraced both physics and biology. But he had once been professor of moral philosophy, an appropriate subject for this educator who was also a clergyman and became the first Episcopal bishop of Virginia. At various stages of his career, he taught mathematics, chemistry, and international law. He also taught "the first regular lecture course on political economy in the United States."[2]

When Madison was made president of the college in the midst of the Revolution, the board had to waive the age requirement for the job. He was two years short of the prescribed minimum of thirty. In his administration, William and Mary added schools of medicine and modern languages, and inaugurated elective courses and the first student honor system in an American institution of higher learning.

We may be sure that Marshall was exposed to Madison's ardent republicanism. Even his parishioners were. He instructed them to omit references to the "Kingdom of Heaven," and substitute the phrase "that great Republic where there is no distinction in class, and . . . all men are free and equal."[3]

At William and Mary and on return trips to Williamsburg, Marshall was exposed to an intellectually exciting society. As for his legal studies per se, he seems to have received a surprisingly extensive grounding in a short time. At first glance, the most notable feature of Marshall's class notes, now preserved in the archives of the college, is the appearance in them of the names "Polly" and, in one instance with elaborate flourishes, "Polly Ambler." Polly, more formally Mary Ambler, was the young woman with whom he was infatuated and who later became his wife.[4] Was Young Marshall paying attention to his professor's lectures? One recalls the fact that, as a famous jurist, he defined a successful judicial demeanor as "the ability to look a lawyer straight in the eyes for two hours and not hear a damned word he says." But an examination of the notes resolves doubts. Nearly two hundred close-packed pages cover a great variety of legal matters.

Before leaving William and Mary, Marshall was inducted into Phi Beta Kappa. The college boasted another fraternity, F.H.C., officially organized "that youth may perfect the cultivation of virtue and invigorate learning." But, in a too literal imitation of the ancient Greek symposia, the organization became a drinking society, and eventually faded away.[5] Not so, Phi Beta Kappa. Its founders and their successors adhered earnestly to intellectual life, flourishing on the Williamsburg campus and sponsoring additional chapters in Harvard and Yale, which in turn sponsored others, so that the little society at William and Mary eventually became one of the world's leading scholastic fraternities.[6]

Marshall carried away from his alma mater even more important, if less tangible, gifts than his Phi Beta Kappa key. J. E. Morpurgo suggests that there may be significance in the fact that "just two years after Marshall had left his classroom Wythe handed down in the case of Commonwealth v. Caton, one of his most profound judgments." As chancellor of the high court of Virginia, Wythe warned:

> if the whole legislature, an event to be deprecated, should attempt to overleap the bounds prescribed to them by the people, I, in administering the public justice of the country, will meet the united powers at my seat in this tribunal; and pointing to the Constitution, will say to them, "Here is the limit of your authority; and hither shall you go but no farther."[7]

As has often been pointed out, in the United States whenever anyone refers to "the great Chief Justice," the reference to John Marshall is unmistakable. And though his predecessors, John Jay and Oliver Ellsworth, had distinguished careers even apart from filling the top judicial office, the popular assumption today is that Marshall was the first chief justice of the United States. This circumstance is not surprising when one considers that, next to James Madison, he did more to determine the character of the United States government than any other individual, and that his influence in this respect was exerted during thirty-four years as head of the judicial system.

Yet Marshall did not march unswervingly by a series of appropriate way-stations to the juridical summit. After he served in the Virginia legislature that called for a ratification convention to consider the proposed Constitution of the United States, and served also in that convention, President Washington offered him an appointment as United States attorney for Virginia. He declined, going instead for another term in Virginia's lower house. In 1795, when Marshall was one of the Federalist Party's principal leaders in the Old Dominion, Washington proffered the post of attorney general in his cabinet. Again, Marshall chose to return to the state legislature instead.

Finally, he accepted from President John Adams a temporary federal appointment. He was one of three members of an American commission sent to Paris in search of better relations with France. Their efforts were in vain, but they became heroes in their homeland when they rebuffed three Frenchmen's demands for large bribes. "Not a sixpence, sir!" was the immediate reply of one of Marshall's colleagues, Charles Cotesworth Pinckney. Marshall wrote the more formal response, which said the same thing in diplomatic language. At a banquet in Marshall's honor upon his return, Congressman Robert Goodloe Harper toasted him with the words "Millions for defense, but not one cent for tribute." Through confusion, the ringing phrase came to be attributed to Pinckney. One thing that survived all the confusion was the enhancement of Marshall's image.

Adams offered him appointment to the Supreme Court, but again he declined. Former President Washington did persuade him to seek election to Congress as a Federalist. Marshall won. Though he ran under the Federalist banner, he opposed the Alien and Sedition Acts. Adams offered appointment as secretary of war, but Marshall refused this too. Beset by conflicts within his party and his administration, Adams entreated Marshall to become his secretary of state. Reluctantly, he accepted. And the Virginian who had been declining administrative responsibilities for years suddenly found himself in an extraordinary position. Adams went back to Massachusetts for several months. Since Vice President Jefferson was not in the capital, Marshall, under the rules of succession, became the acting head of government.

Late in 1800 as Adams' administration drew to a close, Chief Justice Ellsworth resigned because of health problems. Though a lame-duck president, at odds with many even in his own party, Adams had one more opportunity to extend his influence into the administration of his successor. He proposed to John Jay that this retired Chief Justice return to his former office. The New Yorker declined. Adams then offered the appointment to his factotum, John Marshall. The Virginian accepted and was confirmed on January 27, 1801, by the last Federalist Senate. To gratify the outgoing president, Marshall continued to serve as secretary of state for the remaining month of Adams' term.

When Marshall became chief justice, the powers and limits of the judiciary, especially of the Supreme Court, were not as clearly defined as those of the executive and the legislature. Furthermore, legislators and jurists still were debating a question that had occupied some of the best minds in the Constitutional Convention of 1787 and in the state ratifying conventions that followed: Was the United States a federation of sovereign states or a truly national government? When he retired thirty-four years later, the authority of the Supreme Court had been tremendously increased and sharply defined through his leadership. And an impressive body of precedent supported Marshall's concept of a supreme national government.

When he took over, the style of the Supreme Court changed abruptly, and the change of style was a key to a change in substance. Hitherto, the justices of the Supreme Court, like their counterparts in England, had delivered separate opinions in every important case. Of course, the majority opinion prevailed, but in instances of considerable disagreement its force was weakened by the method. Under Marshall, the majority opinion was delivered by one person, the chief justice. Thus each ruling carried the force of a monolithic majority. Such a practice would have tended to increase the prestige of almost any court. With a still amorphous high court in a young republic seeking stability, the difference was crucial.

Add to this method the presence of a chief justice with strangely magnetic eyes, a terse and lucid writing style honed on Alexander Pope and other worthy models, an intellectual grasp of the most complicated issues, and a personality running the gamut from awe-inspiring to charismatic, and you have the makings of a judicial revolution.

"Inevitability" is a word frequently used in discussing Marshall's opinions. His command of both logic and persuasion was such that his arguments projected that quality. He did not begin with precedent and build an opinion. He began with what he considered reasonable within his concept of what was necessary to bolster the federal government and increase its ability to protect individual liberty and the national economy. He seemed to believe that a good lawyer could find precedents to support either side of almost any question. Frequently, as the years passed, when he had wrought the logic of his opinion, he would turn to scholarly Justice Joseph Story of Massachusetts and say, "Find me a precedent, Brother Story. Find me a precedent."

Marshall's early years as chief justice were made more challenging and more historic by the conflict between him and President Jefferson. The two men were cousins through the aristocratic Randolph bloodlines of their mothers. The relationship intensified their rivalry as exponents of opposing constitutional views, with Jefferson being a cofounder of the Republican Party and Marshall formerly secretary of state and acting president in a Federalist administration.

The cousins locked horns in the simultaneous beginnings of their tenures as heads of two of the federal government's three branches. In the dying hours of his administration, Adams had tried to pack the judiciary with Federalists through a series of "midnight appointments." Among these was William Marbury, named a justice of the peace for the District of Columbia. When Secretary of State James Madison, in accord with the wishes of President Jefferson, refused to deliver the eleventh hour appointments, Marbury sued him. Through the case of *Marbury* v. *Madison*, the name of this relatively obscure citizen is not only remembered when a host of more prominent jurists of his era have been forgotten but has come down in history linked with one of the most prominent founders of the Republic.

Marbury's attorney argued that the Supreme Court had the authority to issue a writ of mandamus requiring the administration to deliver his client's appointment. Not only did the court have the power, he insisted; it also had the duty. Once the appointment had been granted by one administration before expiration of its tenure, the succeeding administration had no right to with-hold it.

Marshall believed that failure to deliver the appointment to Marbury was an unlawful act. Furthermore, as a Federalist he would not have been loath to compel the compliance of a Republican administration, especially one headed by his rival. But the matter was not that simple. If the court issued a writ of mandamus commanding the secretary of state to deliver the commission to Marbury, the president surely would instruct his secretary of state to ignore the order. And who could compel the president to do otherwise? Determined to build up the prestige and authority of the Supreme Court, Marshall certainly did not want to demonstrate its impotence by issuing a decree that could be successfully flouted. But what alternative did the chief justice have? Even if Marshall could conscientiously have ruled that Marbury did not have a vested right to the appointment, such an assertion would have been tantamount to claiming that Jefferson from the first had been right in the dispute.

On February 24, 1803, the date on which Marshall delivered the opinion of the court, eager Republicans and anxious Federalists wondered on which horn of the dilemma the chief justice would choose to be gored. They thought they knew when he asked, "Is it to be contended that the heads of departments are not amenable to the laws of their country?" They were sure that the chief justice was deliberately headed for a collision with the president when Marshall concluded that Marbury was entitled to remedy under the law.

His audience was astonished when Marshall then said that, although Marbury was entitled to remedy under the law, the Supreme Court could not provide it because, regardless of any enactments by Congress, it lacked the constitutional authority to intervene.

Many did not immediately appreciate the significance of Marshall's ruling. His opinion is a masterpiece of suspense and sophisticated reasoning. There is no need here to examine the subtle effect of his reversing the order of the questions asked by the plaintiff's attorney. There are two essential points. First, Marshall contrived to present the president and secretary of state as lawbreakers without committing himself to the frustrating procedure of commanding the president or his agent to deliver the commission. Second, in humbly stating that the Court lacked the constitutional authority to intervene, he by implication claimed for the bench the sweeping power to determine what was constitutional and what was not. He concluded "that a law repugnant to the Constitution is void, and that courts, as well as other departments, are bound by that instrument."

Marshall did not snatch this concept from the void. As we have seen, his law professor, George Wythe, just two years after Marshall had left his classroom, declared as chancellor of Virginia's high court that, if even "the whole legislature" should seek to exceed its constitutional authority, he would "meet the united powers . . . in this tribunal; and pointing to the Constitution, [would] say to them, 'Here is the limit of your authority; and hither shall you go but no farther.' " And, of course, the justices of Virginia's counties of Northampton and Accomack in 1766 had declared the Stamp Act void and therefore unconstitutional. Edmund Pendleton, presiding justice of the court in Caroline County, Virginia, and later the state's highest judge, had refused to rule on any contentions arising out of the Stamp Act, saying that the act was not law, owing to "want of power (I mean constitutional authority) in the Parliament to pass it."[8] In 1798, the Kentucky Resolutions, drafted by Jefferson, and the Virginia Resolutions, composed by Madison, asserted the right of state legislatures to declare acts of Congress unconstitutional.

The power to decide that a law or government action was unconstitutional was accepted by many thinkers, but they could not agree where the power resided. Some thought in the courts, others in the executive, and still others in the legislature. Marshall's extraordinary creativity was demonstrated by the ingenuity with which he turned a professional dilemma into an instrument for his concepts of constitutional government and judicial authority. By his persistence and consistency in a series of rulings over the years, opinions whose influence was magnified by his force of intellect and personality, the shape of the United States government was altered. So was that of other governments influenced by the American model.

In *Martin* v. *Hunter's Lessee* (1816), the Marshall Court reiterated and amplified the principle of judicial review. Marshall recused himself from the case because it involved ownership of an estate in which he had a large interest, but the court acted in accordance with his philosophy. In a decision delivered by Justice Story, it overruled the high Court of Virginia, which had held that the United States Supreme Court did not have appellate jurisdiction over state courts even when federal matters were concerned. Thus the nation's high court declared its role as the sifter and synthesizer of decisions from inferior courts, whether federal or state.

Marshall both bolstered the role of the Supreme Court and expanded that of Congress when he rendered a decision in *McCulloch* v. *Maryland* (1819). A Maryland law provided for state taxation of the Bank of the United States operating in Maryland. The Baltimore branch of the national bank ignored the state requirement on grounds that the law was unconstitutional. The state then sued James W. McCulloch, cashier of the branch. The resulting case before the Supreme Court involved an imposing array of legal talent, including Daniel Webster as an attorney for the bank. Counsel for the state of Maryland argued that Congress lacked the authority to create a federal bank.

The Supreme Court's decision was unanimous for the bank. In delivering it, Marshall freely admitted that the Constitution of the United States did not explicitly empower Congress to create a corporation or a bank. But Congress had been explicitly empowered to "regulate commerce . . . among the several states" and to borrow money, collect taxes, and pay and support troops. It may be assumed, he said, that when a government is granted certain powers it is also allowed suitable and effective means for their exercise. It was at this point that he made one of the most famous statements in constitutional law: "Let the end be legitimate, let it be within the scope of the Constitution, and all means which are appropriate, which are plainly adapted to that end, which are not prohibited, but consist with the letter and spirit of the Constitution, are constitutional."

This declaration of Marshall's was anticipated in our discussion of the views that Alexander Hamilton expressed in *The Federalist*. The chief justice's argument owed much to Hamilton's doctrine of implied powers, a theory with which Jefferson had flirted even before Hamilton became its public champion. Of course, Jefferson and his followers were soon claiming that Hamilton, Marshall, and other Federalists had carried the argument much too far.

Marshall's declaration, however, was no mere footnote to Hamilton's theory. The chief justice accompanied his ruling with a brilliant and detailed analysis of his own philosophy of constitutional law. He discussed the origin of the federal union as a means of revealing its essence. He asserted that the powers of the national government were derived directly from the people, not from the states, and illustrated the theory with references to the history of the founding. He gave to his personal view of constitutionalism something that Hamilton could not—the authority of the Supreme Court of the United States, an authority vastly augmented by Marshall's careful nurturing and bold assertion.

A pivotal case, *Cohens* v. *Virginia*, originated when members of the Cohen family were convicted of selling lottery tickets in violation of Virginia law. The Cohens appealed to the United States Supreme Court. The Commonwealth of Virginia claimed exemption from federal jurisdiction in this case, citing the eleventh amendment to the Constitution of the United States: "The judicial power of the United States shall not be construed to extend to any suit in law or equity, commenced or prosecuted against one of the United States by citizens of another state, or by citizens or subjects of any foreign state." Delivering the Court's opinion, which favored Virginia, the chief justice was at pains to insure that this decision was not misread as a weakening of the doctrine that decisions of state courts were subject to review by the Supreme Court. He forcefully reiterated that doctrine and buttressed it with a detailed analysis of federal jurisdiction, culminating in a vigorous assertion of national supremacy.

Gibbons v. *Ogden* in 1824 afforded Marshall the opportunity to reaffirm the national government's supremacy and dramatically widen congressional power under the commerce clause. The decision invalidated a monopoly granted by New York State for the operation of steamboats in its waters. The ruling was important immediately because it curbed state issuance of stultifying monopolies, freeing transportation from such restraints at the very time that the national impulse was to expand and improve communication. But in the long run it was even more significant for two other reasons. First, it declared that congressional authority to regulate interstate and foreign commerce "does not stop at the jurisdictional lines of the several states." Second, it did not accept the narrow definition of commerce as the exchange or sale of goods but instead defined the term to include "every species of commercial intercourse," including navigation. It left the door open for consideration of other processes and technologies not yet envisioned by most inventors.

Marshall's proud record as chief justice was marred by only one event, his conduct in 1807 in the treason trial of Aaron Burr. In those days, individual justices of the Supreme Court presided over United States circuit court sessions in the various districts. Marshall presided over the sessions that convened in Richmond, Virginia. During Burr's trial, Marshall dined with the defendant at the home of one of the defense attorneys. The chief justice explained that when he had accepted the invitation, he had no idea that Burr would be present. When he discovered that the accused was among the guests, he refrained from injuring the host's feelings by withdrawing.

Though Burr was acquitted, there is no reason to suppose that Marshall's social association with him had anything to do with it. Nevertheless, Marshall's action was indecorous. But it was no more so than President Jefferson's attempts to influence public opinion against Burr during the trial. The rival cousins were great and good men, but neither was at his best at this historic juncture. Even in this instance, the opinion rendered by Marshall set a useful precedent, giving the definitive interpretation of the United States law for treason—a strict constructionist one.

The judicial revolution wrought by Marshall in the thirty-four years from 1801 to 1835 is particularly remarkable in view of the fact that it was accomplished among a people sensitized to judicial tyranny by a host of pre-Revolutionary decisions rendered by royal tribunals in London and the colonies. The fact that he always had in mind a large design for the Republic and pursued it persistently and ingeniously accounts for a large measure of his success. So does his mastery of the English language, particularly his ability to write clearly and tersely in a manner often as understandable to the layperson as to the lawyer.

But another factor also deserves consideration: Marshall was a Federalist, but his personality was republican in the lowercase sense favored in his day. On the bench, he was the august embodiment of justice. Off the bench, there was about him an apparently uncontrived, and certainly uncute, folksiness that became the stuff of popular lore. When he was not in the robes of office, anyone who did not engage his luminous eyes but casually noted the rumpled attire of the tall, rawboned man might have assumed that he was a person of no particular distinction.

Persistent tradition accepted as fact by some historians and biographers says that a young dandy was once about to leave a Richmond market with a trussed turkey when he spotted an ill-dressed old man. The young man explained to his elder that he was reluctant to carry the fowl himself for fear of soiling his elegant coat, but would be grateful if the stranger would carry it for him. When the two arrived at their destination, the shopper thanked his helper and handed him a tip. The helpful stranger declined, saying that he had adequate employment. And indeed he did because, as you have already guessed, he was Chief Justice John Marshall.

Another anecdote about Marshall reinforces the picture of a man who on the bench had the majesty of Jove but in the ordinary affairs of life inspired little awe. Once Marshall, it is said, was driving his buggy along a narrow road when his progress was obstructed by a fallen tree. He had no ax, but turned hopefully to a young black boy and offered him a dollar to solve the problem.

This the youngster promptly did by taking the horse's bridle and leading him off the road and around the obstacle.

Reaching into his pocket, Marshall was embarrassed to discover that he lacked the money to pay the boy. But he wrote a note to a local tavern keeper, asking him to reward the lad and promising to remunerate the man the next time he visited his establishment. When the boy collected his money, the tavern keeper asked, "Do you know who that man was?" "No, sir," said the youngster. "He's a nice old man, but he ain't got much sense."

The story effectively illustrates this titan's nonthreatening appearance when outside the forum and the court. But it is misleading evidence indeed if regarded as an index to the professional operations of his mind. Marshall went directly to the point when unswerving directness would suffice. But when the only feasible course around the pitfalls of popular prejudice and entrenched privilege was a circuitous one, he could pick it out with the same assiduity he had shown on the forest trails of his native Fauquier.

It is only a slight exaggeration to say that Marshall is the man who rewrote the Constitution. If it is accurate to say that James Madison was the Father of the Constitution, albeit with the help of skilled obstetricians, it is reasonable to say that Marshall helped the child to its mature character by intervention at crucial times. Madison was the chief author of a master plan for the Republic. Marshall altered it in significant ways through a long, patient, and resourceful process of judicial amendment. Together, the two did more than anyone else to determine the shape of the United States government.

39

FROM JAMES TO JAMES

LITTLE JEMMY MADISON in the Executive Mansion. Face like a dried apple. He appears sour and far older than his fifty-eight years as he looks between the long rows of seated diplomats and officials toward his wife, Dolley, at the other end, seventeen years his junior, abloom with health and charm, chatting captivatingly to all within hearing. Little Jemmy—indecisive, so some say, because he too easily sees every side of every question, stumbling along as a wartime leader in a struggle for which he did not properly arm the nation. Heroic Dolley, moving quickly when the British burn Washington, saving some government documents and a portrait of President Washington before she abandons a home destined for the flames. The revered Father of the Constitution reduced to an inept executive whose chief claim to respect seems to be that he has won the undying love of the fascinating and capable Dolley and the enduring friendship of Thomas Jefferson.

Such is the impression of Madison the president that prevailed for many years. And it still remains among too many people despite Irving Brant's magisterial six-volume biography of the fourth president, published in 1941–1961. The stereotype of Dolley Madison as one of the most capable and charming first ladies in American history is founded in fact. But the stereotype of her husband is grossly unfair. Madison did look dry and ancient and he was shy in the presence of strangers, but his acerbic wit was the delight of close friends. More important, he was not an ineffectual president. Too often he has been pictured as a chief executive who had to be dragged into defense preparations by an aggressive Congress that prepared the United States to win the War of 1812. Brant showed that Madison, faced with a Congress jealous of executive power, worked through key members to create demands for ships and armament that he believed necessary. The president was willing to appear a reluctant agent if in so doing he could fill the nation's defense needs. Brant also showed that Madison resourcefully influenced public opinion to change the composition of Congress in the election of 1810.

Madison was not a creatively great president, though he was a good one. His greatest creativity was demonstrated as Father of the Constitution, and to a lesser extent as a critic of constitutional government. But creativity in the executive branch of the federal government did not die with Madison's inauguration. The Marshall Court was a source of creativity in the nation's capital from 1801 to 1835. But it was not the sole source after Jefferson's retirement in 1809 at the end of his second term. There was intellectual stimulus in an administration headed by James Madison. One member who profited from this association, as well as from his personal friendship with both the president and Jefferson, was Madison's second secretary of state, James Monroe. When Madison's two terms ended in 1817, he was succeeded by Monroe. Though not possessed of the genius of a Madison or Jefferson, Monroe was a highly intelligent man who deserves recognition as one of the constructively creative presidents.[1]

When Monroe became president, crusty old John Adams complained that his own brilliant son John Quincy would never attain the office as long as any Virginians remained in public life. In 1825, at the end of Monroe's two terms, Virginians had been chief executive for thirty-two of the first thirty-six years of the Republic. John Adams' single term had provided the only interruption of what some Americans were calling the "Virginia Dynasty."

Monroe's victory in 1816 was no last gasp for the Virginians. He received 183 electoral votes to 34 for his Federalist opponent, Rufus King of New York, and carried all but three states—Delaware, Connecticut, and Massachusetts. But former President Adams could find some comfort in the Virginian's inaugural address, which embraced wholeheartedly the Federalist principle of nationalism, urging the need for a standing army as well as a strong navy, and proposing "the systematic and fostering care of the government for our manufacturers." And there was perhaps even greater consolation for John Adams in the fact that the new president had turned down a native Virginian, now a powerful senator from Kentucky, Henry Clay, an eager suitor for the position of secretary of state, in order to name John Quincy Adams. The new president and the younger Adams would be colaborers in the most noted achievement of the Monroe administration.

In the first year of his presidency, Monroe toured the Eastern seaboard north of Washington. Later he traveled south and west. Various official reasons were given for these tours, but their most important purpose was to cement the president's national following. He was trusted already in the South. He was determined to win the confidence of the North and West. And he succeeded brilliantly. He was the first president of the United States to make a handshaking tour of the nation's towns and hamlets. His personality was well suited for the task. Without abandoning the dignity of office, he talked informally with farmers, lawyers, and businessmen as one of them. A tall man with an open countenance that most people found appealing, he radiated warmth as he registered what seemed to be a genuine liking for almost everyone he met. The cold reserve of New England Federalists, initially suspicious of this southern Republican, warmed to enthusiastic support.

The Boston *Columbian Centinel* saluted the advent of the Monroe years as the "Era of Good Feelings." The phrase appealed at once to the wishful thinking of many Americans and has found a place in many history books. Actually, it is a too patly optimistic label for a period that incubated regional conflicts and fostered the development of fierce factions whose arguments sometimes erupted in the cabinet itself. But the label has a modicum of truth. Monroe was a master politician as well as a statesman, a consensus builder who enlisted broad support for the subsidizing of roads, canals, and a wide range of internal improvements. When he was reelected in 1820, he received 231 electoral votes out of 235. There were three abstentions and only one opposing vote.

His preparation for the presidency was superb. Though familiar with large cities, he had a rural background. He received a good education from parents well versed in traditional culture. He had entered the College of William and Mary at sixteen. Two years later, in 1776, he had left to become an officer in the Revolution, wounded at Trenton, and a veteran of Brandywine, Germantown, and Monmouth. When he resumed his studies, he read law under the tutelage of Thomas Jefferson. He imbibed a good deal of history and philosophy in the process, and won a lifelong friend and political ally.

Nobody has ever come to the presidency with experience in a greater number and variety of public offices. Monroe became a Virginia legislator and at twenty-four a member of the Governor's Council. He served three terms as a prominent member of the Continental Congress. At one time, voters in his district had the difficult but enviable task of choosing between him and James Madison. He was a member of the Virginia convention to ratify the Constitution, opposing ratification because of the lack of certain safeguards. Nevertheless, he became a United States senator in the new government. Then he was minister to France under Washington, governor of Virginia, envoy extraordinary under Jefferson in the Louisiana Purchase negotiations, minister to Great Britain, special envoy to Spain, secretary of state under Madison, and for a time simultaneously secretary of war.

His extraordinary record of success in an impressive variety of posts was seriously marred only by his recall by President Washington from the position of minister to France. He had made many friends in Paris, but Federalist leaders in the United States thought he was getting too close to his French hosts. Monroe was so carried away that he even persuaded the French government that the hated Jay Treaty with Great Britain would never be ratified by the United States because George Washington would be ousted. Though Washington was not aware of this serious infraction, he had lost confidence in Monroe as a representative of United States interests in France.

Returning to France as a special envoy under Jefferson, Monroe erased the onus of failure in Paris by his association with the greater success of the Louisiana negotiations. By the time he became president, he was known as a man of sound judgment, one not to be led astray by unreasonable antipathies or excessive enthusiasms.

Was the mature Monroe too good to be true? Jefferson, who knew him from well before Monroe's twenty-second year until Jefferson's own death forty-six years later, said that he believed his protégé could be turned inside out without revealing any serious character flaw. Even with allowances for some hyperbole, the recommendation is an impressive one.

Certainly Monroe was an effective president. When the tenuous peace between Great Britain and the United States was threatened by a naval armaments race on the Great Lakes, Monroe and Foreign Minister Castlereagh negotiated a disarmament treaty that probably saved lives and certainly saved money. The product of their diplomatic labors bears the name Rush-Bagot Agreement, for acting United States Secretary of State Richard Rush and British Minister Charles Bagot, although it was almost completely the work of the president and the foreign secretary. Because of Andrew Jackson's military successes and Secretary of State John Quincy Adams' skillful diplomacy, the United States was able to annex East Florida. The Monroe administration, accepting the certainty of angering Spain, recognized newly pledged Latin American republics that had won their independence from her.

The most creative action of the Monroe administration, and altogether the most memorable one, was intimately connected with United States policy toward these newly independent governments. In 1822 Austria, Russia, Prussia, and France, in the name of the Holy Alliance, agreed to intervene in Spain to restore the powers of King Ferdinand VII. He was chafing under the restrictions of a recently imposed constitutional monarchy, and some of his fellow sovereigns feared the contagion of restrictive constitutionalism. High-ranking ministers of the various crowns dreaded the spreading infection of democracy. The Alliance endorsed France's proposal to invade Spain, but deferred action on its proposal for armed intervention in South America to restore Spain's American empire.

British Foreign Secretary George Canning broke with the representatives of the Holy Alliance at the Congress of Verona. He was not overjoyed at the sprouting of republics in the New World, but he believed that Great Britain would be safer with a fractured South America divided among sovereign states than if most of the continent were once again a monolithic Spanish empire. He sought from France a renunciation of plans to acquire any territory in Spanish America, not only by conquest but by any means, however peaceful. This assurance France refused.

Canning was anxious not only because of the threat to the balance of power if Spain should regain, or France should win, domination of Spanish America. He was also concerned about the potential closing of South America to British commerce. Canning wished to warn the Holy Alliance against military attempts to regain or build an empire in Latin America. He invited United States participation in such a warning.

Monroe was already deeply concerned about the potential harm to United States interests. The newly independent South American nations were alternately pleading and demanding in their efforts to obtain recognition from Washington. There the eloquent Henry Clay was leading the battle for them in the House of Representatives. Monroe sent special agents to Latin America and, careful to coordinate his efforts with those of Congress, moved toward recognition. He prudently halted his efforts so as not to disturb negotiations with Spain on the Florida treaty, and then resumed. On March 8, 1822, by presidential decree, in association with Congress, the President recognized the independence of Spain's former colonies in the Americas.

With the United States thus committed, there was considerable anxiety in Washington when United States Minister Richard Rush reported from London news suggesting that Spain and France, probably with allies, pondered the reconquest of Hispanic America. Secretary of State John Quincy Adams, a brilliant diplomat albeit far less diplomatic with fellow Americans than with foreign nations, brought a wealth of knowledge and resourcefulness to cabinet discussions of the problem. He had already said, while negotiating with Russia over the Northwest Coast, that the American continents should no longer be regarded as appropriate subjects for European colonization.

Monroe consulted with Jefferson and Madison, both of whom urged him to accept Canning's offer of an Anglo-American declaration. Monroe and Adams favored a unilateral declaration instead. If the United States issued the statement jointly with Great Britain, the Republic still might seem a mere diplomatic appendage of the British Empire. But if the United States acted alone, it would gain stature among nations and, without the least show of belligerence, would be implying a warning to Britain as well. True, the United States Navy would not be strong enough to enforce the declaration alone against a combination of continental powers. But Britain's self-interest would guarantee its naval support of United States efforts to thwart a continental reconquest.

Adams recommended that the declaration be transmitted to foreign governments in individual diplomatic communications. But Monroe preserved dignified restraint while enhancing the announcement's forcefulness. This he accomplished by including the warning in his next regularly scheduled message to Congress and seeing that it was widely disseminated internationally.

Included in the presidential message of December 2, 1823, the announcement was fourfold. The first point echoed Adams' statement to Russia in the Northwest Coast controversy, that "the American continents were no longer to be considered" as fields for colonization by European nations. Second, the political system prevalent in the Americas was distinctly different from that prevailing in Europe. Intimately tied to this point was a third, that the United States would view as a threat to its own security any efforts by European powers to plant their system anywhere in the Western Hemisphere. Fourth, the United States pledged not to interfere with existing European colonies in the Western Hemisphere, nor to intervene in the domestic affairs of any European nation or in any European wars where only foreign interests were at stake.

The Monroe Doctrine was not immediately so labeled. Indeed the name attained wide use only about a quarter century later. The declaration was not ratified by either house of Congress and attained no formal status in international law until 1919 when President Woodrow Wilson requested an exception for it in the Covenant of the League of Nations.

But its influence in American foreign policy was considerable at a number of historic junctures. President James Polk cited it in 1845 and 1848 in opposition to British claims in Oregon, British and French efforts to thwart United

States annexation of Texas, and European efforts to dominate Yucatan. In Grant's administration, the Monroe Doctrine was amplified to include the assertion that no territory in the Western Hemisphere could be transferred from one European nation to another. Another expansion of the doctrine came in 1895 when President Cleveland insisted that a boundary dispute between British Guiana and Venezuela be submitted to arbitration.

President Theodore Roosevelt in 1904 expanded the doctrine in a reflection of "big stick" diplomacy, saying that continued misconduct of a Latin American nation or conflict within its borders might necessitate intervention by the United States to prevent its being taken over by a European power. A benign amplification of the Monroe Doctrine came under President Franklin D. Roosevelt, who emphasized Pan-Americanism and sought to make enforcement of the doctrine a responsibility shared by all the nations of the Western Hemisphere. The Monroe Doctrine was cited in the John F. Kennedy Administration during tense days of the crisis occasioned by the placement of Russian missiles in Cuba.

The 1823 declaration has proved a remarkably flexible instrument of foreign policy, whether in the hands of those who have used it effectively for the common good or those who have misused it. It was the creation of two American statesmen who accurately reflected the creativity of the United States in the Revolutionary and Early National periods.

Adams was reared to be a leader of distinguished intellect. Fortunately his genetic endowment was equal to the heavy responsibilities envisioned for him by his ambitious parents, John and Abigail, who repeatedly warned him that he must not disgrace them. At the age of ten, he accompanied his father on a diplomatic mission to France. Abigail said that thus she lost not only her "better half" but also "a limb lopped off to heighten the anguish."[2] Nevertheless, she wanted her son to have the advantage of seeing France. He also had the advantage of being with the man then being idolized by France, his fellow American Benjamin Franklin. Abigail had instructed her son, "[I]mprove your understanding for acquiring useful knowledge and virtue, such as will render you an ornament to society, an honor to your country, and a blessing to your parents."

Later, accompanying his father on a mission to the Netherlands, John Quincy was enrolled in the Latin School of Amsterdam. Still later, when John Adams, serving again in France, had his wife and children with him, Jefferson was a familiar guest in the household. The elder Adams once told Jefferson that seventeen-year-old John Quincy spent so much time talking with the Virginian that the lad "appeared to me to be almost as much your boy as mine."[3] The youngster expressed his admiration for Jefferson as a "man of universal learning." And he also profited from association with Franklin and Lafayette. Not a little of his learning also came from the theaters and public assemblies of Paris. And one should not underestimate the advantages of association with his own father, a man of diverse learning and independent mind, or his mother, a remarkably progressive thinker.

John Quincy was reluctant to leave the delights of Paris for the discipline of Harvard. When he did, his proud father wrote, "If you were to examine him in English and French poetry, I know not where you would find anybody his superior."[4] In addition to the prescribed studies at Harvard, he independently took "lessons on the flute, for you must know we are all turning musicians." Initially worried that his preparation in Greek would be inadequate, he soon complained that his Harvard teacher was "so ignorant in Greek that he displays it sometimes in correcting a scholar that is right."[5]

After graduation from Harvard as a Phi Beta Kappa, John Quincy began the study of law, but for the rest of his life pursued the study of the classics on his own.

In 1780 John Adams had written, "I must study politics and war that my sons may have liberty to study mathematics and philosophy. My sons ought to study mathematics and philosophy, geography, natural history, naval architecture, navigation, commerce, and agriculture, in order to give their children a right to study painting, poetry, music, architecture, statuary, tapestry, and porcelain."[6] When he wrote those words, he did not realize that the most gifted of his sons would in a single lifetime achieve the progression that the senior Adams had anticipated for the third generation. John Quincy became something of a polymath, an enthusiastic amateur musician, and not only a dedicated student of poetry but also a writer of poems, one of which still survives in some anthologies.

John Quincy Adams had a naturally superior mind. By environment and training, it benefited both from solid indoctrination in traditional learning and an adventurous curiosity about the new and the foreign. It is not surprising that he is acknowledged as one of the most creative figures in the history of international diplomacy. His record tells much about the creative society of which he was a part.

Monroe's record tells even more. He was a highly intelligent person, but not an outstanding scholar among the public men of his time. Yet he had benefited from a traditional education at the hands of his parents and broader liberal arts training at the College of William and Mary. Afterwards, he had the intellectual stimulus of frequent conversation with both Jefferson and Madison. He read Latin, Greek, Italian, and Spanish, and was fluent in French. He was knowledgeable in geography, history, and military science, and was keenly interested in art and architecture. He so profited by association with geniuses that his own intellectual development in most periods in the history of American politics would have been regarded as scholarly, perhaps even profoundly so. Sometimes the creativity of an age is best demonstrated by the influence of its geniuses on those who, though gifted, are not themselves intellectual giants.

TOO MUCH CREDIT?

T HOUGH JAMES MADISON was shy, he was not given to false modesty. It was a passion for truth and justice that impelled him in 1796 to declare that he and his associates at the Constitutional Convention a decade before had been given too much credit. Not that he doubted the importance or innovative character of the Constitution but that he insisted a large share of the credit was due men who had not even set foot in Philadelphia in 1787, much less participated in the historic convocation. "Whatever veneration might be entertained for the body of men who wrote the Constitution," he said,

> the sense of that body could never be regarded as the oracular guide in expounding the Constitution. As the instrument came from them it was nothing more than a draft of a plan, nothing but a dead letter, until life and validity were breathed into it by the voice of the people, speaking through the several State Conventions. If we were to look, therefore, for the meaning of the instrument beyond the face of the instrument, we must look for it, not in the General Convention, which proposed, but in the State Conventions, which accepted and ratified the Constitution.[1]

Enlivening the debates in the state ratifying conventions and enlightening their fellow citizens were a host of characters now largely forgotten except by scholarly specialists and local historians cherishing the records of community heroes. But legends clustered about their names even in their lifetimes, and several succeeding generations enthusiastically polished the tables of memory. Aside from participation in ratification, what did most of them have in common? Whether from New England, the middle colonies, or the South, they tended to be versatile, intellectually inquisitive, and patriotic.[2]

In most states, though the opponents of ratification were overshadowed by its supporters, they nevertheless played valuable roles. They were explicators of complex issues, worthy antagonists of the Federalist victors, and spirited opponents who, far from sulking in defeat after ratification, successfully worked to have safeguards of liberty added to the Constitution.

In Virginia, many of the "second team" men who opposed ratification were overshadowed not only by the triumphant Federalists but also by leaders of their own faction. How many Masons and Henrys could one expect to find in a single colony to oppose a Washington and a Madison?

One of the most remarkable secondary figures of the Virginia convention for ratification was Spencer Roane, the possessor of talents that would have placed him among the preeminent in most eras of American history. The son of a burgess, he learned about current issues from discussions at home. Home tutoring and courses at William and Mary, where he was active in Phi Beta Kappa, grounded him in the classics and in British political philosophy. He was attracted to the cause of individual liberty by his father's discourses on Patrick Henry and his own reading of Mason's Declaration of Rights and Jefferson's Statute of Virginia for Religious Freedom, which he pronounced "sublime." George Wythe's lectures provided a learned underpinning for his enthusiastic support of liberty.

As a youthful member of the Virginia House, he roomed with Richard Henry Lee and served on committees with John Marshall and Patrick Henry. Little did he dream then that he would become the son-in-law of the great orator who had been one of his first heroes. Of course, it was somewhat easier to have Henry for a father-in-law than to claim any other Founding Father. Henry had twenty-one children. When Roane was only twenty-two years old, he was elected to the Council of State.

He preferred to amend the Articles of Confederation rather than trust a new federal government without specific constitutional guarantees of individual freedom. But, after ratification of the Constitution and amendments to protect civil rights, he gave his wholehearted support. After two terms as a state senator and service as a judge, he was named to the Virginia Supreme Court. At thirty-two, he was its youngest member. He served twenty-seven years, favoring liberty above property rights but generally striking a balance between tradition and experiment.

Federalists thwarted Jefferson's efforts to make Roane chief justice of the United States, but through widely reprinted articles under the pseudonyms "Amphictyon," "Hampden," and "Algernon Sydney," he exerted a stronger influence than some chief justices. The first pen name reflected classical Greek traditions of democratic organization; the other two were reminders of English struggles for liberty. A strict constructionist, he promulgated opinions that made deeper thinkers of the broad constructionists. In one of his most famous declarations, he said, "There is no difference between an *unlimited* grant of power and a grant limited in its terms but accompanied with unlimited means of carrying it into execution." Some praised the penetration of the observation. Roane himself said it should have been obvious to everyone but "a deplorable idiot."

Another skilled opponent of ratification, Joseph McDowell, though born in Virginia, grew up in North Carolina. He fought against Carolina Loyalists in the Revolution. Eventually, he commanded a regiment in the famous battle of King's Mountain and led a detachment of 190 mounted riflemen at Cowpens. After the war, he served in the North Carolina House of Commons. As a delegate to the North Carolina convention on ratification, he opposed the Constitution because it had no bill of rights. After serving in the state senate, he was elected to Congress. There, believing that the Federalists were moving toward the tyranny that he had foreseen as a danger from centralized government, he vigorously opposed the Alien and Sedition Acts.

Another North Carolina opponent of ratification, David Caldwell, was born in Lancaster County, Pennsylvania. He worked as a carpenter and graduated from the College of New Jersey (later Princeton University), where he was a friend of the brilliant Benjamin Rush. Ordained as a Presbyterian minister, he went to North Carolina as a missionary, and was the pastor of churches in Buffalo and Alamance. The area profited from his versatility. Besides preaching and farming, he conducted a highly regarded classical school and practiced medicine. In 1771, as the conflict between Tories and rebels exploded into civil strife in the area, Caldwell negotiated with both royal governor Tryon and the Regulators, but could not prevent the Battle of Alamance. In 1776 he was a member of the state constitutional convention. Later, as a member of the ratification convention, he opposed the proposed Constitution of the United States. A little later, he was offered the presidency of the University of North Carolina. He declined because of his age, but continued to direct his own preparatory school and continued to preach into his ninety-fifth year—equivalent in his time to well over a hundred by present-day standards. He died at ninety-nine.

Not all of North Carolina's ablest men were in the antiratification camp. One of its most precocious leaders was James Iredell, whose name is still legendary in Edenton, where he spent most of his life. As a young man, he began studying law with the town's most prominent citizen, Samuel Johnston, whose sister he married. But the most important part of his education was derived from his far-ranging, self-directed reading.

In 1772, when he was twenty-one, he began writing on issues dividing Great Britain from her colonies. His arguments were widely circulated to other audiences by some of his prominent readers. He also began making speeches that gained recognition throughout the colony for him and his ideas.

Despite differences with England, Iredell hoped as late as June 1776 for reconciliation. But when independence came the next month he accepted the reality and, at age twenty-five, was chosen one of the commissioners to draft laws for the new state government. At twenty-eight, he became attorney general.

In 1787, the year of the Constitutional Convention in Philadelphia, he was named to the North Carolina Council of State. In the same year, the state legislature appointed him to "collect and revise all laws then in force."

He was enthusiastic over the new federal Constitution. Under the signature "Marcus," he published "Answers to Mr. [George] Mason's Objections to the New Constitution." Iredell's arguments reached a national audience. When the ratification convention met in North Carolina, he was the floor leader for the Constitution's advocates. He helped to get the debates published and thus brought public pressure to bear for ratification.

George Washington appointed Iredell to the United States Supreme Court. At thirty-eight, he was the youngest justice. He proved to be a jurist of great vision. In 1792, he wrote Washington that, in his opinion, the act of Congress of that year requiring the justices to serve as pension commissioners was unconstitutional and therefore void. In so doing, he followed the same doctrine that he later enunciated in his opinion in *Calder* v. *Bull*: that a legislative act, unauthorized in the Constitution, or in violation of it, was void, and that the courts had the responsibility of checking its execution. This, of course, was years before the decision in *Marbury* v. *Madison* made the doctrine the law of the land.

Iredell was celebrated for his dissents. The one he issued in *Chisholm v. Georgia* in 1793 was used in support of the Eleventh Amendment to the Constitution, ratified in 1798. The amendment provides: "The judicial power of the United States shall not be construed to extend to any suit in law or equity, commenced or prosecuted against [one of the states of the Union] by citizens of another state, or by citizens or subjects of any foreign [nation]."

Fully as precocious as Iredell was a future convention delegate from neighboring South Carolina. Rawlins Lowndes grew up in Charleston. When he was about fourteen years old, his father died and his mother moved away, leaving him in the care of the colony's provost marshal, Robert Hall. The marshal became his tutor in the law, and Hall's extensive library became the young man's university.

When Hall died, Lowndes, though only nineteen, was named acting provost marshal. He functioned so successfully in this role that he soon was given the permanent appointment. Without relinquishing the post, he was elected to the legislature, and was several times Speaker of the House.

At thirty-three, he resigned as provost marshal to practice law. As a judge in 1766, he refused to enforce the provisions of the Stamp Act, defying the colony's chief justice. In a habeas corpus case in 1773, he boldly denied the right of the royal Council to function as the upper house of the assembly. But there were limits to his defiance. He opposed rebellion, and deplored the idea of separation from Great Britain.

As a member of South Carolina's ratification convention, Lowndes opposed the Constitution because he believed it would not protect the rights of minorities and, among other reasons, because it gave too much power to the Senate. Even though his constituents favored the Constitution, he would not yield an inch. In his last public appearance, delivering a speech against ratification, he said he would like for his epitaph to be "Here lies the man that opposed the Constitution because it was ruinous to the liberty of America."

A foil for the uncompromising Lowndes was Connecticut's Oliver Ellsworth, who made his chief contribution through compromise. But make no mistake about it. Ellsworth was more formidable in compromise than most people were in defiance. After education at Yale and Princeton, where he was awarded the B.A., he studied theology for a year with a view to fulfilling his father's hopes by entering the ministry. But he decided that it was not the career for him and studied law for four years.

He taught part of the time. Disappointed that he was not preparing for the pulpit, his father gave him little or no financial support. When he was admitted to the bar, Ellsworth was too poor to keep a horse. He walked to and from the courthouse every work day, a round-trip of twenty miles. He augmented his income by farming and woodcutting, but still lived near the poverty level.

Despite his lack of financial success, he ran for the legislature and was elected. In 1775 he moved to Hartford. There his law practice made him rich. Noah Webster, who studied in his office, said that Ellsworth usually had between a thousand and fifteen hundred cases on his list.

After service as a judge, Ellsworth was elected to the Continental Congress. As we have seen in an earlier chapter, he was one of four delegates from his state to the Continental Convention of 1787. Though overshadowed by another Connecticut delegate, Roger Sherman, he played a significant part in working out the Connecticut Compromise between the large and small states. Taking a position between those assumed by the two groups, he drew the fire of both. But he stood his ground. He initiated the discussion that preceded the compromise. His use of the words "United States" in a resolution "fixed the name" of the new federal government. He was a member of the Committee of Five, headed by South Carolina's John Rutledge, that was instructed by the Convention to prepare the "first official draft of a Constitution."

One of the most remarkable of the secondary leaders in the ratification contest pursued five careers in three states. A native of Pennsylvania, Hugh Williamson (1735–1819) was a member of the first class graduated by the College of Philadelphia (now the University of Pennsylvania). Afterwards he studied theology in Connecticut and entered the ministry there. A few years later, though, he went back to Philadelphia to study medicine and pursued the subject further in Edinburgh, London, and Utrecht, receiving his medical degree from the Netherlands university. When his Philadelphia practice proved too great a strain for a none too robust constitution, he became a businessman. He also pursued successfully many scientific inquiries. A member of the American Philosophical Society from his thirty-third year, he researched and wrote its official report on the transits of Venus and Mercury. He participated in electrical experiments with Benjamin Franklin. Invited to read a paper to Great Britain's Royal Society, he compiled a report on the electric eel, which was published in 1775.

Williamson moved to Edenton, North Carolina, and established himself as a prominent merchant trading with the West Indies. He also was able to resume the practice of medicine, becoming in 1779 surgeon general for North Carolina's Revolutionary troops. He had a lively time in the Dismal Swamp, studying the effects on health of diet, dress, shelter, and drainage.

He became a state legislator, then a member of the Continental Congress. Based on his experience as a congressman appointed to negotiate a settlement of accounts between the federal government and the states, Williamson advocated a stronger national government. He was an active member of the Constitutional Convention of 1787. As a published essayist and a member of the North Carolina convention of 1789, he worked effectively for ratification. For four years he served as a congressman under the new Republic.

When he married a New York woman, he moved to New York City and produced scholarly works on history, science, and literary topics. But he did not forget North Carolina. One of his principal writings was a history of his old home state.

In his patriotism, his versatility, and his appetite for both traditional learning and exciting experiment, Hugh Williamson was representative of the generation that won American independence and established a government that played a pioneering role in world history. He was a worthy companion in arms or opponent of many other talented people—Spencer Roane, Joseph McDowell, David Caldwell, James Iredell, Rawlins Lowndes, Oliver Ellsworth—and a host of others whose names crowd our awareness but cannot be permitted to crowd our pages. They did not rival Washington, Franklin, Adams, Hamilton, Jefferson, Madison, James Wilson, or John Dickinson. But these secondary leaders deserve remembrance. They were statesmen such as Americans might well have wished for many times since in dry seasons.

FINDING NATIVE MUSES

"I COULD WRITE you a better book than that myself," said Mr. Cooper.[1] He was impatient with his wife's absorption in a current English novel that he had found boring. "Why don't you?" she challenged.

Many men have made similar comments, but few have written books to prove their point. And, of those few, scarcely any have in the process revolutionized their country's literature. Yet that is precisely what James Fenimore Cooper did. In so doing, he became the subject of excited conversations among the literary-minded throughout the Western world.

Cooper began writing a novel immediately. It was published and sold well, but it was not markedly superior to the book he had criticized: indeed, it imitated the model he scorned. But two years later, in 1821, having learned that he could write a commercially successful novel in the English mode then popular, he dared to write a novel that was boldly different. *The Spy* was an adventure story set in America at the time of the Revolution. Its hero was a brave man, but one different from the swashbuckling or aristocratic protagonists of currently favored fiction. He was a peddler like some of those Cooper had known in upstate New York, where he had grown up. The book made the author famous in America, and soon also in many other countries where a growing interest in democracy made a humble hero appealing.

Cooper was not one of those writers who had determined upon a literary career from childhood or youth upward, but the experiences of his early life had provided abundant grist for his literary mill. He grew up in Cooperstown, a New York community dominated in feudal fashion by his father, William Cooper, who was not only the judge but the principal landowner, a self-made entrepreneur with a hunger for aristocracy. The town was on the edge of the frontier. Pioneer hunters and trappers with tales of adventures among the Indians were occasional visitors. At thirteen, James Fenimore Cooper was the youngest member of his freshman class at Yale. He was so juvenile, in fact, that he indulged in one too many boyish pranks and was dismissed in his junior year. Despite his mischief making and his youth, he stood first in his Latin class.

Sailing to England as an apprentice seaman in the merchant marine, he returned two years later to become a midshipman in the United States Navy. Marrying at age twenty-two, he retired from the service. When his father was assassinated by a political opponent, Cooper, as his heir, settled easily into the role of squire.

Writing his first novel at the age of thirty, he produced fifty more works during the thirty-two years remaining to him. Thirty-one of these were novels. An American had brought to literature the same energy with which his countrymen were well on the way to transforming a continent.

Cooper was untiring in researches to insure the historical accuracy of his writings, but his amazing production rate militated against careful craftsmanship. He unwittingly changed a major character's name midway in one novel. There were other flaws in his writing. Mark Twain ridiculed them in a humorous essay quoted more often than anything by Cooper.

But the unevenness of Cooper's writing should not blind us to his considerable achievement. Long passages are sheer melodrama, clichéd melodrama at that. But often we are swept along by a torrent of action while our critical faculties, snagged on some minor quibble, are left far behind. Many times his dialogue is wooden, but at other times it is lively and thoroughly believable. The natural setting is intensely real to virtually any reader with a modicum of imagination. This factor alone goes a long way toward achieving verisimilitude. A cloud-world mirrored in Lake Glimmerglass, the rugged grandeur of a brown cliff touched with the roseate glow of sunset, a forest stillness so complete that the fall of a leaf is noticed and the snap of a twig startles—such things hold the reader captive in Cooper's world. Alexandre Dumas père honored the American as one of the world's great masters of scenic description.

Probably Cooper's greatest gift was for characterization. Admittedly, his minor characters are stereotypical, and most of the women are no more individualized than those in most male-written novels of the period. But Cora in *The Last of the Mohicans* and Hetty and Dew of June in *The Pathfinder* are convincing in their individuality, and most of the major characters are vivid in their vitality. In Natty Bumppo, also known as Leatherstocking and Deerslayer, Cooper created one of the memorable characters of world literature. To many people, he is more real than such real-life frontiersmen as Daniel Boone and Kit Carson. Like Don Quixote and Sherlock Holmes, he was an authentic human being. An author may claim credit for discovering him but, many readers feel, should not presume to call him his personal creation.

When Sir Walter Scott was idolized as the greatest living novelist in the English language, Cooper was regarded by the public and many critics as his greatest rival. Indeed, William Makepeace Thackeray, one of England's most sophisticated nineteenth-century novelists, wrote of Cooper's characters:

> Leatherstocking, Uncas, Hardheart, Tom Coffin, are quite the equals of Scott's men; perhaps Leatherstocking is better than anyone in "Scott's lot." *La Longue Carabine* is one of the great prizemen of fiction. He ranks with our Uncle Toby, Sir Roger de Coverley, Fals-

taff—heroic figures, all—American or British, and the author has deserved well of his country who devised them.[2]

In at least one genre, Cooper certainly did surpass Scott. The American's third novel, *The Pilot*, was inspired in part by dinner-party criticism of Scott's *The Pirate* as a work not true to the realities of maritime life. Cooper's service at sea was an apprenticeship for the writing of a nautical narrative with the ring of truth. He was one of the foremost developers of the genre.

He carried an aging Leatherstocking into the westward migration and, in so doing, invented the western novel, spawning a thousand mediocrities and some masterpieces that have captured the imagination of serious readers and filmgoers around the world. In *The Prairie*, the final volume of the Leatherstocking Series in the chronology of Natty Bumppo's life though not in the actual order of composition, Cooper wrote about a frontier that he had not personally observed. Also his research was less thorough than for some other novels in the series. As a result, some details did not ring true for those familiar with the territory. His descriptions of tribal peculiarities of the Pawnees and the Sioux derived more from imagination than study. But his imagination supplied a surprising prescience. In 1827 he placed covered-wagon trains on the prairie before those great flotillas under full canvas began navigating the vast seas of grass.

Cooper was a keen observer of society, and his travels in England and France widened his perspective. Half a century before Henry James, he explored the relative strengths and weaknesses of the Old World and the New by placing Americans in Europe and Europeans in America. His personal combination of admiration for venerable European traditions and excitement over the American experiment in democracy prepared him well for this task. His promotion in both essays and fiction of the ideal of the "democratic gentleman," the man who recognizes the full dignity of the individual human being regardless of race or occupation but champions cultural heritage in art and intellect, made him vulnerable to charges of elitism. But his views supplied a needed reminder amid the excesses of Jacksonian democracy and have deserved the attention of serious American thinkers ever since.

Cooper was one of the world's most inventive writers. He was a pioneer of the sea story, a genre that has flourished from Herman Melville to Patrick O'Brien and seems to have endless vitality. He was *the* pioneer of the frontier romance. He brought to global attention a world as distinctive as Dickens' London, Balzac's or Proust's Paris, Joyce's Dublin, or Faulkner's Yoknapatawpha. Moreover, it was a realm whose physical scope matched its broad humanity. In it, Indians were presented not as distorted creatures always "better dead than alive" or as "nature's noblemen" free of all the vices of civilization, but as widely varying human beings presenting as many differences as any collection of Caucasians. In the lifetime of one character, Natty Bumppo, Cooper presented the transition of an individual and a nation.

As a great writer of fiction and a master of risibility, Mark Twain commented, unerringly and devastatingly, on Cooper's weaknesses. Twain's points are valid. But his assault should not blind us to the judgment of other titans—some still high in the Pantheon—who have honored Cooper as a transforming genius of literature. Balzac took him for a model in the writing of his own novel *Les Chovans*, borrowing the American's techniques in describing frontier warfare to present his peasants ambushing soldiers and to describe the fights between Parisian criminals and detectives. Victor Hugo called Cooper greater than Scott when Sir Walter was in his prime. Incidentally, like Scott, Cooper had become a historian as well as a novelist, producing the very creditable first history of the United States Navy. Goethe enjoyed his books. Both Herman Melville and D. H. Lawrence praised him as *"the* American novelist." Joseph Conrad, who also presented psychological truths through human action at sea and in the wilderness, saluted him as "a rare artist . . . one of my masters."

While famous writers' enthusiasm for Cooper is impressive, the quickness and extent of his popular reception in the centers of Western civilization seem almost to smack of the miraculous. In 1829, just six years after he began the Leatherstocking Series that is his chief claim to fame, his first six novels had been published in six languages. Only two years later, his works were in the bookstores of thirty-four European cities.

Actually, this achievement, though remarkable, was not miraculous. Cooper did not grow in a petri dish as an isolated specimen. Contrary to an impression all too prevalent even among the well educated, not all the eloquence exhibited in the early days of the Republic issued from political debaters and pamphleteers. The political writings of Madison and Hamilton in *The Federalist,* and of Jefferson, Mason, and James Wilson in their great documents, surpassed contemporary works of the same character anywhere in the Western world. They certainly surpassed any other genre of literature then being produced in America. But even in those days, before Cooper had brought forth his first book, Americans were creating an imaginative literature.

When Philip Freneau was not lambasting the Federalists through the columns of the *National Gazette*, he frequently wrote poetry.[3] Much of it was derivative and some of it was diatribe against the British, who had held him captive during the Revolution and who still seemed to hold the United States in literary thrall. But, at his best, Freneau produced the most original poems to come out of America in his time. A few were among the most original then being produced anywhere in the English-speaking world and are favorites today in distinguished anthologies.

The Connecticut Wits—John Trumbull, Timothy Dwight, and Joel Barlow—were the stars of a galaxy that faded before the rising sun of a truly American literature of universal appeal. All three deserve honor for significant achievements—John Trumbull as a prominent jurist, Joel Barlow as a journalist and diplomat, Timothy Dwight as a Congregational minister and president of Yale. But their labored verses are more important as evidence of the variety of their interests than as contributions to literature. Of course, their work compared favorably with the patriotic jingles and tributes to anonymous ladies appearing in the newspapers of Boston, New York, Annapolis, Richmond, and

Charleston. But the literary reputations of the Connecticut, or Hartford, Wits suffer from a reading of their rhymes.

Freneau's reputation is enhanced by contrast with these American contemporaries, but he will also stand comparison with some international figures of his time and later generations. He was born in New York City, educated at Princeton, where he was Madison's classmate; edited newspapers in Philadelphia; and later returned to New Jersey. He was steeped in English literature. Critics have found in his early work "echoes of young Milton and promise of young Keats."[4] Study for the ministry probably deepened a disposition toward philosophical musing.

The American Revolution put an end to Freneau's ministerial studies. At first he waged war with a savage pen against redcoats and Tories. In fact, he spent two years in the Caribbean, writing poetry. But in 1778 he joined the New Jersey militia, and sailed in Caribbean waters as a privateer preying on the British. Captured by them in 1780, he built up a full head of hatred and upon release produced in *The British Prison-Ship* one of the most vitriolic poems ever written by an American.

When the war ended, he returned to the role of sea captain. In 1790, however, he left his ship to accept a Philadelphia editorship and tell politicians how to steer the ship of state. In a different metaphor, Jefferson once praised him for saving the Republic when it was "galloping fast into monarchy."

For a few years, he alternated between periods on land when he fought furious journalistic battles and times at sea when he wrote poetry. Eventually, he settled for the life of a farmer-poet in New Jersey.

Though the variety of his activities enriched the range of his poetry, his frenetic pursuit of them often crippled his poetic efforts. Nevertheless, he produced, among his volumes of verse, a handful of poems that inspired admiration among famous British writers. His "To the Memory of the Brave Americans" influenced canto 3 of Sir Walter Scott's *Marmion*, and "The Indian Burying Ground" inspired imitation by Thomas Campbell.

In "The Indian Burying Ground" in 1787, Freneau shows himself as much a pre-Romantic as William Blake or Robert Burns. He uses native materials and a wilderness setting, and makes a hero of the natural man, in this case the American Indian. Impressed with the aboriginal custom of burying their braves in a sitting posture with tomahawks, bows and arrows, and other accoutrements of the chase, he contrasts the habit favorably with the Caucasian Christian practice of recumbent burial:

> In spite of all the learned have said,
>   I still my old opinion keep;
>   The posture that we give the dead
> Points out the soul's eternal sleep.
>
> Not so the ancients of these lands—
> The Indian, when from life released,

> Again is seated with his friends,
> And shares again the joyous feast.

After six more verses in a similar vein, the poet concludes:

> By midnight moons, o'er moistening dews;
> In habit for the chase arrayed,
> The hunter still the deer pursues,
> The hunter and the deer, a shade!

> And long shall timorous fancy see
> The painted chief, and pointed spear,
> And Reason's self shall bow the knee
> To shadows and delusions here.

Here is full-blown Romanticism. A sense of mystery is evoked, and Reason genuflects to emotions.

In "On a Honey Bee Drinking from a Glass of Wine and Drowned Therein," Freneau addresses an even humbler creature than the subject of Burns' "To a Mouse" and, like the Scottish poet, finds a parallel with the human condition.

In "The Wild Honey-Suckle," Freneau salutes a native American plant in mood and phraseology that anticipate William Wordsworth. In true Romantic fashion, he ponders the transitory nature of life. Literary historians have noted that this "Wordsworthian" poem anticipates by twelve years the publication of *Lyrical Ballads*.[5]

Freneau also wrote creative prose, inventing characters to comment on the world about him. One was Tomo-Cheeki, a Creek Indian looking at Philadelphia through the eyes of a natural man. Another was Hezekiah Salem, a defrocked New England deacon who saw some aspects of the United States through jaundiced eyes. Most popular was Robert Slender, a stocking-weaver largely innocent of formal education, viewing the foibles of society through ostensibly naive eyes but with the wisdom of common sense. He was the ancestor of a succession of such commentators, some literary and some journalistic, ranging from Oliver Wendell Holmes' Hosea Biglow to Will Rogers.

But Freneau's most important contribution to literature was his poetry. Often called the "Father of American Poetry," he was also the father of the Romantic movement in American literature. He offered indigenous subjects and settings in place of the Old World shepherds and shepherdesses and castled hills. In America, the neatly tended gardens of neoclassical verse, hedged in by old rules, would never be quite the same again after his "Wild Honey-Suckle" had been planted in them.

In 1808, when Freneau was throwing satirical thunderbolts at Jefferson's enemies, a thirteen-year-old boy in Massachusetts aimed shafts of satire at the President himself. William Cullen Bryant was a child prodigy.[6] His neoclassical couplets were imitation Pope at a time when the prevalent literary style was moving toward Romanticism. But the imitation was clever, and the fact that the charges against Jefferson were unproven and unfair mattered not one whit to some of the more zealous Federalists. A review for Boston's influential *Monthly Anthology* praised Bryant's "The Embargo" as having "no small amount of fire and some excellent lines." Few people in the area, where Jefferson's embargo glutted the harbor with anchored commercial vessels, resented the juvenile's calling the polymath president an "imbecile."

Bryant became a tortured teenager. Bereft of the certainties that had caused him at age eleven to call confidently for the resignation of the president of the United States, he was torn between the traditional Puritanism of his mother and maternal grandfather on one hand and his father's liberal theology and receptivity to scientific discovery on the other. Death was constantly talked about in his mother's family. His father, Dr. Peter Bryant, was a physician dedicated to the saving of life. Though a political conservative, he was a liberal in the pursuit of knowledge who considered no intellectual inquiry off limits. The father's wide-ranging library, filled with the traditional lore of Western civilization but also boasting new volumes challenging the old verities, reinforced in the son both the power of heritage and the pull of experiment.

In his sixteenth year, Cullen Bryant approached a crisis of faith. On long, lonely walks within sight of the Berkshires, he turned, like the psalmist, "to the hills whence comest my help." But his refuge was not so much the God of the Old Testament, or even the New, as it was the "Nature and Nature's God" addressed in the Declaration of Independence.

The fruit of this soul-searching was a remarkable poem, "Thanatopsis," to this day one of the most famous in the English language. Only minor changes were made between its composition in 1811 and its publication six years later in the *North American Review*. It was his father who took the poem to the magazine. Publication brought instant fame. Readers were enthusiastic, none more so than Richard Henry Dana, Sr., a leader of Boston's Anglophile literary circle. Nevertheless, Dana told one of the editors, "Ah, you have been imposed upon." It was not the youth of the contributor, whether or not Dana was aware of it, that aroused his doubts. "No one on this side of the Atlantic," he said, "is capable of writing such verses."

The poem is a masterpiece of stoic Deism with a few notes of pantheism. Nothing could be more Wordsworthian than the declaration: "To him who in the love of nature holds/Communion with her visible forms, she speaks/a various language." Or: "Go forth, under the open sky, and list to nature's teachings."

After lines reminding the reader of the common fate of all, to return to the earth from whence they came, the poet says:

> Yet not to thine eternal resting-place
> Shalt thou retire alone, nor couldst thou wish
> With patriarchs of the infant world—with kings,
> The powerful of the earth—the wise, the good,
> Fair forms, and hoary seers of ages past,
> All in one mighty sepulchre.

All the earth, including "Old Ocean's gray and melancholy waste," was the "great tomb of man."

After nearly three score powerful lines on the universality of death, the poem concludes with neoclassical lines that would not have seemed exotic to Aristo, Cicero, Seneca, or Marcus Aurelius:

> So live that when thy summons comes to join
> The innumerable caravan, which moves
> To that mysterious realm, where each shall take
> His chamber in the silent halls of death,
> Thou go not, like the quarry-slave at night,
> Scourged to his dungeon, but, sustained and soothed
> By an unfaltering trust, approach thy grave,
> Like one who wraps the drapery of his couch
> About him, and lies down to pleasant dreams.

The arresting imagery, lofty concept, and precise vocabulary of "Thanatopsis," impressive as they are, are not so wonderful as the chasteness and restraint of this poem written by a boy in his midteens. Almost always, such precocious works of genius are marred by a self-conscious grandiosity that betrays the adolescence of their author.

Bryant's poetry is often described as "a bridge between Romanticism and neoclassicism." This individual poem might be so described.

Cullen Bryant wanted to study at Harvard or Yale, but his mother's family insisted that he settle for the much more economical and conventional Williams College. Because of his advanced learning, he was enrolled as a sophomore. Irritated by what he deemed a shallow intellectual environment, he quit before completing the year, firing a salvo of satiric verses as he left. He was now resolved to educate himself.

Bryant studied law, but was more influenced by his readings in Wordsworth. It became increasingly apparent that the bridge between neoclassicism and Romanticism was a pontoon structure that he had pulled up after him upon gaining the shore of Romance.

At twenty-one, determined to begin anew but apprehensive about starting alone with slender resources, he left his boyhood home in December 1815 to open a law office in a crossroads village. Apprehensive and suffused with melancholy, he paused at sunset on this dying day of a dying year. A flying waterfowl was silhouetted against the sunset. Bryant felt an instant kinship with the bird. His spirits were lifted by a sudden surge of faith. Out of this experience came "To a Waterfowl," one of the most famous poems ever written by an American. The first verse asks:

> Whither, midst falling dew,
> While glow the heavens with the last steps of day,
> Far, through their rosy depths, dost thou pursue
> Thy solitary way?

The third verse replies:

> There is a Power whose care
> Teaches thy way along that pathless coast—
> The desert and illimitable air—
> Lone wandering, but not lost.

Following two verses of vivid imagery, the lyric concludes:

> Thou'rt gone, the abyss of heaven
> Hath swallowed up thy form; yet, on my heart
> Deeply has sunk the lesson thou hast given,
> And shall not soon depart.
> He who, from zone to zone,
> Guides through the boundless sky thy certain flight,
> In the long way that I must tread alone,
> Will lead my steps aright.

Some critics might now feel that the point would have been made subtly and more effectively if the last two verses had been omitted. But Bryant's generation did not think so.

At twenty-seven, Bryant published the first collected edition of his poetry. His allusions were drawn from the Bible, Shakespeare, Milton, the poets of Rome's and of England's Augustan Age, and from the face of nature as it appeared in America. He then was still practicing law in rural courts. But four years later he changed careers and locations. He moved to New York City to accept an editorial position on the *New York Evening Post*. New York State was moving toward the forefront in American literature, and New York City was surpassing even Philadelphia as a journalistic center.

He continued to write poetry. "A Forest Hymn," with the opening line "The graves were God's first temples," was a notable work in Wordsworthian vein. A more original one, "A Meditation on Rhode Island Coal," managed simultaneously to find inspiration in the ancient Roman Catullus and in the machinery of modern industry. Bryant salutes the fuel that can

> . . . make mighty engines swim the sea,
> Like its own monsters—boats that for a guinea
> Will take a man to Havre—and shalt be
> The moving soul of many a spinning-jenny,
> And ply thy shuttles, till a bard can wear
> As good a suit of broadcloth as the mayor.

In spirit, Bryant anticipated Walt Whitman's praise of the "many-cylinder'd steam printing-press" and "the strong and quick locomotive as it departs, panting, blowing the steam-whistle."[7] And his was the forerunner of a succession of industrial paeans reaching to, and beyond, John Masefield's "Cargoes," with its celebration of a

> Dirty British coaster with a salt-caked smokestack,
> Butting through the Channel in the mad March days,
> With a cargo of Tyne coal,
> Road rail, pig lead,
> Firewood, ironware, and cheap tin trays.

Bryant was the first American-born poet to achieve world fame in his lifetime. He was not one of the rare ones, like Goethe and Robert Penn Warren, who write some of their best poetry in their last years. He was rather one of those who, like Matthew Arnold, when Calliope visits less often, turn to literary criticism and efforts to reform society.

For years, he had been, like Freneau, a newspaper editor of national influence. In fact, his influence was exerted on behalf of the same sort of Jeffersonian program that Freneau had so vigorously supported. Looking back, Bryant must have thought it ironic that his first published work had been an anti-Jefferson diatribe. He fought black slavery and also a form of supposedly free labor that he saw as another kind of slavery. When tailors who formed a union were fined for conspiracy in restraint of trade, he declared editorially, "If this is not slavery, we have forgotten its definition." He also was one of his era's greatest champions of free expression.

As both editor and literary critic, Bryant promoted economic and cultural exchange between the United States and Europe. No one worked harder than he to remind Americans of the traditions of the Founding Fathers. But no one was more insistent that the United States be an enterprising participant in the international commerce of ideas. He himself brought back valuable information from travels in Europe and the Near East. This versatile autodidact became the instructor of a nation.

As America's premier poet, its first systematic critic of poetry, its foremost editorial crusader, and the educator of the public in history, government, and classical lore, besides being a bona fide power at points where the politics and the idealism of the nation met, Bryant came to be revered as a seer by many of his countrymen.

Even before attaining that status, he constituted with Philip Freneau and James Fenimore Cooper a triumvirate that was the focus of America's literary pride. The three had noteworthy predecessors, one of whom for a while enjoyed sufficient prestige to make the American pantheon a quartet, and another of whom is taken much more seriously by critics of our day than by readers of his own time.

The writer who now seems to have been underestimated by his contemporaries was Charles Brockden Brown.[8] In the 1963 edition of their *Literary History of the United States*, Robert E. Spiller and Willard Thorp sought to make amends for earlier critics' neglect, devoting nearly four pages to him, calling him "the first [American writer] to approach the stature of a major novelist," and commenting, "Few have failed of greatness by so narrow a margin."⁹ In 1991, Richard Ruland and Malcolm Bradbury, in *From Puritanism to Modernism: A History of American Literature*, wrote of "the distinctive character of the American fictional tradition," and said, "There can be no doubt that that tradition starts with the work of Charles Brockden Brown."¹⁰ He was being called "America's first important novelist." Those who said so usually used quotation marks. Many professors of American literature were already using the same designation.

Though neglected in the long gap between his era and the late years of the twentieth century, Brown did not lack admirers in his own time. One of England's most stimulating critics, William Hazlitt, praised his work, as did Thomas Hood, William Godwin, Sir Walter Scott, and John Keats. Percy Bysshe Shelley was so captivated by Brown's fictional characters that he playfully applied their names to many of his own friends. Commenting on Brown's extraordinary influence on Shelley, Thomas Love Peacock, one of the poet's more famous biographers, wrote that "nothing so blended itself with the structure of his interior mind as the creations of Brown."

Brown was a product of the intellectual ferment that distinguished Philadelphia in the early years of the Republic, and of the city's Quaker society with its emphasis on moral and philosophical questions. He was born in 1771 as America moved toward revolution. He published his four most memorable novels in 1798–1799, in the administration of John Adams, as his countrymen helped to define the Republic as they battled over the Alien and Sedition Acts and the Kentucky and Virginia Resolutions. He died in 1810, as James Madison approached his second year as president.

Brown brought to his writing a rich store of varied learning. Besides being well acquainted with great literature, he had early in life read extensively in geography and political philosophy. He was fascinated by psychological theory. Once, with Elizabethan scope and daring reminiscent of Francis Bacon, he planned to classify all knowledge. After brief service as a lawyer, he devoted himself to literary study and creation.

The strongest contemporary influence on Brown's fiction was the Gothic novel of England and Germany, the tale of the macabre heightened by vivid description of ancient ruins, medieval legends, and haunted landscapes. The foremost Gothic influences on Brown were Godwin and Mrs. Ann Radcliffe, then the leading writer in the genre. But Brown transformed the Gothic novel, producing a version that not only made full use of his American background but also provided a psychological and philosophical depth that made each work a mind stimulator as well as a spine-chiller. He himself said: "Puerile superstition and exploded manners, Gothic castles and chimeras, are the materials usually employed. . . . The incidents of Indian hostility, and the perils of the Western wilderness, are far more suitable; and for a native of America to overlook this would admit of no apology."¹¹

Many students of the Gothic genre think it more than likely that Mary Shelley's *Frankenstein* was influenced by Brown's novels. The psychological and philosophical implications that give depth to her story were not to be found in examples of the genre before Brown's. Her husband's enthusiasm for the American's novels increases the likelihood of Brown's influence.

While the Promethean and Faustian themes of *Frankenstein* match Brown's in philosophical depth, they do not equal them in psychological subtlety. Brown was a pioneer not only in American literature but in literature in the English language.

One of the most unusual aspects of his works is that their philosophical and psychological subtlety is usually presented though a series of melodramatic incidents, sometimes climaxing in bloody violence. In *Wieland*, which many consider his best novel, he explores the influence of obsession on a conscientious but precariously poised mind. The title character, living in a realistically depicted Philadelphia environment, hears the voice of an itinerant ventriloquist and assumes it to be supernatural. He accepts repeated projections from the ventriloquist as the voice of God. Eventually he "hears" the "heavenly" voice even when the ventriloquist is not speaking. When Wieland thinks that he receives a divine commandment to kill his wife and children, he obeys. When he becomes aware of the magnitude of his crime, he commits suicide.

Brown has been praised highly for his perceptive, pioneering fictional presentation of dementia. The tragedy is presented as a disaster not only for Brown and his family but also for Carwin, the ventriloquist. Carwin has his own obsession, a Faustian curiosity about all things. To gratify this, he experiments with the effect of his ventriloquism on the law-abiding Wieland. After the carnage, weighed down with guilt, Carwin asks, "Had I not rashly set in motion a machine, over whose progress I had no control, and which experience had shown me was infinite in power?" Of the novel's climactic scene, John Greenleaf Whittier wrote, "In the entire range of English literature, there is no more thrilling passage. . . . The masters of the old Greek tragedy have scarcely exceeded the sublime horror of this scene from the American novelist."

In contrast to Wieland, Constantia, the heroine of Brown's novel, is a rationalist with high standards of conduct, but also becomes a killer.

In *Edgar Huntly*, Brown produced America's first detective novel. He set it in the wilderness of the Delaware valley and included Indians in the cast. Edgar Allan Poe is hailed internationally as the "Father of the Detective Story," and probably rightly so because of his development of the genre, but in this field too Brown was a pioneer. In *Edgar Huntly*, the exposition of the criminal mind is more fascinating to many readers than the unraveling of the plot. So is the detective, a sleep walker in search of his friend's murderer.

Though Brown was masterly in the depiction of rural and even frontier scenes, he was also the originator of urban fiction in America. In *Ormond* and *Arthur Mervyn*, the cities are as menacing as the wilderness.

Brown's multitude of interests, as reflected in his fiction, helped to educate his readers. He ventured upon such subjects as new scientific theories, votes for women, liberal theology, increased opportunities for the underprivileged, prison reform, and liberalized divorce.

For the most part, Brown's heroes and heroines were not so much embattled with external enemies as with the dark sides of their own personalities.

Such giants of the next generation of American writers as Poe, Hawthorne, and Melville would be his heirs.

Brown drew upon both traditional and new sources to produce a body of work that was powerfully original. Richard Ruland and Malcolm Bradbury do not exaggerate in saying, "When modern critics began seeking the origins of the powerful tradition of American fiction that still serves today, they soon learned to look to Brown."[12]

In spite of his accomplishments, Brown was never so popular a writer as Washington Irving.[13] For Irving is the writer once raised in popular estimation to the American Pantheon of Freneau, Cooper, and Bryant.

Irving lacked the genius of a Brown, the epic scope of a Cooper, and the versatility of a Bryant or Freneau. But he had charm, in person and on the printed page. He raised few dark questions to haunt his readers. He never put them through an emotional wringer. He did lighten their hours with gentle humor and a refreshing sense of the ridiculous.

Many of us today feel that he was overrated by his contemporaries. But he had anecdotal and narrative gifts that have made Rip Van Winkle, Diedrich Knickerbocker, and Ichabod Crane enduring, if artificially created, figures of American folklore. And he has made Sleepy Hollow one of the seemingly permanent landscapes of the American mind.

Irving was born in New York City. His prosperous parents indulged his cultural enthusiasms. Childhood health problems hindered his participation in active sports, and he spent many hours in reading. When he reached an age when good conversation became more important in social relationships than the ability to run and jump, he became hugely popular. His affability and sense of humor were the delight of drawing rooms in both his hometown and Philadelphia, especially among those enthusiastic about literature and the arts.

He read law but became bored with the legal profession. He took his niche in the family hardware business, but was bored there too. Though he published some whimsical essays and some satire, there was little to distinguish his writing from that of other gentleman amateurs.

He seemed to have settled into the role of charming dilettante, when a sharp downturn in the family business sent him to Europe in an attempt to save the firm from bankruptcy. His business efforts failed, but in Great Britain he met Sir Walter Scott, publisher John Murray, and others who persuaded him to concentrate on a literary career, both as a means of realizing his talent and of making a living.

Impressed by the interest of these people in American subjects, he began a systematic exploitation of native material. Under the pseudonym Diedrich Knickerbocker, he composed a mock heroic *History of New York from the Beginning of the World to the End of the Dutch Dynasty*. The public delighted in its humor.

Irving's first writings, when he was merely pursuing a gentlemanly avocation, had been lifeless imitations of English neoclassicism. Now, however, he took his inspiration principally from Romantic works. He took the plots of "Rip Van Winkle" and "The Legend of Sleepy Hollow" from German folklore, but placed Rip and Ichabod Crane in rural New York. The woods, roads, and streams of the setting were vividly portrayed. The man who slept twenty years and the schoolmaster frightened by the headless horseman both live on, for Europeans as well as Americans. A person unaware of changing times is frequently derided as a Rip Van Winkle. And tourists in the Sleepy Hollow country of New York still ask to see the exact spot where the headless horseman rode across the river.

Irving's charm and fluency, combined with his literary fame, eventually led him into a diplomatic career including service in London and climaxed by appointment as United States minister to Spain. But he had been a diplomat long before he was officially commissioned by his government. Referring only to the friends abroad won by Irving's published works and by his mingling with the literati of other nations, William Makepeace Thackeray called him "the first Ambassador whom the New World of Letters sent to the Old."

Irving was the first American writer of fiction to earn an international reputation. His polished style in both composition and conversation helped to dispel the European idea that Americans were inevitably backwoodsmen or urban vulgarians. In addition to carrying a positive image of America to Europe, he introduced many of his fellow Americans to the riches of European culture. His wide reading had steeped him in many elements of Old World literary tradition. In *Bracebridge Hall*, he introduced his countrymen to the English country house and the life of rural England. His diplomatic service in Spain whetted his appetite for Spanish studies, and he produced a biography of Christopher Columbus, a history called *A Chronicle of the Conquest of Granada*, and a minor classic, *The Alhambra*. His last literary work was a five-volume life of George Washington.

Though Irving was not especially profound, he was broadly cultured, eminently civilized, frequently subtle, and the possessor of a smoother and more consistently good style than could be boasted by some who excelled him in their most inspired flights. He also was more creative than is now generally recognized. Though he loved the writings of Addison, Goldsmith, and Lamb, his style was recognizably his own. He brought to his tales not only a sound narrative sense but also a unity and compression that helped to develop the short story as a disciplined literary genre. He produced American literature that in his own lifetime was discussed with respect in London, Paris, and Dresden. At their best, his works are a stimulating blend of Old World and New, of tradition and experiment.

Another early American writer, Hugh Henry Brackenridge, had none of Irving's reluctance to wrestle with the great problems of his day.[14] Also, unlike Irving, he really did grow up in a backwoods community, one in western Pennsylvania. He was the first significant American writer to come from west of the mountains. But the environment was not nearly so devoid of cultural opportunity as many would suppose. He apparently made a good start in a frontier school and was tutored in Greek and Latin by a clergyman.

He was well enough prepared to be an outstanding student at Princeton, where he studied theology and participated in literary activities. When he graduated at eighteen, he read as part of the commencement program a poem that he had written in collaboration with Philip Freneau. Appropriately, it was titled "The Rising Glory of America," and asserted, " 'Tis but the morning of the world with us."

After taking a master's degree at Princeton and teaching school for a while, in the fateful year of 1776 Brackenridge became a chaplain in Washington's army. Some said that he sermonized more about love of country than he did about the love of God. Nevertheless, his militant patriotism still required other outlets. He published two plays based on the Revolution and *Six Political Discourses*, essays attacking Tory foes of American independence.

Apparently without abandoning his faith, he left the ministry to become a lawyer in the small frontier town of Pittsburgh. He was elected to the state legislature. After he lost his seat, he became the party chief for the Jeffersonians in western Pennsylvania and became for the rest of his life a justice of the state supreme court.

He wrote a great many things besides judicial opinions. The parade of humanity before the bench furnished an ample cast for his literary imagination. He wrote a huge, multi-volume novel, *Modern Chivalry*, which, starting in 1793, he published in installments, concluding with a revised version of the whole in 1815.

Though Brackenridge deeply loved his country, he did not love it uncritically. And though he was devoted to democracy, his devotion was not blind. He believed that the greatest threat to democracy was the leap from conviction that all people should be equal in the eyes of the law to the assumption that most people were virtually equal in capability. In *Modern Chivalry*, he says, "The great moral of this book is the evil of men seeking office for which they are not qualified."

Modern Chivalry is a lively picaresque novel that might find more readers today if it were not so long and did not contain so many allusions to persons and events unfamiliar in our time. The style does not seem dated, chiefly because of the author's adherence to his own principle that effective writing is such "that when you read the composition, you think of nothing but the sense."

The style is plain—Brackenridge hoped that his work would be understood by "Tom, Dick, and Harry in the woods"—but the fare he serves is rich. Familiarity with classical literature is not essential to understanding of the novel, but it will enhance the reading experience. The many unobtrusive allusions to Greek and Roman writings reveal a mind that has absorbed the richest nutriment of those two great ancient civilizations.

The two principal characters are a fifty-three-year-old squire, Captain Farrago, and his servant, Teague O'Regan, who experience one adventure after another as they roam the roads of Pennsylvania. The reader will immediately be reminded of Don Quixote and Sancho Panza. But the parallel does not hold in important particulars. In Cervantes' book, the practical servant is always rescuing his blundering master. In *Modern Chivalry*, the master is perpetually rescuing his blundering servant.

Thus Brackenridge reverses a stereotype already old in the times of Plautus and Terence, but in so doing serves his purpose well. The servant, Teague, is an illiterate of no discernible gifts and no moral allegiance. As such, he is enthusiastically seized upon by a succession of democrats eager to prove that virtually any man can be anything that he wants to be.

There are those who try to push Teague into the ministry although he cannot read the Bible and has no qualifications other than the dubious one of being able to rant and shout. Others want to induct him into a philosophical society because he and his master are carrying the carcass of a large owl, a circumstance that suggests a serious interest in natural history. Captain Farrago not only prevents Teague's induction but rebukes his sponsor, saying that "it lessens the incentive of honor, to have the access made so easy that everyone may obtain admission. It has been a reproach to some colleges that a diploma could be purchased for half a crown. This [learned] society [is] still more [generous]; for the bare scratching of the backside of a member has been known to procure a fellowship."

Captain Farrago also tells the society's representative, "If you knew what trouble I have lately had with a parcel of people that were for sending him to Congress, you would be unwilling to draw him from me for the purpose of making him a philosopher."[15]

The captain himself, however, is an "itinerant philosopher"; some of his comments remind us of the observations of Plato and other renowned thinkers. Apart from its picaresque structure, the novel sometimes suggests in its satire the influence of Cervantes. There are also echoes of Jonathan Swift, worthy emulations far removed from the elephantine efforts of most of the Dean's imitators.

But all of Brackenridge's intellectual and literary sources are well assimilated, and his characters move through an authentic eighteenth-century Pennsylvania landscape. His novel is at once distinctly American and manifestly universal.

One important writer in the period of the founders stands apart from both the creators of imaginative literature and the political philosophers. This writer bridges the gap between political commentary and history, but with major emphasis on history. She also deserves a separate category for another reason: she triumphed over all the impediments to literary success with which American women had to contend in her time.

Admittedly, Mercy Otis Warren's family connections made the victory easier for her than for most of her sex.[16] She was the sister of James Otis, the great Massachusetts orator of opposition to the Stamp Act, and the widow of Dr. Joseph Warren, the venerated Massachusetts physician and author of the patriotic Suffolk Resolves, who had been killed as a volunteer in the Battle of Bunker Hill just before he was to have received a commission as major general.

The victims of her well-sharpened quill pen ranged from Tory Governor Thomas Hutchinson to patriot John Adams. She was actually a deeper thinker and better scholar than her eloquent brother, and her *History of the Rise, Progress, and Termination of the American Revolution*, published in 1805, was much respected at that time and is still a valuable source book for historians. She was also a poet and playwright of regional prominence, but her work in these categories was mediocre whereas the history is still respected.

Many of her fellow Americans were also writing plays, most no better than her own, if as good. Their efforts, however, were evidence of a creative ferment in drama. The activities of one remarkably versatile American, William Dunlap, a native of New Jersey, have earned him the title of "Father of American Drama."[17] The first American theatrical performance of record was in 1665 in Accomack County on the Eastern Shore of Virginia.[18] Theaters were popular institutions in both Charleston, South Carolina, and Williamsburg, Virginia, in colonial days. Theatrical entertainment spread northward as Puritan influence faded. But high professionalism in production begins in America with Dunlap. Flourishing between 1790 and 1820, he was a painter, biographer, fiction writer, and essayist. More important to the earning of his sobriquet, he was a playwright, theater manager, producer, designer, and historian of the theater. He wrote *André*, the first tragedy based on American materials. British spy John André was the protagonist, and George Washington was a principal. To productions of plays ranging from Shakespeare's to ambitious young Americans', Dunlap gave a technical polish and tastefulness not then expected so far from the metropolises of Europe. He made New York City the theatrical capital of the nation, but went bankrupt in the process. Fortunately, he found financial salvation in his painting.

One young American wrote a play that survives on its own merits, not just as an historical curiosity for dissection in master's theses. Royall Tyler was the author of *The Contrast*, the earliest American comedy to have survived the era of its creation.[19] Presented in New York City in 1787, it contrasted English sophistication with the usage of a rustic New England society in a way that foreshadowed Henry James. Ultimately, however, the play sheds a more favorable light on the Americans, while realistically admitting some of their flaws. Blessed by a writer with good stage sense and an excellent ear for dialogue, it still delights audiences. And it presents at least one memorable character, Jonathan, a complex combination of naïveté and shrewdness. The role became a stereotype of American comedy.

Some books published during the great creative period were not strictly literary works, but they influenced the way people wrote and had a strong impact on education in the appreciation of literature. These works were dictionaries and textbooks. A Connecticut man, Noah Webster, was by far the most innovative and successful in this field.[20] Some of the finest dictionaries now published still bear the name *Webster* as part of their titles, and some poor ones also include *Webster* in their names in order to appropriate the prestige of the designation. In careless popular ways, *Webster* has become synonymous with *dictionary*.

A graduate of Yale who interrupted his education to serve in the Revolution, Webster was an ardent patriot and a zealous nationalist. Early in life he lived in Connecticut, but moved to New York City, where he founded and briefly edited a magazine and later two newspapers, the *American Minerva* and the *Herald*. Afterwards, he returned to Connecticut. At various stages of his life, he was a teacher and a lawyer, but his true vocations were lexicographer and textbook author.

He produced serially a set of books that he called *A Grammatical Institute of the English Language*. The first volume, published in 1783, was *The American Spelling Book*, more familiarly known to successive generations of teachers and pupils as "Webster's old blue-backed speller." It eventually sold more than seventy million copies and was used in some schools as late as the first decade of the twentieth century.

The second volume of the series was a grammar. Webster was more perceptive than many grammarians of his time, noting that "grammar is formed on language, and not language on grammar." The third volume was a reader consisting largely of selections from American literature, including portions of patriotic speeches. Besides learning to read, some pupils acquired a taste for good literature. Some carried in their minds ever afterward quotations that they cited in conversation with their neighbors or in political speeches of their own. In various writings and in lectures that he delivered in many parts of the Union, Webster insisted, "Customs, habits and language, as well as government, should be national."

He exemplified this principle not only in the selections for his reader, but also in his speller. He attempted to simplify spelling, omitting many letters used in English orthography. More than anyone else, he is responsible for such transatlantic differences in spelling as *colour* and *color*, or *kerb* and *curb*.

His magnum opus, of course, was his *Compendious Dictionary of the English Language*. Published in 1806, it contained five thousand more words than Dr. Samuel Johnson's famous *Dictionary* a half century earlier. Webster's work bristled with prejudices but not so many as Dr. Johnson's. Perhaps the New Englander's most obvious prejudice was shown in his habit of listing as the most favored pronunciation whatever prevailed among educated people in Hartford, Connecticut. Self-confident, well-educated people in other places continued to pronounce words in their accustomed fashion, but the less sure sometimes were intimidated into meekly following Webster's choices. Thus his home area exercised a disproportionate influence on American speech.

Webster's determination to pioneer was exercised more fruitfully in other directions. He added to the lexicon many words that had sprung into existence to meet the needs of American life and that had not before been recognized in any dictionary. His first edition sold even more copies in England than in the United States. Successive editions paved the way for the times when the *Oxford English Dictionary*, reflecting the changed conditions of linguistic commerce, would carry more new words from the United States than any American dictionary carried from Great Britain.

Webster also had the imagination and perspicacity to include in his dictionary words of the workshop and the marketplace hitherto deemed too unliterary for a lexicographer's attention.

He was aided by the breadth of his interests. He was the author of scholarly studies in constitutional law, in the kinship of Asiatic and European languages, and in mythology, meteors, and epidemic diseases. He deepened his linguistic scholarship, traveling to England and France for research that could not be done in the United States. Noah Webster finished revising the last edition of the dictionary in his lifetime just a few days before his death in New Haven at age eighty-five. He had created a distinctly American institution that was also an international one.

The fact that Webster—like Benjamin Franklin, Philip Freneau, and William Cullen Bryant—was a newspaper editor points up an important aspect of America's print culture in the great age of creativity. There was no sharp line between journalism on one side and literature and scholarship on the other. There were some editors of little education, either formal or informal. But a surprising number of newspapers were guided and written by people of some literary or scholarly achievement, and sometimes by those with superb credentials in one or both of these categories. This circumstance was advantageous in two ways. It gave to some commentary on current events a depth and breadth rescuing the particular from the transitory and the superficial. And it supplied the scholar and the literary person with hundreds of points of reference to the society in which they lived.

The creativeness of American literature between 1770 and 1830 is truly astounding. The writings of Benjamin Franklin, John Adams, Thomas Jefferson, James Madison, Alexander Hamilton, John Jay, John Dickinson, and Gouverneur Morris form a library of which a nation several times as populous as America might boast as the accomplishments of a century. Though distinguished chiefly for knowledge, philosophical depth, and ingenuity, some of these works are also models of eloquence.

Even if our consideration of the period's literature is restricted entirely to the incontestably belletristic, the national achievement is still astonishing. In 1820, in the *Edinburgh Review*, Sydney Smith asked, "In the four quarters of the globe, who reads an American book . . . ?"[21] This clever critic was behind the times. Washington Irving's *Sketch Book* was a best-seller in Smith's own Great Britain, and the author was being praised by some of its leading writers. James Fenimore Cooper, already launched upon his career as a novelist, soon would achieve both best-sellerdom and critical celebration in the principal literary capitals of Europe. Philip Freneau had influenced some of England's leading poets, William Cullen Bryant had published some of his most famous poems, and the next year a volume of his collected verse would be published to European acclaim.

The Americans were creating new genres of verse and fiction. Stories, novels, poems, and dramas molded from American materials energized the imaginations of some of Europe's best literary minds. Hugh Henry Brackenridge brought surprising depth to the psychological novel, and Charles Brockden Brown transformed the Gothic novel, giving it new vitality.

Another generation of Americans and Europeans would see the Flowering of New England, distinguished by the genius of Nathaniel Hawthorne, Ralph Waldo Emerson, Henry David Thoreau, and Herman Melville. At the same time, Edgar Allan Poe and William Gilmore Simms would appear in the South.

Later, Walt Whitman, Mark Twain, and Henry James would loom as giants on the world stage and Edith Wharton would reveal a brilliance that, though acclaimed, only recently has come to be fully appreciated. Another period of great literary creativity would begin in the 1920s with the triumvirate of F. Scott Fitzgerald, Ernest Hemingway, and William Faulkner. And this era would be followed by the Southern Renascence, with Faulkner as presiding elder and young writers of distinction springing up in great profusion. But the achievements of these richly creative literary ages have not put in the shade the literary accomplishments of the Revolutionary and Early National periods.

Indeed, when one considers how much of America was either frontier or recently frontier at the birth of the Republic, and how unimaginatively imitative of English models most colonial literary effusions had been, for sheer creativity the literary achievements of the founding period have never been matched by any succeeding era. The United States since has produced greater poets, fiction writers, and dramatists, but it has never again made such creative strides in a few decades.

BOLD BRUSHES

One of the persistent stereotypes of American culture is that any pioneer stealing time for artistic pursuits was regarded as a traitor to the general welfare. Even today we think of the Revolutionary and Early National periods as barren of any artistic achievement comparable to those of contemporaries in the Old World. True, the realities of frontier life were such that the skilled user of a gun or an ax was more valued in a wilderness settlement than the most accomplished wielder of a paintbrush. But by the time of the Revolution, and especially in the subsequent decades of nation building, American society was sufficiently diverse, and sufficiently ambitious for success in all civilized pursuits, to produce artists celebrated on both sides of the Atlantic.

That early American contributions to the fine arts should still be undervalued by many generally well-educated United States citizens is especially surprising in view of James Thomas Flexner's *America's Old Masters*, published in 1939 and in an expanded edition in 1980. In the years since, other scholars and many museum directors have done much to increase awareness of the importance of American painters who flourished between the 1770's and 1820's. Nevertheless, many people still suppose that the historian of creativity in the society of the founders must be hard pressed for examples from the fine arts.

The truth is far from this assumption. Like many other historians, Flexner noted the extraordinary creativity that in America preceded and accompanied the birth of the Republic. He marveled at "a period of great flowering," saying:

> Seeds that had been planted when Columbus discovered a continent and European exiles colonized it, roots that had been growing obscurely for hundreds of years burst suddenly into blossom. The revolution and the founding of a new nation were only symptoms of a fundamental deepening of the American spirit, for in diverse fields the colonies harvested glorious fruits.[1]

Then this versatile scholar, an analyst of American contributions to government, science, and invention, turned to the fine arts for examples.

In no field other than political philosophy and the art of governance was American creativity in the era of the founders more strikingly demonstrated than in the fine art of painting. The explosive flowering of great art among colonial painters of signs for inns and shops was one of the most startling cultural phenomena of the eighteenth century.

The first American artist to be acclaimed as the equal or superior of his most gifted English contemporaries was Benjamin West.[2] He was also the first notable painter among his countrymen to study art abroad. He was, however, a professional before he made the pilgrimage to European mentors. West was born in 1737 in Springfield Townships, Chester County, Pennsylvania, an area of bucolic charm but only ten miles west of the American metropolis, Philadelphia. His father was an innkeeper whose triple-storied stone mansion was both his home and his place of business.

Benjamin's birth was preceded by the sudden onset of labor pains while his mother sat in a Quaker meeting listening to an evangelist's prophecy that in America "the forests shall be seen fading away, cities rising along the shores, and the terrified nations of Europe flying out of the smoke of . . . burning to find refuge here." The preacher "with emphatic solemnity said that a child sent into the world under such remarkable circumstances would prove no ordinary man."

The story comes to us from Benjamin West himself. It may have been embellished unconsciously through the years, but almost surely was not a deliberate invention. Perhaps the most significant thing about the anecdote is that the boy was reared with a sense of destiny that he appears never to have lost. This belief could have been a curse to an ungifted person; to him it was the inspiration for a great career. He saw his own fate as inextricably bound up with the singular destiny of America, an increasingly reiterated theme since the days of Jamestown and Plymouth, a growing national faith that helped to fuel the extraordinary period of creativity accompanying the birth and nurturing of the Republic.

When Benjamin was six years old, his mother instructed him to watch over his sister's infant daughter. To relieve the tedium, the boy sketched the baby. On her return, Mrs. West exclaimed over the picture and kissed the sketcher. "That kiss," the mature artist said, "made me a painter."

One afternoon when he was drawing alone in the woods, his work drew the attention of some passing Indians who, though they clung to their tribal customs, lived in mutual tolerance with the Quaker community. When one asked why the artist did not give the robin in his picture a red breast, he replied that he didn't have any colors. Several tribesmen immediately showed him how they mixed red and yellow earths to paint their own skins. When he told his mother what he had learned, she added the third primary color, giving him indigo for blue skies with the possibility of blending with each of the first two to make green and purple.

But now how could he apply the paints to paper? If the idea of finger painting occurred to him, it had no appeal. Some adult told him that a paintbrush could be made by inserting camel's hair in a quill. Frustrated by the lack of a camel, he cast a covetous eye on the fur of his father's black cat. A quick snip with his mother's scissors deprived kitty of her tail's terminal tuft, but solved Benjamin's problem.

When he was eight years old, a tavern guest from Philadelphia was so impressed with his paintings that he sent him from the city a box of paints, some prepared canvases, and a half dozen engravings by a professional. Until that moment, he later said, he had not known that the genre existed. Yet his awe was not so great as to discourage experimentation. Though daily he appeared to leave for school at the usual hour, he actually returned to the inn and furtively climbed to the attic. There he painted with a passion, uniting, in one brightly colored canvas, elements of two of the engravings.

Benjamin's secret life ended when the schoolmaster asked his parents if the boy was sick. With what trepidation Benjamin must have heard his mother searching! How he must have held his breath at the sound of her footsteps on the attic stairs!

She was prepared to find her son, but was astonished by his painting. Her indignation melted in the warmth of paternal pride. The eight-year-old, far from being in disgrace, was hailed as a genius by family and neighbors.

Many years later, when West was one of the world's most admired artists, he did not view this juvenile achievement with condescending amusement. Seeing in it the creative synthesis that all invention, whether in the arts or sciences, must be, he repeatedly showed it to visitors. Sometimes, his eyes moist with emotion, he would declare that it displayed "inventive touches of art . . . which with all my subsequent knowledge and experience I have not been able to surpass."

He was selling his work by age twelve, and at eighteen was a portrait painter patronized in substantial numbers not only by his fellow townsmen but also by prosperous businessmen two days' journey away. When the subject of one portrait asked him why he did not paint more elevated scenes, such as the death of Socrates, Benjamin confessed that he had never heard of the event. His sitter then read him the story of the philosopher's demise and showed him the illustration in the book. Benjamin made it the basis for a painting of his own showing Socrates placidly drinking the hemlock. But he multiplied the surrounding figures and regrouped them to contrast the teacher's grieving disciples on one side with helmeted, spear-carrying soldiers on the other. In so doing, he anticipated the crowded, classically inspired canvases, filled with faces of widely varying features and expressions, with which he would lead Europe and America into a great era of neoclassical art.

When the Reverend Dr. William Smith, provost of the College of Philadelphia, saw the picture, he was so impressed with the young man's interpretation of a classical subject that he offered him private lessons in the classics. Not only Dr. Smith but the city of Philadelphia itself became Benjamin's teacher. The metropolis was the hometown of Benjamin Franklin and one of the principal American centers of the Enlightenment. Much nearer his own age were some gifted young men headed for distinguished careers in varied fields. There was Francis Hopkinson, an attorney who would become a member of the Continental Congress, a signer of the Declaration of Independence, and the first judge of the Admiralty Court of Pennsylvania. But he became even more famous as America's first native professional composer and the author of satirical poems and essays. There was Thomas Godfrey, son and namesake of a famous mathematician and inventor, and himself a lyricist, narrative poet, and America's first native professional dramatist, whose *Prince of Parthia* is now a landmark in the history of the stage. And there was Joseph Reed, attorney, a graduate of Princeton and alumnus of London's Middle Temple, the future adjutant general of the Continental Army and president of the Supreme Executive Council of Pennsylvania. Philadelphia society in that creative era encouraged versatility.

West was not a scholar, and would never be, but his imagination fed on the tales of antiquity, and he painlessly absorbed elements of a productive culture through association with intellectual and artistic friends. In a less creative society, his own rare gifts would have found neither inspiration nor encouragement. One of his multitalented friends, Hopkinson, saluted West in verse as a "sacred genius." Philadelphia's society honored him as a most accomplished artist who reassuringly retained his Quaker sobriety.

Seeing a painting by Murillo, part of the prize cargo of a captured Spanish ship, awakened in West a hunger for the centuries-old art treasures of Europe. A Philadelphia merchant offered him free passage on a ship bound for Italy, and a New Yorker financed his stay in Rome.

In the ancient city, he had the strange experience of being introduced to the famous statue of the *Apollo Belvedere* by one of Europe's most celebrated art critics, a blind man. Cardinal Alessandro Albani, nephew to Pope Clement XI, relied on his sensitive fingers to supply the information denied his sightless eyes. Those same fingers explored West's head and pronounced it that of an artist. When the young Quaker beheld the *Apollo*, his first nude statue, he exclaimed, "My God, how like a Mohawk warrior!" At first, this comment shocked and offended his audience. But it was an age when Rousseau had saluted the "noble savage." West immediately praised the Mohawks as a noble people, superb examples of the natural man uncontaminated by civilization. Roman pride was caressed. The American became the hero of the city's artistic circles.

West's good looks, pleasing personality, and sensitivity to others' feelings eased the way for his genius in Rome. But immediate introduction to such disparate models for emulation as Rembrandt, Titian, Correggio, and Raphael, together with sudden lionization and the dramatically raised expectations of his patrons, proved too much for the young provincial's nerves and he suffered a breakdown. Such was his prestige, however, that a procession of elegant carriages escorted him to his retreat. He gained perspective during the period of rest, sufficiently losing his awe for the old masters to see how he could select from them the elements congenial to him and synthesize them to serve his own chosen manner of expression.

After three years in Rome, where he was called "the American Raphael," he prepared to return to his native land. But he acted on his father's suggestion that he visit England first. He even toyed with the idea of launching a career in London. Just two miles from the center of the capital, he stopped at a cheap tavern and sat trembling in the taproom. He had conquered Rome, but the colonial in him still was in awe of the British metropolis.

In truth, the competition was daunting. Britain's first great native painter of modern times, William Hogarth, was passing from the scene, but he was succeeded by the greatest aggregation of painters in the country's history—such luminaries as Richard Wilson, Sir Joshua Reynolds, Thomas Gainsborough, and fast-rising young George Romney.

Twenty-five-year-old Benjamin West literally skated into British consciousness. The fancy maneuvers on the ice that he had learned in Philadelphia seemed amazingly sophisticated to British spectators. Curiosity arose about the artistic productions of this talented performer, and he glided into success in artistic circles. When he entered the Society of Artists Exhibition of 1764, his paintings were rated best by both published critics and the general public.

West appealed to Elizabeth Shewell, his fiancée, to leave Philadelphia and sail to England to become his wife. But her brother, determined to save her from what he saw as the insecure life of an artist's spouse, locked her in her bedroom. West's American friends came to the rescue. In on the plot were William White, destined for a future career as the sedate Episcopal bishop of Philadelphia; the ever resourceful Francis Hopkinson; and that practical thwarter of tyranny Benjamin Franklin. They got the young lady's maid to smuggle a rope ladder to her and, when she descended to the ground, spirited her away to a ship bound for England.

West had no more devoted fan than King George III, who soon provided him a studio in the palace. The king once offered him a knighthood, but the painter declined the honor, reportedly because he thought he deserved a peerage instead.

After much success in painting scenes of ancient Greece and Rome, West rendered a large-scale American subject and wrought a revolution in British painting. On a huge canvas, he depicted the death of General James Wolfe on the Plains of Abraham at the very moment that his troops succeeded in taking Quebec. He painted the figures with the solidity that he and some contemporary Americans gave their work. But it was their clothing, rather than their bodies, that excited wonder and even angry opposition as word of the painter's proceedings leaked out. He was not painting Wolfe and his soldiers in classical armor or drapery, but in red coats such as they had actually worn.

The king added his pleas to those of Sir Joshua Reynolds and the archbishop of York that West reconsider his radical course and give the heroes appropriate classical costumes. West replied, "The event to be commemorated took place on the thirteenth of September, 1759, in a region of the world unknown to the Greeks and Romans, and at a period of time when no such nations, nor heroes in their costumes, any longer existed. . . . The same truth that guides the pen of the historian should govern the pencil of the painter."

When the painting was completed, Reynolds, despite his earlier protests, generously proclaimed, "Mr. West has conquered. I foresee that this picture will not only become one of the most popular, but will occasion a revolution in art." The king was delighted. More people thronged to see West's canvas than had ever viewed any other painting in the history of England. The engraving made from it is believed to have sold in greater numbers than "any similar engraving in modern times." West followed the death of Wolfe with another great masterpiece of American inspiration executed in the same style, *William Penn's Treaty with the Indians*. Eventually the French would imitate his realism.

From the pinnacle of his eminence, West saluted other bold innovators whose originality was not at first appreciated by most art critics. Notable among these pioneers were William Blake and Joseph M. W. Turner.

Flexner concludes that

> West was perhaps most important to the history of art as a teacher. Since almost every distinguished American artist of the next generation studied in his studio, he was incontrovertibly the father of American painting. Copley, Stuart, Charles Willson Peale, Rembrandt Peale, Pratt, Trumbull, Allston, Morse, Malbone, Leslie, Earle, Dunlap, Sully—West trained them all and many more besides. English painting too owed him a great debt. Contemporary art chroniclers tell us that every important British painter of the generation after Reynolds received instruction from West.[3]

John Constable, who with Turner was one of the two major British precursors of the great French school of impressionists, was always grateful for West's encouragement of his youthful efforts. He said that West taught him his most important lesson in art, one that the teacher summarized by saying, "Remember that light and shadow never stand still."

West's influence in developing the creative talents of other artists was increased by his freedom from dogmatism. He tried to help each student express his own mind and personality rather than imitate the master. He made loans to impecunious students and gave free lessons to the talented poor. He even removed three of his own paintings from a Royal Academy exhibition so that some young artists could display their work.

When West was at the height of his career, his accomplishments were attributed to many factors. Foremost was his native genius, whose existence West himself appears never to have doubted. But he also believed that his being an American had played a vital role in the development of his originality. He said, "My having no other assistance but what I drew from nature (the early part of my life being quite obscured from art), this grounded me in the knowledge of nature, while had I come to Europe sooner in life, I should have known nothing but the receipts of the masters." Certainly the shocked reaction of British artists and critics to West's determination to paint eighteenth century soldiers in their actual uniforms rather than in the habiliments of ancient Roman warriors was a striking illustration of the degree to which even England's most skilled painters were in bondage to tradition. West, product of a venturesome society, struck a happy balance between heritage and experiment. In so doing, he freed his own creativity and stimulated that of others.

The American society that produced West made another important contribution to his development as an artist. It fed his sense of destiny—not a destiny irrevocably written in the stars but one promised if he fulfilled his contract with fate by conscientiously developing his potential. West's writings, and those of his associates, are filled with a conviction that the time had arrived for Americans not only to join the honored procession of the world's artists but to lead it.

Of all the young American painters whom West helped to develop, none was more talented than John Singleton Copley (1738–1815).[4] Though West was internationally famous while Copley was still unknown at any distance from his native Boston, the two were by birth almost exact contemporaries. As a boy Copley lived over his mother's tobacco shop on Boston's Long Wharf. Tied up only fifteen feet from his home were ships with slave cargoes from Africa and rum from the West Indies. Neither this view nor sailor customers' tales of exotic lands stimulated a desire for travel. The few seascapes that he ever painted were suffused with horror, and he shrank from travel by water even more than from extended journeys by land. Indeed, Copley both aspired to excellence in his art and cowered from the responsibilities that came with public notice. As the Revolution approached, the pressure to take sides mounted in Boston, the most revolutionary of American cities. The whole conflict was to Copley an agony of the soul.

In at least one thing, though, he was bold. In art he asserted his individuality. Like most of his contemporaries who painted, he concentrated on portraits. But his methods were different. He became "the first important American draughtsman in pastel."[5] To obtain the necessary crayons, he wrote to Jean-Etienne Liotard, a Swiss artist he had never met who was generally regarded as the foremost living master of the medium. Though most New England artists and virtually all of his own clients were satisfied so long as a likeness was obtained, Copley strove for something more. When he asked for Liotard's help in obtaining crayons, Copley lamented the paucity of artistic resources in Massachusetts, but added, "However, America, which has been the seat of war and desolation, I would fain hope will one day become the school of fine arts." Like West before him, and like other creative workers in the American colonies, he was inspired by a growing faith in American potential.

For years, he knew the works of more sophisticated artists only from engravings. These revealed none of the secrets of the brushstrokes used in the originals. He had to devise his own technique and in so doing created his own style. The solidity of his figures went beyond anything of the sort in West's work. As Flexner has said, "they looked as if they had been hewn with an ax from the hard wood of American forests."[6]

There has been much speculation as to how he was influenced to create such forms. It seems possible that, consciously or subconsciously, he was inspired by the figureheads of ships that rode at anchor fifteen feet from his boyhood home on the Long Wharf. This characteristic of his art attracted great admiration in his lifetime and still excites enthusiasm. Nor has it always been admired only in historical context. In 1930 another American artist's work, *American Gothic* by Grant Wood, burst upon the American consciousness. In developing his personal version of this kind of solid realism, Wood was influenced by Memling's, Holbein's, and Durer's portraits, which he had seen in Munich. But some of his subsequent work in the same vein seems even closer to Copley's than to the Flemish and German masters.

Seeking a more sophisticated judgment of his work, Copley, in 1766 at age twenty-eight, submitted a painting to the Society of Artists in London. Called *Boy with Squirrel*, the canvas depicted a child with a pet flying squirrel.

When he saw the picture, Sir Joshua Reynolds, who had ambivalent feelings about his American rival, said emphatically, "It exceeds any portrait Mr. West ever drew!" Nevertheless, he asked Benjamin West to look at this canvas from his unknown fellow American. West excitedly praised the "delicious color worthy of Titian." The picture was not only exhibited to admiring crowds, but this single work gained Copley election to the Society of Artists, an honor that many well-trained English professionals had for years sought in vain. Both Reynolds and West urged Copley to come to Europe. "Nothing is wanted to perfect you now," said West, "but a sight of what has been done by the great masters. . . . You may depend on my friendship in any way that's in my power to serve."

Despite encouragement from the two famous artists, followed by an offer from West to take him into his own household and introduce him to leading connoisseurs, Copley could not summon the courage to sail for Europe. Marriage to a wealthy merchant's daughter accustomed to living in elegant style gave him an additional reason for remaining at home where he was assured of demand as a portraitist. But soon life in Boston threatened to become as dangerous as a European adventure. Copley's father-in-law was an agent for the East India Company, the organization that shipped to Boston the cargo dumped overboard in the famous tea party. Because of his combination of Tory in-laws and Whig blood relatives, Copley was pressed into service as an intermediary. In this role, he found himself threatened by a mob. Torn between duty and physical fear, he obeyed the dictates of duty but at great cost to his nerves. A few weeks after this excitement, he sailed for England.

Shortly before, he had visited Philadelphia and found laymen there more discerning about art than their Boston counterparts. "The gentry of this place distinguish very well," he had written, "so I must slight nothing." Nevertheless, he was surprised by the sophistication of London artists, and amazed to see a nude model at the Royal Academy.

In London, after a slow start, he would become an acclaimed example for other painters. He would follow West in the painting of huge historical scenes, and in the eyes of some would excel the master. In *The Death of Chatham*, to which he devoted two years, he depicted the dramatic demise of the prime minister in the House of Lords. The canvas was crowded with individual portraits of more than fifty peers. To this day, some critics consider it "the greatest historical painting ever done in England."[7]

Many of us, however, prefer his portraits of single individuals or small family groups. Some of these seem as good as anything of the sort done in any country in the eighteenth and nineteenth centuries. Contemporaries testified to the faithfulness of his likenesses, but beyond this are the corporeal realism and the penetrating revelation of personality.

Copley remained in England until his death in 1815. Gradually, his portraiture declined in quality. A failure of health was doubtless partly to blame. But, even before the onset of illness, the distinction of early portraits was lost amid a myriad of facile gimmicks that he learned from fashionable society painters. Some contact with the world of traditional painting and cosmopolitan tastes had aided his development. But eventually the strength of tradition outweighed the individuality of his genius, and his art suffered. He had a bold imagination, but he was a timid executioner. Surrounded by colleagues of impressive reputations, he became more an imitator than an independent venturer. The imbalance was inhibiting to his creativity. Nevertheless, the work of his prime still captivates. Then he was following his own genius because he had no other genius to follow. Some critics still consider him "the greatest painter America has ever produced."[8]

No teacher of art in the English-speaking world inspired and trained a more remarkable band of artists than did Benjamin West. Of this impressive company, none was more versatile than his countryman Charles Willson Peale.[9]

West had students whose performance over the years was far more consistent. Peale's portraits ranged from stiff, reverential depictions of George Washington and a morbid but ineffective picture of the artist's wife weeping over their dead child, to brilliant portrayals of his brother James and such luminaries as Benjamin Rush, David Rittenhouse, and Benjamin Franklin.

Peale had many distractions to prevent him from concentrating on techniques as much as some of his rivals, but the breadth of his interests enlivened his art and enriched many aspects of life in America. At various times (and in the case of some occupations, simultaneously) he was a political activist, watchmaker, saddler, upholsterer, carriage maker, officer in Washington's army, silversmith, legislative leader, founder and operator of America's first public art gallery and first significant museum of natural history, inventor of animated dioramas, botanist, ichthyologist, entomologist, taxidermist, medical theorist, paleontologist, father of the Pennsylvania Academy of the Fine Arts, coperfecter (with Jefferson) of the polygraph, innovative bridge designer, and improver of the windmill water pump.

In some ways, Peale was more representatively American than most of his colleagues in the first great age of American painting. He drew from and touched his country at more points geographically. Born in Queen Annes County, Maryland, he grew up principally in Chestertown and Annapolis, spent some time in Accomack County on the Eastern Shore of Virginia as well as in Boston, and finally settled in Philadelphia.

Some would say that painting was Peale's destiny, others that he came to it by chance. While in Norfolk, Virginia, to secure leather for saddle making, he saw some "miserably done" pictures. Confident that he could do better, he bought instruction books.

At first Peale used the same paints for portraits that he applied to the carriages he built. Like other Americans, he graduated to portraiture by way of sign painting. Learning that there were paints better suited for the fine arts, he traveled to Philadelphia to obtain some. There he visited the studio of a mediocre painter. Despite the owner's limitations, the experience was an educational one. Peale not only obtained his first view of a studio but for the first time saw a palette and an easel. He bought a book on painting and returned to Annapolis. He traded a saddle to another mediocre painter, one not too distant from Annapolis, for the privilege of watching him paint one portrait and helping him to finish a second.

In December 1776, when Peale was twenty-five years old, the governor of Maryland and ten members of the council personally financed a trip to London where he might learn from Benjamin West and others. West's success encouraged their belief that Americans would soon lead the international world of art and that so talented a fellow as Peale would be among them. The young artist suffered terribly from seasickness while crossing the Atlantic, but in intervals of freedom from the malady, characteristically acquired a new skill, making a violin.

Though West was particularly kind to his countrymen, the teacher unintentionally led the student away from the robust realism that was his greatest strength. West was in the heyday of his own neoclassical period, filling his canvases with togaed figures in the classical mode.

Peale's most interesting meeting with an American in London came when, unannounced, he called on Benjamin Franklin for the first time and a servant directed him to the great man's laboratory. The experiment in progress was not what he had anticipated. Dr. Franklin was occupied with a fashionably dressed "young lady on his knee." They were too absorbed in each other to notice the visitor. Stepping back from the door, Peale quickly sketched the scene on a page of his account book. Withdrawing a little, he approached again—this time quite noisily. The amorous scene had yielded to decorum. But Peale had captured the informal moment in a sketch that survives to this day.[10]

With his voracious appetite for experiment, Peele devoured lessons in oil painting, miniature work, plaster modeling, and mezzatint scraping. "I was not content to learn to paint in one way," he said, "but engaged in the whole circle of arts, except painting on enamel."

Two years after arriving in London, Peale had exhibited five works at the Royal Academy. Eagerly, he returned to Annapolis, his faith in himself and in America strengthened by the English experience. On the trip back, he wore only American-made clothes he had brought with him, leaving his entire English wardrobe behind. He believed that the colonies should learn to rely on their own manufactures and become economically independent of the mother country.

He found patronage and praise not only in Annapolis but also in Philadelphia. Exulting in the reception of his work, he wrote, "The people here have a growing taste for the arts, and are becoming more and more fond of encouraging their progress among them." Encouragement came from Benjamin Franklin, who we may be sure was still unaware that he was featured in an informal sketch by Peale, the double portrait with the "young lady." "The arts," said Franklin, "have always traveled westward, and there is no doubt of their flourishing hereafter on our side of the Atlantic as the number of wealthy inhabitants shall increase." Franklin, Peale, and thousands of other Americans were sublimely confident that they were Destiny's children.

Before Peale retired from portrait painting to devote himself to scientific pursuits and the development of museums, he left behind several portraits considered milestones of the art in America. One of his techniques in portraiture was his apparently unique practice of using six-foot brushes so that both subject and canvas would be equidistant from him. In Philadelphia he taught a life class in painting. When a nude model became too bashful to step from behind the screen, Peale kept his promise to his class by disrobing and filling in. Thus he became the first nude model to sit for a class in Philadelphia, and surely one of the first anywhere in America.

He taught art to his brothers and some of his seventeen children. One son, Rembrandt Peale, became a world-class portraitist. He combined with the traditional coloring of Rubens and Van Dyck the innovative practice of integrating the figure with the landscape. His paintings of Thomas Jefferson shortly before his first and second inaugurations as president are among the most celebrated examples of historical portraiture. When in Paris, he was offered the post of portrait painter to Napoleon's court, but chose to return to the United States. He was a greater painter than his father, but did not make his mark in as many fields. Nevertheless, he exemplified the versatility encouraged in his America. On subjects ranging from Italian travels to art to personal reminiscence, he produced three books and various articles that still merit attention. Like his father, Rembrandt created a museum, establishing his in Baltimore.

While the elder Peale enjoyed vicariously the artistic triumphs of his son, he brought to his own scientific activities as much energy as he had ever devoted to his art, and even more creativity. He was the world's pioneer in creating the habitat groups that have become standard in museums of natural history. Instead of simply stuffing the skins of birds and other animals for display, he sculpted reproductions of their forms to which the pelts could be fitted. He displayed small insects under the lenses of microscopes and mounted scientific information beside specimens of flora and fauna, practices that since have become almost universal. His museum evolved in relation to the needs and demands of a changing society, and was designed to serve both scholars and the public. Even in his scientific lectures, he was an innovator, becoming the first American to use actual specimens to illustrate his message. Frederic A. Lucas, director of the American Museum of Natural History in the second quarter of the twentieth century, said: "Had Peale lived a hundred years later, he would have been a leader in museum methods."[11]

Peale's museum played an international role in the acquisition and dissemination of knowledge. Virtually all naturalists in the United States studied his specimens. Eighty-five species described by the ornithologist Alexander Wilson were first seen by him at Peale's museum.

Seeking prehistoric specimens, Peale not only brought much greater efficiency to the excavation of ancient bones but became the first person in the world to reconstruct the skeletons of mastodons. He has been called "the Father of American Vertebrate Paleontology."[12] Such accomplishments helped to make his institution, in terms of the fulfillment of its educational mission, one of the leading museums in the world. When a dinner party was held within one of the mastodon skeletons in Peale's exhibit, one of the toasts proposed exemplified the patriotism and confidence that spurred Americans of the Early National period to surprising triumphs in the arts and sciences: "The American people—may they be as pre-eminent among the nations of the earth as the canopy we sit beneath surpasses the fabric of the mouse."

Immersed as he was in scientific studies and museum administration, Peale nevertheless in his seventieth year returned to his first love—painting. Excited by new techniques brought by his son Rembrandt from Jacques Louis David's studio in Paris, he worked out a new style for himself and produced canvases at a prodigious rate. Some critics agree with the artist's own estimate that his septuagenarian art was his best. Others dispute that conclusion, but agree that his rapid development of a new style at an age comparable to ninety in our time was an amazing achievement.

Into his eighties, Peale continued to use his inventive skills. Even the ravages of age were stimulants to his resourcefulness. When he had to have false teeth, he developed better ways of glazing the porcelain imitations and affixing them to the plate. He immediately disseminated his discoveries far and wide. "It will hurt my feelings," he said, "to refuse my aid to others."

In his eighty-sixth year, he died peacefully in bed. But as he had approached his eightieth year, he had taken to building fast-rolling velocipedes on which, to the anxiety and embarrassment of his children, he sped along the roads and highways with a delight approaching adolescent glee. The image lingers. Peale seems always to have been speeding along exuberantly, far ahead of his time.

As Dr. Lillian B. Miller makes abundantly evident in her fascinating book *The Peale Family: Creation of a Legacy*, he was the founder of a family of painters whose familial record of achievement in art is unmatched in America. Two nieces, Ann Claypool Peale and Sarah Miriam Peale, were both elected academicians of the Pennsylvania Academy of the Fine Arts, and were the first women so honored.

John Walker, director emeritus of America's National Gallery of Art, wrote in 1975, "In two hundred years America has produced several great painters, and among them at least one innovator of genius, Gilbert Stuart."[13] Unlike Charles Willson Peale, who proved his patriotism by entering the Revolution as a common soldier and becoming a captain celebrated for maintaining his men's morale, Stuart sailed from Boston for England the day before the Battle of Bunker Hill. Ironically, Stuart's name, more than that of any other painter, has become closely associated with those of America's Founding Fathers.

This connection springs from Stuart's popular portraits of such statesmen as Thomas Jefferson, John Adams, and above all George Washington. The depiction of Adams, in which the man's intelligence and strong character shine through the vanity and irritability, is a brilliant psychological study. The *Edgehill* portrait of Jefferson has the postal-slot mouth that Stuart put on many of his male subjects, but the liveliness of the eyes must faithfully reproduce a characteristic frequently noted by those who met the Virginian but seldom captured by artists. Stuart's three life portraits of Washington, however, give scarcely a hint of the painter's genius. His most famous rendering of the first president, the *Athenaeum Head*, has the postal-slot mouth and a general look of rigor mortis. Admittedly, Washington's acute discomfort in posing, coupled with the awe that he inspired in most of his limners, seems to have made him an extraordinarily difficult subject.

This artistically unsuccessful portrait, nevertheless, is the one on which Stuart's popular fame is based. This is partly because of the veneration in which Washington was held by generations of Americans before the public formed the habit of equating virtue with dullness, and partly because of Stuart's extraordinary skills in marketing and promotion. The *Athenaeum Head* portrait was commissioned by the president's wife, but she had to accept one of seventy-five replicas while the artist kept the original in his studio for further copying. The demand for copies by the original artist was insatiable. Stuart's contract called for him to relinquish the original to Mrs. Washington when it was finished, but he carefully left part of the background incomplete. Mass-produced copies were favorite icons of American classrooms well into the twentieth century. Reproductions of the portrait on the United States dollar bill made it the most familiar likeness in the nation.

Stuart's embarkation for Britain was the second of his career. Born in 1755 in an apartment over his father's place of business, a snuff mill near Narragansett, Rhode Island, he had moved with his family to Newport at age six. There as a teenager he had received instruction in painting from a visiting Scotsman. When his teacher returned to Edinburgh, sixteen-year-old Gilbert accompanied him. Within a year, however, his instructor died and the boy returned to Rhode Island.

When twenty-year-old Stuart sailed for Britain at the beginning of the Revolution, he headed for London. For about six years he worked in Benjamin West's studio, learning much from him and almost as much from the works of Thomas Gainsborough and Sir Joshua Reynolds.

During this period, Stuart produced his first famous work, a portrait that is still regarded as one of the world's great masterpieces of that genre. It had its genesis in Stuart's refusal to accept the consensus that he could create "a tolerable likeness of the face, but as to the figure he could not get below the fifth button." He resolved to do a full-length portrait of a handsome subject, William Grant of Congalton. But, when Grant appeared for his first sitting, the subject said that the day seemed far more suitable for ice skating than for posing indoors. Stuart, who was an enthusiastic skater, agreed. Off they went to skate in Hyde Park. But the ice cracked, and they went back to the studio for the sitting. Stuart then conceived the idea of painting Grant in the act of skating. And so, with a wintry landscape as backdrop, Grant skates toward us with effortless grace, his arms nonchalantly folded, his wide-brimmed hat at a rakish angle. At the Royal Academy it was the wonder of critics and the delight of the public.

Almost a hundred years later, it was exhibited again at the academy. As the canvas was unsigned, a controversy ensued over attribution until it was proved to be Stuart's work. Meanwhile the *Daily Telegraph* insisted that it must be the work of the great George Romney, but the *Times* replied that Romney was incapable of so splendid an achievement. Noting the sketchiness of the background, some suggested that Gainsborough was the painter. To this supposition, the *Art Journal* replied: "A more graceful and manly figure was surely never painted by an English artist, and if Gainsborough were that artist, this is unquestionably his masterpiece."[14]

In 1793, having drawn huge sums for his work but having wasted his earnings in conspicuous consumption, Stuart returned to America to recoup his fortunes. After a year in New York, he lived twelve years in Philadelphia, a city of great creative energy. But he spent the last twenty-three years of his life in Boston, by that time a city appreciative of true artistic distinction.

Though Stuart's own fame was increased by pictures of the famous, some of his best portraits are of less celebrated patrons. The portrait of Mrs. Richard Yates is a remarkable example of painterly dexterity combined with penetrating insight. Apparently, with the exception of *The Skater*, his finest and most original work was done after his return to the United States. Now back among his countrymen after profiting from lessons in the artistic traditions of Europe, he was free to experiment boldly without feeling that London critics were looking over his shoulder. He perceived something that his greatest contemporaries of the Old World had not, that "good flesh coloring partook of all colors, not mixed, so as to be combined in one tint, but shining through each other, like the blood through the natural skin."[15] This observation, and its exemplification in many of Stuart's paintings, caused John Walker to write, "Had there been the artists and the tradition of painting in America that there were in France, these innovations of Stuart's might have caused Impressionism to appear in the New World generations before it revolutionized art in Europe."[16]

One group of painters created a distinctively American school not in portraiture but in landscape. The three leaders of this bold contingent, which became known as the Hudson River school, were Thomas Doughty, Asher Brown Durand, and Thomas Cole. They brought respectful recognition to a genre long regarded as inferior to portraiture and historical painting.

Most gifted of the trio was Thomas Cole.[17] After working as an engraver's assistant and apprentice to a designer of calico prints, he worked on his own as an engraver in Philadelphia. Later, while living in Ohio, he took a few lessons from an itinerant artist in oils. A little later, in Pittsburgh, he became fascinated with capturing on canvas the forms of trees.

Emphatically not one who could not see the forest for the trees, he began painting landscapes with vast vistas of lush forests and towering mountains. Their scope was great in another sense. He described his paintings as "compositions" made from observed aspects of nature combined into a transcendent whole expressive of much more than the sum of their literally rendered details. "The finest pictures which have been produced," he said, "both Historical and Landscapes, have been compositions. . . . If the imagination is shackled, and nothing is described but what we see, seldom will anything truly great be produced in either Painting or Poetry."[18]

His paintings were outstanding examples of the interaction of literature and the fine arts. Notable are his three versions of *The Last of the Mohicans*, inspired by Cooper's novel. And on a grander scale are his *Garden of Eden* and *Expulsion*, for which he drew heavily on Genesis and Milton's *Paradise Lost*. Cole wrote, "We are still in Eden; the wall that shuts us out of the Garden is our own ignorance and folly."

Franklin Kelly, in a particularly insightful study of Cole's art, comments:

> There can be, of course, no single myth or belief that explains the origin and development of a complex political and social entity like America. But certainly one of the most persistent ideas in art and literature of the first half of the nineteenth century concerns the identification of America as a new Eden and of Americans as new Adams. If the vast, unspoiled territories of the New World represented not just physically a new Eden but spiritually a place where man could redeem himself, what guarantee was there that Americans might not also fall victim to temptation? That Cole saw the need to create the *Expulsion* as a pendant to his *Garden of Eden* suggests that he wanted to make the ever-present possibility of loss absolutely apparent to his audience.[19]

Some of us who greatly admire Cole's landscapes wish that he had omitted human figures from many of them. The extremely small figures are acceptable, but the larger ones reveal an ineptitude strangely contrasting with his brilliant representation of trees. One of his principal patrons, however, demanded figures. For some of us, too, Cole's famous *Voyage of Life* series is too obviously allegorical. But in the 1820's, when he was painting the Eden pictures, and at other times in his career, he limned the natural world with a subtlety and sublimity that not only raised landscape art to a new level in the United States but also challenged some of the world's best artists in that genre.

What a glorious galaxy of artists exploded into the firmament at the birth of the American Republic! Not only Benjamin West, John Singleton Copley, Gilbert Stuart, Charles Willson Peale and his son Rembrandt, and Thomas Cole. In their lifetime there were many others who gained international reputations. The roster of students of West alone yields—besides Copley, the two Peales, and Stuart—the names of John Trumbull, Washington Allston, Samuel F. B. Morse, Edward G. Malbone, Ralph Earle, William Dunlap, and Thomas

Sully—any one of whom, had he appeared in an earlier generation of Americans and gotten Europeans to look at his work, would have been hailed as a prodigy.

Virtually all were as imbued with the spirit of their native soil as those who, like West in his early efforts, quite literally drew their colors from the clay underfoot. Yet most drew inspiration as well from the riches of Western civilization, some acquiring classical educations and others learning much from converse in a society that was expanding intellectually as well as artistically.

The creativity of many was stimulated by a diversity of interests and activities extending far beyond the graphic arts. One thinks immediately of Charles Willson Peale, the polymath who enjoyed the friendship and admiration of Franklin and Jefferson. But there were others remarkable for their creative involvement in a variety of disciplines and activities. Dunlap, besides his visual art, is known as the "Father of American Drama" and the author of histories of the American theater and of the art of design. Allston was a poet and novelist. Trumbull is famous chiefly for such large-scale historical pictures as *The Signing of the Declaration of Independence*, but he was also a businessman and diplomat. Though Morse has an honored place in the history of art, he is best known as inventor of the telegraph. Even Stuart, not thought of as exceptionally versatile, had been in London a professional musician and aspiring composer.

These artists were as bright and as richly varied as their palettes. Like the statesmen who were their contemporaries, they epitomize the creative vitality of America at the time of the Revolution and the building of the Republic. They, and the society of which they were both the creatures and the creators, exemplified the same tension between heritage and experiment, the same self-confidence and patriotic pride, the same fruitful cross-fertilization of disciplines and profitable exchange of ideas with other societies, that distinguished Renaissance Florence and Elizabethan England.

43

TINKERERS AND TITANS

NECESSITY MADE many an American frontiersman an inventor. Even as the frontier moved westward, leaving a second or third generation on family farms and in villages and small towns, Americans living far from factories and dependent on stores with a limited range of products were forced to "make do" with what they had.

Sometimes considerable ingenuity was involved in converting a simple tool to do the work of a complex one. Sometimes the local blacksmith was an ingenious mechanic who welcomed a challenge beyond shoeing a horse, mending a wagon, or making simple andirons. Sometimes he might alter designs of farm machinery to improve performance. There were many inventors who never received a patent, never sold their designs to a factory owner. Often they earned small profits by selling their creations one by one to neighbors, meanwhile earning large rewards in the general admiration of their wizardry.

Such was the creative spirit of men and women seeking ways to improve the machinery of life about them that people whose principal occupations were not mechanical were sometimes the authors of important inventions. Washington and Jefferson each won international recognition for the design of a new moldboard for plowing. Jefferson was responsible for improvements on much existing machinery, including the polygraph. Franklin, of course, was one of the great inventors of his time, with the glass harmonica, Franklin stove, lightning rod, and bifocals to his credit.

Not only did some scientists become inventors, but some inventors, through study and experiment, became scientists. The Enlightenment made little distinction between science and mechanics, just as medieval Europeans did not separately categorize arts and crafts. The great French Encyclopédie's subtitle described it as a dictionary "of sciences, of arts, and of trades."[1] One of its editors, Denis Diderot, criticized distinctions between the fine and mechanical arts. Another editor, Jean Le Rond d'Alembert, made the same complaint in a preface.

American intellectuals in various areas organized to pursue mechanical invention, scientific experiment, and artistic creation within the same organization. So many members were interested in all three that there was little chance

of interesting only one segment while the rest of the audience was bored. John
Adams was the prime mover in 1780 in founding in Boston the American Academy of Arts and Sciences. Five years later the society began publishing its *Memoirs*. In 1781, the New Jersey Society for the Promotion of Agriculture, Commerce, and Art was founded. The Chemical Society of Philadelphia was
organized in 1792.

Before the Revolution, some colonies occasionally had granted patents for
inventions to their residents. Massachusetts had issued one to Samuel Winslow
as early as 1641 for a new process of making salt. After the Declaration of
Independence, some patents were granted through special acts of individual
state legislatures. The Constitution of the United States empowered Congress
"to promote the progress of science and useful arts by securing for limited
times to authors and inventors the exclusive right to their respective writings
and discoveries." In Washington's administration, the responsibility for issuing
patents was placed in the State Department. The situation was most appropriate
as the secretary of state, Thomas Jefferson, was himself an enthusiastic inventor.

The federal government issued its first patent July 31, 1790, after a three-
month hiatus following advent of the service. After this slow beginning, patents
were issued in rapidly increasing volume, reflecting an increase that eventually
placed the United States in the forefront of the world in number of inventions.[2]

Two Revolutionary patriots were responsible for a development that would
revolutionize American industry. In his copper manufacturing, Paul Revere of
Massachusetts inaugurated systems that paved the way for assembly-line work.
In Virginia, Colonel Fielding Lewis, Washington's brother-in-law, instituted
an assembly line for gun manufacture to supply the soaring demands of the
Continental Army.

The idea of building a submarine had long engaged ingenious minds. There
were long-forgotten plans for one in the notebooks of Leonardo da Vinci. People in different nations tried their hand at creating underwater vessels. One of
the most promising was the *American Turtle*, the aptly named invention of
David Bushnell. He used the vessel, built in 1775, in a nearly successful attempt
the next year to blow up the British frigate *Eagle* in New York harbor. He did
succeed in startling the enemy fleet into flight. Bushnell's submarine was the
first ever to be used in battle anywhere in the world.

American inventors did even more impressive things with surface ships.
The change was startling when sailing vessels sprouted smokestacks, even
though they still prudently retained their sails in case the newfangled method
of propulsion failed. The rapid development of the steamboat was one result of
the tremendous contemporary interest in the development of steam power for
a multitude of industrial purposes.

As early as the second century B.C., Hero of Alexandria, in his *Pneumat-
ica*, described two kinds of steam engines. Neither, however, had an industrial
use. The first, called an aeoliphile, was a steam reaction turbine, a hollow glove
rotated by escaping steam. It seems to have been only a toy. The other was a
primitive pressure engine used to open and close the doors of a shrine.

Strangely, though others experimented with steam through the centuries, it was not put to industrial use until 1698 when Thomas Savery, an English military engineer, patented an atmospheric engine for pumping water. Much more sophisticated versions of the steam engine were invented by James Watt, a Scotsman, between 1763 and 1781. Commercial demand for his engines kept a Birmingham factory busy turning them out.

American inventors made the next really important improvements in the steam engine after Watt. John Stevens, a native of New York City, patented the first multitubular boiler in 1783. Oliver Evans, a Delaware man, invented a noncondensing, high-pressure steam engine.

John Fitch, a Connecticut native and New Jersey veteran of the American Revolution, invented a steamboat, which he operated in 1787 on the Delaware River before an audience including members of the Constitutional Convention. Though he had had only six years of formal education, he had taught himself a tremendous amount about steam power. He used metalworking techniques learned as an apprentice to a brass founder and clock maker. He built several kinds of steamboats, with the propulsion ranging from paddle wheels to a screw propeller. Unfortunately, Fitch never had sufficient capital to make a commercial success of his steamboats and thus prove their utility. He did, however, for a while, operate one of them as a regularly scheduled ferry between Philadelphia and Trenton, New Jersey. Discouraged after a decade and a half of business failures, he took his own life in 1798.

Another claimant to the honor of inventing the steamboat was James Rumsey, a mechanical engineer from Maryland, who launched his steamboat on the Potomac River in December 1787, about four months after Fitch launched his vessel on the Delaware. Apparently, neither man had borrowed ideas from the other. As happens so often in the field of invention, various fertile minds were at work on the same problem at a nexus between demand and opportunity. Rumsey's boat was propelled by streams of water forced though the stern by a steam pump. He invented an improved steam boiler, patenting it in both the United States and England, and began work on a second steamboat, but died before it was finished.

Neither Fitch nor Rumsey had built the first successful steamboat. That distinction belongs to a Frenchman, Jacques C. Périer, who in 1775 launched on the Seine a small boat propelled a short distance by steam. In 1783, the Marquis Claude de Jouffroy d'Abbans built the first steamboat to be truly successful in demonstration. But after these initial experiments, the French lagged and the British hesitated, while Americans moved to the fore. After Fitch and Rumsey, other Americans—Samuel Morey, Nathan Read, and John Stevens—invented steamboats of different designs. Stevens built the world's first seagoing steamship. Americans were in the lead in the development of the steamboat even before Robert Fulton in 1807 launched his *Clermont*, the first steam-powered vessel to be a conspicuous success both nautically and commercially.

In his versatility and wide range of activities, Fulton was a representative American of his time. Born on a Pennsylvania farm in 1765, he became a jeweler's apprentice in Philadelphia. The city was hospitable to ideas, and Fulton thrived mentally in that environment. When he was twenty years old, he became a painter of miniatures. In the pursuit of excellence, he joined the trek of young American artists to London to study painting under their fellow countryman Benjamin West. Fulton became a good enough portraitist and landscape artist (not then a generally popular genre) to win favorable notice in both England and France.

Even as he forged ahead in art, he found himself spending increasing time in engineering studies. He made engineering his principal profession in 1793. Three years later, Fulton's *Treatise on the Improvement of Canal Navigation* attracted some notice in both the United States and France, but not enough to cause either country to launch a canal-building program of the scope that he advocated.

He invented a submarine that was an improved version of David Bushnell's craft, and it performed successfully in 1800. Despite this achievement, Fulton was not able to sell his submarine to the United States, France, or Great Britain. Even President Jefferson, that lover of invention and experiment, was not interested.

While in Paris, Fulton teamed up with the American minister to France, Robert Livingston, to produce and operate another kind of ship. Livingston had wealth, position, and contacts. The scion of a family prominent in New York since the seventeenth century, he had been John Jay's law partner, and a member of the Continental Congress and of the committee to produce a Declaration of Independence. He was the first chancellor of New York State. Equally important for Fulton's needs, Livingston was the brother-in-law of John Stevens and had assisted him in his experiments in steam navigation. Topping it all off, Livingston held a legal monopoly of steam transportation on New York waters. Fulton could not have found a better partner for his project to produce the world's first commercially successful steamboat.

Fruition came in August of 1807 when both Livingston and Fulton were back in the United States. More than any of his predecessors, Fulton combined the best features of steamboat building in both Europe and America. The *Clermont*, about a week after a short trial run, made the 150-mile voyage from New York City to Albany. Regular commercial schedules were established, and Fulton built other steamboats, including steam ferries for inland waterways. He even built a mobile "floating fort," a steam warship, for the defense of New York harbor in the War of 1812.

Fulton was responsible for many other inventions and mechanical improvements. At an early age, he became one of America's most expert gunsmiths. Many of his inventions were related to transportation. One was the double inclined plane, an apparatus for raising and lowering canal boats. Out of a need to dig canal channels faster came his power shovel. To transport water, he built cast-iron aqueducts. To move people and carriages, he built cast-iron bridges. He experimented with the destruction, as well as the construction, of ships, inventing a self-propelled submarine torpedo.

Some of his important inventions had nothing to do with water—floating ships on it, channeling it, or crossing it with prefabricated bridges. He invented one machine for sawing marble, another for spinning flax. In Paris, he combined his talents as artist and inventor to produce what is believed to be the world's first panorama.

But the last decade of Fulton's life, which ended in 1815, was concentrated on steamships—inventing, building, and improving them, and organizing and managing companies to operate them. Though his accomplishments were diverse, his fame is inseparable from the steamboat. When the American ship *Savannah* in 1819 made the first transatlantic crossing by a steamboat, Robert Fulton had been four years in his grave, but he shared in the glory.

For the nearly four decades from 1781 to 1819, the most impressive and significant industrial inventions throughout the world centered on the development of steam power. The most dramatic part of this development was the application of steam power to water transportation. Great Britain, through the genius of James Watt, held the lead at the start, but American inventors soon moved into the forefront and stayed there. The achievement was a remarkable one for any country, but an astonishing one for a nation so young.

Concurrent with advances related to steam power was what is sometimes described as a kaleidoscope of inventions in other fields. But kaleidoscope implies a series of discernible patterns, whereas American inventiveness, aside from the concentration on steam, expressed itself in so many seemingly disparate ways that the scene is more that of a rapidly shifting montage. A lengthy list would only be confusing, but a cursory view of some of the developments may give a hint of their variety.

Some of the steam-power researchers invented sophisticated things not even imagined by mainstream inventors concerned with water transportation. Jacob Perkins of Massachusetts originated the bathometer, a device for measuring the depth of water; the plenometer, to record the speed of ships; and in his eighty-second year the piezometer, to measure the compressibility of water. But Perkins also was among the great number of Americans creating machines to accelerate processes commonly used in manufacturing. In 1790 he brought forth a machine to cut and head nails in a single operation.

Few inventions were so influential as Eli Whitney's cotton gin. The Massachusetts native, a 1792 graduate of Yale, had shown inventive precocity as a young boy in his father's metalworking shop. He was studying law and working as a tutor on the Georgia plantation of General Nathanael Greene's widow when his hostess appealed to him to solve a problem. Separating the fiber of short-staple cotton from the seed was so slow and tedious a process that cotton cultivation was unprofitable. Concentrating on the problem, Whitney constructed a model gin within ten days.

Later he completed a larger, improved model. With this machine, a single worker could produce daily fifty pounds of cleaned cotton. Ample fields whitened with the "Snow of Southern Summers."[3] Plantations grew larger. Westward expansion was encouraged.

Whitney's invention made many people rich, but he was not one of them. Most of his profits were consumed in legal battles to protect his patent. When he obtained it in 1794, imitations were already on the market. Not until 1807 did he receive judicial confirmation of his priority. Even so, claims have been put forth through the years in behalf of others ranging from businessmen to a laborer. Most historians have concluded that, whatever contributions may have been made by others, the prime credit for the gin belongs to Whitney.

Even if he were not its creator, he still would have high rank among American inventors. When he returned to New Haven, Connecticut, he obtained a federal contract for ten thousand muskets and built an innovative plant for their manufacture. His muskets were the first with standardized, interchangeable parts. Later he built machinery for producing such muskets with precision parts, not only accelerating manufacture but also making it possible for ordinary laborers to duplicate the work of the highly skilled.

One of the important developments in firearms was John Hall's invention of the breech-loading flintlock in 1819. American improvements in guns had begun in colonial days with the development of the long rifle in Pennsylvania. They continued through various nuances as the Republic expanded westward.

There was an explosion of inventions for the building trade. Jesse Reed of Connecticut in 1807 created machinery to make tacks, a fitting companion to Jacob Perkins' machine for cutting and heading nails. Abel Stowel of Massachusetts brought forth a screw-cutting machine in 1809; David Melville the circular saw in 1814; and Thomas Blanchard of Massachusetts, the profile lathe in 1818.

In a nation still predominantly agricultural, inventive skills were frequently turned to agricultural tasks. Whitney's cotton gin was only the most spectacular production in this category. Eliakim Spooner devised a seeding machine in 1799. And Thomas Jefferson and George Washington were not the only Americans to make historic improvements in the plow. Charles Newbold made the first cast-iron plow in 1797. Jethro Wood of New York in 1819 made a cast-iron, three-piece plow with standardized interchangeable parts. In 1822 a Vermonter, John Conant, invented a lock colter, a device attached to the beam of a plow to cut the earth in advance of the plowshare.

In 1826, John Stevens used the multitubular steam engine, his earlier invention, to propel a locomotive.

A multitude of inventions, many minor, some major, were reported in the nation's newspapers. Beginning in 1816, such news was printed on presses invented by Pennsylvanian George Clymer, and in 1817 on improved versions by Samuel Rust.

The field of mechanical invention provided one of the most impressive exhibitions of American creativity in the Revolutionary and Early National periods. Its most important creations were the work of versatile men who observed the needs of the society in which they lived and endeavored to meet them through imaginative synthesis, and sometimes venturesome extension, of the work of their fellow countrymen and of innovative people overseas. From the ranks of the tinkerers had come a generation of titans.

AUDACIOUS IMAGINATIONS

WHEN WE CONSIDER the scientists who helped to make the era of the founders so richly creative in America, we are dealing with many people that we have encountered in earlier chapters. Some we have seen as statesmen, others as inventors, writers, or artists. Some keep reappearing in the habiliments of several different occupations, like a quartet of actors presenting Edgar Lee Masters' *Spoon River Anthology*. Actually, the variety of their activities was not a response to a labor shortage. This variety was both evidence and (in part) cause of their creativity. Their versatility testified to the energy and richness of their creativeness. At the same time, the variety of their interests and activities provided the cross-fertilization for energized originality.

Benjamin Franklin, statesman, diplomat, and writer, was honored as a scientist as much as any person in the world in his generation. We have seen how his scientific achievements gained powerful friends for him when he was representing his country in London, and how his diplomatic role in Paris was helped by the French image of him as the man who "snatched the lightning from the sky." Many people—Americans and Europeans—believed that the most important scientific discoveries were being made in electricity, and it was generally acknowledged that Franklin was foremost in this field. He discovered the existence of plus and minus charges. When French scientists demonstrated the identity of lightning and electricity, they did so by following his suggestions with great fidelity. He personally furnished a more dramatic proof when he flew his kite in a thunderstorm. For three decades, Europe's greatest experimenters with electricity—Italy's Galvani and Volta, Denmark's Oersted, France's Ampère and Arago, Germany's Schweigger and England's Sturgeon—followed the self-educated American.

Thomas Jefferson—statesman, writer, political philosopher, architect, landscaper, educator, and inventor—also rejoiced in the label "scientist." True, when he said that he would have liked to devote his life to science, he was using the word in its broad, eighteenth-century sense to denote all forms of scholarship, his researches into American aboriginal tongues and into classical architecture as well as into paleontology. But, even in the narrower sense of our own day, Jefferson was a scientist. Because of his systematic study of finds in Virginia and Kentucky and reports on them to the American Philosophical Society, he is honored as the "Father of American Paleontology." As president, he planned, and sent Meriwether Lewis and William Clark on, one of the most famous and most efficient scientific expeditions in history.

Rembrandt Peale, the great painter whose most famous works are two portraits of Jefferson, followed his hero into paleontology, producing a study of the mammoth. Of course, he had an even closer example in his father, Charles Willson Peale, "the Father of American Vertebrate Paleontology" and then the world's most innovative science museum creator.

Jefferson, Franklin, and Washington helped to raise funds by subscription for publication in 1791 of botanist William Bartram's *Travels through North and South Carolina, Georgia, East and West Florida.* The author had grown up amid the intellectual ferment of Philadelphia and had accompanied his father, John, royal botanist of the Floridas, on field trips. The son's book contains not only accounts and illustrations of a great many botanical discoveries but also important observations on zoology and the life of the Indians. After being reprinted in London and Dublin, the book found a still wider audience through translations into German, Dutch, and French.

The work is a strange amalgam of reports in conventional scientific language and passages of throbbing lyricism. Chateaubriand borrowed heavily from it without acknowledging his indebtedness. Wordsworth, Coleridge, and Southey found inspiration in its pages, and Carlyle praised its "wondrous kind of flowering eloquence." Bartram, now included in some survey courses in American literature, is regarded by some critics as one of the pioneers of romantic literature. He is another example of the versatility of his generation. In this book, I was briefly undecided whether to introduce him among the scientists or the writers.

Other American botanists did impressive work. Gotthilf Mühlenberg in 1813 produced a catalog of 2,800 species of North American plants. Five years later Thomas Nuttall published his *Genera of North American Plants.* John Torrey in 1824 brought forth a classic compendium on the plants of the northern and middle states.

Nor were the fauna of the nation neglected. William Peck, writing on New Hampshire fish, initiated systematic zoology in America. Zoology seemed to be advancing through competitive ichthyology. Samuel Latham Mitchell, professor of natural history at Columbia University, produced in 1814 a study of New York fishes that brought him recognition as a zoologist of the first rank. Constantine Samuel Rafinesque also made a reputation in fish; his *Ichthyologia Ohiensi* (1820) was quickly recognized as one of the most important works in the field. But he produced studies of other things as well, such as sponges, foxes, and equine salivation. No mean botanist, he later published *Medical Flora of the United States.* John D. Godman was even more inclusive, publishing a three-volume *American Natural History.*

Outstanding work was done with birds. Inspired by association with William Bartram, Alexander Wilson, between 1808 and 1813, published the nine volumes of his *American Ornithology*. And John James Audubon, whose name is synonymous with the study of birds, began the work as a naturalist and artist that would culminate in his monumental *Ornithological Guide*.

The earth itself was the subject of important studies. Amos Eaton in 1815 produced his landmark *Index* to the geology of the northern states. Edward Hitchcock in 1818 and 1823 presented outstanding reports on the geology of New England. Denison Olmsted, a Yale professor known also for studies of meteors, hailstorms, and auroras, produced in North Carolina the "first official state geological survey in the United States." In 1809, William Maclure published the first geological map of the United States. The work of these scientists gained the respect not only of their countrymen but also of fellow scientists in other lands.

While many scientists were studying the earth, some were still looking heavenward. Foremost of these was David Rittenhouse. He was born in Pennsylvania in the year of Washington's birth, 1732. A successful clock maker, he also became an expert maker of engineering and scientific instruments. As his reputation grew, he was asked to use instruments of his own manufacture to determine the boundaries of several states. He became interested in telescopes, and by wide and intensive reading of scientific treatises educated himself in astronomy.

Association with leading intellectuals of Philadelphia, especially Benjamin Franklin, and eventually with such other American thinkers as Jefferson, extended the framework of his inquiries. He combined his knowledge of clock making and astronomy to construct an orrery—the first in America and one of the most celebrated in the world. His observations of the transits of Venus and Mercury, and of Lexell's comet, attracted international notice. He succeeded Franklin as president of the American Philosophical Society, and was made a fellow of Britain's Royal Society.

The accuracy of his astronomical observations, and later those of others following his lead, was increased by his use of measured grating intervals and spider threads to attain precise focus.

During most of his scientific career, Rittenhouse was also busy in public life, serving successively as a member of Pennsylvania's constitutional convention, as state treasurer for twelve years, and as director of the United States Mint. Fearful that a great scientist was spending too much time in politics, Jefferson reminded him that society had many people fit for office but only one Rittenhouse.

Another of Jefferson's Philadelphia friends had America's foremost reputation in another scientific field. Dr. Benjamin Rush was sometimes called "the American Sydenham" and, just as Sydenham had been called "the English Hippocrates," so Rush was called "the Hippocrates of Pennsylvania." Though Dr. Robley Dunglison, the physician in Jefferson's last illness, was a cherished friend, the president tended to doubt the professional competence of most practitioners. He used to say that, when he saw two doctors in conference, he expected to see buzzards circling overhead. He had, however, great respect for Dr. Rush.

In ways both bad and good, Rush was very much a man of his times. He accepted without question the contemporary medical practices of bloodletting and purging and thus exhausted his share of patients struggling for life. But he was also representative of his times in love of learning and appetite for experiment. A College of New Jersey (Princeton) graduate at fifteen, he obtained his medical degree from Edinburgh and became professor of chemistry at the College of Philadelphia. Later, he was professor of the institute of medicine and clinical practice at the University of Pennsylvania. Rush's most important medical contribution was to the psychology of mental illness. His *Medical Inquiries and Observations upon the Diseases of the Mind,* published in 1812, was one of the few truly influential books on the subject. In his own practice, he brought more humane and rational methods to the treatment of confined patients. His reports on cholera infantum and dengue were also valuable, and his study of the relationship between rheumatism and dental disease was important. While preparing his medical reports, he also found time to write literary and philosophical essays.

Rush also carried on a multitude of public duties. In the Revolution, he served in both the Continental Army and the Continental Congress. He was also a member of the Pennsylvania convention to ratify the Constitution. For the last sixteen years of his life, he was treasurer of the United States Mint at Philadelphia. He was a founder of Dickinson College and of the first antislavery society in the United States. He campaigned vigorously for prison reform, abolition of capital punishment, free public schools for the poor, and higher education for women.

Joseph Priestley, the great English chemist and controversial preacher, found in the United States the freedom he craved. In return, he was the catalyst for chemical studies in this country. Princeton established a separate chair of chemistry in 1795.

Thomas Cooper, professor of chemistry at Dickinson College beginning in 1811, at the University of Pennsylvania beginning in 1817, and finally at the University of South Carolina from 1819 to 1834, was one of America's most versatile scientists. He taught mineralogy as well as chemistry in all three schools. Jefferson tried to recruit him to teach both subjects at the University of Virginia. He also tried to engage him as professor of law. Jefferson believed, though, that Cooper's real preeminence was in economics. The Virginian considered him the nation's leading writer on the subject. Jefferson was recruiting faculty members from Europe as well as the United States.

In the early years of the Republic, science was an increasingly important part of the curricula of higher learning. This was to be expected in a society strongly interested in Enlightenment ideas. But many people would probably be surprised to learn of the hospitality to science even in theological seminaries and other church-supported colleges. E. Brooks Holifield notes that when John Holt Rice became the first professor of theology in the Presbyterian Seminary at Virginia's Hampden-Sydney, "he was officially charged with the task of raising up a generation of scientifically minded clergymen." He was told this "branch of knowledge should form a part of that fund of information which every minister of the Gospel should possess." Holifield assures us that "the charge embodied a consensus among the educated clergy of the Old South."[1]

Benjamin Thompson had one of the strangest careers of any American scientist. Born in North Woburn, Massachusetts, in 1753, he was apprenticed at age thirteen to a storekeeper in Salem. He attended some lectures at Harvard and tried his hand at engraving and experiments in chemistry and mechanics. A lover of America but not a friend of American independence, he sailed for London when the British evacuated Boston in 1776. He found employment as a clerk in the office of Britain's secretary of state.

At twenty-three, he was alone in a strange city, one of the world's great metropolises, full of talented, well-educated men striving for preferment. Within several months, he advanced within the Foreign Office to the post of Secretary for the Colony of Georgia. Four years later, at the age of twenty-seven, he was Great Britain's undersecretary of state.

All the while that he was climbing politically, Thompson found time to continue his self-instruction in science as well as increasingly innovative experiments in chemistry and physics. When he was twenty-six years old, he was elected a fellow of the Royal Society. He was knighted, and began to harvest other British honors.

He resigned his civil posts, however, and with the king's permission, accepted an offer from Prince Maximilian, elector of Bavaria, to serve his government. There Thompson spent eleven years as minister of war, minister of police, and grand chamberlain. He instituted reforms benefiting the poor and reorganized the army. Meanwhile, he enlivened the intellectual life of Europe with his contributions to *Philosophical Transactions*. At thirty-eight, he was made a count of the Holy Roman Empire. He chose the title Count Rumford, taking the name from his wife's native township in Massachusetts. He decided to return to England. A grateful Bavaria erected a monument to him in Munich.

His researches in the explosive force of gunpowder, the problems of communication at sea, and the cohesion of bodies attracted favorable attention. But he gained his place in the world history of science in 1798, when he presented to the Royal Society his "Enquiry concerning the Source of Heat Which is Excited by Friction." He successfully maintained, against the general assumption that heat was a material substance, his own revolutionary theory that it was "a mode of motion." Thompson is universally credited with this discovery.

He used his prestige to secure reforms in Dublin hospitals and workhouses and among London's laboring poor. He turned his inventive genius to improving fireplaces and reducing (albeit not sufficiently) the smoke from urban chimneys. When he endowed a medal to be presented by the Royal Society for outstanding achievement in science, they promptly named it the Rumford Medal and made him the first recipient.

Thompson's thoughts turned back to his native land. As one who had left it for London in 1776, he could not count on a warm welcome if he returned. But he did want to do something for the United States. He endowed a medal for the American Academy of Arts and Sciences. Like its counterpart for the

Royal Society, it is known as the Rumford Medal. He also endowed a professorship at Harvard, which is known as the Rumford Professorship.

Even though Sir Benjamin Thompson, Count Rumford, has an honored place in the world history of science, the amount of space devoted to him in these pages may seem disproportionate. But some people still wonder how much impact American scientists would have had on world awareness if they had arrived on "the vaunted scene of Europe"[2] to compete without the full armor of home-built reputations. It is worthwhile to recall the career of a small town storekeeper's apprentice from Massachusetts who arrived in London in 1776 without academic credentials, prominence, or helpful connections.

John Dewey wrote, "Every great advance in science has issued from a new audacity of imagination." In the early days of the Republic, when each dawn brought a new horizon and each horizon a new challenge, there was no lack of audacious imaginations.

MUSIC—FROZEN AND OTHERWISE

GOETHE AND Friedrich von Schelling both called architecture "frozen music." Certainly architecture and music have a great deal in common. They are the most mathematical of the arts. The relationship is even closer than that. The golden section, or divine proportion, of mathematics that prevails in many great architectural monuments prevails also in famous symphonies. And the Fibonacci sequence, a standard part of mathematics since the thirteenth century, defines a spiraling musical segment as well as it does a spiral tower or stairway.

This chapter will deal with both music and architecture in the early days of the Republic, partly because musical advances in the period were insufficient to merit a separate chapter and partly because the mathematical links between the two arts produce an appropriate pairing.

There is nothing strange about the fact that so great a field of human endeavor as music should not have made impressive advances when creativity was burgeoning in virtually every other. The remarkable thing is that there were so few lacunae among the arts and sciences.

The period, however, was not devoid of musical accomplishment. There was nothing in American music comparable to contemporary European achievements, but there was for the first time a stirring of creativity in formal musical composition in the United States. Some of this work was of high caliber.

America's first native-born professional composer was Francis Hopkinson.[1] Reared in the cultural environment of the privileged classes of Philadelphia, the son of the first president of the American Philosophical Society, he came to music as part of a whole spectrum of artistic and public service activities. He received both the bachelor's and master's degrees from the College of Philadelphia (University of Pennsylvania) and became a lawyer. He was a leader in the Continental Congress and used his pen to fight for ratification of the Constitution. He became a federal judge. As we have seen, his poems and satires were admired by many of his contemporaries. He was esteemed as a proficient musician. He published *A Collection of Psalm Tunes* and *Seven Songs for the Harpsichord or Forte Piano*. Perhaps his best known single composition was a secular song, "My Days Have Been So Wondrous Free."

Hopkinson had no exaggerated idea of his ability as a composer, modestly claiming only that in the United States he was first in the field. But until well into the twentieth century, even musical historians regarded him as the best example of musical creativity in the early days of the Republic.

Now, however, the palm for excellence as an early American composer is posthumously awarded to William Billings.[2] This Boston native grew up in a New England still inhospitable to secular music except patriotic pieces that, being anthems, were considered not too far removed from church music. A tanner by trade, he received little musical education but began writing hymns and patriotic songs and eventually made composing and choir directing his chief occupation. Blind in one eye, cursed with legs grossly unequal in length and a partially withered arm, he seemed severely handicapped until, with unerring ear and stentorian voice, he took command of a chorus.

Musicians better versed than he in European musical traditions deplored his parallel fifths and other rough departures from polished custom. This attitude prevailed into the twentieth century, but has been reversed in our time. Critics and music historians now praise the "rough-hewn strength" and "pioneer freshness" of these devices. They consider it fortunate for his art that he had enough of the rudiments of traditional learning to profit in the development of his talent, but was not sufficiently imbued with European ways to lose his artistic independence. They call his work "splendid" and "powerful."

Billings himself said, "Nature must lay the foundation, Nature must inspire the thought. For my own part, . . . I don't think myself confined to any rules for composition laid down by any that went before me. . . . Art is subservient to genius." Billings would be gratified to know that in 1971, under the editorship of Geoffrey Hindley, the first American edition of the *Larousse Encyclopedia of Music* said of him, "In many of his works the spark of genius did indeed burn brightly." It cited "David's touching lamentation for Absalom, the tender melody of the canon *When Jesus wept* . . . , the rousing hymn-tune 'Chester' [and] the grandiose anthem 'Be Glad Then, America.'" Hindley speculated that, had America then been freer of the influence of European musical fashion, Billings' works "might have been a point of departure of an early indigenous American Style."[3]

For his hymn "Chester," Billings wrote patriotic lyrics defiantly proclaiming, "Let tyrants shake their iron rods and slavery clank her galling chains." He published songbooks, notable among them *The New England Psalm Singer*, *The Singing Master's Assistant*, and *The Continental Harmony*.

Billings was innovative as a church choir director as well as a composer. He used both a pitch pipe and a violoncello to achieve better tonal effects, and in this practice was emulated by other directors.

Beginning in the 1960s, publication of books on Billings and his works has reflected the greatly increased appreciation of his art.

At least one other composer in eighteenth century America deserves indi-

vidual consideration. Johann Friedrich Peter (whose name is sometimes anglicized as John Frederick Peter) was part of the great Moravian migration to the
United States.[4] Born in Holland of German stock, he brought with him a solid
grounding in the art and science of music. He composed excellent music, including eighty sacred compositions for chorus and orchestra and a half dozen
string quintets.

Bitter experience with persecution in Europe and a desire to avoid what
they considered corrupting influences in contemporary society caused the Moravians in America to stand aloof from other elements of society. Otherwise,
Peter and some of his coreligionists might have greatly enriched the mainstream
of early American music and perhaps, in turn, have found stimulus in native
influences.

Some of the most impressive church music in the United States was presented in the Moravian Church in Bethlehem, Pennsylvania. As early as 1756,
Franklin reported that the congregation augmented its organ with flutes, oboes,
French horns, and trumpets. Building on this level of sophistication, the Moravians in Pennsylvania and elsewhere were performing at an outstanding level in
the latter part of the eighteenth century and the opening years of the nineteenth. But, of course, they were seldom heard by non-Moravians. Musical societies, however, sprang up in Charleston, South Carolina; New York City; Dartmouth College in New Hampshire; Fredericksburg, Virginia; and Philadelphia.
Most emphasized classical music, presenting an annual concert series of instrumental and vocal music.

Of course, these performances were not accessible to people in most parts
of the United States. Thomas Jefferson said he would rather live on his mountaintop in Albemarle County, Virginia, than anywhere else in the world, but
admitted he missed one thing there—the music of Europe's symphony orches-
tras. A violinist himself, he usually had to be content with informal amateur
productions presented with the help of family and friends. During the Revolution, he recruited a classical orchestra from good German musicians among
Hessian prisoners of war. Some enjoyed so much the friendly associations born
of this activity that, after peace was concluded, they settled down in Albemarle
County.[5]

Often, in some American cities, more artistry was exhibited in the audito-
riums themselves than in the musical performances they housed. Architecture
was far more advanced than the sibling mathematical art.

It got a head start in the frontier days. During the early years of settlement,
even those who felt guilty about taking time for the fine arts amid the pressing
demands for mere survival could feel that substantial housing was essential. As
we have seen, the first settlers in Virginia and Massachusetts built mostly in
medieval styles, the taste of private homeowners tending characteristically
toward long-familiar designs rather than the latest developments in contemporary architecture. In the eighteenth century, Georgian designs predominated
among the affluent.

As a rule, the builder, whether amateur or professional, was also the architect. For inspiration, he depended upon English books of architectural sketches.

Some architects, however, had enough originality and boldness to leave their personal stamp on the buildings that they constructed. Even as early as 1693, it will be recalled, some Virginians "adapted to the nature of the country," a building "first modeled by Sir Christopher Wren," as the central structure of the College of William and Mary. In the eighteenth century, the Governor's Palace in Williamsburg, Virginia, and the Tryon Palace in North Carolina attained a high standard of elegance. But even though some locally designed additions were made (at least in the Old Dominion), neither building could be cited as an example of native architecture. The early eighteenth century capitol in Williamsburg, the old statehouse in Boston, and Carpenter's Hall and Independence Hall in Philadelphia were all esthetically pleasing buildings, but they were not examples of American originality.

The Maryland statehouse, in Annapolis, was different from the other capitols. It was surmounted by a huge dome. The dome was an ancient European form, but its use on a state capitol was a Maryland innovation, one that started a fashion in the United States.

The eighteenth century did see in America some regional interpretations of Georgian ranging from great mansions along the James River in Virginia, to handsome urban homes in the Massachusetts towns of Marblehead and Cambridge, to a more baroque style in Annapolis, and Doric-doorwayed versions in Philadelphia. Stone houses of a different design appeared in western Pennsylvania, but they too were imitative of European models. Their style was brought by settlers from Germany's Upper Rhine valley, and it followed the southward progress of Pennsylvania Dutch migration down the Great Valley into Maryland, Virginia, and the Carolinas.

The American Revolution, and particularly the surge of patriotic pride after victory, prompted self-conscious demands for a new American style of architecture. Jefferson was sympathetic and was quite ready for a break with the Georgian style that seemed to predominate in contemporary construction of English mansions, churches, and government buildings. But he was not ready for something radically new.

Earlier, in observing his political career, we have seen him turn to the problem of constructing government buildings in the District of Columbia, telling President Washington, "Whenever it is proposed to prepare for the Capitol, I should prefer the adoption of some one of the models of antiquity, which have had the approbation of thousands of years." As one of the Founding Fathers, Jefferson was of the generation of American leaders who saw themselves as successors to the statesmen of ancient Greece and Rome.

But he did not advocate a slavish reproduction of ancient structures. Jefferson wanted instead to adapt their design for use in his own time and country. He wished to do for the national capitol what he had done for the new state capitol in Richmond, Virginia. There he had taken as a model the old Roman temple in Nimes, itself adapted from Greek predecessors, but had so varied the fenestration and other aspects that the structure completed in 1789 was, however subtly, his own creation. It inaugurated the Roman Revival in America. The movement's greatest triumph was the execution of Jefferson's design for the University of Virginia, a marvelously integrated work of architecture and landscaping as it stood at the time of his death in 1826. Of course, it was this design that a distinguished jury of architects, architectural critics, and architectural historians cited in 1976 as the greatest single achievement of any architect in American history.[6]

But Jefferson as an architect had other triumphs of innovation and adaptation. On the top of a mountain, he built his mansion, Monticello, first leveling the mountaintop, and in a later stroke of inspiration surmounting the house with a low dome so that the building and the peak were one integrated form. Today the structure is studied throughout the world as a brilliant example of Palladian style. And Poplar Forest, the retreat he built near Lynchburg, Virginia, is a remarkable example of the adaptation of Palladian elegance to the domestic requirements of families of moderate means.[7]

The Roman Revival in the United States declined rapidly after 1826, yielding to the Greek Revival, which in its beginning (about 1820) overlapped the earlier movement. The popularity of the Greek Revival was derived in part from the Americans' habit of seeing themselves as classical heroes, but probably owed even more to the immigration of foreign architects caught up in the latest Continental enthusiasm. Nevertheless, the ablest American architects brought some individuality to their creations in this mode. Probably no foreigner did more for American architecture than the English architect who kept postponing his arrival in America to plan Monticello until Jefferson intensified his own study of the building art and undertook the task himself.

One of Jefferson's architectural disciples was General John H. Cocke, a Jeffersonian statesman, and an unusually versatile man, one who in eras less distinguished for creative genius would have been of the first rank. Cocke, self-taught in architecture, planned and erected handsome buildings in the Jeffersonian Palladian style. But he was no knee-jerk imitator. After all, didn't he warn Jefferson (correctly, as it turned out) that the roof he was planning for one of the University of Virginia buildings would leak?

One architect who profited from Jefferson's advice was Charles Bulfinch, a Bostonian whose nephew married the Virginian's niece.[8] While making a tour of England and the Continent in 1785–1786, Bulfinch followed Jefferson's suggestion that he study the classical architecture of France and Italy. At first, he filtered the classical images through Great Britain's Adamesque neoclassicism, designing highly derivative but handsome mansions for rich Bostonians. More than anyone else, he determined the characteristics in New England of what came to be called the Federal style of residential architecture.

Later, however, Bulfinch followed the classical styles of Greece and Rome in designing public buildings, drawing his inspiration directly from original structures but proceeding with an independence of interpretation that marked his creations as distinctly his own. As chairman of the Boston Selectmen, a position corresponding to that of mayor in other cities, he led a transforming program of renovation and redevelopment. He personally created most of the program's architectural gems, such as a courthouse, the new South Church, the Boylston Market, and additions to Faneuil Hall. Particularly impressive was one creation suggested by a continuous block of houses designed by Robert Adam and some of his colleagues. In Boston, Bulfinch erected a worthy coun-ᵗerpart, Franklin Crescent, a gracefully curving row of sixteen houses.

Other Bulfinch works regarded as monuments of American architecture are University Hall at his old alma mater Harvard, the Massachusetts General Hospital, and the statehouse in Boston. He also designed the Connecticut state-house at Hartford and the capitol of Maine at Augusta. He designed, too, the west portico of the United States Capitol in Washington, providing an approach distinguished by the majesty and restrained exuberance of its stairs and terraces.

In these four government buildings, Bulfinch set the style for state capitols in many parts of the United States. Jefferson's design for the Virginia capitol set a fashion for banks and schools and for buildings housing various government departments. But for state capitols and even many courthouses, Bulfinch fur-nished the most popular model. Everybody had to have a dome, and the dome would be approached through impressive stairways and terraces.

Though Bulfinch designed the west portico of the United States Capitol, the north and south wings adjacent to the central rotunda were designed by William Thornton.[9] Like Jefferson and England's great Sir Christopher Wren, Thornton was a versatile man of formal learning in several fields but a self-trained architect. A native of the Virgin Islands, he studied at the University of Edinburgh and earned an M.D. from Aberdeen University. After travel on the Continent and a return to his birthplace, he visited the United States in the exciting year of 1787, when the Constitution of the Republic was being written in Philadelphia. The freedom and the ferment of ideas appealed to him. Within a year, he became a citizen of the new nation and a resident of Philadelphia.

He tried his hand at inventing and became John Fitch's associate in experi-ments with paddle steamboats. He also tried his hand at architecture and in 1789, despite his lack of formal training, won the Library Company of Phila-delphia's competition for the design of a new building. When he learned of a competition for design of the United States Capitol in Washington, he entered. Even though his entry was received after the formal close of competition, his designs were accepted. As a leader in the Roman Revival, Thornton was second only to Jefferson. In addition to his work on public buildings, he designed for John Tayloe in Washington, D.C., the Octagon House, now cherished by the American Institute of Architects as a monument of domestic architecture.

Though Thornton became the official architect of the Capitol, Bulfinch and others made important contributions. Stephen Hallet is credited in large part with the concept of a central rotunda flanked by the two houses of Con-gress. Benjamin Henry Latrobe, a civil engineer as well as an architect, altered the plan in the interest of sound engineering and practical building needs.[10] He also included decorative details inspired by the Greek orders, but cleverly substituted native American plants for such embellishments as the acacia leaves in Corinthian capitals.

Educated in Germany and England, Latrobe received engineering and ar-chitectural instruction from leaders of those professions. He was the leader of the Greek Revival in the United States, and more than anyone else was responsible for raising architecture in America to the status of a profession. His first public building was the state penitentiary in Virginia. His second was the Bank of Pennsylvania in Philadelphia. Besides its handsome architecture, the bank is distinguished by two priorities, the first stone vault and the first Greek detail in the United States. Latrobe's neoclassical Roman Catholic Cathedral in Baltimore, though it shows the influence of the Pantheon in Paris, nevertheless has considerable originality. It is studied today as a structure of international importance in the history of architecture. In 1800, Latrobe designed Sedgeley, a home near Philadelphia that was in the Gothic style forty years before the Gothic Revival.

While he was designing his architectural masterpieces, Latrobe was busily at work as one of the nation's leading civil engineers. He improved the navigation of the Appomattox, James, and Susquehanna Rivers, served as engineer of the Chesapeake and Delaware Canal, built the Washington City Canal, redesigned the waterworks of New Orleans, and in Jefferson's presidency served as surveyor of public buildings for the District of Columbia.

Other architects made praiseworthy contributions to the Republic's urban landscapes—men such as John McComb, Jr., Joseph F. Mangin, and James Hoban, any one of whom could have been the leading American architect of his day if he had arrived on the scene before the great era of creativity.

The burgeoning architecture of the early Republic exemplified the vitality of the nation. The creations of its architects symbolized the blend of traditional strengths and bold experiment that characterized every field of creative growth in that exciting time.

46

SUMMING UP
THE AMERICAN CASE

"I KNOW OF ONLY two occasions in history when the people in power did what needed to be done about as well as you can imagine its being possible." The speaker was Alfred North Whitehead, answering the questions of an American interviewer.[1] Few people in the world could have created such suspense by that statement. The great ornament of the mathematical faculty at Cambridge University and of the philosophy department at Harvard; coauthor with Bertrand Russell of the *Principia Mathematica*, "one of the great intellectual monuments of all time";[2] maker of "one of the outstanding attempts in his generation to produce a comprehensive metaphysical system which would take account of scientific cosmology";[3] brilliant analyst of societies in his "philosophy of organism"—how many could match his credentials? What were "the two occasions in history when the people in power did what needed to be done about as well as you can imagine its being possible"?

"One," said Whitehead,

> was the framing of your American Constitution. They were able statesmen, they had access to a body of good ideas; they incorporated these general principles into the instrument without trying to particularize too explicitly how they should be put into effect; and they were men of immense practical experience themselves. The other was in Rome and it undoubtedly saved civilization for, roughly, four hundred years. It was the work of Augustus and the set around him.[4]

No mere human being is an unfailing well of wisdom. But, as with wells of all kinds, the deepest tend to be the most dependable. It is not surprising that Whitehead should have so accurately and concisely summarized the elements of greatness in the work of America's Constitution makers. And, while even a little intellectual training teaches us to be skeptical about lists of the top two or top ten of all time in any category, Whitehead's giving dual primacy to the

founders of the American Republic and the Augustan Romans for jobs respon-
sibly and efficiently done deserves some consideration. He was both philosopher and scientist, and far above both geographical and temporal parochialism.

Certainly Washington, Franklin, Adams, Jefferson, Madison, Hamilton—
indeed, the whole panoply of American founders—would have been pleased by
the comparison. Some had received classical educations under the tutelage of
prestigious masters, but even those (like Washington and Franklin) who had
limited formal education were so imbued with the traditions of ancient Greece
and Rome that references abound not only in their public utterances but also
in their private correspondence and personal journals. The books and newspapers they read, the sermons they heard, the conversation of neighbors and fellow businessmen or politicians—all reinforced their awareness of Greek and
Roman predecessors. Washington was viewed as a Cincinnatus, Franklin as a
Nestor, Patrick Henry as a Demosthenes, Richard Henry Lee as a Cicero.
When the founders addressed public issues under a pen name, they chose one
with classical resonance—"Publius" for Hamilton, "Fabius" for John Dickinson, "Cato" and "Caesar" for still unidentified writers in New York newspapers. The era was one in which some people received no formal education but
in which the graduate of a good grammar school had a far better grounding in
the classics than the average holder of a doctorate today.

Delegates to the Constitutional Convention of 1787 and members of the
Congress of the new Republic saw themselves as successors to the Roman senators. Even some of the buildings in which they performed the functions of
government resembled Greek and Roman temples. As the architectural influence of Jefferson and William Thornton spread through the land, these legislators, in increasing numbers, made their homes behind the columned porticoes
of facades no less classical than those of the capitols where they labored.

But these Americans were not mere mimics of their classical predecessors.
If they had been, they would have been greatly inferior to both the Greeks and
the Romans because in imitation they would have forsworn the creativity that
distinguished those ancient peoples.

The Americans performed brilliantly in responding to the crises of revolution and nation building, not because they met the challenge as good Greeks or
Romans but because they filled their minds and fired their imaginations with
the experiences of these earlier societies and then, working in the context of
their own times, brought forth original solutions to old problems. One of
Whitehead's countrymen who possessed the combination of extensive theoretical knowledge and "immense practical experience" that he praised so much in
America's Founding Fathers paid tribute to their originality. As is pointed out
in chapter 34, William Ewart Gladstone, on the centennial of the United States
Constitution, wrote, "I have always regarded that Constitution as the most
remarkable work known to me in modern times to have been produced by the
human intellect, at a single stroke (so to speak), in its application to political
affairs." The statement is not one of the most graceful ever phrased by the
prime minister, but it carries the full weight of any such judgment from one of

the ablest statesmen in English history, who was also a voluminous scholar of political philosophy and an adroit practical politician.

My principal purpose at this time is not to celebrate American achievements in the great era of creativity, though they are certainly worthy of celebration. Nor is it to claim for them uniqueness of significance. In fact, such a claim would be counter to my purpose. If American experience in this regard were truly singular, it would be only marginally instructive. Its chief value for consideration lies in the fact that it parallels the experience of other societies notable for creativity. The period of fruitful innovation that began about 1765 had counterparts in other times and places. It is reasonable to assume that what has happened repeatedly can happen again.

It must be admitted, however, that such periods of creativity have not occurred sufficiently often in the past five thousand years for us to become blasé about them. Indeed, when we consider those that were as fruitful in any particular field as the great American period of creativity was in statesmanship, with that fruitfulness spectacularly evident simultaneously in a wide spectrum of other cultural activities, and with innovation over the whole scope of achievement exercising measurable influence on other societies, we must conclude that such efflorescences are extremely rare.

Development of an American philosophy of government and the machinery to implement it may be followed along a paper trail of great documents. Even if one notices only the few markers indisputably of international influence, the series is extraordinary. The year 1776 brought forth two—the Virginia Bill of Rights and the Declaration of Independence. The years 1787 and 1788 produced the Statute of Virginia for Religious Freedom, the Northwest Ordinance, the Constitution of the United States, and *The Federalist.* The United States Bill of Rights was enacted in 1791. The opinions of Chief Justice John Marshall in *Marbury v. Madison* (1803), asserting the right of judicial review of executive and legislative actions, and in *Fletcher v. Peck* (1810), the *Dartmouth College Case* (1819), *McCulloch v. Maryland* (1819), and *Gibbons v. Ogden* (1824) have become part of the essential lore of the law in the United States and have influenced international events. The Monroe Doctrine, promulgated in 1823 as a bold stroke of diplomacy, proved an evolving organism influencing world affairs for generations.

As remarkable as the documents themselves and even more revelatory of the society from which they issued are the circumstances under which they were produced.

The Virginia Bill of Rights is a far more eloquent document than the first ten amendments that constitute the Bill of Rights added to the Constitution of the United States. Indeed, the Virginia document is usually conceded to be both an important philosophical statement and the finest literary production among all the bills of rights in the world. It is a profoundly original document. Though no single idea appears for the first time in its pages, its comprehensiveness and conscious universality are unprecedented. The Magna Carta of 1215 and the English Declaration of Rights of 1689 are only partial precedents. The agreement signed at Runnymede was concerned primarily with relations between the king and his barons, not with assertions of universal right. It has been made comprehensive by what successive generations have read into it. The English Declaration of Rights chiefly addressed a specific crisis.

Because of its universality and its eloquence, the Virginia Bill of Rights has been the inspiration of many similar documents adopted in other nations and has strongly influenced the United Nations Declaration for Human Rights. Yet George Mason composed the Virginia Bill of Rights at white heat during the same legislative session in which he prepared the first draft of the Constitution of the Commonwealth of Virginia.

In the same year, 1776, his fellow Virginian, Thomas Jefferson, alone in a rented room in Philadelphia, without any books or pamphlets for reference, produced the first draft of the Declaration of Independence. This, too, is a remarkable composite of the most enlightened political thought of the eighteenth century, a literary masterpiece, and one of the great state documents of world history. It has been quoted repeatedly by generations of government leaders and their opponents on six continents.

Both Mason's and Jefferson's seemingly facile feats of composition were made possible by decades of intensive study and thought. In reality, they began preparing for their great tasks long before they knew that they would pen such documents. They had ingested the political thought of some of the best minds of ancient Greece and Rome, medieval Europe, and the French and Scottish Enlightenment, and had analyzed this information in terms of their own political experience in their America.

Mason and Jefferson were extraordinary figures in their own society; they would have been extraordinary in any time or place. But though they were not typical of their society, they were representative of it. In most parts of America in the Revolutionary Period and the days of the early Republic, leaders from the village level up respected both learning and practical experience. The most proficient leaders in each state drew their learning from a spacious intellectual landscape dotted with landmarks erected by people of many cultures. And they put a premium on the ability to express ideas in clear and forceful language.

Delegates from New England, the middle states, and the Deep South were able through argument and compromise to produce in four months a Constitution of the United States unique in the priority of key provisions and, of all workable instruments of government, the most original in human history. New York's Gouverneur Morris, following the instructions of his fellow delegates, wrote the Constitution in two days, producing a masterpiece of clarity. The accomplishment on the part of the delegates as a whole, and of Morris specifically, was possible because the assembled representatives of the separate colonies shared a culture of common tradition and contemporary experiment, one that prized language as an instrument of elucidation rather than obfuscation.

The Federalist has long been hailed not only as "the best theoretical justification for the federal system" and "the best exposition of political thought in its era" but also as the world's "most comprehensive analysis" of the problems and advantages of republican government. The laudatory phrases have been used so often that it is impossible to give a specific attribution for each. Yet the authors of *The Federalist*—Madison, Hamilton, and Jay—did not set out to produce a monument of scholarship and philosophy. There was no time for lengthy conferences directed toward a specific goal, with precise subjects prescribed and research responsibilities carefully apportioned.

Writing under the pseudonym "Publius," often associated with Hamilton, all three statesmen produced a rapid-fire sequence of newspaper articles designed to increase public support for ratification of the Constitution. Seventy-seven of these appeared in New York papers between October 27, 1787 and April 2, 1788 and were reprinted in other states. It was soon realized that these essays would be of more than transient interest. In the spring of 1788, with eight more added, they were published in two volumes titled *The Federalist.*

Five essays were written by the legally learned John Jay. All the rest were by Hamilton and Madison, with Hamilton writing by far the greater number and Madison producing those most highly praised by political scientists and philosophers. Both men were geniuses. They were heirs to a common culture that included knowledge of classical republics and of modern European movements toward self-government. Both were experienced in American politics. Sometimes the more trenchant writer of the two, Hamilton nevertheless was eclipsed by the same diversity of knowledge and persuasive reasoning power that made Madison the strongest influence in the Convention of 1787 and earned him the title "Father of the Constitution."

Both agreed that self-interest was the chief political motive of most people and that virtually no one was completely rational. Republican institutions, they argued, should be so framed that a sophisticated system of checks and balances would offset the tyranny or conflict threatened by individual and collective selfishness and occasional irrationality. In the great number 10, Madison countered the prevalent supposition that republican government was feasible only for small states by presenting evidence that it would be even more workable in a large nation with geographic and demographic diversity. He emphasized that a heterogeneous majority of shifting composition, such as could be attained in a large republic, would be far less of a threat to individual liberty than a monistic majority of the sort found in small political entities.

Since the birth of the American Republic, political theorists, practical politicians, and media commentators throughout the world have debated its effectiveness vis-à-vis both a centralized republic and the parliamentary system so prevalent in Europe. Woodrow Wilson, who was statesman, historian, and political scientist, effectively restated one of Madison's *Federalist* arguments for federation with dual sovereignty of both the Union and component states. The twentieth-century president said that the states were "laboratories" for political experiment, making it possible to try out ideas safely on a smaller scale before adopting them nationally. Though some political scientists argued later that the potential dangers of such a system were demonstrated by the rise of Hitler through Bavarian autonomy under a German version of America's federal system, most students of government have continued to agree with Wilson.

There also have been claims that the parliamentary system, especially as practiced in Great Britain, by insuring that the de facto head of government is always representative of a dominant legislative party or coalition, guarantees smoother-functioning government and a much smoother transition of power, especially in a crisis. The argument regarding transition in crisis has been all but silenced by the easy transfer of power in the constitutional crisis precipitated by Richard Nixon's resignation from the presidency under threat of impeachment. At that time, some British political scientists said that such a political crisis might not have been handled as efficiently under their system.

Certainly the American system of a federated republic is flawed, as are all institutions of human origin. The situation recalls Sir Winston Churchill's assertion that "Democracy is a very bad form of government, but all the others are worse." Recognition of the knowledge, acuity, imagination, and originality of the Founding Fathers is in no way dependent upon a conception that their work was perfect. They were the primary architects and initial builders of the first viable constitutional republic in modern times. Their creation was severely tested by the Civil War of 1861–1865, from which it emerged to become not only one of the strongest nations in history but also one of the most influential by example.

In writing *The Federalist*, three prominent politicians were practicing journalism, contending with all the exigencies of demanding deadlines. The fact that in so doing they simultaneously found an enthusiastic audience of newspaper readers and created an enduring masterpiece of scholarship says something remarkable about the society they served.

No statesman was more aware of the relationship between education and democracy than Thomas Jefferson. He, of course, said, "If a nation expects to be ignorant and free, in a state of civilization, it expects what never was and never will be."[5] And he evidenced his belief by proposing a detailed plan of public education from the first grade through the university, and by his long and devoted struggle to found the University of Virginia, a pacesetter for the English-speaking world in the inauguration of the elective system, teaching across the curriculum, and foreign language dormitories.[6] At the time of that university's founding in 1819, there were operating in the United States under their present or antecedent names, besides three other state universities, such now distinguished institutions of higher learning as Harvard (founded in 1636), William and Mary (1693), Yale (1701), Princeton (1746), the University of Pennsylvania (1751), Columbia (1754), Rutgers (1766), Dartmouth (1769), and Brown (1804).

Just as forward-looking as his plans for the University of Virginia were Jefferson's proposals for public education embodied in the Northwest Ordinance of 1787. Passage of this measure, based on a plan advocated by Jefferson in 1784, was the most important accomplishment of the Congress under the Articles of Confederation. This achievement, registered at the very time that members of the Constitutional Convention were citing examples of the Confederation's ineptitude, is sufficient to offset its shortcomings and demonstrate what can be accomplished by enlightened minds even in an inadequate system.

The ordinance was a plan for government of the vast territory north of the Ohio River. Provisions were made for the formation of new states whenever there were sixty thousand free inhabitants within given boundaries. As we have seen in chapter 34, the regulations prohibited involuntary servitude except as punishment for a crime and guaranteed freedom of religion, right of trial by jury, and support of public education. Each township would be divided into thirty-six lots of 640 acres each, and one of these lots would be set aside for the maintenance of public schools. An even more unusual feature of the ordinance was its provision that newly organized states be admitted to the Union "on an equal footing with the original states in all respects whatever." Few nations or empires have voluntarily followed such an enlightened policy in admitting new members.

It is not surprising that Jefferson should have included in the ordinance a guarantee of religious freedom. After all, he was the author of the Statute of Virginia for Religious Freedom, the first official document of its kind in history. Jefferson's proposal for the Virginia law was first presented to the state legislature in 1779 and finally was passed, with Madison's help, in 1785. It became the basis for the first amendment to the Constitution of the United States, was much admired in Europe, and long has been recognized as one of the world's great title deeds of freedom.

But not in legislative action only was the bold creativity of American government demonstrated. In seven major decisions, from *Marbury v. Madison* in 1803 to *Gibbons v. Ogden* in 1824, John Marshall in effect amended the Constitution, asserting the principle of judicial review and subtly altering the checks and balances both within the three branches of the federal government and between the federal and state governments. The man who often told an associate justice, "Find me a precedent, Brother Story," and who wrote his opinions in a style inspired by Alexander Pope, was as much creative artist as statesman. His influence on American history, and by indirection on world history, is incalculable.

The executive branch, too, had a strong creative influence in development of the United States government. Washington was fully conscious of his role in setting precedents for all successive presidents of the United States. He exercised his own judgment in evaluating the often conflicting opinions of his two brilliant cabinet members, Secretary of State Jefferson and Secretary of the Treasury Hamilton. But he relied on their impressive knowledge and venturesome imaginations. The precedents set by the Washington administration influenced foreign governments as well. Witness especially the statement of George Canning, one of Great Britain's most brilliant foreign ministers, that in a major crisis for his country he based policies and procedures on the actions of Washington and Jefferson in 1793 during the war between Britain and France.

In 1823 another United States president and secretary of state, James Monroe and John Quincy Adams, made diplomatic history more dramatically. Adams, who was truly brilliant and scholarly, and Monroe, who was intelligent without brilliance but had learned much from association with such geniuses as Jefferson and Madison, worked together to produce one of the most influential declarations in the history of diplomacy. They were very different personalities, and with differing gifts, but the Massachusetts man and the Virginian were products of the same highly creative society, one now fully American in scope.

Between 1765 and the mid-1820's, American statesmanship at its best was marked by thoughtful weighing of centuries of human experience while acting innovatively to address current problems. The wealth of talent is amazing.

Careful evaluation of the accomplishments of Franklin, Jefferson, Madison, Hamilton, and Marshall reveals that they were as brilliant as they are generally thought to have been. Examination of Washington's writings and contemporary accounts of him by observers of proven shrewdness reveals that he was a great deal more than the stuffy squire of unlimited courage, but severely limited education, that he is too often presumed to have been. His years of formal education were few, but he had read intensively in military science, government, and agronomy, and he was able to manage the most complicated syntax without lapse of clarity or logic. In both military tactics and land cultivation, he was inventive; and he brought imagination and a subtle regard for psychology to his precedent-setting administrations as president. As is commonly supposed, his most outstanding characteristic was strength of character, but his moral and practical decisions alike were guided by a finely attuned mentality.

George Mason, James Wilson, and Gouverneur Morris, though frequently omitted from lists of the giants, deserve inclusion. Mason's genuine and perhaps also imagined illnesses limited the scope of his action except when he was deeply moved by patriotism. Wilson's patriotism, in minor matters, sometimes was deflected or hobbled by self-interest. Morris sometimes was irritable and arrogant. But each of these men gave of his best for his country in crucial hours, and each was in intellect and precision of expression a worthy ally or antagonist for such as Jefferson, Hamilton, and Madison.

John Adams is often only grudgingly admitted to the company of giants. It is easy to deride his vulnerable vanity and his tendency "to generate more indignation than he could properly contain." But his passionate patriotism was enduring, and his private correspondence, even more than his public papers, reveals impressive learning and a rare mastery of the English language. He sometimes suffered lapses of judgment, but never of devotion to liberty.

We sometimes forget about such "little giants" as Roger Sherman, Elbridge Gerry, William Paterson, and Rufus King but, if they had been absent at certain crucial moments, the Constitution of the United States would have been a poorer instrument.

Monroe and John Quincy Adams brought forth the Monroe Doctrine in one of the last bursts of innovative energy that characterized the creative era. But their perception and readiness in grasping the opportunity presented have earned them the recognition that they have received. They are not responsible for any misuses of the Monroe Doctrine by leaders in subsequent generations.

Laboring a little below the level of the Titans during the entire creative era were generations of subordinate leaders who, as we have seen, in some periods would have towered above the monuments of mediocrity dominating the monotonous flatness of the plains.

In view of the roster of great talents in American government between

1765 and the mid-1820's, it is not surprising that most people should think first of that field when reference is made to the creativity of the founders. Properly so. The innovations of American statesmen have been more influential in the world than those of any other American workers in that period. But too many people, in considering the creativity of that age, think of statesmanship not only first but also last.

Even specialists in American history tend to forget the wide range of American creativity in the period. They know that some of the statesmen, most conspicuously Jefferson and Franklin, were leaders in other professions as well, but they forget that many other Americans were internationally famous principally for their achievements in the arts and sciences.

It is unnecessary to detail here the achievements in arts and sciences that have been reviewed in other chapters. But a brief reminder may be desirable. For the period 1765 to the mid-1820's, the record of American accomplishments in literature, the fine arts, invention, science, and architecture is sufficient to mark the era as one of unusual creativity—even without the celebrated contributions to government and political philosophy.

Not surprisingly, in an era so noted for political achievement, many of the literary classics were primarily expressions of political philosophy. In considering the Declaration of Independence, the Constitution of the United States, *The Federalist*, the Statute of Virginia for Religious Freedom, and the Virginia Bill of Rights, we have discussed world-renowned American literature. In the same category are the eloquent published letters of Thomas Jefferson and John Adams. There are also patriot memoirs, such as *The Autobiography of Benjamin Franklin*. And at least one writer, Mercy Otis Warren, effectively combined political commentary with history.

Often overlooked is the brilliantly original imaginative literature created by Americans between 1765 and the mid-1820's. Many people, when they think of such work in the Revolutionary and post-Revolutionary periods, refer to the poems of the Connecticut Wits and of Phillis Wheatley. The Wits—primarily John Trumbull, Joel Barlow, and Timothy Dwight—deserve credit for commendable service in a variety of occupations, but while their sentiments are American, their literary styles are imitative of England's Augustans. Miss Wheatley was a precocious child. Sixteen months after arriving in Boston from her native Africa to work as a slave, she had mastered the English language, "to which she was an utter stranger before," sufficiently to read "the most difficult parts of the sacred writings." Jefferson, however, had a better ear for poetry than George Washington, who greatly admired her verse; the Sage of Monticello pronounced truly that she lacked the originality associated with poetic excellence. Though occasionally she speaks for herself, as in the reminder that "Negroes, black as Cain, may be refin'd and join th' angelic train," most of her poems seem to have borrowed their sentiments, as well as their vocabulary and versification, from Alexander Pope.

For imaginative literature expressive of originality in the Revolutionary and Early National periods, one must turn to such writers as Philip Freneau, founder of the Romantic movement in American literature. He decorated his poetic landscapes with wild honeysuckle instead of English primroses and peopled them with American Indians instead of neoclassical shepherds. Indeed, his poem titled "The Wild Honey-Suckle" anticipates by a dozen years the publication of Wordsworth's similarly Romantic verses in *Lyrical Ballads.* In short, Freneau was as much a pre-Romantic as William Blake or Robert Burns, not as great a poet as either, but as much a pacesetter.

Another American poet, William Cullen Bryant, produced "Thanatopsis," one of the world's most famous poems, when he was twenty-one years old. In a long literary career, he abandoned his initial neoclassicism for full-blown Romanticism, and still later became an international pioneer in writing poetry on industrial subjects. He also became America's first systematic critic of poetry.

James Fenimore Cooper made the wilderness areas of America part of the landscape of the world's imagination. In the Leatherstocking Series of novels, a multivolumed work of epic proportions, he began a new genre in world literature. Tales of pioneer life and Indian exploits have fired the imaginations of readers around the globe. Among Cooper's great admirers were such international literary luminaries as Balzac, Victor Hugo, and Goethe. Later, Joseph Conrad saluted him as "a rare artist . . . one of my masters."

Another American writer who drew high praise from European authors and critics in his own time was not so fortunate as Cooper in consistently retaining his reputation through successive generations. But in the 1960's he began regaining lost ground, not regaining popular success but again winning critical plaudits. Charles Brockden Brown, saluted as "Father of the American Novel," numbered among his most enthusiastic admirers William Hazlitt, Thomas Hood, William Godwin, Sir Walter Scott, and John Keats. Thomas Love Peacock, in his biography of Shelley, said that "nothing so blended itself with the structure of his interior mind as the creations of Brown." For philosophical and psychological depth and richness of varied learning, Brown has few equals among fiction writers.

A Brown contemporary, Washington Irving, won easy acceptance and has remained popular ever since. Though he included some eerie tales amid his humorous stories and sunlit romances, they are a far cry from the dark psychology of Brown's American Gothic, more like ghost stories told in fireside comfort. Irving borrowed the legends of Europe and made them live again in American settings. Though he no longer excites the extravagant praise that he once received from critics on both sides of the Atlantic, he is justly honored internationally as one of the molders of the modern short story and the creator of the unforgettable Rip Van Wrinkle and Ichabod Crane.

Cutting much deeper than the probing humor of Irving's *Diedrich Knickerbocker* is the sharp satire of Hugh Henry Brackenridge's *Modern Chivalry.* This picaresque novel, superficially reminiscent of Cervantes' *Don Quixote,* reverses the convention, antedating Plautus, of the obtuse master and perceptive servant. This innovation facilitates pointed reminders as valid today as in earlier democratic societies.

In the great creative period, some Americans were writing plays. William

Dunlap—playwright, producer, stage designer, theater historian, and portrait painter—is honored as the "Father of American Drama." Royall Tyler wrote *The Contrast*, a play still studied in literature classes and still presented on the stage. Anticipating Henry James, it depicted social relations between Americans and Europeans.

As we have seen, the great creative period was also rich in adjuncts to literature. Noah Webster was a one-man intellectual factory, producing dictionaries, grammars, and spelling and reading texts. They expressed their maker's dictum: "Grammar is formed on language, and not language on grammar." They declared the linguistic independence of America while, at the same time, recognizing that American writers were citizens of a great republic of letters extending across the boundaries of nations. American and British dictionaries were regularly enlarged and enlivened by the borrowing of neologisms from each other. Soon the number of new American words exported to Great Britain outnumbered the new words from Britain exported to the United States.

American authors were creating a vital literature in a growing language. Many of them were journalists as well as makers of books, so that the language of literature became familiar even to many not attracted to literary studies. Though the United States has since produced even greater literature, it has never again made such literary progress within a half century.

Benjamin West, the first American-born painter to win international recognition, was hailed in Rome as "the American Raphael." In London's Society of Artists Exhibition of 1764, his paintings were rated best by published critics and the viewing public. He not only became the English-speaking world's most admired painter of historical scenes when that genre was most in vogue; he also changed the course of historical painting by delineating eighteenth-century heroes in the garb of their own time rather than the classic robes and helmets of ancient Greeks and Romans. His influence was magnified by the fact that he was the English-speaking world's foremost teacher of painting in his day.

A West protégé, John Singleton Copley, became the first American to do significant work in pastels. Then he went on to paint oil portraits of such corporeal realism and penetrating insight that they are the equal of any painted anywhere in the eighteenth or nineteenth centuries.

Another of West's students was Charles Willson Peale who, amid a career as active patriot, inventor, scientist, and the world's most innovative museum director, worked unevenly as a portrait painter, turning out some stiff, imitative portraits, but also producing some robust likenesses that today are prized possessions of leading museums. His son Rembrandt Peale fulfilled the hopeful prophecy implicit in his name and produced, among other distinguished works, two paintings of Jefferson that rank among the finest portraiture of the nineteenth century.

Gilbert Stuart was a far greater painter than those familiar only with his famous portrait of Washington might assume. John Walker has cited him as America's foremost "innovator of genius" in two hundred years of art. His full-length portrait of William Grant, in which the subject skates toward the viewer instead of standing in a conventional pose, started a new fashion on both sides of the Atlantic. Henceforth, "sitters" were often depicted actually doing something connected with their recreation and, if they were sufficiently confident of their social positions, with their work. The Grant picture is celebrated as one of the world's great masterpieces of portraiture.

Stuart was equally innovative in using many tints to produce flesh color, letting the viewer's eye blend the separate colors into a harmonious whole. It was primarily this method that led Walker to write, as previously noted: "Had there been the artists and the tradition of painting in America that there were in France, these innovations of Stuart's might have caused Impressionism to appear in the New World generations before it revolutionized art in Europe."

A small revolution of sorts was wrought by Thomas Cole, Thomas Doughty, and Asher Brown Durand, of the Hudson River school. Cole, particularly, brought an age that exalted portraiture and scorned landscape to an appreciation of artistic representation of nature's beauties. His works were distinguished by scope and symbolism that lifted them to the sublime.

Other distinguished American artists were at work in the great creative age. Though they were not as innovative as West, Copley, Rembrandt Peale, Stuart, or Cole, their work is still appreciated today. Among them were John Trumbull, Washington Allston, Samuel F. B. Morse, Edward G. Malbone, Ralph Earle, William Dunlap, and Thomas Sully. During this period, the most exciting art work in the English-speaking world—and some of the most exciting anywhere on the planet—was being done by American artists.

In a time that valued individual versatility so highly, some of these artists were even better known for other fields of accomplishment. One of the most striking examples was Samuel F. B. Morse. Avidly pursuing art from the time of his graduation from Yale in 1810 at the age of nineteen, he was recognized as one of America's best portraitists by 1818 and won lasting fame in 1825 with two portraits of Lafayette. He later plunged into politics, and still later into science and invention. Today, of course, he is best known as the inventor of the telegraph and of a system of electromagnetic relays to carry messages to widely separated points by means of many branch lines.

Morse, as a creator, comes well within our limits for the great age of creativity in the United States, having attained fame as an artist by the mid-1820's. But, strictly speaking, his career as scientist and inventor, for which he is most celebrated, began beyond the limits of this period. He poured into these occupations the same intensity of creative energy that he earlier had devoted to art.

In embracing both art and science, Morse was representative of the creative age that produced him. There was then nothing like our latter-day concept of these two great fields of human endeavor as separate worlds without a shared vocabulary. The early days of the American Republic were reminiscent of Renaissance Florence, when those who worked out mathematically the laws of perspective also used them in painting realistic interiors and street scenes, a time when Leonardo would sometimes draw on the same page a character-laden face and a projected machine.

The great creative age in America was a time when men famous as statesmen and diplomats also proudly called themselves scientists. Franklin and Jefferson immediately spring to mind. As for invention, a society of tinkerers was virtually certain to produce inventors. Some communities seemed to regard inventing as one of the essential skills, like riding a horse well or shooting on target, one of the rites of passage into adulthood.

Many inventions were the work of factory owners attempting to improve the rate or quality of production. Thus Paul Revere in his copper manufactory in Massachusetts and Colonel Fielding Lewis in his gun factory in Virginia paved the way for the modern assembly line.

The American colonies, later the United States, were blessed with many miles of coastline and many penetrating rivers. It is therefore not at all surprising that a great deal of American inventive genius was concentrated on ships. David Bushnell produced a submarine in 1775. John Fitch brought forth a steamboat in 1787. It was the first of several that he produced, with the propulsion ranging from paddle wheels to a screw propeller. James Rumsey, working completely independently of Fitch and his ideas, launched a steamboat of his invention about four months after Fitch's first. In connection with the building of his vessel, Rumsey invented an improved steam engine.

Actually a Frenchman, Jacques C. Périer, had invented the first steamboat in history, but it was not successful in operation. One invented in 1783 by another Frenchman, the Marquis de Jouffroy, was successful. But after these two inventions, European developments in steam navigation lagged, while Americans moved to the front. Americans Samuel Morey and Nathan Read invented steamboats of new designs. Another citizen of the United States, John Stevens, built the world's first seagoing steamship. In 1807 Robert Fulton launched the *Clermont*, the first steam-powered vessel to be a conspicuous success both nautically and commercially.

Inventions of steamboats and of steam engines for water navigation and other purposes went hand in hand. Just as France had led at first in the development of steam-driven ships, Great Britain, largely through James Watt's genius, had led in the development of steam power. But here, too, American inventors wrested the lead from their European rivals. As these were the world's two most exciting fields of invention in the last years of the eighteenth century and early decades of the nineteenth, American attainment of primacy in both was an astonishing feat for so young a nation.

American inventions related to agriculture won international recognition for Thomas Jefferson, George Washington, Charles Newbold, Jethro Wood, John Conant, and Eli Whitney.

American inventors produced a host of devices used in their country and Europe. The list of these creators in chapter 43 is long, but still far from exhaustive. Many other American inventors lived in obscurity while their creations won the tribute of use and imitation throughout the Western world. And many inventors were scientists in an age when the labels *mechanical science* and *mechanical arts* paid tribute to the dignity of invention.

True to the versatility fostered by the times, many of the scientists were also statesmen, diplomats, authors, or artists. Benjamin Franklin was considered foremost in the world in the study of electricity at a time when many believed that the most important scientific discoveries were being made in that field. He perceived the identity of lightning and electricity and demonstrated it in his famous experiment with a kite. He discovered the existence of plus and minus charges.

Jefferson was the Father of American Paleontology and successfully refuted one of the Comte de Buffon's pet theories, that all forms of life tended to degenerate in the New World. The Lewis and Clark expedition sent out by President Jefferson in 1803 was more than an epic adventure in the wilderness. William Clark was a cartographer and skilled sketcher of natural phenomena, and Meriwether Lewis had received vigorous training in preparation for his role. The enterprise that bears their name is one of history's greatest fact-finding expeditions, an epic of intellectual discovery. It is recognized as such by scholars throughout the world. The great painter Rembrandt Peale was also famous for his paleontological study of the mammoth.

William Bartram's writings about his botanical discoveries, as well as his observations in zoology and the life of the Indians, were published in English, German, Dutch, and French. Three other botanists, Gotthilf Mühlenberg, Thomas Nuttall, and John Torrey, produced scientific classics that won an international audience. Their success was matched by that of three zoologists, William Peck, Samuel Latham Mitchell, and Constantine Samuel Rafinesque, while John D. Godman embraced both botany and zoology in his three-volume *American Natural History*. Alexander Wilson produced his classic, nine-volume *American Ornithology*, and the even more famous John James Audobon brought forth his monumental *Ornithological Guide*.

Three Americans, Edward Hitchcock, Amos Eaton, and William Maclure, earned international praise for pioneer work in geology. David Rittenhouse, an astronomer admitted to Britain's Royal Society, was internationally honored for his observations of the transits of Venus and Mercury and of Lexell's comet. He constructed one of the most celebrated orreries in the world. He pioneered in the use of measured grating intervals and spider threads to attain precise focus in telescopes.

Dr. Benjamin Rush, a Philadelphia physician, was famous for his study of the relationship between rheumatism and dental disease and especially for his *Medical Inquiries and Observations upon the Diseases of the Mind,* a truly influential investigation of the psychology of mental illness.

Benjamin Thompson, a self-taught scientist, rocked the scientific world with his discovery that heat was not a material substance but a "mode of motion." In a career of amazing variety, which we have already followed, he was elected to Britain's Royal Society and knighted by the king, and was made a count of the Holy Roman Empire.

Perhaps no scientific discovery by any individual American was so wonderful as the fact that between the 1780's and the early 1800's many scientists in the North American aggregation of former colonies had become the instructors, as well as the pupils, of Europe.

To what music did Americans march so confidently into the future? Ironically, for the most part they still were listening to "the stately muses of Europe." Both their folk and their chamber music were imparted from the Old World. In folk songs, sometimes the rendering was faithful to the original import. At other times, the mutilated form remained, and the singers themselves could not translate the meaning. In one instance, "Sir Ronald stood at his castle gate combing his milk-white steed" became "Sir Ronald stood at his castle gate, coming his mule white stee." Classical favorites and new songs from England were presented in the parlors of New York, Philadelphia, Williamsburg, and Charleston in a manner familiar to English society of the same period.

There were exceptions. Though few, they were noteworthy. Francis Hopkinson, famous chiefly as a leader of the Continental Congress and a skilled satirist, deserves remembrance also as his country's first native professional composer. His work was highly derivative, as he himself realized, but it was of acceptable quality.

Foremost among early American composers was William Billings, a New England tanner self-taught in music. He began writing hymns and patriotic songs, the only kind of music acceptable to most of his neighbors. Though he conformed in genre, he was bold in experimentation within those limits. His parallel fifths and other departures from tradition were decried by critics in his own day and later, but now are honored as innovations of "pioneer freshness." Musical historian Geoffrey Hindley has speculated that, had America been freer of the influence of European musical fashion, Billings' works "might have been a point of departure for an early indigenous American style." Billings himself had no doubts, declaring, "I don't think myself confined to any rules for composition laid down by any that went before me. . . . Art is subservient to genius."

Another noteworthy composer in eighteenth-century America was Johann Friedrich Peter (sometimes anglicized to John Frederick Peter). A Moravian born in Holland of German stock, he came to America with a solid grounding in the art and science of music. He composed eighty sacred compositions for chorus and orchestra and six string quintets—all of it quality music.

If memories of persecution in Europe and fears of corruption from contemporary society had not kept Peter and his fellow Moravians from mingling freely with other Americans, they might greatly have enriched the new land's musical culture and in turn been stimulated by other cultural currents.

Nevertheless, musical culture was moving forward in America at an accelerated rate during the period of great creativity. Musical societies sprang up in Charleston; New York City; Dartmouth College in New Hampshire; Philadelphia; and Fredericksburg, Virginia. Their appearance, together with that of such talented composers as Billings and Peter, signaled the beginning of a new creativity in American music. Polyhymnia lagged behind most of her sister Muses, and Euterpe trudged along even farther in the rear, but America was on the way to making its own music, borrowing notes from woodland birds and automobile horns, finding its rhythms in the roar of mighty waters or of city traffic.

American architecture burgeoned in the last years of the eighteenth century and the first decades of the Republic. At its best, as in Thomas Jefferson's designs, it was a happy blend of traditional forms and adaptation to local or regional needs. Some professional architects protest that the president was an amateur, and hence below professional standards, citing the narrow stairways at Monticello as an example. Others recall that Jefferson wanted narrow, half-hidden stairways by means of which he could escape guests in his overcrowded house, and that he considered broad stairways a waste of space. In 1976 a distinguished jury of architects, critics, and historians from the American Institute of Architects, feeling completely unthreatened by the performance of so talented an amateur, voted that Jefferson's integrated plan of buildings and landscapes for the University of Virginia was the finest architectural creation by a citizen of the United States. One of the leading competitors for the honor was the same amateur's design of Monticello. His plans for Poplar Forest and the state capitol in Virginia are also notable.

Charles Bulfinch, in his best works, followed the classical styles of Greece and Rome that recalled to Americans the glory days of their republican predecessors. He transformed the face of Boston with such outstanding creations as the courthouse, the New South Church, the Boylston Market, additions to Faneuil Hall, and impressive Franklin Crescent. In each case, the buildings bore both classical hallmarks and the stamp of his own individuality. Also notable among Bulfinch's works are the Boston General Hospital, the statehouses of Massachusetts and Connecticut, and the capitol of Maine. His designs were copied in the building of state capitols and courthouses throughout the United States.

Bulfinch also designed the west portico of the Capitol in Washington. The north and south wings were designed by William Thornton. As a leader in the Roman Revival, Thornton was second only to Jefferson.

The man who raised architecture to the status of a profession in America was Benjamin Henry Latrobe. The leader of the Greek Revival, he designed the Bank of Pennsylvania in Philadelphia and the Roman Catholic Cathedral of Baltimore, which is studied today as a structure of international importance in the history of architecture. His designs for Sedgeley, a home near Philadelphia, anticipated the Gothic Revival by forty years. Each of his best works was an example at once of his mastery of a traditional genre and of the vitality of his own originality.

Other architects exemplified the creativity of this period: Stephen Hallet, John H. Cocke, John McComb, Jr., Joseph F. Mangin, and James Hoban. Architecture was an integral part of the creative revolution transforming the young Republic.

Another aspect of America's creative society will surprise many people. John J. McCusker and Russell R. Menard in their *Economy of British America* estimate that the gross national product of Britain's North American colonies multiplied about twenty-five times between 1650 and 1770, and that their real per capita growth rate may have been twice that of Britain itself. Economic historian Alice Hanson Jones suggests, and social historian Jack P. Greene concludes, that "By the time of the American Revolution, this vigorous economic growth had produced a standard of living that may have been the highest achieved for the great bulk of the [free] population in any country up to that time."[7]

We should not glide thoughtlessly over the word "free." In 1770 slavery existed in every one of the thirteen colonies except New Hampshire. It was by no means purely a Southern phenomenon. Indeed, as late as 1770, Rhode Island, New York, New Jersey, and Pennsylvania all had more slaves per capita than Maryland and Virginia had had in 1710, and the institution was still expanding in every northern colony.[8] Slavery existed throughout the British Empire and would remain legal in Britain itself for six more decades. Slavery or a system close to it existed virtually everywhere in the civilized world. Indenture, which in the American colonies opened doors of opportunity to many men and women and could even be a benign intrafamily arrangement of service to an uncle or senior sibling, was sometimes instead an oppressive instrument of servitude. Serfdom existed in Russia and elsewhere. So-called free labor was not always all that free; the Industrial Revolution sometimes brought oppressive labor conditions more disregardful of worker welfare than slavery, where even unkind masters had a property interest in the health and welfare of their workers.

There was no such thing as a truly "free" civilized society. Some were much freer than others, but none was free for every segment of society. Specific ethnic or economic groups were oppressed in every civilized country. And the position of women was inferior in virtually all except Tibet, where they were even free to practice polyandry.

But the average citizen of the American Republic was freer than his or her counterpart in any other nation, and also almost surely enjoyed a higher standard of living than prevailed anywhere else in the world. Social analysts sometimes have said that the United States has never created a cultural legacy to equal those of great nations of the Old World but that it can plead in extenuation before the bar of history that, more than any other country, it has made the fruits of culture and material well being available to the mass of its citizens. The young Republic could have declared that it had achieved a wider distribution of the blessings of civilization than other countries, and then could have added that it also had achieved an unusually high degree of creativity. It could have recited a roll call of evidence: Exhibit A, statesmanship and political philosophy; Exhibit B, the fine arts; Exhibit C, invention; Exhibit D, science; Exhibit E, architecture.

CONCLUSION

SIX KEYS

THE CREATIVE PERIOD in American history that began in the mid-1760's, peaked about 1787, and declined after the mid-1820's is one of the world's great epochs of creativity. As such, it is comparable to the experience of Renaissance Florence from the 1440's to 1492, and of Elizabethan England beginning with the queen's accession in 1558 and extending to the 1630's, in what may be called the Elizabethan Afterglow.

In the last years of the eighteenth century and first years of the nineteenth century, America was the cynosure of European thinkers. Leaders of the Enlightenment in Great Britain, France, and Italy hailed the dawn of American independence as if its glow were fresh from the torch of Prometheus. Alarmed royalists in old European kingdoms thought the torch was now in the hands of arsonists. Centrists in many nations believed that some of the American experiments might be helpful, some harmful. A wise person, in either case, would watch them intently. The coming of Romanticism, with its emphasis on nature and the natural man, focused the attention of the world's artists and poets on the young Republic that had sprung from a wilderness. Even the most prominent economist of the age, England's Adam Smith, in his *Wealth of Nations,* published in 1776, the very year of the Declaration of Independence, wrote that "the seat of the empire would . . . naturally remove itself to" America.[1] And in 1782, one year after Yorktown, the famous Frenchman Saint Jean de Crèvecoeur wrote that America seemed to have "the most perfect society now existing in the world."[2]

Renaissance Florentines and Elizabethan Englishmen had no greater hold upon the minds of contemporaries in other societies than did Americans in the age of the founders. And they could not match the hold of the Americans on their contemporaries' imaginations. Europeans debated over the writings of Jefferson, Madison, Hamilton, and Mason; devoured the novels of James Fenimore Cooper and the short stories of Washington Irving; marveled at the scientific wizardry of Benjamin Franklin; acclaimed the paintings of Benjamin West, the Peales, and Gilbert Stuart; and traveled about the world through the magic of American inventions. Foreigners are still debating over the writings of Jefferson and other founders of the Republic, but the theater of discussion extends beyond the Atlantic world. It includes six continents.

Major differences distinguished the three societies. England in the Age of Elizabeth was a monarchy in every sense of the word. No monarchy in a civilized nation, however, is absolute. In a complex society, the ruler must always make concessions to some subjects. Renaissance Florence was a republic in name only. The Medici were as much a dynasty as any family in history. The American Republic was truly republican in form but with an occasional vestigial or sentimental squinting toward monarchy that worried some of its founders.

Each of the three societies is associated with preeminence in a different field or fields. With Renaissance Florence, it is always art and architecture. With Elizabethan England, it is literature and exploration. With America, it is government and political philosophy.

The Florentine city-state, though an independent nation, was a compact entity, a metropolitan area dwarfed by such population concentrations in our times as metropolitan Mexico City, Tokyo, London, or New York. Elizabethan Great Britain, though less compact, was roughly equal in area to the present State of California. In contrast, the United States, when it declared its independence in 1776, stretched along the Atlantic coast from Canada to Florida, and with the Louisiana Purchase in 1803 became half a million square miles larger than the combined area of Great Britain, France, Spain, and Portugal.

Some see other differences that they consider significant. Some say that America, in contrast to Renaissance Florence, Elizabethan England, and other European countries, was geographically isolated from major centers of power and culture. Others say that, unlike other nations noted for cultural creativity, Americans from Jamestown on simply brought their culture with them as part of their baggage from Europe.

Some of the differences cited are more apparent than real. Others existed, but were less pronounced than usually supposed and therefore less consequential. America was indeed far removed from Europe's shores and, as a new nation, counted unrealistically on this "isolation" to separate it from Europe's wars. But America became so much a meeting place of colonizing British, Dutch, and Swedes and fleeing Germans that it was not truly isolated from continental currents. Furthermore, the North American continent was so much the target of European aspiration, either imperial or reformist, that England's colonies and the Republic that they became were integrally involved in movements that transformed the whole Atlantic world. As Jack P. Greene has said, "Except for the island colonies in the Atlantic and the Caribbean . . . virtually every one of the new English colonies established in America after Virginia represented an effort to create in some part of the infinitely pliable world of America . . . some specific Old World vision for the recovery of an ideal past in a new and carefully constructed society."[3]

It is also a mistake to assume that Florence and England were intimately involved with daily events in the great cultural capitals of Europe before the beginning of their own extraordinary creativity. Before its great awakening, Florence was one of the least promising city-states of Italy. Lacking a seaport and far from the principal routes of overland travel, it seemed badly positioned to become a major importer or exporter of ideas. And continental Europe, at the start of Elizabeth's reign, regarded the British Isles as offshore stepping-stones into ocean wastes. England's own most eloquent voice portrayed the Channel not as an avenue to other countries but as a "moat defensive to a house, against the envy of less happier lands."[4]

To imply that the American experience in cultural creativity was less original than that of other nations because the Republic's founders or their ancestors brought an advanced culture with them from the Old World is to ignore the fact that the builders of all advanced and complex societies have inherited vital elements of their civilization. Indeed, starting anew, working with the old tools in a new environment, undoubtedly was a stimulus to American creativity. The movement from cultural colonialism to cultural pioneering is one of its most exciting aspects. No successful colony is a fissiparous reproduction of the parent nation. Not only will changed environment work changes in the organism. Also there is something akin to genetic selection. Those impelled to move out and colonize will not be a perfect sample of the parent society.

The disparate disciplines in which the three societies have been accorded preeminence do not indicate differences as great as are commonly assumed. While the immediate association with Renaissance Florence is with art and architecture, as is not the case with Elizabethan England or the American Republic, it must be remembered that in America's great creative era her artists were pacesetters for the English-speaking world and some of her architects designed buildings now studied internationally. While literature and exploration were the great glories of Elizabethan England, Renaissance Florence produced some of the world's great literature, and the American Republic influenced European literature and conducted one of the greatest expeditions of exploration in world history. American preeminence in statesmanship and political philosophy in the time of the founders is generally conceded, but should not blind us to the political reforms inaugurated in Florence by Lorenzo de' Medici or the efficiencies in administration introduced by Elizabeth and her ministers or the growth of English law through the decisions of Lord Coke. Though different fields of primacy are emphasized in the separate nations, in each of them creativity in the categories for which they are most celebrated is accompanied by increased inventiveness in other arts and sciences.

The most striking differences among the three nations are those of geographical area. These differences would suggest that there is no special correlation between acreage and creativity. The comparatively great size of the American Republic did lead one of its greatest thinkers, James Madison, into one of his most original lines of thought. The most seminal pages of *The Federalist* are those in which he refutes the notion that a republican government is practicable only in a small state, and argues that such a government is most effective and most valuable in an extensive domain.

As creativity even under the strongest group stimulus is so largely an individual activity, it is not surprising that outstandingly creative societies should differ in many ways. Nevertheless, they tend also to be alike in some ways that, for our purposes, are more important than the differences. The fact of their extraordinary creativity is itself a major point of likeness and is productive of many minor points of similarity.

A legitimate question at this point is how one determines which societies are especially creative. There is no formula for rendering a completely objective decision. Beware of anybody who claims to have completely eliminated subjectivity from the process. But there are some cultures on which there will be nearly universal agreement. Certainly Renaissance Florence is one of these. When creativity in Western civilization is discussed, the example of Renaissance Italy is usually the first to spring to mind. And when pressed to name a particular center, most informed people cite Florence. The society of Elizabethan England is among those most often put forth as examples of Western cultural efflorescence. And the creativity of America in the time of the founders, even among those aware only of its political accomplishments, is widely acknowledged not only throughout the Western Hemisphere but in Europe and Asia as well.

For a serious study, criteria other than general acknowledgment also are needed. A society producing an unusual number of ideas, inventions, works of art or science, and institutional innovations valued by other societies, contemporary and subsequent, is certainly highly creative. Distinguished anthropologists have found, in "clusters of genius" distinguishing some societies, a convenient index to high creativity. A. L. Kroeber, in 1944 in his *Configurations of Culture Growth*, points out that even the most advanced civilizations have for only fragments of their existence been marked by the productions of such "clusters of genius." Yet the appearance of great geniuses in particular generations indicates that the genetic raw material of genius was present in all. He says, "it follows that more individuals born with the endowment of genius have been inhibited by the cultural situations into which they were born than have been developed by . . . [such] situations."[5] Therefore, he concludes, when many geniuses produce proofs of talent in a particular society, much of their achievement should be credited to that society.

Kroeber's method of measuring the creativity of a society by determining the number of its creative geniuses and their working accomplishment has been adopted also by such distinguished anthropologists as Pitirim A. Sorokin[6] and Charles Edward Gray.[7] In 1955 anthropologist Clyde Kluckhorn called Kroeber's work "the outstanding anthropological study of the great civilizations of the world."[8] Kroeber's method has enjoyed more than half a century of scientific endorsement. It has not been used as often as it might have been, however, because in recent decades anthropologists have been less interested in surveying advanced civilizations than in studying more primitive societies.

Anyone using Kroeber's method of assaying the creativity of a particular society is faced with the problem of determining which of its members were authentic creative geniuses and then assessing the status of each. Gray formularized Kroeber's method of solving this problem and applied it in a survey of Western civilization from 850 A.D. past the first third of the twentieth century. In appraising each creator's work, he asked four questions that he defined as major criteria, five designated as intermediate criteria, and two as minor.[9]

Before learning of Gray's eleven questions, I had asked six of them in substantially the same form in completing my own evaluations of creative geniuses. I claim no special perspicuity in arriving at these questions. They seem to be the sort likely to occur to any reasonable person considering the subject after some study. Gray's first question, and mine, was whether the person's creations were still appreciated long after the creator's own time. This is simply the familiar "test of time," itself time-honored. Two other questions sought to determine whether the creator rose above contemporary limitations and the extent to which he or she influenced "contemporary and subsequent creators." Gray classified these questions as "primary criteria."

Among the five questions that Gray listed as "intermediate criteria" were "How original was [the creator]?" and "How great was [the creator's] competence in techniques?" These questions I, too, asked, but I did not classify them as "intermediate." Gray listed with "minor criteria" the question "Was [the creator's] work admired beyond his [or her] own country?" This query I also used, but did not classify as "minor." In fact, I considered all six of the questions that I used major.

Gray sought to quantify his data to an extent that has proved impracticable for me. From information ranging from biographies to length of encyclopedia entries to frequency of references in general histories, Gray compiled a numerically weighted list of creative geniuses. For example, among composers of the same era, he assigned a seven to Jean-Baptiste Lully and a six to Arcangelo Corelli. Of dramatists flourishing between 1500 and 1620, both Shakespeare and Ben Jonson rated a seven, with Christopher Marlowe a six, Thomas Dekker a five, and Thomas Heywood a four. Among painters from 1910 to 1935, Pablo Picasso and Sir William Newenham Montague Orpen were each counted as a seven. A seven was the highest possible rating.

Gray defended these lists as objective, saying that "in the statistical handling of thousands of names there is an evening-out process that eradicates almost all errors and distortions." He insisted that the few points by which one creator in a given society would be overrated would be offset by the points by which another was underrated, thus leaving the composite score for a particular society a true indication of its creativity. He saw himself as "very much like a physicist operating an instrumental panel with a series of dials, reading them simultaneously and correlating them to arrive at a composite figure." He added, "with careful use this method should yield empirical results, and the objective name lists that result make it possible for others to review or revise them and repeat the experiment."[10]

I doubt the possibility of operating with such precision in a world where much creative accomplishment is in fields, such as philosophy and the arts, that defy quantification. I certainly am sure of my own inability to make such empirical calculations.

I find it easier to agree partially with Kroeber's statement: "I don't think we can really measure creativity objectively. We can more or less measure opinions of it—the ratings are subjective, but their number or strength is more or less measurable. We're then dealing with 'reflections' of the phenomena themselves; but that's something. It is empirical and naturalistic." Kroeber's statement is not contradictory to Gray's explanation. Indeed, Gray quotes it approvingly.[11] But Kroeber's claims for the method seem to me more modest.

Like many other scholars, I am indebted to Kroeber, Gray, and Sorokin for their stimulating thoughts on the measurement of creativity. And my methods are not radically different from theirs. I am encouraged that the musings of a humanist and the researches of these distinguished scientists are so much in accord. I, too, evaluate creative geniuses in terms of others' estimates as well as my own analysis. But I do not make the number of references in general histories part of a formula by which I can assign the geniuses numerical weights. Though I cite some as being of greater magnitude than others, I cannot weigh them satisfactorily on any scale that will produce a numerical result. I am careful in the case of each genius to study evaluations over successive generations, well aware that while the passage of time is necessary to attain perspective, there is no reason to assume that the latest appraisals are necessarily more valid than earlier ones.

While I believe that I bring a reasonable degree of objectivity to many aspects of the measurement, I realize that the most subjective statement I could make would be a claim to complete objectivity. Some of my evidence is statistical, but even more is anecdotal.

The artistic productions of an advanced society are cultural clues as legitimate and as pertinent as those of a primitive society. And the tools of an advanced culture, including books, are informative artifacts no less than the bone knives and stone axes of a Neanderthal tribe. Physical evidence from the arts is essential when societal creativity is the subject of investigation. But even when the subject is not so concentrated, literary and pictorial evidence is important in penetrating to the ethos of a time and place. Jacob Burckhardt, in the introduction to his *Greek Cultural History,* argued for the use of literary and pictorial clues as keys to the thoughts and attitudes of people in earlier times. He used such information to great advantage not only in that book but also in his famous *Civilization of the Renaissance in Italy.* Philologists attacked his employment of such resources but, as Lionel Grossman points out, fellow historians defended him.

Huizinga, in *Autumn of the Middle Ages,* a masterpiece often compared with Burckhardt's great work, used the same method. And Grossman reminds us that the great French historian Jules Michelet used "evidence of literature, painting, and architecture to reconstruct 'mentalities.' "[12] Similarily, one of the twentieth century's great thinkers, Wittgenstein, as Professor Richard Rorty has neatly summarized, "thought that we got lots of our most useful ideas from areas of culture—religion, poetry, philosophy, psychoanalysis—which cannot claim anything like the sort of knowledge that physics offers."[13]

Even physics is not always consistent in offering "the sort of knowledge that physics offers." Witness the current state of quantum physics, whose calculations are based on holding two inherently contradictory concepts. At the beginning of the eighteenth century, physicists argued over two theories of light deemed incompatible. Newton advanced a corpuscular theory. He conceived of a beam of light as a succession of tiny bullets. Other scientists, most notably Christian Huygens, but also Robert Hooke, Leibniz, and Leonhard Euler, saw light as a wave, spread out in space at a given moment, not composed of discrete particles. Twentieth-century physicists agreed to accept the particle theory of light for some purposes and the wave theory for others. In 1924 Albert Einstein acknowledged, "There are . . . now two theories of light, both indispensable and—as one must admit despite twenty years of tremendous effort on the part of the theoretical physicists—without any logical connection." Sir William Bragg bluntly said that physicists used "the wave theory on Mondays, Wednesdays and Fridays, and the quantum theory on Tuesdays, Thursdays and Saturdays."[14]

Cliometrics was already dominating many fields of history before the computer revolution brought the technology that tempted many people into trying to tell all stories in terms of statistics. Some educators who should have known better confused facts with understanding and spoke of a millionfold increase in the world's store of wisdom.

Some brilliant cliometrists were responsible for important revisions of views long held by responsible historians. In some cases, their arguments were provocative. In a few, they were irrefutable. Perhaps the most spectacular example was that of Robert Fogel, whose book *Railroads and American Economic Growth* examined the commonly accepted premise that in the 1890's railroads had determined the economic survival of the United States and the commercial health or sickness of its major cities. Fogel proved statistically that railroads probably had not been indispensable to the nation's economy in the last decade of the nineteenth century. Some of his findings are valuable not only for helping to correct the historical record but also because they suggested remedies for current problems.

Inasmuch as Fogel had been a leader in the use of quantitative methods in historical scholarship, his receiving the Nobel Prize in economic science in 1993 was hailed by many as a vindication of cliometrics as the chief tool for recovering historical truth. In fact, some saw it as the universal tool. But the award's peculiar appropriateness sprang from the fact that it was an economic prize presented in recognition of work in economic history that itself made economic history because of special contemporary relevance. It confirmed the great value of cliometrics in the writing of economic history.

It does not, however, indicate that unaided cliometrics offers a suitable method for writing the cultural history of a complex civilization. How does one quantify the stature of a play by Shakespeare, a quartet by Mozart, or a painting by Rembrandt? Statistical research can be a valuable adjunct in comparative studies in cultural history, but some major insights are best conveyed in terms of individual experiences, intellectual and emotional. If anecdotal evidence is insufficient without statistics, it is also true that statistics are insufficient without anecdotal evidence.

So, in this book, I have used as examples of especially creative societies those of Renaissance Florence, Elizabethan England, and the founders of the American Republic. And the most important single category of evidence for the appropriateness of the designation is in each case the list of individual creators. Who would deny inclusion to a small city-state that in a half-century was home to Lorenzo de' Medici, Fra Filippo Lippi, Leonardo da Vinci, Michelangelo, Raphael, Botticelli, Ghiberti, Giordano Bruno, Verrocchio, Toscanelli, Brunelleschi, Alberti, Machiavelli, Guicciardini, and Donatello? And who would exclude from any honor roll of creativity Elizabethan England, which, if we include the Elizabethan Afterglow, embraced within about six decades such creative giants as Elizabeth herself, Sir Walter Ralegh, Shakespeare, Marlowe, Sir Philip Sidney, Edmund Spenser, Sir Thomas More, Sir Francis Drake, Sir William Gilbert, Thomas Harriot, Inigo Jones, Richard Hakluyt, William Harvey, Sir Edward Coke, William Byrd, Orlando Gibbons, and Sir Francis Bacon?

For that matter, who, reviewing a sixty-year roster including Jefferson, Madison, Franklin, Hamilton, Marshall, James Wilson, Gouverneur Morris, John Quincy Adams, James Monroe, Robert Fulton, Samuel F. B. Morse, Eli Whitney, Charles Willson Peale, Rembrandt Peale, Benjamin West, Gilbert Stuart, James Fenimore Cooper, and William Cullen Bryant, would deny creative recognition to the American society that produced them?

But such creative giants do not alone escort their communities into the rarefied circle of creative societies, though their unamplified presence would be sufficient to gain admission. They are, in each case, augmented by outstanding talents just below their level that in ordinary societies would reign supreme.

Inseparable from the roster of creators is the list of their creations. The ideas, art, literature, discoveries, and inventions that a society produces are a surer index to its general health than the gross national product is to the economic health of a nation.

What do these three creative societies—Renaissance Florence, Elizabethan England, and the America of the founders—have in common other than their uncommon creativity?

One of the most striking things in each is the *healthy tension between heritage and the urge to experiment*. This was true of the Renaissance throughout Italy and everywhere else that it spread subsequently. The common assumption is that the principal factor in the Renaissance was the invigorating effect of newly rediscovered knowledge. True, new influences worked a transformation in society. But newness was only one part of the equation. If native traditions had suddenly been wiped out by the force of the new, there would have been no healthy tension between the pull of heritage and the urge to experiment. One might as well hope to have a functioning physical system based on centrifugal force alone with no countervailing centripetal.

Though the causes and effects of the Renaissance were much the same throughout Italy, the example of Florence is a particularly instructive one. The changes were more dramatic there than elsewhere, partly because of the cultural primacy that Florence gained over the other Italian states but equally because of the unpromising obscurity from which the city of the Medici moved to that exalted position.

I have followed well-worn paths in affirming that three simultaneous factors, in addition to the enthusiastic rediscovery of classical writing, promoted the Renaissance in Italy. They were the rise of city-states ruled by merchant princes; the need and the stimulus for seeking different markets, which furnished new ideas as well as new products; and the inclination of the chiefs of state to become patrons of art and scholarship.

Normally one would expect the effect of such factors to be much less in Florence than in many of her sister states. With sea-lanes the most important avenues, she was about as far removed from both the Mediterranean and the Adriatic as the geography of the Italian boot would permit. Built in a valley surrounded by mountain heights, one of them commanded by the rival city of Fiesole, Florence was not even well placed to command principal land routes. She had a poverty of natural resources. Yet Florence rose above her more advantaged sisters. Virtually all of them thrived on a healthy tension produced by currents pulling them out of inertia, but in Florence the sense of excitement was highest. Though all Italian (indeed, virtually all European) cities were inheritors of Roman civilization, Florentines thought of themselves as special heirs. Ferdinand Schevill's studies convinced him that this belief "became the first and outstanding article of the civic faith with which Florence began her existence."

Florence's passionate attachment to tradition was much more than a force for inertia. It was a soul-felt tug that provided an antithesis to exciting change, producing a healthy tension between heritage and experiment. Some of her sister cities who not only lacked natural advantages but also lacked a strong sense of heritage succumbed early to the waves of change sweeping over Italy with the coming of the Renaissance.

Florence's greatest leader, Lorenzo de' Medici, personified the two forces. He encouraged artistic experiment and scholarly exploration but also, in tournaments and pageantry rich in symbolism reminded the Florentines of their heritage. For Florentines, the Renaissance had a special source of vitality in that, through the rediscovery of classical literature, some of the most important "new" elements in their culture were also reinforcements of the sense of heritage.

So long as the forces of heritage and discovery were in a nearly even but precarious balance, cultural vitality was strong. The productions of Florence's native artists, writers, and thinkers became models for all of Europe and drew to the city talented creators from other societies.

Toward the end of Lorenzo's life, he and his coterie of artists and intellectuals began to lose affection and respect for their traditions and even to make sly fun of their religious heritage, at the same time seeming to celebrate newness principally for the sake of novelty. The beneficial tension between the two forces lapsed, and the intellectual leaders found that not only the less privileged classes but even the prosperous and politically influential middle classes had ceased to follow them. Florence's cultural vitality suffered.

But then Savonarola eloquently summoned the Florentines to renewed appreciation of their medieval Christian heritage and attracted, among many other adherents, some of the younger geniuses clustered about Lorenzo. With the balance restored, a new vitality surged through the arts.

This vitality died, however, when the balance between heritage and experiment so shifted that only what was regarded as native and medieval prevailed. Great works of art and literature were ritually consumed in the Bonfires of the Vanities, and even Savonarola himself, when he sought to mediate between the old and the new, was consigned to the flames. When these excesses brought the inevitable reaction, the quest for glory became an attempt to repeat the past. Some great talents nurtured by Florence continued to flourish, but in environments more hospitable and more stimulating.

The waxing and waning of creativity in England's great era of genius, the Elizabethan Age, followed a pattern roughly analogous to the record of creativity in Renaissance Florence. England, like the city-state of Florence, was a small nation lacking many obvious natural advantages. Unlike Florence, it had direct access to the sea, but it suffered a disadvantage that the Italian state did not. It was removed from the Mediterranean world that was the cradle of civilization and whose classical culture had been a vital part of the heritage of all the most advanced nations of the West.

Like her Italian counterpart, England was inspired to mental adventuring by the coming of the Renaissance. Florence had been stirred by the rediscovery of Greek and Roman culture. England was stirred not only by the same classical heritage but also by the artistic and intellectual achievements of the Florentine Renaissance. In England, as in Florence, the process was marked at its zenith by a healthy tension between tradition and experiment.

Just as the leadership of two generations of Medici patrons of art and learning paved the way for the great efflorescence under Lorenzo, so similar patronage under Henry VIII prepared for the great flowering under Elizabeth. Excited by the teachings of English scholars returned from the Continent, the English upper and middle classes supported the new learning and stimulating developments in art with their pocketbooks and by example. Geographical exploration opened the New World, and science discovered a new world even within the old. Everywhere adventure awaited the adventurous. Poets and dramatists explored new techniques, scholars delved into rediscovered documents that held the excitement of buried treasure, scientists tackled old problems with new methods, and world maps were revised repeatedly as new place names replaced a shrinking terra incognita.

Like Lorenzo, Elizabeth fostered revitalizing change while using pageantry to dramatize her people's heritage. Sir Francis Bacon, who with true Elizabethan daring took all knowledge for his province, stated the ideal in his *Novum organum*:

> There are found some minds given to an extreme admiration of antiquity, others to an extreme love and appetite for novelty; but few so duly tempered that they can hold the mean, neither carping at what has been laid down by the ancients, nor despising what is well intro-

duced by the moderns. This [imbalance], however, turns to the great injury of the sciences and philosophy. . . .[15]

The greatest poet and dramatist of the age exclaimed, "O brave new world . . . !"[16] and eulogized with equal fervor the ancient virtues of "This blessed plot, this earth, this realm, this England, This nurse, this teeming womb of royal kings, Feared by their breed and famous by their birth."[17]

The same devotion to heritage and experiment that created a healthful tension in Renaissance Florence and Elizabethan England was also an important factor in the era of the founders of the American Republic. It was illustrated almost ideally in the career of Thomas Jefferson. His correspondence yields hundreds of examples of this tension as an energizing agency in his personal and public decision making.

It is soberly argued in his admonition that, while we should avoid "frequent and untried changes in laws and constitutions, . . . laws and constitutions must go hand in hand with the progress of the human mind." It was illustrated strikingly by the combination of two statements. One was his exuberant claim that "this whole chapter in the history of man is new. The great experiment of our Republic is new." The other was his advice to President Washington regarding the buildings that would house the new government: "Whenever it is proposed to prepare for the Capitol, I should prefer the adoption of some one of the models of antiquity, which have had the approbation of thousands of years."

This same view was illustrated by Jefferson's plans for the Virginia state capitol, based on a Roman ruin but modified for modern needs, and his design of Monticello, true to Palladian tradition but embodying the inventions of his experimental mind. It was demonstrated when he boldly pioneered with the University of Virginia a new curriculum, but insisted that Latin and Greek, as the bearers of so much of the heritage of Western civilization, be given even stronger emphasis than was the common in the universities of the Anglo-American world. It was shown when, as an old man, he reluctantly lessened his readings in those classical tongues to make more time for the perusal of new publications in experimental science, lest his intellectual development suffer from an imbalance of old and new.

The philosophy of the coexistence of reliance on tradition and experiment with the new was implied or voiced by Chief Justice John Marshall many times, and was formally expressed by him in such judicial pronouncements as that in *McCulloch v. Maryland*: "This proposition is made in a Constitution, intended to endure for ages to come, and consequently, to be adapted to the various *crises* of human affairs." The italics were his. He was trained to value precedents, and he realized that change for the sake of change could destroy life-giving continuity. But he realized also that the preservation of institutions was dependent on change for growth and adjustment.

Benjamin Franklin was a great cherisher of American tradition, devoted not only to the heritage from the early European settlers but also to that from the country's aboriginal inhabitants. Some of his favorite ideas of government were borrowed from the American Indians. He valued the ancient wisdom of Europe, but no one was more eager than he to read the latest news from the laboratories of the world. His own experiments were, of course, pacesetters, especially in electricity. The dispenser of Greek, Roman, and traditional American wisdom through *Poor Richard's Almanac* also wrote reports and produced inventions that brought significant change to life in both the Old World and the New. It was Franklin's deliberate habit to rephrase Athenian proverbs in the accents of contemporary American folk wisdom and to express revolutionary ideas in pithy slogans that bore the stamp of ancient rhetoric. He, too, realized that risk is essential to preservation, writing, "He that's secure is not safe."

John Adams walked boldly into the future, but his correspondence affords abundant proof that he was aware of being part of a procession of greatness whose earliest marchers wore prophets' robes or statesmen's togas and whose future ones would find inspiration in his example. Edmund Burke himself was not more aware than he that a healthy society is a compact among past, present, and future generations, nor a more ardent believer that "People will not look forward to posterity who never look backward to their ancestors."

Yet, as we have emphasized before, John Adams envisioned changing roles for the generations, writing in 1780, "I must study politics and war that my sons may have liberty to study mathematics and philosophy. My sons ought to study mathematics and philosophy, geography, natural history, naval architecture, navigation, commerce, and agriculture, in order to give their children a right to study painting, poetry, music, architecture, statuary, tapestry, and porcelain."

Such evidences of simultaneous enthusiasm for tradition and experiment are representative of the three great creative societies with which we are immediately concerned. Though most memorably revealed in the writings and activities of the giants, this attitude is found also among the secondary leaders. In Revolutionary and Early Federal America, it is discoverable in local newspapers from New England to Georgia, not only in the editorial columns but also in letters to the editor.

One may ask if such expressions are not common in most societies whether notable for cultural fecundity or not. Intensity sets the quotations from these golden societies apart from the comments spawned by more common eras. In Renaissance Florence, Elizabethan England, and America in the time of the founders, such quotations are not just endorsements of "the happy medium" and "golden mean," or something akin to Alexander Pope's measured admonition "Be not the first by whom the new are tried, nor yet the last to lay the old aside."[18] They are instead fervent expressions of devotion to heritage and passion for exploration. And the force of the quotations is made evident in the actions of the authors. In each of the three societies, the waxing and waning of creativity were synchronous with the rise and decline in passionate pursuit of these antitheses. Granted, similar statements can be extracted from speeches, publications, and the correspondence of leaders in societies of only ordinary creativity. So can actions expressive of that philosophy be discovered in the records of political, business, or cultural leaders in any society. The three especially creative ones under consideration are distinguished by the frequency, and especially the intensity, of such evidence.

Closely related to the heritage component is another characteristic of the three creative societies—*patriotism*. Heritage involves both the broad legacy that comes from earlier cultures of disparate origins on the one hand, and on the other the traditions of a peculiarly native culture defining a specific society. Leaders of the three societies consciously used reminders of native traditions to strengthen national unity and build confidence in the ability to meet challenges.

Lorenzo, in contrast to the austere simplicity of his clothing and manner within the walls of his private apartments, appeared before the citizens of Florence in elaborate regalia symbolic of his city's great past. Though he seems to have found little personal pleasure in tournaments, he performed in them regularly, staging processions replete with colorful armorial emblems and other reminders of a proud civic history with which his family's story was intimately interwoven.

In Elizabethan England, the queen made full use of pageantry to reinforce patriotic sentiments. On public occasions she sallied forth in farthingale and ballooning, pearl-festooned skirts like some great ship floating on the waves of cheers from her worshiping subjects. And she could trust their loyalty and patriotism on that August day of 1588 when, with Spain's Armada offshore, she addressed them from the saddle on a threatened beach: "I have the heart and stomach of a king, and of a king of England too."

The founders of the American Republic preached the patriotic faith in which they had been reared. Even before the leaders of Massachusetts proclaimed the likeness of that colony to the biblical "city set upon a hill," Captain John Smith and other leaders of Virginia were insisting that the settlement on the James was part of a New World reserved for the happiest experiments of the Old. The speeches and papers of the founders stressed that the North American continent had remained a virgin land until it became a refuge for freedom seekers prepared to build a new reality from humankind's noblest dreams. Many saw the United States as a successor to the old Roman republic, as a reincarnation of antique glory, one last opportunity for humanity to enjoy republican freedoms without degenerating into corrupt imperialism. Like the citizens of Renaissance Florence, but by an even more tenuous succession, they saw themselves as the heirs of ancient Rome.

The leaders of Renaissance Florence, Elizabethan England, and the newborn American Republic consciously used tradition to build patriotism, but for the most part they did not use it cynically. They themselves responded emotionally to the same stimuli.

In each of the three societies, people believed in themselves because they believed in their countries. Residents of Renaissance Florence expected to triumph over handicaps that others could not surmount. They expected to accomplish the seemingly impossible because they were Florentines, just as Elizabethan Englishmen expected to overcome all obstacles precisely because they were Englishmen. Edmund Spenser, Michael Drayton, and Samuel Daniel wrote verses glowing with patriotic fervor. Some of Shakespeare's most memorable lines shine with love of country. One thinks especially of passages in *Richard II* and in *Henry V*, a work whose durable patriotism proved as inspirational to Englishmen of World War II as to their Elizabethan ancestors. Love of country and a concomitant faith in themselves were so strong in citizens of the young United States as to provoke the irritation, ridicule, or envy of foreign visitors.

Without unusually strong patriotism, the geographically disadvantaged little city-state of Florence would never have become the cultural leader of Europe, a small island kingdom off the western edge of the Continent would not have produced the glories of the Elizabethan Age, and a New World republic so recently carved from a wilderness would not have challenged, and in some cases, surpassed, the artistic and scientific achievements of the seats of empire.

Each of these three societies, at the height of its creativity, had an *economy well above the subsistence level.* Many people assume that periods of unusual cultural vitality coincide with economic booms. This is not always true. When Florentine creativeness was at its height, the economy was in decline. Complex factors relating to trade throughout the Mediterranean and with northern Europe played a part. Another influence, some analysts think, was the fact that Lorenzo was so absorbed in diplomacy and the arts that he neglected his family's vast financial interests. Circumstances were different with Elizabethan England. English exploration and success on the high seas brought an economic boom. For America, the evidence is mixed. In the late colonial period, the North American colonies had prospered so much (especially the Chesapeake colonies) that the standard of living for average citizens was higher than in England and may well have been higher than anywhere else in the world. It is also true, though, that in Jefferson's presidency the embargo on shipping because of the war between Great Britain and France depressed the economy. Nevertheless, this was the same highly creative administration that fostered science and the arts, promoted education, and sponsored one of the most creatively conceived and resourcefully conducted expeditions of exploration in the history of the world.

While a period of great cultural creativity may not be concurrent with an economic boom, it is emphatically true that the economy must be well above the subsistence level. Just as barbarians advance into civilization only when they have time, energy, and resources beyond the elementary requirements for food and shelter, so civilized societies achieve the most notable advances in philosophy, science, and the arts only when a substantial element of the population has time and energy to spend beyond the acquisition of what are regarded as material necessities.

One of the most impressive features of each of the three creative societies is *the intellectual example set by the leaders.*

Lorenzo's grandfather, Cosimo the Elder, called *Pater patriae* (Father of His Country), encouraged the intellectual and artistic development of Florence by sponsoring its first public library, generously supporting artists and humanists with praise and pay, and protecting the deliberations of the Platonic Academy. He also magnified his cultural influence by showing his delight in the conversation of scholars and creators and by his personal enthusiasm for the Greek language and intense interest in the revelations of Greek literature. Cosimo's son, Piero, during his brief rule, showed the same intellectual enthusiasm that had characterized his father. Piero's son, Lorenzo, leading at the peak of Florence's cultural influence, not only was the patron of some of the world's greatest artists and scholars but opened his splendid private library and art collection to the public. A reputable scholar, he participated in the lively discussions of the Platonic Academy. He was a creator as well as an appreciator, becoming one of the notable Italian poets of his day. Florentine political and business leaders contemporaneous with Lorenzo were involved in intellectual activity in degrees ranging from dilettantism to dedication.

Elizabethan English leaders set equally good examples of intellectual involvement. Elizabeth's father, Henry VIII, paved the way. Before his appetite for food, drink, and women eclipsed his appetite for learning, his writing in theology earned him papal designation as "defender of the faith." He conversed with learned men knowledgeably in four languages and was a good musician and an acceptable composer.

Elizabeth herself was an excellent scholar in Latin, Italian, and French classics, a writer of acceptable verse, and a brilliant master of English prose. Her successor, James I, who presided over most of the Elizabethan Afterglow, combined pedantic scholarship and impracticality in a way that earned him designation as "the wisest fool in Christendom." Leaders of practical affairs in both reigns were distinguished by impressive intellectual achievements. Sir Walter Ralegh, courtier, explorer, and popular hero, was also a prominent poet in an era of great poetry and author of a *History of the World* honored as a masterpiece of both scholarship and prose. Lord Chancellor Francis Bacon was, in his generation, England's greatest essayist and Europe's most comprehensive scholar.

Certainly some of the most prominent founders of the American Republic were conspicuous for intellectual accomplishment, not only among their countrymen but on the world stage. Thomas Jefferson and Benjamin Franklin were deferred to as leaders of the Enlightenment by noted scholars in Europe. James Madison, Alexander Hamilton, and John Jay coauthored one of the greatest classics of political philosophy. John Adams, George Mason, Richard Henry Lee, James Wilson, and Gouverneur Morris were all exceptionally learned men. When the brilliant American dawn was beginning to fade but was still effulgent, an important role was played by the literary and scholarly John Quincy Adams. Learning was in vogue in the infant republic. Those ambitious to lead cultivated their minds; even the losers at least cultivated the appearance of learning.

One of the most impressive aspects of all three creative societies was the intellectual preeminence of many of their leaders. The most successful business and political leaders were as intent upon increasing their learning as upon enlarging their fortunes or their constituencies. And in none of the three did aspiring politicians find it necessary to feign ignorance in cultural matters in order to sustain a reputation for practicality.

Every bit as impressive as the respect for learning in the three societies was *the interdisciplinary character of learning.* In each, narrow specialization fell away with the waxing of creativity, returning only with creativity's decline.

In the case of Renaissance Florence, the intellectual versatility of its geniuses is a matter of common knowledge. Florentine culture was the epitome of the Italian Renaissance. And the terms *Renaissance man* and *Renaissance woman* are firmly rooted in the English language. Definitions vary slightly, ranging from the *Random House* designation of one "who has acquired profound knowledge or proficiency in more than one field" to the *American Heritage* reference to one "who has broad intellectual interests and is accomplished in both the arts and the sciences." In all instances, the reference is to interdisciplinary learning. The first name that commonly springs to mind at reference to a Renaissance person is that of a leader of the Florentine Renaissance, Leonardo da Vinci. It is not necessary to repeat his accomplishments as painter, sculptor, architect, engineer, scientist, and inventor.

Renaissance Florence furnishes many other examples of interdisciplinary activities. Botticelli was not only a great painter but also a serious student of classical literature and Platonic and neoplatonic philosophy. Michelangelo, besides being a great painter, sculptor, and architect, was an important poet, a serious student of theology and Christian Platonism, and an expounder of Dante's *Divine Comedy.* Machiavelli, the famous writer in political theory, was also a poet, diplomat, public official, and military officer. The annals of Florence are crowded with the names of those who had national or international reputations in more than one field. Lorenzo de' Medici was himself a distinguished poet and active humanist scholar as well as one of Europe's ablest diplomats and chiefs of state.

Often, when people are asked to name a non-Italian Renaissance man, they think first of Francis Bacon. The man who proclaimed that he took all knowledge for his province was the most conspicuous example of interdisciplinary learning in Elizabethan and Jacobean England. His eminence in literature, law, government, science, and philosophy certainly makes him one of history's most versatile figures. But he had impressive competition in his own time and country.

Among them are some of those, like Bacon himself, that we have discussed as exemplifying the intellectual involvement of political leaders or those close to the seats of power. Sir Walter Ralegh, as courtier, soldier, vice admiral, explorer, member of Parliament, prose master, poet, and historian on a grand scale, was extraordinarily versatile. Sir Philip Sidney, now famous chiefly as a poet and literary critic, was prominent in his own day as courtier, soldier, linguist, translator, and diplomat. Edmund Spenser was not only a great poet but also a linguist and theologian as well. Thomas Harriot was famous not solely as an explorer of the North Carolina coast but also as a chronicler, pioneer statistical reporter, inventor, and astronomer and as one of the most creative mathematicians in Europe. William Gilbert, now most famous for his experiments with magnetism and electrical attraction, was also celebrated as a physician and astronomer.

Shakespeare, though not a formal scholar (as Ben Jonson often emphasized), nevertheless exemplifies the intellectual versatility so prized in his day. Besides being a supremely great poet and playwright, he was a prominent actor and successful businessman. But his versatility exceeds this listing. He took life for his subject and made the world his open book. His works suggest such a detailed knowledge of horses, sailing, soldiering, royal courts, and an almost infinite variety of other subjects that biographers and speculative literary critics have imagined for him a variety of careers and identities.

Americans in the time of the founders valued versatility as much as Renaissance Florentines and Elizabethan Englishmen had. Frontier life in Virginia, beginning in 1607, and Massachusetts, beginning in 1620, fostered the multitalented development encouraged by the Elizabethan ethos.

For most settlers, it was a matter of plying strictly practical and at least partly manual tasks—building houses and boats, farming, hunting, fishing, using native herbs for healing. But some managed to include the practice of arts and scholarship as well, as with George Sandys at Jamestown, laying aside his pen to take up his musket against attacking tribesmen and afterward resuming work on his famous translation of Ovid's *Metamorphoses.* In 1687 the Huguenot exile Durand de Dauphiné wrote of the Virginia "gentlemen called cavaliers" who "hold most of the offices in the country, consisting of twelve seats in . . . [the Council], six [customs] collectors, the rank of colonel in each county, and captains of each company," and who "sit in judgment with girded sword."[19] He meant that some individuals performed all of these functions.

Nearly a century later, a continued tradition of diverse accomplishment had been nurtured to remarkable fruition by Enlightenment influences. In 1782 another Frenchman visiting in Virginia, the Marquis de Chastellux, described his host as "an American who, without ever quitting his country, is at once a musician, skilled in drawing, a geometrician, an astronomer, a natural philosopher, legislator, and statesman. . . . [I]t seemed as if from his youth he had placed his mind, as he had done his house, on an elevated situation from which he might contemplate the universe."[20] The Frenchman's host was, of course, Thomas Jefferson. Chastellux could have added that this American was also an architect, landscape artist, horticulturist, and inventor.

When Jefferson finally did leave his country in order to serve it as a diplomat, he not only furthered his learning in Europe but excited in Chastellux' compatriots an admiration equal to the marquis' own. The Virginian had eagerly anticipated listening to the brilliant talk of Paris salons. He was surprised when he found himself the center of attention in these fabled precincts. He concluded that conversations in those gilded surroundings were indeed brilliant, but no more so than in Williamsburg.

Parisians were accustomed to the brilliance of an American polymath even before they met Jefferson. Benjamin Franklin gloried in being the center of attention at salons crowded with savants of international reputation. He had added to his roles as writer, publisher, canny businessman, inventor, eminent scientist, sage statesman, and consummate diplomat. The "early to bed and early to rise" man had become a celebrated bon vivant.

In discussing the intellectual leadership of political chiefs, we have covered the versatility of the two principal authors of *The Federalist,* James Madison and Alexander Hamilton. With Jay, they were co-authors of a great international classic. Both were accomplished in statesmanship and practical politics. Madison was also learned in theology, and Hamilton was expert in finance.

George Mason was not only one of the ablest writers and statesmen of his generation, but also a man of richly various learning.

George Washington is not generally regarded as an intellectual, partly because he is compared with so many associates famous for intellectual accomplishment. But his range of activities was wide. He was a surveyor, a large-scale farmer, an inventor, a student of agronomy, a leading businessman, and a talented though amateur architect, besides being one of history's famous generals and a great statesman.

As we have seen, many political leaders below the great pantheon exhibited a versatility that in some other periods would have excited wonder. Some Virginians chided Jefferson for supporting his old friend John Page for governor, saying that the candidate was a splendid fellow but lacked the intellectual stature to be expected of one in that office. They said that, except for being learned in the law, delighting in complicated Latin puns, and working abstruse mathematical problems for recreation, he evinced almost no intellectual interests at all.

Intellectual diversity was by no means confined to political leaders. Think of the scholarly versatility of American newspaper editors from Philip Freneau to William Cullen Bryant. Most did not, like them, win durable reputations as poets, but many were well versed in several disciplines. And what of Charles Willson Peale, celebrated painter, great teacher, inventor, scientist, and the world's most creative museum curator in his time? Or Samuel F. B. Morse, who was both a famous painter and the inventor of the telegraph. Men of such abilities are never typical of any period, but they were certainly representative of the era of the founders. And each of these names can be matched by others equally honored and just as closely associated with interdisciplinary accomplishments.

The record is remarkable even in comparison with the diverse accomplishments of many contemporary western Europeans stimulated by the Enlightenment. Americans seemed more daring than their Old World counterparts in exploring many fields. American pioneers' habits of self-sufficiency in practicing many crafts to supply their wants, and later the American tradition of the jack-of-all-trades (and possibly master of one or two), prepared people to accept the notion that a person could be accomplished in more than one thing. There was not only the Renaissance ideal of the polymath but also the American tradition of versatility.

There was a direct relationship between the creativity of the three societies under consideration and the *interdisciplinary studies* that they encouraged. If originality expresses itself chiefly in the drawing of fresh analogies, as many psychologists, laboratory scientists, and critics of the arts maintain, it is obvious that a respectable knowledge of several fields provides many more possibilities for meaningful analogues, and hence greater creativity, than an almost exclusive concentration on a single discipline. Some prominent interdisciplinarians are found in virtually every advanced civilization, but their abundance in Renaissance Florence, Elizabethan England, and the founders' America is an extraordinary feature of those societies.

Another kind of exchange is important to the development and vitality of creative societies. The psychologist George W. Crane recognized its significance at almost any level when he called salesmen "the spark plugs of civilization" because they carry ideas as well as physical products from one society to another. Sociologists and cultural historians have noted it by references to the *cross fertilization of cultures*. It takes place in several ways, principally through commercial relations: communication through the arts and printed matter (with the addition in recent generations of increasingly sophisticated technological means), recreational travel, and the influx as permanent residents of people from other cultures.

The Italian Renaissance, which reached its height of creativity in Florence, was born largely amid the rediscovery of ancient Greek and Roman manuscripts, and expanding trade with Eastern societies that became a commerce of ideas as well. Of course, strictly speaking, the acquisition of classical ideas was not a trade but an importation. Outside science fiction, there could be no two-way communication between past and present.

Elizabethan England was revitalized by communication with the Italian Renaissance through trade, the consultation of scholars, and its people's travel and study in Italy and elsewhere on the Continent.

First successfully colonized by Elizabethan and Jacobean Englishmen, America was the heir to the English Renaissance and through it to the Italian Renaissance and its heritage of classical lore. Books and magazines from Great Britain, and to a lesser extent from France, challenged the reason and the imagination of builders of the new Republic. Travel, residence, and study in Europe broadened and stimulated many Americans, notably Franklin and Jefferson among statesmen, Washington Irving among writers, and among artists Benjamin West and a host of painters trained in his London studio. Even more than Renaissance Florence and Elizabethan England, both of which experienced an influx of artists and scholars, the American Republic was culturally vitalized by immigration. Some were famous intellectuals such as Joseph Priestley and Samuel Du Pont de Nemours, others as nearly anonymous as the Moravians from Germany who brought their high standards of musicianship. Particularly enriching in the pre-Revolutionary era and early years of the Republic were immigrants from all over the British Isles, France, Holland, Sweden, and the German states. A few Italians, such as Philip Mazzei, exercised an influence disproportionate to their small numbers.

The substantial immigration into the United States did not result in a balkanization. Most of the newcomers were drawn to the country by a promise of economic opportunity or freedom, or both, not available to them in their homelands. Those from the British Isles, and some others, already spoke English. Those immigrants who did not were quite prepared to learn the English language, and to see that their children did. They cherished certain elements of their native cultures and introduced the citizens of the Republic to new foods, unfamiliar music, and sometimes fresh esthetic visions. But most of them did not seek to replace the society they found or even to remain apart from it. By their own desire and the generally ready acceptance of neighbors already in residence, they enriched the existing Anglo-American environment and were assimilated by it.

A society that attempts to isolate itself from external influences will diminish its creativity. One of the most impressive illustrations of this fact is the experience of China, once one of the world's most creative societies, which deliberately tried to exclude all foreigners and in the process lost the stimulus of new ideas and products. Not all of the decline in creativity was attributable to this self-segregation. Isolationism was as much symptom as cause, reflecting a serious imbalance between adherence to tradition and an impulse to experiment.

And, of course, any decline in the creativity of an entire society, is so complex as to involve many factors. On the other hand, history affords examples of societies so inundated by immigration that they failed to assimilate the newcomers and lost communication among their people, a sense of unity, and of course patriotism. Needless to say, such a situation saps a society's creativity and virtually every other form of vitality. Some homogeneity is necessary to progress.

It might be well to amend our statement about the cross-fertilization of cultures to say that attainment of maximum creativity depends partly on *cultural exchange with other societies, but not inundation of native culture by foreign.*

So, from the experience of Renaissance Florence, Elizabethan England, and America in the era of the founders, we have culled six common characteristics:

1. Tension between heritage and the urge to experiment.
2. Patriotism.
3. An economy well above the subsistence level, though an economic boom is not essential.
4. Intellectual example set by leaders.
5. Interdisciplinary studies emphasized rather than narrow specialization.
6. Cultural exchange with other societies, including the stimulus of immigration, but not inundation of native culture by foreign. Some homogeneity is necessary to progress.

The next (and final) chapter will examine the possible significance of these things.

48

SALVATION THROUGH ADVENTURE

I N PONDERING THE significance of the six points, the immediate consideration is their possible importance to the three societies with which we
are primarily concerned. That the three, Renaissance Florence, Elizabethan
England, and the America of the founders, are among the most creative in history derives significance from the fact that the cultures are highly atypical and
yet alike in the nature of their atypicality. The fact that all six characteristics
were most prominent in all three societies at the height of their creativity, waxing in approach to the apogee and waning in decline, suggests that the similarity
may not be accidental.

It may be argued that the coexistence of certain characteristics with a state
of extraordinary creativity is not in itself proof of cause and effect. The point
is valid. But even synchronicity is a relationship sufficiently intimate to merit
study. Not only is this synchronicity strikingly apparent in the three extraordinarily creative societies that are the principal objects of this study, but it is
conspicuously lacking in the case of any uncreative societies of which I have
sufficient knowledge to judge. Furthermore, there is reason to believe that this
remarkable simultaneity exists in other unusually creative societies in other
times and places. But more of them later.

Some may object that few reliable statistics are available for meaningful
comparison of many aspects of the societies whose similarities are stressed.
They may say that, given this deficiency and the lack of any means of analysis
comparable to those available in analytical chemistry, any inquiry must be
largely dependent on anecdotal evidence.

In the preceding chapter, I have already conceded the limitations of the
anecdotal method, while nevertheless pointing out that it has proven useful to
distinguished sociologists and cultural historians, particularly in dealing with
the sort of questions that I am addressing here. Statistics may mark a path to
the truth, but seldom with the clearly defined exactitude of the trails of pebbles
in the old fairy tales. Sometimes a writer will find false comfort in clinging to
a bundle of ill-assorted statistics as he hurls himself through the air in a wild

flight of fancy, like the trapeze artist in the animated cartoon who happily clasps the now detached bar as he hurtles to his doom.

Only a fool would refuse to use statistics when they are abundant enough and reliable enough to be enlightening. But a wise person will not neglect anecdotal evidence when it is the best evidence available. We must never forget that generations of Western scientists derided the "superstition" of the Chinese in touting powdered seaweed as a cure for goiter. Only later did scoffing pathologists discover that hyperthyroidism resulted from a deficiency of iodine, a substance abundant in seaweed. The Chinese arguments had been too anecdotal to be taken seriously by Western physicians.

Anyone entertaining the idea that the six characteristics of creative societies treated here may be examples of cause and effect must also admit that, granted the hypothesis, it is sometimes difficult to determine which factor is the cause and which the effect. Does the tension between heritage and experiment produce creativity, or does creativity automatically find itself in conflict with the status quo? Does the emphasis on interdisciplinary studies breed creativity, or does free-ranging creativity awaken interest in a variety of disciplines?

It seems most likely that these attributes of the creative society work both ways, that they may be simultaneously causes and results. Such would be in accordance with a principle at work both in human activities and in the natural world, to follow a categorical distinction that we humans customarily make but that might not be apparent to some sentient being from another universe. Even if some of the characteristics are principally or entirely results rather than causes, the cultivation of them may be useful as a pump-priming measure to stimulate creativity.

In Renaissance Florence, *the tension between heritage and the urge to experiment* stimulated, in demonstrable ways, the imaginations of Leonardo da Vinci, Michelangelo, Machiavelli, Lorenzo de' Medici, and a host of other shapers of that extraordinarily productive society. Here the interaction was especially complex because the classical sources, never wholly lost in the medieval period, were both part of the Western heritage and at the same time, with the emphasis of rediscovery in the Renaissance, representative of the new and challenging.

In Elizabethan England, the Renaissance itself, coming from the Continent, presented the challenge of the exotic as well as emphasizing the ancient heritage of classical civilization, which had flourished in Britain in the eighth century, and after near destruction by the Vikings had been revived by Alfred late in the ninth. England's traditions were compounded of these sources as well as of a native Anglo-Saxon culture that had survived the Norman Conquest. Spenser, Bacon, Ralegh, Queen Elizabeth, and many more molders of England's arts and nationhood in the critical period reflect the tension between heritage and experiment.

So, too, with America in the era of the founders. The tension between heritage and experiment was not only evident at almost every level of political, intellectual, and artistic leadership in the society. It was articulated individually by such notable leaders as Jefferson, Franklin, John Adams, Madison, James

Wilson, Freneau, Benjamin West, and William Cullen Bryant. Jefferson is one of history's supreme examples of this binary tension, consciously expressing it in government and architecture. J. E. Morpurgo has pointed out that even his plans for public education, often called his most progressive scheme, "involved in almost every function . . . some element of compromise between conservative prejudices and reforming zeal."[1] Of Marshall, Lord Bryce said that "the Constitution seemed not so much to rise under his hands to full stature, as to be gradually unveiled by him till it stood revealed in the harmonious perfection of the form which its framers designed."[2] Commenting on Bryce's observation, historian Joseph J. Ellis says, "An essential feature of Marshall's genius . . . was to claim that he was not creating anything."[3]

In all these societies, this tenuous balance, when successfully maintained, permitted the advantages of both continuity and change. As Alfred North Whitehead has said, "The art of progress is to preserve order amid change and to preserve change amid order."[4] The proponent of change who asserts that his proposal is revolutionary engenders fear and hostility. History affords numerous examples of people who were educated enough and clever enough to call for worthwhile reforms but lacked the wisdom and restraint to forgo such claims. All beneficial change has in it some element of tradition. Emphasizing continuity not only makes change more acceptable; it also makes it more valuable.

It cannot be urged too strongly, however, that a balance of heritage and experiment benefits society not only because it preserves valuable elements in the midst of mutability and facilitates popular acceptance but also because the tension between these two forces in balance is a great energizer. Arnold Toynbee accustomed historians, sociologists, and political analysts to thinking of the survival or death of civilizations in terms of challenge and response. But these thoughts were almost always on an epic scale, whereas civilizations, and especially subordinate cultures within great civilizations, have been more likely to die by inches, by evasion of responsibility in one instance, timidity in another, lassitude in still another. The fall of the Roman Empire was actually a slow motion descent through three centuries.

Sometimes those who endorse the idea of experiment as a means of keeping a society vital impose restrictions that impede that aim. They regard pure science as wasteful and demand that every experiment be directed toward a practical objective, whether it be the conquest of disease, increased efficiency in manufacturing or communication, or the making of a great deal of money. Actually, this pragmatic course is not very practical. In the Stalin years, when the Soviet Union required scientists to work only in fulfillment of specific projects to answer well-defined needs, there was a decrease in practical results. In Western Europe and North America, many practical products are actually by-products of pure science.

As a reflection of the vitality of a society, adventuring in research or exploration is as important as any synthetic products emerging from the laboratory or any exotic fruits brought back from the Caribbean or Cathay. In the Elizabethan Age, some captains sailed forth in search of gold or ambergris or new lands for the Crown they served, but others were lured by insatiable curiosity and the promise of adventure in terra incognita. In our own time, the urge to explore celestial space instead of concentrating solely on terrestrial problems is evidence of the adventuring spirit essential to the vitality of a society.

Sometimes the healthful tension between heritage and experiment is lacking because a society's leaders prefer to live entirely in the past, seeking to duplicate the achievements of former generations admired for their accomplishments. And they seek in vain, because the generations they admired maintained societies benefiting from the tension created by the simultaneous pull of tradition and lure of adventure. In trying to become mere imitators of revered forebears, they have renounced the pioneering proclivities that helped to make their heroes great.

Other societies, like our own American society at this juncture, seem determined to cut loose from their heritage. They try to forget their past, thereby losing the opportunity to build on it or even to learn from it. Articles revealing popular ignorance of history are staple newspaper fare in the United States. Amnesia can be as disorienting to a society as to an individual.

Though some pseudosophisticates decry *patriotism* as an outmoded sentiment, it remains a necessity in building a great society. It is not surprising that many people regard patriotism with a jaundiced eye. Too often flag-waving is used to divert attention from personal and societal failings, and the flag itself is sometimes used to blanket dissent or cover disgraceful situations. Dr. Samuel Johnson, in 1775, said, "Patriotism is the last refuge of a scoundrel." And in every generation there have been scoundrels to prove him right.

But patriotism also sometimes inspires noble sacrifice by the advantaged and noble aspirations among the disadvantaged. What passes for love of country is sometimes a self-indulgent tribal sense of superiority to all strangers. It then discourages, rather than encourages, endeavor. All passions are two-edged swords. But soaring patriotism can sometimes lift an unpromising community, local or national, to heights not easily reached by the measured tread of unheartened logic.

When Philip spoke of the greatness of Jesus, Nathaneal asked, "Can anything good come out of Nazareth?"[5] Varieties of the incredulous question have been asked through the ages whenever some hitherto unpromising community was stirring with the first signs of greatness. Before the last quarter of the eighteenth century, Weimar was the "obscure capital of a petty Duchy in the heart of Germany."[6] Yet the patriotism of Anna Amalia, who was ultimately responsible for bringing Christoph Martin Weiland, Friedrich von Schiller, Johann Gottfried von Herder, and Goethe to the mediocre city-state, initiated a series of events that built pride and confidence sufficient for great achievements. Toward the close of the eighteenth century, the city that believed in itself had inspired the belief of others. It was often saluted as a second Athens.

Of the three creative societies that are our special concern in this book, patriotism fueled the rise of Renaissance Florence from obscurity, Elizabethan England from second-class nationhood, and the United States from colonial status. In the Revolution, perhaps only a third of the American people were truly patriots, but their fervor sustained nationhood, and a subsequent growth in national pride and confidence fed creativity that made the Republic the cynosure of nations. Patriotism can become arrogance; but properly bridled, it can be a pegasus. The society that loses pride in its achievements soon has no achievements of which to be proud.

Closely allied to patriotism is the matter of heroes, national or otherwise. Societies often indulge in the debunking of heroes because gaining relative equality with the great by pulling them down is easier than exerting ourselves to climb to the heights. In our time, in the United States and Europe, vilification of the hero has become a passionate pastime. Any of the departed great retaining a shred of earthly vanity must dread the recurrence of anniversaries providing excuses for renewed attacks. Objective examination of heroes is a duty of scholarship and an obligation to realism. But the systematic denigration of heroes mirroring a society's virtues saps a people's inspiration and energy.

About no factor in the building of a creative society is there more popular misunderstanding than concerning *the role of the economy.* The general assumption is that an economic boom is essential to creative leadership. There is an intimate relationship between the economy and an artistically and scientifically inventive society: cultural development and intellectual pioneering do not flourish in a community that must concentrate virtually all its faculties on providing food and shelter. But sometimes too great a concern with affluence can cause connoisseurship to degenerate into mere conspicuous consumption.

Minor financial reverses need not curb creativity in a society accustomed to intellectual adventure. We have seen how Florence reached the peak of its cultural leadership during a recession and how Jefferson's presidency provided vital intellectual leadership during an economic crisis. It is also worth remembering that it was during a recession that Jefferson persuaded his fellow Virginians to appropriate the necessary funds and spend sufficient energy to help him found the University of Virginia in a bold experiment in higher education.

Too often even a brief downturn in the economy is thought sufficient to justify jettisoning the arts and intellectual experiments to prepare for a rough voyage. The truth of the matter is that fertile imaginations and questioning intellects are the best long-time guarantees of a reviving economy. Stockbrokers are fond of saying that, regardless of short-term losses, investment in diversified stocks can be depended upon to pay off in the long run. The same can be said about societal investment in diversified intellectual potential.

Crucial to a society's support of creativity is the *example of its leaders in both government and business.* Such an example is particularly effective if the head of government, like Lorenzo, Elizabeth I, or Jefferson, is not only a patron but also a practitioner of the arts. But even the chief of state who is merely an enthusiastic spectator can exercise a beneficent influence. President Harry S. Truman is not generally thought of as a crusader for the arts or intellectual creativity, but his intelligent appreciation of classical music and competence as an amateur pianist, as well as his knowledgeable interest in American history, had an influence on culture in his presidency.

Even a feigned interest in an art can have a positive effect. Though in recent years, the public has learned that President John F. Kennedy disliked ballet, media coverage of his frequent visits to performances influenced some of his fellow Americans to attend.

Of course, this influence is magnified when the president is a skilled professional in an artistic or intellectual field. President Theodore Roosevelt was a successful writer and historian. His publicly declared interest in certain writers, including poet Edwin Arlington Robinson, produced an eager audience for their works.

Political and business leaders at almost every level in Renaissance Florence, Elizabethan England, and the Republic of the founders were not only strong supporters of artists and intellectuals, but often proud to claim membership in their ranks. This is almost always effective. The average person fears that neither scholarship nor the arts are sufficiently practical to justify the wholehearted appreciation of a responsible adult. This fear is allayed when interest in such activities is manifested by those skilled in garnering either votes or money.

Perhaps no example from former periods of great creativity is more needed in our time than their *emphasis on interdisciplinary studies* rather than narrow specialization. Another discussion of this emphasis would be redundant at this point. It is the most conspicuous difference between those superbly creative societies and those of Western civilization today. Contemporary societies have not only suffered from an absence of intellectual virtuosity. They actually have been as proud of their narrow specialization as Renaissance Florence, Elizabethan England, and the early American Republic were of their versatility. There seems to have been an assumption that narrowness would automatically guarantee thoroughness.

In a primitive culture, the advent of specialization frees individuals from the necessity of performing so many functions "to keep body and soul together" that there is little or no opportunity for cultural advance. What we have generally failed to realize is that, although specialization can be an aid to cultural progress in a primitive society, it can be an impediment in a more complex one.

There are encouraging signs that in some quarters the need for interdisciplinary studies is beginning to be recognized. Medical associations and some broader-based scientific organizations have faced the fact that a professional worker cannot truly master a specialty without acquiring knowledge of many other related specialties.

Scientists, more than any other group, have urged the value of specialization. But in recent years the appearance of new disciplines, each a combination of two previous disciplines, affords evidence of a tacit recognition that professional preparation cannot be simultaneously separate and complete. So we have biochemistry, bioengineering, biomechanics, biomathematics, bionics, biotechnology, biophysics, biogeography, bioethics, chemurgy, chemosurgery, astrophysics, molecular biology, and ekistics. Specialization becomes its own enemy. Advances in complexity necessitate a breaching of barriers between fields of knowledge.

Education in recent years has paid lip service, and sometimes serious attention, to the interdisciplinary ideal. But too often it is merely a trendy, superficial endeavor. In the humanities, it sometimes degenerates into a struggle between those who would not add a single item to the cultural canon and those who would junk the cultural canon altogether. We prate about diversity, but confine our awareness of it to matters of ethnicity.

Certainly, however, *the interaction of different cultures* can be an important factor in stimulating creativity. The society without diversity is doomed. Like the asexual reproduction of an extremely simple organism, its means of reproduction precludes evolutionary adjustment to a changing environment. There is no creative future in any approach to universal cloning.

To be fully creative, a society must be aware of ideas current in other societies as well as of important ideas from the past that deserve analysis and reevaluation. But such acquaintance is not sufficient to achieve diversity. Constant additions to the population through the immigration of persons of varied cultural heritage is a necessary enlivening force.

Here, once again, as in so many matters, a fine balance is important. The existing culture of an entity can sometimes be swamped by too great a tide of unrestricted immigration. Under such circumstances, a nation can become the victim of a cultural version of guerilla warfare. Immigration then becomes a vitiating, rather than a vitalizing, experience.

The researches and writings of Jack P. Greene, especially *Pursuits of Happiness,* have made many scholars aware of the degree to which immigrants from varying national backgrounds were assimilated into America's growing population both in colonial days and in the early days of the Republic.[7] Like the annual rising of the waters of the Nile that nourished civilization in ancient Egypt, the tides of immigration were life-giving, rather than overwhelmingly destructive, floods. A strong factor was the basic linguistic unity that was consciously sought after and preserved.

Of course, the influence of some groups within Renaissance Florence, Elizabethan England, and the early American Republic was greatly reduced by prejudice, the encrustations of custom, and the effects of previous discrimination on the fitness of some persons for full participation. Elizabethan England refused the potential contributions of Catholics and Jews. Renaissance Florence also lost some talents because of religious infighting. The American colonies, and later the states, North and South, found little use for any higher talents of Indians or blacks. All three societies wasted the intellectual talents of women. Yet, deplorable as this record is, each of the three afforded opportunities for personal development to a larger proportion of its citizens than was the case in most contemporary societies.

The six major points of similarity I have stressed in discussing three extraordinarily creative societies (tension between heritage and experiment, patriotism, an economy well above subsistence, intellectual example set by leaders, interdisciplinary pursuits, cultural exchange with other societies) are, of course, not the only ones they have in common. They are not even the only ones distinguishing them from less creative societies.

There are related and auxiliary points. In contemplating them, it seems impossible to separate synchronicity from cause and effect, or even, positing a case of cause and effect, to determine which is which. One of these points is the existence of keen creative competition. This is related to the role of heritage because some of the greatest creators in all three societies revealed their sense of competition not only with contemporaries but also with predecessors, sometimes from distant eras. Another auxiliary point is the strong emphasis on individualism in Renaissance Florence, Elizabethan England, and the America of the founders. Since creativity is dependent on originality, it is intimately related to individuality. Creativity begets individualism, and individualism begets creativity. Who can say which comes first?

There is some absurd talk in our time about humanity having reached the end of history and even the end of science. History and science both teach us that unanticipated discoveries are constantly forcing us to reevaluate the possibilities of the universe and of human potential. It is rash to say that either history or science will end while there are sentient beings. And, so long as civilizations remain, history will help to preserve their heritage, and science will prompt experiment; and both will provide vital perspectives.

Surely the societies of Renaissance Florence, Elizabethan England, and the early American Republic share with other creative societies the six major points that I have discussed. I have chosen them from a number of outstanding examples because they were diverse specimens of which I had some knowledge. My writings and researches in the history of colonial North America and the early American Republic, in Anglo-American cultural history, in Elizabethan literature, and in the contributions of the Italian Renaissance to Western civilization provided a foundation for the studies involved in this book. On each of these topics, I have worked among both original and secondary sources for a long time, in fact among the English and American sources for forty years.

Regarding creative societies about which I lack the personal expertise to write, I have consulted enough experts and studied enough secondary works to suspect that they share the six characteristics that I have found so strongly evident in the three societies discussed in this book. Among likely prospects are Egypt under the fourth dynasty, Babylonia under Hammurabi, France (despite tragic waste of men and material) under Louis XIV, China in the Sung Renaissance of the eleventh and twelfth centuries, India in the reigns of Samadragupta and several successive Guptas, and Japan in the Engi period of the tenth century. There are, I am sure, others of which I know too little even to conjecture.

Some may say that evidence regarding the significance of our six major characteristics of creative societies is offset by the record of ancient Athens. The linchpin of our whole structure of a half-dozen prominent features is the tension between heritage and experiment. Yet we think of Athenian civilization as, like Athena herself, springing into existence full grown. Edith Hamilton said of the Greeks, "They were the first Westerners."[8] We think of the great Greeks of the fifth century B.C. as having no antecedent models, no heritage sufficient to meet the demands of their own questioning minds. We too readily assume that there was no intellectual tradition of sufficient strength to create a healthy tension with the drive to experiment.

Certainly there has been no more richly creative society on earth than that of Periclean Athens. But Athens did not invent itself out of nothing. Heed the words of Tatian, who in the second century A.D. wrote:

> The Greeks claim, without reason, the invention of the arts. Be not, O Greeks, so very hostilely disposed towards the Barbarians, nor look with ill will on their opinions. For which of your institutions has not been derived from the Barbarians? . . . To the Babylonians you owe astronomy; to the Persians, magic; to the Egyptians, geometry; to the Phoenicians, instruction by alphabetic writing. Cease, then, to miscall these imitations inventions of your own. The Tuscans taught you the plastic art; from the annals of the Egyptians you learned to write history; you acquired the art of playing the flute from Phrygians. The Tyrrhenians invented the trumpet. . . .[9]

We may be sure that the civilized predecessors of the Greeks learned from still earlier cultures nurtured by the traditions of those who were truly barbarians, but nevertheless skillful and inventive people.

Can creativeness be induced by cultivating, through education and other societal institutions, some of the same factors prominent in highly creative societies since the dawn of civilization? The experiment is certainly worth trying. Societies of rich and dynamic culture may arise in places as unlikely as Florence before the days of Medici leadership or Weimar before Anna Amalia burned with inspiration.

And we need not assume that civilizations that have blazed with glory and then subsided to pulsing embers can never again be lights to the world. Many people have been made unduly pessimistic by Arnold Toynbee's and Oswald Spengler's assumption that a society cannot be revived, that it is allotted only one life. As they have defined societies, their premise is supported by history. But their theories, even if true, do not preclude the flourishing of a national entity in another guise, the reincarnation of a society. The Egypt that flourished under the fourth dynasty flourished again under the eighteenth. Frankish culture that rose to international influence under Charlemagne and then subsided rose again eight centuries later under Louis XIV. But if these paired societies are so far apart in time and character that they seem to have little connection beyond geographical location, consider the vibrant culture of Victorian England that energized so much of the Western world only about two centuries after the fading of the Elizabethan Afterglow.

In a controversial book, *Out of Control: The New Biology of Machines,* Kevin Kelly says that evolution "is a technological, mathematical, informational, and biological process rolled into one."[10] One need not accept all of his theories to agree that, as summarized by Anson Rubinbach (who disagrees with Kelly on many points), "This logic of evolution can be applied to any living system when it is neither 'stagnant' with too little communication nor 'gridlocked' with too much."[11] Historians and philosophers need to think boldly about the possibilities.

Scholars should not pride themselves on sticking entirely to the accumulation of minute facts without venturing to draw conclusions of extensive significance. Historians of the particular who never make syntheses are like the medieval hermits who lived atop poles or in desert caves. They may have preserved their purity undefiled by the errors incident to participation in the normal traffic of human life, but there must be more useful ways of promoting virtue. Accumulations of discrete data have little significance until someone connects them. The very boldness necessary to do so is part of the boldness that can revitalize a society. And the accumulation of meaningful knowledge should not lead to a dead end and, as some timid spirits have feared, the death of history and science, the demise of vitalizing curiosity. Each of us can say with Isaac Newton: "The more I enlarge the island of knowledge, the more I increase the shoreline of wonder."

Some people despair of finding meaningful order in a world that seems increasingly chaotic. The inventiveness of our era seems to be attested by great technological progress, but is it merely accidental that the semichaos of Christopher Rouse's symphonic *Infernal Machine* seems more appropriate to our time than the ordered busyness of Johann Strauss's *Perpetual Motion*? The increasingly complex technology of the industrial revolution inspired many musical representations of *perpetuum mobile.* Paganini's compositions on the theme were distinguished by a vivacious regularity. Strauss' music rolled through the landscape like a horse-drawn barouche, up hill and down dale, but conveying always a sense of the orderly revolution of the wheels. Rimsky-Korsakov's *Flight of the Bumblebee* discovered perpetual motion in nature with all the movements as divinely ordered as Fibonacci's spirals.

Though a single composition does not necessarily reflect the spirit of the era in which it is created, there is significance when audiences see in the semichaos of such a work as Rouse's *Infernal Machine* an accurate reflection of their world.[12] This significance is magnified when prominent works of painting, sculpture, and fiction mirror the same turbulence.

Artists who portray contemporary society are obligated to present it accurately, insofar as they can perceive it, whether the picture be one of order or disorder. But, elsewhere in the full spectrum of their works, they also have the responsibility of imposing order on chaos.

Scientists, too, have the responsibility of finding order amid apparent chaos. They do so whenever they formulate a law. They approach the possibility whenever they posit a theory. Some of the most prominent ones even go beyond the traditional processes of controlled experiment, as in work by mathematicians, meteorologists, and physicists on the chaos theory. Physicist Mitchell Feigenbaum, mathematician James York, and meteorologist Edward Lorenz have sought evidence of structure even in aperiodic dynamic systems long conceded to be unpredictable. Mathematician Benoit Mandelbrot, inventor of fractal geometry, has found geometrical patterns in irregular shapes and surfaces and in seemingly erratic processes. We cannot predict the general evaluation of their researches a generation hence.

But we historians are far more inhibited than scientists. All too often, we fear to use anecdotal evidence, although it is quite acceptable among many psychologists and psychiatrists. Feigenbaun daringly admitted that his calculation of a universal constant was prompted by meditation on the art of Van Gogh, Ruysdael, and Turner. Cocksureness is both foolish and dangerous in any search for truth, but some speculation is also necessary. It always has been. If scientists can search for patterns where all seems chaos, surely we historians can examine them when they are discernible. Unlike chemists, physicists, and medical scientists, historians cannot conduct controlled experiments, but we can assess empirical evidence and thereby stumble toward some portion of the truth. Cognitive scientist Douglas Hofstadter has said, "It turns out that an eerie type of chaos can lurk just behind a facade of order—and yet, deep inside the chaos lurks an even eerier type of order."[13]

Great poets and great scientists succeed by making metaphors, by pointing out relationships between things hitherto not perceived as related.[14] Through creativity in arts, science, and scholarship, we find connections that give meaning to society and to the universe. Einstein conveyed the kindred esthetics and creativity of great science and great art when he said that a clearly stated mathematical theorem and a beautiful poem produced in him the same sensation. And, of course, he found in great music an expression of the laws of the universe.

Creativity alone cannot save a society. Societies rich in creativity have fallen because of a lack of moral fiber. But neither can a society save itself solely by the cultivation of individual virtues apart from knowledge and creativity. Even the combination of virtue and creativity is not sufficient to save us without perspective. Like the boys in Graham Greene's "Destructors," who engaged our attention in the beginning of this book, we may cultivate sacrifice, ingenuity, and industry, and yet, without perspective, use them as tools of destruction. We need to acquire perspective by studying the recurring patterns of vital communities whose creativity has enriched humankind.

Henry Kissinger is a professional historian who left his Harvard post to become a political leader intimately involved in decision making on an international level. One does not have to agree with all of his personal applications of the lessons of history to admire the effective phrasing of his admonition about the process: "History is not, of course, a cookbook offering pretested recipes. It teaches by analogy, not by maxims. It can illuminate the consequences of actions in comparable situations, yet each generation must discover for itself what situations are in fact comparable."[15]

To accomplish that purpose, we must search among the patterns of our worldwide heritage, and we must bring to that search an adventurous spirit of experiment.

NOTES

Throughout this book, in some quotations from former centuries, spelling and punctuation have been modernized for clarity.

CHAPTER 2, THE BOW AND THE LYRE

1. The story was one of Sir Winston Churchill's favorites. I remember the essentials quite well, but cannot vouch for the accuracy of the precise colors of the multihued butterfly. Sir Winston expresses the idea behind the anecdote in *My Early Life: A Roving Commission* (New York, 1930), 117: "The idea that nothing is true except what we comprehend is silly, and that ideas which our minds cannot reconcile are mutually destructive, sillier still."

2. Alf J. Mapp, Jr., *Frock Coats and Epaulets: The Men Who Led the Confederacy* , 4th ed. (Lanham, Md., New York, and London, 1996), 481–486.

3. Quoted in Karl Joachim Weintraub, *Visions of Culture* (Chicago, 1966), 135.

4. Alfred North Whitehead, *Adventures of Ideas* (New York, 1933), 380.

5. Goethe to Wilhelm von Humboldt, March 17, 1832. Johann Wolfgang von Goethe, *Letters from Goethe*, trans. M. von Herzfeld and C. A. M. Sym (New York, 1957), 537.

CHAPTER 4, WAKING THE DEAD

1. Ciriaco di Filippo Pizzicolli (1391–?), known also as Cyriacus of Ancona.

2. Jacob Burckhardt, *The Civilization of the Renaissance in Italy*, trans. S. G. C. Middlemore (New York, 1954), 136.

3. Daniel J. Boorstin, *The Discoverers*, 1st ed. (New York, 1983), 612.

4. Eugene F. Rice, Jr., "The Renaissance and Reformation in Europe," *The Columbia History of the World*, ed. John Arthur Garraty and Peter Gay (New York, 1972), 485.

5. Ibid., 486.

6. Ibid., 487.

7. Burckhardt, 4.

8. Ibid., 11–13.

9. Ibid., 30.

10. Psalms 19:1–2

CHAPTER 5, LORENZO THE MAGNIFICENT

1. If it is a rule of ecclesiastical law that Ascension is preceded by rogation, it is equally true in the world of secular heroes that ascension is inevitably followed by derogation. After enjoying a

lengthy elevation by the almost common consent of scholars, Lorenzo is now under attack not only as a despot but also as one less generous to the arts than some of his Florentine predecessors. But study of his career suggests that it is no mere coincidence that his leadership coincides with Florence's period of most intense and varied creativity. When the whole spectrum of creativity is examined, the world of literature, science, and scholarship as well as the graphic arts, and when Lorenzo's contributions are measured in hours of personal activity as well as monetary donations, his role appears pivotal.

Terra-cotta bust by Andrea del Verrocchio and bronze medallion by Bertoldo di Giovanni in the Kress Collection, National Gallery of Art, Washington, D.C. Also Nicola Valori's manuscript portrait in Charles L. Mee, *Lorenzo de' Medici and the Renaissance,* 1st ed. (New York, 1969), 91.

2. Vincent Cronin, *The Florentine Renaissance* (New York, 1967), 222.

3. Mee, 12.

4. Edward Armstrong, *Lorenzo de' Medici and Florence in the Fifteenth Century* (New York and London, 1914), 74.

5. Mee, 37–38.

6. George Frederick Young, *The Medici* (New York, 1933), 153, with slight variations.

7. Information on the Medici family is derived primarily from the following sources: Cecilia Mary Ady, *Lorenzo de' Medici and Renaissance Italy* (New York, 1952); Edward Armstrong, *Lorenzo de' Medici and Florence in the Fifteenth Century* (New York and London, 1914); Selwyn Brinton, *The Golden Age of the Medici: Cosimo, Piero, Lorenzo de' Medici, 1434–1494* (London, 1925); Alison Brown, *Languages and Images of Renaissance Italy* (New York, 1995); James Cleugh, *The Medici: A Tale of Fifteen Generations,* 1st ed. (Garden City, N.Y., 1975); Janet Cox-Rearick, *Dynasty and Destiny in Medici Art* (Princeton, 1984); Vincent Cronin, *The Florentine Renaissance* (New York, 1967); Raymond De Roover, *The Rise and Decline of the Medici Bank, 1397–1494* (Cambridge, Mass., 1963); Caroline Elam, "Lorenzo de' Medici and the Urban Development of Renaissance Florence," *Art History* 1 (March 1978): 43–66; Sir John Rigby Hale, *Florence and the Medici: The Pattern of Control* (London, 1977); Christopher Hibbert, *The House of Medici: Its Rise and Fall* (New York, 1980); Judith Hook, *Lorenzo de' Medici: An Historical Biography* (London, 1984); Philip Jones, *The Italian City-State from Commune to Signoria* (New York, 1997); Luca Landucci, *A Florentine Diary from 1450 to 1516* (1927; reprint, New York, 1969); Angelo Lipari, *The "Dolce Stil Nove" According to Lorenzo de' Medici* (New Haven and London, 1936); Niccolò Machiavelli, *History of Florence and of the Affairs of Italy, from the Earliest Times to the Death of Lorenzo the Magnificent* (New York, 1960); Lauro Martines, *The Social World of the Florentine Humanists, 1390–1460* (Princeton, 1963); Lorenzo de' Medici, *The Political Philosophy of the Great de' Medici As Revealed by Their Correspondence,* 2 vols. (Albuquerque: Institute for Economic and Political World Strategic Studies, 1985); Charles L. Mee, *Lorenzo de' Medici and the Renaissance,* 1st ed. (New York, 1969); William Roscoe, *The Life of Lorenzo de' Medici, Called the Magnificent,* 9th ed. (London, 1847); Janet Ann Duff-Gordon Ross, trans. and ed., *Lives of the Early Medici As Told in Their Correspondence* (London, 1910); Nicolai Rubinstein, *The Government of Florence under the Medici, 1434–1494* (Oxford, 1966), and *The Palazzo Vecchio, 1298–1532: Government, Architecture, and Imagery in the Civic Palace of the Florentine Republic* (New York, 1995); Walter B. Scaife, *Florentine Life during the Renaissance* (Baltimore, 1893); Ferdinand Schevill, *History of Florence: From the Founding of the City through the Renaissance,* 1st ed. (New York, 1936), and *The Medici* (New York, 1949); Evelyn Welch, *Art and Society in Italy, 1350–1500* (New York, 1997); and George Frederick Young, *The Medici* (New York, 1933).

8. "Pater Patriae," Inscription on medallion in Kress Collection, National Gallery of Art, Washington, D.C.

9. Portrait by Domenico Ghirlandaio in Mee, 33, and portrait by Sandro Botticelli in Armstrong, 45.

10. Giovanni di Bicci de' Medici.

11. Mee, 17.

12. Young, 150.

13. Ibid., 134–135.

14. Schevill, *History of Florence,* 379–380, and Young, 157–159.

15. Mee, 47.

16. According to some accounts, Francesco playfully punched Giuliano in the side to see whether he was armored. Cleugh, 134.

17. For a contemporary account of the conspiracy, see Landucci, 15–20.

18. Schevill, *History of Florence*, 387.

19. Ibid.

20. Mee, 69–70.

CHAPTER 6, SAINTS, SINNERS, AND SEERS

1. Ferdinand Schevill, *History of Florence: From the Founding of the City through the Renaissance*, 1st ed. (New York, 1936), 286–287.

2. Ibid., 287.

3. Ibid., xiii.

4. Ibid., 368.

5. Petrarch (Francesco Petrarca), *Letters of Old Age: Rerum Senilium Libri, 1–18*, Aldo S. Bernardo, Saul Levin, and Reta A. Bernardo, vol. 1, books 1–9 (Baltimore and London, 1992), 160–161.

6. Eugenio Garin, *Italian Humanism: Philosophy and Civic Life in the Renaissance*, trans. Peter Munz (Oxford, 1966), 57.

7. Giuseppe Martinelli, ed., *The World of Renaissance Florence* (New York, 1968), 92–98.

8. Information on Lorenzo is derived primarily from the following sources: Cecilia Mary Ady, *Lorenzo de' Medici and Renaissance Italy* (New York, 1952); Edward Armstrong, *Lorenzo de' Medici and Florence in the Fifteenth Century* (New York and London, 1914); Selwyn Brinton, *The Golden Age of the Medici: Cosimo, Piero, Lorenzo de' Medici, 1434–1494* (London, 1925); James Cleugh, *The Medici: A Tale of Fifteen Generations*, 1st ed. (Garden City, N.Y., 1975); Janet Cox-Rearick, *Dynasty and Destiny in Medici Art* (Princeton, 1984); Vincent Cronin, *The Florentine Renaissance* (New York, 1967); Raymond De Roover, *The Rise and Decline of the Medici Bank, 1397–1494* (Cambridge, Mass., 1963); Caroline Elam, "Lorenzo de' Medici and the Urban Development of Renaissance Florence," *Art History*, 1 (March 1978), 43–66; Sir John Rigby Hale, *Florence and the Medici: The Pattern of Control* (London, 1977); Christopher Hibbert, *The House of Medici: Its Rise and Fall* (New York, 1980); Judith Hook, *Lorenzo de' Medici: An Historical Biography* (London, 1984); Angelo Lipari, *"The Dolce Stil Nove" according to Lorenzo de' Medici* (New Haven and London, 1936); Niccolò Machiavelli, *History of Florence and of the Affairs of Italy, from the Earliest Times to the Death of Lorenzo the Magnificent* (New York, 1960); Lorenzo de' Medici, *The Political Philosophy of the Great de' Medici As Revealed by Their Correspondence,* 2 vols. (Albuquerque: Institute for Economic and Political World Strategic Studies, 1985); Charles L. Mee, *Lorenzo de' Medici and the Renaissance*, 1st ed. (New York, 1969); William Roscoe, *The Life of Lorenzo de' Medici, Called the Magnificent*, 9th ed. (London, 1847); Janet Ann Duff-Gordon Ross, ed. and trans., *Lives of the Early Medici As Told in Their Correspondence* (London, 1910); Nicolai Rubinstein, *The Government of Florence under the Medici, 1434–1494* (Oxford, 1966); Walter B. Scaife, *Florentine Life during the Renaissance* (Baltimore, 1893); Ferdinand Schevill, *History of Florence: From the Founding of the City through the Renaissance*, 1st ed. (New York, 1936), 374–407, and *The Medici* (New York, 1949); and George Frederick Young, *The Medici* (New York, 1933), 149–224. See also Luca Landucci, *A Florentine Diary from 1450 to 1516*, reprint of 1927 ed. (New York, 1969), a contemporary source, for appropriate references, especially to the embassy to the Pope, the Pazzi conspiracy, the mission to Naples, and the death and funeral of Lorenzo. See also Lauro Martines, *The Social World of the Florentine Humanists, 1390–1460* (Princeton, 1963) for Lorenzo's relations with the literati.

9. Schevill, *History of Florence*, 397–398, and Mee, 78–79.

10. Schevill, *History of Florence*, 396.

11. Ibid., 398–399.

12. Young, 199.

13. Ibid., 192–193.

14. Ibid., 198.

15. Ibid.

16. Ibid., 201.

17. Angelo Poliziano (1454–1494).

18. Pico della Mirandola (1463–1494).

19. Quoted in Schevill, *History of Florence*, 409.

20. Hebrews 11:1; 2 Corinthians 4:18; 1 Corinthians 13:2.

21. Cleugh, 177.

22. Ibid., 178.

23. Petrarch, vol. 1, books 1–9, 25.

CHAPTER 7, GOLD COINS AND A GOLDEN AGE

1. Ferdinand Schevill, *History of Florence: From the Founding of the City through the Renaissance*, 1st ed. (New York, 1936), 289.

2. Ibid., 288.

3. John Adams to Abigail Adams, May 12, 1780. *Letters of John Adams, Addressed to His Wife*, ed. Charles Francis Adams (Boston, 1841), 1:68.

4. Giuseppe Martinelli, ed., *The World of Renaissance Florence* (New York, 1968), 167.

5. Trewin Copplestone, ed., *World Architecture* (1966; reprint, London and New York, 1973), 239.

6. Schevill, 330.

7. Glenn M. Andres, John M. Hunisak, and A. Richard Turner, *The Art of Florence*, 1st ed. (New York, 1988), 2:870–872.

8. Ibid., 2:870.

9. Ibid., 2:871.

10. As summarized by Schevill, 431.

11. Jean Paul Richter, ed., *The Notebooks of Leonardo da Vinci*, trans. Mrs. R. C. Bell (New York, 1970), 2:397–398. (Translations are accompanied by parallel columns of the original Italian.)

12. Ibid., 1:19.

13. Eugene Hecht, *Physics in Perspective* (Reading, Mass, 1980), 464.

14. Abraham Pais, *Niels Bohr's Times: In Physics, Philosophy, and Polity* (Oxford and New York, 1991), 52–88, 275–315.

15. James Cleugh, *The Medici: A Tale of Fifteen Generations*, 1st ed. (Garden City, N.Y., 1975), 184.

16. Charles L. Mee, *Lorenzo de' Medici and the Renaissance*, 1st ed. (New York, 1969), 133; and Giorgio Vasari, *The Lives of the Painters, Sculptors, and Architects*, trans. A. B. Hinds (London and New York, 1927), 4:111.

17. Ralph Roeder, *The Man of the Renaissance: Four Lawgivers: Savonarola, Machiavelli, Castiglione, Aretino* (New York, 1933), 6.

18. Ibid., 5.

19. Savonarola's 28th Sermon on Ezekiel.

20. Matthew Arnold, "Hebraism and Hellenism," in *Culture and Anarchy*, ed. John Dover Wilson (Cambridge, 1932).

21. Cleugh, 107.

CHAPTER 8, BONFIRE OF THE VANITIES

1. Luca Landucci, *A Florentine Diary from 1450 to 1516* (1927; reprint, New York, 1969), 130–131.

2. Marcia B. Hall, "Savonarola's Preaching and the Patronage of Art," in *Christianity and the Renaissance: Image and Religious Imagination in the Quattrocento*, ed. Timothy Verdon and John Henderson, 1st ed. (Syracuse, N.Y., 1990), 493–522.

3. Ibid., 514–515 n. 7.

4. Jacob Burckhardt, *The Civilization of the Renaissance in Italy*, trans. S. G. C. Middlemore (New York, 1954), 161.

5. Eugenio Garin, "Gian Francesco Pico della Mirandola: Savonarolan Apologetics and the Critique of Ancient Thought," in *Christianity and the Renaissance: Image and Religious Imagination in the Quattrocento*, ed. Timothy Verdon and John Henderson, 1st ed. (Syracuse, N.Y., 1990), 525–527.

6. Geoffrey Hindley, ed., *Larousse Encyclopedia of Music* (New York, 1971), 125.

7. Salvatore Camporeale, "Humanism and the Religious Crisis of the Late Quattrocento: Giovanni Caroli, O.P., and the *Liber Dierum Lucensium*," in *Christianity and the Renaissance: Image and Religious Imagination in the Quattrocento*, ed. Timothy Verdon and John Henderson, 1st ed. (Syracuse, N.Y., 1990), 456–457.

8. Primarily the *Liber dierum lucensium* and the *Vitae nullorum fratrum veate Marie Novelle*.

9. The excellent summary phrase is Camporeale's, 458.

10. Accounts of the actual words spoken by Savonarola vary slightly, but virtually all agree on the content to the extent that the quotation here may at least be regarded as a free translation into English.

11. The best list of troops and order of the march is in Cerretani, *Storia di Firenze*, quoted in George Frederick Young, *The Medici* (New York, 1933), 245.

CHAPTER 9, CYCLE OF FIRE

1. Information on Savonarola is derived primarily from the following sources: Lorenzo Polizzotto, *The Elect Nation: The Savonarlan Movement in Florence, 1494–1545* (New York, 1995); R. Richard Renner, *Savonarola: The First Great Protestant*, 1st ed. (New York, 1965); Roberto Ridolfi, *The Life of Girolamo Savonarola*, trans. Cecil Grayson, (New York, 1959); Ralph Roeder, *The Man of the Renaissance: Four Lawgivers: Savonarola, Machiavelli, Castiglione, Aretino* (New York, 1933); Joseph Schnitzer, *Savonarola*, 2 vols. (Milan, 1931); Ronald M. Steinberg, *Fra Girolamo Savonarola, Florentine Art, and Renaissance Historiography* (Athens, Ohio, 1977); Pasquale Villari, *The Life and Times of Girolamo Savonarola*, 2 vols. (London, 1890); and Donald Weinstein, *Savonarola and Florence: Prophecy and Patriotism in the Renaissance* (Princeton, 1970).

CHAPTER 10, AGE OF GENIUS

1. Salone del Cinquecento.

2. Marcia B. Hall, "Savonarola's Preaching and the Patronage of Art," in *Christianity and the Renaissance: Image and Religious Imagination in the Quattrocento*, ed. Timothy Verdon and John Henderson (Syracuse, N.Y., 1990), 511.

3. Ronald M. Steinberg, *Fra Girolamo Savonarola, Florentine Art, and Renaissance Historiography* (Athens, Ohio, 1977), 86.

4. The reader is free to read what significance he or she will into the fact that neither Leonardo nor Michelangelo completed his fresco. Perhaps it is best not to strain for further symbolism. Failure to complete work was a habit with Leonardo. The cartoons preliminary to his frescoes exerted great influence on other artists.

5. Hall, 510–511.

6. Ibid., 501–502.

7. Ibid., 512.

8. Ibid., 514.

9. Steinberg, 39.

10. Information on Machiavelli is derived primarily from the following sources: Niccolò Machiavelli, *The Discourses of Niccolò Machiavelli*, trans. Leslie J. Walker and ed. W. Stark, 2 vols. (London, 1950); *History of Florence and of the Affairs of Italy, from the Earliest Times to the Death of Lorenzo the Magnificent* (New York, 1960), and *The Prince*, trans. and ed. David Wootton

(Indianapolis and Cambridge, 1995); J. G. A. Pocock, *The Machiavellian Moment: Florentine Political Thought and the Atlantic Republican Tradition* (Princeton, 1975); Ralph Roeder, *The Man of the Renaissance: Four Lawgivers: Savonarola, Machiavelli, Castiglione, Aretino* (New York, 1933); and Pasquale Villari, *The Life and Times of Niccolò Machiavelli*, trans. Linda Villari, 2 vols. (New York, 1878).

11. "Canto degli spiriti beati."

12. Machiavelli to Vettori, December 10, 1513. Villari, 2:158.

13. Machiavelli, *The Discourses,* vol. 1, book 1, discourse 11, paragraph 5, p. 242.

14. Ibid., vol. 1, book 1, discourse 10, paragraph 1, p. 236.

15. To Machiavelli, as to many of the ancient Greeks, a virtuous person was not simply one inclined to the good but one also capable of distinguishing it.

16. Machiavelli, *The Prince*, chapter 25, 74.

17. Machiavelli, *The Prince*, chapter 26, 78.

18. Ibid., chapter 18, 54.

19. Ibid., chapter 19, 56.

20. Machiavelli, *The Discourses*, vol. 2, Book 1, discourse 16, paragraph 1, p. 252.

21. Giorgio Nicodemi, "The Portrait of Leonardo," in *Leonardo da Vinci* (New York, nd.), 14–15.

CHAPTER 11, WHY THE RENAISSANCE LEFT HOME

1. Ferdinand Schevill, *History of Florence: From the Founding of the City through the Renaissance*, 1st ed. (New York, 1936), xiii.

2. Vincent Cronin, *The Florentine Renaissance* (New York, 1967), 266.

CHAPTER 12, SAINTS AND SINNERS—ENGLISH STYLE

1. Vincent Cronin, *The Florentine Renaissance* (New York, 1967), 268.

2. Ibid.

3. Daniel J. Boorstin, *The Discoverers,* 1st ed. (New York, 1983), 424.

4. Albrecht Dürer to Herr Pirkheimer, October 16, 1506, *The Writings of Albrecht Dürer*, trans. and ed. William Martin Conway (New York, 1958), 58.

5. Alf J. Mapp, Jr., *The Golden Dragon: Alfred the Great and His Times* (Lanham, Md., New York, and London, 1987), 85–150.

6. Information on More is derived primarily from the following sources: Sir Thomas More, *Utopia*, trans. and ed. Robert M. Adams (New York, 1975); *Utopia*, trans. Ralph Robinson and ed. Edward Arber, 1551; revised (London, 1869); and William Roper, "The Life of Sir Thomas More, Knight," in *Lives of Saint Thomas More*, ed. E. E. Reynolds (New York, 1963).

7. Roper, 3.

8. The first four editions of *Utopia* were published in Latin in Louvain (1516), Paris (1517), and Basle (twice in 1518). Sir Thomas More or those directly responsible to him were engaged in the preparation of all of these texts. English translations subsequently were based on the Latin texts, but More had no part in these. In variety they range from the 1551 and 1556 translations of Ralph Robinson to the much more idiomatic rendering by Robert M. Adams in 1975. While I admire the Adams Englishing, I have chosen to use the 1556 translation by Robinson, altering it in some places to remove impediments for readers in our time. This does no violence to More's language, as he wrote the work in Latin, not in English. Latin and English syntax are so different that an attempt at transliteration from the ancient tongue to the vernacular would fail to convey the spirit and character of the original. The much more inflected nature of the classical language gives coherence to sentences that, to be easily comprehensible in English, must be tightened up and subjected to well-defined subordination. I have sought to retain the fidelity of the Robinson translation while occasionally approaching the fluency of the Adams version. This attempt necessarily

falls short of the goal. I recommend that the truly enterprising student of *Utopia* read both the Robinson and the Adams translations.

9. Latin *servus* meant either "slave" or "one who serves."

10. Desiderius Erasmus to Ulrich von Hutten, *The Epistles of Erasmus: From His Earliest Letters to His Fifty-First Year, Arranged in Order of Time,* trans. and ed. Francis Morgan Nichols (New York, 1962), 3:390–391.

CHAPTER 13, GLORIANA

1. Information on Elizabeth I is derived primarily from the following sources: Lucy Aikin, *Memoirs of the Court of Elizabeth, Queen of England* (New York, 1870); John Bennett Black, *The Reign of Elizabeth, 1558–1603,* 2d ed. (Oxford, 1959); Lisa Hopkins, *Elizabeth I and Her Court* (New York, 1990); Joel Hurstfield, *Elizabeth I and the Unity of England* (New York, 1960); Elizabeth Jenkins, *Elizabeth the Great,* 1st American ed. (New York, 1959); Paul Johnson, *Elizabeth I: A Biography* (New York, 1974); Carole Levin, *The Heart and Stomach of a King* (Philadelphia, 1991); Wallace T. MacCaffrey, *Elizabeth I* (London and New York, 1993), *Queen Elizabeth and the Making of Policy, 1572–1588* (Princeton, 1981), and *The Shaping of the Elizabethan Regime* (Princeton, 1968); Conyers Read, *Lord Burghley and Queen Elizabeth* (New York, 1960), *Mr. Secretary Cecil and Queen Elizabeth* (New York, 1960), and *Mr. Secretary Walsingham and the Policy of Queen Elizabeth* (Oxford, 1925). Francis Teague, in "Queen Elizabeth in Her Speeches" (in *Dissing Elizabeth: Negative Representations of Gloriana* [Durham, N.C., 1998], 63–78), questions the authenticity of Elizabeth's Tilbury speech as the Spanish Armada approached.

2. Ben Jonson, "Ben Jonson's Conversations with William Drummond," in *Ben Jonson,* ed. C. H. Herford and Percy Simpson (1925; reprint, Oxford, 1954), 1:142; Sir John Ernest Neale, *Elizabeth I and Her Parliaments,* 2 vols. (New York, 1953–1958), and *Queen Elizabeth I* (London, 1959); A. L. Rowse, *The England of Elizabeth: The Structure of Society,* 2 vols. (New York, 1951); Anne Somerset, *Elizabeth I* (New York, 1991); Neville Williams, *The Life and Times of Elizabeth I* (London, 1972).

3. James Anthony Froude, *History of England from the Fall of Wolsey to the Death of Elizabeth* (New York, 1870), 12:393.

4. A. W. Ward, G. W. Prothero, and Stanley Leathes, eds., *The Cambridge Modern History,* planned by the late Lord Acton (Cambridge, 1969), 3:289.

5. *Hamlet* 2. 2.

6. *Richard* 2. 1.

7. Though Sir Walter's name today is commonly spelled Raleigh, he himself customarily spelled it Ralegh. Information on Ralegh is derived primarily from the following sources: Jack H. Adamson and H. F. Folland, *The Shepherd of the Ocean: An Account of Sir Walter Ralegh and His Times* (Boston, 1969); Donald Barr Chidsey, *Sir Walter Raleigh: That Damned Upstart* (New York, 1931); Philip Edwards, *Sir Walter Raleigh* (London, 1953); Margaret Irwin, *That Great Lucifer: A Portrait of Sir Walter Raleigh* (New York, 1960); Sir Walter Ralegh, *The History of the World,* Extracts from the 1st ed., ed. C. A. Patrides (Philadelphia, 1971), and *The Poems of Sir Walter Ralegh,* ed. Agnes M. C. Latham (Cambridge, Mass., 1951); A. L. Rowse, *Raleigh and the Throckmortons* (London, 1962); Ernest Albert Strathmann, *Sir Walter Ralegh: A Study in Elizabethan Skepticism* (1953; reprint, New York, 1973); Willard Mosher Wallace, *Sir Walter Raleigh* (Princeton, 1959); and Norman Lloyd Williams, *Sir Walter Raleigh* (Philadelphia, 1962).

8. Chidsey, 40.•

9. Samuel Eliot Morison, *The European Discovery of America, The Northern Voyages A.D. 500–1600* (New York, 1971), 651.

10. Ibid., 657–658.

11. Strathmann, 251.

12. Ibid.

13. *Henry VI,* part 2, act 3, sc. 1.

14. From Ralegh's "Nature, That Washed Her Hands in Milk."

15. Sometimes quoted as "So long as the heart is right, it is no matter which way the head lies."

16. Albert C. Baugh, ed., *A Literary History of England* (New York, 1988), 625.

CHAPTER 14, "ALL KNOWLEDGE FOR MY PROVINCE"

1. Information on Bacon is derived primarily from the following sources: Fulton Henry Anderson, *The Philosophy of Francis Bacon* (Chicago, 1948); Francis Bacon, *Essays of Bacon*, ed. Henry Morley (Cleveland, 1946); *The New Organum and Related Writings,* ed. Fulton Henry Anderson (New York, 1960); *The Philosophical Works of Francis Bacon*, ed. John M. Robertson (London, 1905), and *The Works of Francis Bacon*, ed. James Spedding, Robert Leslie Ellis, and Douglas Denon Heath, 15 vols. (Boston, 1860–1864); Charlie Dunbar Broad, *The Philosophy of Francis Bacon* (Cambridge, 1926); Benjamin Farrington, *Francis Bacon: Philosopher of Industrial Science* (New York, 1949), and *The Philosophy of Francis Bacon: An Essay on Its Development from 1603 to 1609*, with new translations of fundamental texts (Liverpool, 1964); Paolo Rossi, *Francis Bacon: From Magic to Science* (Chicago, 1968); Alfred Edward Taylor, "Francis Bacon," *Proceedings of the British Academy* (1927), 12:273–294; and Charles Whitney, *Francis Bacon and Modernity* (New Haven, 1986).

2. Hazelton Spencer, *British Literature* (Lexington, Mass, 1974), 1:509–510.

3. Comparison of the first and final versions of the *Essays* is possible because both were printed in *Essays of Bacon,* Introduction by Henry Morley (Cleveland, 1946).

4. *De principiis atque originibus secundum fabulas cupidinis et coeli.*

5. Sir Thomas Littleton, *Littleton's "Tenures" in English*, ed. Eugene Wambaugh (1903; reprint, Littleton, Colo., 1985), lix–lxiv.

6. Ibid., lxiii.

7. Rossi, 186–189, 219–223.

8. Farrington, *The Philosophy of Francis Bacon*, 63–64. Also Rossi, 195.

9. *The Works of Francis Bacon*, ed. Spedding, Ellis, and Heath, 13:155–156.

10. Anderson, 9.

11. Ibid., 10.

12. *The Works of Francis Bacon*, ed. Spedding, Ellis, and Heath, 6:168.

CHAPTER 15, THE GRAND DESIGN

1. Title page for *The Great Instauration,* in *The Works of Francis Bacon*, ed. James Spedding, Robert Leslie Ellis, and Douglas Denon Heath (Boston, 1860–1864), 1:194.

2. Ibid., 8:17–18.

3. Anthony Grafton, *New Worlds, Ancient Texts: The Power of Tradition and the Shock of Discovery* (Cambridge, Mass., 1992), 3.

4. Quoted in Grafton, 1, from *Historia natural y moral de las Indias,* trans. E. Grimston, n.d.

5. *The Works of Francis Bacon,* ed. Spedding, Ellis, and Heath, 8:76. Subsequent translations are also from Spedding.

6. Some have suggested that the choice was not Bacon's, but strong tradition asserts otherwise.

7. Bacon's attitude toward classical fables is discussed in Paolo Rossi, *Francis Bacon: From Magic to Science* (Chicago, 1968), 73–134.

8. Quoted in Rossi, ix.

9. Ibid., 146.

10. Alf J. Mapp, Jr., *Thomas Jefferson: A Strange Case of Mistaken Identity* (Lanham, Md., New York, and London, 1987), 3, 19, 20, 194, 417, and *Thomas Jefferson: Passionate Pilgrim* (Lanham, Md., New York, and London, 1991), 208, 297, 321.

CHAPTER 16, THE GREAT MAGICIAN

1. Aside from Shakespeare's own work, information on him is derived primarily from the following sources: Joseph Quincy Adams, *A Life of William Shakespeare* (Boston and New York, 1925); Peter Alexander, *Shakespeare's Life and Art* (New York, 1961); Henry R. D. Anders, *Shakespeare's Books: A Dissertation on Shakespeare's Reading and the Immediate Sources of His Works* (Berlin, 1904); Thomas Whitfield Baldwin, *William Shakespeare's Small Latine and Lesse Greeke . . .*, 2 vols. (Urbana, Ill., 1944); Gerald Eades Bentley, *Shakespeare: A Biographical Handbook* (New Haven, 1961), and *Shakespeare and Jonson: Their Reputations in the Seventeenth Century Compared* (Chicago and London, 1965); Geoffrey Bullough, ed., *Narrative and Dramatic Sources of Shakespeare*, 8 vols. (New York and London, 1957–1975); E. K. Chambers, *William Shakespeare: A Study of Facts and Problems*, 2 vols. (Oxford, 1930); H. B. Charlton, *Shakespearian* [sic] *Comedy* (London and New York, 1938), and *Shakespearian Tragedy* (Cambridge and Toronto, 1948); Leonard Fellows Dean, ed., *Shakespeare: Modern Essays in Criticism* (New York, 1967); Michael Dobson, *The Making of the National Poet: Shakespeare, Adaptation, and Authorship, 1660–1769* (Oxford, 1992); Katherine Duncan-Jones, ed., *Shakespeare's Sonnets* (Walton-on-Thames, 1997); Russell Fraser, *Shakespeare: The Later Years* (New York and Oxford, 1992); Edgar Innes Fripp, *Shakespeare: Man and Artist*, 2 vols. (London, 1938); Harley Granville-Barker and G. B. Harrison, eds., *A Companion to Shakespeare Studies* (Cambridge, 1959); G. B. Harrison, *Shakespeare at Work, 1592–1603* (Ann Arbor, 1958); William Allan Neilson and Ashley Horace Thorndike, *The Facts about Shakespeare* (New York, 1961); M. Reese, *Shakespeare: His World and His Work* (London and New York, 1953); Anne Ridler, ed., *Shakespeare Criticism, 1919–1935* (London, 1936); A. L. Rowse, *Shakespeare: The Man*, 1st American ed. (New York, 1973), *Shakespeare the Man*, rev. ed. (New York, 1988), and *William Shakespeare: A Biography*, 1st ed. (New York, 1963); Samuel Schoenbaum, *Shakespeare's Lives* (Oxford and New York, 1970); William Shakespeare, *Mr. William Shakespeare's Comedies, Histories, and Tragedies*, facsimile of 1st folio, ed. H. Kökeritz and C. T. Prouty (New Haven, 1954); *The Riddle of Shakespeare's Sonnets: The Text of the Sonnets*, ed. Edward Hubler et al., 1st ed. (New York, 1962), and *The Sonnets*, ed. William Burto with introduction by W. H. Auden (New York, 1965); Peter Thomson, *Shakespeare's Professional Career* (Cambridge and New York, 1992); Stanley W. Wells, ed., *Current Approaches to Shakespeare: Language, Text, Theatre and Ideology* (New York, 1988), and *William Shakespeare: A Textual Companion* (Oxford and New York, 1987); John Dover Wilson, *The Essential Shakespeare: A Biographical Adventure* (Cambridge and New York, 1932). Fairness requires a notation that Professor Richard Wilson of England's Lancaster University, and some other Shakespearean scholars, hold that John Shakespeare, the playwright's father, lived out his life in prosperity. In their view, his excuse that he did not attend Anglican services for "fear of process of debt" was a cover for the fact that he was secretly a Catholic.

2. *Henry V*, 4. 1.

3. *King Lear*, 4. 7.

4. *Macbeth*, 1. 5.

5. Thomas De Quincey, "On the Knocking at the Gate in *Macbeth*," 1823.

6. Commonly seen busts of Shakespeare are based principally on the bust by Gerard Jansson, which was placed at his burial place in Stratford Church, Stratford-upon-Avon before 1623, and on the frontispiece to the folio of 1623, which was engraved by Martin Droeshout.

7. *The Sonnets*, ed. Burto, xvii.

8. Rowse, *Shakespeare: The Man* (1973), 87–113.

9. Ben Jonson, "To the Memory of My Beloved, the Author, Mr William Shakespeare," 1623.

CHAPTER 17, BENIGN CONTAGION

1. Information on Spenser is derived primarily from the following sources: Paul J. Alpers, *The Poetry of the "Faerie Queene"* (Princeton, 1967); Tucker Brooke, "Edmund Spenser" and "The Faerie Queene: The Spenserian," in *A Literary History of England*, ed. Albert C. Baugh (New York, 1948); Bernard Eustace Cuthbert Davis, *Edmund Spenser: A Critical Study* (New York, 1962);

Richard C. Frushell and Bernard J. Vondersmith, *Contemporary Thought on Edmund Spenser* (Carbondale and London, 1975); Harrie Stuart Vedder Jones, *A Spenser Handbook* (New York, 1930); William Nelson, *The Poetry of Edmund Spenser: A Study* (New York, 1963); David Hill Radcliffe, *Edmund Spenser: A Reception History* (Columbia, S.C., 1996); James A. Riddell and Stanley Stewart, *Jonson's Spenser: Evidence and Historical Criticism* (Pittsburgh, Pa., 1995); William Lindsay Renwick, *Edmund Spenser: An Essay on Renaissance Poetry* (London, 1925); James A. Riddell and Stanley Stewart, *Jonson's Spenser: Evidence and Historical Criticism* (Pittsburgh, Pa., 1995); Edmund Spenser, *Poetical Works*, ed. J. C. Smith and Ernest De Selincourt (New York, 1961), and *Works: A Variorum ed.*, ed. Edwin Greenlaw et al., 9 vols. (Baltimore, 1932–1949); Gary Waller, *Edmund Spenser: A Literary Life* (New York, 1994); and John Watkins, *The Specter of Dido: Spenser and Virgilian Epic* (New Haven and London, 1995).

2. Brooke, "Edmund Spenser," *A Literary History of England*, ed. Albert C. Baugh (New York, 1948), 483–495.

3. Brooke, "The Faerie Queene: The Spenserian," 501 n. 9.

4. Information on Sidney is derived primarily from the following sources: Alfred Hoyt Bill, *Astrophel* (New York and Toronto, 1937); Tucker Brooke, "Sidney and the Sonneteers," in *A Literary History of England*, ed. Albert C. Baugh (New York, 1948); John Buxton, *Sir Philip Sidney and the English Renaissance*, 3d ed. (London, 1987); Dorothy Connell, *Sir Philip Sidney: The Maker's Mind* (Oxford, 1977); Sherod M. Cooper, *The Sonnets of "Astrophel and Stella": A Stylistic Study* (Paris, 1968); Walter R. Davis and Richard A. Lanham, *Sidney's "Arcadia"* (New Haven, 1965); Katherine Duncan-Jones, *Sir Philip Sidney, Courtier Poet* (New Haven and London, 1991); Fulke Greville, "The Life of the Renowned Sir Philip Sidney," in *The Prose of Fulke Greville, Lord Brooke*, ed. Mark Caldwell, Renaissance Imagination Series, vol. 26 (New York and London, 1987); Roger Howell, *Sir Philip Sidney: The Shepherd Knight* (Boston and Toronto, 1968); David Kalstone, *Sidney's Poetry: Contexts and Interpretations* (Cambridge, Mass., 1965); Dennis Kay, ed., *Sir Philip Sidney: An Anthology of Modern Criticism* (Oxford and New York, 1987); Jon Sherman Lawry, *Sidney's Two "Arcadias": Pattern and Proceeding* (Ithaca, N.Y., 1972); James Marchall Osborn, *Young Philip Sidney, 1572–1577* (New Haven and London, 1972); Forrest G. Robinson, *The Shape of Things Known: Sidney's Apology in its Philosophical Tradition* (Cambridge, Mass., 1972); Neil L. Rudenstine, *Sidney's Poetic Development* (Cambridge, Mass., 1967); Irene Samuel, "The Influence of Plato on Sir Philip Sidney's *Defense of Poesy*," *Modern Language Quarterly* 1 (September 1940), 1:383–391; Sir Philip Sidney, *The Prose Works of Sir Philip Sidney*, ed. Albert Feuillerat, 4 vols. (Cambridge, 1962); Malcolm William Wallace, *The Life of Sir Philip Sidney* (1915; reprint, New York, 1967); Mona Wilson, *Sir Philip Sidney* (1950; reprint, Folcroft, Pa., 1971); and Reinard W. Zandvoort, *Sidney's "Arcadia": A Comparison Between the Two Versions* (Temecula, Calif., 1992).

5. Brooke, "Sidney and the Sonneteers," 479.

6. Published in 1596 in two slightly different versions: *Apologie for Poetrie* and *Defense of Poesie*.

7. Walter Jackson Bate, ed., *Criticism: The Major Texts* (New York, 1952), 77.

8. Information on Jonson is derived primarily from the following sources: Jonas A Barish, *Ben Jonson and the Language of Prose Comedy* (Cambridge, Mass., 1960); Gerald Eades Bentley, *Shakespeare and Jonson: Their Reputations in the Seventeenth Century Compared* (Chicago and London, 1965); T. S. Eliot, "Ben Jonson," in *Selected Essays*, ed. T. S. Eliot (London, 1951); John Jacob Enck, *Jonson and the Comic Truth* (Madison, 1957); Gabriele Bernhard Jackson, *Vision and Judgment in Ben Jonson's Drama* (New Haven, 1968); Ben Jonson, *Ben Jonson*, ed. C. H. Herford and Percy Simpson, 11 vols. (1925; reprint, Oxford, 1954); L. C. Knights, *Drama and Society in the Age of Jonson* (New York, 1937); Edward Bellamy Partridge, *The Broken Compass: A Study of the Major Comedies of Ben Jonson* (New York, 1958); and Algernon Charles Swinburne, *A Study of Ben Jonson* (New York, 1968).

9. Thomas Fuller, *Worthies of England*, ed. John Freeman, abridged 1st ed. (London, 1952), 590–591.

10. Information on Donne is derived primarily from the following sources: R. C. Bald, *John Donne: A Life* (New York and Oxford, 1970); John Donne, *The Poems of John Donne*, ed. Sir Herbert J. C. Grierson, 2 vols. (London, 1912); T. S. Eliot, "The Metaphysical Poets," *Selected Essays*, ed. T. S. Eliot (London, 1951); Sir Herbert J. C. Grierson, ed. Introduction to *Metaphysical*

Lyrics and Poems of the Seventeenth Century: Donne to Butler, 1st ed. (Oxford, 1921); Stanley Johnson, "John Donne and the Virginia Company," *Journal of English Literary History* 14 (1947): 127–138; James Blair Leishman, *The Monarch of Wit* (London, 1965); Derek Parker, *John Donne and His World* (London, 1975); "Dr. Donne to Preach Annual Service," in Edward D. Neill, *History of the Virginia Company of London* (Albany, N.Y., 1869); Murray Roston, *The Soul of Wit: A Study of John Donne* (Oxford, 1974); A. J. Smith, ed., *John Donne: Essays in Celebration* (London, 1972); Joan Webber, *Contrary Music: The Prose Style of John Donne* (Madison, 1963); and George Williamson, *The Donne Tradition: A Study in English Poetry from Donne to the Death of Cowley* (New York, 1958). I am grateful to George Holbert Tucker for the use of some materials relating to John Donne.

11. Samuel Johnson, "Cowley," in *Lives of the English Poets*, ed. George Birkbeck Hill, vol. I (Oxford, 1905), 21.

12. T. S. Eliot, "The Metaphysical Poets," *Selected Essays*, ed. T. S. Eliot (London, 1951), 281.

13. Information on Hakluyt is derived primarily from the following sources: Richard Hakluyt, *The Original Writings and Correspondence of the Two Richard Hakluyts*, ed. E. G. R. Taylor, vol. 2 (London, 1935), and *The Principal Navigations, Voyages, Traffiques, and Discoveries of the English Nation*, 12 vols. (Glasgow, 1903–1905) (Short-titled *Hakluyt's Voyages* in various editions); Samuel Eliot Morison, The *European Discovery of America, The Northern Voyages, A.D. 500–1600* (New York, 1971); George Bruner Parks, *Richard Hakluyt and the English Voyages*, ed. James A. Williamson, 2d ed. (New York, 1961); and Richard Hakluyt, *Richard Hakluyt and His Successors*, ed. Edward Lynam (London, 1946).

14. "The Epistle Dedicatory to Sir Francis Walsingham, in the First Edition, 1589," in *The Principal Navigations*, 1:xvii–xviii. (The quoted version of the Psalm is slightly different from the King James Version, which was not published until 1611.)

15. Parks, 162–163.

16. Ibid., 205.

17. Fuller, 224.

18. James Anthony Froude, *Short Studies on Great Subjects* (London, 1870), 361.

CHAPTER 18, EXPLORERS ALL

1. Information on Harvey is derived primarily from the following sources: William Harvey, *The Circulation of the Blood, and Other Writings*, ed. Kenneth J. Franklin (London and New York, 1963); Kenneth D. Keele, *William Harvey: The Man, the Physician, and the Scientist* (London, 1965); Sir Geoffrey Keynes, *The Life of William Harvey* (Oxford, 1966); Walter Pagel, *William Harvey's Biological Ideas: Selected Aspects and Historical Background* (New York, 1967); and Gweneth Whitteridge, *William Harvey and the Circulation of the Blood* (London and New York, 1971).

2. Information on Gilbert is derived primarily from the following sources: I. Bernard Cohen, "Gilbert and His Successors," in *Benjamin Franklin's Experiments: A New Edition of Franklin's "Experiments and Observations on Electricity,"* ed. I. Bernard Cohen (Cambridge, Mass., 1941); and William Gilbert, *De magnete*, trans. P. Fleury Mottelay (1893; reprint, New York, 1958), and *De magnete*, trans. S. P. Thompson (1901; reprint, New York, 1958).

3. Cohen, 21–37.

4. Daniel J. Boorstin, *The Discoverers*, 1st ed. (New York, 1983), 311.

5. Information on Harriot (Hariot) is derived primarily from the following sources: Thomas Hariot [cq], *A Briefe and True Report of the New Found Land of Virginia*, facsimile of the 1st ed. of 1588 (New York, 1903); Muriel Rukeyser, *The Traces of Thomas Hariot* [cq], 1st ed. (New York, 1971); Henry N. Stevens, *Life of Thomas Hariot* [cq] (London, 1900); and examination of original drawings by Harriot.

6. Information on Jones is derived primarily from the following sources: John Alfred Gotch, *Inigo Jones* (New York, 1968); Norbert Lynton, "Renaissance Architecture," in *World Architecture*, ed. Trewin Copplestone (1966; reprint, London and New York, 1973); Stephen Orgel and Roy Strong, *Inigo Jones*, 2 vols. (London, 1973); Sir John Newenham Summerson, *Architecture in Brit-*

ain, 1530–1830 (London and Baltimore, 1953); and Margaret Whinney, *Renaissance Architecture in England* (London, New York, and Toronto, 1952).

7. Lynton, 280.

8. Information on Byrd and the "Golden Age" of English music is derived primarily from the following sources: Edmund Horace Fellowes, *English Cathedral Music*, 5th ed. (London, 1969); *The English Madrigal Composers*, 2d ed. (London and New York, 1948); *Orlando Gibbons: A Short Account of his Life and Work* (Oxford, 1925); *William Byrd*, 2d ed. (London and New York, 1948); Sir George Grove, *The New Grove Dictionary of Music and Musicians*, ed. Stanley Sadie (London, 1980), 3:537–545; Geoffrey Hindley, ed., *Larousse Encyclopedia of Music* (New York, 1971); Joseph Kerman, *The Masses and Motets of William Byrd, Music of William Byrd Series*, vol. 1 (London and Boston, 1981); O. W. Neighbour, *The Consort and Keyboard Music of William Byrd, Music of William Byrd Series*, vol. 3 (London and Boston, 1978); and listening to and analyzing Byrd's music.

9. Information on Coke is derived primarily from the following sources: Sir Edward Coke, *The First Part of the Institutes of the Laws of England, or, A Commentary upon Littleton*, 1st American ed. (Philadelphia, 1853); Sir William Searle Holdsworth, *A History of English Law*, ed. A. L. Goodhart and H. G. Hanbury, 2d ed., vol. 5 (London, 1936–1966); and Samuel Edmund Thorne, *Sir Edward Coke, 1552–1952* [sic] (London, 1957).

10. Stephen Charlton, Levin Denwood, John Nuthall, William Whittington, John Ellis, and Stephen Horsey.

11. Alf J. Mapp, Jr., *Thomas Jefferson: A Strange Case of Mistaken Identity* (Lanham, Md., New York, and London, 1987), 48, and *The Virginia Experiment: The Old Dominion's Role in the Making of America*, 2d ed. (Lanham, Md., and New York, 1987), 131–132; Nora Miller Turman, *The Eastern Shore of Virginia, 1603–1964* (1964; reprint, Bowie, Md., 1988), 54–55; Ralph T. Whitelaw, *Virginia's Eastern Shore: A History of Northampton and Accomack Counties* (Richmond, 1951), 1:28–31, 528–529; Jennings Cropper Wise, *Ye Kingdome of Accawmacke, or The Eastern Shore of Virginia in the Seventeenth Century* (Richmond, 1911), 139–140; Elizabeth S. Haight, "The Northampton Protest of 1652: A Petition to the General Assembly from the Inhabitants of the Eastern Shore," *American Journal of Legal History* 28 (1984): 364–375.

12. Sir Thomas Littleton, *Littleton's Tenures in English*, ed. Eugene Wambaugh (1903; reprint, Littleton, Colo., 1985), lxiii.

13. Ibid., lxii.

14. Ibid., lxvii–lxxxiv.

15. Jefferson to John Page, December 25, 1762, *The Papers of Thomas Jefferson*, ed. Julian P. Boyd, L. H. Butterfield, and Charles T. Cullen (Princeton, 1950–1992), 1:3–4; Mapp, *Thomas Jefferson: A Strange Case of Mistaken Identity*, 25–27.

16. Information on Edwin Sandys is derived primarily from the following sources: Matthew Page Andrews, *Virginia: The Old Dominion* (Richmond, 1949); Alexander Brown, *The Genesis of the United States: A Narrative of the Movement in England, 1605–1616*, 2 vols. (New York, 1964); Edward Channing, *A History of the United States* (New York, 1933), 1:190–93; Wesley Frank Craven, *Dissolution of the Virginia Company: The Failure of a Colonial Experiment* (New York, 1932), 27–28, 41–44, 46, 67, 136–139, 154–162; Mapp, *The Virginia Experiment, The Old Dominion's Role in the Making of America*, 2d ed., 13–80; J. Hall Pleasants, "The Lovelace Family and Its Connections," *The Virginia Magazine of History and Biography* 29 (1921): 231–242; William Stith, *The History of the First Discovery and Settlement of Virginia* (Williamsburg, 1747); and Virginia Company of London, *The Records of the Virginia Company of London*, ed. Susan Myra Kingsbury (Washington, D.C., 1906–1935), 1:212, 4:94.

17. Andrews, *Virginia: The Old Dominion*, 43.

18. Matthew Page Andrews, *Virginia Magazine of History and Biography* 52:91.

19. James Truslow Adams, *The March of Democracy* (New York and London, 1932–1933), 1:22.

20. John Fiske, *Old Virginia and Her Neighbours* (Boston, 1899), 1:187.

CHAPTER 19, "WESTWARD THE COURSE"

The chapter title is from George Berkeley, *On the Prospect of Planting Arts and Learning in America*, 1752.

1. Information on George Sandys is derived primarily from the following sources: Richard Beale Davis, *George Sandys, Poet Adventurer: A Study in Anglo-American Culture in the Seventeenth Century* (London and New York, 1955); Jonathan Haynes, *The Humanist as Traveler: George Sandys' Relation of a Journey Begun an. Dom. 1610* (Rutherford, N.J., 1986); Boies Penrose, *Urbane Travelers, 1591–1635* (Philadelphia, 1942); George Sandys, *The Poetical Works of George Sandys*, with introduction and notes by Richard Hooper, 2 vols. (London, 1872); and Geoffrey Tillotson, *On the Poetry of Pope*, 2d ed. (Oxford, 1950).

2. Alf J. Mapp, Jr., *The Virginia Experiment: The Old Dominion's Role in the Making of America*, 2d ed. (Lanham, Md., and New York, 1987), 77.

CHAPTER 20, "WHERE NONE BEFORE HATH STOOD"

The chapter title is from Richard Rich, *Newes from Virginia*, 1610.

1. Alf J. Mapp, Jr., *The Virginia Experiment: The Old Dominion's Role in the Making of America*, 2d ed. (Lanham, Md., and New York, 1987), 495–496 n. 11.

2. Ibid., 64; Captain John Smith, *Travels and Works of Captain John Smith*, ed. Edward Arber (New York, 1967), 2:572–578, 582–583; Alexander Brown, *The First Republic of America: An Account of the Origin of This Nation* (Boston and New York, 1898), 468, 511, and *The Genesis of the United States: A Narrative of the Movement in England, 1605–1616* (New York, 1964), 2:971.

3. William Bradford, *Of Plymouth Plantation, 1620–1647*, ed. Samuel Eliot Morison (New York, 1963), 34, 39, 60, 75–76; Samuel Eliot Morison, "The Plymouth Colony and Virginia," *Virginia Magazine of History and Biography*, 62 (April 1954): 154–158.

4. Virginia M. Meyer and John Frederick Dorman, *Adventurers of Purse and Person: Virginia, 1607–1624/5*, 3d ed. (Richmond, 1987), entries for Bagwell, Cocke, Cary, Barkham-Jenings, Bayly, Bennett, Bland, Buck, Burwell, Calthorpe, Chaplaine, Claiborne, Cole, Croshaw, Curtis, Macock, Martiau, Mason, Bacon, Mathews, Menefie, Littleton, Robins, Thorowgood, Osborne, Peirce, Peirsey, Perry, Savage, Scarburgh, Harmar, Southey, Strachey, Michael, West, Yeardley, Wilkins, Willoughby, Woodhouse, and Wyatt; Matthew M. Wise, *The Littleton Heritage: Some American Descendents of Col. Nathaniel Littleton (1605–1654) of Northampton Co., Virginia and His Royal Forebears* (West Columbia, S.C., 1997) (contains information not only on the Littletons but on the ancestry of many lines of early Virginia settlers allied with them).

5. Louis B. Wright, *The First Gentlemen of Virginia: Intellectual Qualities of the Early Colonial Ruling Class* (San Marino, 1940), 77; and Mapp, 207.

6. Frederick Lewis Weis and Walter Lee Shepperd, Jr., *Ancestral Roots of Sixty Colonists Who Came to New England Between 1623 and 1650*, 6th ed. (Baltimore, 1988).

7. Ibid., 58.

8. Reverend Robert Hunt and George Thorpe. See Mapp, 9, and 63.

9. William Bennett.

10. Robert C. Winthrop, *Life and Letters of John Winthrop, 1630–1649* (reprint, New York, 1971), 2:430.

CHAPTER 21, WHERE THEY WERE IN 1760

1. Thomas Jefferson, *Memoir, Correspondence and Miscellanies from the Papers of Thomas Jefferson*, ed. Thomas J. Randolph (Charlottesville, 1829), 1:2; Alf J. Mapp, Jr., *Thomas Jefferson: A Strange Case of Mistaken Identity* (Lanham, Md., New York, and London, 1987), 18–20; J. E. Morpurgo, *Their Majesties' Royall Colledge: William and Mary in the Seventeenth and Eighteenth Centuries*, 1st ed. (Williamsburg, 1976), 133, 136–140.

2. Crane Brinton, "The Enlightenment," in *The Encyclopedia of Philosophy*, ed. Paul Edwards, vol. 2 (New York and London, 1967), 519–525.

3. Douglas Southall Freeman, *George Washington: A Biography* (New York, 1951), 3:7, n. 11. Freeman points out that this anecdote, probably transmitted to William Wirt through two generations of oral tradition, may not be accurate in every particular.

4. John Adams, *The Selected Writings of John and John Quincy Adams*, ed. Adrienne Koch and William Peden (New York, 1946), 7.

5. Jack Shepherd, *The Adams Chronicles: Four Generations of Greatness* (Boston and Toronto, 1975), 19.

6. Unpublished manuscript of John Mason, c. 1832, quoted in Brent Tarter, "George Mason and the Conservation of Liberty," *Virginia Magazine of History and Biography* 99 (July 1991): 280. The article presents unusually valuable insights.

7. Mapp, 18. *Memoir, Correspondence, and Miscellanies from the Papers of Thomas Jefferson*, ed. Thomas J. Randolph, 1:2.

8. Ibid.

9. For evidence of this wording, see Alf J. Mapp, Jr., *The Virginia Experiment: The Old Dominion's Role in the Making of America*, 2d ed. (Lanham, Md., and New York, 1987), 529–530, n. 87, and Mapp, *Thomas Jefferson: A Strange Case of Mistaken Identity*, 33–35, 426, n. 44; and Edmund S. Morgan and Helen M. Morgan, *The Stamp Act Crisis: Prologue to Revolution* (Chapel Hill, 1953), 89–91.

CHAPTER 22, "BEFORE WE WERE THE LAND'S"

The chapter title is from Robert Frost, "The Gift Outright."

1. Carl Bridenbaugh and Jessica Bridenbaugh, *Rebels and Gentlemen: Philadelphia in the Age of Franklin* (New York, 1962), 3.

2. See Henry Chandlee Forman, *Virginia Architecture in the Seventeenth Century*, Jamestown—350th Anniversary Historical Booklet, no. 11 (Williamsburg, 1957), 19–50.

3. Hugh Jones, *The Present State of Virginia*, ed. Richard Lee Morton (Chapel Hill, N.C., 1956), 67. Some doubt that Wren made the original design. See J. E. Morpurgo, *Their Majesties' Royall Colledge: William and Mary in the Seventeenth and Eighteenth Centuries*, 1st ed. (Williamsburg, 1976), 36–38.

4. Robert Frost, "The Gift Outright."

CHAPTER 23, THE VIRGINIA PATH

1. Alf J. Mapp, Jr., *The Virginia Experiment: The Old Dominion's Role in the Making of America*, 2d ed. (Lanham, Md., and New York, 1987), 3–4.

2. Major events in Virginia in 1619 are discussed in ibid., 41–57.

3. Ibid., 83–115. Other sources are: Samuel Mathews, "The Mutiny of Virginia, 1635: Letter from Capt. Sam'l Mathews Concerning the Eviction of Harvey, Governor of Virginia," *Virginia Magazine of History and Biography* 1 (1894): 416–420; and Thomas Jefferson Wertenbaker, *Virginia under the Stuarts, 1607–1688* (Princeton, 1914), 73–74.

4. Ralph T. Whitelaw, *Virginia's Eastern Shore: A History of Northampton and Accomack Counties* (Richmond, 1951), 1:30.

5. Though not there analyzed in terms of development of a creative society, the chief events of Berkeley's administration are narrated in Mapp, 119–172. Other sources are: Robert Beverley, *The History and Present State of Virginia*, ed. Louis B. Wright (1705; reprint, Chapel Hill, N.C., 1947); Philip Alexander Bruce, *Economic History of Virginia in the Seventeenth Century: An Inquiry into the Material Condition of the People, Based upon Original and Contemporaneous Records*, 2 vols. (New York, 1895–1896); George MacLaren Brydon, *Virginia's Mother Church and the Political Conditions under Which it Grew, 1607–1727*, vol. 1 (Richmond, 1947–1952); Peter Force, comp., *Tracts and Other Papers Relating Principally to the Origin, Settlement, and Progress of the Colonies in North America, from the Discovery of the Country to the Year 1776*, vol. 1 (Washington, D.C., 1836–1846); *Journals of the House of Burgesses of Virginia 1619–1776*, 13 vols., Richmond, 1905–1915; and Thomas Jefferson Wertenbaker, *Torchbearer of the Revolution: The Story of Bacon's Rebellion and Its Leader* (Princeton and London, 1940), and *Virginia under the Stuarts, 1607–1688*.

6. Mapp, 119–172. Other sources are: John B. Frantz, comp., *Bacon's Rebellion: Prologue to the Revolution?* (Lexington, Mass., 1969); and Wilcomb E. Washburn, *The Governor and the Rebel: A History of Bacon's Rebellion in Virginia* (Chapel Hill, N.C., 1957).

CHAPTER 24, ROYAL ROAD TO LEARNING

1. Alf J. Mapp, Jr., *The Virginia Experiment* (Lanham, Md., and New York, 1985), 175–184.

CHAPTER 25, "ARISTOCRACY WITH THE DOORS OPEN"

1. John M. Jennings, *The Library of the College of William and Mary in Virginia, 1693–1793*, quoted in Wilford Kale, *Hark upon the Gale* (Norfolk, Va., 1985), 19.

2. J. E. Morpurgo, *Their Majesties' Royall Colledge: William and Mary in the Seventeenth and Eighteenth Centuries*, 1st ed. (Williamsburg, 1976), 34.

3. For information on Williamsburg planning and Nicholson's achievements, see Alf J. Mapp, Jr., *The Virginia Experiment: The Old Dominion's Role in the Making of America*, 2d ed. (Lanham, Md., and New York, 1987), 175–190. Other sources are: Matthew Page Andrews, *Virginia: The Old Dominion* (Richmond, 1949); Robert Beverley, *The History and Present State of Virginia*, ed. Louis B. Wright (1705; reprint, Chapel Hill, 1947); Philip Alexander Bruce, *Economic History of Virginia in the Seventeenth Century: An Inquiry into the Material Condition of the People, Based upon Original and Contemporaneous Records*, vol. 2 (New York, 1895–1896); Henry Hartwell, James Blair, and Edward Chilton, *The Present State of Virginia and the College*, ed. H. D. Farish (Princeton, 1940); Richard Lee Morton, *Colonial Virginia*, 2 vols. (Chapel Hill, N.C., 1960); Parke Rouse, Jr., *James Blair of Virginia* (Chapel Hill, N.C., 1971); Virginia, *Journals of the House of Burgesses, 1659/60–1693* (Richmond, 1905–1915); and Thomas Jefferson Wertenbaker, *Virginia under the Stuarts, 1607–1688* (Princeton, 1914).

4. Information on Spotswood is derived primarily from the following sources: Leonidas Dodson, *Alexander Spotswood: Governor of Colonial Virginia, 1710–1722* (New York, 1969); Walter Havighurst, *Alexander Spotswood: Portrait of a Governor* (Williamsburg, 1967); Mapp, 213–220; and Alexander Spotswood, *The Official Letters of Alexander Spotswood, Lieutenant-Governor of the Colony of Virginia, 1710–1722*, 2 vols, with introduction and notes by R. A. Brock (Richmond, 1882–1885).

5. Thomas Tileston Waterman, *The Mansions of Virginia, 1706–1776* (Chapel Hill, N.C., 1946), 61.

6. Ibid., 31.

7. Burke Davis, *A Williamsburg Galaxy* (Williamsburg, 1968), 31.

8. Also Thorowgood and Thoroughgood. Virginia M. Meyer and John Frederick Dorman, *Adventures of Purse and Person: Virginia 1607–1624/5*, 3d ed. (Richmond, 1987), 607.

9. Ibid., 322–323.

10. Durand de Dauphiné, *A Huguenot Exile in Virginia, or Voyages of a Frenchman Exiled for His Religion with a Description of Virginia and Maryland* (1687; reprint, with an introduction and notes by Gilbert Chinard, New York, 1934), 117. Information on the Virginia elite may be found in Mapp, 193–220. Other sources are: William Byrd, *Natural History of Virginia*, trans. and ed. R. C. Beatty and W. J. Mulloy (Richmond, 1940), v–xxv, and *The Secret Diary of William Byrd of Westover, 1709–1712*, ed. Louis B. Wright and Marion Tinling (Richmond, 1941); Douglas Southall Freeman, *George Washington: A Biography* (New York, 1951), 1:1–47, 2:279–290; Hartwell, Blair, and Chilton, xxii–xxxv; Burton J. Hendrick, *The Lees of Virginia: Biography of a Family* (Boston, 1935), 3–57; Dumas Malone, *Jefferson the Virginian* (Boston, 1948), 3–16; David John Mays and Edmund Pendleton, *Jefferson and His Time*, vol. 1, *1721–1803: A Biography* (Cambridge, Mass., 1952), 1:3–12; Charles S. Snydor, *Gentlemen Freeholders* (Chapel Hill, 1952), 1–10; Thomas Jefferson Wertenbaker, *The Planters of Colonial Virginia* (New York, 1959); Louis B. Wright, *The First Gentlemen of Virginia: Intellectual Qualities of the Early Colonial Ruling Class* (San Marino, 1940), in its entirety but especially 63–94; together with such sources as the Robert Carter Letter

Books in the archives of the Virginia Historical Society, the Richard Corbin Letter Book in the Virginia State Library, and the official records of Lancaster, Middlesex, Norfolk, and Northampton Counties.

11. Mapp, 280. The information and ideas presented in the last five paragraphs of this chapter are presented also in Chapter 8 of my *Virginia Experiment*. Inevitably, there are similarities between the two presentations.

CHAPTER 26, PURITAN COMMONWEALTH

1. Information on Winthrop is derived primarily from the following sources: Richard S. Dunn, *Puritans and Yankees: The Winthrop Dynasty of New England, 1630–1717* (New York, 1962); Samuel Eliot Morison, *Builders of the Bay Colony* (Boston and New York, 1930), 51–104; Joseph Hopkins Twichell, *John Winthrop: First Governor of the Massachusetts Colony* (New York, 1891); Thomas Franklin Waters, *A Sketch of the Life of John Winthrop the Younger, Founder of Ipswich, Massachusetts, in 1633* (Cambridge, Mass., 1899); John Winthrop, *Winthrop's Journal: History of New England, 1630–1649*, ed. James Kendall Hosmer, 2 vols. (New York, 1908); Robert C. Winthrop, *Life and Letters of John Winthrop, 1588–1649,* 2 vols. (New York, 1971); and Winthrop Family, *Winthrop Papers, 1498–1630,* coauthored by Massachusetts Historical Society, 2 vols. (Boston, 1929–1931).

2. James Truslow Adams, *The Founding of New England* (Boston, 1921), 136–137.

3. Robert C. Winthrop, vol. 1: 296.

4. Morison, 66.

5. Ibid., 72.

6. Ibid., 73.

7. "John Winthrop to His Wife," March 28, 1630, Winthrop Family's *Winthrop Papers, 1498–1630,* 2:224–226.

8. "Journal," John Winthrop, ibid., 2:259.

9. Morison, 84.

10. Description by Governor William Bradford of Plymouth. William Bradford, *Of Plymouth Plantation, 1620–1647*, ed. Samuel Eliot Morison (New York, 1963), 205–206.

11. Adams, 142.

12. Robert C. Winthrop, Vol. II, 430.

13. Thomas Hutchinson, *The History of the Colony of Massachusetts-Bay*, reprint ed., vol. 1 (New York, 1972), Appendix, 497.

14. Terms as Governor 1629–1634, 1637–1640, 1642–1644, 1646–1649.

15. Morison, 87–88.

16. Albert Bushnell Hart, ed., *Commonwealth History of Massachusetts*, vol. 1 (New York, 1966), 108.

16. Ibid., 111–112.

17. Ibid., 112.

18. Ibid., 116.

19. Ibid., 117.

20. Journal entry dated April 13, 1645, *Winthrop's Journal*, James Kendall Hosmer, ed., vol. 2, 225.

21. Morison, 120.

22. Quoted in Morison, 120.

23. The Hutchinson episode is reported in Robert C. Winthrop, vol. 2, 203–215; John Stetson Barry, *The History of Massachusetts: The Colonial Period* (Boston, 1855), 244–266; and Morison, 119–126. Governor Vane is quoted in Barry, 250, and Morison, 120.

24. Morison, 121.

25. Ibid., 98.

26. Ibid., 124–125.

27. Herbert L. Osgood, *The American Colonies in the Seventeenth Century*, vol. 1 (New York, 1904), 377. Opinion endorsed by Adams, 216–217.

28. Figure from Adams, 210.

29. Massachusetts (Colony), *Records of the Governor and Company of the Massachusetts Bay in New England: Printed by Order of the Legislature*, Nathaniel Bradstreet Shurtleff, ed., vol. 1 (Boston, 1853–1854), 109.

30. Quoted in Adams, 172.

31. Adams, 172–173.

32. Ibid., 173.

33. Robert C. Winthrop, "Arbitrary Government Described," vol. 2, Appendix, 448.

34. Morison, 218.

35. Ibid., 219.

36. Ibid., 218.

37. Ibid., 219.

38. Nathaniel Ward, *The Simple Cobler of Aggawam in America*, ed. P. M. Zall (Lincoln, 1969), 29.

39. Ibid., 12–14.

40. Morison, 231.

41. Ibid., 232.

42. Ibid., 234.

43. Adams, 147.

44. Arnold J. Toynbee, *A Study of History,* Abridgement of Vols. I–VI by D. C. Somervell (New York and London, 1947).

45. Thomas Hutchinson, *Hutchinson Papers*, Series: Burt Franklin Research and Source Works, Reprint of 1865 ed., vol. 1 (New York, 1967), 174.

46. Learned Hand (1872–1961) in *The Faith We Fight For.*

47. Hart, vol. 1, 483.

48. Ibid., 483–484.

49. Morison, 188–189.

50. Jack P. Greene, *Pursuits of Happiness: The Social Development of Early Modern British Colonies and the Formation of American Culture* (Chapel Hill, N.C., and London, 1988), 38.

CHAPTER 27, THE CLOUD-VEILED SUN

1. William Hubbard, *The Happiness of a People, In the Wisdome of Their Rulers Directing and in the Obedience of their Brethren Attending Unto What Israel Ought to Do: Recommended in a Sermon* (Boston, 1676), 36.

2. Samuel Eliot Morison, *The Founding of Harvard College* (Cambridge, Mass., 1935), 228–240.

3. Samuel Torrey, *An Exhortation unto Reformation* (Cambridge, Mass., 1674), 16–17.

4. Thomas Jefferson Wertenbaker, *The Puritan Oligarchy: The Founding of American Civilization* (New York and London, 1947), 149.

5. Ibid.

6. Ibid., 150.

7. Ibid., 151.

8. See Increase Mather's presidency in Samuel Eliot Morison, *Harvard College in the Seventeenth Century,* vol. 2 (Cambridge, Mass., 1936), 472–536.

9. Wertenbaker, 154.

10. Ibid.

11. Ibid., 161–162.

12. Ibid., 164.

13. Testimony of Henry Newman, secretary of the Society for the Promotion of Christian Knowledge in London. Quoted in Morison, *Harvard College in the Seventeenth Century*, vol. 2, 505–506.

14. Samuel Eliot Morison, *Three Centuries of Harvard, 1636–1936* (Cambridge, Mass., and London, 1936), 46.

15. Jack P. Greene, *Pursuits of Happiness: The Social Development of Early Modern British Colonies and the Formation of American Culture* (Chapel Hill, N.C., and London, 1988), xiii.

16. Ibid., 81.

17. Ibid., 60, 101.

18. Ibid., 64.

19. Ibid., 176.

20. Increase Mather, *An Essay for the Recording of Illustrious Providences* (1684) (New York, 1977), Preface.

21. Milton R. Stern and Seymour L. Gross, *American Literature Survey: Colonial and Federal to 1800*, vol. 1 (New York, 1975), 109.

22. Wertenbaker, 271–280, 282–288.

23. Ibid., 265.

24. Samuel Eliot Morison, *The Intellectual Life of Colonial New England*, 4th ed. (New York, 1970), 252.

CHAPTER 28, SCIENCE ENSLAVED

1. Charles Francis Adams, *Massachusetts: Its Historians and History, an Object Lesson* (Boston, 1893), 59.

2. Samuel Eliot Morison, preface to *The Intellectual Life of Colonial New England*, 4th ed. (New York, 1970).

3. Ibid., 35.

4. Ibid., 113–118.

5. Information on Bradstreet is derived primarily from the following sources: Anne Bradstreet, *The Tenth Muse*, ed. Josephine K. Piercy (Gainesville, 1965); Anne Bradstreet, *The Works of Anne Bradstreet*, ed. Jeannine Hensley (Cambridge, Mass., 1967); and Elizabeth Wade White, *Anne Bradstreet, "The Tenth Muse"* (New York, 1971).

6. Account of Taylor largely based on my reading of his poetry.

7. Mary White Rowlandson, *The Soveraignty and Goodness of God, Together with the Faithfulness of his Promises Displayed, Being a Narrative of the Captivity and Restauration of Mrs. Mary Rowlandson* (Boston, 1682).

8. Ibid., 3.

9. Ibid., 12.

10. Ibid., 76.

11. Morison, 123–124.

12. Ibid., 195.

13. Ibid., 127.

14. From "The Garrison of Cape Ann," quoted by Morison, 196.

15. Also called *Compendium Physicae*.

16. Psalm 19.

17. George L. McMichael, ed., *Anthology of American Literature* (New York, 1974), 1:224 ("the first modern American" and "America's" last medieval man); Nathan O. Hatch and Harry S. Stout, eds., *Jonathan Edwards and the American Experience* (New York and Oxford, 1988), 3 ("a prophet of modernity" and "a great anachronism"). Information on Edwards is derived primarily from the following sources: Alfred Owen Aldridge, *Jonathan Edwards* (New York, 1966); Jonathan Edwards, *Benjamin Franklin and Jonathan Edwards: Selections from Their Writings*, ed. Carl Van Doren (New York and Chicago, 1920), *Representative Selections*, ed. Clarence Henry Faust and Thomas Herbert Johnson, revised ed. (New York, 1962), and *Scientific and Philosophical Writings, Works of Jonathan Edwards*, ed. Wallace E. Anderson, vol. 6 (New Haven and London, 1980); Terrence Erdt, *Jonathan Edwards: Art and the Sense of the Heart* (Amherst, Mass., 1980); Norman Fiering, *Jonathan Edwards' Moral Thought and Its British Context* (Chapel Hill, N.C., 1981); Edward M. Griffin, *Jonathan Edwards* (Minneapolis, 1971); Nathan O. Hatch and Harry S. Stout, eds., *Jonathan Edwards and the American Experience* (New York and Oxford, 1988); Perry Miller,

Jonathan Edwards (New York, 1949); and Ola Elizabeth Winslow, *Jonathan Edwards, 1703–1758: A Biography* (New York, 1941).

18. Miller, 36.

19. Edwards, *Scientific and Philosophical Writings*, ed. Anderson, 6:1–6, 147–153.

20. Jonathan Edwards, *Personal Narrative*.

21. Winslow, 147–148.

22. Phrase used in lecture by Dr. Ramona H. Mapp.

23. Quoted in Miller, 301.

24. Francis A Christie, "Jonathan Edwards," in *Dictionary of American Biography*, ed. Allen Johnson and Dumas Malone (New York, 1959), vol. 3, part 2, 36.

25. Aldridge, 1.

26. Moses Coit Tyler, *A History of American Literature, 1607–1765* (Ithaca, N.Y., 1949), 422, 1878.

CHAPTER 29, THE PHILADELPHIA WIZARD

1. Information on Franklin is derived primarily from the following sources: Alfred Owen Aldridge, *Benjamin Franklin and Nature's God* (Durham, N.C., 1967), *Benjamin Franklin: Philosopher and Man* (Philadelphia and New York, 1965), and *Franklin and His French Contemporaries* (New York, 1957); Douglas Anderson, *The Radical Enlightenments of Benjamin Franklin* (Baltimore and London, 1997); John Hardin Best, *Benjamin Franklin on Education* (New York, 1962); Roger Burlingame, *Benjamin Franklin: Envoy Extraordinary* (New York, 1967); I. Bernard Cohen, *Benjamin Franklin: Scientist and Statesman* (New York, 1975), and *Science and the Founding Fathers: Science in the Political Thought of Jefferson, Adams, Franklin, and Madison* (New York and London, 1995); I. Bernard Cohen, ed. *Benjamin Franklin's Experiments: A New Edition of Franklin's "Experiments and Observations on Electricity"* (Cambridge, Mass., 1941); Verner W. Crane, *Benjamin Franklin and a Rising People* (Boston, 1954); Cecil B. Currey, *Road to Revolution: Benjamin Franklin in England, 1765–1775* (Garden City, N.Y., 1968); Max Farrand, *Benjamin Franklin's Memoirs* (Cambridge, Mass., 1936), reprinted for private circulation by the *Huntington Library Bulletin*, no. 10 (October 1936): Thomas J. Fleming, *The Man Who Dared the Lightning: A New Look at Benjamin Franklin* (New York, 1971); Paul Leicester Ford, *The Many-Sided Franklin* (1898; reprint, Freeport, N.Y., 1972); Benjamin Franklin, *Benjamin Franklin and Jonathan Edwards: Selections from Their Writings*, ed. Carl Van Doren (New York and Chicago, 1920); *Educational Views of Benjamin Franklin*, ed. Thomas Woody (New York, 1971), and *The Writings of Benjamin Franklin*, ed. Albert Henry Smyth, vol. 1 (New York, 1905); Bruce Ingham Granger, *Benjamin Franklin: An American Man of Letters* (Ithaca, N.Y., 1964); Claude-Anne Lopez, *Mon Cher Papa: Franklin and the Ladies of Paris* (New Haven and London, 1966); Robert Middlekauff, *Benjamin Franklin and His Enemies* (Berkeley, Los Angeles, and London, 1996); Richard D. Miles, "The American Image of Benjamin Franklin," *American Quarterly* 9 (Summer 1957): 117–143; David T. Morgan, *The Devious Dr. Franklin, Colonial Agent* (Macon, Ga., 1996); Carl Van Doren, *Benjamin Franklin* (New York, 1938); and Dilys P. Winegard, *The Intellectual World of Benjamin Franklin* (Philadelphia, 1990).

2. Van Doren, 220–223.

3. *The Writings of Benjamin Franklin*, ed. Smyth, 1:388.

4. Alan Tully, *Forming American Politics: Ideas, Interests, and Institutions in Colonial New York and Pennsylvania* (Baltimore and London, 1994), 200. The friend was John Hughes, leader of the Quaker Party. Franklin's own newspaper refused to print his recommendation that Hughes be appointed.

5. Farrand, 53.

6. Ibid., 53.

7. John Adams, *The Works of John Adams, Second President of the United States: With a Life of the Author, Notes, and Illustrations*, ed. Charles Francis Adams (Boston, 1856), vol. 1, appendix, 660.

8. Van Doren, 713.

CHAPTER 30, "THE GREAT LITTLE MADISON"

1. Property of the Library of Congress, reproduced in Conover Hunt-Jones, *Dolley and "the Great Little Madison"* (Washington, D.C., 1977), 6.

2. Hunt-Jones, *Dolley and "the Great Little Madison,"* 12.

3. Information on Madison is derived primarily from the following sources: Henry Adams, *History of the United States during the Administrations of Jefferson and Madison*, 9 vols. (New York, 1891–1893); Lance Banning, *The Sacred Fire of Liberty: James Madison and the Founding of the Federal Republic* (Ithaca, N.Y., 1995); Samuel Flagg Bemis, ed., *The American Secretaries of State and Their Diplomacy*, vol. 3 (New York, 1958); Irving Brant, *James Madison: Commander-in-Chief, 1812–1836*, James Madison Series, vol. 6 (Indianapolis and New York, 1961), *James Madison: Father of the Constitution, 1787–1800*, James Madison Series, vol. 3 (Indianapolis and New York, 1950), *James Madison: The Nationalist, 1780–1787*, James Madison Series, vol. 2 (Indianapolis and New York, 1948), *James Madison: The President, 1809–1812*, James Madison Series, vol. 5 (Indianapolis and New York, 1956), *James Madison: Secretary of State, 1800–1809*, James Madison Series, vol. 4 (Indianapolis and New York, 1953), and *James Madison: The Virginia Revolutionist, 1751–1780*, James Madison Series, vol. 1 (Indianapolis and New York, 1941); Edmund C. Burnett, ed., *Letters of Members of the Continental Congress*, 8 vols. (1921; reprint, Gloucester, Mass., 1963); *Journal of the Federal Convention, The Debates in the Federal Convention of 1787*, ed. Gaillard Hunt and James B. Scott (Westport, Conn., 1970); Sydney Howard Gay, *James Madison* (Boston, 1898); Hugh Blair Grigsby, *The History of the Virginia Federal Convention of 1788*, ed. R. A. Brock, 2 vols. (Richmond, 1890–1891); Gaillard Hunt, *The Life of James Madison* (New York, 1902); Hunt-Jones, *Dolley and "the Great Little Madison"*; Thomas Jefferson, *The Papers of Thomas Jefferson*, ed. Julian P. Boyd, L. H. Butterfield, and Charles T. Cullen, 25 vols. (Princeton, 1950–1992), and *The Republic of Letters: The Correspondence between Thomas Jefferson and James Madison, 1776–1826*, ed. James Morton Smith, 3 vols. (New York and London, 1995); Adrienne Koch, *Jefferson and Madison: The Great Collaboration* (New York, 1950); Adrienne Koch and Harry Ammon, "The Virginia and Kentucky Resolutions: An Episode in Jefferson's and Madison's Defense of Civil Liberties," *William and Mary Quarterly*, 3d series, 5 (April 1968); *James Madison: A Biography in His Own Words*, ed. Merrill D. Peterson, (New York, 1974), James Madison Papers, Presidential Papers, Library of Congress, microfilm, 28 reels (Washington, D.C., 1964), *Letters and Other Writings of James Madison*, published by order of Congress, 4 vols. (Philadelphia, 1867), *The Papers of James Madison*, ed. William T. Hutchinson, William M. E. Rachal, and Robert A. Rutland, 15 vols. (Chicago, 1962–1985), *The Papers of James Madison*: Presidential Series, ed. Robert A. Rutland et al., 2 vols. (Charlottesville, Va., 1984), *The Papers of James Madison*: Secretary of State Series, ed. Robert J. Brugger et al., 3 vols. (Charlottesville, Va., 1986), and *The Writings of James Madison*, ed. Gaillard Hunt, 9 vols. (New York, 1900–1910); James Madison, Alexander Hamilton, and John Jay, *The Federalist*, ed. Benjamin Fletcher Wright (Cambridge, Mass., 1961); Richard K. Matthews, *If Men Were Angels: James Madison and the Heartless Empire of Reason* (Lawrence, Kans., 1995); Jack N. Rakove, *James Madison and the Creation of the American Republic*, ed. Oscar Handlin (Glenview, Ill., and London, 1990); William C. Rives, *History of the Life and Times of James Madison*, 3 vols. (Freeport, N.Y., 1970); Robert A. Rutland, *James Madison: The Founding Father* (New York and London, 1987), and *The Presidency of James Madison* (Lawrence, Kans., 1990); Robert A. Rutland, ed., *James Madison and the American Nation, 1751–1836: An Encyclopedia* (New York and London, 1994); and Margaret Bayard Smith, *The First Forty Years of Washington Society, Portrayed by the Family Letters of Mrs. Samuel Harrison Smith from the Collection of Her Grandson, J. Henly Smith* (New York, 1906).

4. Thomas Jefferson to James Madison, December 8, 1784, *The Papers of Thomas Jefferson*, ed. Boyd, Butterfield, and Cullan, 8:558.

5. Brant, *James Madison, Father of the Constitution*, 15.

6. Ibid., 26.

7. Ibid., 11.

8. Ibid., 17.

9. *The Republic of Letters*, ed. Smith, 1:15, 380–383, 440–441.

CHAPTER 31, THE OTHER JAMES

1. Information on Wilson is derived primarily from the following sources: Randolph Greenfield Adams, *Political Ideas of the American Revolution: Britannic-American Contributions to the Problem of Imperial Organization, 1765–1775* (New York, 1939); Charles Page Smith, *James Wilson: Founding Father, 1742–1798* (Chapel Hill, N.C., 1973); and James Wilson, *Selected Political Essays of James Wilson*, ed. Randolph Greenfield Adams (New York, 1930), *The Works of James Wilson*, ed. Robert Green McCloskey, 2 vols. (Cambridge, Mass., 1967), *The Works of James Wilson, Associate Justice of the Supreme Court of the United States*, ed. James DeWitt Andrews, 2 vols. (Chicago, 1896).

2. Page Smith, *A New Age Now Begins: A People's History of the American Revolution* (New York, 1976), 1:544.

3. Perhaps the best portrait illustrative of this description is by Albert Rosenthal. It appears in Irving Brant, *James Madison: Father of the Constitution, 1787–1800*, James Madison Series (Indianapolis and New York, 1950), vol. 3, opposite 33.

4. Alf J. Mapp, Jr., *The Virginia Experiment: The Old Dominion's Role in the Making of America*, 2d ed. (Lanham, Md., and New York, 1987), 131–132; Ralph T. Whitelaw, *Virginia's Eastern Shore: A History of Northampton and Accomack Counties* (Richmond, 1951), 1:28–31; Jennings Cropper Wise, *Ye Kingdome of Accawmacke*, or, *The Eastern Shore of Virginia in the Seventeenth Century* (Richmond, 1911), 134–140; Elizabeth S. Haight, "The Northampton Protest of 1652: A Petition to the General Assembly from the Inhabitants of the Eastern Shore," *American Journal of Legal History* (1984): 364–375; James R. Perry, *The Formation of a Society on Virginia's Eastern Shore, 1615–1655* (Chapel Hill, N.C., 1990), 214–217, 227, 236; Nora Miller Turman, *The Eastern Shore of Virginia 1603–1964* (1964; reprint, Bowie, Md., 1988). Johnson was the chief orator and was singled out for special punishment. His chief associates were Stephen Charlton, Llevyne Denwood, John Nuthall, William Whittington, John Ellis, and Stephen Horsey.

5. Northampton and Accomack county information from Whitelaw, 1:40–41, and Mapp, 318. Frederick County information from Charles Albro Barker, *The Background of the Revolution in Maryland* (New Haven and London, 1940), 305–310; and James McSherry, *History of Maryland* (Baltimore, 1904), 130–133.

CHAPTER 32, HEROIC HYPOCHONDRIAC

1. Information on Mason is derived primarily from the following sources: Florette Henri, *George Mason of Virginia* (New York, 1971); George Mason, *The Papers of George Mason, 1725–1792*, ed. Robert A. Rutland, 3 vols. (Chapel Hill, N.C., 1970); Helen Hill Miller, *George Mason: Gentleman Revolutionary* (Chapel Hill, N.C., 1975); Kate Mason Rowland, *The Life of George Mason, 1725–1792*, 2 vols. (New York, 1892); and Robert A. Rutland, *George Mason: Reluctant Statesman* (Charlottesville, Va., 1963).

2. *Virginia Cavalcade*, 1:14.

3. Alf J. Mapp, Jr., *The Virginia Experiment: The Old Dominion's Role in the Making of America*, 2d ed. (Lanham, Md., and New York, 1987), 430.

4. Edmund Randolph, "Manuscript History of Virginia," Virginia Historical Society Archives.

CHAPTER 33, THE SUN ON THE PRESIDENT'S CHAIR

1. Irving Brant, *James Madison: Father of the Constitution, 1787–1800*, James Madison Series (Indianapolis and New York, 1950), 3:19.

2. Sir Winston Churchill's particularly apt phrase in another context.

3. Information on Randolph is derived primarily from the following sources: Moncure Daniel Conway, *Omitted Chapters of History Disclosed in the Life and Papers of Edmund Randolph* (New York, 1888); Hamilton James Eckenrode, *The Randolphs: The Story of a Virginia Family*, 1st

ed. (Indianapolis and New York, 1946); and Hugh Blair Grigsby, *The History of the Virginia Federal Convention of 1788* (Richmond, 1890–1891), vols. 1 and 2, especially 1:83–86.

CHAPTER 34, "THE MOST REMARKABLE WORK"

1. William Ewert Gladstone, Statement on the celebration of the centennial of the Constitution of the U.S., July 20, 1887.
2. Silvano Arieti, *Creativity: The Magic Synthesis* (New York, 1976), 323.
3. Mortimer Sellers, "American Republicanism," in *Great American Presidents*, ed. Kenneth W. Thompson (Lanham, Md., and New York, 1995), 1:207–223. Professor Sellers discusses the significance of Latin pseudonyms as evidence of Americans' thinking of themselves as Romans.
4. Douglas Adair, "The Disputed Authorship of the Federalist Papers," *William and Mary Quarterly*, April–July 1944.
5. Charles, Baron de Montesquieu, *Spirit of Laws*, vol. 1, book 9, chapter 1.
6. Irving Brant, *James Madison: Father of the Constitution*, 1787–1800, James Madison Series (Indianapolis and New York, 1950), 3:173.
7. Bernard Bailyn, ed., *The Debate on the Constitution: Federalist and Antifederalist Speeches, Articles, and Letters during the Struggle over Ratification* (New York, 1993), 1:1159.

CHAPTER 35, A GENIUS FOR GOVERNMENT

1. Hugh Blair Grigsby, *The History of the Virginia Federal Convention of 1788* (Richmond, 1890), 67–69.
2. Ibid., 81.
3. Ibid., 96–97.
4. Ibid., 96–97.
5. Irving Brant, *James Madison: Father of the Constitution 1878–1800,* James Madison Series (Indianapolis and New York, 1950), 3:173.

CHAPTER 36, WAS WASHINGTON IGNORANT?

1. Alf J. Mapp, Jr., *The Virginia Experiment*, 3d ed. (Lanham, Md., New York, and London), 360. Other sources on Washington, both primary and secondary, are listed in the bibliography.
2. Jack Shepherd, *The Adams Chronicle* (Toronto, 1975), 68.
3. Those who lack the leisure or inclination to study Washington's correspondence may consult Paul A. Rake, *Republics Ancient and Modern: Classical Republicanism and the American Revolution* (Chapel Hill, N.C., 1993).
4. Douglas S. Freeman, *George Washington*, 64 n.112.
5. J. E. Morpurgo, *Their Majesties' Royall Colledge* (Williamsburg, 1976), 97, 112.
6. Ibid., 214.
7. Statue in the rotunda of the state capitol in Richmond, Virginia.
8. James Thomas Flexner, *Washington: The Indispensable Man* (Boston and Toronto, 1974), 94–95.
9. Ibid., 360.
10. Thomas Tileston Waterman, *The Mansions of Virginia, 1706–1776* (Chapel Hill, N.C., 1946), 275. Architectured features of Mount Vernon are discussed on pp. 268–299.
11. Researchers for the Mount Vernon Ladies' Association of the Union, *Mount Vernon, An Illustrated Handbook* (Fairfax, Va., 1974), 40.
12. Flexner, 52.
13. Ibid., 48.
14. Ibid., 52.
15. Jefferson to Dr. Walter Jones, January 2, 1814. The circumstances of the correspondence

are discussed in Alf J. Mapp, Jr., *Thomas Jefferson: Passionate Pilgrim* (Lanham, Md., New York, and London, 1991), 239–241.

16. The term *cabinet* was not used at first in reference to the United States government, but came into use during Washington's presidency.

17. Dumas Malone, *Jefferson and His Time* (Boston, 1962), 3:79–80.

18. Jefferson's career as secretary of state is discussed in some detail in Alf J. Mapp, Jr., *Thomas Jefferson: A Strange Case of Mistaken Identity* (Lanham, Md., New York, and London, 1987), 275–342.

19. The conflict between Jefferson and Hamilton is discussed more extensively in ibid., 283–343. Jefferson's letter to Washington is dated September 9, 1792.

CHAPTER 37, THE PHILOSOPHER-KING AND THE NEW REPUBLIC

1. Alf J. Mapp, Jr., *Thomas Jefferson: A Strange Case of Mistaken Identity* (Lanham, Md., New York, and London, 1987), 370.

2. Thomas Jefferson to Joseph Priestley, March 12, 1801. Paul Leicester Ford, ed., *The Writings of Thomas Jefferson* (New York, 1892), 8:22.

3. Jefferson's presidency is covered in Alf J. Mapp, Jr., *Thomas Jefferson: Passionate Pilgrim* (Lanham, Md., New York, and London, 1991), 1–190.

4. Mapp, *Thomas Jefferson: A Strange Case*, 207.

CHAPTER 38, HOMEGROWN SOLOMON

1. Information on Marshall derived primarily from: Harry Ammon, "Agricola versus Aristides: James Monroe, John Marshall, and the Genet Affair in Virginia," *Virginia Magazine of History and Biography* 71 (1963): 395–418; Albert J. Beveridge, *The Life of John Marshall*, 4 vols. (Boston, 1916); Donald O. Dewey, *Marshall versus Jefferson* (New York, 1970); George L. Haskins, *The Foundations of Power: John Marshall, 1801–1815* (New York, 1981); Charles F. Hobson, *The Great Chief Justice: John Marshall and the Rule of Law* (Lawrence, Kan., 1996); Herbert Alan Johnson, "John Marshall," in *The Justices of the United States Supreme Court, 1789–1978: Their Lives and Major Opinions* (New York and London, 1980), 1:285–351; John Marshall, law notes, account books, and other papers in Special Collections (Archives), Earl Gregg Swem Library, College of William and Mary, Williamsburg, Virginia, and *The Papers of John Marshall*, ed. Charles F. Hobson, vols. 1–7 (Chapel Hill, N.C., 1974–1995); Jean E. Smith, *John Marshall: Definer of a Nation* (New York, 1996); and G. Edward White, *The Marshall Court and Cultural Change, 1815–1835* (Oxford, 1991). I have also benefited from discussions with Professor Charles F. Hobson, one of the best of Marshall biographers and editor of *The Papers of John Marshall*.

2. Burke Davis, *A Williamsburg Galaxy* (Williamsburg and New York, 1968), 212.

3. Ibid.

4. John Marshall's law notes. Polly's name is written in a fancier hand than the rest of the notes. This could mean that a teasing friend or even Polly herself added her name, or that Marshall wrote her name in a fancier style because of his love for her.

5. J. E. Morpurgo, *Their Majesties' Royall Colledge* (Williamsburg, 1976), 133–134, 180.

6. Ibid., 182.

7. Ibid., 187.

8. David John Mays, *Edmund Pendleton 1721–1803: A Biography* (Cambridge, Mass., 1952), 1:168–169.

CHAPTER 39, FROM JAMES TO JAMES

1. Information on Monroe, John Quincy Adams, and the Monroe Doctrine is derived principally from: John Quincy Adams, *Diary of John Quincy Adams, 1794–1845*, ed. Allan Nevins (New

York, 1951), and *Writings*, ed. W. C. Ford, vols. 1 and 3 (New York, 1914); Alejandro Alvarez, *The Monroe Doctrine: Its Importance in the International Life of the States of the New World* (New York, 1924); Harry Ammon, *James Monroe: The Quest for National Identity*, 1st ed. (New York, 1971); Samuel Flagg Bemis, *John Quincy Adams and the Foundations of American Foreign Policy* (New York, 1949), and *John Quincy Adams and the Union* (New York, 1956); Stuart Gerry Brown and Ronald G. Baker, eds., *The Autobiography of James Monroe* (Syracuse, N.Y., 1959); William Penn Cresson, *James Monroe* (Chapel Hill, N.C., 1946); Frederick Merk, *The Monroe Doctrine and American Experiences* (New York, 1966); James Monroe, *Writings*, ed. Stanislaus M. Hamilton, 7 vols. (New York, 1898–1903); Paul Nagel, *Descent from Glory: Four Generations of the John Adams Family* (New York, 1983), and *John Quincy Adams: A Public Life, A Private Life* (New York, 1997); Dexter Perkins, *A History of the Monroe Doctrine*, rev. ed. (Gloucester, Mass., 1963), and *The Monroe Doctrine, 1823–1826* (Gloucester, Mass., 1927); Daniel Preston, "James Monroe, National Boundaries, and the Monroe Doctrine," Monroe Lecture, Mary Washington College, Oct. 15, 1997; Arthur Styron, *The Last of the Cocked Hats: James Monroe and the Virginia Dynasty* (Norman, Okla., 1945); and C. M. Wilson, *The Monroe Doctrine; An American Frame of Mind* (Princeton, 1971). I have also benefited from discussions with Professor Daniel Preston, of the College of William and Mary, judicious editor of *The Monroe Papers*, and Paul C. Nagel, distinguished biographer of John Quincy Adams and foremost chronicler of the long line of famous Adamses.

2. Jack Shepherd, *The Adams Chronicles: Four Generations of Greatness* (Boston and Toronto, 1975), 87.

3. John Adams to Jefferson, January 22, 1825. Lester J. Cappon, ed., *The Adams-Jefferson Letters* (Chapel Hill, N.C., 1958), 606–607.

4. Shepherd, *Adams Chronicles*, 140.

5. Ibid., 142.

6. John Adams to Abigail Adams, May 12, 1780, *Letters of John Adams, Addressed to His Wife*, ed. Charles Francis Adams (Boston, 1841), 1:68.

CHAPTER 40, TOO MUCH CREDIT?

1. Readers interested only in major American figures of the Early National Period may safely skip the rest of this chapter. But those wishing to gauge the creative quality of the age should find it helpful.

2. Bernard Bailyn, *The Ideological Origins of the American Revolution*, enlarged edition (Cambridge, Mass., and London, 1977), 321.

CHAPTER 41, FINDING NATIVE MUSES

1. Discussion of Cooper is based principally on his novels and on the following sources: Charles Haniford Adams, *The Guardian of the Law: Authority and Identity in James Fenimore Cooper* (University Park, Pa., 1990); Martin Barker, *"The Last of the Mohicans": History of an American Myth* (Jackson, Miss., 1995); James Franklin Beard, ed., *The Letters and Journals of James Fenimore Cooper*, 6 vols. (Cambridge, Mass., 1960–1968); James Fenimore Cooper, *Gleanings in Europe: Italy*, ed. Constance A. Denne (Albany, N.Y., 1980), and *Gleanings in Europe: The Rhine*, ed. Ernest Redskop et al. (Albany, N.Y., 1980); Alexander Cowie, *The Rise of the American Novel* (New York, 1948), 115–164; Donald Darnell, *James Fenimore Cooper: Novelist of Manners* (Newark, Del., and London, 1993); Wayne Fields, ed., *James Fenimore Cooper: A Collection of Critical Essays* (Englewood Cliffs, N.J., 1979); Philip Gould, *Covenant and Republic: Historical Romance and the Politics of Puritanism* (Cambridge, 1996), 133–171; James Grossman, *James Fenimore Cooper* (New York, 1949); William P. Kelly, *Plotting America's Past: Fenimore Cooper and the Leatherstocking Tales* (Carbondale, Ill., 1983); William P. Kelly, *Plotting America's Past: Fenimore Cooper and the Leatherstocking Tales* (Carbondale, 1983); Thomas R. Lounsbury, *James Fenimore Cooper* (New York, 1910); Warren Motley, *The American Abraham: James Fenimore Cooper and the Frontier Patriarch* (Cambridge, 1987); Blake Nevius, *Cooper's Landscapes: An Essay on the Picturesque*

Vision (Berkeley, 1976); Orm Overland, *James Fenimore Cooper's "The Prairie": The Making and Meaning of an American Classic* (Oslo, 1973); H. Daniel Peck, *A World by Itself: The Pastoral Moment in Cooper's Fiction* (New Haven and London, 1977); H. Donald Peck, ed., *New Essays on "The Last of the Mohicans"* (Cambridge, 1992); Thomas Philbrick, *James Fenimore Cooper and the Development of American Sea Fiction* (Cambridge, Mass., 1961); Stephen Railton, *Fenimore Cooper: A Study of His Life and Imagination* (Princeton, 1978); Donald A. Ringe, *James Fenimore Cooper* (New York, 1962); and Robert E. Spiller, *Fenimore Cooper: Critic of His Time* (New York, 1931).

2. Discussion of Philip Freneau is based principally on personal study of his published poems and prose and on the following sources: Nelson F. Adkins, *Philip Freneau and the Cosmic Enigma* (New York, 1949); Mary S. Austin, *Philip Freneau: The Poet of the Revolution* (New York, 1901); Jacob Axelrad, *Philip Freneau: Champion of Democracy* (Austin, Tex., and London, 1967); Mary Weatherspoon Bowden, *Philip Freneau* (Boston, 1976); Lewis G. Leary, *That Rascal Freneau* (New Brunswick, N.J., 1941); Philip M. Marsh, *Philip Freneau: Poet and Journalist* (Minneapolis, 1967); Fred Lewis Pattee, "Life of Philip Freneau," in *The Poems of Philip Freneau*, ed. Fred Lewis Pettee (Princeton, 1902–1907), 1: xiii–cxii; and Richard C. Vitzhum, *Land and Sea: The Lyric Poetry of Philip Freneau* (Minneapolis, 1978).

3. Robert E. Spiller et al., *Literary History of the United States*, 3d ed. (New York and London, 1963), 170.

4. Ibid., 172.

5. Information on Bryant derived principally from study of his own writings and from the following sources: William Cullen Bryant, *The Letters of William Cullen Bryant*, ed. William Cullen Bryant II and Thomas B. Voss (New York, 1975); Parks Godwin, *A Biography of William Cullen Bryant, with Extracts from His Private Correspondence*, 2 vols. (New York, 1883; reprint 1967); Curtiss Johnson, *Politics and a Belly-full: The Journalism Career of William Cullen Bryant* (Westport, Conn., 1974); Albert F. McLean, Jr., *William Cullen Bryant* (New Haven, 1975); H. H. Peckham, *Gotham Yankee, A Biography of William Cullen Bryant* (reprint, New York, 1950); Spiller et al., *Literary History of the United States*, 294–305, 775; and James Grant Wilson, *Bryant and His Friends: Some Reminiscences of the Knickerbocker Writers* (New York, 1886).

6. "Song of Myself" stanza 18.

7. Comments on Brown are based principally on a study of his writings and on the following sources: Paul Allen, *The Life of Charles Brockden Brown* (Delmar, N.Y., 1975); David Lee Clark, *Charles Brockden Brown: Pioneer Voice of America* (Durham, N.C., 1966); Cowie, 69–104; William Dunlop, *The Life of Charles Brockden Brown*, 2 vols. (Philadelphia, 1815); William Dunlop, *The Life of Charles Brockden Brown*, 2 vols. (Philadelphia, 1815); F. L. Pattee, introduction to *Wieland* (New York, 1926), ix–xxv; and Harry R. Warfel, *Charles Brockden Brown: American Gothic Novelist* (New York, 1974).

8. Spiller et al., *Literary History of the United States*, 181.

9. Richard Ruland and Malcolm Bradbury, *From Puritanism to Modernism* (New York, 1991), 85.

10. Charles Brockden Brown, introduction to *Edgar Huntley*.

11. Ruland and Bradbury, 89.

12. Discussion of Irving is based principally on his published literary works, and on Van Wyck Brooks, *The World of Washington Irving* (New York, 1944); and Stanley T. Williams, *The Life of Washington Irving*, 2 vols. (New York, 1935).

13. Discussion of Brackenridge is based principally on his published literary works and on Claude Milton Newlin, *The Life and Writings of Hugh Henry Brackenridge* (Princeton, 1932); and Cowie, 43–60.

14. Brackenridge, *Modern Chivalry*, vol. 2, chapter 1.

15. Mercy Otis Warren's letters afford the liveliest examples of her style. Her *History of the Rise, Progress, and Termination of the American Revolution* is well worth mining, but the sort of work that few will read from cover to cover. A biography attuned to recent scholarship on the Revolutionary era is Jeffrey H. Richards, *Mercy Otis Warren* (New York, 1995).

16. Information on Dunlap is derived principally from a study of his writings and from Wil-

liam Dunlap, *Diary of William Dunlap*, 3 vols. (New York, 1931); and Oral Sumner Coad, *William Dunlap: A Study of His Life Works and of His Place in Contemporary Culture* (New York, 1962).

17. The playwright was John Martin, a resident of the county. Nora Miller Turman, *The Eastern Shore of Virginia, 1603–1964* (Bowie, Md., 1988), 66–67; and Ralph T. Whitelaw, *Virginia's Eastern Shore* (Richmond, 1951), 1:712–713.

18. Information on Tyler is derived principally from his writings and from Ada Lon Carson and Herbert L. Carson, *Royall Tyler* (Boston, 1979).

19. Information on Webster is derived principally from E. Jennifer Monaghan, *A Common Heritage: Noah Webster and His Blue-Back Speller* (New Haven, 1982); John S. Morgan, *Noah Webster* (New York, 1975); *Noah Webster's First Edition of an American Dictionary of the English Language*, facsimile of 1828 (San Francisco, 1987); H. E. Scudder, *Noah Webster* (Boston, 1881); and Harry R. Warfel, *Noah Webster: Schoolmaster to America* (1936; reprint, New York, 1953).

21. Sydney Smith, *Edinburgh Review* (Jan.–May 1820).

CHAPTER 42, BOLD BRUSHES

1. James Thomas Flexner, foreword to 1st. ed. of *America's Old Masters* (Garden City, N.Y., 1980), no pagination.

2. Account of Benjamin West is derived principally from personal study of his original paintings and from the following: Wayne Craven, *American Art: History and Culture* (Oxford, 1994), and *Colonial American Portraiture: The Economic, Religious, Social, Cultural, Philosophical, Scientific, and Aesthetic Foundations* (New York, 1986); Flexner, 19–97, 315–340; J. E. Hodgson and Frederick A. Eaton, *The Royal Academy and Its Members, 1768–1830* (London, 1905); Robert Hughes, *American Visions: The Epic History of Art in America* (New York, 1997), 69–81; Henry E. Jackson, *Benjamin West: His Life and Work* (Philadelphia, 1900); Helmut Von Erffa and Allen Staley, *The Paintings of Benjamin West* (New Haven, 1986); and John Walker, *National Gallery of Art* (New York, 1975).

3. Flexner, 74.

4. Sketch of Copley is derived principally from personal study of the artist's original work and from the following: John Singleton Copley, *The Letters and Papers of John Singleton Copley and Henry Pelham, 1739–1776*, ed. Massachusetts Historical Society (Boston, 1904); Craven, *Colonial American Portraiture*; William Dunlap, *History of the Rise and Progress of the Arts of Design in the United States*, 3 vols. (Boston, 1918); Flexner, 101–167; Neil Harris, *The Artist in American Society: The Formative Years, 1790–1860* (New York, 1966); Robert Hughes, *American Visions: The Epic History of Art in America* (New York, 1997), 81–93; Ellen G. Miles, ed., *The Portrait in Eighteenth Century America* (Newark, Del., and London, 1993); Neville Parker and A. B. Wheeler, *John Singleton Copley: American Portraits in Oil, Pastel, and Miniature* (Boston, 1938); and Carrier Rebora et al., *John Singleton Copley in America* (New York, 1995).

5. Flexner.

6. Ibid., 120.

7. Ibid., 154.

8. Ibid., 167.

9. Account of Charles Willson Peale, Rembrandt Peale, and other Peale family painters is based principally on personal study of their original paintings and on the following sources: Dunlap, 1:136–142; 2:50–58; Dorinda Evans, "Survival and Transformation: The Colonial Portrait in the Federal Era," in *The Portrait in Eighteenth Century America*, ed. Ellen G. Miles, 123–137; Flexner, 171–244; Sidney Hart, "Charles Willson Peale and the Theory and Practice of the Eighteenth Century Family," in *The Peale Family*, ed. Miller, 100–117; Anne Sue Hirshorn, "Anne Claypoole, Margaretta, and Sarah Miriam Peale: Modes of Accomplishment and Fortune," in *The Peale Family*, ed. Miller, 220–247; David C. Miller, ed., *American Iconology: New Approaches to Nineteenth Century Art and Literature* (New Haven and London, 1993); Lillian B. Miller, *In Pursuit of Time: Rembrandt Peale, 1778–1860* (Seattle, 1992), and *Patrons and Patriotism: The Encouragement of the Fine Arts in the United States, 1790–1860* (Chicago, 1966, 1974); "The Peales and Their Legacy, 1735–1885," in *The Peale Family: Creation of a Legacy, 1770–1870*, ed. Lillian

B. Miller (Washington, D.C., 1996), 16–97; Lillian B. Miller et al., eds., *The Selected Papers of Charles Willson Peale and His Family*, vols. 1–4 (New Haven, 1983–1996); Laura Rigal, "Peale's Mammoth," in *American Iconology: New Approaches to Nineteenth Century Art and Literature,* ed. David C. Miller (New Haven and London, 1993), 18–38; Saunders and Miles, *American Colonial Portraits, 1700–1776,* 33–36, 282–295; David Steinberg, "Charles Willson Peale Portrays the Body Politic," in *The Peale Family,* ed. Miller, 150–167; and David C. Ward, "Democratic Culture: The Peale Museums, 1784–1850," in *The Peale Family,* ed. Miller, 260–275. I have also benefited from consultation with Dr. Lillian B. Miller, Historian of American Culture at the National Portrait Gallery of the Smithsonian Institution, editor of the Peale Family Papers, and curator of the great "Peale Family" exhibits of 1996–97 at the Philadelphia Museum of Art, the Fine Arts Museums of San Francisco, and the Corcoran Gallery of Art in Washington, D.C. She was the world's foremost authority on the ten most famous artists of the Peale family.

10. According to some accounts, Peale made the sketch after returning from his visit, but his family believed that he had sketched on the spot.

11. Flexner, 229.

12. Flexner, 227.

13. Walker, 380.

14. Ibid. My estimate of Stuart's work, especially of the George Washington portraits, is based largely on personal study of the original canvases. Other sources for Stuart are Dunlop; Flexner, 247–312; John Hill Morgan, *Gilbert Stuart and His Pupils* (New York, 1939); and William T. Whitley, *Gilbert Stuart* (Cambridge, Mass., 1932).

15. Walker, 384.

16. Ibid.

17. Information on Cole is derived principally from personal study of his original works and from Brigitte Bailey, "The Protected Witness: Cole, Cooper, and the Tourist's View of the Italian Landscape," in *American Iconology: New Approaches to Nineteenth Century Art and Literature,* ed. David C. Miller (New Haven and London, 1993), 92–111; Dunlop, 2:350–368; Franklin Kelly, *Thomas Cole's Paintings of Eden* (Fort Worth, Tex., 1994); Hughes, 141–157; Howard S. Merritt, ed., *Thomas Cole* (Rochester, N.Y., 1969); Miller, *Patrons and Patriotism,* 37, 54–55, 150–156, 160–166, 207–210; William H. Truettner, "Nature and the Native Traditions: The Problem of Two Thomas Coles," in *Thomas Cole,* ed. Truettner and Wallach, 137–158; and Wallach, "Thomas Cole: Landscape and the Course of American Empire," in *Thomas Cole: Landscape into History,* ed. William H. Truettner and Alan Wallach (New Haven and London, 1994), 23–111. I have also benefited from consultations with Franklin Kelly on Cole and other aspects of American art history. He is curator of American and British Painting at the National Gallery of Art, Washington, D.C.

18. Kelly, 19.

19. Ibid., 43.

CHAPTER 43, TINKERERS AND TITANS

1. *Dictonnaire raisonné des sciences, des arts, et des matière.*

2. Frederic J. Haskins, *The American Government* (Washington, D.C., 1924), 202.

3. Henry Timrod, "Ethnogenesis," stanza 1, line 24.

CHAPTER 44, AUDACIOUS IMAGINATIONS

1. E. Brooks Holifield, "Science and Religion," *The Encyclopedia of Southern Culture,* ed. Charles Reagan Wilson and William Ferris (New York and London, 1989), 4:161–162.

2. Jefferson's phrase.

CHAPTER 45, MUSIC—FROZEN AND OTHERWISE

1. Information on Hopkinson is derived principally from the following sources: Francis Hopkinson, *The Miscellaneous Essays and Occasional Writings of Francis Hopkinson,* eq., vols. 1–3,

(Philadelphia, 1792); and George Everett Hastings, *The Life and Works of Francis Hopkinson* (New York, 1968).

2. Information on Billings is derived principally from the following sources: James Murray Barbour, *The Church Music of William Billings* (1960; reprint, East Lansing, 1972); Nathaniel D. Gould, *Church Music in America* (1853; reprint, New York, 1972), 43–46; C. Lindstrom, "William Billings and His Times," *Musical Quarterly* 25 (1939):479–497; David McKay and Richard Crawford, *William Billings of Boston: Eighteenth Century Composer* (Princeton, 1975) and; Stanley Sadie, ed., *The New Grove Dictionary of Music and Musicians* (London and New York, 1995), 2:703–705.

3. Geoffrey Hindley, ed., *Larousse Encyclopedia of Music* (New York and Cleveland, 1971), 434.

4. Information on Peter is derived principally from A. G. Rau, "John Frederick Peter," *Musical Quarterly* 23 (1937): 306–313; W. E. Schnell, "The Choral Music of Johann Friedrich Peter" (dissertation, University of Illinois, 1973; includes autobiography); and C. Daniel Crews, *Johann Friedrich Peter and His Times* (Winston-Salem, N.C., 1990).

5. Alf J. Mapp, Jr., *Thomas Jefferson: Passionate Pilgrim* (Lanham, Md., New York, and London), 130–131.

6. *AIA Journal* (July 1976): 91; Alf J. Mapp, Jr., *Thomas Jefferson: A Strange Case of Mistaken Identity* (Lanham, Md., New York, and London, 1987), 162–163.

7. Jack McLaughlin, *Jefferson and Monticello*, 1st ed. (New York, 1988); Ihna Thayer Frary, *Thomas Jefferson: Architect and Builder* (Richmond, Va., 1939); and Mapp, *Thomas Jefferson: Passionate Pilgrim*.

8. Information on Bulfinch is derived principally from Harold Kirker, *The Architecture of Charles Bulfinch* (Cambridge, Mass., 1969), and *Bulfinch's Boston* (New York, 1964); Charles A. Place, *Charles Bulfinch: Architect and Citizen* (New York, 1968); and Charles Bulfinch, *The Life and Letters of Charles Bulfinch, Architect, with Other Family Papers*, ed. Ellen Susan Bulfinch, with introduction by Charles A. Cummings (Boston, 1973).

9. Information on Thornton is derived principally from personal study of his work at the U.S. Capitol and at the Octagon House (Taylor Town House), Washington, D.C.; from study of his original architectural drawings in the collection of the American Institute of Architects; Orlando Rideout, *Building the Octagon Museum* (Washington, D.C., 1989); and from William Thornton, *The Papers of William Thornton*, ed. C. M. Harrris, vol. 1 (1781–1802) (Charlottesville, Va., 1995). The value of the papers is equaled by that of Harris' introduction, xxxi–lxxv.

10. Information on Latrobe is derived principally from Talbot Faulkner Hamlin, *Benjamin Henry Latrobe* (New York, 1955); Lee W. Formwalt, *Benjamin Henry Latrobe and the Development of Internal Improvements in the New Republic* (New York, 1977); Benjamin Henry Latrobe, *The Engineering Drawings of Benjamin Henry Latrobe, Architect*, ed. David H. Stapleton (New Haven, 1980); and *The Correspondence and Miscellaneous Papers of Benjamin Henry Labrobe*, ed. John C. Van Horn and Lee W. Formwalt (New Haven, 1984).

CHAPTER 46, SUMMING UP THE AMERICAN CASE

1. Lucien Price, ed., *Dialogues of Alfred North Whitehead* (New York, 1956), 132–133.

2. Appraised by W. V. Quine, "Whitehead and the Rise of Modern Logic," *The Philosophy of Alfred North Whitehead*, ed. Paul A. Schilpp, 2nd ed. (New York, 1951).

3. Dorothy M. Emmett, "Alfred North Whitehead," *The Encyclopedia of Philosophy*, 8:290.

4. Price, 132–133.

5. Thomas Jefferson to Col. Charles Yancy, January 6, 1816. *The Writings of Thomas Jefferson*, ed. Paul Leicester Ford (New York, 1892), 10:1–4.

6. Roy J. Honeywell, *The Educational Works of Thomas Jefferson* (Cambridge, Mass., 1931), 113–115, 123–124, 130–131, 134–135; and Alf J. Mapp, Jr., *Thomas Jefferson: Passionate Pilgrim* (Lanham, Md., New York, and London, 1991), 370–371.

7. Jack P. Greene, *Pursuits of Happiness: The Social Development of Early Modern British Colonies and the Formation of American Culture* (Chapel Hill, N.C., and London, 1988), 181–182.

8. Ibid., 176.

CHAPTER 47, SIX KEYS

1. Cited by Jack P. Greene, *The Intellectual Construction of America* (Chapel Hill, N.C., 1993), 123.

2. Ibid., 122.

3. Ibid., 54–55.

4. William Shakespeare, *King Richard the Second*, II, i.

5. A. L. Kroeber, *Configurations of Culture Growth* (Los Angeles, 1944), 840. Also quoted in Charles Edward Gray, "A Measurement of Creativity in Western Civilization," *American Anthropologist* 68 (1966): 384.

6. Pitirim A Sorokin, *Social Philosophies of an Age of Crisis* (Boston, 1950).

7. Gray, 1384–1417.

8. Ibid., 1385. Elsewhere Kluckhorn said of Kroeber, "He has contributed to all branches of anthropology and is generally regarded as the leading anthropologist in the world today." Clyde Kluckhorn, "Anthropology," in *What Is Science?*, ed. James R. Newman (New York, 1955), 319–357. Specific quotation on p. 339, n. 13.

9. Gray, 1384–417. Gray's questions, listed on pp. 1391–1392, were all stated in masculine terms, as was customary with many scientists in the 1960's. These were the major criteria:

> 1. Have a man's creations continued to be appreciated long after his era?
> 2. Did his work reveal universal qualities of humanism?
> 3. Did he rise above the limitations of his era?
> 4. How influential was he on contemporary and subsequent creators?

Then there were five intermediate criteria:

> 1. How original was he?
> 2. How versatile and many-sided was he (that is, active in different fields)?
> 3. How prolific and sustained was his productivity?
> 4. How great was his competence in the techniques of his art?
> 5. In addition to form and beauty, did his work show social consciousness?

And two minor criteria:

> 1. Was his work admired beyond his own country?
> 2. Did he communicate, so that his work was contemporaneously popular?

10. Ibid., 1392.

11. Ibid., 1390–1391.

12. The interdisciplinary relationships are sometimes more clearly demonstrable than one might imagine. William Empson introduced a new style of literary interpretation in his landmark work *Seven Types of Ambiguity* (London, 1930). He conceived the new frame of reference because he was reading Shakespeare's *Measure for Measure* while taking a physics course at Cambridge University, center for study of the new physics with its ambiguous use of both wave and corpuscular theories. Jonathan Bate, "Words in a Quantum World: How Cambridge Physics Led William Empson to Refuse 'Either/Or,' " *Times Literary Supplement* (London), July 25, 1997, 14–15.

13. Richard M. Rorty, "Sigmund on the Couch," *New York Times Book Review*, Sept. 22, 1996, 42.

14. David Dietz, *The New Outline of Science* (New York, 1972), 309–310.

15. Sir Francis Bacon, *Novum organum*, "The Idols," paragraph 56, in *The Works of Francis Bacon*, trans. and ed. James Spedding, Robert Leslie Ellis, and Douglas Deron Heath (Boston, 1860–1864).

16. William Shakespeare, *The Tempest*, V, i.

17. William Shakespeare, *King Richard the Second*, II, i.

18. Alexander Pope, *An Essay on Criticism*, 1:135.

19. Durand de Dauphiné, *A Huguenot Exile in Virginia* (1687; reprint, New York, 1934).

20. Marquis de Chastellux, *Travels in North America, in the Years 1780, 1781, and 1782* (Chapel Hill, N.C., 1963).

CHAPTER 48, SALVATION THROUGH ADVENTURE

1. J. E. Morpurgo, *Their Majesties' Royall Colledge* (Williamsburg, Va., 1976), 185.

2. Bryce said of Marshall, "No other man did half as much either to develop the Constitution by expounding it, or to secure for the judiciary its rightful place in the government as the living voice of the Constitution." James Bryce, *The American Commonwealth* (Philadelphia, 1906), 121.

3. Joseph J. Ellis, *New York Times Book Review*, December 1, 1996, 14.

4. Alfred North Whitehead, *The Process of Reality* (New York, 1978), 339.

5. John 1:46.

6. W. F. Bruford, "Goethe's Weimar," in *Cities of Destiny*, ed. Arnold Toynbee (London, 1967), 88.

7. Persuasive arguments for this conclusion are also presented in Jack P. Greene, *The Intellectual Construction of America: Exceptionalism and Identity from 1492 to 1800* (Chapel Hill, N.C., and London, 1993).

8. See Edith Hamilton, *The Greek Way* (New York, 1993), chapter 1.

9. Tatian, "Address to the Greeks," in *Three Thousand Years of Educational Wisdom in Selections from Great Documents*, ed. Robert Ulich (Cambridge, Mass., 1905), 137.

10. Kevin Kelly, *Out of Control: The New Biology of Machines* (Indianapolis, 1994).

11. Anson Rubinbach, *Times Literary Supplement* (London), September 9, 1994, 3–4.

12. For an understanding of Rouse's purpose, I am indebted to his own explanation printed in the Virginia Symphony program for 1996 and the interpretation, both musical and verbal, by Dr. JoAnn Falletta, musical director of the Virginia Symphony and Buffalo (New York) Symphony.

13. Most helpful to me as an introduction to chaos theory has been James Gleick, *Chaos: Making a New Science* (New York, 1987).

14. This point is effectively made by Arthur Koestler in *The Act of Creation* (New York, 1964).

15. Henry Kissinger, quoted in *The Virginian-Pilot* (Norfolk, Va.), May 27, 1995, E3.

BIBLIOGRAPHY

I. RENAISSANCE FLORENCE

Primary Sources

Landucci, Luca. *A Florentine Diary from 1450 to 1516.* New York, 1969.

Leonardo da Vinci. *The Notebooks of Leonardo da Vinci.* Edited by Jean Paul Richter and translated by Mrs. R. C. Bell. 2 vols. New York, 1970.

Machiavelli, Niccolò. *The Discourses of Niccolò Machiavelli.* Translated by Leslie J. Walker and edited by W. Stark. 2 vols. London, 1950.

————. *History of Florence and of the Affairs of Italy from the Earliest Times to the Death of Lorenzo the Magnificent.* New York, 1960.

————. *The Prince.* Translated and edited by David Wootton. Indianapolis and Cambridge, 1995.

Medici, Lorenzo de'. *The Political Philosophy of the Great de' Medici As Revealed by Their Correspondence.* 2 vols. Albuquerque: Institute for Economic and Political World Strategic Studies, 1985.

Michelangelo Buonarroti. *The Poetry of Michelangelo.* Translated by James M. Saslow. New Haven, 1991.

Nicodemi, Giorgio. *Leonardo da Vinci.* New York, n.d.

Petrarch, Francesco (Petrarca, Francesco). *Letters of Old Age: Rerum Senilium Libri, 1–18.* Translated by Aldo S. Bernardo, Saul Levin, and Reta A. Bernardo. 2 vols. Baltimore and London, 1992.

Ross, Janet Ann Duff-Gordon, trans. and ed. *Lives of the Early Medici As Told in Their Correspondence.* London, 1910.

Vasari, Giorgio. *Lives of the Artists.* Edited by E. L. Seeley. New York, 1963.

————. *The Lives of the Painters, Sculptors, and Architects.* Translated by A. B. Hinds. 4 vols. London and New York, 1927.

Welch, Evelyn. *Art and Society in Italy, 1350–1500.* New York, 1997.

Secondary Sources

Ady, Cecilia Mary. *Lorenzo dei Medici and Renaissance Italy.* New York, 1952.

Andres, Glenn M., John M. Hunisak, and A. Richard Turner. *The Art of Florence.* 1st ed. 2 vols. New York, 1988.

Antal, Frederick. *Florentine Painting and its Social Background: The Bourgeois Republic before Cosimo de' Medici's Advent to Power, Fourteenth and Early Fifteenth Centuries.* London, 1948.

Armstrong, Edward. *Lorenzo de' Medici and Florence in the Fifteenth Century.* New York and London, 1914.

Baron, Hans. *The Crisis of the Early Italian Renaissance: Civic Humanism and Republican Liberty in an Age of Classicism and Tyranny.* 2 vols. Princeton, 1966.

Baxandall, Michael. *Painting and Experience in Fifteenth Century Italy: A Primer in the Social History of Pictorial Style.* 2d ed. Oxford and New York, 1972.

Becherucci, Luisa. *Botticelli: La Primavera.* Firenze, 1965.

Berenson, Bernard. *The Florentine Painters of the Renaissance.* 3d ed. New York and London, 1909.

———. *The Italian Painters of the Renaissance.* New York, 1952.

———. *The Study and Criticism of Italian Art.* London, 1901.

Brinton, Selwyn. *The Golden Age of the Medici: Cosimo, Piero, Lorenzo de' Medici, 1434–1494.* London, 1925.

Brown, Alison. *Languages and Images of Renaissance Italy.* New York, 1995.

Brucker, Gene A. *Renaissance Florence.* New York and London, 1969.

———. *Florentine Politics and Society, 1343–1378.* Princeton, 1962.

———, ed. *Society of Renaissance Florence: A Documentary Study.* New York, 1971.

Bullard, Melissa Meriam. *Filippo Strozzi and the Medici: Fever and Finance in Sixteenth Century Florence and Rome.* Cambridge, 1980.

———. "Marsilio Ficino and the Medici: The Inner Dimensions of Patronage." In *Christianity and the Renaissance: Image and Religious Imagination in the Quattrocento.* Edited by Timothy Verdon and John Henderson. 1st ed. Syracuse, N.Y., 1990.

Burckhardt, Jacob. *The Civilization of the Renaissance in Italy.* Translated by S. G. C. Middlemore. New York, 1954.

Butterfield, Andrew. *The Sculptures of Andrea del Verrocchio.* New Haven and London, 1997.

Butters, H. C. *Governors and Government in Early Sixteenth Century Florence, 1502–1519.* Oxford and New York, 1985.

Camporeale, Salvatore. "Humanism and the Religious Crisis of the Late Quattrocento: Giovanni Caroli, O.P., and the *Liber dierum lucensium.*" *Christianity and the Renaissance: Image and Religious Imagination in the Quattrocento.* Edited by Timothy Verdon and John Henderson. 1st ed. Syracuse, N.Y., 1990, 445–466.

Cleugh, James. *The Medici: A Tale of Fifteen Generations.* 1st ed. Garden City, 1975.

Cox-Rearick, Janet. *Dynasty and Destiny in Medici Art.* Princeton, 1984.

Cronin, Vincent. *The Florentine Renaissance.* New York, 1967.

Dempsey, Charles. *The Portrayal of Love: Botticelli's Primavera and Humanist Culture at the Time of Lorenzo the Magnificent.* Princeton, 1992.

De Roover, Raymond. *The Rise and Decline of the Medici Bank, 1397–1494.* Cambridge, Mass., 1963.

Durant, Will. *The Renaissance: A History of Civilization in Italy from 1304–1576 A.D.* New York, 1953.

Einem, Herbert von. *Michelangelo.* Translated by Ronald Taylor. London, 1973.

Elam, Caroline. "Lorenzo de' Medici and the Urban Development of Renaissance Florence." *Art History,* Vol. 1 (March 1978): 43–66.

Field, Arthur. *The Origins of the Platonic Academy of Florence.* Princeton, 1988.

Field, J. V., and Frank A. J. L. James, eds. *Renaissance and Revolution: Humanists, Scholars, Craftsmen, and Natural Philosophers in Early Modern Europe.* Cambridge, 1993.

Garin, Eugenio. "Gian Francesco Pico della Mirandola: Savonarolan Apologetics and the Critique of Ancient Thought." In *Christianity and the Renaissance: Image and Religious Imagination in the Quattrocento.* Edited by Timothy Verdon and John Henderson. 1st ed. Syracuse, N.Y., 1990.

———. *Italian Humanism: Philosophy and Civic Life in the Renaissance.* Translated by Peter Munz. Oxford, 1966.

Goldthwaite, Richard A. *The Building of Renaissance Florence: A Social and Economic History.* Baltimore, 1980.

———. *Wealth and the Demand for Art in Italy, 1300–1600.* Baltimore and London, 1993.

Grendler, Paul. *Critics of the Italian World, 1530–1560.* Madison and London, 1969.

Hale, Sir John Rigby. *The Civilization of Europe in the Renaissance.* New York, 1995.

———. *England and the Italian Renaissance: The Growth of Interest in its History and Art*. 2d ed. London, 1954.

———. *Florence and the Medici: The Pattern of Control*. London, 1977.

Hall, Marcia B. "Savonarola's Preaching and the Patronage of Art." In *Christianity and the Renaissance: Image and Religious Imagination in the Quattrocento*. Edited by Timothy Verdon and John Henderson. 1st ed. Syracuse, N.Y., 1990.

Hay, Denys, ed. *The Age of the Renaissance*. London, 1986.

Hibbert, Christopher. *Florence: The Biography of a City*. New York and London, 1993.

———. *The House of Medici: Its Rise and Fall*. New York, 1980.

Holmes, George, ed. *Art and Politics in Renaissance Italy*. New York, 1995.

———, ed. *Art and Politics in Renaissance Italy: British Academy Lectures*. Oxford, 1993.

Hook, Judith. *Lorenzo de' Medici: An Historical Biography*. London, 1984.

Jones, Philip. *The Italian City-State from Commune to Signoria*. New York, 1992.

Levey, Michael. *Florence: A Portrait*. Cambridge, Mass., 1996.

Lipari, Angelo. *The "Dolce Stil Nove" according to Lorenzo de' Medici*. New Haven and London, 1936.

Lynton, Norbert. "Renaissance Architecture." In *World Architecture*. Edited by Trewin Copplestone. 1966, Reprint, London and New York, 1973.

Martinelli, Giuseppe, ed. *The World of Renaissance Florence*. New York, 1968.

Martines, Lauro. *Power and the Imagination: City-States in Renaissance Italy*. New York, 1979.

———. *The Social World of the Florentine Humanists, 1390–1460*. Princeton, 1963.

Mee, Charles L. *Lorenzo de' Medici and the Renaissance*. 1st ed. New York, 1969.

Phillips, Mark. *The Memoir of Marco Parenti: A Life in Medici Florence*. Princeton, 1987.

Pocock, J. G. A. *The Machiavellian Moment: Florentine Political Thought and the Atlantic Republican Tradition*. Princeton, 1975.

Polizzotto, Lorenzo. *The Elect Nation: The Savonarolan Movement in Florence, 1494–1545*. New York, 1995.

Renner, R. Richard. *Savonarola: The First Great Protestant*. 1st ed. New York, 1965.

Rice, Eugene F., Jr. "The Renaissance and Reformation in Europe." *The Columbia History of the World*. Edited by John Arthur Garraty and Peter Gay. New York, 1972.

Ridolfi, Roberto. *The Life of Girolamo Savonarola*. Translated by Cecil Grayson. New York, 1959.

Roeder, Ralph. *The Man of the Renaissance: Four Lawgivers: Savonarola, Machiavelli, Castiglione, Aretino*. New York, 1933.

Roscoe, William. *The Life of Lorenzo de' Medici, Called the Magnificent*. 9th ed. London, 1847.

Rubinstein, Nicolai. *The Government of Florence under the Medici, 1434–1494*. Oxford, 1966.

———. *The Palazzo Vecchio, 1298–1532: Government, Architecture, and Imagery in the Civic Palace of the Florentine Republic*. New York, 1995.

Ruggiers, Paul G. *Florence in the Age of Dante*. 1st ed. Norman, Okla., 1964.

Scaife, Walter B. *Florentine Life during the Renaissance*. Baltimore, 1893.

Schevill, Ferdinand. *History of Florence: From the Founding of the City through the Renaissance*. 1st ed. New York, 1936.

———. *The Medici*. New York, 1949.

Schnitzer, Joseph. *Savonarola*. 2 vols. Milan, 1931.

Steinberg, Ronald M. *Fra Girolamo Savonarola, Florentine Art, and Renaissance Historiography*. Athens, Ohio, 1977.

Stern, Laura Ikins. *The Criminal Law System of Medieval and Renaissance Florence*. Baltimore and London, 1994.

Stephens, J. N. *The Fall of the Florentine Republic, 1512–1530*. Oxford, 1983.

Taylor, Rachel A. *Leonardo the Florentine: A Study in Personality*. New York and London, 1928.

Trexler, Richard C. *Public Life in Renaissance Florence*. New York and London, 1986.

Turner, A. Richard. *Inventing Leonardo*. 1st ed. New York, 1993.

Verdon, Timothy, and John Henderson, eds. *Christianity and the Renaissance: Image and Religious Imagination in the Quattrocento*. 1st ed. Syracuse, N.Y., 1990.

Villari, Pasquale. *The Life and Times of Girolamo Savonarola*. 2 vols. London, 1890.

———. *The Life and Times of Niccolò Machiavelli.* Translated by Linda Villari. 2 vols. New York, 1878.

Waley, Daniel P. *The Italian City-Republics.* London and New York, 1988.

Weinstein, Donald. *Savonarola and Florence: Prophecy and Patriotism in the Renaissance.* Princeton, 1970.

Whitcomb, Merrick. *A Literary Source-Book of the Italian Renaissance.* Philadelphia, 1898.

Young, George Frederick. *The Medici.* New York, 1933.

II. ELIZABETHAN ENGLAND

Primary Sources

Aikin, Lucy. *Memoirs of the Court of Elizabeth, Queen of England.* New York, 1870.

Bacon, Sir Francis. *Essays of Bacon.* Edited by Henry Morley. Cleveland, 1946.

———. *The New Organum and Related Writings.* Edited by Fulton Henry Anderson. New York, 1960.

———. *The Philosophical Works of Francis Bacon.* Edited by John M. Robertson. London, 1905.

———. *The Works of Francis Bacon.* Edited by James Spedding, Robert Leslie Ellis, and Douglas Denon Heath. 15 vols. Boston, 1860–1864.

Coke, Sir Edward. *The First Part of the Institutes of the Laws of England, or, A Commentary upon Littleton.* 1st American ed. Philadelphia, 1853.

Donne, John. *The Poems of John Donne.* Edited by Sir Herbert J. C. Grierson. 2 vols. London, 1912.

Drake, Sir Francis. *The World Encompassed, and Analogous Contemporary Documents.* Edited by Sir Richard Carnac Temple. London, 1854.

Frushell, Richard C., and Bernard J. Vondersmith. *Contemporary Thought on Edmund Spenser.* Carbondale, Ill., and London, 1975.

Fuller, Thomas. *Worthies of England.* Edited by John Freeman. Abridged 1st ed. London, 1952.

Gilbert, William. *De Magnete.* Translated by P. Fleury Mottelay. 1893. Reprint, New York, 1958.

———. *De Magnete.* Translated by S. P. Thompson. 1901. Reprint, New York, 1958.

Greville, Fulke. "The Life of the Renowned Sir Philip Sidney." In *The Prose of Fulke Greville, Lord Brooke.* Edited by Mark Caldwell. Renaissance Imagination Series, vol. 26. New York and London, 1987.

Grierson, Sir Herbert J. C., ed. *Metaphysical Lyrics and Poems of the Seventeenth Century: Donne to Butler.* 1st ed. Oxford, 1921.

Hakluyt, Richard. *The Original Writings and Correspondence of the Two Richard Hakluyts.* Edited by E. G. R. Taylor. 2 vols. London, 1935.

———. *The Principal Navigations, Voyages, Traffiques, and Discoveries of the English Nation.* 12 vols. Glasgow, 1903–05. (Short-titled *Hakluyt's Voyages* in various editions.)

Hariot (cq), Thomas. *A Briefe and True Report of the New Found Land of Virginia.* Facsimile of the 1st edition of 1588. New York, 1903.

Harvey, William. *The Circulation of the Blood, and Other Writings.* Edited by Kenneth J. Franklin. London and New York, 1963.

Jonson, Ben. *Ben Jonson.* Edited by C. H. Herford and Percy Simpson. 1925. 11 vols. Reprint, Oxford, 1954.

Littleton, Sir Thomas. *Littleton's "Tenures" in English.* Edited by Eugene Wambaugh. 1903. Reprint, Littleton, Colo., 1985.

Marlowe, Christopher. *The Jew of Malta.* Edited by N. W. Bawcutt. Manchester and Baltimore, 1978.

More, Sir Thomas. *Utopia.* Translated and edited by Robert M. Adams. New York, 1975.

———. *Utopia.* Translated by Ralph Robinson and edited by Edward Arber. 1551. Revised, London, 1869.

Neill, Edward D. "Dr. Donne to Preach Annual Service." In *History of the Virginia Company of London.* Albany, N.Y., 1869.

Ralegh, Sir Walter. *The History of the World*. Edited by C. A. Patrides. Philadelphia, 1971.

———. *The Poems of Sir Walter Ralegh*. Edited by Agnes M. C. Latham. Cambridge, Mass., 1951.

Roper, William. "The Life of Sir Thomas More, Knight." In *Lives of Saint Thomas More*. Edited by E. E. Reynolds. New York, 1963.

Sandys, George. *The Poetical Works of George Sandys*. With introduction and notes by Richard Hooper. 2 vols. London, 1872.

Shakespeare, William. *Mr. William Shakespeare's Comedies, Histories, and Tragedies*. Edited by H. Kökeritz and C. T. Prouty. Facsimile of 1st folio ed. New Haven, 1954.

———. *The Riddle of Shakespeare's Sonnets: The Text of the Sonnets*. Edited with interpretive essays by Edward Hubler et al. 1st ed. New York, 1962.

———. *Shakespeare's Sonnets*. Edited by Katherine Duncan-Jones. Walton-on-Thames, 1997.

———. *The Sonnets*. Edited by Stephen Booth. New York, 1977.

———. *The Sonnets*. With an introduction by W. H. Auden. Edited by William Burto. New York, 1965.

Sidney, Sir Philip. *The Prose Works of Sir Philip Sidney*. Edited by Albert Feuillerat. 4 vols. Cambridge, 1962.

Spenser, Edmund. *Poetical Works*. Edited by J. C. Smith and Ernest De Selincourt. New York, 1961.

———. *Works*. Edited by Edwin Greenlaw et al. Variorum ed. 9 vols. Baltimore, 1932–1949.

Secondary Sources

Adams, Joseph Quincy. *A Life of William Shakespeare*. Boston and New York, 1925.

Adamson, Jack H., and H. F. Folland. *The Shepherd of the Ocean: An Account of Sir Walter Ralegh and His Times*. Boston, 1969.

Alexander, Peter. *Shakespeare's Life and Art*. New York, 1961.

Alpers, Paul J. *The Poetry of the "Faerie Queene."* Princeton, 1967.

Anders, Henry R. D. *Shakespeare's Books: A Dissertation on Shakespeare's Reading and the Immediate Sources of His Works*. Berlin, 1904.

Anderson, Fulton Henry. *The Philosophy of Francis Bacon*. Chicago, 1948.

Anglo, Sidney. *Spectacle, Pageantry, and Early Tudor Policy*. 2d ed. New York, 1997.

Bald, R. C. *John Donne: A Life*. New York and Oxford, 1970.

Baldwin, Thomas Whitfield. *William Shakespeare's Small Latine and Lesse Greeke*. . . . 2 vols. Urbana, Ill., 1944.

Barish, Jonas A. *Ben Jonson and the Language of Prose Comedy*. Cambridge, Mass., 1960.

Bate, Walter Jackson, ed. *Criticism: The Major Texts*. New York, 1952.

Baugh, Albert C., ed. *A Literary History of England*. New York, 1988.

Bawcutt, N. W. "Machiavelli and Marlowe's *The Jew of Malta*." In *Renaissance Drama*. Edited by Samuel Schoenbaum. N.s. 3, Evanston, Ill., 1970.

Bentley, Gerald Eades. *Shakespeare: A Biographical Handbook*. New Haven, 1961.

———. *Shakespeare and Jonson: Their Reputations in the Seventeenth Century Compared*. Chicago and London, 1965.

Bill, Alfred Hoyt. *Astrophel*. New York and Toronto, 1937.

Black, John Bennett. *The Reign of Elizabeth, 1558–1603*. 2d ed. Oxford, 1959.

Broad, Charlie Dunbar. *The Philosophy of Francis Bacon*. Cambridge, 1926.

Brooke, Tucker. "Edmund Spenser," "The Faerie Queene: The Spenserian," and "Sidney and the Sonneteers." In *A Literary History of England*. Edited by Albert C. Baugh. New York, 1988.

Bullough, Geoffrey, ed. *Narrative and Dramatic Sources of Shakespeare*. 8 vols. New York and London, 1957–1975.

Buxton, John. *Sir Philip Sidney and the English Renaissance*. 3d ed. London, 1987.

Cerasano, S. P., and Marion Wynne-Davies, ed. *Gloriana's Face: Women, Public and Private, in the English Renaissance*. Detroit, 1992.

Chambers, E. K. *William Shakespeare: A Study of Facts and Problems*. 2 vols. Oxford, 1930.

Charlton, H. B. *Shakespearian* [cq] *Comedy*. London and New York, 1938.

———. *Shakespearian* [cq] *Tragedy*. Cambridge and Toronto, 1948.

Chidsey, Donald Barr. *Sir Walter Raleigh, That Damned Upstart.* New York, 1931.

Connell, Dorothy. *Sir Philip Sidney: The Maker's Mind.* Oxford, 1977.

Cooper, Sherod M. *The Sonnets of "Astrophel and Stella": A Stylistic Study.* Paris, 1968.

Cummins, John G. *Francis Drake: The Lives of a Hero.* New York, 1995.

Davis, Bernard Eustace Cuthbert. *Edmund Spenser: A Critical Study.* New York, 1962.

Davis, Richard Beale. *George Sandys, Poet Adventurer: A Study in Anglo-American Culture in the Seventeenth Century.* London and New York, 1955.

Davis, Walter R., and Richard A. Lanham. *Sidney's "Arcadia."* New Haven, 1965.

Dean, Leonard Fellows, ed. *Shakespeare: Modern Essays in Criticism.* New York, 1967.

Dobson, Michael. *The Making of the National Poet: Shakespeare, Adaptation, and Authorship, 1660–1769.* Oxford and New York, 1992.

Duncan-Jones, Katherine. *Sir Philip Sidney, Courtier Poet.* New Haven and London, 1991.

Edwards, Philip. *Sir Walter Raleigh.* London, 1953.

Eliot, T. S. "Ben Jonson" and "The Metaphysical Poets." In *Selected Essays.* Edited by T. S. Eliot. London, 1951.

Enck, John Jacob. *Jonson and the Comic Truth.* Madison, 1957.

Farrington, Benjamin. *Francis Bacon: Philosopher of Industrial Science.* New York, 1949.

———. *The Philosophy of Francis Bacon: An Essay on Its Development from 1603 to 1609.* With new translations of fundamental texts. Liverpool, 1964.

Fellowes, Edmund Horace. *English Cathedral Music.* 5th ed. London, 1969.

———. *The English Madrigal Composers.* 2d ed. London and New York, 1948.

———. *Orlando Gibbons: A Short Account of His Life and Work.* Oxford, 1925.

———. *William Byrd.* 2d ed. London and New York, 1948.

Fraser, Russell. *Shakespeare: The Later Years.* New York and Oxford, 1992.

Fripp, Edgar Innes. *Shakespeare: Man and Artist.* 2 vols. London, 1938.

Froude, James Anthony. *History of England from the Fall of Wolsey to the Death of Elizabeth.* 12 vols. New York, 1870.

———. *Short Studies on Great Subjects.* London, 1870.

Gotch, John Alfred. *Inigo Jones.* New York, 1968.

Granville-Barker, Harley, and G. B. Harrison, eds. *A Companion to Shakespeare Studies.* Cambridge, 1959.

Grove, Sir George. *The New Grove Dictionary of Music and Musicians.* Edited by Stanley Sadie. 20 vols. London, 1955.

Harrison, G. B. *Shakespeare at Work, 1592–1603.* Ann Arbor, 1958.

Haynes, Jonathan. *The Humanist as Traveler: George Sandys' Relation of a Journey Begun an. Dom. 1610.* Rutherford, 1986.

Holdsworth, Sir William Searle. *A History of English Law.* Edited by A. L. Goodhart and H. G. Hanbury. 2d ed. 16 vols. London, 1936–1966.

Hopkins, Lisa. *Elizabeth I and Her Court.* New York, 1990.

Howell, Roger. *Sir Philip Sidney: The Shepherd Knight.* Boston and Toronto, 1968.

Hurstfield, Joel. *Elizabeth I and the Unity of England.* New York, 1960.

Irwin, Margaret. *That Great Lucifer: A Portrait of Sir Walter Raleigh.* New York, 1960.

Jackson, Gabriele Bernhard. *Vision and Judgment in Ben Jonson's Drama.* New Haven, 1968.

Jenkins, Elizabeth. *Elizabeth the Great.* 1st American ed. New York, 1959.

Johnson, Paul. *Elizabeth I: A Biography.* New York, 1974.

Johnson, Samuel. "Cowley." In *Lives of the English Poets.* Edited by George Birkbeck Hill. 3 vols. Oxford, 1905.

Johnson, Stanley. "John Donne and the Virginia Company." *Journal of English Literary History,* 14 (1947):127–138.

Jones, Harrie Stuart Vedder. *A Spenser Handbook.* New York, 1930.

Jones, Norman L. *The Birth of the Elizabethan Age: England in the 1560s.* Oxford and Cambridge, Mass., 1993.

Kalstone, David. *Sidney's Poetry: Contexts and Interpretations.* Cambridge, Mass., 1965.

Kay, Dennis, ed. *Sir Philip Sidney: An Anthology of Modern Criticism.* Oxford and New York, 1987.

Keele, Kenneth D. *William Harvey: The Man, the Physician, and the Scientist*. London, 1965.

Kerman, Joseph. *The Masses and Motets of William Byrd*. Music of William Byrd Series, vol. 1. London and Boston, 1981.

Keynes, Sir Geoffrey. *The Life of William Harvey*. Oxford, 1966.

Kiernan, Pauline. *Shakespeare's Theory of Drama*. Cambridge, Eng., 1996.

Knights, L. C. *Drama and Society in the Age of Jonson*. New York 1937.

Lawry, Jon Sherman. *Sidney's Two "Arcadias": Pattern and Proceeding*. Ithaca, N.Y., 1972.

Leishman, James Blair. *The Monarch of Wit*. London, 1965.

Levin, Carole. *"The Heart and Stomach of a King": Elizabeth I and the Politics of Sex and Power*. Philadelphia, 1994.

Lloyd, Christopher. *Sir Francis Drake*. London, 1957.

Lynton, Norbert. "Renaissance Architecture." In *World Architecture*. Edited by Trewin Copplestone. 1966. Reprint, London and New York, 1973.

MacCaffrey, Wallace T. *Elizabeth I*. London and New York, 1993.

———. *Queen Elizabeth and the Making of Policy, 1572–1588*. Princeton, 1981.

———. *The Shaping of the Elizabethan Regime*. Princeton, 1968.

Morison, Samuel Eliot. *The European Discovery of America*. Vol. 1, *The Northern Voyages A.D. 500–1600*. New York, 1971.

Neale, Sir John Ernest. *Elizabeth I and Her Parliaments*. 2 vols. New York, 1953–1957.

———. *Queen Elizabeth I*. London, 1959.

Neighbour, O. W. *The Consort and Keyboard Music of William Byrd*. Music of William Byrd Series, vol. 3. London and Boston, 1978.

Neilson, William Allan, and Ashley Horace Thorndike. *The Facts about Shakespeare*. New York, 1961.

Nelson, William. *The Poetry of Edmund Spenser: A Study*. New York, 1963.

Orgel, Stephen, and Roy Strong. *Inigo Jones*. 2 vols. London, 1973.

Osborn, James Marshall. *Young Philip Sidney, 1572–1577*. New Haven and London, 1972.

Pagel, Walter. *William Harvey's Biological Ideas: Selected Aspects and Historical Background*. New York, 1967.

Parker, Derek. *John Donne and His World*. London, 1975.

Parks, George Bruner. *Richard Hakluyt and the English Voyages*. Edited by James A. Williamson. 2d ed. New York, 1961.

Partridge, Edward Bellamy. *The Broken Compass: A Study of the Major Comedies of Ben Jonson*. New York, 1958.

Penrose, Boies. *Urbane Travelers, 1591–1635*. Philadelphia, 1942.

Pulling, Alexander. *The Order of the Coif*. Classics in Legal History, vol. 28. Buffalo, 1975.

Raab, Felix. *The English Face of Machiavelli: A Changing Interpretation, 1500–1700*. London and Toronto, 1965.

Radcliffe, David Hill. *Edmund Spenser: A Reception History*. Columbia, S.C., 1996.

Read, Conyers. *Lord Burghley and Queen Elizabeth*. New York, 1960.

———. *Mr. Secretary Cecil and Queen Elizabeth*. New York, 1960.

———. *Mr. Secretary Walsingham and the Policy of Queen Elizabeth*. Oxford, 1925.

Reese, M. M. *Shakespeare: His World and His Work*. London and New York, 1953.

Renwick, William Lindsay. *Edmund Spenser: An Essay on Renaissance Poetry*. London, 1925.

Riddell, James A., and Stanley Stewart. *Jonson's Spenser: Evidence and Historical Criticism*. Pittsburgh, 1995.

Ridler, Anne, ed. *Shakespeare Criticism, 1919–1935*. London, 1936.

Robinson, Forrest G. *The Shape of Things Known: Sidney's "Apology" in Its Philosophical Tradition*. Cambridge, Mass., 1972.

Rossi, Paolo. *Francis Bacon: From Magic to Science*. Chicago, 1968.

Roston, Murray. *The Soul of Wit: A Study of John Donne*. Oxford, 1974.

Rowse, A. L. *The England of Elizabeth: The Structure of Society*. 2 vols. New York, 1951.

———. *Raleigh and the Throckmortons*. London, 1962.

———. *Shakespeare: The Man*. 1st American ed. New York, 1973.

———. *Shakespeare the Man*. Rev. ed. New York, 1988.

———. *William Shakespeare: A Biography*. 1st ed. New York, 1963.

Rudenstine, Neil L. *Sidney's Poetic Development.* Cambridge, Mass., 1967.

Rukeyser, Muriel. *The Traces of Thomas Hariot* (cq). 1st ed. New York, 1971.

Samuel, Irene. "The Influence of Plato on Sir Philip Sidney's *Defense of Poesy.*" *Modern Language Quarterly* vol. 1 (September 1940): 383–391.

Schoenbaum, Samuel. *Shakespeare's Lives.* Oxford and New York, 1970.

Seward, Desmond. *Prince of the Renaissance: The Golden Life of François I.* New York, 1973.

Shakespeare Quarterly. Folger Shakespeare Library, Washington, D.C., vol. 39 (1988)–vol. 49 (Summer 1998).

Smith, A. J., ed. *John Donne: Essays in Celebration.* London, 1972.

Somerset, Anne. *Elizabeth I.* New York, 1991.

Spencer, Hazelton. *British Literature.* 2 vols. Lexington, Mass., 1974.

Stenton, F. M. *Anglo-Saxon England.* 3d ed. Oxford, 1971.

Stephen, Sir Leslie, and Sir Sidney Lee, eds. *Dictionary of National Biography.* 24 vols. London, 1937–1939.

Stevens, Henry N. *Life of Thomas Hariot* (cq). London, 1900.

Strathmann, Ernest Albert. *Sir Walter Raleigh: A Study in Elizabethan Skepticism.* 1953. Reprint, New York, 1973.

Summerson, Sir John Newenham. *Architecture in Britain, 1530–1830.* London and Baltimore, 1953.

Swinburne, Algernon Charles. *A Study of Ben Jonson.* New York, 1968.

Taylor, Alfred Edward. "Francis Bacon." *Proceedings of the British Academy* 12 (1927): 273–294.

Thomson, Peter. *Shakespeare's Professional Career.* Cambridge and New York, 1992.

Thorne, Samuel Edmund. *Sir Edward Coke, 1552–1952* (sic). London, 1957.

Tillotson, Geoffrey. *On the Poetry of Pope.* 2d ed. Oxford, 1950.

Trevelyan, George Macaulay. *History of England.* New and enlarged ed. London, 1960.

Walker, Julia M., ed. *Dissing Elizabeth: Negative Representations of Gloriana.* Durham, N.C., 1998.

Wallace, Malcolm William. *The Life of Sir Philip Sidney.* 1915. Reprint, New York, 1967.

Wallace, Willard Mosher. *Sir Walter Raleigh.* Princeton, 1959.

Ward, A. W., G. W. Prothero, and Stanley Leathes, eds. *The Cambridge Modern History.* Planned by the late Lord Acton. 13 vols. Cambridge, 1969.

Watkins, John. *The Specter of Dido: Spenser and Virgilian Epic.* New Haven and London, 1995.

Webber, Joan. *Contrary Music: The Prose Style of John Donne.* Madison, 1963.

Wells, Stanley W. *William Shakespeare: A Textual Companion.* Oxford and New York, 1987.

———, ed. *Current Approaches to Shakespeare: Language, Text, Theatre, and Ideology.* New York, 1988.

Whinney, Margaret. *Renaissance Architecture in England.* London, New York, and Toronto, 1952.

Whitelock, Dorothy. *Changing Currents in Anglo-Saxon Studies.* Cambridge, 1958.

Whitney, Charles. *Francis Bacon and Modernity.* New Haven, 1986.

Whitteridge, Gweneth. *William Harvey and the Circulation of the Blood.* London and New York, 1971.

Williams, Neville. *The Life and Times of Elizabeth I.* London, 1972.

Williams, Norman Lloyd. *Sir Walter Raleigh.* Philadelphia, 1962.

Williamson, George. *The Donne Tradition: A Study in English Poetry from Donne to the Death of Cowley.* New York, 1958.

Williamson, James A. *The Age of Drake.* 4th ed. London, 1960.

———. "Richard Hakluyt." In *Richard Hakluyt and His Successors.* Edited by Edward Lynam. London, 1946.

Wilson, Derek A. *The World Encompassed: Francis Drake and His Great Voyage.* New York, 1977.

Wilson, John Dover. *The Essential Shakespeare: A Biographical Adventure.* Cambridge and New York, 1932.

Wilson, Mona. *Sir Philip Sidney.* 1950. Reprint, Folcroft, Pa., 1971.

Wrong, George M. *The British Nation: A History.* New York, 1903.

Zandvoort, Reinard W. *Sidney's "Arcadia": A Comparison Between the Two Versions.* Temecula, Calif., 1992.

III. THE FOUNDING OF THE UNITED STATES

Official and Semiofficial Collections

Commager, Henry Steele, ed. *Documents of American History.* 3d ed. New York, 1944.

Continental Congress. *The Debates in the Federal Convention of 1787.* Edited by Gaillard Hunt and James B. Scott. Westport, Conn., 1970.

Continental Congress. *Journals of the Continental Congress, 1774–1789.* Edited from the original records in the Library of Congress. 34 vols. Washington, D.C., 1904–1937.

Daniel, James Randolph Vivian, and Everard Kidder Meade, eds. *A Hornbook of Virginia History.* Richmond, 1949.

Massachusetts. *Records of the Colony of New Plymouth in New England.* Edited by Nathaniel Bradstreet Shurtleff and David Pulsifer. 12 vols. Boston, 1855–1861.

Massachusetts. *Records of the Governor and Company of the Massachusetts Bay in New England.* Edited by Nathaniel Bradstreet Shurtleff. 5 vols. Boston, 1853–1854.

Ohio Company of Virginia. *George Mercer Papers relating to the Ohio Company of Virginia [in the Darlington Memorial Library].* Edited by Lois Mulkearn. Pittsburgh, 1954.

Sowerby, E. Millicent, ed. *Catalogue of the Library of Thomas Jefferson.* 5 vols. Charlottesville, Va., 1983.

United States. Congress. *American Archives.* Compiled by Peter Force. 9 vols. Washington, D.C., 1837–53.

United States. Congress. *American State Papers.* 38 vols. Washington, D.C., 1832–1861.

Virginia. *Calendar of Virginia State Papers and Other Manuscripts . . . Preserved in the Capitol at Richmond.* 11 vols. Richmond, 1875–1893.

Virginia. *Executive Journals of the Council of Colonial Virginia.* Edited by H. R. McIlwaine. 3 vols. Richmond, 1925–1928.

Virginia. *Journal of the House of Delegates of the Commonwealth of Virginia.* Richmond, 1828–.

Virginia. *Journals of the Council of the State of Virginia, 1776–1781.* Edited by H. R. McIlwaine. 2 vols. Richmond, 1931–1932.

Virginia. *Journals of the House of Burgesses of Virginia, 1619–1776.* Edited by H. R. McIlwaine. 13 vols. Richmond, 1905–1915.

Virginia. *Legislative Journals of the Council of Colonial Virginia.* Edited by H. R. McIlwaine. 3 vols. Richmond, 1918–1919.

Virginia. *Official Letters of the Governors of the State of Virginia.* Edited by H. R. McIlwaine. Richmond, 1926–.

Virginia. *The Official Records of Robert Dinwiddie, Lieutenant-Governor of the Colony of Virginia, 1751–1758.* Edited by R. A. Brock. 2 vols. Richmond, 1883–1884.

Virginia. *The Statutes at Large: Being a Collection of All the Laws of Virginia, From the First Session of the Legislature, in the Year 1619, Published Pursuant to an Act of the General Assembly of Virginia, Passed on the Fifth Day of February, One Thousand Eight Hundred and Eight.* Edited by William Waller Hening. 13 vols. New York, 1819–1923.

Virginia Company of London. *The Records of the Virginia Company of London.* Edited by Susan Myra Kingsbury. 4 vols. Washington, D.C., 1906–1935.

Other Primary Sources

Adams, Henry, ed. *Documents Relating to New-England Federalism, 1800–1815.* Boston, 1877.

Adams, John. *The Adams-Jefferson Letters: The Complete Correspondence between Thomas Jefferson and Abigail and John Adams.* Edited by Lester J. Cappon. 2 vols. Chapel Hill, N.C., 1959.

———. *Letters of John Adams, Addressed to His Wife.* Edited by Charles Francis Adams. 2 vols. Boston, 1841.

———. *The Spur of Fame: Dialogues of John Adams and Benjamin Rush.* Edited by John A. Schutz and Douglass Adair. San Marino, 1966.

——. *The Works of John Adams, Second President of the United States: With a Life of the Author, Notes and Illustrations*. Edited by Charles Francis Adams. 10 vols. Boston, 1856.

Adams, John, and John Quincy Adams. *The Selected Writings of John and John Quincy Adams*. Edited by Adrienne Koch and William Peden. New York, 1946.

Adams, John Quincy. *The Diary of John Quincy Adams, 1794–1845: American Political, Social, and Intellectual Life from Washington to Polk*. Edited by Allan Nevins. New York, London, and Toronto, 1928.

——. *Writings of John Quincy Adams*. Edited by Worthington Chauncey Ford. 7 vols. New York, 1913–1917.

Ames, Fisher. *Works of Fisher Ames*. Edited by Seth Ames. 2 vols. Boston, 1854.

Anderson, Douglas. *The Radical Enlightenments of Benjamin Franklin*. Baltimore and London, 1997.

Barbour, James Murray. *The Church Music of William Billings*. 1960. Reprint, East Lansing, 1972.

Bemis, Samuel Flagg. *John Quincy Adams and the Foundations of American Foreign Policy*. New York, 1949.

Beveridge, Albert J. *The Life of John Marshall*. 4 vols. Boston, 1916.

Beverley, Robert. *The History and Present State of Virginia*. Edited by Louis B. Wright. 1705. Reprint, Chapel Hill, N.C., 1947.

Bland, Richard. *An Inquiry into the Rights of the British Colonies*. Edited by Earl Gregg Swem. 1776. Reprint, Richmond, 1922.

Boswell, James. *Boswell's London Journal*. Edited by F. A. Pottle. New York, 1950.

Bradford, William. *Of Plymouth Plantation, 1620–1647*. Edited by Samuel Eliot Morison. New York, 1963.

Bradstreet, Anne. *The Tenth Muse*. Edited by Josephine K. Piercy. Gainesville, 1965.

——. *The Works of Anne Bradstreet*. Edited by Jeannine Hensley. Cambridge, Mass., 1967.

Brown, Alexander. *The Genesis of the United States*. Boston, 1891.

Bulfinch, Charles. *The Life and Letters of Charles Bulfinch, Architect, with Other Family Papers*. Edited by Ellen Susan Bulfinch with introduction by Charles A. Cummings. Boston, 1973.

Burnaby, Andrew. *Travels through the Middle Settlements in North America in the Years 1759 and 1760*. 2d ed. London, 1775.

Burnett, Edmund Cody, ed. *Letters of Members of the Continental Congress*. 8 vols. 1921. Reprint, Gloucester, Mass., 1963.

Burr, Aaron. *Memoirs of Aaron Burr with Miscellaneous Selections from His Correspondence*. Edited by Matthew L. Davis. 2 vols. New York, 1836–1837.

——. *Reports of The Trials of Colonel Aaron Burr, on an Indictment for Treason . . . Taken in Shorthand by David Robertson*. 2 vols. New York, 1872.

Byrd, William. *Another Secret Diary of William Byrd of Westover, 1739–1741*. Edited by Maude H. Woodfin and translated by Marion Tinling. Richmond, 1942.

——. *Natural History of Virginia*. Edited and translated by R. C. Beatty and W. J. Mulloy. Richmond, 1940.

——. *The Secret Diary of William Byrd of Westover, 1709–1712*. Edited by Louis B. Wright and Marion Tinling. Richmond, 1941.

Cabell, Nathaniel Francis, ed. *Early History of the University of Virginia, As Contained in the Letters of Thomas Jefferson and Joseph C. Cabell*. Richmond, 1856.

Carter, Landon. *The Diary of Colonel Landon Carter of Sabine Hall, 1752–1778*. Edited by Jack P. Greene. 2 vols. Charlottesville, Va., 1965.

Chastellux, Marquis de. *Travels in North America in the Years 1780, 1781, and 1782*. Edited by Howard C. Rice, Jr. Chapel Hill, N.C., 1963.

Clark, George Rogers. *The Capture of Old Vincennes: The Original Narratives of George Rogers Clark and of his Opponent Gov. Henry Hamilton*. Edited by Milo M. Quaife. Indianapolis, 1927.

Cutler, William Parker, and Julia Perkins Cutler. *Life, Journals, and Correspondence of Reverend Manasseh Cutler, LL.D.* By his grandchildren. 2 vols. Cincinnati, 1888.

Dauphiné, Durand de. *A Huguenot Exile in Virginia*, or *Voyages of a Frenchman Exiled for His*

Religion with a Description of Virginia and Maryland. 1687. Reprint, with an introduction and notes by Gilbert Chinard, New York, 1934.

Dewey, Donald O. *Marshall versus Jefferson.* New York, 1970.

Dunglison, Robley. *The Autobiographical Ana of Robley Dunglison, M.D.* Transactions of the American Philosophical Society. Edited by Samuel X. Radbill. Vol. 53, part 8. Philadelphia, 1963.

Edwards, Jonathan. *Representative Selections.* Edited by Clarence Henry Faust and Thomas Herbert Johnson. Revised ed. New York, 1962.

——. *Scientific and Philosophical Writings.* Edited by Wallace E. Anderson. Works of Jonathan Edwards, vol. 6. New Haven and London, 1980.

Fithian, Philip Vickers. *Journal and Letters of Philip Vickers Fithian, 1773–1774: A Plantation Tutor of the Old Dominion.* Edited by Hunter Dickinson Farish. Williamsburg, 1943.

Fitzhugh, William. *William Fitzhugh and His Chesapeake World, 1676–1701: The Fitzhugh Letters and Other Documents.* Edited by Richard Beale Davis. Chapel Hill, N.C., 1963.

Fontaine, Reverend James. *Memoirs of a Huguenot Family.* Translated and compiled by Ann Maury. New York, 1872.

Force, Peter, comp. *Tracts and Other Papers Relating Principally to the Origin, Settlement, and Progress of the Colonies in North America, from the Discovery of the Country to the Year 1776.* 4 vols. Washington, D.C., 1836–1846.

Forman, Henry Chandlee. *Virginia Architecture in the Seventeenth Century.* Jamestown 350th Anniversary Historical Booklet, no. 11. Williamsburg, 1957.

Formwalt, Lee W. *Benjamin Henry Latrobe and the Development of Internal Improvements in the New Republic.* New York, 1977.

Franklin, Benjamin. *Educational Views of Benjamin Franklin.* Edited by Thomas Woody. New York, 1971.

——. *The Writings of Benjamin Franklin.* Edited by Albert Henry Smyth. 10 vols. New York and London, 1905.

Franklin, Benjamin, and Jonathan Edwards. *Benjamin Franklin and Jonathan Edwards: Selections from Their Writings.* Edited by Carl Van Doren. New York and Chicago, 1920.

Gallatin, Albert. *The Writings of Albert Gallatin.* Edited by Henry Adams. 3 vols. Philadelphia, 1879.

Haight, Elizabeth, "The Northampton Protest of 1652: A Petition to the General Assembly from the Inhabitants of the Eastern Shore." *American Journal of Legal History* 23 (1984): 364–375.

Hamilton, Alexander. *The Papers of Alexander Hamilton.* Edited by Harold C. Syrett and Jacob E. Cooke. 27 vols. New York, 1961–1987.

——. *The Works of Alexander Hamilton.* Edited by John C. Hamilton. 7 vols. New York, 1850–51.

——. *The Works of Alexander Hamilton.* Edited by Henry Cabot Lodge. 12 vols. New York, 1904.

Hartwell, Henry, James Blair, and Edward Chilton. *The Present State of Virginia and the College.* Edited by H. D. Farish. Princeton, 1940.

Hubbard, William. *The Happiness of a People, in the Wisdome of Their Rulers Directing and in the Obedience of Their Brethren Attending unto What Israel Ought to Do: Recommended in a Sermon.* Boston, 1676.

Hutchinson, Thomas. *Hutchinson Papers.* Burt Franklin Research and Source Works. 2 vols. 1865. Reprint, New York, 1967.

Jackson, Andrew. *The Papers of Andrew Jackson.* Edited by Harold D. Moser and Sharon MacPherson. 4 vols. Knoxville, 1984.

Jefferson, Thomas. *Autobiography of Thomas Jefferson, 1743–1790.* Edited by Dumas Malone. Boston, 1948.

——. *The Complete Anas of Thomas Jefferson.* Edited by Franklin B. Sawvel. 1903. Reprint, New York, 1970.

——. *Correspondence between Thomas Jefferson and Pierre Samuel Du Pont de Nemours, 1798–1817.* Edited by Dumas Malone and translated by Ernest L. Lehman. Boston, 1930.

——. *Correspondence of Thomas Jefferson, 1788–1826.* Missouri Historical Society's Glimpses of the Past, vol. 3. St. Louis, 1936.

——. *An Essay towards Facilitating Instruction in the Anglo-Saxon and Modern Dialects of the English Language for the Use of the University of Virginia.* New York, 1851.

——. *The Family Letters of Thomas Jefferson.* Edited by Edwin M. Betts and James A. Bear. Charlottesville, Va., 1986.

——. *Jefferson Himself: The Personal Narrative of a Many-sided American.* Edited by Bernard Mayo. Boston, 1942.

——. *The Living Thoughts of Thomas Jefferson.* Edited by John Dewey. New York, 1940.

——. *Memoir, Correspondence and Miscellanies from the Papers of Thomas Jefferson.* Edited by Thomas J. Randolph. 4 vols. Charlottesville, Va., 1829.

——. *Notes on the State of Virginia.* Edited by William H. Peden. Chapel Hill, N.C., 1955.

——. *The Papers of Thomas Jefferson.* Edited by Julian P. Boyd, L. H. Butterfield, and Charles T. Cullen. 25 vols. Princeton, 1950–1992.

——. *Jefferson's Extracts from the Gospels.* The Papers of Thomas Jefferson, 2d. series, Edited by Charles T. Cullen. Princeton, 1983.

——. *The Republic of Letters: The Correspondence Between Thomas Jefferson and James Madison, 1776–1826.* Edited by James Morton Smith. 3 vols. New York and London, 1995.

——. *Thomas Jefferson and the National Capital.* Edited by Saul K. Padover. Washington, D.C., 1946.

——. *Thomas Jefferson Papers.* Presidential Papers. Library of Congress. Microfilm-65 reels. Washington, D.C., 1974.

——. *Thomas Jefferson's Farm Book.* Edited by Edwin M. Betts. Charlottesville, Va., 1976.

——. *Thomas Jefferson's Garden Book, 1766–1824, with Relevant Extracts from His Other Writings.* Edited by Edwin M. Betts. Philadelphia, 1944.

——. *Writings.* Edited by Merrill D. Peterson. Library of America, vol. 17. New York, 1984.

——. *The Writings of Thomas Jefferson.* Edited by Paul Leicester Ford. 10 vols. New York, 1892–1899.

——. *The Writings of Thomas Jefferson.* Edited by Andrew Adgate Lipscomb and Albert Ellery Bergh. 20 vols. Washington, D.C., 1903.

Jones, Hugh. *The Present State of Virginia.* Edited by Richard Lee Morton. Chapel Hill, 1956.

King, Rufus. *The Life and Correspondence of Rufus King.* Edited by Charles R. King. 6 vols. New York, 1971.

Latrobe, Benjamin Henry. Edited by John C. Van Horn and Lee W. Formwalt. *The Correspondence and Miscellaneous Papers of Benjamin Henry Latrobe.* New Haven, 1984.

——. *The Engineering Drawings of Benjamin Henry Latrobe, Architect.* Edited by David H. Stapleton. New Haven, 1980.

Lewis, Meriwether. *Letters of the Lewis and Clark Expedition with Related Documents, 1783–1854.* Edited by Donald Dean Jackson. 2d ed. 2 vols. Urbana, Chicago, and London, 1978.

——. *Journals of Lewis and Clark.* Edited by Bernard DeVoto. Boston, 1953.

Maclay, William. *Journal of William Maclay, United States Senator from Pennsylvania, 1789–1791.* Edited by Edgar S. Maclay. New York, 1890.

Madison, James. *James Madison: A Biography in His Own Words.* Edited by Merrill D. Peterson. New York, 1974.

——. *James Madison Papers.* Presidential Papers. Library of Congress. Microfilm-28 reels. Washington, D.C., 1964.

——. *Letters and Other Writings of James Madison.* Published by order of Congress. 4 vols. Philadelphia, 1867.

——. *The Papers of James Madison.* Edited by William T. Hutchinson, William M. E. Rachal, and Robert A. Rutland. 15 vols. Chicago, 1962–1985.

——. *The Papers of James Madison.* Presidential Series, edited by Robert A. Rutland et al. 2 vols. Charlottesville, Va., 1984.

——. *The Papers of James Madison.* Secretary of State Series. Edited by Robert J. Brugger et al. 3 vols. Charlottesville, Va., 1986.

——. *The Writings of James Madison.* Edited by Gaillard Hunt. 9 vols. New York, 1900–1910.

Madison, James, Alexander Hamilton, and John Jay. *The Federalist.* Edited by Benjamin Fletcher Wright. Cambridge, Mass., 1961.

Marshall, John. "John Marshall to Charles Cotesworth Pinckney, March 4, 1801." *American Historical Review* 53 (1947), no. 3.

———. Law notes, account books, and other papers in Special Collections (Archives), Earl Gregg Swem Library, College of William and Mary, Williamsburg, Va.

———. *The Life of George Washington.* 5 vols. Philadelphia, 1804–1807.

———. *The Papers of John Marshall.* Edited by Charles F. Hobson. Vols. 1–7. Chapel Hill, N.C., 1974–1995.

Mason, George. *The Papers of George Mason, 1725–1792.* Edited by Robert A. Rutland. 3 vols. Chapel Hill, N.C., 1970.

Mason, John. Unpublished manuscript. c. 1832. Quoted in Brent Tartar, "George Mason and the Conservation of Liberty." *Virginia Magazine of History and Biography* 99 (July 1991): 279–304.

Mather, Increase. *An Essay for the Recording of* Illustrious Providences. 1684. Reprint, New York, 1977.

Mathews, Samuel. "The Mutiny of Virginia, 1635: Letter from Capt. Sam'l Mathews concerning the Eviction of Harvey, Governor of Virginia." *The Virginia Magazine of History and Biography* (1894): 416–420.

Miller, Lillian B., Sidney Hart, et al., eds. *The Selected Papers of Charles Willson Peale and His Family.* Vols. 1–4. New Haven, 1983–1996.

Mitchill, Samuel Latham. "Dr. Mitchill's Letters from Washington, 1801–1813." *Harper's New Monthly* 5 (April 1879).

Monroe, James. *The Writings of James Monroe.* Edited by Stanislaus M. Hamilton. 7 vols. New York, 1898–1903.

Moreau de Saint-Mery, M. L. E. *Moreau de St. Mery's American Journey (1793–1798).* Edited and translated by Kenneth and Anna M. Roberts. Garden City, N.Y., 1947.

Morris, Gouverneur. *The Diary and Letters of Gouverneur Morris.* Edited by Anne Cary Morris. 2 vols. New York, 1970.

Norton, John, and Sons. *John Norton and Sons, Merchants of London and Virginia, Being the Papers from Their Counting House for the Years 1750–1795.* Edited by Frances Norton Mason. New York, 1968.

Oberg, Barbara B., ed. *The Papers of Benjamin Franklin.* Vol. 32. New Haven, 1977.

Oswald, Richard. *Memorandum on the Folly of Invading Virginia, the Strategic Importance of Portsmouth, and the Need for Civilian Control of the Military.* Edited by Walter Stitt Robinson. Charlottesville, Va., 1953.

Quincy, Edmund. *Life of Josiah Quincy of Massachusetts.* Boston, 1868.

Randolph, Edmund. "Edmund Randolph's Essay on the Revolutionary History of Virginia, 1774–1782." *Virginia Magazine of History and Biography* 43 (1953).

Rowlandson, Mary White. *The Soveraignty and Goodness of God, Together with the Faithfulness of his Promises Displayed, Being a Narrative of the Captivity and Restauration of Mrs. Mary Rowlandson.* Boston, 1682.

Rush, Benjamin. *Letters of Benjamin Rush.* Edited by L. H. Butterfield. 2 vols. Princeton, 1951.

Smith, Captain John. *Travels and Works of Captain John Smith.* Edited by Edward Arber. 2 vols. New York, 1967.

Smith, Margaret Bayard. *The First Forty Years of Washington Society, Portrayed by the Family Letters of Mrs. Samuel Harrison Smith from the Collection of Her Grandson, J. Henly Smith.* New York, 1906.

Smith, Paul Hubert, and Gerard W. Gawalt, eds. *Letters of Delegates to Congress, 1774–1789.* 21 vols. Washington, D.C., 1976–90.

Spotswood, Alexander. *The Official Letters of Alexander Spotswood, Lieutenant-Governor of the Colony of Virginia, 1710–1722.* 2 vols. With introduction and notes by R. A. Brock. Richmond, 1882–1885.

Stevens, Benjamin Franklin, ed. *The Campaign in Virginia, 1781: An Exact Reprint of Six Rare*

Pamphlets on the Clinton-Cornwallis Controversy, with Very Numerous Important Unpublished Manuscript Notes by Sir Henry Clinton, K.B. 2 vols. London, 1888.

Stith, William. *The History of the First Discovery and Settlement of Virginia.* Williamsburg, 1747.

Torrey, Samuel. *An Exhortation unto Reformation.* Cambridge, Mass., 1674.

Tucker, George. *The Life of Thomas Jefferson, Third President of the United States.* 2 vols. Philadelphia, 1837.

Tyler, Lyon G. *The Letters and Times of the Tylers.* 3 vols. Richmond, Va., 1884.

Ward, Nathaniel. *The Simple Cobler of Aggawam in America.* Edited by P. M. Zall. Lincoln, Nebr., 1969.

Washington, George. *The Writings of George Washington.* Edited by John C. Fitzpatrick. Published by authority of Congress. 39 vols. Washington, D.C., 1931–1944.

Wilson, James. *Selected Political Essays of James Wilson.* Edited by Randolph Greenfield Adams. New York, 1930.

———. *The Works of James Wilson.* Edited by Robert Green McCloskey. 2 vols. Cambridge, Mass., 1967.

———. *The Works of James Wilson, Associate Justice of the Supreme Court of the United States.* Edited by James DeWitt Andrews. 2 vols. Chicago, 1896.

Winthrop Family, *Winthrop Papers, 1498–1630.* Coauthored by Massachusetts Historical Society. 2 vols. Boston, 1929–1931.

Winthrop, John. *Winthrop's Journal: History of New England, 1630–1649.* Edited by James Kendall Hosmer. 2 vols. New York, 1908.

Winthrop, Robert C. *Life and Letters of John Winthrop.* 2 vols. 1588–1649. Reprint, New York, 1971.

Young, Alexander. *Chronicles of the First Planters of the Colony of Massachusetts Bay.* Boston, 1846.

———. *Chronicles of the Pilgrim Fathers of the Colony of Plymouth, 1602–1625.* Reprint, New York, 1971.

Secondary Sources

Abernethy, Thomas Perkins. *Western Lands and the American Revolution.* New York, 1937.

Adair, Douglas. *Fame and the Founding Fathers: Essays.* New York, 1974.

Adams, Arthur, and Frederick L. Weis. *The Magna Carta Sureties, 1215: The Barons Named in the Magna Carta and Some of Their Descendants Who Settled in America, 1607–1650.* 2d authorized ed. with revisions and corrections by Walter Lee Shepard, Jr. Baltimore, 1968.

Adams, Charles Francis. *Massachusetts: Its Historians and History, an Object Lesson.* Boston, 1893.

Adams, Henry. *History of the United States of America. . . .* 9 vols. New York, 1909–1917.

Adams, James Truslow. *Building the British Empire: To the End of the First Empire.* New York and London, 1938.

———. *The Founding of New England.* Boston, 1921.

———. *The March of Democracy.* 2 vols. New York and London, 1932–1933.

Adams, Randolph Greenfield. *Political Ideas of the American Revolution: Britannic-American Contributions to the Problem of Imperial Organization, 1765–1775.* New York, 1939.

Adams, William Howard, ed. *The Eye of Thomas Jefferson.* An exhibition at the National Gallery of Art, Washington, D.C., 1976.

Aldridge, Alfred Owen. *Benjamin Franklin and Nature's God.* Durham, N.C., 1967.

———. *Benjamin Franklin: Philosopher and Man.* Philadelphia and New York, 1965.

———. *Franklin and His French Contemporaries.* New York, 1957.

———. *Jonathan Edwards.* New York, 1964.

Allen, David Grayson. *In English Ways: The Movement of Societies and the Transferal of English Local Law and Custom to Massachusetts Bay in the Seventeenth Century.* Chapel Hill, N.C., 1981.

Allen, Gardner Weld. *A Naval History of the American Revolution.* 2 vols. New York, 1962.

Ambler, Charles Henry. *Sectionalism in Virginia from 1776–1861.* Chicago, 1910.

Ambrose, Stephen E. *Undaunted Courage: Meriwether Lewis, Thomas Jefferson, and the Opening of the American West.* New York, 1995.

Ammon, Harry. "Agricola versus Aristides: James Monroe, John Marshall, and the Genet Affair in Virginia." *Virginia Magazine of History and Biography,* vol. 71 (1963): 395–418.

———. *James Monroe: The Quest for National Identity.* 1st ed. New York, 1971.

Anderson, Douglas. *The Radical Enlightenments of Benjamin Franklin.* Baltimore and London, 1977.

Andrews, Charles McLean. *The Colonial Period of American History.* 4 vols. New Haven and London, 1934.

Andrews, Matthew Page. *The Soul of a Nation: The Founding of Virginia and the Projection of New England.* New York, 1943.

———. *Virginia: The Old Dominion.* Richmond, 1949.

Arnason, H. Harvard. *The Sculptures of Houdon.* New York, 1975.

Atack, Jeremy, and Peter Passell. *A New Economic View of American History: From Colonial Times to 1940.* New revised ed. New York, 1994.

Bailey, Kenneth P. *The Ohio Company of Virginia and the Westward Movement, 1748–1792: A Chapter in the History of the Colonial Frontier.* Glendale, 1939.

Bailyn, Bernard. *Faces of Revolution: Personalities and Themes in the Struggle for American Independence.* New York, 1992.

———. *The Ideological Origins of the American Revolution.* Cambridge, Mass., 1992.

———. "Jefferson and the Ambiguities of Freedom." *Proceedings of the American Philosophical Society* 137, no. 4 (1993): 498–515.

———. *Realism and Idealism in American Diplomacy: The Origins: Homage to Felix Gilbert 1905–1991.* Princeton, 1994.

Baker-Crothers, Hayes. *Virginia and the French and Indian War.* Chicago, 1928.

Baldwin, Anna, and Sarah Hutton. *Platonism and the English Imagination.* Cambridge and New York, 1994.

Ballagh, James Curtis. *A History of Slavery in Virginia.* Baltimore, 1902.

———. *White Servitude in the Colony of Virginia: A Study of the System of Indentured Labor in the American Colonies.* New York, 1969.

Banning, Lance. *The Sacred Fire of Liberty: James Madison and the Founding of the Federal Republic.* Ithaca, N.Y., 1995.

Barbour, Philip L., comp. *The Jamestown Voyages under the First Charter, 1606–1609.* 2 vols. London, 1969.

———. *The Three Worlds of Captain John Smith.* Boston, 1964.

Barker, Charles Albro. *The Background of the Revolution in Maryland.* New Haven and London, 1940.

Barry, John Stetson. *The History of Massachusetts.* 3 vols. Boston, 1855.

Barton, William. *Memoirs of the Life of David Rittenhouse, LLD., F.R.S.* Philadelphia, 1813.

Bear, James A., Jr. *Jefferson at Monticello.* Charlottesville, 1976.

Becker, Carl Louis. *The Declaration of Independence: A Study in the History of Political Ideas.* New York, 1942.

Bedini, Silvio A. *Thomas Jefferson: Statesman of Science.* New York, 1990.

Bemis, Samuel Flagg. *Jay's Treaty: A Study in Commerce and Diplomacy.* New York, 1924.

———. *John Quincy Adams and the Foundations of American Foreign Policy.* New York, 1949.

———. *John Quincy Adams and the Union.* New York, 1956.

———, ed. *The American Secretaries of State and Their Diplomacy.* 10 vols. New York, 1958.

Benario, Herbert W. "The Classics in Southern Higher Education." *Southern Humanities Review* 11(1977): 15–20.

Benedict, David. *A General History of the Baptist Denomination in America and Other Parts of the World.* New York, 1848.

Berman, Eleanor Davidson. *Thomas Jefferson among the Arts: An Essay in Early American Esthetics.* New York, 1947.

Best, John Hardin. *Benjamin Franklin on Education.* New York, 1962.

Betts, Edwin M. "Ground Plans and Prints of the University of Virginia, 1822–1826." *Proceedings of the American Philosophical Society* 90, no. 2 (1946).

Betts, Edwin M., and Hazelhurst B. Perkins. *Thomas Jefferson's Flower Garden at Monticello.* Richmond, Va., 1941.

Beveridge, Albert J. *The Life of John Marshall.* 4 vols. Boston, 1916.

Bivins, Caroline Holmes. *Dolley and "the Great Little Madison."* Washington, D.C., 1977.

Blanton, Wyndham Bolling. *Medicine in Virginia in the Eighteenth Century.* Richmond, 1931.

———. *Medicine in Virginia in the Seventeenth Century.* Richmond, 1930.

Bolton, Herbert Eugene, and Thomas Maitland Marshall. *The Colonization of North America, 1492–1783.* New York, 1971.

Bourne, Edward Gaylord. "The Authorship of the Federalist." *American Historical Review* (April 1897): 443–460.

Bowen, Catherine Drinker. *John Adams and the American Revolution.* Boston, 1950.

Bowers, Claude Gernade. *Jefferson and Hamilton: The Struggle for Democracy in America.* New York, 1925.

Boyd, Julian P., ed. *The Declaration of Independence: The Evolution of the Text as Shown in Facsimiles of Various Drafts by Its Author.* Washington, D.C., 1943.

Brant, Irving. *James Madison: Commander-in-Chief, 1812–1836.* James Madison Series, vol. 6. Indianapolis and New York, 1961.

———. *James Madison: Father of the Constitution, 1787–1800.* James Madison Series, vol. 3. Indianapolis and New York, 1950.

———. *James Madison: The Nationalist, 1780–1787.* James Madison Series, vol. 2. Indianapolis and New York, 1948.

———. *James Madison: The President, 1809–1812.* James Madison Series, vol. 5. Indianapolis and New York, 1956.

———. *James Madison: Secretary of State, 1800–1809.* James Madison Series, vol. 4. Indianapolis and New York, 1953.

———. *James Madison: The Virginia Revolutionist, 1751–1780.* James Madison Series, vol. I. Indianapolis and New York, 1941.

Bridenbaugh, Carl. *Seat of Empire: The Political Role of Eighteenth-Century Williamsburg.* New ed. Williamsburg, 1958.

Bridenbaugh, Carl, and Jessica Bridenbaugh. *Rebels and Gentlemen: Philadelphia in the Age of Franklin.* New York, 1962.

Brinton, Crane. "The Enlightenment." In *The Encyclopedia of Philosophy.* Edited by Paul Edwards. Vol. 2. New York and London, 1967.

Brock, Robert Alonzo. *Virginia and Virginians: Eminent Virginians, Executives of the Colony of Virginia.* 2 vols. Richmond and Toledo, 1888.

Brodie, Fawn M. *Thomas Jefferson: An Intimate History.* New York, 1974.

Brooke, Iris, and James Laver. *English Costume from the Fourteenth through the Nineteenth Century.* New York, 1937.

Brookhiser, Richard. *Founding Father: Rediscovering George Washington.* New York, 1996.

Brown, Alexander. *The First Republic of America: An Account of the Origin of This Nation.* Boston and New York, 1898.

———. *The Genesis of the United States: A Narrative of the Movement in England, 1605–1616.* 2 vols. New York, 1964.

Brown, Robert Eldon, and B. Katherine Brown. *Virginia, 1705–1786: Democracy or Aristocracy?* East Lansing, 1964.

Bruce, Kathleen. *Virginia Iron Manufacture in the Slave Era.* New York and London, 1931.

Bruce, Philip Alexander. *Economic History of Virginia in the Seventeenth Century: An Inquiry into the Material Condition of the People, Based upon Original and Contemporaneous Records.* 2 vols. New York, 1895–1896.

———. "John Randolph." In *Library of Southern Literature,* edited by Edwin Anderson Alderman et al., Vol. 10. Atlanta, 1908–1913.

———. *Social Life of Virginia in the Seventeenth Century.* 2d ed. Lynchburg, Va., 1927.

———. *The Virginia Plutarch.* 2 vols. Chapel Hill, N.C., 1929.

Bruce, Philip Alexander, Lyon G. Tyler, and Richard Lee Morton, eds. *History of Virginia.* 6 vols. Chicago and New York, 1924.

Brumm, Ursula. *American Thought and Religious Typology.* New Brunswick, N.J., 1970.

Brydon, George MacLaren. *Virginia's Mother Church and the Political Conditions under Which it Grew, 1607–1727.* 2 vols. Richmond, 1947–1952.

Bullock, Helen Duprey. *My Head and Heart: A Little History of Thomas Jefferson and Maria Cosway.* New York, 1945.

Burk, John Daly. *The History of Virginia, from its First Settlement to the Present Day.* 4 vols. Petersburg, Va., 1804–1916.

Burke, Sir John Bernard. *A Genealogical History of the Dormant, Abeyant, Forfeited, and Extinct Peerages of the British Empire.* New ed. London, 1883.

Burke's Presidential Families of the United States of America. Edited by Hugh Montgomery-Massingberd. London, 1975.

Burlingame, Roger. *Benjamin Franklin: Envoy Extraordinary.* New York, 1967.

Burns, Edward M. "The Philosophy of History of the Founding Fathers." *The Historian* 16 (Spring 1954): 142–168.

Burt, Alfred LeRoy. *The United States, Great Britain, and British North America from the Revolution to the Establishment of Peace after the War of 1812.* New Haven and Toronto, 1940.

Butt, Marshall W. *Portsmouth under Four Flags.* Portsmouth, Va., 1971.

Butterfield, L. H. "The Dream of Benjamin Rush: The Reconciliation of John Adams and Thomas Jefferson." *Yale Review* 40 (December 1950).

Butterfield, L. H., and Howard C. Rice, Jr. "Jefferson's Earliest Note to Maria Cosway with Some New Facts and Conjectures on His Broken Wrist." *William and Mary Quarterly,* 3d series, 5 (January 1948).

Campbell, Charles. *History of the Colony and Ancient Dominion of Virginia.* Philadelphia, 1860.

Carrier, Lyman. *Agriculture in Virginia, 1607–1699.* Williamsburg, 1957.

Channing, Edward. *A History of the United States.* 5 vols. New York, 1933.

Cherry, Conrad. *Nature and Religious Imagination from Edwards to Bushnell.* Philadelphia, 1980.

Chinard, Gilbert. "Jefferson's Influence Abroad." *Mississippi Historical Review* 30 (September 1943): 171–186.

———. *Thomas Jefferson: The Apostle of Americanism.* 2d ed. Ann Arbor, 1960.

Chitwood, Oliver Perry. *Justice in Colonial Virginia.* Baltimore, 1905.

———. *Richard Henry Lee: Statesman of the Revolution.* Morgantown, W.Va., 1967.

Clark, J. C. D., ed. *The Language of Liberty, 1660–1832: Political Discourse and Social Dynamics in the Anglo-American World.* Cambridge and New York, 1994.

Clebsch, William A. *American Religious Thought: A History.* Series, edited by Martin E. Marty. Chicago History of American Religion. Chicago and London, 1973.

Cohen, I. Bernard. *Benjamin Franklin: Scientist and Statesman.* New York, 1975.

———. *Science and the Founding Fathers: Science in the Political Thought of Jefferson, Adams, Franklin, and Madison.* New York and London, 1995.

———, ed. *Benjamin Franklin's Experiments: A New Edition of Franklin's "Experiments and Observations on Electricity."* Cambridge, Mass., 1941.

Coit, Margaret L. *The Growing Years, 1789–1829.* New York, 1963.

Commager, Henry Steele, and Allan Nevins, eds. *The Heritage of America.* Boston, 1949.

Conway, Moncure Daniel. *Omitted Chapters of History Disclosed in the Life and Papers of Edmund Randolph, Attorney-General.* New York, 1888.

Cramp, J. M. *Baptist History.* Philadelphia, n.d.

Crane, Verner W. *Benjamin Franklin and a Rising People.* Boston, 1954.

Cranston, Maurice. "Liberalism." *The Encyclopedia of Philosophy.* Edited by Paul Edwards. New York and London, 1967.

Craven, Wesley Frank. *Dissolution of the Virginia Company: The Failure of a Colonial Experiment.* New York, 1932.

———. *The Southern Colonies in the Seventeenth Century, 1607–1689.* Baton Rouge, 1949.

Cresson, William Penn. *James Monroe.* Chapel Hill, N.C., 1946.

Cripe, Helen. *Thomas Jefferson and Music.* Charlottesville, Va., 1976.

Cunningham, Noble E. *In Pursuit of Reason: The Life of Thomas Jefferson.* Baton Rouge, La., 1987.

———. *The Jeffersonian Republicans in Power: Party Operations, 1801–1809.* Chapel Hill, N.C., 1963.

———. *The Jeffersonian Republicans: Tthe Formation of Party Organization, 1789–1801.* Chapel Hill, N.C., 1957.

Currey, Cecil B. *Road to Revolution: Benjamin Franklin in England, 1765–1775.* Garden City, N.Y., 1968.

Curti, Merle Eugene. *The Growth of American Thought.* 3d ed. New York, Evanston, Ill., and London, 1964.

Dabney, Virginius. "From Cuckoo Tavern to Monticello." *Iron Worker* 30 (Summer 1966).

———. "Jack Jouett's Ride." *American Heritage* 131 (December 1961).

———. *The Jefferson Scandals: A Rebuttal.* New York, 1981.

———. *Liberalism in the South.* Chapel Hill, N.C., 1932.

———. *Mr. Jefferson's Univeristy: A History.* Charlottesville, Va., 1981.

———. *Virginia: The New Dominion.* Garden City, N.Y., 1971.

Dangerfield, George. *Chancellor Robert R. Livingston of New York, 1746–1813.* 1st ed. New York, 1960.

Daniels, Jonathan. *The Randolphs of Virginia.* 1st ed. Garden City, N.Y., 1972.

Dauer, Manning Julian. *The Adams Federalists.* Baltimore, 1953.

Davidson, Marshall B. *Life in America.* Bicentennial ed. 2 vols. Boston, 1951.

Davis, Burke. *A Williamsburg Galaxy.* Williamsburg and New York, 1968.

Davis, Richard Beale. *Intellectual Life in Jefferson's Virginia, 1790–1830.* Chapel Hill, N.C., 1964.

———. *Intellectual Life in the Colonial South, 1585–1763.* 3 vols. Knoxville, 1978.

———. *Literature and Society in Early Virginia, 1608–1840.* Baton Rouge, 1973.

Dewey, Frank L. *Thomas Jefferson: Lawyer.* Charlottesville, Va., 1986.

———. "Thomas Jefferson's Law Practice." *Virginia Magazine of History and Biography* 85 (July 1977).

Dillenberger, John. *Benjamin West: The Context of His Life's Work. . . .* San Antonio, 1977.

Dodson, Leonidas. *Alexander Spotswood: Governor of Colonial Virginia, 1710–1722.* New York, 1969.

Dowdey, Clifford. *The Golden Age: A Climate for Greatness, Virginia, 1732–1775.* 1st ed. Boston, 1970.

———. *The Great Plantation: A Profile of Berkeley Hundred and Plantation Virginia from Jamestown to Appomattox.* New York, 1957.

———. *The Virginia Dynasties: The Emergence of "King" Carter and the Golden Age.* 1st ed. Boston, 1969.

Draper, Theodore. *A Struggle for Power: The American Revolution.* New York and Toronto, 1996.

Dumbauld, Edward. *Thomas Jefferson: American Tourist.* Norman, Okla., 1946.

Dunn, Richard S. *Puritans and Yankees: The Winthrop Dynasty of New England, 1630–1717.* New York, 1962.

Eckenrode, Hamilton James. *The Randolphs: The Story of a Virginia Family.* 1st ed. Indianapolis and New York, 1946.

———. *The Revolution in Virginia.* Boston and New York, 1916.

Egan, Clifford L. "The United States, France, and West Florida, 1803–1807." *Florida Historical Quarterly* 47 (1968–1969).

Elkins, Stanley M., and Eric L. McKitrick. *The Age of Federalism.* New York, 1993.

Erdt, Terrence. *Jonathan Edwards: Art and the Sense of the Heart.* Amherst, Mass., 1980.

Farrand, Max. *Benjamin Franklin's Memoirs.* Cambridge, Mass., 1936. Reprinted for private circulation in the *Huntington Library Bulletin* 10 (October 1936).

Fiering, Norman. *Jonathan Edwards' Moral Thought and Its British Context.* Chapel Hill, 1981.

Fiske, John. *The American Revolution.* 2 vols. Boston and New York, 1901.

———. *The Beginnings of New England, or The Puritan Theocracy in Its Relations to Civil and Religious Liberty.* Boston, 1902.

———. *Old Virginia and Her Neighbours.* 2 vols. Boston, 1899.

Fitzhugh, Giorgianna. *The Life of Dr. John Tankard*. Hampton, Va., 1907.

Fleming, Thomas J. *The Man Who Dared the Lightning: A New Look at Benjamin Franklin*. New York, 1971.

Flexner, James Thomas. *America's Old Masters*. Garden City, N.Y., 1980.

———. *George Washington in the American Revolution, 1775–1783*. 1st ed. Boston, 1968.

———. *George Washington: The Forge of Experience, 1732–1775*. 1st ed. Boston, 1965.

———. *The Young Hamilton: A Biography*. Boston, 1978.

Flippin, Percy Scott. *The Royal Government in Virginia, 1624–1775*. New York, 1919.

Ford, Paul Leicester. *The Many-Sided Franklin*. 1898. Reprint, Freeport, N.Y., 1972.

Forman, Henry Chandlee. *Virginia Architecture in the Seventeenth Century*. Jamestown 350th Anniversary Historical Booklet, no. 11. Williamsburg, 1957.

Foster, Sir Augustus John. *Jeffersonian America: Notes on the United States of America, Collected in the Years 1805–1807 and 1811–1812*. Edited by Richard Beale Davis. San Marino, 1954.

Frantz, John B., comp. *Bacon's Rebellion: Prologue to the Revolution?* Lexington, Mass., 1969.

Frary, Ihna Thayer. *They Built the Capitol*. Richmond, 1950.

———. *Thomas Jefferson: Architect and Builder*. Richmond, 1939.

Freeman, Douglas Southall. *George Washington: A Biography*. 7 vols. New York, 1948–1957.

Gaines, William Harris. *Thomas Mann Randolph: Jefferson's Son-in-Law*. Baton Rouge, La., 1966.

Gay, Sydney Howard. *James Madison*. Boston, 1898.

Genovese, Eugene D. *The Southern Tradition: The Achievements and Limitations of an American Conservatism*. Cambridge, Mass., 1994.

Gipson, Lawrence Henry. *The British Empire before the American Revolution*. 13 vols. New York, 1936–1967.

———. *The Coming of the Revolution, 1763–1775*. 1st ed. New York, 1954.

Gooch, Robert Kent. *The Government of England*. New York, 1937.

Gould, Nathaniel D. *Church Music in America*. 1853. Reprint, New York, 1972.

Granger, Bruce Ingham. *Benjamin Franklin: An American Man of Letters*. Ithaca, N.Y., 1964.

Green, John Richard. *A Short History of the English People*. New York, 1916.

Greene, Jack P. *The American Colonies in the Eighteenth Century, 1689–1763*. New York, 1969.

———. *The Intellectual Construction of America: Exceptionalism and Identity from 1492 to 1800*. Chapel Hill, N.C., 1993.

———. *Pursuits of Happiness: The Social Development of Early Modern British Colonies and the Formation of American Culture*. Chapel Hill, N.C., and London, 1988.

———. *The Quest for Power: The Lower Houses of Assembly in the Southern Royal Colonies, 1689–1776*. Chapel Hill, N.C., 1963.

Griffin, Edward M. *Jonathan Edwards*. Minneapolis, 1971.

Griffith, Lucille B. *The Virginia House of Burgesses, 1750–1774*. Revised ed. University, Ala., 1970.

Grigsby, Hugh Blair. *The History of the Virginia Federal Convention of 1788*. Edited by R. A. Brock. 2 vols. Richmond, 1890–1891.

———. *The Virginia Convention of 1776*. Richmond, 1855.

Gross, Robert A. *The Minutemen and Their World*. New York, 1976.

Gummere, Richard Mott. "The Classical Ancestry of the U.S. Constitution." *American Quarterly* 14 (Spring 1962): 3–18.

Hamlin, Talbot Faulkner. *Benjamin Henry Latrobe*. New York, 1955.

Harrison, Fairfax. "The Equine F.F.V.'s." *Virginia Magazine of History and Biography* 35 (October 1927).

Hart, Albert Bushnell, ed. *Commonwealth History of Massachusetts*. 5 vols. New York, 1966.

Hart, Freeman Hansford. *The Valley of Virginia in the American Revolution, 1763–1789*. Chapel Hill, N.C., 1942.

Haskins, George L. *The Foundations of Power: John Marshall, 1801–1815*. New York, 1981.

Hastings, George Everett. *The Life and Works of Francis Hopkinson*. New York, 1968.

Hatch, Nathan O., and Harry S. Stout, eds. *Jonathan Edwards and the American Experience*. New York and Oxford, 1988.

Havighurst, Walter. *Alexander Spotswood: Portrait of a Governor*. Williamsburg, 1967.

Hazelton, John H. *The Declaration of Independence: Its History*. New York, 1906.

Hendren, Samuel Rivers. *Government and Religion of the Virginia Indians*. Baltimore, 1895.

Hendrick, Burton J. *The Lees of Virginia: Biography of a Family*. Boston, 1935.

Henri, Florette. *George Mason of Virginia*. New York, 1971.

Henry, William Wirt. *Patrick Henry: Life, Correspondence, and Speeches*. 3 vols. New York, 1891.

Herold, J. Christopher. *The Age of Napoleon*. English-language ed. New York, 1963.

Hiden, Martha. "Education and the Classics in the Life of Colonial Virginia." *The Virginia Magazine of History and Biography* 49 (January 1941): 20–28.

Hindle, Brooke. *The Pursuit of Science in Revolutionary America, 1735–1789*. Chapel Hill, N.C., 1956.

Hobson, Charles F. *The Great Chief Justice: John Marshall and the Rule of Law*. Lawrence, Kan., 1996.

Hofstadter, Richard. *The American Political Tradition and the Men Who Made It*. Twenty-fifth anniversary ed. New York, 1973.

Hogan, Pendleton. *The Lawn: A Guide to Jefferson's University*. Charlottesville, Va., 1987.

Honeywell, Roy John. *The Educational Works of Thomas Jefferson*. Cambridge, Mass., 1931.

Horn, James P. P. *Adapting to a New World: English Society in the Seventeenth-Century Chesapeake*. Chapel Hill, N.C., and London, 1994.

Hornberger, Theodore. *Scientific Thought in the American Colleges, 1638–1800*. New York, 1968.

Howard, George Elliott. *Preliminaries of the Revolution, 1763–1775*. New York, 1907.

Howe, Henry. *Historical Collections of Virginia: Containing a Collection of the Most Interesting Facts, Traditions, Biographical Sketches, Anecdotes, etc., Relating to Its History and Antiquities, Together with Geographical and Statistical Descriptions*. Charleston, 1845.

Huang, Nian-Sheng. *Benjamin Franklin in American Thought and Culture*. Philadelphia, 1997.

Hunt, Gaillard. *The Life of James Madison*. New York, 1902.

Hunt-Jones, Conover. *Dolley and "the Great Little Madison."* Washington, D.C., 1977.

Hutchinson, Thomas. *The History of the Colony of Massachusetts-Bay*. 3 vols. Reprint, New York, 1972.

International Colloquy on Military History (7th: 1982). *Soldier-Statesmen of the Age of the Enlightenment: Records of the 7th Internaitonal Colloquy on Military History*. Edited by Phillip K. Lundenberg and Abigail T. Siddall. Manhattan, Kans., 1984.

Isaac, Rhys. *The Transformation of Virginia, 1740–1790*. Chapel Hill, N.C., 1982.

Jackson, Donald Dean. *Thomas Jefferson and the Stony Mountains: Exploring the West from Monticello*. Norman, Okla., and London, 1993.

James, Alfred Procter. *George Mercer of the Ohio Company: A Study in Frustration*. Pittsburgh, 1963.

James, James Alton. *The Life of George Rogers Clark*. Chicago, 1928.

Jensen, Merrill, John P. Kaminski, and Gaspare J. Saladino, eds. *The Documentary History of the Ratification of the Constitution*. 18 vols. Madison, 1976.

Jester, Annie Lash. *Domestic Life in Virginia in the Seventeenth Century*. Williamsburg, 1957.

Johnson, Herbert Alan. "John Marshall." In *The Justices of the United States Supreme Court, 1789–1978: Their Lives and Major Opinions*. New York and London, 1980.

Johnston, Henry Phelps. *The Yorktown Campaign and the Surrender of Cornwallis, 1781*. New York, 1881.

Jordan, Daniel P. *Political Leadership in Jefferson's Virginia*. Charlottesville, Va., 1983.

Jordan, Winthrop D. *White over Black: American Attitudes toward the Negro, 1550–1812*. Chapel Hill, N.C., 1968.

Kahn, E. J. *Harvard: Through Change and through Storm*. 1st ed. New York, 1969.

Kelly, Franklin. *Thomas Cole's Paintings of Eden*. Fort Worth, Tex., 1994.

Kenyon, Cecelia M., ed. *The Anti-Federalists*. Indianapolis, 1966.

Kerber, Linda K. *Women of the Republic: Intellect and Ideology in Revolutionary America*. New York, 1986.

Ketcham, Ralph. "Thomas Jefferson." In *The Encyclopedia of Philosophy*. Edited by Paul Edwards. Vol. 5. New York and London, 1967.

Kimball, Fiske. "Thomas Jefferson and the First Monument of the Classical Revival in America." *Journal of American Institute of Architects* 3 (September–November 1915): 371–491.

————. *Thomas Jefferson: Architect*. Boston, 1916.

Kimball, Fiske, and Susan Higginson Nash. *The Restoration of Colonial Williamsburg in Virginia*. New York, 1935.

Kimball, Marie G. *Jefferson: The Road to Glory, 1743 to 1776*. New York, 1943.

Kirker, Harold. *The Architecture of Charles Bulfinch*. Cambridge, Mass., 1969.

————. *Bulfinch's Boston*. New York, 1964.

Koch, Adrienne. *Jefferson and Madison: The Great Collaboration*. New York, 1950.

Koch, Adrienne, and Harry Ammon. "The Virginia and Kentucky Resolutions: An Episode in Jefferson's and Madison's Defense of Civil Liberties." *William and Mary Quarterly*, 3d series, 5 (April 1948).

Koontz, Louis Knott. *Robert Dinwiddie: His Career in American Colonial Government and Westward Expansion*. Glendale, 1941.

————. *The Virginia Frontier, 1754–1763*. Baltimore, 1925.

Kraus, Michael. *The Atlantic Civilization: Eighteenth-Century Origins*. Ithaca, N.Y., 1949.

————. *Intercolonial Aspects of American Culture on the Eve of the Revolution, with Special Reference to the Northern Towns*. New York, 1964.

Lanciano, Claude O. *Rosewell, Garland of Virginia*. Gloucester, Va., 1978.

Lasky, Melvin J. "America and Europe: Transatlantic Images." In *Paths of American Thought*. Edited by Arthur Meier Scheslinger, Jr. and Morton Gabriel White. Boston, 1963.

Latané, John H. *The Early Relations between Maryland and Virginia*. Baltimore, 1895.

Lavender, David. *The Way to the Western Sea: Lewis and Clark across the Continent*. New York, 1988.

Lawson-Tancred, Sir Thomas. *Records of a Yorkshire Manor*. London, 1937.

Lehmann-Hartleben, Karl. "Thomas Jefferson: Archaeologist." *American Journal of Archaeology* 47 (April 1943).

Lemay, J. A. Leo, ed. *Essays in Early Virginia Literature Honoring Richard Beale Davis*. New York, 1977.

Levy, Leonard W. *Jefferson and Civil Liberties: The Darker Side*. Cambridge, Mass., 1963.

Lief, Leonard, comp. *The New Conservatives*. Indianapolis, 1967.

Lienesch, Michael. *New Order of the Ages: Time, the Constitution, and the Making of Modern American Political Thought*. Princeton, 1988.

Lindstrom, C. "William Billings and His Times." *Musical Quarterly* 25 (1939):479–497.

Lodge, Henry Cabot. *Life and Letters of George Cabot*. 2d ed. Boston, 1878.

Long, John Cuthbert. *Mr. Pitt and America's Birthright: A Biography of William Pitt, the Earl of Chatham, 1708–1778*. New York, 1940.

Longmore, Paul K. *The Invention of George Washington*. Berkeley, Los Angeles, and London, 1988.

Lonn, Ella. *The Colonial Agents of the Southern Colonies*. Chapel Hill, N.C., 1945.

Lopez, Claude-Anne. *Mon Cher Papa: Franklin and the Ladies of Paris*. New Haven and London, 1966.

Lyon, Elijah Wilson. *Louisiana in French Diplomacy, 1759–1804*. Norman, Okla., 1934.

Maier, Pauline. *American Scripture: Making the Declaration of Independence*. New York, 1997.

Malone, Dumas. *Jefferson and His Time*. 6 vols. Boston, 1948–1981.

Manchester, William Raymond. *American Caesar*. New York, 1978.

Manners, Lady Victoria, and George C. Williamson. *Angelica Kauffmann, R.A., Her Life and Her Works*. New York, 1976.

Mapp, Alf J., Jr. *Frock Coats and Epaulets: The Men Who Led the Confederacy* 4th ed. Lanham, Md., New York, and London, 1996.

————. "Thomas Jefferson and the Language of Liberty." In *Constitutionalism: Founding and Future*. Edited by Kenneth W. Thompson. Charlottesville, Va., 1989.

————. *Thomas Jefferson: A Strange Case of Mistaken Identity*. Lanham, Md., New York, and London, 1987.

————. *Thomas Jefferson: Passionate Pilgrim*. Lanham, Md., New York, and London, 1991.

————. *The Virginia Experiment: The Old Dominion's Role in the Making of America*. 2d ed. Lanham, Md., and New York, 1987.

Marckwardt, Albert H., and James L. Rosier. *Old English Language and Literature*. New York, 1972.

Martin, Edwin Thomas. *Thomas Jefferson: Scientist*. New York, 1952.

Mason, George Carrington. *Colonial Churches of Tidewater Virginia*. Richmond, 1945.

Mason, George Champlin. *The Life and Works of Gilbert Stuart*. New York, 1879.

Matthews, Richard K. *If Men Were Angels: James Madison and the Heartless Empire of Reason*. Lawrence, Kans., 1995.

———. *The Radical Politics of Thomas Jefferson: A Revisionist View*. Lawrence, Kans., 1984.

Mays, David John. *Edmund Pendleton, 1721–1803: A Biography*. 2 vols. Cambridge, Mass., 1952.

McClellan, Elisabeth. *History of American Costume*. New York, 1937.

McDonald, Forrest. *The Presidency of Thomas Jefferson*. Lawrence, Kans., 1976.

McKay, David, and Richard Crawford. *William Billings of Boston: Eighteenth Century Composer*. Princeton, 1975.

McKee, Christopher. *Edward Preble: A Naval Biography, 1761–1807*. Annapolis, 1972.

McLaughlin, Jack. *Jefferson and Monticello: The Biography of a Builder*. 1st ed. New York, 1988.

McMichael, George L., ed. *Anthology of American Literature*. 2 vols. New York, 1974.

McSherry, James. *History of Maryland*. Baltimore, 1904.

Meade, Robert D. *Patrick Henry: Patriot in the Making*. Philadelphia, 1957.

———. *Patrick Henry: Practical Revolutionary*. Philadelpia, 1969.

Meade, William. *Old Churches, Ministers and Families of Virginia*. 2 vols. Philadelphia, 1857.

Meyer, Virginia M., and John Frederick Dorman. *Adventurers of Purse and Person: Virginia, 1607–1624/5*. 3d ed. Richmond, 1987.

———. "A Persistent Tradition: The Classical Curriculum in Eighteenth Century New England." *William and Mary Quarterly*, 3d series, 18 (January 1961): 54–67.

Middlekauff, Robert. *Benjamin Franklin and His Enemies*. Berkeley, Los Angeles, and London, 1996.

Middleton, Arthur Pierce. *Tobacco Coast: A Maritime History of Chesapeake Bay in the Colonial Era*. Edited by George Carrington Mason. Newport News, Va., 1953.

Miles, Richard D. "The American Image of Benjamin Franklin." *American Quarterly* 9 (Summer 1957): 117–143.

Miller, Charles A. *Jefferson and Nature: An Interpretation*. Baltimore, 1988.

Miller, F. Thornton. *Juries and Judges Versus the Law: Virginia's Provincial Legal Perspective, 1783–1828*. Charlottesville, Va., 1994.

Miller, Helen Hill. *George Mason: Gentleman Revolutionary*. Chapel Hill, N.C., 1975.

Miller, John Chester. *Origins of the American Revolution*. Boston, 1943.

———. *The Wolf by the Ears: Thomas Jefferson and Slavery*. New York, 1977.

Miller, Lillian B. *In Pursuit of Time: Rembrandt Peale, 1778–1860*. Seattle, 1992.

———. *Patrons and Patriotism: The Encouragement of the Fine Arts in the United States, 1790–1860*. Chicago, 1966.

Miller, Perry. *Jonathan Edwards*. New York, 1949.

Montross, Lynn. *The Reluctant Rebels: The Story of the Continental Congress, 1774–1789*. 1st ed. New York, 1950.

Moody, R. E., ed. *The Mayflower Compact, 1620*. Worcester, Mass., 1970.

Moore, John Hammond. *Albemarle: Jefferson's County*. Charlottesville, Va., 1976.

Morgan, David T. *The Devious Dr. Franklin, Colonial Agent*. Macon, Ga., 1996.

Morgan, Edmund S. "The American Revolution Considered as an Intellectual Movement." In *Paths of American Thought*. Edited by Arthur Meier Scheslinger, Jr. and Morton Gabriel Whites. Boston, 1963.

Morgan, Edmund S., ed. *Prologue to Revolution: Sources and Documents on the Stamp Act Crisis, 1764–1766*. Chapel Hill, N.C., 1959.

Morgan, Edmund S. and Helen M. *The Stamp Act Crisis; Prologue To Revolution*. Chapel Hill, 1953.

Morgan, John Hill. *Gilbert Stuart and His Pupils*. New York, 1939.

Morgan, John S. *Noah Webster*. New York, 1975.

Morison, Samuel Eliot. *Builders of the Bay Colony*. Boston and New York, 1930.

———. *The European Discovery of America.* 2 vols. New York, 1971.

———. *The Founding of Harvard College.* Cambridge, Mass., 1935.

———. *Harvard College in the Seventeenth Century.* 2 vols. Cambridge, Mass., 1936.

———. *The Intellectual Life Of Colonial New England.* 4th ed. New York, 1970.

———. *The Oxford History of the American People.* New York, 1965.

———. "The Plymouth Colony and Virginia." *Virginia Magazine of History and Biography* 62 (April 1954): 154–158.

———. *Three Centuries of Harvard, 1636–1936.* Cambridge, Mass., and London, 1936.

Morison, Samuel Eliot, Henry Steele Commager, and William Edward Leuchtenburg. *The Growth of the American Republic.* 2 vols. New York, 1942.

Morpurgo, J. E. *Their Majesties' Royall Colledge: William and Mary in the Seventeenth and Eighteenth Centuries.* 1st ed. Williamsburg, 1976.

Morton, Louis. *Robert Carter of Nomini Hall: A Virginia Tobacco Planter of the Eighteenth Century.* Williamsburg, 1941.

Morton, Richard Lee. *Colonial Virginia.* 2 vols. Chapel Hill, N.C., 1960.

Mount, Charles Merrill. *Gilbert Stuart: A Biography.* New York, 1964.

Mott, Frank Luther. *Jefferson and the Press.* Baton Rouge, 1943.

Munford, Beverley Bland. *Virginia's Attitude toward Slavery and Secession.* New York, 1909.

Nagel, Paul C. *Descent From Glory: Four Generations of the John Adams Family.* New York, 1983.

———. *John Quincy Adams: A Public Life, A Private Life.* New York, 1997.

———. *The Lees of Virginia: Seven Generations of an American Family.* New York, 1990.

Neill, Edward D. *Virginia Carolorum: The Colony under the Rule of Charles the First and Second, A.D. 1625–A.D. 1685, Based upon Manuscripts and Documents of the Period.* Albany, N.Y., 1886.

Nichols, Frederick D., and James A. Bear, Jr. *Monticello.* Charlottesville, Va., 1982.

Nicolson, Nigel. *Great Houses of the Western World.* New York, 1968.

Norton, Mary Beth. *Founding Mothers and Fathers: Gendered Power and the Forming of American Society.* New York, 1996.

Oates, Stephen B. *With Malice toward None: The Life of Abraham Lincoln.* New York, 1977.

Orcutt, Georgia. *Massachusetts: Portrait of the Land and Its People.* 2 vols. Helena, Mont., 1988.

Osgood, Herbert L. *The American Colonies in the Seventeenth Century.* 3 vols. New York, 1904–1907.

Pangle, Lorraine, and Thomas Pangle. *Learning of Liberty: Educational Ideas of American Founders.* Lawrence, Kans., 1993.

Parton, James. *The Life and Times of Aaron Burr: Lieutenant-Colonel in the Army of the Revolution, United States Senator, Vice-President of the United States, ...* 2 vols. Boston, 1890.

Perry, James R. *The Formation of a Society on Virginia's Eastern Shore, 1615–1655.* Chapel Hill, N.C., 1990.

Peterson, Merrill D. *The Jefferson Image in the American Mind.* New York, 1960.

Petrie, Sir Charles. *The Stuart Pretenders: A History of the Jacobite Movement, 1688–1807.* Boston and New York, 1933.

Phelps, Glenn A. *George Washington and American Constitutionalism.* Lawrence, Kans., 1993.

Pierson, Hamilton W. *Jefferson at Monticello: The Private Life of Thomas Jefferson.* New York, 1862.

Place, Charles A. *Charles Bulfinch: Architect and Citizen.* New York, 1968.

Pleasants, J. Hall. "The Lovelace Family and Its Connections." *Virginia Magazine of History and Biography* 29 (1921): 231–242.

Prown, Jules David. *John Singleton Copley.* 2 vols. Cambridge, Mass., 1966.

Quarles, Benjamin. *The Negro in the American Revolution.* Chapel Hill, N.C., 1961.

Quine, W. V. "Whitehead and the Rise of Modern Logic." In *The Philosophy of Alfred North Whitehead.* 2d ed. New York, 1951.

Rakove, Jack N. *The Beginnings of National Politics: An Interpretive History of the Continental Congress.* 1st ed. New York, 1979.

———. *James Madison and the Creation of the American Republic.* Edited by Oscar Handlin. Glenview, Ill., and London, 1990.

Randall, Henry S. *The Life of Thomas Jefferson.* 3 vols. Philadelphia, 1865.

Randolph, Sarah N. *The Domestic Life of Thomas Jefferson: Compiled from Family Letters and Reminiscences by his Great-Granddaughter.* With an introduction by Dumas Malone. New York, 1958.

Richard, Carl J. *The Founders and the Classics: Greece, Rome, and the American Enlightenment.* Cambridge, Mass., and London, 1994.

Richardson, Eudora Ramsay, ed. *Virginia: A Guide to the Old Dominion.* New York, 1941.

Rives, William C. *History of the Life and Times of James Madison.* 3 vols. Freeport, N.Y., 1970.

Roberts, Gary Boyd. *The Royal Descents of Five Hundred Immigrants to the American Colonies of the United States: Who Were Themselves Notable or Left Descendants Notable in American History.* Baltimore, 1993.

Rollins, Richard M. *The Long Journey of Noah Webster.* Philadelphia, 1980.

Rorty, Richard M. "Sigmund on the Couch." *New York Times Book Review*, September 22, 1996.

Rosenberger, Francis Coleman, ed. *Jefferson Reader: A Treasury of Writings About Thomas Jefferson.* 1st ed. New York, 1953.

Rossiter, Clinton Lawrence. *Seedtime of the Republic: The Origin of the American Tradition of Political Liberty.* 1st ed. New York, 1953.

Rothery, Agnes. *Houses Virginians Have Loved.* New York, 1954.

Rouse, Parke, Jr. *James Blair of Virginia.* Chapel Hill, N.C., 1971.

————. *Virginia: The English Heritage in America.* New York, 1966.

Rowland, Kate Mason. *The Life of George Mason, 1725–1792.* 2 vols. New York, 1892.

Rutland, Robert A. *George Mason: Reluctant Statesman.* Charlottesville, Va., 1963.

————. *James Madison: The Founding Father.* New York and London, 1987.

————. *The Presidency of James Madison.* Lawrence, Kans., 1990.

————, ed. *James Madison and the American Nation, 1751–1836: An Encyclopedia.* New York and London, 1994.

Rutman, Darrett B., and Anita H. Rutman. *A Place in Time: Middlesex County, Virginia, 1650–1750.* New York and London, 1984.

Sams, Conway Whittle. *The Conquest of Virginia: The Forest Primeval: An Account, Based on Original Documents, of the Indians in That Portion of the Continent in Which Was Established the First English Colony in America.* New York and London, 1916.

Sanchez-Saavedra, E. M. *A Description of the Country: Virginia's Cartographers and Their Maps, 1607–1881.* Richmond, 1975.

Schachner, Nathan. *Thomas Jefferson: A Biography.* 2 vols. New York, 1951.

Scheer, George F., and Hugh F. Rankin. *Rebels and Redcoats.* 1st ed. Cleveland, 1957.

Schlesinger, Arthur Meier. *The Colonial Merchants and the American Revolution, 1763–1776.* New York, 1957.

Schwartz, Barry. *George Washington: The Making of an American Symbol.* New York and London, 1987.

Sellers, Charles Coleman. *Charles Willson Peale.* 2 vols. New York, 1969.

————. *Portraits and Miniatures by Charles Willson Peale.* Philadelphia, 1952.

Shackelford, George Green. *Thomas Jefferson's Travels in Europe, 1784–1789.* Baltimore and London, 1995.

Sharp, James Roger. *American Politics in the Early Republic: The New Nation in Crisis.* New Haven and London, 1993.

Shepherd, Henry E. "Thomas Jefferson as a Philologist." *American Journal of Philology* 3 (1882): 211–214.

Shepherd, Jack. *The Adams Chronicles: Four Generations of Greatness.* Boston and Toronto, 1975.

Shepperson, Archibald Bolling. *John Paradise and Lucy Ludwell of London and Williamsburg.* Richmond, Va., 1942.

Smith, Abbot Emerson. *Colonists in Bondage: White Servitude and Convict Labor in America, 1607–1776.* Chapel Hill, N.C., 1947.

Smith, Charles Page. *James Wilson: Founding Father, 1742–1798.* Chapel Hill, N.C., 1973.

Smith, Jean E. *John Marshall: Definer of a Nation.* New York, 1996.

Smith, Page. *A New Age Now Begins: A People's History of the American Revolution*. 2 vols. New York, 1976.

Smith, Stuart W., ed. *Douglas Southall Freeman on Leadership*. Shippensburg, Pa., 1993.

Spalding, Matthew and Patrick J. Garrity. *A Sacred Union of Citizens: George Washington's Farewell Address and the American Character*. Lanham, Md., and New York, 1996.

Squires, William Henry Tappey, Francis E. Turin, and Maurice Edward Bennett. *Through the Years in Norfolk*. Portsmouth, Va., 1937.

Stanard, Mary Mann Page Newton. *The Story of Virginia's First Century*. Philadelphia and London, 1928.

Stern, Milton R., and Seymour L. Gross. *American Literature Survey*. 4 vols. New York, 1975.

Storing, Herbert J., ed. *The Complete Antifederalist*. Chicago, 1981.

Sydnor, Charles S. *Gentlemen Freeholders*. Chapel Hill, N.C., 1952.

Tully, Alan. *Forming American Politics: Ideals, Interests, and Institutions in Colonial New York and Pennsylvania*. Baltimore and London, 1994.

Turman, Nora Miller. *The Eastern Shore of Virginia, 1603–1964*. 1964. Reprint, Bowie, Md., 1988.

Twichell, Joseph Hopkins. *John Winthrop: First Governor of the Massachusetts Colony*. New York, 1891.

Tyler, Moses Coit. *A History of American Literature, 1607–1765*. Ithaca, N.Y., 1949.

———. *The Literary History of the American Revolution, 1763–1783*. Vol. 2. New York, 1941.

———. *Patrick Henry*. Ithaca, N.Y., 1962.

Van Doren, Carl. *Benjamin Franklin*. New York, 1938.

Van Tyne, Claude H. *The Causes of the War of Independence*. Boston, 1922.

Walsh, Correa Moylan. *The Political Science of John Adams: A Study in the Theory of Mixed Government and the Bicameral System*. New York and London, 1915.

Walters, Ray. *Albert Gallatin: Jeffersonian Financier and Diplomat*. New York, 1957.

Ward, Christopher. *The War of the Revolution*. 2 vols. New York, 1952.

Washburn, Wilcomb E. *The Governor and the Rebel: A History of Bacon's Rebellion in Virginia*. Chapel Hill, N.C., 1957.

Waterman, Thomas Tileston. *The Mansions of Virginia, 1706–1776*. Chapel Hill, N.C., 1946.

Waters, Thomas Franklin. *A Sketch of the Life of John Winthrop the Younger, Founder of Ipswich, Massachusetts, in 1633*. Cambridge, Mass., 1899.

Weddell, Alexander Wilbourne, ed. *A Memorial Volume of Virginia Historical Portraiture, 1585–1830*. Richmond, 1930.

Weis, Frederick Lewis, and Walter Lee Shepperd, Jr. *Ancestral Roots of Sixty Colonists Who Came to New England between 1623 and 1650*. 6th ed. Baltimore, 1988.

Wells, Robert V. *The Population of the British Colonies in America before 1776: A Survey of Census Data*. Princeton, 1975.

Wertenbaker, Thomas Jefferson. *Norfolk: Historic Southern Port*. Durham, N.C., 1931.

———. *Patrician and Plebian in Virginia, or, The Origin and Development of the Social Classes of the Old Dominion*. Charlottesville, Va., 1910.

———. *The Planters of Colonial Virginia*. New York, 1959.

———. *The Puritan Oligarchy: The Founding of American Civilization*. New York and London, 1947.

———. *Torchbearer of the Revolution: The Story of Bacon's Rebellion and Its Leader*. Princeton and London, 1940.

———. *Virginia Under the Stuarts, 1607–1688*. Princeton, 1914.

Weymouth, Lally, ed. *Thomas Jefferson: The Man, His World, His Influence*. New York, 1973.

Whitaker, Arthur Preston. *The Mississippi Question, 1795–1803*. New York, 1934.

White, Elizabeth Wade. *Anne Bradstreet: "The Tenth Muse."* New York, 1971.

White, G. Edward. *The Marshall Court and Cultural Change, 1815–1835*. Oxford, 1991.

White, Leonard D. *The Jeffersonians: A Study in Administrative History, 1801–1829*. New York, 1951.

Whitelaw, Ralph T. *Virginia's Eastern Shore: A History of Northampton and Accomack Counties*. Edited by George Carrington Mason. 2 vols. Richmond, 1951.

Willcox, William Bradford. *Star of Empire: A Study of Britain as a World Power, 1485–1945.* 1st ed. New York, 1950.

Wills, Garry. *Cincinnatus: George Washington and the Enlightenment.* Garden City, N.Y., 1984.

———. *Inventing America: Jefferson's Declaration of Independence.* New York, 1978.

Wilson, Woodrow. *A History of the American People.* 5 vols. New York and London, 1902.

———. "What Jefferson Would Do." In *Jefferson Reader: A Treasury of Writings about Thomas Jefferson.* Edited by Francis Coleman Rosenberger. New York, 1953.

Winegard, Dilys P. *The Intellectual World of Benjamin Franklin.* Philadelphia, 1990.

Winslow, Ola Elizabeth. *Jonathan Edwards, 1703–1758: A Biography.* New York, 1941.

Wirt, William. *The Life of Patrick Henry.* Revised ed. Philadelphia, 1836.

———. *Sketches of the Life and Character of Patrick Henry.* 15th ed. Hartford, 1854.

Wise, Jennings Cropper. *Ye Kingdome of Accawmacke, or The Eastern Shore of Virginia in the Seventeenth Century.* Richmond, 1911.

Wise, Matthew M. *The Littleton Heritage: Some American Descendants of Col. Nathaniel Littleton (1605–1654) of Northampton Co., Virginia and His Royal Forebears.* West Columbia, S.C., 1997.

Wold, Karl C. *Mr. President—How is Your Health?* St. Paul, 1948.

Wood, Gordon S. *The Radicalism of the American Revolution.* 1st ed. New York, 1992.

Wright, Louis B. *The First Gentlemen of Virginia: Intellectual Qualities of the Early Colonial Ruling Class.* San Marino, 1940.

Writers' Program. Virginia. *The Negro in Virginia, Compiled by Workers of the Writers' Program of the Work Projects Administration in the State of Virginia.* New York, 1940.

Wyllie, John Cook. "Writings about Jack Jouett and Tarleton's Raid on Charlottesville in 1781." *Magazine of Albemarle County History* (1958–1959).

Youngs, J. William T., Jr. *God's Messengers: Religious Leadership in Colonial New England, 1700–1750.* Baltimore and London, 1976.

Zuckerman, Michael, ed. *Friends and Neighbors: Group Life in America's First Plural Society.* Philadelphia, 1982.

IV. GENERAL REFERENCES

Arieti, Silvano. *Creativity: The Magic Synthesis.* New York, 1976.

Arnold, Matthew. "Hebraism and Hellenism." In *Culture and Anarchy.* Edited by John Dover Wilson. Cambridge, 1932.

Asser, John. *Asser's Life of King Alfred.* Edited by William Henry Stevenson and Dorothy Whitelock. Oxford, 1959.

Bate, Jonathan. "Words in a Quantum World: How Cambridge Physics Led William Empson to Refuse 'Either/Or.'" *Times Literary Supplement* (London), July 25, 1997.

Boorstin, Daniel J. *The Creators.* 1st ed. New York, 1992.

———. *The Discoverers.* 1st ed. New York, 1983.

Bruford, W. F. "Goethe's Weimar." In *Cities of Destiny.* London, 1967.

Buell, Frederick. *National Culture and the New Global System.* Baltimore and London, 1994.

Churchill, Sir Winston. *My Early Life: A Roving Commission.* New York, 1930.

Copplestone, Trewin, ed. *World Architecture.* 1966. Reprint, London and New York, 1973.

Dray, William H. *Philosophy of History.* Englewood Cliffs, N.J., 1964.

Dunham, William. *Journey through Genius: The Great Theorems of Mathematics.* New York, 1990.

Dürer, Albrecht. *The Writings of Albrecht Dürer.* Translated and edited by William Martin Conway. New York, 1958.

Einstein, Albert. *Relativity: The Special and the General Theory.* 15th ed. New York, 1961.

Eliade, Mircea. *Cosmos and History: The Myth of the Eternal Return.* Translated by Willard R. Trask. New York, 1959.

Erasmus, Desiderius. *The Epistles of Erasmus, From His Earliest Letters to His Fifty-First Year, Arranged in Order of Time.* Translated and edited by Francis Morgan Nichols. 3 vols. New York, 1962.

Gardiner, Patrick, ed. *The Philosophy of History.* Oxford, 1974.

Gardner, Howard. *Creating Minds: An Anatomy of Creativity, Seen through the Lives of Freud, Einstein, Picasso, Stravinsky, Eliot, Graham, and Gandhi.* New York, 1993.

Goethe, Johann Wolfgang von. *Letters from Goethe.* Translated by M. von Herzfeld and C.A.M. Sym. New York, 1957.

Grafton, Anthony. *New Worlds, Ancient Texts: The Power of Tradition and the Shock of Discovery.* Cambridge, Mass., 1992.

Gray, Charles Edward. "An Analysis of Graeco-Roman Development: The Epicyclical Evolution of Graeco-Roman Civilization." *American Anthropologist* 60 (1958): 13–31.

———. "An Epicyclical Model for Western Civilization." *American Anthropologist* 63 (1961): 1014–1037.

———. "A Measurement of Creativity in Western Civilization." *American Anthropologist* 68 (1966): 1384–1417.

Hadfield, Andrew. *Literature, Politics, and National Identity: Reformation to Renaissance.* Cambridge, 1994.

Hecht, Eugene. *Physics in Perspective.* Reading, Mass., 1980.

Hindley, Geoffrey, ed. *Larousse Encyclopedia of Music.* New York, 1971.

Kapitsa, Peter. *Peter Kapitsa on Life and Science: Addresses and Essays.* Translated and edited with an introduction by Albert Parry. New York and London, 1968.

Kelly, Kevin. *Out of Control: The Rise of Neo-biological Civilization.* Reading, Mass., 1994.

Kroeber, A. L. *Configurations of Culture Growth.* Berkeley and Los Angeles, 1969.

Mahdi, Muhsin. *Ibn Khaldun's Philosophy of History: A Study of the Philosophic Foundation of the Science of Culture.* Chicago, 1971.

Margolis, Howard. *Paradigms and Barriers: How Habits of Mind Govern Scientific Belief.* Chicago, 1993.

Mazlish, Bruce. *The Riddle of History: The Great Speculators from Vico to Freud.* New York, 1966.

McNeill, William Hardy. *The Rise of the West: A History of the Human Community.* Chicago, 1963.

Merson, John. *Roads to Xanadu: East and West in the Making of the Modern World.* Crows Nest, Australia, 1989.

Mokyr, Joel. *The Lever of Riches: Technological Creativity and Economic Progress.* New York and Oxford, 1990.

Pais, Abraham. *Niels Bohr's Times: In Physics, Philosophy, and Polity.* Oxford and New York, 1991.

Rahe, Paul. *Republics Ancient and Modern: Classical Republicanism and the American Revolution.* Chapel Hill, N.C., 1993.

Rice, Eugene F., Jr. "The Renaissance and Reformation in Europe." In *The Columbia History of the World.* Edited by John Arthur Garraty and Peter Gay. New York, 1972.

Shlain, Leonard. *Art and Physics: Parallel Visions in Space, Time, and Light.* New York, 1991.

Simonton, Dean Keith. *Scientific Genius: A Psychology of Science.* Cambridge, 1988.

Sorokin, Pitirim Aleksandrovich. *Social Philosophies of an Age of Crisis.* Boston, 1950.

Tatian. "Address to the Greeks." In *Three Thousand Years of Educational Wisdom in Selections from Great Documents.* Edited by Robert Ulich. Cambridge, Mass., 1905.

Thompson, Kenneth W. *Fathers of International Thought.* Baton Rouge, 1994.

———. *Toynbee's World Politics and History.* Baton Rouge, 1985.

Toynbee, Arnold J. *A Study of History.* 12 vols. Oxford, 1934–1961.

———. *A Study of History.* Abridgement of vols. 1–6 by D. C. Somervell. New York and London, 1947.

Vico, Giambattista. *The New Science of Giambattista Vico.* Revised translation by Thomas Goddard Bergin and Max Harold Fisch. Ithaca, N.Y., 1968.

Weintraub, Karl Joachim. *Visions of Culture.* Chicago, 1966.

Wescott, Roger W. "The Enumeration of Civilization." In *History and Theory: Studies in the Philosophy of History.* Vol. 9. Middletown, Conn., 1970.

Whitehead, Alfred North. *Adventures of Ideas.* New York, 1933.

———. *Dialogues of Alfred North Whitehead.* Edited by Lucien Price. New York, 1956.

INDEX

ABOUT THE AUTHOR

A world-renowned expert on Thomas Jefferson and on the society created by America's Founders, Alf J. Mapp, Jr., is also one of the most acclaimed biographers of our time. Circling the globe in nine languages, his sprightly writings have earned the praise of scholarly critics for their literary quality and fresh insight, and have won the plaudits of the public for their high entertainment value. His *Thomas Jefferson: A Strange Case of Mistaken Identity* and *Thomas Jefferson: Passionate Pilgrim* have been cited for depth of research among thousands of records. Both also were featured selections of the Book-of-the-Month Club and best-sellers.

In thirty-one years at Old Dominion University, where he lectured in history, literature, creative writing, and an interdisciplinary course in western civilization, Mapp earned the institution's highest academic honors and today bears the titles Eminent Scholar Emeritus and Louis I. Jaffe Professor Emeritus.

The scope of his scholarly and artistic activities has increased steadily and his audience has expanded correspondingly. National honors include the Outstanding American Educator Award twice and the National Bicentennial Medal of the National Bicentennial Administration, while international recognition includes the Medal Comité Français du Bicentenaire from the Republic of France and (in England) inclusion in special manuscript collections of the Manchester Central Library and Cambridge University. Professor Mapp is included in twenty-eight encyclopedias and biographical directories published in four nations.

On radio and TV, nationally and internationally, he is a much sought-after interpreter of current events in the light of history. It is almost as if his whole professional career had been building toward the production of *Three Golden Ages: Discovering the Creative Secrets of Renaissance Florence, Elizabethan England, and America's Founding.*